THE VICTORIA HISTORY
OF THE
COUNTIES OF ENGLAND

—

A HISTORY OF
STAFFORDSHIRE

VOLUME V

THE VICTORIA HISTORY
OF THE
COUNTIES OF ENGLAND

EDITED BY R. B. PUGH

THE UNIVERSITY OF LONDON
INSTITUTE OF
HISTORICAL RESEARCH

Oxford University Press, Amen House, London, E.C.4

GLASGOW NEW YORK TORONTO MELBOURNE WELLINGTON
BOMBAY CALCUTTA MADRAS KARACHI KUALA LUMPUR
CAPE TOWN IBADAN NAIROBI ACCRA

PRINTED IN GREAT BRITAIN

INSCRIBED TO THE

MEMORY OF HER LATE MAJESTY

QUEEN VICTORIA

WHO GRACIOUSLY GAVE THE TITLE TO

AND ACCEPTED THE DEDICATION

OF THIS HISTORY

STAFFORD CASTLE FROM THE SOUTH-EAST

A HISTORY OF THE COUNTY OF STAFFORD

EDITED BY L. MARGARET MIDGLEY

VOLUME V

EAST CUTTLESTONE
HUNDRED

PUBLISHED FOR
THE INSTITUTE OF HISTORICAL RESEARCH
BY THE
OXFORD UNIVERSITY PRESS
AMEN HOUSE, LONDON
1959

CONTENTS OF VOLUME FIVE

LIST OF ILLUSTRATIONS

The two photographs by Dr. St. Joseph are reproduced by permission of the Air Ministry, Crown Copyright reserved. Thanks are due to Lord Hatherton, Mr. T. A. W. Giffard, Mr. P. H. Jennings, Mr. R. Webb, *Country Life*, the Wolverhampton *Express and Star*, the Staffordshire Record Office, the Vicar and Churchwardens of Brewood, and the Clerk to the Staffordshire County Council, for permission to reproduce paintings, drawings, and photographs; to the Staffordshire Record Society and Messrs. Cassell & Co. Ltd. for the loan of the blocks of Blackladies Chapel and Thomas Giffard on pages 34 and 132; and to the Trustees of the William Salt Library, Stafford, for granting facilities for making reproductions from 'Staffordshire Views' and other works in their possession.

xi

LIST OF ILLUSTRATIONS

xii

LIST OF MAPS AND PLANS

The eight church plans and the sectional drawings of Brewood Church were measured and drawn by M. Edwards; the maps of Cannock and Rugeley were drawn by G. R. Versey; and Old Smithy Cottages were measured and drawn by S. R. Jones.

EDITORIAL NOTE

T HIS volume, the third in the Staffordshire series to appear, is, like its predecessor, Volume IV, the outcome of a partnership between the University of London and a group of Local Authorities in Staffordshire. For some explanation of the nature of that partnership and a description of the editorial arrangements the reader is referred to the Editorial Note prefixed to Volume IV. It only remains for the University of London to reiterate its gratitude to the Local Authorities for the continuation of their much valued financial assistance. Sincere thanks must also again be returned to those who have helped in the work of compilation, especially to Miss Marguerite Gollancz and Mr. F. B. Stitt (successively Librarians of the William Salt Library, Stafford, and County Archivists), the members of their staff, Mr. M. B. S. Exham (Lichfield Diocesan Registrar), and Mr. S. A. H. Burne.

LIST OF CLASSES OF PUBLIC RECORDS
USED IN THIS VOLUME
WITH THEIR CLASS NUMBERS

Chancery
C 1 Proceedings, Early
C 2 Proceedings, Series I
C 3 Proceedings, Series II
C 5 Proceedings, Six Clerks' Series, Bridges
C 54 Close Rolls
C 60 Fine Rolls
C 66 Patent Rolls
C 93 Proceedings of Commissioners for Charitable Uses, Inquisitions and Decrees
C 131 Extents for Debts
Inquisitions post mortem, Series I:
C 135 Edw. III
C 136 Ric. II
C 137 Hen. IV
C 138 Hen. V
C 139 Hen. VI
C 140 Edw. IV
C 142 Inquisitions post mortem, Series II
C 143 Inquisitions ad quod damnum
C 145 Inquisitions, Miscellaneous

Court of Common Pleas
C.P. 34 King's Silver Books
C.P. 25 (2) Feet of Fines, Series II
C.P. 40 Plea Rolls
C.P. 43 Recovery Rolls

Exchequer, Queen's Remembrancer
E 101 Accounts, Various
E 122 Customs Accounts
E 134 Depositions by Commission
E 164 Miscellaneous Books, Series I
E 178 Special Commission of Enquiry
E 179 Subsidy Rolls

Exchequer, Augmentation Office
E 315 Miscellaneous Books
E 317 Parliamentary Surveys

Home Office
H.O. 129 Various, Census, Ecclesiastical Returns

Duchy of Lancaster
D.L. 30 Court Rolls

Court of Requests
Req. 2 Proceedings

Special Collections
S.C. 6 Ministers' Accounts
S.C. 11 Rentals and Surveys Rolls

Court of Star Chamber
Sta. Cha. Proceedings

Court of Wards and Liveries
Wards 7 Inquisitions post mortem

LIST OF CLASSES OF DOCUMENTS IN THE STAFFORDSHIRE RECORD OFFICE
USED IN THIS VOLUME
WITH THEIR CLASS NUMBERS

Court of Quarter Sessions

Q/SR   Sessions Rolls.

Q/SB   Sessions Bundles, 1768 and after.

Q/SBe Early Sessions Bundles, to 1767.

Q/SM Sessions Minute Books.

Q/RDc Inclosure Awards.

Q/FA   Finance, General Accounts.

Q/RGd Gamekeepers' Deputations.

Parish Records

A/PC   Churchwardens' Accounts.

A/PO   Overseers of the Poor Accounts.

NOTE ON ABBREVIATIONS

Among the abbreviations and short titles used the following may require elucidation:

Erdeswick, *Staffs.*	S. Erdeswick, *Survey of Staffordshire*, ed. T. Harwood (1844).
Lich. D. and C.	Lichfield Dean and Chapter.
Lich. Dioc. Regy.	Lichfield Diocesan Registry.
Pitt, *Staffs.*	W. Pitt, *Topographical History of Staffordshire* (Newcastle under Lyme, 1817).
Plot, *Staffs.*	R. Plot, *Natural History of Staffordshire* (Oxford, 1686).
S.H.C.	Staffordshire Record Society (formerly the William Salt Archaeological Society), *Collections for a History of Staffordshire*.
S.R.O.	Staffordshire Record Office.
Shaw, *Staffs.*	S. Shaw, *History and Antiquities of Staffordshire* (2 volumes, 1798–1801).
Trans. Birm. Arch. Soc.	Birmingham and Midland Institute: Archaeological Society, *Transactions and Proceedings*.
Trans. N. Staffs. Field Club	*Transactions of the North Staffordshire Field Club*.
W.S.L.	William Salt Library, Stafford.

ANALYSIS OF SOURCES

PRINTED IN *STAFFORDSHIRE HISTORICAL COLLECTIONS* AND USED IN VOLUMES IV AND V OF THIS HISTORY

Vol.	*Pages*	*Subject-matter or title of article*
i	1–144	Pipe Rolls, 1130, 1155–89.
,,	145–240	Liber Niger Scaccarii, 1166.
,,	241–88	Register of Roger de Norbury, Bishop of Lichfield and Coventry, 1322–58.
,,	289–384	'History of Blymhill' (part I).
ii (1)	1–177	Pipe Rolls, 1189–1216.
,,	178–276	Staffs. Deeds, 1072–*c.* 1237.
ii (2)	3–22	Knighthood Composition List, *temp.* Charles I.
,,	69–147	'History of Blymhill' (part II).
iii (1)	1–165	Curia Regis (including Eyre) Rolls, 1194–1215.
,,	166–77	Final Concords, 1196–1213.
,,	178–231	Staffs. Deeds, *c.* 1120–*c.* 1272.
iii (2)	1–155	Heraldic Visitation, 1583.
iv (1)	1–217	Pleas coram rege, de banco, and before itinerant justices, 1219–72.
,,	218–63	Final Concords, 1218–72.
iv (2)		'History of Church Eaton.'
v (1)	1–104	Burton Abbey Cartulary.
,,	105–22	Hundred Rolls, *temp.* Henry III, Edward I.
,,	123–80	Pleas of the Forest, 1262–1300.
v (2)		Heraldic Visitations, 1614, 1663, 1664.
vi (1)	1–28	Stone Priory Cartulary.
,,	29–36	Pleas (coram rege, de banco, and before itinerant justices) from B.M. Add. MS. 12269 (abstract of pleas 4–24 Hen. III believed to have been compiled by Bracton).
,,	37–300	Pleas coram rege, de banco, and before itinerant justices, 1271–94.
vi (2)	5–104	Catalogue of Muniments of the Dean and Chapter of Lichfield.
vii (1)	1–192	Pleas coram rege, de banco, and before itinerant justices, 1293–1307.
,,	193–255	Subsidy Roll, 1327.
vii (2)		'History of the Swynnerton family.'
viii (1)	1–124	'Military service of Staffs. tenants, 13th and 14th centuries.'
,,	125–201	Cartulary of the Priory of St. Thomas the Martyr near Stafford.
viii (2)		'History of Castle Church.'
ix (1)	1–119	Pleas coram rege, de banco, and before itinerant justices, 1307–27.
x (1)	1–78	Pleas coram rege, and before itinerant justices, 1307–26.
,,	79–132	Subsidy Roll, 1332–3.
xi	1–126	Pleas de banco and before itinerant justices, 1327–41.
,,	127–294	Final Concords, 1327–1547.
xii (1)	1–173	Pleas de banco and before itinerant justices, 1341–59.
,,	177–235	Final Concords, mixed counties including Staffs., 1492–1558.
,,	235–9	Final Concords, 1558–9.
,,	242–336	Chetwynd Cartulary.

ANALYSIS OF SOURCES

THE HUNDRED OF CUTTLESTONE

(continued)

EASTERN DIVISION

NOTE. The broken lines show the boundaries of civil parishes, other than ancient parishes, as they existed in 1956

BASWICH OR BERKSWICH

THE ancient parish of Baswich, lying immediately east-south-east of Stafford, contained Baswich with Weeping Cross, Walton and Milford, the township of Brocton and the joint township of Acton Trussell and Bednall. Acton Trussell and Bednall were severed from Baswich for civil purposes by the mid-17th century.[1] Their history will be treated after that of Baswich.

The boundaries of the ancient parish of Baswich, after the separation of Acton Trussell and Bednall, as defined in 1671 and 1796,[2] were on the west the River Penk at Radford Bridge, on the north the

---

[1] The boundaries of the parish of Baswich as perambulated in 1671 did not include Acton Trussell and Bednall: *Berkswich with Walton Parish Register* (Staffs. Par. Reg. Soc.), 42–43. Acton Trussell and Bednall formed a separate constablewick in 1666 (*S.H.C.* 1927, 27–28), and the

township was not included in the Accounts of the Overseers for the Poor for either Brocton or Berkswich at this date; therefore it presumably had its own poor law administration.

[2] *Berkswich w. Walton Par. Reg.* 42–43, 140–1.

River Sow, and on the east the line of the Sherbrook valley running southward across Cannock Chase to an old waymark known as Cank Thorn[3] near the war cemetery. At this point the three ancient parishes of Rugeley, Penkridge, and Cannock converge with Baswich.

This area was divided by 1666 into two separate constablewicks,[4] Walton and Brocton, the constables being appointed in the court of the manor of Haywood as late as 1841.[5] The surviving accounts of the overseers of the poor for the constablewick of Walton, which included Baswich and Radford, date from 1699[6] and those for the constablewick of Brocton from 1759.[7] The constable's accounts for Walton date from 1699 and those for Brocton from 1736.[8] Baswich and Brocton have formed separate civil parishes since 1871.[9] The civil parish of Baswich was encroached upon by the extension of Stafford Borough as far as Stockton Lane in 1934,[10] so that its area in 1951 was 1,194 acres with a population of 1,096, while the area of the civil parish of Brocton was then 2,318 acres and its population 572.[11]

Two important trunk roads cross the parishes. The road from Lichfield to Stafford enters at Satnall Hills and runs due west to Stafford crossing the River Penk at Radford Bridge. This road was of great importance in the Middle Ages as is shown by the fact that the liability for the maintenance of Radford Bridge fell upon the hundred.[12] The bridge was re-built in 1771 and 1799,[13] and by 1830 responsibility for its maintenance had been fixed on the county.[14] It was again rebuilt c. 1825 and is of stone ashlar with three rusticated elliptical arches, between which are paired Tuscan columns supporting a modillion cornice. According to Dugdale, the river marked the western limit of the forest of Cannock until the 17th century. In King John's time Hugh de Loges, the royal forester of Cannock, held his fee by the serjeanty of meeting the Earl of Chester at Radford Bridge and conveying him across the forest.[15] This Lichfield–Stafford road is joined at Weeping Cross, where an island at the junction is preserved as a war memorial, by the road from Birmingham running via Cannock to Stafford, Newcastle under Lyme, and the north. The Industrial Revolution has made this road one of the most heavily burdened in the country. From Weeping Cross a minor road leads north, past the church and over the River Sow to the site of the Augustinian priory of St. Thomas (in St. Mary's parish, Stafford, Pirehill hundred), and on to Weston upon Trent, Chartley, and Uttoxeter. St. Thomas Bridge carrying this road over the Sow was a county bridge by 1830.[16] It appears to be contemporary with Radford Bridge and has a single elliptical arch and a

parapet terminating in small octagonal piers.[17] The main line of the former L.M.S.R. crosses the northern tip of the parish of Baswich. Milford and Brocton Station was opened for passenger traffic in 1877, and for goods traffic in 1882; it was closed for passenger traffic in 1950 but in 1956 was still used for goods.[18]

The Staffordshire and Worcestershire Canal, which follows the line of the River Penk to the confluence with the Sow where it turns eastwards alongside the Sow to the terminus at Haywood, was constructed under an Act of 1766[19] and completed in 1772.[20] There was formerly a wharf at Radford Bridge, connected with Stafford by a tramway, where, it was stated in 1851, considerable business in coal, lime, &c., was carried on.[21] The canal is largely disused but still navigable.

Baswich church stands in an isolated position at the extreme northern tip of the parish, and there has never been a village to which the name Baswich as a geographical term can be applied, the old centres of population in the parish being the villages of Walton and Brocton. Several old houses remain in both Walton and Brocton (see below) but in the former, which was still expanding rapidly in 1956, most of the building has taken place since 1920. In Pool Lane, leading to Milford, there are several larger houses of the 19th and 20th centuries, and further building was in progress in 1956. Sawpit Lane is entirely built up with 20th-century houses, many of them semi-detached. There are three pairs of council houses in Oldacre Lane dating from c. 1950, and the police house in Sawpit Lane was built in 1949.[22] The school and the vicarage are at Walton. At Weeping Cross, north of the church and at the junction of the Lichfield to Stafford and the Cannock to Stafford roads, a wooden cross stood in Edward VI's reign[23] and by 1747 an inn of that name[24] on a site now occupied by Baswich House (see below). Weeping Cross became a favourite residential area in the 19th century and by 1834 there were 'several neat villas' on or near the Lichfield road.[25] Ribbon development took place here, mainly between the two world wars, down Baswich Lane almost as far as the church, down Stockton Lane in Radford Rise, and along the Lichfield and Cannock roads as far as the borough boundary. Since the Second World War large compact blocks of detached and semi-detached houses have been erected here, so that the greater part of the present parishes of Baswich and Brocton form a dormitory for Stafford.

Milford, now a hamlet in the south-east of the parish on both sides of the Lichfield road, first occurs in the late 18th century and grew up around

[3] 'Naughmarethorn' in the 13th cent.: Dugd. *Mon.* vi. 1253. The present thorn tree is said to be a North American species and probably not more than 100 years old: *Trans. N. Staffs. Field Club,* lxxxiv. 123.

[4] *S.H.C.* 1927, 40.

[5] W.S.L., D. 1734, Minutes of court proceedings, Haywood manor, 1841–9.

[6] S.R.O., D. 114/A/PC 1699–1828.

[7] W.S.L., Brocton Parish Records, 1736–1806.

[8] Ibid. 1759–1812; they include some churchwarden's accounts: S.R.O., D. 114/A/PC, 1699–1828.

[9] *Census,* 1871, Staffs.

[10] Staffs. Review Order, 1934. This area now forms part of the Baswich Ward in the borough of Stafford.

[11] *Census,* 1951, Staffs.

[12] *S.H.C.* 1948–9, 82; ibid. 1934(1), 144.

[13] Ibid. 1934 (1), 89.

[14] J. Potter, *List of Bridges which the inhabitants of the County of Stafford are bound to repair* (1830), 3.

[15] Dugd., *Warws.* i. 213.

[16] Potter, *List of Bridges,* 3.

[17] Compare Bull Bridge, Penkridge, p. 105.

[18] Ex inf. Public Relations Officer, London Midland Region, British Railways.

[19] Staffs. and Worcs. Canal Act, 6 Geo. III, c. 97 (priv. act).

[20] *S.H.C.* 1934 (1), 111.

[21] White, *Dir. Staffs.* (1851).

[22] Local inf.

[23] C 1/1219, nos. 20–23.

[24] At the county election of 1747 100 horses were baited at this inn: W.S.L., Hand Morgan Coll., election expenses.

[25] White, *Dir. Staffs.* (1834).

the Milford Hall estate, many of the cottages along the main road being built by the Levett family from the late 18th century onwards.[26]

Despite modern development Brocton and Baswich still preserve a certain rural setting, particularly Brocton where there are over 2,000 acres of unenclosed uplands on Cannock Chase and of common at Milford, acquired in 1956 by the Staffordshire County Council from the Earl of Lichfield.[27] In the First World War there were extensive army camps in Brocton, a military burial ground for both British and German troops being consecrated there in 1917 on land given by the Earl of Lichfield.[28] During the Second World War the area of the Chase known as Anson's Bank was used as a bombing range.[29]

About 1890 Stafford Salt and Alkali Company opened the Common Salt Works on Stafford Common, north of the town. About 1900 the works were extended by a building at Baswich so that the canal could be used, and a wharf was then constructed. The brine was brought by pipeline down Greengate Street, supplying the Brine Baths which were opened at this date, and thence along the canal to Baswich. Salt continued to be manufactured at Baswich by the open-pan method until 1945 when Messrs. Geo. Hamlett & Sons, Cheshire, the Stafford Salt and Alkali Company, and Messrs. Manger & Son (Crown Salt Works, Stafford Common) put up the capital for a new salt-works, Vacuum Salt Ltd. This stands in Baswich Lane, opposite the old salt-works, and uses vacuum pans. A second pipeline from Stafford Common was laid to supply these works. In 1950 the three companies concerned merged as Amasal.[30]

Stafford Concrete Buildings Ltd. established their factory in Baswich Lane opposite the new salt-works in 1950 and 1951. It manufactures the smaller type of prefabricated building, using sand and gravel from Brocton.[31] Brick-making was formerly carried on in Brocton in 1851[32] and there is now a large disused brick-works just west of the Cannock road. On the Chase the Bunter Pebble Beds are worked for gravel.

In 1801 about 781 acres of arable land were under cultivation in Baswich, roughly 197 acres sown with wheat, 298 acres with barley, 165 acres with oats, 27 acres with potatoes, 2 acres with peas, 3 acres with beans, 96 acres with turnips or rape, 3 acres with rye.[33] Most of the agricultural land is now used as pasture, especially near the Sow and Penk on account of flooding. In 1297 or 1298 some 180 acres of demesne lay in open fields, the largest block, 48 acres, being in 'campo de Halseyley' i.e. Haseley.[34] In 1357 there were three open fields in Baswich.[35]

In the old hamlet now called Walton on the Hill there are several houses dating from before the 19th century. Parts of nos. 9 and 11 were formerly one timber-framed house and the building retains original beams, a large fireplace, and a four-centred

door head. No. 14 is a thatched house of three bays with some of its timber-framing still exposed externally. It has large back-to-back fireplaces between the two west bays. Congreve House opposite, the home of Sir William Congreve,[36] is a T-shaped brick house dating from the late 17th century.[37] Next to No. 14 is the former smithy. Walton Lodge and the vicarage were built in the early 19th century and both enlarged later. The former infant school near the vicarage is now used as a parish room;[38] there are older cottages adjoining it on the east side. The village hall is a wooden building erected c. 1933 on land given by Mrs. G. Haszard.[39] There is one old timber-framed cottage on the west side of Stockton Lane.

A timber-framed house, of which only the stone chimneys are still standing, formerly lay 200 yds. south of the present Brocton Hall. This may well have been the capital messuage held by Matthew Cradock in 1584;[40] its features suggest that it dates from the second half of the 16th century. It was later known as Brocton Farm. Drawings made in 1847 and 1849,[41] before the house was demolished, show a central block flanked by cross wings with overhanging gable-ends. There is a porch in the angle of the north wing and a massive chimney at the north end of the central block. The chimney, which is still in existence, has a stone base and brick shafts. On the ground floor are back-to-back fireplaces, one, in a good state of preservation, having a four-centred arch and a stone lintel enriched with late 16th-century ornament. The second standing chimney belonged to the kitchen and appears to have been on the back wall of the north wing. It retains a very long oak lintel and the remains of baking ovens. Both chimneys carry fireplaces on the upper story. In 1666 George Launder, then owner of the manor, was assessed for nine hearths.[42]

Brocton Hall, now the clubhouse of the Brocton Hall Golf Club, may incorporate an 18th-century house but dates largely from c. 1815. It has a fine circular entrance hall and a stone staircase with an iron balustrade. There is a semicircular colonnade to the bowed entrance front. The house formerly had three stories above the basement, but the top floor was damaged by fire in 1939[43] and has been largely removed. A pointed stone arch, not in situ, and two large carved gargoyles form a garden feature to the north of the park. Near the south-west corner of the park is an octagonal brick dovecot, probably dating from the late 18th or early 19th century. It is decorated externally with recessed panels in the form of pointed arches and quatrefoils.

Brocton Lodge, formerly Brocton Villa,[44] is a white stucco house with a Tuscan colonnade between flanking bays dating from the early 19th century. It lies on the west side of the road to Milford and originally formed part of the Brocton Hall estate.

The Cottage, Park Lane, is a small timber-framed house on a cruciform plan with a large central

[26] Ex inf. Mrs. G. Haszard, Milford Hall.
[27] Ex inf. Staffs. C.C. Planning Dept.
[28] Lich. Dioc. Regy., Bp's. Reg. Bk. V, pp. 660–4.
[29] Ex inf. Staffs. C.C. Planning Dept.
[30] Ex inf. Mr. J. J. Etridge, Vacuum Salt Works.
[31] Ex inf. Stafford Concrete Buildings Ltd.
[32] White, Dir. Staffs. (1851).
[33] S.H.C. 1950–1, 243.
[34] W.S.L., C.B. Baswich, copy of Bodl. MS. Ashmole 864, p. 15.
[35] H. L. Gray, English Field Systems (1915), 497.
[36] See p. 4.
[37] W.S.L., Staffs. Views, i, p. 147.
[38] Local inf.
[39] Ex inf. Mrs. Haszard.
[40] See p. 6.
[41] At Milford Hall.
[42] S.H.C. 1927, 26.
[43] Official Handbook, Brocton Hall Golf Club.
[44] Estate Map (1812–35) at Milford Hall.

chimney. A projecting wing in the centre of the front probably once formed its porch. This wing has exposed framing of quadrant and chevron design and is said formerly to have borne the date 1616.[45] The base of the central chimney is of stone and has back-to-back fireplaces serving the two bays of the central portion. Beyond the chimney is a staircase with flat wavy balusters. The kitchen wing at the rear, which has a lower roof line, was once a single-story structure. Moulded and curved posts at the farther end, interrupted by a large stone kitchen chimney, and a single curved windbrace suggest that this wing may have been an earlier hall, altered and shortened in 1616.

At Brocton Green there is a small nucleus of timber-framed houses dating from the 16th and early 17th centuries. Village Farm has a stone plinth and a timber-framed west wing with the date 1646 scratched in modern plaster at the gable-end. On the dividing wall between this wing and the brick-faced main block is a large stone and brick chimney with back-to-back fireplaces. Green Farm, a timber-framed structure, is now roughcast externally. The cottage on the corner of Oldacre Lane has exposed framing to the front consisting of square panels with straight braces. The eaves level has been raised. At the east gable-end is the base of a stone chimney, and the framing of the end truss is visible. Between this cottage and Green Farm is a timber-framed barn. On the corner of Chase Road is another partly timber-framed cottage. Bank Farm is a brick house dating from c. 1700.

Weeping Cross Inn at the junction of the Stafford–Lichfield and Stafford–Cannock roads was rebuilt or converted into a private residence known as the White House by John Stevenson Salt, probably soon after 1813.[46] About 1850 it was demolished, and Baswich House was built by Thomas Salt (d. 1871) on or near the site. It is an irregularly planned mansion of red brick with oriel windows of wood and many small gables, and is a good building of its period. A single-story picture gallery and a billiard room were added by Thomas's son Thomas (d. 1904).[47] The property was in use as a preparatory school before the Second World War. In 1952 it was acquired by the Staffordshire County Council for a Police Motor Training Centre.[48] Barnfields is a dignified red-brick house built by Samuel Twigg[49] early in the 19th century. The large stone barn to the south was already in existence and may be partly of 16th-century origin. This barn has been added to at various times and may incorporate stone from old Baswich church[50] (demolished 1740). At its northern end a game larder was added by John Twigg in 1841,[51] taking the form of a stone porch in the Norman style. Here, as elsewhere in the district, the garden contains dressed and carved stones, some of medieval origin, said to have come from St. Mary's Church, Stafford (restored in 1844–5). Weeping Cross House was built by a member of the Twigg

family[52] in the middle of the 19th century. The Shawms in Radford Rise is a good example of the domestic architecture of its time. It was built in 1905 by H. J. Bostock, the architect being Henry T. Sandy,[53] and has roughcast gables, stone mullioned windows, a steep roof, and battered chimneys.

Milford Hall is an 18th-century house enlarged in 1817 and later. The principal front, facing east, originally had a central doorway and Ionic pilasters supporting a pediment at eaves level.[54] Adjoining the south side is an orangery with five tall windows. The east front was altered in 1817 by Richard Levett, the pilasters and pediment being removed and the central block set forward. The entrance was moved to the west side and the window arrangement altered.[55] Further additions, including upper stories to a service wing at the rear, date from later in the 19th century. East of the house there is an ornamental water supplied by the former mill stream. Near its north end is a small brick bath house dating from c. 1803.[56] In front of the building an oval stone bathing pool, screened by high walls, was supplied by pipes from the stream. The garden contains a circular colonnaded summerhouse which is thought to have been built by the Revd. Richard Levett in the late 18th century. It may have been suggested to him by the 'temples' in West Wycombe Park (Bucks.). Ionic capitals, probably from the east front of the house, are preserved in the garden, together with medieval stone fragments believed to have come from St. Mary's Church, Stafford.

The Old Dame Coffee House forms the east range of a three-sided block of farm buildings opposite Milford Hall dating from c. 1800. It was used as a dame school until 1879, after which hot drinks were served there to wagon drivers and tramps.[57] Milford Lodge, the only other large house in the village, dates from the early 19th century. In the extreme north-east corner of the parish are twin lodges at one of the entrances to Shugborough Park. These were designed by Samuel Wyatt c. 1800 and are contemporary with the diversion of the Lichfield road.[58]

North-west of Milford station the Staffordshire and Worcestershire Canal is carried over the River Sow by a stone aqueduct of four segmental arches. It was first erected on the south bank of the river, the water course being diverted southwards as soon as the building was complete.[59]

Holdford Bridge is a narrow humped bridge with four segmental arches, probably dating from the 18th century. It is of stone ashlar, and its parapets terminate in square piers.

Sir William Congreve (1772–1828), Comptroller of the Royal Laboratory, Woolwich (1814–28), and inventor of the Congreve rocket and brimstone matches, lived at Congreve House, Walton.[60]

MANORS. *BASWICH* or *BERKSWICH* both before and after the Conquest was one of the manors of the bishopric. In 1086 it was assessed at 5 hides,

[45] Ex inf. the owner (1956).
[46] The inn was up for auction in that year: *Story of Berkswich*, compiled by Baswich Women's Institute (copy in W.S.L.), 5. For drawings of the White House see W.S.L., Staffs. Views, i, pp. 149–50.
[47] Ex inf. Mr. R. J. Salt.
[48] Ex inf. Chief Insp. R. N. Buxton.
[49] *Story of Berkswich*, 6.
[50] Ex inf. Dr. G. R. Rigby.
[51] Date over door.

[52] *Story of Berkswich*, 19.
[53] Ex inf. Mr. H. J. Bostock.
[54] Sketch at Milford Hall.
[55] Building Accounts and drawings at Milford Hall.
[56] Ibid.
[57] Ex inf. Mrs. Haszard.
[58] *Country Life*, Apr. 1954.
[59] Plan at Milford Hall.
[60] See p. 3; *D.N.B.*; *Story of Berkswich*, 30.

and with Walton, which belonged to it, was then valued at 15s., 5s. more than in King Edward's time.[61] Also belonging to it were the vills of Brocton and Bednall, then waste,[62] but by 1297 or 1298 they were dependent upon the manor of Haywood.[63] The manor of Baswich remained with the bishop until 1546.[64] It held its own courts until at least 1360,[65] but by 1473 was being administered as part of the bishop's manor of Haywood,[66] the courts of which were held until at least 1869.[67] The bishop surrendered Baswich, with other manors, in 1546 to the Crown in exchange for certain benefices.[68] The lands, which had formed the bishop's demesne manor of Baswich, were granted in the same year to Sir William Paget[69] with whose descendant, the Marquess of Anglesey, any surviving lordship remains.[70]

In 1893 the Marquess of Anglesey conveyed to Lord Lichfield 1,784 acres of uninclosed land on Cannock Chase lying in Baswich and Brocton together with all manorial rights, except the coal and mineral rights, over this land.[71] Consequently, after the dispersal of the Chetwynd estates in Brocton and elsewhere in 1921, Lord Lichfield is frequently referred to as lord of the manor of Brocton.[72] The land conveyed comprised Satnall Hills, Milford Common, Spring Hill, Oat Hill, Broc Hill, Brocton Coppice, Coppice Hill, Hollywood Slade, Sherbrook Banks, Dry Pits, Tar Hill, Old Acre Valley, Sycamore Hill, Brocton Field, Anson's Bank, and various pools. In 1956 Lord Lichfield conveyed all this land to the Staffordshire County Council.[73]

Land in Baswich was granted c. 1199 by Geoffrey de Muscamp, Bishop of Coventry and Lichfield, to Simon the cook who later granted all his land described as in Stockton to the nearby Priory of St. Thomas.[74] About 1272 Avice, widow of Peter of Brocton, gave to the same priory land known as 'Smithemore', part of her dower.[75] The lands of the priory in Baswich and elsewhere were granted in 1539 to Bishop Roland Lee,[76] who in 1540 settled them on his nephew Brian Fowler.[77] Brian Fowler also held the demesne lands of the manor of Baswich, the warren and a house situated at the Baswich end of Radford Bridge on a 90 years lease beginning 1539.[78] These Fowler lands although occasionally called the

manor of Baswich were subsequently usually referred to as the manors of SOWE and BROCTON.[79] On the death of Brian Fowler in 1587 they passed to his son Walter.[80] He died in 1621 and was succeeded by his son Edward,[81] who died in 1624 leaving as his heir a son Walter aged three years.[82] Walter Fowler was succeeded in 1681 by his son Walter[83] who died without male issue in 1684.[84] The lands then passed to his younger brother, William Fowler, who died without male issue in 1716.[85] Under a settlement of 1712 the estate then passed to John Betham, husband of Mary, daughter of Magdalen, youngest sister of William Fowler.[86] As John Betham Fowler[87] he died in 1719, and from then the lands were held in trust for his daughter Catherine, then aged nine, until her marriage with Viscount Fauconberg in 1726. In 1728 the beneficial interest was disputed by Robert Fitzgerald, his wife Rebecca, granddaughter of Dorothy, eldest sister of William Fowler, and the trustees.[88] The Fowler lands were finally partitioned in 1734, Baswich falling with the manor or lordship of Sowe and the capital messuage of St. Thomas to Lord Fauconberg, but by 1744 the lands south of the Sow in Baswich and Brocton had been acquired by Sarah Dowager Duchess of Marlborough, who in her will of that year disposed of them to her grandson John Spencer.[89] George Earl Spencer[90] transferred his interest in 1785 to George Anson of Shugborough (Pirehill hundred), the area conveyed being slightly more than 300 acres and the price £7,500.[91]

In 1086 Brocton was a member of the manor of Baswich.[92] By 1242 or 1243 Brocton formed with Bednall ¼ knight's fee then held of the bishop by John de Acton[93] of Acton Trussell. The overlordship of the bishop in Brocton continued until at least 1523.[94] The mesne lordship of the Trussells of Acton Trussell and their descendants in Brocton continued until at least 1569.[95]

In 1221 John de Acton granted a virgate of land and the capital messuage in Brocton to Avice and Benigna, daughters of Nicholas of Brocton, of which Bella their mother was to hold one-third, on condition that they relinquished their claim to another virgate.[96] In 1227 half of this other virgate was acquired by their brother John,[97] believed dead in 1221,[98] who had already successfully claimed the

[61] V.C.H. Staffs. iv. 41, no. 67.
[62] Ibid. no. 69.
[63] W.S.L., C.B. Baswich, copy of Bodl. MS. Ashmole 864, p. 15.
[64] S.H.C. 1939, 110–11.
[65] W.S.L., D. 1734, Ct. R. of manor of Haywood, 34 Edw. III.
[66] W.S.L., S. MS. 335/1, Compotus R. of Bpric of Cov. and Lich. Mich. 12–Mich. 13 Edw. IV, m. 15. The farm of demesne lands in Baswich is accounted for by the bailiff of Haywood.
[67] W.S.L., D. 1611, D. 1734.
[68] S.H.C. 1939, 110–11.   [69] Ibid. 111.
[70] Complete Peerage, i. 138–141; ibid. x. 276–289; W.S.L., D. 1734, Haywood Ct. Rolls and Bks., passim.
[71] Ex inf. Staffs. County Archivist (1955).
[72] Kelly's Dir. Staffs. (1924; 1928; 1932; 1940).
[73] Ex inf. Staffs. C.C. Planning Dept.
[74] S.H.C. viii (1), 142, 143.   [75] Ibid. 148.
[76] L. & P. Hen VIII, xiv (2), g. 435 (12).
[77] C 142/69, no. 119.
[78] W.S.L., D. 1734, Compotus of lands of William Paget 2–3 Edw. VI, Haywood manor.
[79] S.H.C. xvi. 166; C.P. 25(2)/486, 19 Chas. I East.; C.P. 25(2)/724, 18 Chas. II East.; C 142/393, no. 154; C 142/404, no. 126; C.P. 43/238, rot. 46.

[80] C 142/216, no. 21.   [81] C 142/393, no. 134.
[82] C 142/404, no. 126.
[83] S.H.C. v (2), 136.
[84] Berkswich w. Walton Par. Reg. 50.
[85] S.H.C. v (2), 137.
[86] Appeals to the House of Lords, 1730, Fauconberg v. FitzGerald.
[87] He assumed the name Fowler under the terms of the settlement.
[88] Appeals to the House of Lords, 1730, Fauconberg v. FitzGerald.
[89] W.S.L., Hand Morgan Coll., Anson Papers, Abstract of Title of Lord Spenser to Wm. Fowler's Estate in Baswich; S.R.O., D. 260/M, box 12, bdle. b.
[90] Grandson of John Spencer: Complete Peerage, vii. 153–5.
[91] W.S.L., Hand Morgan Coll. Anson, Papers, Spencer title.
[92] V.C.H. Staffs. iv. 41, no. 69.
[93] Bk. of Fees, 969.
[94] W.S.L., C.B. Baswich, Copy of Bodl. MS. Ashmole 864, p. 15.
[95] C 142/152, no. 149.
[96] S.H.C. iv. 221.
[97] Ibid. 43, 65.
[98] Ibid. 221.

previous virgate from his sisters after his return from overseas.[99] This was probably the estate[1] granted by Thomas, son of Peter lord of Brocton, to Roger de Aston in 1295,[2] sometimes but doubtfully called the manor of *BROCTON*. Roger de Aston, still living in 1306 or 1307,[3] was succeeded by John de Aston who was dead before 1353.[4] His son and heir, Roger de Aston, died before 1364 or 1365[5] leaving as his heir a son Thomas, then under age and in ward to William de Chetwynd and his wife Isabel, formerly wife of Roger de Aston.[6] Thomas Aston had been succeeded by Roger Aston, probably his son, before 1413.[7] Roger Aston died in 1447 or 1448[8] and was succeeded by Robert Aston who died in 1467.[9] His heir, John Aston, died seised of lands and tenements in Brocton in 1484[10] and was succeeded by his son John who died in 1523, when his tenements in Brocton were assigned as dower to his widow Joan,[11] daughter of Sir James Littleton,[12] who died in 1526.[13] The Brocton lands then passed to her son Edward Aston who died in 1569, leaving to his son and heir Walter tenements and messuages in Brocton.[14] In 1584 Walter Aston settled on his son and heir Edward what may have been this manor of Brocton.[15]

In 1544 or 1545 Thomas Cradock of Stafford purchased from Stephen Ward 2 messuages and 60 acres of land, 10 acres of pasture and 6s. rent in Brocton.[16] His son Matthew at his death in 1584 held a capital messuage in Brocton of the heirs of Thomas son of Peter of Brocton,[17] presumably acquired therefore from the Aston family. This fell to Francis, younger son of Matthew Cradock, and on his death in 1594 to his son Edward.[18] By 1611 it had reverted to the senior branch of the Cradock family,[19] being held at his death in that year by George Cradock of Caverswall, eldest son of Matthew, and then described as 'a capital messuage in Brocton called Brocton Hall, 3 other messuages, 3 cottages, 1 dovecot, 130 acres of land in Brocton' held of William Lord Paget in fee and common socage.[20] In 1638 it was conveyed by this George Cradock to Thomas Aston and John Saunders.[21] By 1679 the owners were George and Elizabeth Lander who conveyed what was described as the manor to William Milward,[22] a step in the process of sale to Walter Chetwynd of Ingestre (Pirehill hundred).[23] In 1692 Walter Chetwynd left the manor of Brocton

to Walter, son of Richard Chetwynd of Rugeley,[24] with whose descendants, a junior line of the Grendon and Rugeley branch of the Chetwynds,[25] the land remained until the sales between 1920 and 1922.[26] In 1851 William Fawkener Chetwynd owned 700 acres in Brocton.[27] In 1920 the Brocton Hall Estate consisted of 834 acres, the rental being £1,831 4s. 6d.; 131 acres were attached to Brocton Hall and 21 acres to Brocton Lodge, and there were six farms, namely Bednall Farm (75 a.), Brocton Gate Farm (68 a.), Road Farm (156 a.), Cottage Farm (15 a.), Brocton Bank Farm (131 a.), and Village Farm (129 a.).[28] The major part of the estate was then sold by Mrs. Mary Chetwynd, the farms mainly to the tenants.[29] Brocton Hall with its land was sold a short while afterwards to the Brocton Hall Golf Club,[30] the course being laid out in 1923 and the Hall used as the club house.[31]

LESSER ESTATES. In 1474 or 1475 a so-called manor of Haseley was in dispute between Robert and Humphrey Barbour, sons of John Barbour of Stafford who had died seised of it.[32] Robert Barbour at his death on 25 February 1531 or 1532 was seised of half a virgate of land and houses in Baswich called Haseley held of the Bishop of Lichfield and valued at 40s.[33] In 1732 Haseley manor or farm lying south-south-east of Radford Bridge was owned by Richard Drakeford.[34] An 18th-century brick barn still stands near the site of Haseley manor-house, south-south-east of Radford Bridge and 150 yds. east of the canal.

Milford Hall formed part of the estate of Ellen and Lucy Byrd, daughters and coheirs of John Byrd, in 1771 on the marriage of Lucy to the Revd. Richard Levett, Vicar of West Wycombe (Bucks.), in which county the Byrds also had estates.[35] In 1810 there were 43 acres attached to Milford Hall. By private act the entail was cut, and the Byrd lands in Shropshire, Cheshire, and Buckinghamshire were subsequently sold,[36] the proceeds being invested in land in Baswich and in extending Milford Hall.[37] By c. 1830 the Levetts had acquired land in Brocton, mostly lying immediately south of the present Brocton Hall, and including the site of the old Brocton Hall.[38] This was exchanged with Sir George Chetwynd (d. 1869) for the Barley Mow Inn, Milford, in 1849. Between 1900 and 1929 Capt. W. S. B.

[99] *S.H.C.* iv. 225.
[1] In 1568 the Aston estate in Brocton was said to be held of Edward Earl of Oxford as of his manor of Acton Trussell: Clifford, *Tixall* (1817), 251.
[2] B.M. Harl. MS. 506, pp. 226, 227.
[3] *S.H.C.* xii (1), 287.
[4] Ibid. 119.
[5] Ibid. 134.
[6] Ibid. 257.
[7] Ibid. xvii. 47.
[8] Clifford, *Tixall*, 146.
[9] Ibid. 147.
[10] C 141/2.
[11] C 142/40, no. 132.
[12] Clifford, *Tixall*, 147.
[13] C 142/45, no. 53.
[14] C 142/152, no. 149.
[15] C 142/222, no. 43. It may, however, have been the Aston manor of Brocton or Broughton (in Longdon) which occurs as late as 1629: C.P. 25(2)/484, 5 Chas. I Mich.
[16] *S.H.C.* xi. 287.
[17] C 142/239, no. 97.
[18] Ibid.
[19] *S.H.C.* 1920, 6.
[20] C 142/337, no. 83.

[21] W.S.L. 74/50.
[22] C.P. 25(2)/484, 3 Chas. I Trin.
[23] Walter Chetwynd's will recites the purchase: *S.H.C.* 1920 and 1922, 125.
[24] Ibid.
[25] Burke, *Peerage* (1949), 398; C.P. 43/622, rot. 417; C.P. 43/724, rot. 33.
[26] Ex inf. Messrs. Hand, Morgan, and Owen, Solrs., Stafford.
[27] Ibid.
[28] Sale Catalogue *penes* Messrs. Hand, Morgan, and Owen.
[29] Ex inf. Messrs. Hand, Morgan, and Owen.
[30] Ibid.
[31] Local inf.
[32] *S.H.C.* n.s. vii. 269.
[33] C 142/52, no. 45.
[34] W.S.L., Map 12/30.
[35] Pedigree of the Byrd family, *penes* Mrs. G. Haszard, Milford Hall.
[36] Act for vesting and selling estates in the Counties of Stafford, Salop., Chester and Buckingham, late of Revd. Richard Levett, Lucy his wife and Ellen Byrd, spinster, 50 Geo. III, c. lxxx (priv. act).
[37] Estate papers, *penes* Mrs. Haszard.
[38] Estate map, *penes* Mrs. Haszard.

Levett extended the estate to nearly 1,000 acres. He was succeeded by his daughter Mrs. Gerald Haszard, in 1956 still the owner of the estate, which was then about 600 acres and comprised Stockton, Walton, and the Home Farms.[39]

MILLS. In 1279 18d. was accounted for by the bailiff of Baswich for the carrying of the mill stones to the mill.[40] In 1472 there was a water-mill and a fulling mill at Baswich.[41] In 1732, although the mill had disappeared, its site was identified as on the River Penk about half a mile west of Radford Bridge.[42] There is considerable evidence that there was formerly a mill in what are now the grounds of Milford Hall. About 1845 a field south of the park was known as 'Mill Dam Field',[43] and traces of a water-wheel have been found at the upper end of the lake.[44] A small red-brick building 100 yds. south-west of Brocton Hall stands above the stream and is said to have been a mill. A field west of the park was known at one time as Mill Croft.[45]

CHURCHES. There was a priest on the bishop's manor of Baswich in 1086.[46] By 1255 at the latest the benefice had been appropriated to the prebend of Baswich in Lichfield Cathedral and was then subject to the peculiar jurisdiction of the prebendary.[47] Dependent chapels of Baswich were founded in Acton Trussell and Bednall during the Middle Ages,[48] a chantry chapel existed in Brocton by 1549, and mission churches were established from Baswich at Walton and Brocton in 1842 and 1890 respectively (see below).

The income of the prebend from the rectorial tithes and incidents of Baswich in 1291 was £20.[49] At some time between 1529 and 1532 the right to the great tithes of Baswich, which had been leased by Richard Egerton, Prebendary of Baswich, to Edmond Warde, was being disputed by the Prior of St. Thomas, apparently unsuccessfully.[50] In 1535 the income of the prebend of Whittington and Baswich from tithes and other spiritual emoluments was £13 6s. 8d.[51]

A vicarage had been ordained by the time of Bishop Roger de Meuland (1258–95), and in 1341 the Bishop of Coventry and Lichfield successfully claimed the right of presentation.[52] In 1407 the advowson was granted to the Prior and Convent of

St. Thomas, a pension of 20d. being reserved.[53] In 1539, after the dissolution of St. Thomas's Priory, the canons' rights in the church of Baswich with its dependent chapels were granted to Bishop Roland Lee.[54] On his death in 1542 they passed to Brian Fowler his nephew.[55] The advowson of what was by the 18th century called a perpetual curacy[56] and only again in 1867 a vicarage[57] remained with the Fowler family of Brocton[58] and their descendants[59] until 1912,[60] when the Revd. (later the Very Revd.) W. R. Inge and J. H. H. V. Lane, then the alternate patrons, transferred the advowson to the bishop.[61]

In 1535 the income of the vicarage was £5 6s. 8d.[62] Mrs. C. B. Inge of Oxford, by will proved 1931, left £800 for the augmentation of the income of the minister of Baswich with Walton.[63] By 1933 the incumbent received £67 10s. a year from this source.[64]

Miss S. J. Smith, by will proved 1938, left £100 to the Vicar and Churchwardens of Baswich for keeping the graveyard in good order; this has been invested in stock.[65] Sermons are still preached by the Vicar of Baswich under the terms of the Twigg Charity at Christmas and Easter for which he receives 10s.[66]

A chapel at Brocton, mentioned as 'one wherein service was sometimes kept and sometimes not', was standing in 1549,[67] but the site is unknown. Chantry lands consisting of 2 messuages and a garden, belonging to the late chapel of Brocton, were granted in the same year to Roger Ackroyd, Geoffrey Harrison, and Thomas Burnet.[68]

A mission church was erected in Brocton in 1890,[69] and in 1951 was dedicated to All Saints.[70]

The church of HOLY TRINITY, Baswich, which is of 12th-century origin, was largely rebuilt in 1740.[71] It consists of a chancel with a porch on its north side, a nave slightly wider than the chancel, and a west tower. It retains good Georgian features internally, including two double-tier family pews which occupy most of the chancel and a three-decker pulpit.

The earliest parts of the church are the jambs of the chancel arch and the footings of the external east wall both of which date from the 12th century. Late-12th- or early-13th-century masonry is also visible above the chancel arch on its east side. The north jamb of the arch has a circular shaft and

[39] Ex inf. Mrs. Haszard.
[40] Lichfield D. and C. MSS., N. 1.
[41] W.S.L., S. MS. 335/1, Compotus R. of Bpric. of Cov. and Lich., Mich. 12–Mich. 13 Edw. IV, m. 15.
[42] W.S.L., Map 12/30.
[43] Tithe Maps and Appt., Baswich (copy in W.S.L.).
[44] Ex inf. Col. Haszard.
[45] Tithe Maps and Appt., Baswich (copy in W.S.L.).
[46] V.C.H. Staffs. iv. 41, no. 67.
[47] Dugd. Mon. vi. 1245. Of the prebendal churches mentioned in the confirmatory charter of Bishop Robert de Weseham that of Baswich was assigned to the prebendaries: S.H.C. 1924, no. 24.
[48] See pp. 15, 16.
[49] Tax. Eccl. (Rec. Com.), 247.
[50] C 1/688, no. 33. In 1535 the income of the vicarage of Baswich did not include the great tithes: Valor Eccl. (Rec. Com.), iii. 112.
[51] Ibid. iii. 130.
[52] S.H.C. xi. 117.
[53] Cal. Pat. 1405–8, 445; S.H.C. viii. 143.
[54] L. & P. Hen. VIII, xiv, p. 156.
[55] C 142/69, no. 119.
[56] W.S.L. 11/41; Berkswich w. Walton Par. Reg. 140;

Ecton, Thesaurus (1742), 114.
[57] Lich. Dioc. Ch. Cal. (1867).
[58] C 142/216, no. 21; C 142/393, no. 154; C 142/404, no. 126; Berkswich w. Walton Par. Reg. 77, 140.
[59] Berkswich w. Walton Par. Reg. 1. In 1857 it lay with J. N. Lane Esq. and Revd. C. Inge alternately: Lich. Dioc. Ch. Cal. (1857).
[60] In 1911 the patrons were still the Rev. W. R. Inge and J. H. H. V. Lane: Lich. Dioc. Ch. Cal. (1911). In 1912 the bishop was patron: ibid. (1912).
[61] Note by W. R. Inge in The Story of Berkswich, compiled by Baswich Women's Inst., 11.
[62] Valor Eccl. (Rec. Com.), iii. 112.
[63] Charity Com. files.
[64] Ibid.
[65] Ibid.
[66] See p. 11.
[67] S.H.C. 1915, 25.
[68] Cal. Pat. 1549–51, 127–8.
[69] Kelly's Dir. Staffs. (1940).
[70] Ex inf. the Vicar of Baswich (1956).
[71] Berkswich w. Walton Par. Reg. 1, is incorrect in stating that it had been burnt down: see p. 8.

curious superimposed capitals, one of which is probably reset. The lower capital is circular, the upper is of a crude Corinthian type with a cable moulding below it. The square abacus is chamfered along its lower edge. The south jamb has been cut back and has no distinctive features.

windows in the east and south walls. The east gable of the nave is truncated, and the roof line is evidently lower than that of the medieval church.[76] The belfry stage of the tower was rebuilt in stone, each face having a round-headed window. It terminates in a straight parapet which formerly carried urns at the

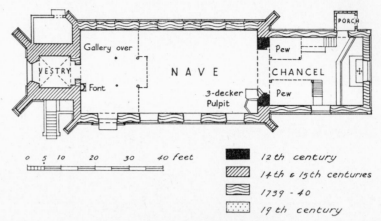

0 5 10 20 30 40 feet

12th century
14th & 15th centuries
1739 - 40
19th century

PLAN OF HOLY TRINITY CHURCH

The church appears to have been extensively altered in the 14th century, the east and west walls of the nave, both with angle buttresses, and the pointed chancel arch being of this period. The lower stages of the tower, also with angle buttresses, are of 14th- or 15th-century masonry. The blocked west doorway, the window above it, and the string-course are of Perpendicular type.

In 1733 Quarter Sessions authorized an application for a brief for rebuilding.[72] The precedent certificate described the walls as bulging at the foundations, the roof rotted and in danger of falling in, and the steeple, being too high and too heavy for its foundations, as held with iron cramps. In 1739 an agreement was made with Richard Trubshaw and Richard Jackson, builders, to undertake the work of pulling down and rebuilding the church and steeple.[73] Their account for £336 was settled in 1742.[74] It may be assumed that Richard Trubshaw (1689–1745), master builder and quarry owner of Haywood,[75] was responsible for the design. The east and west walls of the nave and the base of the tower were left standing; the other walls were demolished to ground level and rebuilt in brick above a few courses of stone laid on the old foundations. The south nave wall has three round-headed windows with brick aprons and plain stone archivolts with key-blocks. There is a stone band at impost level and a moulded cornice. The square-headed south doorway, above which is a circular window, has rusticated jambs and voussoirs. In the north wall are four round-headed openings with blind panels below and semicircular lights above. The chancel has rusticated quoins and single round-headed

four corners.[77] A branching external stair gives access to the ringing-chamber and to the west gallery of the nave. The base of the tower, used as a vestry, is entered from the church by an 18th-century doorway. In 1771 the roof was retiled at a cost of £18, and the vestry was repaired and whitewashed.[78]

Many of the interior fittings, including the three-decker pulpit,[79] the altar rails, the original west gallery, and the small font against the west wall of the nave date from the 18th-century rebuilding. The lower stage of the pew on the south side of the chancel, formerly belonging to the Chetwynds of Brocton Hall, is probably of the same period. In 1812 a faculty was granted to Richard Levett of Milford Hall for erecting a two-tiered pew on the north side of the chancel for the accommodation of his family and servants.[80] The 16th-century altar tomb of Brian Fowler was cut away to give room for its staircase. The upper stage of the Chetwynd pew opposite, which is fitted with a fireplace, is similar in style and is of the same date.[81] Also early in the 19th century an eastward extension was made to the west gallery.[82] In 1894 a new lychgate in the churchyard was given by Mrs. Spooner, mother-in-law of the Revd. F. G. Inge, in memory of her husband.[83] A new altar was presented and alterations made to the chancel in 1899; the north door was raised and a wooden porch outside it rebuilt in brick at the expense of Capt. Levett.[84] In 1900 the nave was repewed, the chancel arch scraped and heating installed.[85] The chancel ceiling was removed in 1935 and the roof timbers exposed.[86] Electric lighting was installed in 1953, and a portable oak font was introduced in 1956.[87] The Royal Arms of George III

[72] Copy of application in parish safe.
[73] S.R.O., D. 114/A/PC 1.
[74] W.S.L., S. MS. 436, loose sheets inserted pp. 167–8.
[75] H. M. Colvin, *Biog. Dict. of Eng. Architects*, 627–8.
[76] Weather marks visible on tower and nave walls.
[77] W.S.L., Staffs. Views, i, pp. 147–8 (1831, 1841).
[78] S.R.O., D. 114/A/PC 1.
[79] See plate opposite.
[80] *Penes* Mrs. G. Haszard, Milford Hall.
[81] Copy of Faculty of Dec. 1812 in parish safe.

[82] The original gallery front is in position behind the front seats.
[83] *Lich. Dioc. Mag.* (1894), 204.
[84] Ibid. (1899), 47.
[85] Ibid. (1900), 197; Lich. Dioc. Regy., Consist. Ct. Act Bk. 1899–1903, p. 115, faculty 31 Aug. 1900.
[86] Lich. Dioc. Regy., Consist. Ct. Act Bk. 1934–8, p. 120, faculty 13 June 1935.
[87] Ex inf. the vicar (1956).

BASWICH: Georgian fittings in the church

BREWOOD: Tombs of Sir Thomas Giffard (d. 1560) and John Giffard (d. 1615)

Cannock Chase from Broc Hill

Sherbrook Valley

hang on the north nave wall. Nearby is a marble tablet inscribed with details of the Twigg and Harding charities. Stained glass in the east window was inserted in 1935 in memory of William S. B. Levett (d. 1929). A south window contains stained glass given in 1950 by Eleanora and H. J. Bostock.

The oldest memorial is an altar tomb against the north chancel wall dated 1587 and inscribed to Brian, son of Roger Fowler, and his wife Joan. The angle pilasters have Renaissance ornament and the top bears a cross moline. The sides and front of the tomb have rows of shields bearing the arms of various families impaled with Fowler.[88] Nearby is a wall tablet erected in 1700 by William Fowler commemorating members of his family and Mr. Daniel Fitter, 'his virtuous friend'; also one in memory of William Fowler (d. 1716/17), his wife Catherine, and others. Above the Levett pew is a tablet to William Swynnerton Byrd Levett (d. 1929) and a cartouche on which his initials and those of his wife are entwined. Above the Chetwynd pew are several uniform tablets to members of the family including Walter Chetwynd (d. 1750), William Chetwynd (d. 1778), George Chetwynd (d. 1824), and William Fawkener Chetwynd (d. 1873). Elsewhere in the church are tablets in memory of Joseph Ellerton, (d. 1856) and Francis George Inge (d. 1923), vicars.

In the earlier 19th century vicars of Baswich were living at Weeping Cross.[89] When St. Thomas's Church was built at Walton in 1842 a house was already in existence on the adjoining site.[90] It was enlarged and converted into a vicarage soon afterwards.[91]

In 1553 there was a silver chalice with paten, two candlesticks, and a latten cross at Baswich church.[92] The plate included in 1956 a flagon, a two-handled cup, a paten and a salver, all Sheffield plate, purchased by the inhabitants of Baswich in 1798; a silver almsdish, 1809, the gift of Richard Byrd Levett in 1843; a silver chalice, undated, and a silver paten, both marked I.J.K.; a silver chalice with three garnets in knop, 1916, given in memory of Algernon Harold Baillie; a silver paten, 1917–18, given in memory of Aubrey Norman and Basil Norman, grandsons of William Grindley of Weeping Cross; a silver flagon and lid, a silver chalice, undated;[93] a silver chalice and paten given in memory of Norman Jones, 1956.[94]

In 1553 there were three bells and one little bell.[95] There are now three bells: (i) cast by John of Stafford, early 14th century, inscribed 'In Onore Sancte Trenete'; (ii) early 14th century, inscribed 'Missi decelis [sic] vos salvet vox Gabrielis'; (iii) 1591, Henry Oldfield of Nottingham.[96]

The registers date from 1601. Those for 1601–1812 are printed.[97]

The church of *ST. THOMAS*, Walton, was built in 1842 as a chapel-of-ease to Baswich. The architect was Thomas Trubshaw[98] (1802–42), and the Early English style of the building is said to have been suggested by Thomas Salt of Weeping Cross.[99] It is a small cruciform church built of purple brick with stone dressings. The base of the tower, in the west angle of the north transept, serves as a porch. Access to the west gallery of the nave is obtained by a projecting turret at the south-west corner of the church. The tower formerly had a stone spire, but this was struck by lightning and destroyed in 1845.[1] It was replaced by the existing tall lead-covered spire.

Internally there is an open hammer-beam roof to the chancel and a king-post roof to the nave. The font is of stone and the pulpit of stone and coloured marble. The pierced alabaster chancel screen was presented in 1888,[2] and the carved oak reredos was erected in 1889 in memory of Col. Richard Byrd Levett.[3] In 1919 the north transept was converted into a war memorial chapel,[4] the architect being Cecil Hare.[5] A stained-glass window, said to be by Pugin, in memory of the Revd. Richard and Louisa Frances Levett was moved to the chapel from the south side of the church.[6] Other windows commemorate R. B. Levett (d. 1888), Mary Hitchings (d. 1922), Herbert T. and Edith Mary Allsopp (inserted 1937), and Major H. Pye (d. 1944). Electric light was installed in 1934.[7] The oak altar rails were presented in 1945 in memory of the Revd. Gerard Hitchings, late incumbent.[8] In 1956 a new organ was installed in the west gallery, the former instrument having been removed from a small organ chamber at the side of the chancel.[9]

On the south nave wall is a marble tablet in memory of the Revd. Richard Levett (d. 1843) and Louisa Frances, his wife (d. 1864). There are also tablets to Lt. Richard B. Wilton (d. 1917) and Lt. M. A. McFerran (d. 1918). An altar tomb bearing a recumbent effigy in alabaster in memory of Lt. Richard Byrd Levett (d. 1917) is placed at the entrance to the north transept.[10] Above it is a bronze Madonna and Child by Albert Roze. The carved oak canopy, designed by Cecil Hare, was added when the transept became a memorial chapel in 1919.[11] Other tablets in the church commemorate William Morgan of Walton Lodge (d. 1924), Herbert T. Allsopp and his wife Edith Mary (d. 1920 and 1935), and Louisa Mary and Evelyn Honora Levett (d. 1939 and 1946).

The plate consists of a silver chalice and paten

[88] For details of heraldry see *Trans. Birm. Arch. Soc.* lxix. 13.
[89] Parson and Bradshaw, *Dir. Staffs.* (1818); White, *Dir. Staffs.* (1834; 1851).
[90] Tithe Maps and Appt., Baswich (copy in W.S.L.).
[91] Ex inf. the vicar (1956).
[92] *S.H.C.* 1915, 24.
[93] Ex inf. the Archdeacon of Stafford (1956).
[94] Ex inf. the vicar (1956).
[95] *S.H.C.* 1915, 24.
[96] C. Lynam, *Church Bells of Staffs.* 3 and plates 11, 12, 13, 14, 43, 44; A. E. Garbett, 'Church Bells of Staffs.' (*Trans. Old Stafford Soc.* 1953–4), 8, 9, 31.
[97] Staffs. Par. Reg. Soc. 1905.
[98] *Illus. Lond. News*, 24 May 1845. He was a great-grandson of Richard Trubshaw, builder of Baswich church.

[99] W.S.L. 89/50; *Story of Berkswich*, 35.
[1] *Illus. Lond. News*, 24 May 1845.
[2] *Lich. Dioc. Ch. Cal.* (1889), 160.
[3] Lich. Dioc. Regy., Consist. Ct. Act Bk. 1879–91, p. 588, faculty 15 Jan. 1889.
[4] Ibid. 1914–20, p. 361, faculty 8 Jan. 1919.
[5] *Story of Berkswich*, 37.
[6] Ibid.
[7] Lich. Dioc. Regy., Consist. Ct. Act Bk. 1934–8, p. 62, faculty 13 Dec. 1934.
[8] Ibid. 1938–47, p. 369, faculty 12 May 1945.
[9] *Stafford Newsletter*, 3 Nov. 1956.
[10] Lich. Dioc. Regy., Consist. Ct. Act Bk. 1914–20, p. 267, faculty 9 Nov. 1917.
[11] Ibid. p. 361, faculty 8 Jan. 1919.

given in memory of Marjorie Gibson, 1916.[12] There is one bell, 1842, Thomas Mears.[13]

There are no remains of the ancient chapel at Brocton, but field names occurring c. 1845 north of the lane to Walton may indicate its approximate position.[14] The present church of All Saints is a plain rectangular brick building erected as a mission room in 1891 at a cost of £200.[15] It was dedicated to *ALL SAINTS* by the Bishop of Lichfield in 1951 and enlarged by the addition of a south bay in 1955. The crucifix above the altar dates from 1951, and the oak pews, of local workmanship, date from between 1950 and 1956.[16]

The plate consists of a silver chalice and paten given in memory of Mrs. Mary Chetwynd, 1951, and a modern brass alms dish.[17] In 1553 there was one bell and ornaments worth 16*d.* in the chapel at Brocton.[18] There is one modern bell in the present chapel.

NONCONFORMITY. In 1690 the house of James Twigg of 'Baswidge' was certified as a nonconformist place of worship under the Toleration Act.[19] In 1812 the house of a Mr. Browne at Walton on the Hill[20] and in 1826 the house of Thomas Saint were registered as meeting-houses for nonconformists.[21]

PRIMARY SCHOOLS. Dorothy Bridgeman (d. 1697), widow of Sir Orlando Bridgeman of Weston under Lizard (d. 1671) and formerly wife of George Cradock of Caverswall and Brocton Hall,[22] by will dated 10 January 1694 (or 1695), left two-tenths of £200 towards the schooling of poor children of Brocton.[23] It was possibly not until 1726, as in the case of her similar bequest to Castle Church,[24] that the money was made available.[25] Land in Baswich parish known as School Leasow and two doles in the 'town hills' believed to have been bought for this charity and let before 1778 for £2 10*s.*, paid for the schooling of six children; after the raising of the rent in 1778 to £3 a seventh child was taught, and from about 1800 to at least 1823, when the rent was £6 6*s.*, nine poor children were sent to a mistress in Brocton who taught the boys to read and the girls to read and sew.[26] The attendance at this private school on the day of inspection in 1871 was five boys and seven girls.[27]

All these charity lands have been sold, some part to the Staffordshire and Worcestershire Canal Co., by whom a rent-charge of 14*s.* 8*d.* was still paid in 1905; some to the Trent Valley Railway Co.; and

the rest under Orders of the Charity Commissioners of 1894 and 1895 and of the Board of Education of 1903.[28] The proceeds of sale and accumulated income, by 1905 invested in £369 4*s.* 2*d.* stock, produced an income of £18 4*s.* 4*d.* which was 'applied towards the remuneration of a school dame'.[29]

There is no longer a school in Brocton, but the charity, which is administered by a scheme under the Charitable Trusts Acts, may be applied partly for the benefit of children resident in Brocton parish and attending a public elementary school, either in providing facilities for conveyance to school or in providing spectacles or surgical appliances or other aids to health; partly in helping such children towards higher education, by payment of fees and travelling or maintenance allowances, or alternatively in otherwise promoting the education of the boys and girls of the poorer classes in Brocton.[30] The annual income in 1954 was £41 16*s.* 4*d.* interest on stock and 8*s.* 1*d.* from Docks and Inland Waterways.[31]

Another dame school was founded at Milford by Richard Levett of Milford Hall and his wife Louisa, niece of Lord Bagot, who were married in 1804.[32] Elizabeth Dean, schoolmistress, was a resident of Milford by 1834.[33] The Levett family continued to finance the school, providing even the girls' dresses which, within the memory of those living in 1949, were grey and white gingham with goffered white linen tippets for summer and red and black plaid for winter, with scarlet cloaks and hoods.[34] The children were taught reading, writing, and arithmetic, the youngest prepared wool for the older girls to spin, and both boys and girls knitted their own stockings. This little dame school closed down in 1879 on the death of Mrs. Betty Dean.[35]

A National school for boys and girls of Baswich parish was built at Walton on the Hill in 1838, with a house for the master and mistress.[36] It received an annual parliamentary grant from 1855.[37] From at least 1865 the standard of work seems to have been very low, and a reduction of the government grant was threatened in 1872.[38] Attendance between 1863 and 1894 was irregular,[39] being about 50 in 1871.[40] After the appointment of William and Annie Longson as master and mistress in 1893, the school began to improve.[41] By 1894, when average attendance was 105,[42] it had probably already absorbed the infant school. This, founded in Walton c. 1860 in a building adapted from several cottages and supported entirely by Miss Salt of Weeping Cross, had places for 40 children and an average attendance

[12] Ex inf. the vicar (1956).
[13] Lynam, *Church Bells of Staffs.* 31.
[14] 'Chapel Hill' and 'Chapel Leasows': Tithe Maps and Appt., Baswich (copy in W.S.L.), nos. 128, 129, and 130.
[15] *Lich. Dioc. Ch. Cal.* (1892), 172.
[16] Ex inf. the vicar (1956).
[17] Ex inf. the vicar (1956).
[18] *S.H.C.* 1915, 25.
[19] A. G. Matthews, *Cong. Churches of Staffs.* 125; S.R.O., Q/SM 1, Ep. 1 Wm. and Mary.
[20] S.R.O., Q/SB, Ep. 1812.
[21] Lich. Dioc. Regy., Bp's Reg. Bk. H, p. 57.
[22] *S.H.C.* N.S. ii. 248, 249, and pedigree facing p. 238.
[23] *Staffs. Endowed Char. Elem. Educ.* [Cd. 2729], p. 13, H.C. (1906), xc.
[24] See p. 98.
[25] *Staffs. End. Char.* 13, 112–13, citing decree of 20 June 1726.
[26] *11th Rep. Com. Char.*, H.C. 433, p. 508 (1824), xiv, where the benefactress is referred to as 'Mrs.' Dorothy Bridgeman.

[27] *Returns relating to Elem. Educ.*, H.C. 201, pp. 358–9 (1871), lv.
[28] *Staffs. End. Char.* 14.
[29] Ibid.
[30] Ex inf. Mr. H. J. Bostock (1954).
[31] Ex inf. Mr. Bostock.
[32] *Story of Berkswich*, 45.
[33] White, *Dir. Staffs.* (1834; 1851).
[34] *Story of Berkswich*, 49; local inf.
[35] *Story of Berkswich*, 49.
[36] White, *Dir. Staffs.* (1851); *P.O. Dir. Staffs.* (1854; 1868).
[37] *Mins. of Educ. Cttee. of Council, 1855* [2058], p. 148, H.C. (1956), xlvi.
[38] *Story of Berkswich*, 33, quoting from School Log Book, 1863–94.
[39] Ibid. 33.
[40] *Returns relating to Elem. Educ.*
[41] *Story of Berkswich*, 34.
[42] *Returns of Schools, 1893* [C. 7529], pp. 538–9, H.C. (1894), lxv.

in 1884 of 20.[43] The National school building was enlarged in 1894 and again in 1907.[44] It had an average attendance of 93 boys and girls and 52 infants in 1910.[45] There were 129 in the school in 1931, when it was limited to junior children and infants, the seniors being transferred to Stafford borough.[46] It became a controlled school in 1949[47] and is now Baswich Church of England Voluntary Primary (Controlled) School (Junior Mixed and Infants).[48] The average attendance in 1955 was 150 children.[49]

The interest on a sum of £35, being the surplus of 'The Revd. Joseph Ellerton Memorial Fund', was assigned in 1891 for the provision of rewards, at Christmas, for 'the best conducted children at Berkswich National School.'[50] In 1918 the principal was used to buy £37 0s. 1d. stock, and in 1954 the income, £1 5s. 10d., was still spent on school prizes.[51]

CHARITIES FOR THE POOR. Dorothy Bridgeman (d. 1697)[52] left to the poor of Brocton township land there which was yielding 10s. in 1786[53] and 20s. in 1823. The income in 1823 was distributed on St. Thomas's Day (21 Dec.) in sums of 2s. 6d. or 3s. among the poorest parishioners in the township.[54] This charity was subsequently lost.

Thomas Twist of Walton, by will of 1683, left £10, the interest to be spent on cloth for the poor of the liberty of Walton, i.e. all the parish except Brocton township.[55] In 1786 the interest was 8s.[56] and from at least 1816 10s. which was laid out in flannel given away at a vestry meeting in October.[57] The annual income, 7s. 4d., was being paid to the poor in cash in 1954.[58]

George Baddeley of Weeping Cross, by will dated 1717, gave a rent of 6s. charged on land at Weeping Cross to be distributed in bread to the poor of Walton liberty on Palm Sunday and on the first Sunday of each of the following two months.[59] Payment had ceased some years before 1823, and attempts then made to recover the charity seem to have been unsuccessful.[60]

Roger Twigg of Walton, by will of 1726, left £40, the interest to provide 'bread-corn' for the poor of Walton constablewick on 25 March and at Midsummer, Michaelmas, and Christmas.[61] On Roger's death in 1733[62] the £40 passed to his brother Samuel, who, by will of October, charged two closes with a rent of 32s., being interest at 4 per cent on £40. Samuel added a rent of 40s. of which 8s. was to be added to the four distributions laid down in his brother's will, 10s. was to be paid to the minister at Baswich for sermons on St. Thomas's Day and Good Friday, 10s. was to be distributed in 'household bread' on these two days at the church and the remaining 12s. was to be given away in 'penny bread' on the first Sunday of every month.[63] By 1823 £2 was distributed in bread-corn to twelve of the poorest in the constablewick of Walton, most of them widows, 10s. in sixpenny loaves on Good Friday and St. Thomas's Day, and 12s. in twelve-penny loaves on the first Sunday of the month, and 10s. was paid to the vicar for the two sermons.[64] In 1954 10s. of this £3 12s. was still paid to the vicar for sermons at Easter and Christmas, and the rest went to the poor.[65]

Esther Harding of Weeping Cross, by will of 1830, left £50, the interest to be used to purchase warm clothing for the poor of the parish.[66] In 1918 the principal was invested in £52 16s. 2d. stock, and in 1954 the income of £1 16s. 10d. was still paid to the poor.[67]

ACTON TRUSSELL AND BEDNALL

ACTON TRUSSELL and Bednall, formerly two joint townships and chapelries within the ancient parish of Baswich,[1] now form a single civil parish,[2] the area of which is 2,594 acres and the population of which was 432 in 1951.[3]

In shape a rough parallelogram, this parish is bounded on the west by the River Penk, and to the east it extends to the uncultivated upland of Cannock Chase. On the north lies Baswich, and the southern boundary abuts on the formerly extraparochial area of Teddesley Hay. The ground is very low lying but rises in the north-east at Acton Hill to 375 ft. and in the south-east to 600 ft.

The Staffordshire and Worcestershire Canal runs from south to north through the western edge of the parish. The parish is also crossed by the Stafford–Cannock road in the north-east on which there was formerly a toll-gate and toll-house, 600 yds. north-east of Acton Hill.[4]

Of the two villages Acton is situated 2½ miles north-east of Penkridge and three miles south-east of Stafford. Bednall lies due east of Acton. Both villages lie somewhat isolated from main roads, the shortest access being over the canal and then by way of a bridge at Acton Mill. John Linacres of Forebridge (in Castle Church parish) left a yearly rent in 1577 for the repair and maintenance of this bridge,[5] which was ruinous in 1609[6] and was

[43] P.O. Dir. Staffs. (1868); Kelly's Dir. Staffs. (1884).
[44] Kelly's Dir. Staffs. (1896; 1912).
[45] Staffs. Educ. Cttee. List of Schools, corrected to 1910.
[46] Staffs. Educ. Cttee. Mins. 30 May 1931.
[47] Rep. Staffs. Educ. Cttee. Oct. 1949.
[48] Staffs. Educ. Cttee. List of Schools, 1951, corrected to 1955.
[49] Lich. Dioc. Dir. (1955–6).
[50] Ex inf. Mr. H. J. Bostock, from Acct. Bk. 1891–1932 in parish chest. Ellerton d. 17 May 1836: tablet in Baswich church.
[51] Ex inf. Mr. H. J. Bostock (1954).
[52] See p. 10.
[53] Abstract of Returns of Charitable Donations, 1786–8, H.C. 511, pp. 1118–19 (1816), xvi (2).
[54] 11th Rep. Com. Char. 508.   [55] Ibid.
[56] Abstract, 1786–8, 1118–19.
[57] S.R.O., D. 114/A/PC1.

[58] Ex inf. Mr. H. J. Bostock (1954).
[59] 11th Rep. Com. Char. 508–9.   [60] Ibid. 509.
[61] Ibid.; marble slab on N. wall of Baswich church, erected by Samuel Twigg.
[62] Berkswich v. Walton Par. Reg. 91.
[63] 11th Rep. Com. Char. 509.
[64] Ibid. 509–10.
[65] Ex inf. Mr. H. J. Bostock.
[66] Marble slab on N. wall of Baswich church.
[67] Ex inf. Mr. H. J. Bostock.
[1] White, Dir. Staffs. (1834).
[2] In pursuance of the Poor Law Amendment Act of 1834 Acton and Bednall were assigned to Penkridge Union whereas Baswich was placed in Stafford Union.
[3] Census, 1951, Staffs.
[4] Tithe Maps and Appt., Baswich (copy in W.S.L.).
[5] S.H.C. 1926, 33.
[6] Ibid. 1948–9, 81, 133.

frequently the subject of indictments at Quarter Sessions for non-repair.[7] In 1648 liability for its repair was found to lie upon the inhabitants of Acton Trussell, Burton and Rickerscote (in Castle Church parish), and Dunston (in Penkridge parish), Acton being responsible for the maintenance of the first two arches, Burton and Rickerscote for the fifth, and Dunston for the sixth. As it was not known with whom liability for the third and fourth lay, responsibility for the maintenance of the bridge was then fixed on Acton, Bednall, Burton, Rickerscote, and Dunston.[8] It was rebuilt in 1726 in stone.[9] In 1830 it was said to be new, and liability for its maintenance then lay with the county.[10] These references to the upkeep of six arches suggest that there was formerly one long bridge, but the main bridge now has two semicircular and one segmental arch, while the smaller bridge over the relief stream to the west has a single segmental arch. Both structures appear to have been rebuilt in the early 19th century. The relief stream, which forms the parish boundary, may represent the original course of the River Penk.

By the mid-16th century some arable land in the parish had been inclosed by private agreement,[11] a process which was completed before 1827 when meadowland and commonland were inclosed under an Act of 1814.[12]

The Moat House, Acton, stands on the site of the former manor-house of the Trussells at the south end of Acton Trussell village on low ground in the river valley. In 1666 Mrs. Dickenson of the Moat House was charged for six hearths, the largest assessment in the parish.[13] The oldest part of the present house is on the east side and probably dates from the early 16th century. It consists of a two-story timber-framed wing of four bays. The upper story, originally open to the roof, has had a floor inserted to form attics. The roof has curved windbraces and three original trusses. Two large external chimneys with stone bases and later brick stacks may be contemporary or additions of the early 17th century. Much of the exterior has been faced with brickwork, and there are low brick additions to the south. A brick wing at right angles to the original block was added at the west side c. 1700. This has two stories, attics, and cellars. It may have replaced an early timbered hall. Internally it has a contemporary staircase and panelling. Some earlier panelling may have been removed from the 16th-century wing. The moat, originally large and curved, was probably of early medieval date. The west side was destroyed by the construction of the canal and a depression in the ground indicates the eastern arm. Only part of the north side, fed from the canal, is now wet. The moat was formerly supplied by a small stream from the east which entered the Penk at this point. In 1752 Edward Dickenson was the plaintiff in an action against his neighbour whom he accused of diverting the stream, thus causing his moat, in which he kept fish, to become stagnant.[14] A barn lying north-east of the house is partly of masonry of comparatively modern date.

Old Croft Cottage and The Old Homage are two thatched and timber-framed houses at the north end of Acton Trussell village. Both probably date from the 16th century but have been largely faced with later brickwork. The former has a timber-framed central bay in which the roof level has been raised and a ceiling inserted. The Old Homage consists of a central block of two bays with a cross wing at its north end and a later hipped bay to the south. Between the central bays is a large chimney with back-to-back fireplaces. These have moulded and embattled oak lintels. The ceiling of the north bay is clearly a later insertion.

The Old Schoolhouse lies 200 yds. north-east of Moat House Farm. It is a T-shaped timber-framed house of the late 16th or early 17th century with much brickwork facing of later dates. It has a central chimney with large back-to-back fireplaces, one retaining an original oak lintel with a chamfered three-centred arch. The cross wing was restored and reroofed in the mid-19th century. The original framing in a herringbone design and an early blocked window are visible in the gable-end of the back wing. On the west side the oversailing upper story formerly had decorative framing in a quadrant pattern.[15] Within living memory a Sunday school was held there, but it is not known whether it was ever in use as a day school.[16]

Many of the cottages in Acton Trussell village were built or restored in the middle of the 19th century by the 1st Lord Hatherton. Two pairs of council houses were built at the south end of the village c. 1950. Near this site several old cottages have been demolished.[17]

A village institute of corrugated iron was erected soon after the First World War. Previously a small reading-room, now a cottage, was used for a Sunday school and for parish activities.[18]

Bednall Hall dates from the first half of the 19th century. This and the vicarage are the only houses of any size in Bednall. The post office, Hollybush Farm, and Lower Farm are timber-framed houses of the late 16th or early 17th century, much altered. At Lower Farm there is a 17th-century timber-framed barn with brick panels. Three pairs of council houses opposite the church date from 1953. In a drawing of c. 1840 several old timber houses, now demolished, are shown east of the church.[19] The buildings at Gipsy Green in the extreme south of the parish are mostly Teddesley Estate cottages of the mid-19th century.

MANORS. In 1086 *ACTON* (Actone) was held under the Bishop of Chester by one Robert,[20] and remained within the leet of the bishop's manor of Haywood until at least 1841.[21]

[7] S.R.O., Q/SB, M. 1639, T. 1636, Ep. 1649, Ep. 1655, Ep. 1726, E. 1726, E. 1797, Ep. 1798, Ep. 1808.
[8] S.H.C. 1934, 43–44.   [9] Ibid. 81.
[10] Potter, List of Bridges, 3.
[11] As indicated in Littleton and Dickenson deeds: S.R.O., D. 260/M, box 20, bdles. a, b; box 3, bdle. d; box 4, bdle. a.
[12] S.R.O., Q/RDc, 22 a, b.
[13] S.H.C. 1927, 27.
[14] W.S.L., Hand Morgan Coll., Acton Trussell box,

Dickenson v. Seavill.
[15] W.S.L., Staffs. Views, i, p. 16 (1841).
[16] Local inf.
[17] Local inf. Several are shown on the Tithe Map, c. 1850: Tithe Maps and Appt., Baswich (copy in W.S.L.).
[18] Local inf.
[19] W.S.L., Staffs. Views, i, p. 164, a.
[20] V.C.H. Staffs. iv. 41, no. 68.
[21] W.S.L., D. 1734, Minutes of Court Proceedings, Haywood manor, 1841–9.

Robert the tenant of Acton in 1086[22] was probably Robert de Stafford founder of the Stafford barony, since Robert de Stafford (II) held 1 fee under the bishop in 1166,[23] and in 1242 or 1243 Acton was held as ⅔ fee of the barony of Stafford.[24] The mesne lordship remained with the barony of Stafford until 1501.[25]

In 1206 John de Acton was defending his claim to ⅔ fee in Acton against Philip de Wastenys,[26] possibly the same John de Acton who held ⅔ fee in Acton in 1242 or 1243.[27] In 1342 John Trussell, described as of Acton, and Alice Trussell his wife settled the manor (with Bednall and Brocton) on themselves for life with remainder to William Trussell of Kibblestone in Stone (Pirehill hundred),[28] but Acton appears to have passed to another William, the son of John Trussell,[29] who in 1371 settled it on Margaret, daughter of Sir William Trussell of Kibblestone (d. 1363)[30] and her husband Fulke Pembrugge,[31] Margaret Pembrugge was dead before 17 February 1400[32] leaving her husband with a life interest under the settlement of 1371 and also under a later one of 1383.[33] On his subsequent marriage Fulke appears to have secured another settlement[34] which, after providing for the joint life interests of himself and his wife Isabel, created a remainder in favour of William Trussell, son of a Lawrence Trussell and grandson of a Warin Trussell, who acquired Acton on the death of Isabel in 1446, he being then 60 years old.[35] Richard Vernon, a cousin on the Pembrugge side, successfully dispossessed him by an action of novel disseisin in 1448, but an appeal brought by William Trussell in 1450[36] was apparently successful, for in 1464 on his death he held the manor.[37] It then passed to his son Thomas who had been succeeded, before 1480, by a William Trussell who died in that year.[38] Edward Trussell, his heir, died in 1499 being succeeded by his son John,[39] who died in infancy in 1500 and whose heir was his sister Elizabeth,[40] subsequently married to John de Vere, Earl of Oxford.[41] The manor descended with the Earldom of Oxford[42] until 1575 when Edward Earl of Oxford

conveyed it to trustees,[43] probably for the purpose of sale. The manor was divided into three main estates at this date, all subsequently designated the manor of Acton Trussell and Bednall. The manorial rights and much of the land but not the capital messuage (see below) passed to Thomas Fowke and William Hankyn in whose names the court was held in 1575.[44] Thomas Fowke was holding what was described as half the manor at his death in 1586.[45] The other half, held by William Hankyn,[46] was acquired by Thomas Fowke's son and heir John who appears as sole lord in 1591.[47] By 1658 this manor was held by William Anson of Shugborough[48] and has descended in that family,[49] the Earl of Lichfield holding such manorial rights as still existed in 1956 as well as owning 659 acres within the parish.[50] A court was last held there in 1811.[51]

In 1086 *BEDNALL* was waste and formed part of the bishop's manor of Baswich.[52] The overlordship of the bishop continued until at least 1507,[53] Bednall being held of his manor of Haywood from at least 1295.[54]

By 1243 a mesne lordship lay with the barony of Stafford[55] with which it descended until at least 1523[56] when on the attainder of Edward Duke of Buckingham the lordship escheated, and in 1604 John late Earl of Oxford was said to have held a ware of land in Bednall of the king as of his manor of Stafford.[57]

By 1243 Bednall was held with Brocton by John de Acton as ¼ fee of the barony of Stafford.[58] In 1297 or 1298 it was held with land in Brocton by John Trussell as ¼ fee owing suit twice a year at the bishop's court of Haywood.[59] It has since descended with Acton Trussell (see above), the courts of the two manors being held jointly from at least 1557.[60]

In 1574 this joint manor of Acton Trussell and Bednall was coextensive with the present civil parish of Acton Trussell and Bednall. In Acton Trussell there were 9 freeholds while the manorhouse was leased to Henry Webb with part of the demesne land. Of 22 other tenancies of demesne land within Acton Trussell, 17 were leaseholds and

[22] *V.C.H. Staffs.*, iv. 41, no. 68.
[23] *Red Bk. Exch.* (Rolls Ser.), 263.
[24] *Bk. of Fees*, 967.
[25] *Complete Peerage*, xii. 168–201; C 137/73; C 140/9; C 140/78; *Cal. Inq. p.m. Hen VII*, ii, nos. 408, 415.
[26] *S.H.C.* iii (1), 135; [F. P. Parker], *Some Account of Colton and of the de Wasteneys Family* (1897), 27.
[27] *Bk. of Fees*, 967.
[28] *S.H.C.* xi. 151.
[29] Wrottesley, *Pedigrees from the Plea Rolls*, 384; Dugd. *Warws.* ii. 716.
[30] *Cal. Inq. p.m.* xi, no. 533.
[31] *S.H.C.* xi. 179.
[32] *Cal. Fine R.* 1399–1405, 52.
[33] *S.H.C.* xi. 206.
[34] C 139/125; *Cal. Close*, 1447–54, 12; *S.H.C.* N.S. iii. 189, where the date of the settlement is given as 1409.
[35] C 139/125.
[36] *S.H.C.* N.S. iii. 188–91.
[37] *Cal. Fine R.* 1461–71, 137.
[38] C 140/78.
[39] *Cal. Inq. p.m. Hen. VII*, ii, nos. 408, 415; C 142/20, no. 47.
[40] *Cal. Inq. p.m. Hen. VII*, iii, no. 233.
[41] *Complete Peerage*, x. 247.
[42] Ibid. 245–50. Courts of the manor of Acton Trussell were held regularly for the earls of Oxford between 1512 or 1513 and 1568: W.S.L., D. 1765/3–21. A survey of the manor was made for Edward Earl of Oxford in 1574: W.S.L., D. 1765. One Fowke of Penkridge paying rent to Lord Stafford in 1532 or 1533 for water for the mill at

Acton was said to be lord of Acton: W.S.L., Stafford Barony, Mins. Accts. 1532–3, m. 11d.
[43] *S.H.C.* xiv. 179.
[44] W.S.L., D. 1765/23, Acton Ct. R.
[45] C 142/213, no. 133.
[46] C 142/213, no. 116.
[47] W.S.L., D. 1765/23.
[48] C.P. 25(2)/597, 1658 Mich.
[49] *Complete Peerage*, i. 172–4; ibid. vii. 647, 649; C.P. 25(2)/724, 18 and 19 Chas. II Hil.; C.P. 43/838, rot. 147; C.P. 43/942, rot. 351.
[50] Ex inf. the Earl of Lichfield's Estate Office, Eccleshall (1956).
[51] W.S.L., Hand Morgan Coll., Anson Papers, Bill of Costs of Collins and Keen, 1811.
[52] *V.C.H. Staffs.*, iv. 41, no. 69.
[53] *Cal. Inq. p.m. Hen VII*, iii, no. 233.
[54] W.S.L., C.B. Baswich, copy of Bodl. MS. Ashmole 864, p. 15.
[55] *Bk. of Fees*, 967.
[56] *Complete Peerage*, xii. 168–201; S.C. 11/604, m. 2. In 1481, 1499, and 1507 Bednall was said to be held directly of the Bishop of Lichfield: *Cal. Inq. p.m. Hen. VII*, iii, nos. 233, 235.
[57] C 142/284, no. 30. Bednall remained, however, within the leet of Haywood: W.S.L., D. 1734, Haywood.
[58] *Bk. of Fees*, 967.
[59] W.S.L., C.B. Baswich, copy of Bodl. MS. Ashmole 864, p. 15.
[60] W.S.L., D. 1765/20.

only 5 tenancies-at-will. In Bednall there were 6 freeholds and 8 tenancies of demesne land, 6 of which were leaseholds and 2 tenancies at will. A rent of 2s. was then said to be due from the lord of Acton Trussell to the queen as to her manor of Penkridge. At this date there were 4 common fields in Acton Trussell, namely Mylfield, Churchfield, Harpemore or Harpemyrefield and Highfield, and 5 common pastures, High Meadow, Mylholme, Boothmeadowe, Overmeadowe, and Churchmeadowe. There were three common fields in Bednall, namely Bednall (Beddingale) Field, Lower Field, and Ridgefield, and two common pastures, Stockinge Meadow and Harde Meadow.[61]

In 1569 the tenants of the Earl of Oxford in Acton Trussell were said to have rights of pasture in Teddesley Hay of which Sir Edward Littleton had inclosed the greater part and which he was then ordered to throw open.[62] These rights were still claimed in 1574, while the survey of the manor then made also set out the rights of the tenants of the manor in Deepmore and Sidnall Commons, both of which lay within the manor of Acton Trussell and Bednall. The maintenance of Deepmore Gate and the draining of Deepmore Ditch were a charge on the parish of Baswich at least by 1700, and in 1797 a meeting of parishioners of Baswich resolved to dispose of Deepmore Common with the concurrence of all landowners interested in it and to use the money to erect a house of industry.[63] This common was surveyed in 1798 and had been inclosed and sold by 1814, the house of industry having been opened in 1801, but in rented premises.[64] The four commons in Acton Trussell and Bednall, namely Shuthill Common, Lords Wood Common, Old Sydnall Common, and Bednall Head Common were inclosed in 1814.[65]

In 1575 the trustees of Edward Earl of Oxford conveyed to Matthew Moreton of Engleton (in Brewood parish) the capital messuage and manor of Acton Trussell with messuages and tenements there.[66] In 1593 Edward Moreton of Engleton sold to Lewis Dickenson the messuage and tenements then in his occupation.[67] In 1650 a Lewis Dickenson, Margaret his wife and Lewis Dickenson his son, a minor, settled what was described as a manor of *ACTON TRUSSELL* and *BEDNALL*, the capital messuage called the Moat and various lands.[68] On his marriage in 1655 the estate was settled on Lewis Dickenson the younger for life with remainder to Jane his wife for life.[69] Settlements were made in 1674 by Lewis and Jane on their son Lewis and

Elizabeth his wife[70] and in 1718 on Lewis, son of Lewis and Elizabeth, on his marriage to Mary, daughter of Edward Ward of Stafford.[71] Edward, eldest son and heir of Lewis and Mary,[72] was dead by 1753[73] when his sister Mary and her husband Thomas Spicer were in possession of the manor.[74] By his will, dated 1767, Thomas Spicer devised the manor to his wife Mary who, by her will of 1776, left it to her nephew Edward Dickenson, son of Lewis Dickenson, her younger brother,[75] but after her death it was sold by her trustees in 1778 to John Barlow.[76] John Barlow, by his will dated 1804, left the Moat House, the so-called manor and all his lands in trust to his grandson John Barlow, son of his son John, deceased,[77] who came of age in 1818[78] and in 1819 sold them to Edward John Littleton of Teddesley, retaining, however, the rights of common.[79]

Members of the Littleton family had already acquired land in Acton Trussell in 1541,[80] 1547,[81] 1624,[82] and 1634,[83] and in 1635 William, son of a Sir Edward Littleton, made a settlement of what was called the manor or manors of Acton Trussell and Bednall[84] which he sold in 1637 to his brother, Sir Edward Littleton.[85] The Littleton family bought other land here in 1636, 1638, and 1668.[86] All of this then descended with Pillaton (in Penkridge parish) in the main line of the Littleton family,[87] who in 1819 also purchased the Moat House estate (see above). In 1947 the Littleton estates in Acton Trussell and Bednall were sold. They then consisted of the Moat House Farm (208 a.), Plashes Farm, Bednall (172 a.), Church Farm, Bednall (34 a.), Lower Farm, Bednall (41 a.), Holly Bush Farm, Bednall (68 a.), Belt Farm, Bednall (63 a.), with cottages and other small pieces of land in the parish.[88] Moat House Farm and Plashes Farm were bought by Lotus Ltd. of Stafford.[89]

A fishery in the River Penk was attached to Lord Oxford's manor of Acton Trussell and Bednall by at least 1574.[90] The fishing rights apparently passed to Lewis Dickenson with the Moat House (c. 1593), and in 1819 John Barlow sold them to Edward John Littleton of Teddesley.[91] They then extended from the Swan Inn to Radford Bridge.[92]

MILL. There was a mill in Acton in 1086.[93] In 1449 the lord of Acton was paying 5½d. rent to the free tenants of Dunston (in Penkridge parish) for a watercourse leading to his mill.[94] In 1533 one Fowke of Penkridge, said to be lord (but probably then lessee) of Acton, was paying a rent to Lord Stafford for

[61] W.S.L., D. 1765, Survey of the manor of Acton Trussell and Bednall.
[62] W.S.L., C.B. Littleton transcripts.
[63] S.R.O., D. 114/A/PC, 1, Accts. of Churchwardens and of Overseers of the Poor for the liberty of Walton, 1701, 1797.
[64] Ibid. 1798, 1801.
[65] S.R.O., Q/RDc, 22 a, b.
[66] S.H.C. xiv. 179; S.R.O., D. 260/M, box 4, bdle a.
[67] S.R.O., D. 260/M, box 4, bdle. a.
[68] Ibid.
[69] Ibid.
[70] Ibid.
[71] Ibid.
[72] Ibid., box 20, bdle. b.
[73] Ibid.
[74] Ibid.
[75] Ibid.
[76] Ibid.
[77] Ibid.
[78] Ibid.
[79] Ibid.
[80] Ibid., box 3, bdle. d.
[81] Ibid.
[82] Ibid.
[83] Ibid.
[84] Ibid.
[85] Ibid.
[86] Ibid., box 4, bdle. d; box 3, bdle. d.
[87] See p. 119.
[88] W.S.L., Sale Cat. B/2/10.
[89] Ex inf. Teddesley and Hatherton Estate Office, Penkridge.
[90] W.S.L., D. 1765, Survey of the manor of Acton Trussell and Bednall.
[91] S.R.O., D. 260/M, box 20, bdle. a.
[92] Ibid.
[93] V.C.H. Staffs. iv. 41, no. 68.
[94] W.S.L., D. 1721/1/8.

leave to turn the Penk to his mill.[95] The rent was paid in 1574 by Richard Dickenson, then the lessee of the mill.[96] By 1645 the mill had been separated from the manor, and £12 rent was paid for it by Richard Thomason to Sir Edward Littleton.[97] In 1653 or 1654 the mill was regranted from his forfeited property to Sir Edward Littleton,[98] whose descendents paid suit silver for it to Lord Somers from 1713 to 1723,[99] to Sir Joseph Jekyll, husband of one of the coheirs of Lord Somers,[1] from 1724 to 1739, to Lady Jekyll in 1739, and to James Cocks from

to Baswich, but Acton Trussell and Bednall formed a separate parish by at least 1671,[11] each chapel presumably having all rights of a parish church. The parish was described as a joint chapelry in 1834[12] and 1851,[13] the benefice remaining a perpetual curacy until 1867 when it was declared a vicarage.[14]

The advowson of Acton Trussell was presumably included in the grant of the advowson of Baswich to the priory of St. Thomas (St. Mary's parish, Stafford) in 1407.[15] On the dissolution of St. Thomas's it was granted to Roland Lee, Bishop of

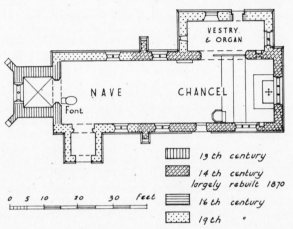

PLAN OF ST. JAMES'S CHURCH

1743 to 1755.[2] In 1775 Sir Edward Littleton bought the fee farm rent of Acton Mill from Sir Charles Cocks.[3] In 1827 the mill was owned by E. J. Littleton,[4] in whose possession it remained until at least 1845.[5]

The site of the mill is about 100 yds. south of Actonmill Bridge. It was still in use in 1878[6] but had been demolished by 1900.[7] The farmhouse of Actonmill Farm, formerly the mill-house, dates from the first half of the 19th century. The mill pool has been partly filled in and the river bank straightened.

CHURCHES. The chapel of Acton Trussell was built in the 13th century, presumably as a dependent chapel of Baswich, and was consequently appropriated to the prebend of Whittington and Baswich in Lichfield Cathedral.[8] Although the church of Baswich was claiming 4s. in respect of corn tithe from Acton Trussell and Bednall between 1547 and 1551[9] the chapel was still said to be appropriated to the prebend of Whittington and Baswich in 1563.[10] In 1604 Acton Trussell chapel was described as a chapel in Baswich and c. 1690 as a chapel annexed

Lichfield, in 1539[16] and subsequently descended with the Fowler manor of Brocton until at least 1695.[17] By 1834 it had been transferred to the Revd. W. H. Molineux, who was himself the incumbent but served the church by a deputy.[18] The joint advowson was held in 1851,[19] and is still held, by the Hulme Trustees.[20]

The vicarage of Acton Trussell and Bednall was endowed out of the Common Fund in 1877 with £100 and with £120 a year for a curate.[21]

Miss L. E. Johnson, by will proved 1917, left £500, the income to be applied for general parochial purposes. In 1936 the yield from stock was £18 10s. 2d. The charity was still in being in 1954.[22]

The church of ST. JAMES, Acton Trussell, stands a quarter of a mile south of the village. Before the middle of the 19th century it was approached by a footpath only.[23] The original structure dates from the 13th and 14th centuries, but the church was enlarged and partly rebuilt in 1870 under the direction of G. E. Street.[24] It now consists of a structurally undivided nave and chancel, a south porch, and a combined vestry and organ chamber.

95 W.S.L., Stafford Barony, Mins. Accts. 1532–3, m. 11d.
96 W.S.L., D. 1765, Survey of the manor of Acton Trussell and Bednall.
97 S.R.O., D. 260/M, box 25, bdle. k, f. 116b.
98 Ibid. box 3, bdle. e.
99 Ibid. box 4, bdle. n.
1 Complete Peerage, xii. 29–36.
2 S.R.O., D. 260/M, box 3, bdle. d.
3 Ibid. box 10, bdle. h.
4 S.R.O., Q/RDc 22.
5 Tithe Maps and Appt., Baswich (copy in W.S.L.).
6 P.O. Dir. Staffs. (1876).
7 Local inf.
8 The original structure dates from the 13th and 14th cents.
9 C 1/1219, nos. 20–23.
10 S.H.C. 1915, 3.

11 Ibid.; W.S.L. Hand Morgan Coll., (Shorthand) Diocesan Survey, c. 1690; see p. 1.
12 White, Dir. Staffs. (1834).
13 Ibid. (1851).
14 Lond. Gaz. 1867, p. 4476.
15 See p. 7.
16 L. & P. Hen. VIII, xiv (2), g. 435(12); C 1/1219, nos. 20–23.
17 See p. 5.
18 White, Dir. Staffs. (1834), where the initials are given in error as G. F.
19 Ibid. (1851).
20 Lich. Dioc. Dir. (1955–6).
21 Lond. Gaz. 1877, p. 2689.
22 Charity Com. files.
23 Tithe Maps and Appt., Baswich (copy in W.S.L.).
24 Lich. Dioc. Ch. Cal. (1871), 73.

The base of the tower is of 13th-century masonry, and until the alterations of 1870 the west ends of both north and south nave walls were of the same date. There were formerly lancet windows and a north doorway in this part of the nave.[25] The east end of the church appears to have been remodelled and extended in the 14th century, probably by a member of the Trussell family. The walling is either of this period or is a 19th-century reconstruction in which much of the old material was reused. An external view of the north side of the church drawn before the vestry addition[26] shows a large blocked arch near the east end. Further east is a small recess, probably a piscina.[27] These features suggest that there was formerly a projecting chapel in this position. In the masonry which blocks the arch a two-light 14th-century window is shown. It seems probable that when the chapel was demolished, possibly in the 16th century, one of its windows was reused here to light the chancel. Both north and south nave walls have 14th-century buttresses. Other features of this date are the three-light east window and two windows in the south wall of the chancel. Near the middle of the south wall is a 'low side' window with an ogee head externally and a flat sill within. A small square recess, now blocked, lies a few inches to the west. East of the window is a priest's door with a simple pointed head. The position of these features indicates that the original division between nave and chancel was farther west than at present, giving a chancel rather longer than the nave. A piscina in the south wall of the sanctuary and an aumbry opposite have recut ogee heads and have been much restored.

Alterations to the tower took place in the 16th century when an embattled parapet with pinnacles, a string course with central gargoyles, and a short stone spire were added. This work and the tower windows, one square-headed, the others pointed with simple tracery, may all be of 1562, a date which appears above the lowest west window. Similar pointed windows appear in the body of the church, and the north doorway was also renewed in the 15th or 16th century.

Drawings and plans of the church made in the first half of the 19th century[28] show the lancet windows and north doorway near the west end of the nave. The tower arch had been partially blocked and there was a plain gabled porch outside the south door.

By 1867 there was considerable pressure to increase the seating in the church. A scheme for enlargement in that year included the addition of a north aisle as well as a north vestry.[29] In 1869 and 1870 the vestry, but not the aisle, was built and the whole church thoroughly restored. The cost was between £1,000 and £1,200.[30] The west end of the nave was entirely

renewed, all its features disappearing in the process. The tower arch was opened up and probably raised in height, and the south porch was rebuilt. The 14th-century window, formerly in the north wall of the chancel, was reset in the east vestry wall. The piscina was restored and left in position. The original jambs and four-centred head of the north doorway were utilized as a vestry door. In 1869 the Incorporated Church Building Society contributed £25 towards adding 58 seats to the church.[31] The opening-up of the base of the tower and the eastward extension of the nave were probably expedients for increasing the seating space.[32] In 1895 a new organ was dedicated and in 1937 electric heating and lighting were installed.[33]

The present stone font is of the 19th century, but an early tub-shaped bowl is preserved in the churchyard. In 1841 the church contained an 18th-century pedestal font.[34] An old bassoon is preserved below the tower. Three shields of arms of the Trussell family have been reset in the east window of the vestry as a memorial to John Higgot of the Moat House (d. 1862). These were formerly in the east window of the chancel[35] and may well be contemporary with the 14th-century rebuilding. Other windows contain 19th-century memorial glass to members of the Price, Alsop, and Locker families. The glass in the 'low side' window commemorates Lt. J. M. Lees (d. 1916).

A marble wall tablet with fluted pilasters and a segmental pediment commemorates Richard Nevil of Rickerscote (d. 1728). Other tablets commemorate Ann Richards (d. 1821), and Richard Locker (d. 1886) and Arthur Richard Alsop (d. 1928), vicars. There is also an undated 19th-century tablet to members of the Wright family.

The plate includes a silver chalice set with six amethysts and a paten on a foot.

In 1553 there were three bells and a sacring bell.[36] There are now three bells: (i) no date; (ii) 15th century, 'Sancta Maria Ora pro nobis'; (iii) 1630.[37]

The four volumes of registers for the joint parishes of Acton Trussell and Bednall cover the years 1571–1625, 1704–50, 1721–50, 1783–1813; from 1813 each church had its own register.[38]

There was a chapel at Bednall by the 12th century.[39] It was presumably included among the dependent chapels of Baswich in 1535[40] and subsequently had the same institutional history as the chapel of Acton Trussell (see above).

Although included in Baswich in the Valor of 1535, Bednall church in 1549 and 1553 was described as immemorially in receipt of tithes, then worth 40s. a year.[41] The incumbent of Bednall benefits under the Alport Charity on condition of attending an annual service in Cannock parish church on the Feast of St. Barnabas (11 June),

[25] S.R.O., D. 260/M/E 417 a, b; W.S.L., S. MS. 433, p. 315.
[26] W.S.L., S. MS. 433, p. 315.
[27] W.S.L., S. MS. 436, p. 170. William Salt assumed it to be a holy water stoup.
[28] S.R.O., D. 260/M/E 417 a, b; W.S.L., S. MS. 443, p. 315; W.S.L., Staffs. Views, i, pp. 13–15.
[29] S.R.O., D. 260/M/E 417 b.
[30] Lich. Dioc. Ch. Cal. (1871), 73.
[31] Inscription in church.
[32] Lich. Dioc. Mag. (1895), 122.
[33] Lich. Dioc. Regy., Consist. Ct. Act Bk. 1934–8, p. 382, faculty 30 July 1937.

[34] W.S.L., Staffs. Views, i, p. 15, b.
[35] S.H.C. 1919, 238.
[36] Ibid. 1915, 3.
[37] C. Lynam, Church Bells of Staffs., pp. ix–x, 1, and plates 19, 74; A. E. Garbett 'Church Bells of Staffs.' (Trans. Old Stafford Soc. 1953–4), 6.
[38] Ex inf. the Vicar of Acton and Bednall (1956).
[39] The former chapel appears to have incorporated 12th-century features: see p. 17.
[40] Valor Eccl. (Rec. Com.), iii. 112.
[41] W.S.L., Hand Morgan Coll., (Shorthand) Diocesan Survey, c. 1690.

preaching a sermon at this in rotation with seven other beneficiaries, and residing in his benefice for at least ten months a year.[42]

The rents of three pieces of land applied for the repair of Bednall chapel amounted to £8 by 1823. The sum of £2 a year was added in 1827 from allotments awarded to the parishioners in respect of this land on the inclosure of Teddesley Hay and Bednall Field.[43] The rent paid in 1937 was £15 14s., and the charity was still in being in 1955.[44]

The present church of *ALL SAINTS* dates from 1846.[45] The former chapel, on or near the same site, appears to have been of 12th-century origin. It consisted of nave and chancel, the nave being slightly higher and wider than the chancel and having a wooden bell turret at its west end. The north doorway had an enriched 12th-century arch with heavy chamfered imposts. Small 12th-century windows survived in both nave and chancel. The remaining windows were insertions of the 17th or 18th century, and the south doorway was dated 1707. The chapel also retained angle buttresses, a 'low side' window, and a priest's door.[46]

The present stone church originally consisted of a nave, a chancel, and a south aisle of three bays. A late 13th-century style was adopted, and the cost was about £1,100.[47] A tower and spire in the same style, the base forming a north porch, was added in 1873 at the expense of Mrs. Heath of Bednall Hall.[48] The clock was presented by her sister, Miss Stokes, in 1874.[49] The organ dates from 1887.[50] Stained glass was inserted in the east and west windows c. 1862 and in 1894 in memory of Mrs. and Miss Stokes respectively.[51] The glass in the north windows, together with the desk and lectern, date from 1915.[52] Electric light was installed in 1937.[53]

Mural tablets include those to Arthur Richard Alsop, vicar (d. 1928), and to William Rogers (d. 1889), for 46 years forester on the Teddesley Estate.

A parsonage house was in existence at Bednall in the early part of the 19th century, but it was considered unfit for habitation by the incumbent. The licensed curate who performed the duty lived at Cannock.[54] A 'parsonage house and garden', let to a tenant, is shown on the tithe map near the site of the present school.[55] In 1842 a large red-brick vicarage was built half a mile south-east of the church at a cost of £1,600.[56]

The plate includes a silver chalice, 1946; a silver paten, 1946; a paten, no date; a flagon inscribed 'Acton Trussell cum Bednall', 1846; and an electroplated chalice and paten. In 1553 there were two bells and two sacring bells.[57] There are now one ringing bell, 1681, and one clock bell, 1874.[58]

The earlier registers are described under Acton Trussell. From 1813 Bednall has kept its own registers.[59]

PRIMARY SCHOOLS. There was said to be a dayschool at Acton in 1818.[60] A day-school master, George Oldford, was among the Acton Trussell residents in 1834,[61] and in 1854 there were said to be two schools in Acton and Bednall, supported by annual subscriptions.[62] A National school for boys and girls at Bednall under a master and mistress was built by subscription in 1856[63] and by 1884 had average attendances of 60 older children and 24 infants.[64] In 1894 the average attendance was 88,[65] in 1931 54,[66] and in 1937 44.[67] It became an aided school from November 1952[68] and is now Acton Trussell and Bednall Church of England Voluntary Primary (Aided) School (Junior Mixed and Infants), under a mistress.[69] The average attendance in 1955 was 15.[70]

CHARITIES FOR THE POOR. By 1786 rent charges of 12s. and 6s. had been given by an unknown benefactor for bread for the poor of Acton Trussell and Bednall respectively.[71] The land on which the rents were charged was known in 1823 as White Bread Piece, and the owner was then sending 12 penny loaves to Acton Trussell Chapel and 6 to Bednall Chapel on the first Sunday of every month.[72]

By 1786 there were rents of 10s. and 4s. charged on land in Acton Trussell for the poor by an unknown benefactor and 5s. and 4s. on land in Bednall.[73] A benefaction, also of unknown origin, in aid of the poor rate in Acton Trussell and Bednall was yielding £3 a year by 1786, apparently from land,[74] but by 1823 the overseer and chapel wardens were paying 12s., for the poor of Acton only, as interest on a sum of £15.[75] In 1823 all this money was distributed on Good Friday at the two chapels after divine service to such poor as were not receiving parish relief, in sums of 3s. and under in Acton Trussell and 1s. 6d. and under in Bednall, according to size of family.[76]

All these charities have long since lapsed.[77]

[42] See pp. 64, 96.
[43] *11th Rep. Com. Char.* H.C. 436, p. 510 (1824), xiv. The Inclosure Act was 1814 and the award 1827: S.R.O., Q/RDc 22a, pp. 63, 124 (allotment no. 375 was probably also no. 66).
[44] Charity Com. files.
[45] White, *Dir. Staffs.* (1851).
[46] W.S.L., S. MS. 433, p. 315, reproduced facing p. 25; W.S.L., Staffs. Views, i, p. 164, a, b (c. 1838 and 1841).
[47] White, *Dir. Staffs.* (1851).
[48] *Lich. Dioc. Ch. Cal.* (1875), 73.
[49] Ibid.
[50] Ibid. (1888), 149.
[51] Lich. Dioc. Regy., Consist. Ct. Act Bk. 1891–9, p. 173, 28 Aug. 1894.
[52] Ibid. 1914–20, p. 37, faculty 6 Apr. 1915.
[53] Ibid. 1934–8, p. 382, faculty 30 July 1937.
[54] Lich. Dioc. Regy., Non-Residence Licences, ii, iii, B and C (1808–21).
[55] Tithe Maps and Appt., Baswich (copy in W.S.L.).
[56] White, *Dir. Staffs.* (1851).
[57] *S.H.C.* 1915, 23.
[58] Lynam, *Church Bells of Staffs.* 3.
[59] Ex inf. the vicar (1956).

[60] *Digest of Returns to Sel. Cttee. on Educ. of Poor,* H.C. 224, p. 854 (1819), ix (2).
[61] White, *Dir. Staffs.* (1834).
[62] *P.O. Dir. Staffs.* (1854).
[63] Ibid. (1860); tablet *in situ*.
[64] *Returns relating to Elem. Educ.* H.C. 201, pp. 364–5 (1871), lv; *Kelly's Dir. Staffs* (1884).
[65] *Returns of Schools, 1893* [C. 7529], pp. 538–9, H.C. (1894), lxv.
[66] Staffs. Educ. Cttee. Mins. 25 Apr. 1931.
[67] Ibid. 29 May 1937.
[68] Ibid. 7 Feb. 1953.
[69] Staffs. Educ. Cttee., *List of Schools, 1951,* corrected to 1955.
[70] *Lich. Dioc. Dir.* (1955–6).
[71] *Abstract of Returns of Charitable Donations 1786–8,* H.C. 511, pp. 1118–19 (1816), xvi (2).
[72] *11th Rep. Com. Char.* 510. Nos. 1951 and 1952 on Baswich Tithe Map (copy in W.S.L.), are named White Bread Piece and lie east of Acton mill Bridge.
[73] *Abstract, 1786–8,* 1118–19.
[74] Ibid.
[75] *11th Rep. Com. Char.* 510.
[76] Ibid.
[77] Ex inf. the vicar (1956).

BREWOOD

THE ancient parish of Brewood lies in the south-west corner of the hundred on the Shropshire border. Its northern boundary is formed by nearly four miles of Watling Street while the Stafford–Wolverhampton road runs through the eastern part of the parish. The River Penk, joined by a number of tributaries, flows north through the parish, also on the eastern side, and with the Moat Brook, a tributary, also forms part of the southern boundary. The ground rises from below 300 ft. in the north-east to over 500 ft. on the western boundary to the north of Chillington Park. The soil is fertile but varied, being mainly stiff in the north and west and lighter in the south and east.[1] The parish to the west of the Penk lay within the royal forest of Brewood until its disafforestation by King John in 1204, while the part to the east of the river was within the royal forest of Cannock between at least 1167 and 1301.[2] In 1940 there were eleven farms of over 150 acres.[3] The geological formation is Keuper Sandstone,[4] which lies near the surface in and around the town itself so that the earth tremors noticed along the west of England in 1678, 1852, and 1863 were strongly felt in Brewood.[5]

By 1834 the ancient parish was divided into the eight liberties or constablewicks of Brewood town, Chillington, Coven, Engleton, Gunstone and the Hattons, Horsebrook, Kiddemore, and Somerford, which maintained their poor jointly and their roads separately.[6] There were 305 households in the parish in 1666,[7] and the population was 2,960 in 1931 and 3,576 in 1951.[8] The area was increased from 12,152 acres to 12,517 acres under the Staffordshire Review Order of 1934 when Coven Heath and Brinsford were transferred from Bushbury (Seisdon hundred) to Brewood.[9]

The nucleus of the town of Brewood is the market-place and the four streets radiating from it, Bargate, Newport and Stafford Streets, and Sandy Lane, with a fifth, Dean Street, leading south-east from the parish church. The township had some 60 houses c. 1680[10] and by 1811 210 inhabited houses with a population of 919.[11] It was described in 1834 as 'a small but well-built market town, with several good streets and a spacious market-place'.[12] Chillington, to the south-west of Brewood, contained 30 houses c. 1680,[13] but in 1834 and 1851 it had only five farms, in addition to the Hall.[14] Coven, two miles

to the south-east of Brewood town, had 40 houses c. 1680,[15] and by 1851 covered 1,750 acres with 650 inhabitants, being 'a large liberty, with a considerable village'.[16] Engleton, about 1½ mile to the north-east of Brewood, had 5 or 6 houses c. 1680[17] but was only 'a small estate' in 1834.[18] Gunstone, some two miles to the south-west of Brewood, had 10 houses c. 1680, the Hattons being two farms there.[19] In 1834 Hatton and Gunstone were described as adjoining hamlets with four farms and a few cottages.[20] Horsebrook, a mile to the north of Brewood, with 30 houses c. 1680,[21] was described as 'a small hamlet' in 1834.[22] Kiddemore Green, some 2 miles west of Brewood, had 30 houses c. 1680, with 'a good farm' called Hawkshead House belonging to Edward Moreton of Engleton,[23] and in 1834 was described as 'a hamlet of scattered houses'.[24] Bishop's Wood, c. 1680 'a little vill a little beyond Kiddemore Green',[25] was, in 1834, an open common with a few cottages built on encroachments upon the waste[26] but had been inclosed by 1851.[27] Somerford, a mile east of Brewood, with 30 houses c. 1680,[28] had a population of 578 in 1811.[29] Standeford, described as a vill in Somerford c. 1680,[30] seems to have been attached to Coven by 1834.[31] The hamlet of Four Ashes, which existed by 1775[32] and was part of Somerford in 1834,[33] is said to have taken its name from a former cluster of trees in front of the inn of the same name on the Stafford–Wolverhampton road.[34]

This main road to Wolverhampton was turnpiked under an Act of 1760.[35] The present dual carriageway was constructed between 1936 and 1939.[36] The road from Brewood formerly joined this main road at Standeford, passing close to Somerford Hall, but the Hon. Edward Monckton c. 1781 closed the section by the Hall and built the present road which, running farther to the north, goes direct to Four Ashes.[37] Between at least 1730 and 1750 Brewood town had two separate overseers of the highways, one for the 'High Town' and one for the 'Deanery'.[38]

The first mail coach between Birmingham and Liverpool, which began running in 1785, passed through Four Ashes at night, while the mail coach between Bristol and Manchester, started in 1810, passed through by day.[39] With the opening of the railway in 1837, out of several coaches calling at

---

[1] Kelly's Dir. Staffs. (1940).
[2] S.H.C. 1923, 294, 300–1; ibid. v (1), 179; Select Pleas of the Forest, ed. G. J. Turner (Selden Soc. xiii), p. cv.
[3] Kelly's Dir. Staffs. (1940).
[4] Ibid.
[5] R. Plot, Staffs. (1686), 143; J. Hicks Smith, Brewood (1874), 1; Anon. Notes and Collections relating to Brewood (Wolverhampton, 1860), 10.
[6] White, Dir. Staffs. (1834).
[7] S.H.C. 1927, 54–58.
[8] Census, 1951, Staffs.
[9] Kelly's Dir. Staffs. (1932; 1940).
[10] S.H.C. 1919, 241.
[11] W. Pitt, Staffs. (1817), 253.
[12] White, Dir. Staffs. (1834). The market-place was still unpaved in 1860: P.O. Dir. Staffs. (1860).
[13] S.H.C. 1919, 241.
[14] White, Dir. Staffs. (1834; 1851).
[15] S.H.C. 1919, 240.
[16] White, Dir. Staffs. (1851).
[17] S.H.C. 1919, 241.
[18] White, Dir. Staffs. (1834).

[19] S.H.C. 1919, 241.
[20] White, Dir. Staffs. (1834).
[21] S.H.C. 1919, 241.
[22] White, Dir. Staffs. (1834).
[23] S.H.C. 1919, 241.
[24] White, Dir. Staffs. (1834).
[25] S.H.C. 1919, 241.
[26] White, Dir. Staffs. (1834).
[27] Ibid. (1851).
[28] S.H.C. 1919, 241.
[29] Pitt, Staffs. 255.
[30] S.H.C. 1919, 241.
[31] White, Dir. Staffs. (1834).
[32] Yates, Map of Staffs. (1799), based on a survey made between 1769 and 1775.
[33] White, Dir. Staffs. (1834).
[34] Hicks Smith, Brewood, 54.
[35] Ibid. 53–54.
[36] Ex inf. Staffs. C.C. Roads and Bridges Dept.
[37] Hicks Smith, Brewood, 54–55.
[38] Notes and Coll., Brewood, 93.
[39] Hicks Smith, Brewood, 55.

Four Ashes only the Potteries coach, the Red Rover, was retained, running between Manchester and Birmingham until 1846.[40] The London–Liverpool coach, known as the Emerald, passed through Brewood town daily in each direction by 1834, calling at the Lion Inn, and for many years required an additional pair of horses to take it over the bad road through Bishop's Wood to Ivetsey Bank on Watling Street.[41] A rival coach, the Albion, preferred to go via Gailey with only four horses.[42] Also by 1834 there was a coach from Brewood to Wolverhampton and back each Wednesday and a 'car' there and back from the Fleur de Lis Inn on Wednesdays and Saturdays.[43] The Emerald was replaced in 1837 by a two-horse coach which eventually ran only between Wolverhampton and Kiddemore Green, and for some years after 1855 there was an 'omnibus' from Brewood to Wolverhampton and back twice a week.[44] The post office was at 'The Giffard's Arms' by 1818,[45] and by 1860 there was also a post office at Coven.[46]

The railway between Birmingham and Stafford runs through the eastern part of the parish and has a station at Four Ashes, which was opened in 1837, with two trains a day in each direction by 1838.[47] A further line from Bushbury Junction to the end of Stafford Street in Brewood town was being planned by 1874[48] but was never constructed.

The Staffordshire and Worcestershire Canal, completed in 1772,[49] crosses the south-eastern part of the parish. The Birmingham and Liverpool Junction Canal (now the Shropshire Union), running northward through the middle of the parish, was begun in 1830.[50] It was opened in 1843[51] and in 1851 had 'commodious wharves and warehouses' in Brewood town and Chillington.[52] The wharves were still in existence in 1956 but neither had been in commercial use for the past 30 years.[53] The Belvide reservoir built in connexion with the canal about a mile north-west of the town covers some 208 acres,[54] and by 1860 was noted for its pike,[55] the Giffards of Chillington having the fishing and shooting rights by at least 1876.[56]

Somerford Bridge (formerly Stone Bridge), carrying the road from Brewood to Four Ashes over the Penk, was repaired at the expense of the parish in 1605[57] and at the expense of the county in 1711.[58] Rebuilt in 1796,[59] it was described in 1830 as 'old but in good repair'.[60] An attempt by the Hon. Edward Monckton to divert the road from Brewood to cross the Penk at Somerford Mill farther south was defeated at a vestry meeting in 1781; the foot-

bridge at the mill, apparently the responsibility of the lord of Somerford, would have had to be replaced by a carriage bridge, the cost of maintaining which would have fallen upon the parish.[61] Somerford Bridge is a stone bridge of four segmental arches, splayed piers, and refuges at parapet level. The core is probably of the 17th century, but there has been much rebuilding, and the bridge has been widened on its north side. Standeford Bridge, carrying the Stafford–Wolverhampton road over the Saredon Brook before it enters the Penk, is mentioned in 1630[62] and was rebuilt as a cart bridge c. 1757.[63] It was widened by the county in 1823[64] and stated to be in good repair in 1830.[65] A bridge at Gunstone was repaired by the parish in 1663 at a cost of £1 5s. 4d. It then seems to have been of timber,[66] but was rebuilt as a stone bridge in 1682 at a cost to the parish of £2 10s.[67] Lows Bridge over the Penk near Brewood Lower Forge (see below) occurs in 1724.[68] King's Bridge, now Jackson's Bridge, carrying the road from Brewood to Coven over the Penk, and possibly to be identified with 'the bridge of Coven, near the Park of Brewood' mentioned in 1286,[69] was rebuilt by the county in 1824.[70] Two bridges over Dean's Hall Brook and Brewood Hall Brook were repaired by the parish in 1663.[71] There are also thirteen bridges in the parish over the Shropshire Union Canal and five over the Staffordshire and Worcestershire Canal. Avenue Bridge, carrying Chillington Lower Avenue over the Shropshire Union Canal about 500 yds. north of Chillington Wharf, dates from c. 1830 and is of rustic-faced stone ashlar with long curved balustraded parapets.

The workhouse, formerly in the lane leading to Kiddemore between the Churchfields and Hockerill, was moved at some time between 1795 and 1801 to premises in Bargate which in 1837 became the workhouse for the Penkridge Union.[72] Extensions made between 1838 and 1842 gave it a capacity of 200,[73] but in 1872 the poor of the Union were moved to the new workhouse in Cannock.[74] The house and garden in Brewood were sold in 1878 to Major J. E. Monckton and the proceeds added to the Workhouse Charity.[75] Since 1920 the building has been a Dominican convent.[76] It is a long two-story brick range with projecting side wings and a five-sided porch. Large extensions were made at the rear in 1956.

There were gas-works, owned by a private company, in the town between at least 1872 and 1912,[77] but by 1916 gas was provided by the Stafford

[40] Ibid.
[41] Ibid. 56.
[42] Ibid.
[43] White, *Dir. Staffs.* (1834).
[44] Hicks Smith, *Brewood*, 56.
[45] Parsons and Bradshaw, *Dir. Staffs.* (1818).
[46] *P.O. Dir. Staffs.* (1860).
[47] J. C. Tildesley, *Penkridge* (1886), 73, 74.
[48] Hicks Smith, *Brewood*, 57.
[49] *S.H.C.* 1934 (2), 111.
[50] Hicks Smith, *Brewood*, 56.
[51] White, *Dir. Staffs.* (1834).
[52] Ibid. (1851).
[53] Ex inf. the Clerk, Brewood Parish Council (1956).
[54] *Kelly's Dir. Staffs.* (1940).
[55] *P.O. Dir. Staffs.* (1860).
[56] Ibid. (1876).
[57] *Notes and Coll., Brewood*, 85.
[58] *S.H.C.* 1934 (2), 82.
[59] Ibid. 89.
[60] J. Potter, *List of Bridges which the Inhabitants of the County of Stafford are bound to repair* (1830), 4.

[61] Hicks Smith, *Brewood*, 55, 91.
[62] S.R.O., D. 260/M, box 8, bdle. m, Coven Ct. R.
[63] S.R.O., Bridges Index.
[64] S.R.O., Q/Fa, 1823–4.
[65] Potter, *List of Bridges*, 4.
[66] *Notes and Coll., Brewood*, 87.
[67] Ibid. 89.
[68] W.S.L., D. 1766/35, Ct. Baron and Ct. of Survey of the manor of Brewood, Mar. 1723/4, pp. 2, 10.
[69] *S.H.C.* v (1), 166.
[70] S.R.O., Bridges Index; S.R.O., Q/Fa, 1824–5; Teesdale, *Map of Staffs.* (1832).
[71] *Notes and Coll., Brewood*, 87.
[72] Hicks Smith, *Brewood*, 7; Parsons and Bradshaw, *Dir. Staffs.* (1818).
[73] White, *Dir. Staffs.* (1851), 439.
[74] Hicks Smith, *Brewood*. 7.
[75] Charity Com. files; see p. 48.
[76] See p. 45.
[77] *P.O. Dir. Staffs.* (1872; 1876); *Kelly's Dir. Staffs.* (1880 and later edns. to 1912); Hicks Smith, *Brewood*, 60.

Corporation.[78] Two pumping stations, one at Slade Heath, east of Coven, and the other north-east of Somerford Bridge, were built by the South Staffordshire Waterworks Company in 1922.[79] Electricity was available in the town by 1928[80] and throughout the parish by 1940.[81]

A reading-room, built in 1857 by 'Mr. Swann of this town' at the expense of T. W. Giffard, was mentioned in 1860 and 1868 as possessing 'a small but select library as well as newspapers and periodicals'[82] and was apparently still in existence in 1896.[83] A library of 600 volumes was formed under the auspices of the clergy c. 1842 and was held in 1874 by the Working Men's Institute.[84] This may have been the 'parochial library' of 1860 and 1868, open to subscribers of 4s. a year,[85] and the 'church library of divinity', with some 70 volumes, of 1884, 1892, and 1896.[86]

At the wake held on the Sunday following the September fair horse-racing was substituted for bull-baiting after 1835, and although by 1864 the wake consisted merely of 'two cake-stalls and two public-house balls', 'shows and sports' had been revived by 1874.[87] Before the First World War many visitors came to Brewood from the Black Country during the third week of September travelling by horse-drawn brake, but the wake seems to have lapsed, like the fair, after 1918.[88] The custom of adorning wells, and, at the Gospel places, trees and houses also, with boughs and flowers on Maundy Thursday was noted in 1686[89] and was still practised in 1794.[90]

From time immemorial until the end of 1872 an 8 o'clock curfew was rung each evening from All Hallowtide to Candlemas for about fifteen minutes.[91] The ringing of the 'Pudding Bell' at the end of midday service on Sunday and of the 'Pancake Bell' for a quarter of an hour before 11 a.m. on Shrove Tuesday had both been discontinued by 1874.[92]

There are remains of two sulphur wells in the parish, one in Chillington Park and the other in Gunstone in a field near the Water Splash.[93] Sulphurous waters were used as a remedy for leprosy, and a house for lepers seems to have been built near Gunstone, presumably on or near the site of the present Leper House Farm.[94] In the later 17th century men and animals suffering from scabs or itch were treated with these local waters which were also used by the inhabitants in brewing and cooking.[95]

There was considerable trade in timber here in the 18th century, carried on by the Emery family, one of whom was tenant of Brewood Hall for a few years after its sale to the Hon. Edward Monckton,[96] while the Sansom family had a large tannery in Brewood at some time during the 18th century.[97] By 1817 the chief manufacture was agricultural machinery.[98] There were lockmakers in the parish by at least 1818,[99] and by 1834 there were three in Brewood town and three in Coven.[1] The craft was in decline by 1874,[2] but there was still a locksmith in Brewood town in 1940.[3] Malting was a major occupation between at least 1834 and 1874.[4] Stradsfield Quarry to the west of Somerford Hall and near the Birmingham and Liverpool Junction Canal was being worked by 1834.[5] It was some 4 acres in extent and owned by the Giffards of Chillington.[6] It was disused by 1956. The stone used in the building of the churches at Bishop's Wood and Coven and of the Roman Catholic church in Brewood, as well as for local farm buildings and the restoration of Lapley church, came from this and a neighbouring quarry.[7] By 1924 the Four Ashes Manufacturing Company had opened their carbon works here.[8] The buildings were taken over by the General Electric Company c. 1940 and were occupied in 1956 by Battery Carbons Ltd., a subsidiary of G.E.C., and by G.E.C. Switchgear Works (Four Ashes Iron-clad Factory).[9] Since about 1950 the Midland Tar Distillers also have had a works at Four Ashes on a neighbouring site.[10]

By 1485 there was a forge in Brewood leased by the lord of the manor to Thomas Smith for a rent of 4d.,[11] and there was reference in 1603 to 'hammermen' of Brewood Park.[12] Thomas Chetwynd of Rugeley and Walter Coleman of Cannock built a forge on the Penk, less than a quarter of a mile south of Somerford Hall, c. 1620, and in 1623 Francis Somerford was complaining not only that the working of his water-mill was being impeded and his meadowland flooded but also that the iron-works were disturbing him and his family 'by the usual knocking thereof at several times of the night', by 'the unwholesome smoke, sparks and air . . . and by the ill neighbourhood of disordered and ill-disposed persons usually employed in and repairing unto such iron-works'.[13] There was a furnace in Brewood in 1642,[14] which in 1647 was stated to lie a quarter of a mile from the iron forge adjoining Brewood Park.[15] There was then ironstone also within two miles of

[78] Kelly's Dir. Staffs. (1916).
[79] Dates on buildings.
[80] Kelly's Dir. Staffs. (1928).
[81] Ibid. (1940).
[82] P.O. Dir. Staffs. (1860; 1868).
[83] Kelly's Dir. Staffs. (1884; 1892; 1896).
[84] Hicks Smith, Brewood, 34.
[85] P.O. Dir. Staffs. (1860; 1868).
[86] Kelly's Dir. Staffs. (1884; 1892; 1896).
[87] Hicks Smith, Brewood, 10; Notes and Coll., Brewood, 94–95.
[88] Ex inf. the Clerk, Brewood Parish Council (1956).
[89] Plot, Staffs. 318.
[90] 'Mara' [M. E. Wakefield], Ancient Brewood (1932), 72.
[91] Ibid. 34; Hicks Smith, Brewood, 10, 78.
[92] Hicks Smith, Brewood, 10–11.
[93] 'Mara', Ancient Brewood, 51–52; Teesdale, Map of Staffs. (1832). There is a third at Codsall Wood in the grounds of Pendrell Hall (Codsall parish, Seisdon hundred): 'Mara', op. cit. 51.
[94] Plot, Staffs. 101.
[95] Ibid. 101–2.
[96] See pp. 31, 37.

[97] Hicks Smith, Brewood, 35.
[98] Pitt, Staffs. 254.
[99] Parsons and Bradshaw, Dir. Staffs. (1818).
[1] White, Dir. Staffs. (1834).
[2] Hicks Smith, Brewood, 35.
[3] Kelly's Dir. Staffs. (1940).
[4] White, Dir. Staffs. (1834; 1851); Hicks Smith, Brewood, 35, 86.
[5] White, Dir. Staffs. (1834).
[6] Ibid.; Tithe Maps and Appt., Brewood (copy in W.S.L.).
[7] 'Mara', Ancient Brewood, 4, 6; Notes and Coll., Brewood, supplement, 6, 7.
[8] Kelly's Dir. Staffs. (1924).
[9] Ex inf. the Clerk, Cannock Rural District Council (1956); local inf.
[10] Ex inf. the Clerk, Cannock Rural District Council.
[11] S.H.C. 1912, 254.
[12] Ibid. 1940, 33.
[13] C 2/Jas. I, C 22/51.
[14] Brewood Par. Reg. (Staffs. Par. Reg. Soc.), 121.
[15] Church Comm. MS. 123783, Survey of Brewood 1646/7.

the park.[16] The forge and iron-works known as Brewood Park Forge or Brewood Upper Forge was leased by Walter Giffard of Chillington to Philip Foley of Stourbridge (Worcs.) in 1669, evidently in succession to Thomas Foley, and the lease was renewed for seventeen years at a rent of £20 in 1673 when there was also reference to another forge in the parish known as the Lower Forge, then apparently no longer in use.[17] Brewood Park Forge was still in operation in 1682.[18] The New Forge near Shurgreave Field within the manor of Brewood occurs in 1696.[19] There were two forges in the parish in 1717, the Lower Forge, erected on land inclosed out of Shurgreave Field, and the Upper Forge, and the total output was 100 tons.[20] In 1735 one of these forges, presumably the Lower, was described as in Brewood and the other as in Coven,[21] and both were still in operation in 1750.[22] The Lower Forge was disused by 1753,[23] while that at Coven was worked at some time during the 18th century by Mr. Barker, an iron-master of Congreve[24] (in Penkridge parish). The Upper Forge is probably to be identified with a forge on the site of the 1682 iron-works that was in operation between at least 1747 and 1832,[25] but this was disused by c. 1841 when the pool was owned and held by T. W. Giffard.[26] The building seems to have been used subsequently as a corn mill and was burnt down c. 1869.[27] Low brick footings remain near the pool, which, now silted up, is owned by Mr. T. A. W. Giffard of Chillington Hall.[28] Forge House, on the opposite side of the road, incorporates a large late-16th-century brick chimney with four nibbed shafts and a moulded base. The house itself dates from the early 18th and late 19th centuries.

There was a Roman villa near Engleton on a slight eminence overlooking the Penk some 500 yds. south of Watling Street, inhabited probably between the late 2nd and the 4th centuries.[29]

Henry II visited Brewood probably in September 1165.[30] King John was here in April 1200,[31] January 1206,[32] and August 1207,[33] and Edward I in October 1278.[34] Queen Elizabeth I stayed one night at Chillington Hall on her way south from Stafford in 1575.[35] A proposal in 1585 to lodge Mary Queen of Scots at Chillington Hall was abandoned since the neighbourhood was considered too 'backward in religion' and the house not secure enough.[36]

The greatest concentration of old buildings is in the region of Dean Street and the Market Place which appear to have been built up at an early date. At the lower end of Dean Street, opposite its junction with The Pavement, is a timber-framed building, now four cottages known as Old Smithy Cottages, which retains evidence of a single-story hall of c. 1350. The hall, which is represented by

the two middle cottages, consisted of two bays and covered an area of 28 ft. by 18 ft. The framing of the side walls, which have heavy posts and deep curved braces, is still visible although altered by the insertion of later doors and windows. The wall plates have stopped double chamfers and the cambered tie-beam of the open truss which divided the bays forms part of a later partition between the cottages. The original steeply pitched roof is of the trussed rafter type, having a king-post with four-way struts above the tie-beam of the central truss. All the timbers are smoke-blackened. The partition at the north-west end of the hall roof has evidence on its farther side that there was originally another bay beyond it. The structure now in this position is a timber-framed replacement of the early 17th century. Adjoining the south-east wall of the former hall is a brick addition of c. 1700. A spliced purlin near this end of the roof suggests that there may originally have been an additional bay here also. On the other hand, the timbers in the gable end are heavily weathered, showing that for some considerable period this wall was external and exposed to the elements. About 50 yds. south of this house there was formerly a cottage which stood partly demolished for many years and has now disappeared. Exposed in one gable end was the open truss of a medieval hall, having cruck principals below collar-beam level.[37] This type of truss has been found elsewhere associated with two-bay halls of the 14th century.[38]

Facing The Pavement at its junction with Dean Street is a long timber-framed range. The two cottages at its north-east end have been formed out of a three-bay house probably of the early 16th century. The cottage at the extreme end contains the cross-passage with its original doorhead, the mortices of the buttery partition being visible in a main cross-beam. The second cottage represents the single-bay hall and the solar, the end walls of the former being heavily smoke-blackened. A large fireplace and stack of c. 1600 have been inserted. The south-west end of the range consists of a two-bay cottage added in the early 17th century but incorporating earlier material. The external framing can be distinguished from that of the older structure by its small square panels. The whole range was heightened c. 1700, the roof trusses of both this and the earlier dates being visible internally. Farther along The Pavement a roof truss consisting of cambered tie, collar-beam, and principals remains embedded in the gable end of a later cottage.

On the south-west side of Dean Street are at least five timber-framed houses of the late 16th or early 17th century. In most cases they retain exposed framing on their rear and end elevations and have

[16] Ibid.
[17] Giffard papers at Chillington, bdle. 19.
[18] S.H.C. 1919, 240; Plot, Map of Staffs. (1682).
[19] W.S.L., Brewood Ct. R. 1693–1709, 2 Nov. 1696.
[20] W.S.L., D. 1766/35, pp. 10, 11; E. Wyndham Hulme, 'Statistical History of the British Iron Trade 1717–50' (Newcomen Soc. 1928), 8 (copy in W.S.L.).
[21] Shaw, Staffs. i, table opp. p. (1).
[22] Newcomen Soc. 1928, 8.
[23] W.S.L., Brewood Ct. R. 1753–63, 23 Apr. and 27 Aug. 1753. It was described in 1757 as 'now pulled down in part'; ibid. 4 July 1757.   [24] Pitt, Staffs. 258.
[25] Smith, New Map of Staffs. (1747); Yates, Map of Staffs. (1799); estate maps at Chillington, no. 8 (1808); Greenwood, Map of Staffs. (1820); Teesdale, Map of Staffs. (1832).

[26] Tithe Maps and Appt., Brewood (copy in W.S.L.).
[27] Hicks Smith, Brewood. 59.
[28] Ex inf. Mr. T. A. W. Giffard (1956).
[29] S.H.C. 1938, 267–93.
[30] Cal. Chart R. 1300–26, 438; R. W. Eyton, Itinerary of Henry II (1878), 83.
[31] Cal. Rot. Chart. (Rec. Com.), i. 43.
[32] Rot. Litt. Pat. (Rec. Com.), i. 59.
[33] Rot. Litt. Claus. (Rec. Com.), i. 90, 91–92.
[34] Cal. Fine R. 1272–1307, 100; Cal. Close, 1272–9, 478.
[35] S.H.C. n.s. v. 127.
[36] Ibid. 136–8.
[37] S.H.C. 1939, 225–6, fig. iii.
[38] Cf. house at Weobley, Herefs.: R.C.H.M. Survey Herefs. iii. 199, pl. 38(b).

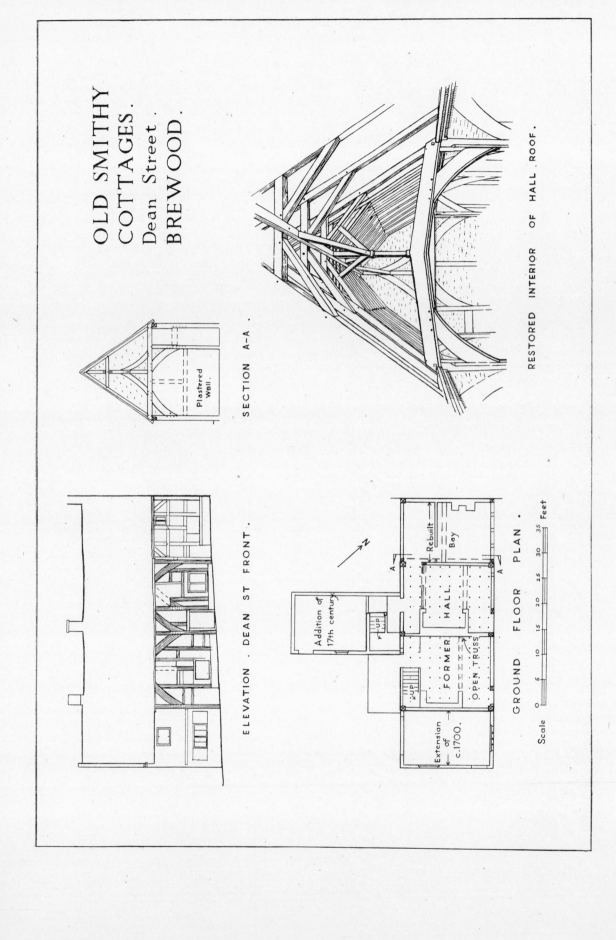

OLD SMITHY
COTTAGES.
Dean Street.
BREWOOD.

SECTION A-A.

Plastered Wall.

RESTORED INTERIOR OF HALL ROOF.

ELEVATION . DEAN ST FRONT .

GROUND FLOOR PLAN .

Addition of 17th century.

UP

FORMER HALL.

OPEN TRUSS.

Extension of c.1700.

UP

Rebuilt Bay

N

A

A

Scale 0 5 10 15 20 25 30 35 Feet

centrally placed chimneys of the original date. They include Dean Cottage at the higher end of the street, Wood End, with a late-18th-century 'Gothic' bay window facing the road, and Old Smithy House, refronted in the 18th century. West Gate on the same side of the street is dated 1723 and has a good brick frontage of the period. The doorcase is original, and the central first-floor window has side scrolls and a grotesque mask below the keystone. The Chantry and The Deanery are slightly later 18th-century houses of similar type, the latter having an imposing façade with angle pilasters and pedimented windows, altered in the 19th century. These houses contain good staircases and other contemporary internal details. The enriched door-hood of Dean Street House is dated 1791. The first-floor windows, which have segmental heads to the lights, are of the type that appears to have been fashionable in Brewood at this period. A girls' school is said to have been held here in the 19th century.[39] Dean House on the opposite side of the street has a good symmetrical front of c. 1800. Other houses and cottages date from the late 18th and early 19th centuries.

The street connecting Dean Street with the Market Place dates from 1864 when a new road was cut.[40] The east side of the Market Place, lying north of the parish church, was traditionally the site of the 14th-century capital messuage of the bishop's manor.[41] An ancient timber building on the site of the house known as The Dreadnought was demolished here in 1896[42] but there is no evidence to connect this with the bishop's messuage. South of this a house with a three-story 18th-century frontage is structurally of c. 1680 and has a good staircase of this period. Farther south the so-called 'Manor House', also refronted, has a late-16th-century rear wing and one of c. 1700. The houses forming the opposite side of the Market Place are timber-framed structures of c. 1600 refronted early in the 18th century with later shop-fronts inserted. The house at the north end has two upper-cruck roof trusses, probably late-17th-century work. The post office, on the north side of the Market Place, formerly had a good pedimented brick frontage of c. 1800.[43] The two-story stucco building at the corner of Sandy Lane, which retains its fluted doorcase and railings, is of similar date. In general the Market Place is Georgian in appearance in spite of alterations and the insertion of later shops.

A timber-framed building at the east end of Newport Street was faced with brickwork in the early 18th century and retains a small open shop of this period under a pentice roof. An adjoining outbuilding with stabling, was at one time the fire station.[44] A group of timber-framed buildings, formerly known as The Mansion House[45] and standing at the junction of Newport Street with School Road, date from c. 1600. They consist of a low cottage range and a small house with two stories, attics, and a centrally placed entrance and chimney.

Most of the houses in Bargate were built after the

beginning of the 19th century, but a few partially timber-framed cottages remain, and Bargate House dates from the mid-18th century. The former pinfold stood on the south side of the street east of the canal bridge.[46] The site is now occupied by a single-story shop. Facing the end of Stafford Street is a tall brick house, now known as Castle Flats, with a very striking and ornate Gothic frontage.[47] It is said to have been built by William Rock, an apothecary (d. 1753),[48] who acquired a large sum at some date before 1740 by backing the racehorse Speedwell.[49] The house was formerly called Speedwell Castle. The building certainly represents an extravagant outlay on a confined site, but the architectural evidence suggests that its date is unlikely to be earlier than 1760. The front has two five-sided bays of three stories flanking a central entrance. The ogee-headed and crocketted porch is supported on shafted columns. The windows of the bays are either round-headed with keystones or ogee-headed with acorn finials. A few of the original Gothic glazing-bars have survived. Internally the staircase has a fretted balustrade of the 'Chinese Chippendale' type and one ground-floor room has an elaborate plaster ceiling and doorhead.

Stafford Street dates in the main from the 18th century. A house near the north end, dated 1715, contains a roof truss in which a medieval tie-beam has been reused. At the south end is a uniform terrace of six mid-18th-century houses. Opposite Stafford House, a brick building of c. 1800, are two early-19th-century stucco fronts applied to a large L-shaped timber-framed house of the early 17th century. Adjoining it to the south and parallel with the street is an outbuilding containing a large medieval cruck truss. The south end of this building was evidently reconstructed in the early 17th century when a second cruck truss was replaced by one having an upper cruck tenoned into a cross beam.

The former smithy in Sandy Lane is a brick house incorporating a chimney and timbers from an earlier structure. The smithy itself has been converted into a living room. In other parts of the town are isolated examples of timber-framed structures of early-17th-century date.

The old grammar school, a building probably of the 17th century, disappeared in a reconstruction of 1856. It stood on the south-west side of School Road with the head master's house adjoining it. An 18th-century drawing[50] shows the latter as a building of the late 17th century with mullioned and transomed windows and a curvilinear central gable. The school itself was a long single-story structure in which both the master's and the usher's classes were taught. In 1799 the master's house was enlarged and refronted.[51] At the same time two attached houses on the opposite side of the road were acquired and converted into an usher's house and a junior school.[52] These buildings, considerably altered, now represent the oldest part of the school. They are said to bear a

[39] Local inf.
[40] Hicks Smith, *Brewood*, 12–13; see p. 18.
[41] See p. 25.
[42] Ex inf. Mrs. M. E. Wakefield, Brewood (1957).
[43] Photograph *penes* Mrs. M. E. Wakefield.
[44] O.S. Map 6", lvi N.W. (1882); local inf.
[45] Hicks Smith, *Brewood: Supplement* (1881), map of Brewood Town, 1680.
[46] Ibid.; local inf.

[47] See plate opposite.
[48] Brewood Par. Reg., from transcript in W.S.L., iv, 9 Dec. 1753.
[49] Hicks Smith, *Brewood*, 34.
[50] W.S.L., Staffs. Views, ii, p. 135.
[51] C. Dunkley, *Brewood Grammar School* (1936), 18; W.S.L., Staffs. Views, ii, pp. 133 (a, 1842), 134 (1844).
[52] Dunkley, *Brewood Grammar School*, 18.

bricklayer's date of 1778.[53] In 1799 School Road was diverted behind these houses, and the original road, by the erection of a wall and gate, became part of the school grounds.[54] In 1830 a portion of the croft or playground was sold to the Birmingham and Liverpool Junction Canal Company.[55] A hall and classrooms replaced the original school building in 1856, and the head master's house was rebuilt in 1863.[56] Further extensions date from 1898, 1926, 1935, and 1952.[57]

Little expansion of the town took place in the late 19th and early 20th centuries, the small residential development being mostly confined to the roads to Kiddemore Green and Coven. By far the largest area of new building is to the north-east, between Deansfield and the Stafford road. Here council and private housing estates have been developed since the Second World War and are still expanding. The police station and three police houses in the Pavement date from 1950.

The outlying parts of the parish also contain buildings of considerable interest. In Chillington Street, a lane that formed the main approach to Chillington Hall before the early 18th century, are several small timber-framed cottages with thatched roofs. They date from c. 1600 and have exposed framing in small square panels.

White House Farm, which internally appears to date from the early 18th century, has a long north elevation evidently designed to screen the farm buildings and present an imposing façade to Chillington Park on the north. The frontage is of brick, now painted white, with stone dressings. The tall central block, masking the farmhouse, is connected by short colonnades to side pavilions. Both the main block and the pavilions have pediments, formerly with ball finials, and a treatment of tall round-headed recessed panels.[58]

Leper House Farm[59] to the east is a timber-framed building of the central chimney type dating from the early 17th century. A later dormer window is dated 1716. One of the barns is partly timber-framed.

Park Lodge, perpetuating in its name the former park of Brewood,[60] is an isolated cottage 150 yds. east of Chillington Wharf. Its older portion is timber-framed and dates from the late 16th or early 17th century.

Grange House Farm at the north end of Coven village retains a two-storied timber-framed cross-wing dating from the later 16th century. The upper floor is jettied on three sides, supported on bull-nosed joists and with a heavy dragon beam at the south-west angle. The framed partition between the two ground-floor rooms contains a Tudor door-head and both rooms have chamfered and broach-stopped beams and joists. The original stair newel is in position, and a first-floor room contains panelling of the late 16th or early 17th century. Coven Farm is a timber-framed two-story house built on a T-shaped plan and probably of the late 16th century. The roof has queen-post trusses, and the upper story was

originally open to the ridge. At the corner of Lawn Lane and attached to the building and engineering works of John McLean & Sons Ltd. is a house originally of the 16th century which has been largely rebuilt in brick. The gable-end facing the road has stone walling and a projecting chimney-stack, probably a partial rebuilding dating from the 17th century. The engineering works occupy a mid-19th-century brick building, formerly a brewery.[61] A colour-washed brick house in the centre of Coven, known as The Homage, has a date stone of 1679. It consists of two stories, attics, and cellars, and has a rectangular plan with a projecting porch wing near the north end of the front. The large central stack contains a cellar fireplace. The eaves cornice, gable parapets, and cellar windows are of stone. The Beeches, a tall brick house in its own grounds, dates from the late 18th century, and there are several other 18th-century houses in the village. Estate cottages built in the mid- and late 19th century by the Moncktons of Stretton occur in Coven village, at Four Ashes, and at Hill Top.

Owing to their position near the main Stafford–Wolverhampton road and the industrial development at Four Ashes, both Coven and Four Ashes have expanded considerably since c. 1930. There are council houses both north and east of the school, near Jackson's Bridge, and at Cross Green. Chambley Green is a three-sided court of fourteen terrace houses built by Cannock R.D.C. in 1955. There are caravan sites in Lawn Lane, at Lower Green, and near Coven Farm.

At Clay Gates, Engleton, are two single-story square brick cottages known locally as the 'pepper-pots'. They were built by Mrs. Monckton of Stretton in the mid-19th century and their design is said to have been suggested by workers' dwellings in Scotland.[62]

Yew Tree Cottage in the hamlet of Horsebrook is a well-preserved example of a small brick house of the late 17th century. It has an L-shaped plan and retains its brick strings, stone eaves cornice, and wood-framed windows with leaded lights. Horsebrook Manor Farm has a 17th-century timber-framed barn. Lea Fields Farm at Shutt Green to the south-west incorporates a late-16th-century timber-framed house with a central chimney. One of the farm buildings contains two upper-cruck trusses, probably work of the late 17th or early 18th century.

At Kiddemore Green and Bishop's Wood are scattered timber-framed cottages of the late 16th and early 17th centuries.

Somerford Grange, a farmhouse in Somerford hamlet, is said to have been built by George Barbor[63] who took possession of the estate in 1761.[64] The three-storied south elevation was designed to present a picturesque front to Somerford park and is of interest as an example of 18th-century Gothic taste. It has a castellated parapet and stone bands, the central windows being circular and the windows of the two projecting bays having trefoil heads. Somer-

[53] Dunkley, *Brewood Grammar School*, 18.
[54] D. Thompson, *Brewood Grammar School* (1953), 21; W.S.L., Staffs. Views, ii, p. 137 (R. Paddy, 1799).
[55] Thompson, *Brewood Grammar School*, 30.
[56] Dunkley, *Brewood Grammar School*, 18.
[57] Thompson, *Brewood Grammar School*, 77–87.
[58] It may be the work of one of the architects employed at Chillington, either James Paine (c. 1770) or Sir John

Soane (c. 1786).
[59] See p. 20 for the existence of a leper hospital in the parish.
[60] See p. 26.
[61] Local inf.
[62] Local inf.
[63] Dunkley, *Brewood Grammar School*, 43.
[64] See p. 35.

'Speedwell Castle'

Dean Street from the church tower

BREWOOD

South East View of BREWOOD CHURCH, Staffordshire 1845

BREWOOD: the church from the south-east in 1845

BEDNALL: the church from the north-east in 1836

ford Farm has a 17th-century timber-framed barn and there is a small timber-framed cottage in the hamlet.

The architecture of the manor-houses and houses attached to lesser estates is treated under the relevant sections.

MARKETS AND FAIRS. In 1221 the Bishop of Coventry and Lichfield was granted a market in Brewood each Friday until the full age of the king.[65] In 1259 the Crown granted the bishop a market to be held in his manor each Monday.[66] The bishop successfully upheld this right in 1293.[67] In 1382 the burgesses of Stafford complained that Brewood market had been held for twenty years past without royal licence and to their prejudice,[68] but at some time between 1387 and 1390 the king confirmed the bishop's right.[69] By 1680 the Monday market had been discontinued,[70] but by 1747 a Tuesday market was being held.[71] The market-cross collapsed in 1810,[72] while by 1817 the decayed market-house had been pulled down and markets were no longer held.[73] The Friday market was revived in November 1833[74] but had been discontinued by 1851, owing to the growing importance of Wolverhampton.[75] The market pump was destroyed in a bonfire on 5 November 1837.[76]

In 1259 the king granted the bishop an annual fair at the manor of Brewood on the vigil, feast and morrow of the Nativity of the Virgin (7, 8, 9 September).[77] The bishop upheld this right in 1293,[78] and at some time between 1387 and 1390 Richard II confirmed it.[79] By 1662, when the fair was held on 8 and 9 September, the main traffic was in horses.[80] After the change of style in the calendar the date was altered to 19 September.[81] An additional fair, free of tolls, held on the second Tuesday in May by at least 1834,[82] had lapsed by 1860,[83] and that on 19 September was gradually discontinued after the First World War.[84]

MANORS. *BREWOOD* was among the possessions of the church of Lichfield before the Conquest and in 1086 was held by the bishop as 5 hides.[85] It was confirmed to the bishop with other temporalities in

1152 by Pope Eugenius III,[86] and Henry II, probably in 1155, granted the bishop 80 acres of assarted land at Brewood taken from the royal forest after 1135.[87] Brewood remained with the bishops of Lichfield[88] until 1852 when it passed to the Ecclesiastical Commissioners.[89]

For some years before 1643 the manor had been leased to the Giffards of Chillington, and Peter Giffard, who was lessee c. 1647 at the time of his sequestration as a papist and for taking arms against Parliament, paid a rent of £58 3s.[90] Although the park was surveyed in 1647, the bounds of the manor could not then be defined since, 'by reason of the unity of possession many ages in Mr. Giffard and his ancestors' of the manor of Chillington and of lands in Brewood, Broom Hall, Hatton, and Chillington, 'the late bishop's lands and his are annexed and for the present not distinguished'.[91] Sir Roland King, who had acquired the manor, was complaining in 1651 that although he had paid for it he was deprived of the rent due from tenants to whom the State had given leases.[92] By 1670 Peter Giffard's son Walter was holding the manor.[93] The Giffards thereafter retained a leasehold which seems to have afforded them a status and rights equivalent to lordship,[94] but in 1758 Thomas, great-nephew of Walter Giffard, made over his lease for lives to Thomas Prowse[95] in order to avoid prosecution as a papist.[96] Courts were held in the name of Thomas Prowse until 1 December 1766, in the name of John Prowse from 20 July 1767 to 16 May 1768 and in the name of Thomas Giffard again from 8 August 1768.[97] Thomas's grandson T. W. Giffard was granted the lease in 1825[98] and is said to have bought the reversionary interest from the Ecclesiastical Commissioners in 1852.[99] In 1956 Mr. T. A. W. Giffard of Chillington owned such manorial rights as still existed.[1]

Bishop Roger de Weseham, who was at Brewood in 1253[2] and 1254,[3] retired there in 1256 and died the next year.[4] The bishops continued to visit Brewood until at least 1305,[5] but by 1321 the capital messuage, with a garden and a close, had been leased out for a rent of 18d. which, it was then estimated, might be increased to 40d.[6] The manor-house

[65] *Rot. Litt. Claus.* (Rec. Com.), i. 466.
[66] *Cal. Chart R.* 1257–1300, 18–19.
[67] *S.H.C.* vi (1), 243–4.
[68] C 145/224, no. 13.
[69] *Cal. Rot. Chart.* (Rec. Com.), 192.
[70] *S.H.C.* 1919, 240.
[71] J. Smith, *New Map of Staffs.* (1747).
[72] Hicks Smith, *Brewood*, 5.
[73] Pitt, *Staffs.* 253.
[74] White, *Dir. Staffs.* (1834).
[75] Ibid. (1851).
[76] Hicks Smith, *Brewood*, 5.
[77] *Cal. Chart. R.* 1257–1300, 18–19.
[78] *S.H.C.* vi (1), 243–4.
[79] *Cal. Rot. Chart.* (Rec. Com.), 192.
[80] Giffard Papers at Chillington, bdles. 2 and 22. There was land called Horse Fair within the manor in 1753: W.S.L., Brewood Ct. R. 1753–63, 23 Apr. 1753.
[81] Pitt, *Staffs.* 253; Hicks Smith, *Brewood*, 10. It may have become a one-day fair by 1741: T. Badeslade and W. H. Toms, *Map of Staffs.* (1741).
[82] White, *Dir. Staffs.* (1834; 1851).
[83] *P.O. Dir. Staffs.* (1860).
[84] Ex inf. the Clerk, Brewood Parish Council (1956).
[85] *V.C.H. Staffs.* iv. 41, no. 66.
[86] *S.H.C.* 1924, no. 262; *S.H.C.* iii (1), 182–4.
[87] *S.H.C.* 1924, no. 19.
[88] Ibid. ii (1), 59, 63–64; *Rot. Hund.* (Rec. Com.), ii.

114; *S.H.C.* vi (1), 243–4; *Cal. Fine R.* 1413–72, 326; E 134, Mich. 3 Jas. II, no. 37.
[89] Dunkley, *Brewood Grammar School*, 31.
[90] *Cal. Cttee. for Compounding*, 2711; *S.H.C.* n.s. v. 177; Church Comm. MS. 123783, copy of Survey of Brewood Manor, 22 Mar. 1646/7.
[91] Ch. Comm. MS. 123783. The 'late bishop' was Robert Wright, who died 1643.
[92] *Cal. Cttee. for Compounding*, 2711.
[93] W.S.L., Brewood Ct. R. 1653/4—1693, 17 Jan. 1669/70.
[94] E 134, Mich. 3 Jas. II, no. 37; E 134, East. 4 Jas. II, no. 32; W.S.L., D. 1766/35, Survey of the manor and its members, Mar. 1723/4.
[95] W.S.L., Brewood Ct. R. 1753–63, under 3 Sept. 1759.
[96] W.S.L., C.B. Brewood, Manorial Fees, &c.
[97] W.S.L., Brewood Ct. R. 1753–63.
[98] Ch. Comm. MS. 123780.
[99] Dunkley, *Brewood Grammar School*, 31.
[1] Ex inf. Mr. T. A. W. Giffard (1956).
[2] *S.H.C.* 1924, no. 667.
[3] Ibid. no. 65.
[4] *Notes and Coll., Brewood*, 108.
[5] *S.H.C.* 1924, nos. 49, 318, 599, 600, 702.
[6] Hicks Smith, *Brewood*, 62. The manor-house is thought to have occupied the east end of the present market-place: ibid. 2–3.

had been leased to the Vicar of Brewood by 1473,[7] but there seems to have been no house in existence by 1538, when a pasture described as the site of the manor was leased to Roger Fowke of Brewood.[8]

In 1321 there was a fishpond within the manor of Brewood valued at 10s., although no rent was received for it as no fish were found there,[9] and by 1473 a fishery within the manor had been leased to Thomas Knightley for 20d.[10]

By c. 1280 the bishop had created burgage tenure in Brewood, the tenement being situated at Woodhouse-end.[11] One of the common fields in the manor was called Burgage Field.[12]

In 1086 the bishop held woodland at Brewood $1\frac{1}{2}$ league long and a league broad.[13] In 1139 and 1144 the Pope confirmed the bishop in his possession of the 'hay and forest' of Brewood.[14] A plot of woodland here called 'Stryfwode' was sold by Sir Fulk Pembrugge, lord of Tong (Salop.), to the bishop in 1314.[15] In 1321 the underwood from a wood in the manor was valued at 51 marks, although only 12s. had been realized by the sale of underwood that year.[16] In 1538 the bishop gave Roger Fowke of Brewood the right to take timber from 'the common wood of Brewood called Bishop's Wood or Kerrimore' for 40 years, the dean and chapter confirming the grant.[17] In 1661 Peter Giffard of Chillington, presumably as lessee of the bishop's manor, had a 'warren of connies' in Bishop's Wood which he then leased to one of his younger sons, John Giffard of Blackladies.[18] By 1724 Bishop's Wood was all waste ground except for the rabbit warren, leased by the Giffards to a John Blakemore.[19]

In 1200 King John, after visiting Brewood, gave the bishop licence to inclose a park 2 leagues in circumference within the woodland of the manor,[20] and, having disafforested the royal forest of Brewood in 1204,[21] allowed the bishop to erect a deer-leap in this park, over against 'the forest' in 1206.[22] This park seems to have lain on the western side of the Penk opposite Coven.[23] The king gave 30 stags from this park to the Archbishop of Dublin in 1213, during a vacancy in the See of Coventry and Lichfield.[24] The deer-leap within the park was said in 1286 to be to the injury of the forest of Cannock.[25] In 1321 the park with a pasture was valued at 100s. though no rent was received because of the tenant's right of turbary.[26] In 1485 a sum of 23s. 4d. was spent on repairing the park palings.[27] Although in

1534 Bishop Rowland Lee, at the request of Thomas Cromwell, appointed a Ralph Sadleyer as keeper of the park and bailiff of the manor,[28] in 1535 Thomas Giffard was receiving a salary of £5 0s. 8d. as bailiff and custodian of the park.[29]

The park was in the tenure of John Giffard in 1609.[30] By 1647 Peter Giffard held it on lease for £8 a year and a brace of bucks and a brace of does in season, but the sequestrators then valued it at a rack rent of £134 13s. 1½d., namely 300 acres at 5s., 300 acres at 3s., and 293 acres at 12d. an acre, while a tenement and land leased by Peter Giffard to a Widow Bumfield for £17 12s. they considered should be worth £23.[31] In assessing the value of the woodland the sequestrators calculated that ironworking in the vicinity would 'advance the sale of the wood'; and they suggested that 'a great part of Brewood Park will bear good corn and may be much improved by ploughing.'[32] In 1649 Peter Giffard, lessee under the former bishop, was farmer of the park from the Committee of the County of Stafford or their lessee and had cut down 110 timber trees, worth £300, of which some were used by him to repair the park-pales, 'in these distracted times . . . so pulled down and stolen', and the rest, worth £102 17s. 8d. or more were disposed of to friends and neighbours; he had sold bark, 'from timber fallen in season for barking', to Francis Spooner of Brewood, tanner, for £5 10s.[33] Only two brace of deer were then left in the park; part of it was already sown with corn, and a further 100 acres was being made ready for ploughing.[34]

Walter Giffard was lessee c. 1680.[35] When the bishop leased the park in 1777 to Frances, widow of Thomas Giffard, the rent was still £8.[36] By 1788 the lessee was Thomas's son, Thomas Giffard.[37]

By 1255 the bishop held a view of frankpledge in the manor of Brewood and its 'members', which were together assessed at 5 hides, geldable,[38] and were described in 1285 as the liberty of Brewood, held in chief by the bishop as of his barony of Lichfield.[39] The temporalities of Brewood, assessed at £38 4s., then included 30s. from perquisites of courts and 15s. from view of frankpledge.[40] In 1293 the bishop defended his right to view of frankpledge, infangthief, and waif in his manor,[41] and in 1316 he was found to have return of writs in his vill of Brewood.[42] A fixed payment of 10s. 4d. for view of frankpledge called frithsilver was made in 1473 by the members of the manor, namely Brewood,

---

[7] W.S.L., S. MS. 335 (1), Compotus R. of Bpric. of Cov. and Lich. 13–14 Edw. IV, m. 17, where there is also mention of the 'porta manerii'.
[8] W.S.L., S. MS. 201 (1), p. 368.
[9] Hicks Smith, *Brewood*, 62.
[10] W.S.L., S. MS. 335 (1), m. 17.
[11] See p. 36.
[12] See p. 38. Parcels of land called Burgage End and The Burgage lay in the Deanery Manor in 1897: W.S.L., D. 1766/33, Deanery Manor Ct. Bks. ii, pp. 105–6.
[13] *V.C.H. Staffs.* iv. 41, no. 66.
[14] *S.H.C.* 1924, nos. 452, 453.
[15] Eyton, *Shropshire*, ii. 237.
[16] Hicks Smith, *Brewood*, 62.
[17] W.S.L., S. MS. 201 (1), p. 368.
[18] Giffard papers at Chillington, tin box, bdle. 1.
[19] W.S.L., D. 1766/35, p. 10. For the inclosing of the and at Bishop's Wood see p. 38.
[20] *Rot. Chart.* (Rec. Com.), i. 43, 60; *S.H.C.* 1924, no. 221.
[21] *Rot. Chart.* (Rec. Com.), i. 122.
[22] *Rot. Litt. Claus.* (Rec. Com.), i. 64.

[23] *S.H.C.* 1924, no. 692; *Notes and Coll., Brewood,* 52; Hicks Smith, *Brewood*, 3. Brewood Park Farm and Park Lodge are situated in this area.
[24] *Rot. Litt. Claus.* (Rec. Com.), i. 139.
[25] *S.H.C.* v (1), 167.
[26] Hicks Smith, *Brewood*, 62.
[27] *S.H.C.* 1912, 254.
[28] *L. & P. Hen. VIII*, vii (1), p. 173.
[29] *Valor Eccl.* (Rec. Com.), iii. 130.
[30] C 66/1790, no. 31.
[31] Church Comm. MS. 123783, Survey of Brewood Mar. 1646/7.
[32] Ibid.; see pp. 20–21 for details of the iron-works.
[33] Ch. Comm. MS. 123783, Resurvey 12 Mar. 1648/9.
[34] Ibid.
[35] *S.H.C.* 1919, 240.
[36] C.P. 43/821, rot. 117–21.   [37] Ibid.
[38] *Rot. Hund.* (Rec. Com.), ii. 114.
[39] *Feud. Aids*, v. 2.
[40] *Tax. Eccl.* (Rec. Com.), 250.
[41] *S.H.C.* vi (1), 244.
[42] *Feud. Aids*, v. 17.

Horsebrook, Engleton, Somerford, Gunstone, Hyde, Broom Hall, and Chillington.[43] The bishop's demesne lands of Kiddemore ('Kyrrymore') were then held on lease by five tenants, and no frithsilver was due from the remaining member, Hatton, because there was no building there.[44] Each brewer in Brewood and Horsebrook was paying 1d. for toll of ale.[45] The townships within the view in 1724 were Brewood, Horsebrook, Kiddemore, Engleton, Somerford, Chillington, the Hattons, and Gunstone.[46]

ASPLEY, within the fee of Coven by 1310,[47] was described as a manor in 1507 when the overlordship was held by Simon Harcourt, mesne lord of Coven.[48]

This manor was held in 1507 by Thomas Ellyngbrigg who was then succeeded by his infant daughter Anne.[49] There was a hall here by the 16th century,[50] and in 1704 the manor and capital messuage were held by Thomas Fowke and Mary his wife who in that year sold them to Thomas Bracegirdle.[51] The manor subsequently passed to Thomas Watson Perks of Shareshill by marriage with one of the daughters of a Henry Bracegirdle[52] and in 1774 seems to have been held by John and Ann Perks and William and Mary Bromley.[53] It was sold soon afterwards to the Hon. Edward Monckton[54] and as Aspley Farm was owned c. 1841 by his son Edward, the tenant then being Michael Lovatt.[55] The farm seems then to have descended with Somerford, being owned by Major R. F. P. Monckton of Stretton Hall in 1956.[56] By 1940 Aspley farm was over 150 acres in size.[57]

The farmhouse has a roughly H-shaped plan with a central block between north and south cross-wings. It incorporates a timber building of the open-hall type, probably dating from the early 16th century. The hall was presumably of two bays and a through passage formerly existed at its north end. The shaped and chamfered head of a post belonging to the open truss dividing the bays is visible in the bedroom above the passage. The insertion of heavy ceiling beams in the hall to form two stories probably took place in the late 16th century when a large chimney was built against the passage. A late 17th-century staircase blocks the passage at the north-west angle. The framed walls were replaced by brick in the 18th and 19th centuries.

BROOM HALL was probably a member of the bishop's manor of Brewood until the grant of the

overlordship at some time between 1155 and 1159 by the bishop to the Dean and Chapter of Lichfield.[58] The overlordship was still held by the dean and chapter in 1317,[59] but by 1473 it had returned to the bishop.[60] Broom Hall descended as part of the liberty of Brewood until at least 1605.[61]

Land in Broom Hall, formerly held by Burtheimer and his sons Edwin, Achi, and Gamel and from about 1149 by William 'Awnoilus' (or 'the uncle') and by the widow of Ailric, was granted, with the services of the last two, by the bishop to his steward Ralph, lord of Harborne (Offlow hundred; now in Birmingham), and his heirs at some time between 1155 and 1159.[62] Ralph was to hold this with other land in Brewood of the dean and chapter at a rent of 4s. for the light of the high altar in the cathedral.[63] The subsequent descent of this intermediate lordship is obscure.

Land in Broom Hall was granted to Thomas de la Hyde and Margaret his wife in 1299 by John son of Ralph of Broom Hall,[64] while in 1303 Adam, son of John, and Adam's wife Lettice conveyed to Thomas a messuage, ½ virgate, 3 acres of meadow, and 4 acres of pasture here.[65] Thomas died in 1314,[66] and in 1315 the dean and chapter granted Broom Hall to his son, also Thomas.[67] Iseult, widow of the elder Thomas, seems to have been holding what was described as the manor of Broom Hall as her dower in 1316 and 1317, paying the 4s. due for the light at the high altar.[68] Thomas de la Hyde leased the manor in 1332 to William de Donyngton of Leicester for nine years, at a rent of 28s. to Thomas and 4s. to the light at Lichfield.[69] In 1342 Thomas settled all his lands in Broom Hall on Nicholas his eldest son, with reversion to Thomas's younger son Giles for life and the right heirs of Thomas.[70] Giles conveyed these lands in 1353 to Ralph his brother,[71] who in 1354 settled them on his own wife Joan and his son Thomas.[72] In 1396 or 1397 Joan acquired from Agnes Somerford, widow of Robert Fowleshurst, all her right in lands of 'the manor of Broom Hall' formerly held by Thomas,[73] but was sued in 1414 for a toft, land, and rent in Broom Hall by Elizabeth, described as daughter and heir of Ralph, and her husband Richard Lane,[74] to whom Joan resigned the manor in 1418 or 1419.[75] Lands here were held by Richard's grandson Ralph in 1477[76] and, described between at least 1577 and 1605 as the manor of Broom Hall, descended in the Lane family with The Hyde[77] until at least 1715.[78] Sir John Giffard, however, at his death

43 W.S.L., S. MS. 335 (1), mm. 17–17d.
44 Ibid. m. 17.
45 Ibid. m. 17d.
46 W.S.L., D. 1766/35, Ct. Baron and Ct. of Survey, Mar. 1723/4, p. 1. An incomplete series of rolls of Courts Leet and Baron from 1329 to 1786 exists at Chillington Hall *penes* Mr. T. A. W. Giffard (1956). Ct. Bks. 1653/4–1814 are at the W.S.L. on deposit from Mr. Giffard. The W.S.L. has also Ct. R. 1729–47 deposited by the Church Commissioners (D. 1766/35, 36).
47 W.S.L., S. MS. 350A/40, f. 38a; *S.H.C.* xvii. 103.
48 C 142/24, no. 64.
49 Ibid.
50 See below; *S.H.C.* 1919, 241.
51 C.P. 25(2)/965, 3 Anne Trin.
52 *Notes and Coll.*, Brewood, 82.
53 C.P. 43/764, rot. 202.
54 *Notes and Coll.*, Brewood, 82; W.S.L., D. 1813, bdle. 31.
55 Tithe Maps and Appt., Brewood (copy in W.S.L.).
56 Ex inf. Major R. F. P. Monckton (1956); see p. 35.
57 *Kelly's Dir. Staffs.* (1940).

58 *S.H.C.* 1924, nos. 337, 582.
59 Ibid. nos. 68, 302.
60 W.S.L., S. MS. 335 (1), m. 17.
61 *S.H.C.* 1910, 158, 162, 166, 174.
62 *S.H.C.* 1924, no. 301.
63 Ibid.
64 W.S.L., S. MS. 350A/40, f. 47a.
65 *S.H.C.* 1911, 60–61.
66 Ibid. ix (1), 123.
67 Ibid. 1924, no. 302.
68 Ibid. ix (1), 58–59; ibid. 1924, no. 68.
69 W.S.L., S. MS. 201 (1), p. 353.
70 W.S.L., S. MS. 350A/40, f. 47a; *S.H.C.* xvii. 50.
71 W.S.L., S. MS. 201 (1), p. 86.
72 W.S.L., S. MS. 350A/40, f. 48a.
73 Ibid.
74 *S.H.C.* xvii. 50–51.
75 W.S.L., S. MS. 350A/40, f. 48a.
76 *S.H.C.* 1910, 157–8.
77 Ibid. 160–2, 164–6, 168–71, 172–4; *S.H.C.* 1919, 241; see p. 34.
78 Giffard Papers at Chillington, bdle. 17.

in 1556 was holding lands in Broom Hall of the bishop,[79] and what was described as a manor of Broom Hall was held of the bishop by Sir John's son and heir Thomas at his death in 1560 when the manor was stated to have been settled on him at the time of his marriage in 1531.[80] Lands in Broom Hall belonging to John, son of Thomas, were confiscated in 1588 because of his recusancy and were still forfeit in 1595,[81] but by 1611 John held a messuage and lands here.[82] His estate passed at his death in 1613 to his son Walter,[83] who died seised of it in 1632[84] and whose grandson Walter was holding part of Broom Hall c. 1680, the other part being 'Captain Lane's'.[85]

In 1715, since the Giffard and Lane shares of what was called Broom Hall farm were so intermixed that neither party could sell or improve, Thomas Giffard of Chillington and John Lane of Bentley agreed to an exchange of various parcels.[86] The house remained with Thomas Giffard,[87] and c. 1841 Broom Hall farm was owned and held by T. W. Giffard,[88] whose nephew W. T. C. Giffard sold it in 1919.[89] In 1956 it was owned by Mr. C. Moreton.[90]

Thomas Careless was tenant of Sir John Giffard's lands in Broom Hall in 1556.[91] In 1599 a John Careless, husbandman, his wife Ellen and his son Edward were granted a lease by John Lane of all his lands in Broom Hall,[92] while in 1611 John, Ellen, and Edward were granted the lease of John Giffard's messuage and lands.[93] John Careless, whose brother William was with Charles II at Boscobel in 1651,[94] was tenant of the Giffards at Broom Hall in 1656, and from 1662 to 1670 he shared the tenancy with his step-father Edward Dearn, who had been tenant in 1653 and 1656.[95] After Edward's death John became sole tenant.[96] In 1704 the Careless estate consisted of 132 acres and included what was described as the hall.[97] John's grandson Edward was tenant at some time after 1707, but by 1715 he had been succeeded by his son Charles, who was then ejected from the share of the estate owned by John Lane and replaced by a Thomas Dearn.[98] In 1724 Charles was ejected from the Giffard share also, on grounds of having impoverished the estate, and Peter Giffard granted the lease to an Adrian Goodluck.[99] Charles died

in 1726,[1] and his son Edward, a Wolverhampton baker, was claiming the land in 1739 after coming of age.[2]

The present farmhouse is a much-altered brick building of late-17th-century origin, and there is a 17th-century timber-framed barn. Pools which have recently been filled in and built over may have formed part of a moat.

In 1086 CHILLINGTON (Cillentone) was held of the king as 3 hides by William son of Corbucion, but it was being claimed by the Bishop of Coventry and Lichfield,[3] who held the overlordship by 1182.[4] Chillington descended as part of the liberty of Brewood between at least 1285[5] and 1724.[6]

Peter Corbesun, apparently William's son,[7] held the manor at some time during the 12th century, and his daughter Margaret had it as her marriage portion.[8] Peter's son, however, Peter (II), after granting the manor to Peter Giffard at some time between 1175 and 1182,[9] retained a mesne lordship which may have passed in 1263 to Sir John Fitz John.[10] John's brother Richard, having succeeded him in 1275, was holding this lordship by 1287,[11] and it passed at his death in 1297 to his sister Maud Countess of Warwick,[12] whose son Guy Earl of Warwick was holding it in 1304.[13] Guy's son Thomas succeeded in 1315,[14] and Thomas's son Thomas was holding the mesne lordship at his death in 1401.[15] William and Roger, sons of a Peter Corbesun, were successively claiming some right in the manor as heirs of their kinswoman Margaret, daughter of Peter Corbesun (I), between 1293 and 1329.[16]

At some date between 1175 and 1182 Peter Corbesun (II) conveyed the manor to his wife's nephew Peter Giffard to hold as ½ knight's fee, and his son William confirmed the grant.[17] The manor then descended in the Giffard family[18] and in 1956 was held by Mr. T. A. W. Giffard.[19]

By 1297 Sir John Giffard's lands in the vills of Chillington and La Hyde included a capital messuage, presumably in Chillington, with a garden and curtilage attached, a carucate of land containing 80 acres under wheat and 40 acres under rye, 12 acres of woodland and pasture and rents from free and villein tenants.[20] Sir John's son John was

---

[79] C 142/110, no. 143.
[80] C 142/127, no. 45.
[81] S.H.C. N.S. v. 139.
[82] Giffard Papers at Chillington, bdle. 20.
[83] S.H.C. 1910, 140.
[84] Ibid. 162.
[85] Ibid. 1919, 241.
[86] Giffard Papers at Chillington, bdle. 17.
[87] Ibid.
[88] Tithe Maps and Appt., Brewood (copy in W.S.L.).
[89] Ex inf. Mr. T. A. W. Giffard (1956).
[90] Local inf.
[91] C 142/110, no. 143.
[92] Giffard Papers at Chillington, bdle. 18.
[93] Ibid. bdle. 20.
[94] D.N.B.; Notes and Coll., Brewood, 36, Appendix; Hicks Smith, Brewood, 40.
[95] Giffard Papers at Chillington, bdle. 27.
[96] Ibid.
[97] Estate maps at Chillington, no. 23; the Lane–Giffard lands at Broom Hall were then divided among eight tenants.
[98] Giffard Papers at Chillington, bdles. 17, 27.
[99] Ibid. bdle. 27.
[1] Brewood Par. Reg. iii, from transcript in W.S.L., 3 Mar. 1725/6.
[2] Giffard papers at Chillington, bdle. 27.
[3] V.C.H. Staffs. iv. 60, no. 305. The entry is misplaced,

in Warwickshire. The bishop is called the Bishop of Chester as the see was then at Chester.
[4] S.H.C. iii (1), 203–4.
[5] Feud. Aids, v. 2.
[6] W.S.L., S. MS. 350A/40, f. 29a; W.S.L., S. MS. 335 (1), m. 17; S.H.C. N.S. v. 162; E 134, East. 4 Jas. II, no. 32; W.S.L., D. 1766/35, p. 1.
[7] S.H.C. iii (1), 202–3.
[8] Ibid. 203.
[9] Ibid. 202–4.
[10] S.H.C. 1911, 134; ibid. vi (1), 65; ibid. N.S. v. 89–90; Complete Peerage, v. 433–5.
[11] S.H.C. vi (1), 168; Complete Peerage, v. 436–8.
[12] Cal. Inq. p.m. iii, pp. 285, 287.
[13] S.H.C. vii (1), 115.
[14] Cal. Inq. p.m. v, pp. 402, 409; Complete Peerage (orig. edn.), viii. 57.
[15] C 137/27–28; Complete Peerage (orig. edn.), viii. 58.
[16] S.H.C. vi (1), 222, 234; ibid. vii (1), 23, 35, 114–15; ibid. xi. 6–7.
[17] Ibid. iii (1), 202–3.
[18] G. Wrottesley, 'The Giffards' (S.H.C. N.S. v), 82–199.
[19] Ex inf. Mr. T. A. W. Giffard (1956). The three-weekly court for Chillington was being held by 1279 (S.H.C. vi (1), 96), and a single court paper, of 1306, survives among the Brewood Ct. R. at Chillington Hall.
[20] S.H.C. 1911, 241–2.

granted free warren in his demesne lands at Chillington for himself and his heirs in 1319.[21] In 1511 a later John Giffard inclosed 5 acres of arable at Chillington to make a park, and the pastures at Chillington in 1650 included the New Park, the Old Park, and the Common Park.[22] By 1851 Chillington Park was open to the public during the summer.[23]

Chillington Hall is largely the work of Sir John Soane *c.* 1786, but it incorporates an early-18th-century wing, and there are traces of the Tudor house which preceded it. The same site appears to have been in use since medieval times. A curved stretch of water south-east of the house, which survived until at least 1756,[24] was probably part of the moat. A complete rebuilding was undertaken by Sir John Giffard (d. 1556), probably after his mother's death in 1537.[25] The Tudor house appears to have been roughly quadrangular in plan with a gatehouse on the east side.[26] The present saloon, of which the walls are unusually thick, is thought to occupy the site of the Great Hall. A stone chimney-piece dated 1547, now in the saloon, may incorporate in a restored form original carved panels which were formerly above the doorway of the Great Hall. It bears shields of arms and a representation of the panther-shooting legend (see below). Some fragments of panelling are the only other survivals from the Tudor house. The building is said to have been 'remarkable for the various forms of its windows and chimneys'.[27]

Peter Giffard, who succeeded his cousin in 1718, demolished some of the Tudor buildings and erected the present three-story brick range on the south side of the quadrangle. Between this and the Hall he inserted a staircase block. The service courtyard behind the house and the stable ranges with their octagonal dovecot are also of his time. The south wing, of which the rainwater heads are dated 1724 with initials P.G·B. (Peter and Barbara Giffard), is of red brick with stone dressings. It is typical good provincial work of its day, thought to have been designed and built by Francis Smith of Warwick (1672–1738).[28] The windows, eight to each story, are uniformly spaced and have segmented heads, keystones, and aprons. Internally several of the rooms are oak-pannelled. The fine staircase has turned balusters, carved strings, and moulded undersides to the treads and risers. The walls of the staircase hall are ornamented with contemporary plasterwork. The kitchen rises to the full height of the service wing and originally had open fireplaces on two opposite walls. In the garden west of the house, laid out by Peter Giffard, is a stone screen which formerly led to a bowling alley. The fine wrought-iron gates have his initials on the overthrow. The Upper Avenue, over a mile long, leading from the house to Giffard's

Cross was described in 1727 as 'lately made by Peter Giffard'.[29] The earlier approach was by the lane still known as Chillington Street.

Between 1756 and his early death in 1776 Thomas Giffard carried out important alterations to the park. He employed 'Capability' Brown and James Paine[30] who had recently collaborated on similar work at Weston under Lizard.[31] A string of three pools, about three-quarters of a mile south-west of the house, was formed into a roughly triangular expanse of water, with a dam at its lower end. The shores were planted with woodland. By 1851 the lake was admired for its 'beautiful fleet of vessels . . . from large yachts to the smallest of skiffs'.[32] A canal or 'private navigation', used for the transport of fuel and building material, leads from the south-east corner of the lake towards the house. Near its west end is a bridge of local stone designed by Paine. It is composed of a single segmented arch and has niches to the piers, roundels in the spandrels, and an iron balustrade.[33] There is said to have been a bridge by Brown at the farther end of the 'navigation'.[34] Across the northern arm of the lake is a sham bridge or causeway, similar in detail to Paine's bridge and having five blind arches. Other features designed to be seen to advantage across the water and probably dating from *c.* 1772 are a Classical and a 'Gothic' temple.[35] The former is a small summerhouse on the east bank with a Roman Doric portico of local stone. The Gothic temple, now partly ruinous, is of brick and stucco. An octagonal room in one of its flanking turrets is decorated with contemporary plasterwork. The so-called Ionic Temple, which masks the back of a gamekeeper's cottage, is possibly the work of Soane some fifteen years later.

Two designs by Adam for rebuilding the house survive from Thomas Giffard's time. One, dated 1772, was for an entirely new mansion probably on a site near the lake. The other was intended to incorporate the wing of 1724.[36] Thomas Giffard the younger,[37] who came of age in 1785, employed Sir John Soane from 1786 onwards. Soane's first design was also for a completely new house, but this was modified to include Peter Giffard's buildings of 1724.[38] Nearly all the remaining Tudor work was demolished. The house now consists of a long rectangle with the 1724 range forming its south end. The intended stucco finish was never applied, possibly to avoid too great a contrast with the older brickwork. The principal two-story front faces east and has a central Ionic portico of Tunstall stone. In order to mask the east end of the earlier and higher range the two end pavilions are carried up an extra story, a feature which did not appear in Soane's original design and which tends to dwarf the central portico. The fine domed saloon is entered through

[21] *Cal. Chart. R.* 1300–26, 409.
[22] *S.H.C.* 1931, 65; Giffard Papers at Chillington, tin box, bdle. 2. There was already a park in 1486: Glos. R.O., D. 340 a/T 208/13.   [23] White, *Dir. Staffs.* (1851).
[24] Plan of 1756 at Chillington.
[25] *Country Life,* 13 Feb. 1948.
[26] Recorded 1663 when the Giffard arms were also noted in a great bay-window in the Hall: W.S.L., S. MS. 252, 69.
[27] Erdeswick, *Staffs.,* ed. Harewood (1844), 159.
[28] *Country Life,* 20 Feb. 1948.
[29] Giffard papers at Chillington, bdle. 18. For a view of the Avenue see plate facing p. 35.
[30] James Paine, *Plans etc. of Noblemen's and Gentlemen's Houses,* ii (1783).

[31] *V.C.H. Staffs.* iv. 170.
[32] White, *Dir. Staffs.* (1851).
[33] Paine, *Plans,* ii, pl. lxxxvii; the executed design differs in several respects from the one illustrated.
[34] Ibid.
[35] Work to the temples was being carried out in 1772: Giffard papers at Chillington, bdle. 27.
[36] *Country Life,* 27 Feb. 1948. The drawings are in Sir John Soane's Museum.
[37] For his portrait see plate facing p. 132.
[38] Soane, *Plans of Buildings* (1788–9), pl. xii–xvi. The original drawings are included in W.S.L., Staffs. Views, iii, pp. 95–98, 105–7.

the portico and a vestibule with Ionic columns. It was originally intended for a chapel[39] and is thought to occupy the site of the Tudor hall. Its only lighting is from a clerestory in the shallow elliptical dome. Once again the design has been modified, the room as executed being asymmetrical and only three-quarters of its intended size. The handling of the dome and coved ceiling foreshadows some of Soane's important later interiors. The first-floor corridor with a small top-lighted dome at each end is also characteristic of this architect's later work. Soane's drawings include an unexecuted design for a bridge with an Ionic pavilion in the centre.[40]

Thomas William Giffard, who succeeded in 1823, completed some interior work, and the staircase window contains armorial glass said to have been designed by his brother Francis.[41] In 1911 a billiard room was added to the house, and the garden screen leading to the bowling alley was restored.[42] In 1957 restoration was in progress under the supervision of the Ministry of Works.[43]

Giffard's Cross, reputedly marking the spot where a panther was shot by Sir John Giffard (d. 1556),[44] is an ancient wooden cross about 6 ft. high. The arms, formerly terminating in trefoils, are much decayed. It now stands in the garden of a small 18th-century brick lodge near the gates at the east end of Upper Avenue.

COVEN was held by Ailric before the Conquest and by Robert de Stafford in 1086 when it was assessed at a hide.[45] The overlordship descended in the Stafford barony until at least 1605.[46]

In 1086 Coven was held of Robert de Stafford by Buered.[47] An intermediate lordship seems to have been held in 1166 by Geoffrey de Coppenhall[48] and to have descended with the mesne lordship of Coppenhall until about 1255 when Robert de Coppenhall surrendered it to Robert de Stafford.[49]

A lordship in Coven, held by the Burnell family, passed to Ralph Purcell with Shareshill on his marriage to Sibyl, sister of Robert Burnell, possibly during Stephen's reign.[50] Otwell Purcell held the vill of Coven c. 1255 of Robert de Coppenhall, and then replaced him as immediate tenant of the Staffords.[51] Otwell's son, Otwell (II), had succeeded to what was called the manor of Coven by 1283,[52] and Thomas, son of Otwell (II), was holding it in 1334 when his homage and services were included in a grant by Ralph de Stafford of 1½ knight's fee here and in Shareshill to Sir William de Shareshill.[53] In 1339 Thomas surrendered to Sir William all the homages and services of his tenants in Coven[54] and in 1340 all his rights and those of his wife Joan in a knight's fee there.[55] This intermediate lordship, covering by 1390 only two-thirds of Coven,[56] descended with Shareshill[57] until at least 1638 when Thomas Leveson conveyed it to Sir Edward Littleton,[58] who made a settlement of it in 1642.[59] Its subsequent descent is obscure.

In 1166 Alan de Coven was holding ⅔ knight's fee, presumably in Coven, of Geoffrey de Coppenhall,[60] and a Ralph de Coven held a fee there in 1242[61] and 1255.[62] Ralph was still living in 1262 but by 1272 had been succeeded by his three daughters, Alice the eldest, Margery, and Philippa.[63] Ralph (II), the son of Alice and Robert de Pendeford, was granted a messuage and ½ carucate there in 1278 by his mother and her second husband Thomas Sany (or Pany),[64] and in 1285 he was said to be holding Coven of Otwell Purcell.[65] A Ralph de Coven was lord until at least 1329.[66] John, son of Ralph, and Juliana, wife of John, granted what was called the manor to Ralph de Coven, probably John's son or perhaps a brother, at some time after 1331, reserving to themselves a chamber in the great hall.[67] The manor was settled on a John de Coven in 1356 by a Richard le Taylor,[68] and in 1366 a Sir Thomas Coven conveyed all his lands and services here to Robert Jones, skinner, of London, who then settled them on a John de Coven.[69] In 1391 or 1392 John held a messuage and lands here[70] and settled the manor in 1394 or 1395[71] on trustees, one of whom conveyed it to John's son, also John, in 1422.[72]

A grant of land in Coven to Richard Lane in 1433 or 1434 by a Thomas Boddesley and his wife Catherine[73] seems to have been confirmed by John Coven,[74] and an estate here, called a manor from 1576, then descended in the Lane family with The Hyde[75] until 1705 when John Lane conveyed the manor to Sir Walter Wrottesley.[76] It seems to have passed to Sir Walter's widow Anne at his death in 1712 and after her death in 1732 to Thomas, their

[39] W.S.L., Staffs. Views, iii, p. 107 (b).
[40] Ibid. p. 98 (b).
[41] Country Life, 20 Feb. 1948.
[42] Ex inf. Mr. T. A. W. Giffard (1956).
[43] Ex inf. Mr. Giffard.
[44] The crest of a panther's head is said to have been granted to Sir John in 1513: S.H.C. N.S. v. 210–11. For a view of the cross in 1838 see plate facing p. 35.
[45] V.C.H. Staffs. iv. 53, no. 217.
[46] S.H.C. i. 150, 181; Bk. of Fees, 543; Rot. Hund. (Rec. Com.), ii. 114; E 361/150; S.H.C. 1910, 166, 172.
[47] V.C.H. Staffs. iv. 53, no. 217.
[48] S.H.C. i. 150, 181–2.
[49] Ibid. N.S. xi. 129; see p. 139.
[50] S.H.C. vi (1), 128–9; B. H. Putnam, Sir William Shareshull (1950), 2.
[51] S.H.C. N.S. xi. 129; S.H.C. vi (1), 128–9.
[52] S.H.C. vi (1), 128–9.
[53] Ibid. xi. 138; Cal. Pat. 1334–8, 11. Thomas seems to have succeeded by 1332: W.S.L., D. 1790/A/8/19.
[54] W.S.L., S. MS. 350A/40, ff. 3a–4a.
[55] S.H.C. xi. 147. [56] Ibid. xv. 30.
[57] Ibid. xi. 208, 215; C 137/4; Cal. Pat. 1339–1401, 417; S.H.C. N.S. iii. 228; W.S.L., S. MS. 201 (1), 306, 319, 320–1; C 140/38; C.P. 43/91, rot. 96; C 142/390, no. 148; C.P. 25 (2)/485, 13 Chas. I Mich.; see p. 175. It was described as the manor by 1486: E 150/1013 (1).
[58] C.P. 25(2)/486, 14 Chas. I Mich.
[59] C.P. 25(2)/486, 18 Chas. I Mich.
[60] Red Bk. Exch. (Rolls Ser.), 267; S.H.C. i. 181.
[61] Bk. of Fees, 967.
[62] Rot. Hund. (Rec. Com.), ii. 114.
[63] S.H.C. i. 313–14.
[64] Ibid. 1911, 32–33; ibid vi (1), 107.
[65] Feud. Aids, v. 1.
[66] Ibid. 16; S.H.C. i. 319–20.
[67] W.S.L., S. MS. 201 (2), p. 10 (2nd nos.); S.H.C. i. 320.
[68] W.S.L., S. MS. 201 (1), p. 84.
[69] Ibid., p. 85.
[70] Ibid.
[71] W.S.L., S. MS. 350A/40, f. 39a.
[72] Ibid. f. 40a.
[73] W.S.L., S. MS. 201 (1), p. 85. In 1457 or 1458 a Catherine Devey, widow, released to a Thomas Astley all her right in the manor of Coven, said to have descended to her by inheritance after the death of a Ralph de Coven: ibid. p. 328.
[74] Ibid. (2), p. 10 (2nd nos.).
[75] S.H.C. 1910, 158, 160–2, 165–6, 169–70, 172–4; C.P. 25 (2)/725, 25 Chas. II Trin.; Shaw, Staffs. ii. 97, Lane pedigree; see p. 34.
[76] C.P. 25 (2)/965, 4 Anne Trin.; C 5/346, no. 30; W.S.L., C.B. Brewood: Coven.

grandson.[77] Thomas still held it in 1735[78] but being childless he devised it to Magdalen Craig, presumably a relative on his mother's side.[79] In 1744 she conveyed it to Robert Barbor of the Inner Temple,[80] and the manor then descended with Somerford.[81] Such manorial rights as still existed in 1956 were then held by Major R. F. P. Monckton.[82]

What was described as one-third of the manor was held of Otwell Purcell by Robert Burnell, Bishop of Bath and Wells, at his death in 1292 and passed to his nephew Philip,[83] whose son Edward was holding rent only in Coven at his death in 1315.[84]

The Coven family were occupying a hall at Coven at some time shortly after 1331,[85] while in 1666 the 'hall house' here, whose owner was not named, was taxable for five hearths.[86] In 1738 the hall was held by William Jellicoe, apparently as tenant of Robert Lillyman, to whom it seems to have been sold by Thomas Wrottesley.[87] No house known as Coven Hall now exists.

A court leet and a court baron were included in the sale by John Lane to Sir Walter Wrottesley in 1705.[88] Records of the manorial court survive from 1520 to 1630.[89]

There was a fishpond in the vill in 1307, and the 'old fishpond' here was mentioned in 1322.[90]

By 1242 *ENGLETON* was held of the Bishop of Coventry and Lichfield as $\frac{1}{4}$ knight's fee[91] and continued to be held of the manor of Brewood until at least 1724.[92]

A Ralph de Engleton occurs at some time between 1149 and 1160,[93] and by 1226 William de Engleton was holding a free tenement here.[94] William's son John[95] held the $\frac{1}{4}$ fee here in 1242,[96] but probably by 1272 and certainly by 1293 he had been succeeded by his son Thomas,[97] who was lord of Engleton until at least 1326.[98] Thomas's eldest son Hugh,[99] who may have succeeded by 1327[1] and was described as lord of Engleton in 1330 or 1331,[2] was alive in 1332[3] but by 1355 had been succeeded as lord of Engleton by Thomas de Levereshoved (or Levershed).[4] Apparently by 1368 an Adam de Wisbrid

and his wife Joan, possibly a daughter of Thomas, had settled what was called the manor on their daughter Joan with successive remainders to the son of Thomas and to Eleanor daughter of Thomas.[5] Eleanor, as a widow, made a settlement of half the manor of Engleton in 1376 or 1377.[6] Edmund Botiler and his wife Iseult likewise made a settlement of half the manor in 1391,[7] while in 1428 Agnes de Bradley and co-parcenors were holding $\frac{1}{2}$ fee in Engleton.[8]

Alan de Withyfield, described as lord of Engleton, and his wife Joan conveyed what was called the manor to Roger Fowke and his wife Elizabeth for their lives in 1446 at a rent of 25s.[9] Roger Fowke, descendant of Roger and Elizabeth,[10] was described as lord of the manor between at least 1582 and 1610,[11] while his son Thomas and Thomas's son Ferrers together made a settlement of the manor in 1641.[12] Thomas died in 1652,[13] and in 1682 Ferrers, with his younger son Thomas, made a further settlement.[14] By 1691 the manor had passed to Phineas Fowke, second cousin of Ferrers,[15] and Phineas was succeeded in 1711 by his nephew Fowke Hussey,[16] who was holding the manor in 1724.[17] Phineas, son of Fowke, held the manor in 1734,[18] and in 1767 he conveyed it to Thomas Plimley,[19] who made a settlement of it in 1778.[20] Plimley conveyed it in 1785 to the Hon. Edward Monckton,[21] who was living at Engleton Hall in 1817[22] and whose son Edward c. 1841 owned the land there, most of which, including the Hall, was in the hands of tenants.[23] The estate seems then to have descended with Somerford, and Major R. F. P. Monckton owned land here in 1956. In 1929 he had sold the Hall to the tenant, R. M. Walley, whose son, Mr. W. Walley, succeeded c. 1953 and still lived there in 1957.[24]

The other half of the manor had been held by William Buckingham, apparently of Wolverley (Worcs.), before 1473, when his daughter and heir Elizabeth, still under age, was in the custody of the Duchess of Buckingham while the bishop, as overlord, was receiving 26s. 8d. rent from a John Hore as lessee.[25] By 1544 this land was held by Thomas

[77] *S.H.C.* n.s. vi (2), 340, 343, 402 (pedigree); W.S.L., C.B. Brewood: Coven.
[78] C.P. 43/610, rot. 401.
[79] *S.H.C.* n.s. vi (2), 402 (pedigree); W.S.L., C.B. Brewood: Coven.
[80] W.S.L., C.B. Brewood: Coven; *S.H.C.* n.s. vi (2), 343.
[81] C.P. 25 (2)/725, 23–24 Geo. II Trin.; C.P. 43/731, rot. 389; C.P. 43/763, rot. 19, 20; W.S.L., D. 1813, bdle. 29; Hicks Smith, *Brewood*, 41; Pitt, *Staffs*. 254; Tithe Maps and Appt., Brewood (copy in W.S.L.); White, *Dir. Staffs*. (1851); *P.O. Dir. Staffs*. (1872); *Kelly's Dir. Staffs*. (1940); see p. 35.
[82] Ex inf. Maj. R. F. P. Monckton (1956).
[83] *Cal. Inq. p.m.* iii, no. 65.
[84] Ibid. v, no. 611. Philip does not appear to have been holding the manor at his death in 1294: ibid. iii, no. 194. Edward's nephew Sir Nicholas Burnell was holding rent here of Sir William de Shareshill in 1354: *Cal. Pat. 1350–4*, 443; *S.H.C.* xiv (1), 83.
[85] W.S.L., S. MS. 201 (2), p. 10.
[86] *S.H.C.* 1927, 54.
[87] W.S.L., C.B. Brewood, Misc. (1).
[88] C 5/346, no. 30.
[89] S.R.O., D. 260/M, box 8, bdle. m.
[90] W.S.L., S. MS. 201 (1), p. 369; W.S.L., S. MS. 350A/40, f. 40a; *S.H.C.* 1928, 114.
[91] *Bk. of Fees*, 969.
[92] *Feud. Aids*, v. 2; W.S.L., S. MS. 350A/40, f. 44a; W.S.L., S. MS. 335 (1), m. 17d.; W.S.L., D. 1766/35, Survey of the manor of Brewood, Mar. 1723/4, pp. 1, 3.
[93] *S.H.C.* iii (1), 183.
[94] Ibid. iv (1), 40.

[95] Ibid. 198; ibid. vi (1), 229.
[96] *Bk. of Fees*, 969.
[97] *S.H.C.* iv (1), 198; ibid. vi (1), 229.
[98] W.S.L., S. MS. 350A/40, f. 47a.
[99] W.S.L., S. MS. 201 (1), p. 364.
[1] *S.H.C.* vii (1), 237.
[2] W.S.L., S. MS. 201 (1), p. 361.
[3] Ibid., p. 353.
[4] Ibid., p. 362.
[5] Ibid., p. 366.
[6] Ibid., p. 362.
[7] *S.H.C.* xi. 148.
[8] *Feud. Aids*, v. 23.
[9] W.S.L., S. MS. 201 (1), pp. 366–7.
[10] Shaw, *Staffs*. ii. 60, Fowke and Hussey pedigree.
[11] C 142/201, no. 114; *S.H.C.* n.s. iii. 43.
[12] C.P. 25(2)/486, 17 Chas. I Mich.
[13] Monuments in Brewood church.
[14] C.P. 25(2)/726, 34 Chas. II East.; Shaw, *Staffs*. ii. 60.
[15] C.P. 43/432, rot. 256, where he is called Phineas Hussey; Shaw, *Staffs*. ii. 60.
[16] W.S.L., Brewood Ct. R. 1709–15, 2 July 1711.
[17] W.S.L., D. 1766/35, p. 1.
[18] C.P. 43/607, rot. 252; W.S.L., Brewood Ct. R. 1731–41, 11 May 1741.
[19] *Notes and Coll.*, Brewood, 78.
[20] W.S.L., D. 1813, bdle. 46.
[21] Ibid.; Monckton held the court rolls in 1811.
[22] Pitt, *Staffs*. 254.
[23] Tithe Maps and Appt., Brewood (copy in W.S.L.).
[24] Ex inf. Maj. R. F. P. Monckton (1957); see p. 35.
[25] W.S.L., S. MS. 335 (1), m. 17d.; W.S.L., S. MS. 201 (1), pp. 367–8.

Moreton and his wife Margery,[26] and their son Matthew was holding a messuage called 'Buckingham's Land' of the bishop at a rent of 2d. at his death in 1582, when his son Edward succeeded.[27] The estate passed in 1630 to Edward's son and heir Matthew,[28] who made a settlement of what was called half of the manor in 1639.[29] He died in 1669,[30] and his son and heir Edward[31] was living at Engleton Hall c. 1680.[32] Edward's son Matthew, who became Lord Ducie of Moreton (in Gnosall) in 1720,[33] succeeded in 1687[34] and in 1724 held the Hall and ancestral lands at a rent of £1 0s. 5d.[35] His son Matthew, who succeeded in 1735 and was created Baron Ducie of Tortworth (Glos.) in 1763,[36] made a settlement of what was called the manor with a dovehouse and a fishery in the Penk in 1767.[37] By his will dated 1768 he devised the manor to his nephew Thomas Reynolds,[38] who succeeded in 1770, and whose brother Francis, having succeeded in 1785,[39] held it in 1797.[40] Francis's son Thomas sold this half of the manor to Edward Monckton in 1811.[41]

The present Engleton Hall, now a farmhouse, was probably built in 1810, a date which appears on the brickwork. Ponds and depressions south-east of the house may indicate the position of a moat surrounding an earlier hall.

A Thomas de Lovers held a fishery in Engleton in 1346,[42] and a fishery in the mill-pond was included in the lease of the mill by the bishop to Robert Knightley in 1467.[43] In 1724 Fowke Hussey and Matthew Ducie each had a fishery appurtenant to their lands in Engleton, Matthew paying a rent of 10d. to the lord of Brewood.[44]

The overlordship of GUNSTONE as a member of Brewood was held by the Bishop of Coventry and Lichfield between at least 1477[45] and 1576.[46]

In 1227 Geoffrey de Thickbroom was found to have been unjustly disseised of 2 virgates in Gunstone by Robert Fulco and his son Walter.[47] A Richard de Thickbroom leased 2 virgates in Gunstone formerly held by Walter de Thickbroom to a Henry de Lilleburn and his wife Isabel at a rent of 12d. in 1240, retaining 1½ virgate.[48] In 1251 what was called the manor of Gunstone was in dispute, except

for 2 virgates, between Richard, described as son of Roger de Thickbroom, and his younger brother Hugh.[49] Richard de Thickbroom was still living in 1283[50] but had been succeeded by his son Simon's son Ralph by 1293.[51] By 1341 Ralph de Thickbroom had granted to Hugh de Gunstone ⅙ knight's fee in Gunstone, 12s. rent and the services of four tenants, including Thomas de la Hyde and Hugh atte Pyrye.[52]

What was called the manor had passed by 1419 or 1420 to Joan, widow of Ralph son of Thomas de la Hyde, who then conveyed all her estate in it to Elizabeth, Ralph's daughter, and her husband Richard Lane.[53] Lands here were held by Richard Lane and his son John in 1434[54] and then descended with Hyde in the Lane family,[55] being described in 1576 and 1589 as a manor.[56] In 1597 John Lane conveyed land there to John Fowke, described as of Gunstone,[57] who made a settlement of an estate there, including the capital messuage, in 1618.[58] John was succeeded in 1641 by his son Roger, who on his death in 1649 was followed by his son John.[59] John was succeeded in 1670 by his son Roger, who was living here c. 1680.[60] The subsequent history of this tenancy is not known.

By c. 1841 T. W. Giffard owned the land at Gunstone, most of which was in the hands of three tenant farmers.[61] The owner in 1956 was Mr. T. A. W. Giffard.[62]

At some time before 1279 one-third of the capital messuage of Gunstone was held by Alice, wife of Henry de la Pyrye of Gunstone, who after Henry's death exchanged it with his son Hugh for a messuage and land in Chillington.[63] Gunstone Hall was held by John Fowke in 1618[64] and was the seat of 'Squire Fowke' in 1666[65] and of his son Roger c. 1680.[66] There is now no trace of the early capital messuage. The present Gunstone Hall is a gabled stucco farmhouse dating from c. 1840.[67]

The overlordship of the manor of HATTON, a member of Brewood, was held by the Bishop of Coventry and Lichfield between at least 1428 and 1477.[68]

A messuage and land in Hatton were held by a Roger de Sparham of Hatton in 1302.[69] Richard

[26] C.P. 40/1123, mm. 12d., 13d.; W.S.L., S. MS. 201 (1), pp. 367–8.
[27] C 142/201, no. 114.
[28] C 142/461, no. 130.
[29] C.P. 25(2)/486, 15 Chas. I Mich.
[30] Brewood Par. Reg., from transcript in W.S.L., iv, 25 Nov. 1667.
[31] W.S.L., Brewood Ct. R. 1653/4–1693, 13 Oct. 1673.
[32] S.H.C. 1919, 241. He died in 1687: floor-slab in Brewood church.
[33] Complete Peerage, iv. 474.
[34] Memorial slab in Brewood church.
[35] W.S.L., D. 1766/35, pp. 3, 10.
[36] Complete Peerage, iv. 474–5.
[37] C.P. 43/738, rot. 265.
[38] W.S.L. 31/50/42, will of Matthew Lord Ducie.
[39] Complete Peerage, iv. 475.
[40] C.P. 43/857, rot. 84.
[41] W.S.L., D. 1813, bdle. 46; Complete Peerage, iv. 476.
[42] C.P. 40/345, m. 198d.
[43] W.S.L., S. MS. 335 (1), m. 17.
[44] W.S.L., D. 1766/35, p. 10; Matthew's predecessors were then stated to have paid the same.
[45] S.H.C. 1910, 158.
[46] Ibid. 166.
[47] Ibid. iv (1), 42.
[48] Ibid. 236–7.
[49] Ibid. 121.
[50] Ibid. vi (1), 130.
[51] Ibid. 212.

[52] Ibid. xi. 111; S.H.C. N.S. v. 222, for what is probably a pedigree of Hugh.
[53] Ibid. i. 324–5.
[54] Ibid. xi. 244.
[55] Ibid. 1910, 157–8, 160–2; see p. 34.
[56] Ibid. 165–6, 169–70.
[57] Ibid. xvi. 169. John Fowke's family seem to have been resident at Gunstone for some generations: Burke, Peerage (1949), 789; S.H.C. xii (1), 211; ibid. xiii. 282; C 1/1243, nos. 3–5.
[58] C 5/483, no. 81.
[59] Ibid.
[60] Ibid.; S.H.C. 1919, 241.
[61] Tithe Maps and Appt., Brewood (copy in W.S.L.); White, Dir. Staffs. (1851).
[62] Ex inf. Mr. T. A. W. Giffard (1956).
[63] S.H.C. vi (1), 139.
[64] C 5/483, no. 81; Brewood Par. Reg. 116.
[65] S.H.C. 1927, 57.
[66] Ibid. 1919, 241.
[67] Gunstone Hall in Virginia, U.S.A., is said to take its name from Gunstone in Brewood, having been built by a Roger Fowke, an active royalist, who settled in Virginia with his friend Col. Mason in the mid-17th century: Hicks Smith, Brewood, 39, 87.
[68] W.S.L., S. MS. 350A/40, f. 31a; S.H.C. 1910, 157–8; ibid. N.S. v. 230; C 1/1243, no. 4.
[69] S.H.C. vii (1), 95. The Sparham family held land in The Hyde in the 14th and 15th cents.: S.H.C. 1910, 200–1.

Lane of Bentley (in Wolverhampton) and Hyde held a close in Hatton in 1423 and 1425,[70] and in 1428 the bishop granted him and his heirs what was described as the manor of Hatton for a rent of 7 marks and two appearances at the great court of Brewood.[71] Lands here descended in the Lane family with Hyde (see below) until at least 1477,[72] but in 1495 the bishop leased all his messuages and lands here to Sir John Giffard and Roger Fowke for 99 years.[73] Sir John's grandson John Giffard made a settlement in 1579 of what was called the manor of Hatton with lands and a fishery[74] and bought a further messuage and lands in Hatton and Brewood from John Lane in 1592.[75] John Giffard was holding lands in Hatton at his death in 1613,[76] and his grandson Peter held the 'manor or lordship of Hatton' in 1633.[77] John, Peter's son, held the manor in 1689,[78] but the subsequent descent is obscure.

In 1540 Bishop Roland Lee seems to have granted to Roger Fowke's son John a messuage and lands in Hatton which John Lane was claiming c. 1547,[79] and in 1571 Roger son of John Fowke made a settlement of lands and a free fishery in Hatton.[80] An estate here then descended in the Fowke family with Gunstone[81] (see above) until at least c. 1680, when Joyce, widow of John Fowke, owned the two farms called The Hattons, devised to her by her husband,[82] and seems to have been living at Hatton House, presumably the present Old Hattons (see below).[83] Part of the estate was subsequently sold to one of the Giffards of Chillington, while the remainder, continuing to be called The Hattons, was sold c. 1698 to a Mr. Nichols, who in turn sold it to a Mr. Stannier c. 1713.[84] By 1728 it was occupied and probably owned by Thomas Plimley, while the Giffard portion was by then divided between two tenants.[85]

Farms on the site of the present Upper Hattons, Hattons, and Old Hattons were owned c. 1841 by T. W. Giffard and occupied by Edward Wilson.[86] The Upper Hattons was sold by W. T. C. Giffard in 1919 to E. J. Morris and subsequently transferred to his sister Mrs. E. M. Cartwright, whose son, Mr. P. H. Cartwright, owned it in 1956.[87] The Hattons was sold, also in 1919, to the late Mr. Williams, who sold it in 1943 to P. H. Cartwright, the owner in 1956.[88] The Old Hattons was sold in 1919 to Major Carr and subsequently to Mr. Crewe of Kiddemore Green, who later sold it to Mr. F. Watson, the owner and occupier in 1956.[89] The oldest of the three farmhouses at The

Hattons is the most northerly. This continued to be known as The Hattons until at least c. 1841[90] but has now been renamed The Old Hattons. The smaller house about 200 yds. to the south was built by 1775,[91] and is now known as The Hattons. The third and most southerly of the farms, described c. 1841 as Lower Hattons,[92] is now called Upper Hattons. It is an 18th-century brick house with later additions at its east end.

The Old Hattons dates in the main from the late 17th century but some of its features may be of earlier origin and there are indications that it was formerly of greater extent. It has a roughly L-shaped plan with wings extending to the east and south. Below the east wing a rock-cut cellar is lighted by windows in the stone plinth. There is a projecting chimney-stack on the north wall. On the west side of the south wing there is a central doorway with brick pilasters. Against the east wall are later additions concealing the features of a large chimney-stack which may have formed part of an older house. Heavy chamfered and moulded ceiling beams are also of earlier character than the rest of the building.

The overlordship of *HYDE*, a member of Brewood, was held by the Bishop of Coventry and Lichfield from before 1292[93] until at least 1605.[94]

What seems to have been a mesne lordship of part at least of Hyde, was held with Chillington as $\frac{1}{2}$ knight's fee by Richard Fitz John at his death in 1297 when the reversion passed to his sister Maud Countess of Warwick.[95] Her son Guy Beauchamp, Earl of Warwick, held the lordship at his death in 1315.[96]

Sir John Giffard held the $\frac{1}{2}$ fee of Richard Fitz John in 1297,[97] and this further intermediate lordship was held by Sir John's son John in 1316.[98]

A Walter de la Hyde, possibly the Walter son of Roger de la Hyde who occurs in 1294 or 1295,[99] conveyed the vill of La Hyde with lands in Chillington and Brewood to John de Sparham (or Sempringham), Canon of Lichfield, who conveyed them to the bishop.[1] Before 1292 the bishop granted them to Margaret, later the wife of Urian lord of Saint Pierre, knight, as the manor of La Hyde consisting of a messuage worth $\frac{1}{2}$ mark, 60 acres of land worth 4d. an acre, and 4 acres of meadow worth 12d. an acre, and subsequently settled the manor on Urian and Margaret jointly.[2] Urian was dead by 1295,[3] with a grandson, Urian son of John, a minor, as his heir,[4] and in this year Margaret, then wife of Ralph Basset, recovered seisin of the manor.[5] She was holding La

[70] Ibid. xvii. 94, 106.
[71] W.S.L. S. MS. 350A/40, f. 31a.
[72] Cal. Fine R. 1437–45, 45; S.H.C. 1910, 154–5, 157–8.
[73] C 1/1243, no. 4; S.H.C. N.S. v. 230–1.
[74] S.H.C. xiv (1), 210–11.
[75] Ibid. xvi. 117.
[76] Ibid. N.S. v. 140.
[77] Giffard Papers at Chillington, bdle. 10.
[78] Ibid., bdle. 11, no. 4.
[79] C 1/1180, nos. 43, 44; C 1/1243, nos. 3–5; C 1/1244, no. 10.
[80] S.H.C. xiii. 282. He died in 1594: Brewood Par. Reg. 50.
[81] C 5/483, no. 81; Lichfield D. and C. MS. Bk. lv, f. 26a.
[82] S.H.C. 1919, 241; C 5/483, no. 81.
[83] E 134, Mich. 2 Geo. II, no. 5.
[84] Ibid.
[85] Ibid.
[86] Tithe Maps and Appt., Brewood (copy in W.S.L.); White, Dir. Staffs. (1834, 1851).

[87] Ex inf. Mr. P. H. Cartwright, The Hattons Farms (1956).
[88] Ex inf. Mr. Cartwright.
[89] Ex inf. Mr. Cartwright.
[90] Tithe Maps and Appt., Brewood (copy in W.S.L.).
[91] Yates, Map of Staffs. (1799), based on a survey made between 1769 and 1775.
[92] Tithe Maps and Appt., Brewood (copy in W.S.L.).
[93] Cal. Inq. p.m. iii, p. 176.
[94] W.S.L., S. MS. 350A/40, f. 32a; S.H.C. 1910, 158, 164, 174.   [95] Cal. Inq. p.m. iii, pp. 285, 287.
[96] Ibid. v, pp. 402, 409.
[97] Ibid. iii, pp. 285, 287.
[98] Ibid. v, pp. 402, 409.
[99] W.S.L., S. MS. 201 (1), p. 83.
[1] Ibid., p. 82.
[2] Cal. Inq. p.m. iii, no. 280; S.H.C. 1911, 237.
[3] W.S.L., S. MS. 201 (1), p. 351; Cal. Inq. p.m. iii, p. 176.
[4] Cal. Inq. p.m. iii, p. 176.
[5] Cal. Gen. ii. 769.

Hyde in 1323 or 1324 as ½ knight's fee[6] but seems to have been succeeded by John de Saint Pierre, son of her son Robert, by 1347.[7] John was still living in 1354,[8] but in 1425 his sister's son Robert de Brinton, described as of Chillington, conveyed lands called 'Seymperesthing' (St. Pierre's Thing) to Joyce wife of William Greville and widow of Thomas Giffard.[9] The land had passed by 1452 to Margaret, daughter of William Greville and Joyce, and Margaret's husband Thomas Corbyn, described as of Chillington,[10] and in 1455, after Margaret's death, Thomas conveyed it to John Lane of Bentley and his wife Margery.[11]

Lands and tenements in La Hyde were conveyed by a Roger son of William de la Hyde to his daughter Parnel, widow of Thomas de Gypwich (or Gypevico), whose settlement of them on her eldest son Thomas was confirmed in 1294 or 1295 by Walter son of Roger.[12] At about the same time Thomas de la Hyde was granted by John de Sparham a further 10 acres here, held of John Giffard,[13] and after Thomas's death c. 1314[14] his widow Iseult sued for dower in La Hyde from his son and heir Thomas,[15] who in 1316 or 1317 was holding what was called the manor of Hyde.[16] It seems to have passed with Broom Hall to his son Ralph whose widow Joan in 1419 or 1420 conveyed all her estate in the manor of Hyde to Elizabeth, daughter and heir of Ralph, and Elizabeth's husband Richard Lane of Bentley,[17] and in 1434 Richard settled it on his son John,[18] who had succeeded by 1439.[19]

The two manors seem to have been united in the hands of John Lane, who was succeeded in 1470 by his son Ralph.[20] He held a messuage and a mill in Hyde called 'le maner' of Hyde with lands here at his death in 1477 when his son Richard succeeded.[21] The manor passed to Richard's son John in 1517[22] and in 1576 to John's son Thomas,[23] who was succeeded in 1589 by his son John.[24] The 'capital messuage called Le Hyde' with lands appurtenant passed in 1605 to John's son Thomas,[25] an active supporter of Charles I and father of Jane who assisted Charles II in part of his flight after the battle of Worcester in 1651.[26] John, son of Thomas, succeeded in 1660[27] and was followed in 1667 by his son Thomas,[28] whose son John succeeded in 1715.[29] The manor, or reputed manor, of The Hyde with the farmhouse called The Hyde, having been settled

in 1732 on John's son Thomas, was conveyed by him in 1747 to Thomas Plimley[30] who in 1757 settled the farm on his son Thomas on his marriage with Catherine Stubbs.[31] This younger Thomas mortgaged the manor and house in 1767[32] and in 1778 leased the house for ten years to Walter Richards of The Hyde.[33]

By 1781 the manor seems to have been in the hands of Frances, widow of Thomas Giffard,[34] and it passed to Thomas's son and heir Thomas when he came of age in 1785.[35] Hyde Farm, with 48 acres of land, was owned c. 1841 by T. W. Giffard, the tenant being George Howell.[36] The owner in 1956 was Mr. T. A. W. Giffard.

The present brick farmhouse was built early in the 18th century. The symmetrical north front was later covered with stucco, the windows altered and a porch added. A ground-floor room contains reset panelling which incorporates carved medallion heads of the mid-16th century and shields bearing the arms of Lane and of Lane impaling Bagot.[37] The former moat has been filled in on the north and east sides. The western arm still contains water and a ditch remains on the south.

SOMERFORD was within the manor of Brewood probably before 1120 and certainly by 1126[38] and remained a member of the Bishop of Coventry and Lichfield's liberty of Brewood between at least 1285 and 1761.[39]

Probably at some date between 1120 and 1126 the bishop gave a Richard de Somerford lordship over Haenilda and the lands which she had inherited from her father Franus, to hold as ½ knight's fee,[40] and this is probably the ½ fee held of the bishop by a Robert fitz Richard in 1166.[41] A Robert son of William de Somerford, who in 1281 was holding a messuage here of the bishop by suit of court and a rent of 4s.,[42] was named as lord of Somerford in 1285[43] and was holding Somerford in 1313 or 1314 by the service of finding a man with a horse worth ½ mark and with a sack of hemp, to follow the lord for 40 days when there was war in Wales; by attendance at the lord's three-weekly courts; by presentation of a tithing man at the twice-yearly great courts of Brewood; and by a rent of 4s. a year.[44] By 1324 Robert had been succeeded by John de Somerford,[45] and he or another John was holding land here in 1346[46] and 1347.[47] A John Somerford

[6] W.S.L., S. MS. 350A/40, f. 32a.
[7] S.H.C. xii (1), 71.
[8] Notes and Coll., Brewood, 76.
[9] W.S.L., S. MS. 350A/40, ff. 26a–27a.
[10] Ibid.
[11] Ibid. ff. 29a–30a.
[12] W.S.L., S. MS. 201 (1), p. 83; W.S.L., S. MS. 350A/40, f. 32a.
[13] Erdeswick, Staffs. ed. Harwood (1844), 160.
[14] Cal. Inq. p.m. v, p. 276.
[15] S.H.C. ix (1), 49–50.
[16] Ibid. 1911, 339.
[17] W.S.L., S. MS. 350A/40, f. 33a; S.H.C. xvii. 50–51.
[18] S.H.C. 1910, 151–2.
[19] W.S.L., S. MS. 201 (1), p. 82.
[20] S.H.C. 1910, 154–5; C 1/1180, no. 43; C 1/1243, no. 3, for pedigree.
[21] S.H.C. 1910, 157–8.
[22] Ibid. 160–2.
[23] Ibid. 164–6.
[24] Ibid. 168–71.
[25] Ibid. 172–4.
[26] Ibid. 176–88; H. M. Lane, Lane of Bentley Hall (1910), 9–18.
[27] S.H.C. 1910, 188.
[28] Lane, Lane of Bentley Hall, 20.
[29] Ibid. 21.
[30] W.S.L., C.B. Brewood, Abstract of Title to The Hyde 1732–79, mm. 1–8.
[31] Ibid. m. 10.
[32] Ibid. mm. 9, 11–12.
[33] Ibid. m. 13.
[34] C.P. 43/793, rot. 264.
[35] C.P. 43/810, rot. 94; S.H.C. N.S. v. 193.
[36] Tithe Maps and Appt., Brewood (copy in W.S.L.); White, Dir. Staffs. (1834).
[37] Thomas Lane m. Anne Bagot: S.H.C. 1910, 174.
[38] Ibid. iii (1), 178–9.
[39] Feud. Aids, v. 2; C 1/1112, nos. 39–42; W.S.L., Brewood Ct. R. 1726–31, 21 Oct. 1728; ibid. 1731–41, 22 Dec. 1737; ibid. 1753–63, 16 July 1761.
[40] S.H.C. iii (1), 178–9.
[41] Red Bk. Exch. (Rolls Ser.), 264; S.H.C. i. 158–9.
[42] S.H.C. vi (1), 96.
[43] Feud. Aids, v. 2.
[44] W.S.L., S. MS. 350A/40, f. 2a.
[45] Ibid.
[46] S.H.C. xii (1), 56.
[47] Ibid. 75.

Blackladies Chapel in 1837

Longbirch in 1838

BREWOOD

Chillington Avenue and Cross in 1838

Somerford Hall in 1820

BREWOOD

of Somerford occurs in 1422[48] and he or another of the same name in 1473.[49] By 1547 a William son of John Somerford of Somerford[50] had been succeeded by his son Humphrey[51] whose eldest son Robert seems to have predeceased him without issue and whose second son Thomas may have been in possession in 1548.[52] Thomas too died without issue, and the third son Geoffrey was holding what was described as the manor of Somerford in 1589[53] and 1594.[54] Geoffrey's eldest son Francis was living at Somerford Hall between at least 1620 and 1623,[55] but Francis's son John was dealing by fine with the manor in 1625, the year of his coming of age,[56] and in 1655.[57] Francis died in 1657,[58] but John was not admitted to his lands until 1661.[59] John's eldest son Francis, who was admitted to his father's lands in 1673,[60] was still living in 1689,[61] but by 1693 he had been succeeded by a John Somerford.[62]

The capital messuage and lands had been conveyed by 1705 to Sir Walter Wrottesley of Wrottesley (in Tettenhall, Seisdon hundred), who was living at Somerford Hall at least in 1707 and, dying there in 1712, was buried in Brewood church.[63] His widow Anne, on whom he had settled the estate[64] and who subsequently married Paul Boyer, was holding part of Somerford in her own right by 1724,[65] and after her death in 1732 the manor with the capital messuage and lands passed to her daughter and others in trust for sale.[66] The estate was bought in 1734 for £5,400 by Robert Barbor, of the Inner Temple,[67] who was living there in 1737.[68] Robert was still alive in January 1761,[69] but his son and heir George was admitted to the Somerford lands in July.[70] A James Barbor suffered recoveries of the manor in 1766 and 1774,[71] and it passed, probably in 1779, to the Hon. Edward Monckton,[72] who was a younger son of Viscount Galway (d. 1751) and had made a large fortune in India.[73] He much improved the estate and made extensive plantations of trees to replace the timber cut by previous owners.[74] He was succeeded in 1828 by his son Edward, who was followed by his brother George in 1848.[75] Francis, nephew of George's younger brother Henry, succeeded in 1858 and was followed in 1926 by his son Major R. F. P. Monckton,[76] the owner in 1956 of the estate and of such manorial rights as still existed.[77]

After the death of George Monckton in 1858 the Hall was held by tenants until at least 1928, but it was unoccupied in 1932 and 1940.[78] It was converted into flats c. 1945.[79]

Somerford Hall stands in a park and consists of a tall three-storied block of seven bays, flanked by single-story pavilions.[80] On the entrance front the pavilions have Venetian windows with blind side lights set in round-headed recessed panels. Above these are pedimented gables with ball finials. The house was built by Robert Barbor[81] in the second quarter of the 18th century. The central hall of this date has contemporary plasterwork and an oak staircase. The building was much altered in the late 18th century by the Hon. Edward Monckton whose additions include the porch, the Adam-type fireplaces, and probably the external stucco. Since 1945, when the building was adapted for use as separate dwellings, alterations to doorways and windows have taken place. In the mid-19th century the domestic offices were considered 'all very excellent and commodious for the purpose of saving manual labour, being supplied by a large reservoir at the top of the house . . . filled by a waterwork invented and erected at great expense by Mr. Monckton on the river at some distance'.[82] The gardens and strawberry beds were served by an irrigation system using surplus water from the house.[83] Extensive stables and outbuildings adjoin the house on the west, incorporating a square dovecot which probably dates from Robert Barbor's time. Farther west the farm buildings are also large and numerous and include a fine Dutch barn of brick with arcaded sides.

An estate in Brewood belonging to the deans of Lichfield included the prebend of Brewood (to which the church of Brewood had already been approximated) in Lichfield Cathedral by episcopal grant c. 1176;[84] half a 'wara' of land and a dwelling-house in Brewood given by the bishop between 1175 and 1182;[85] and a parcel of moor in Brewood granted by Roger de Hyde after 1222.[86] What was called the *DEANERY MANOR* by 1628 remained with the deans of Lichfield[87] until 1868 when, on the death of Dean Howard, the ownership became vested in the Ecclesiastical Commissioners.[88] In 1904 the commissioners conveyed some 24 acres to Francis

[48] Ibid. xvii. 84–85.
[49] W.S.L., S. MS. 335 (1), m. 17.
[50] S.H.C. iii (2), 131; W.S.L., S. MS. 350A/40, f. 1a.
[51] S.H.C. iii (2), 131; C 1/1112, nos. 39–42; C 1/1158, nos. 44–46.
[52] S.H.C. iii (2), 131; ibid. xii (1), 200.
[53] Ibid. ii (2), 131; ibid. xii (1), 200; ibid. xviii (1), 3.
[54] Ibid. xviii (1), 8.
[55] C 2/Jas. I, C. 22/51; S.H.C. iii (2), 131; ibid. v (2), 275–6.
[56] C.P. 25(2)/526, 1 Chas. I Trin.; S.H.C. v (2), 276.
[57] C.P. 25(2)/597, 1655 Mich.
[58] S.H.C. v (2), 276.
[59] W.S.L., Brewood Ct. R. 1653/4–93, 11 Mar. 1660/1.
[60] Ibid. 19 May 1673.
[61] Ibid. 11 Mar. 1688/9, 1 Apr. 1689.
[62] C.P. 25(2)/873, Wm. and Mary Mich.
[63] S.H.C. n.s. vi (2), 340; C.P. 25(2)/873, 5 Wm. and Mary Mich.; C.P. 43/443, rot. 10; C.P. 25(2)/874, 6 Wm. III Hil.; C.P. 43/448, rot. 44.
[64] S.H.C. n.s. vi (2), 342–3.
[65] W.S.L., D. 1766/35, p. 1.
[66] S.H.C. n.s. vi (2), 343; C.P. 25(2)/1205, 7 Geo. II Mich.
[67] S.H.C. n.s. vi (2), 343.
[68] W.S.L., Brewood Ct. R. 1731–41, 23 Dec. 1737.
[69] Ibid. 1753–63, 19 Jan. 1761.
[70] Ibid. 16 July 1761.

[71] C.P. 43/731, rot. 389; C.P. 43/763, rot. 19, 20.
[72] Notes and Coll., Brewood, 104.
[73] Gent. Mag. 1832, cii (2), 80; Notes and Coll., Brewood (1858), 80 and MS. note between pp. 80, 81 in W.S.L. copy.
[74] Pitt, Staffs. 254.
[75] Burke, Land. Gent. (1937), 1614.
[76] Ibid.
[77] Ex inf. Maj. R. F. P. Monckton of Stretton Hall.
[78] P.O. Dir. Staffs. (1860 and later edns. to 1876); Kelly's Dir. Staffs. (1880 and later edns. to 1940).
[79] Ex inf. Maj. R. F. P. Monckton.
[80] See plate facing p. 35.
[81] Notes and Coll., Brewood, 80.
[82] Ibid.   [83] Ibid.
[84] S.H.C. 1924, no. 497; Tax. Eccl. (Rec. Com.), 243; Valor Eccl. (Rec. Com.), iii. 130. For a detailed statement of the value of glebe and tithes owned by the dean as rector in 1535 see Valor Eccl. iii. 102.
[85] S.H.C. 1924, no. 495. Richard Peche, the grantor, was bishop from 1161 to 1182, and Richard de Dalham, the grantee, was dean from 1176 to 1209: Le Neve, Fasti, i. 545, 560.
[86] S.H.C. 1924, no. 498.
[87] Lichfield D. and C. MS. Bk. lv, ff. 27a–29a; W.S.L., D. 1766/33, Ct. Bks. of the Deanery Manor of Brewood 1781–1922.
[88] Hicks Smith, Brewood, 6.

Monckton and in 1911 some 8 acres to the grammar school for sports fields.[89] The manor and its court were still held by the commissioners in 1925,[90] but in 1927 they sold all remaining deanery land in Brewood, some 117 acres, to Mr. T. A. W. Giffard.[91] The Dean of Lichfield still retains the prebend of Brewood.[92]

In 1628 the manor was leased to Isaac Tomkys of Bilston (in Wolverhampton) and his eldest son John, and Isaac was still in possession in 1650.[93] By c. 1680 the rectorial estate at least was held of the dean by a Samuel Whitwick, 'brother of Francis'.[94] A John Whitwick, probably son of Francis, appears as Samuel's executor in 1684,[95] and this John's son John[96] was lessee of the manor in 1724.[97] Mary daughter of this younger John[98] and her husband Peter Calmel conveyed manor, prebend, and tithes in 1780 to Edward Monckton of Somerford.[99] He was holding the manor courts by 1781,[1] and his family retained the lease of the manor[2] until 1903 when it expired and reverted to the Ecclesiastical Commissioners.[3]

A house called Dean's Hall was included in the lease of the manor in 1628 and was valued 'upon improvement' at £6 a year in 1650.[4] It is presumably the 'Dean's Hill in Dean's End' noted by Gregory King c. 1680.[5] As the capital messuage it was included in the leases of the manor to the Moncktons from 1783[6] and it was still held by the family in 1874.[7] As Dean's Hall Farm it was bought in 1927 by Mr. T. A. W. Giffard[8] who sold it in 1950 to Mr. S. Robinson, still the owner in 1956.[9]

In its present form the house dates largely from c. 1700 and is roughly L-shaped on plan. It is built on two levels, the block of c. 1700 facing north-east and having an earlier but much altered service wing at its rear. A large pilastered chimney is common to both wings. Two rooms contain 17th-century panelling, in one case obviously reset. A tall garden wall and a dovecot, the latter much overgrown, date from c. 1700. In the farmyard a barn of five bays retains three cruck trusses of medieval date. These have tie-beams, collar-beams with curved braces, and upper collars. Short spur ties, formerly connecting the principals with the side framing, are still in existence although the side walls have been rebuilt in brick. There is evidence that several other cruck trusses are missing. At the north-west corner of the barn is a 17th-century timber-framed extension of two stories.

LESSER ESTATES. A virgate of land at Ackbury ('Herkebarowe'), with ½ virgate in Hyde, was conveyed c. 1200 by Galopin and his wife Edith, whose mother's marriage portion the land had been, to Hugh son of Peter Giffard for homage, service, and 2 marks.[10] By 1230 Hugh had granted it to his brother Peter to hold of Galopin and his heirs.[11] In 1724 waste land called 'Ackburyes' belonged to Peter Giffard as parcel of the manor of Chillington and was held by four tenants.[12]

Bishop Roger Meuland c. 1280 granted 9 acres in Ackbury ('Eskborrow'), with a burgage in Brewood, to Richard le Mason who in 1315 or 1316 conveyed the estate to Richard of Wolverhampton, and he in return granted these 9 acres, described as 'Eskborrow Heath' near the bishop's park, with the burgage in Brewood in Woodhouse-end, to Thomas de la Hyde.[13]

A formerly moated site at the junction of Port Lane and Chillington Street probably indicates the position of an early messuage. Two cottages on the site, known as Barn Houses, form together a rectangular timber-framed structure of the 17th century, very probably a converted barn.[14] In 1889 the moat was more extensive and the building was described as 'Hackbury Heath'.[15] The house 300 yds. to the north, now known as Ackbury Heath, is not ancient.

The site and lands in Brewood belonging to the Benedictine nunnery of St. Mary, or Blackladies, founded c. 1150 probably on land granted by the bishop out of the manor of Brewood and dissolved in 1538,[16] were sold by the Crown in 1539 to Thomas Giffard of Stretton,[17] who succeeded his father Sir John Giffard as lord of Chillington in 1556.[18] Thomas leased the site to his son Humphrey in 1559 for life with reversion to his eldest son John,[19] and after Humphrey's death, at some time between 1614 and 1632, it passed to Walter Giffard of Chillington, son of John, from whom it descended in 1632 to his son and heir Peter.[20] By 1655 Blackladies had been sequestrated and sold by the Treason Trustees to a Thomas Gookin,[21] and in 1656 it passed to Thomas Harper of London, who conveyed it in 1657 to Francis Page of London.[22] Peter Giffard's fourth son John, on whom it seems to have been settled at his marriage,[23] redeemed it[24] and was living there in 1661.[25] In a dispute lasting from 1680 to 1698 he tried unsuccessfully to maintain the exemption of Blackladies, as an ancient peculiar

[89] Church Comm. files.
[90] W.S.L., D. 1766/33, ii, p. 169.
[91] Ch. Comm. files.
[92] *Lich. Dioc. Dir.* (1955–6), 5.
[93] Lich. D. and C. MS. Bk. lv, ff. 27a–29a.
[94] *S.H.C.* 1919, 241.
[95] Giffard papers at Chillington, bdle. 14; Shaw, *Staffs.* ii. 201.
[96] Shaw, *Staffs.* ii. 201.
[97] W.S.L., D. 1766/35, Ct. of Survey of Peter Giffard for the manor of Brewood, p. 1.
[98] Erdeswick, *Staffs.* ed. Harwood (1844), 240 note.
[99] C.P. 25(2)/1413, 21 Geo. III Mich.
[1] W.S.L., D. 1766/33, i, f. 1a.
[2] Ibid. i, ii, *passim* to 1897; Ch. Comm. MSS. 126189, 126190; W.S.L., D. 1813, bdle. 26.
[3] Ch. Comm. files.
[4] Lich. D. and C. MS. Bk. lv, ff. 13a, 27a–29a.
[5] *S.H.C.* 1919, 240.
[6] W.S.L., D. 1766/33, i, p. 148; W.S.L., D. 1813, bdle. 26.
[7] Hicks Smith, *Brewood*, 41.

[8] Ch. Comm. files.
[9] Ex inf. Mr. T. A. W. Giffard (1956).
[10] *S.H.C.* iii (1), 209.
[11] Ibid. 209–10.
[12] W.S.L., D. 1766/35, Survey of Brewood Manor, March 1723/4.
[13] W.S.L., S. MS. 201 (1), p. 89.
[14] The barn at Brewood Hall is of similar construction.
[15] J. R. Veall, *Old Houses in Wolverhampton and its Neighbourhood* (1889), pl. 14.
[16] *S.H.C.* 1939, 178, 179, 211.
[17] *L. & P. Hen. VIII*, xiv (1), p. 159.
[18] *S.H.C.* n.s. v. 121.
[19] C 142/127, no. 45; C 142/337, no. 113, where the date is given as 1554.
[20] C 142/500, no. 41.
[21] *Cal. Cttee. for Compounding*, 2711.
[22] Giffard Papers at Chillington, bdle. 17.
[23] Hicks Smith, *Brewood*, 44; *S.H.C.* n.s. v. 192; C 5/486, no. 82.
[24] *Notes and Coll., Brewood*, 101.
[25] Giffard Papers at Chillington, bdles. 3, 10.

within the parish, from payment of tithe.[26] His grandson Peter succeeded to Blackladies in 1710 and to Chillington in 1718.[27] Blackladies then descended with Chillington[28] but was sold by W. T. C. Giffard in 1919 to Miss Louise Vaughan, passing a few years later to her brother, Major Ernest Vaughan.[29] His widow occupied it in 1956.[30]

In c. 1841 this farm comprised 206 acres with house and chapel and was tenanted by John Green.[31]

There was a fishpond attached to the nunnery in 1280.[32] The estate in 1710 included a fishpool 'lately made' and a dovecot.[33]

No part of the monastic buildings has survived, the present house having been built late in the 16th or early in the 17th century. It is T-shaped in plan, having two stories and attics, and is a large brick structure with stone dressings. The principal range faces east, and a long rear wing extends to the west. The entrance front has a central porch and two large projecting five-sided bays, each of three stories. The range has crow-stepped gable ends. Both here and in the rear wing some of the original windows have survived. The rear wing retains moulded brick round-headed doorways and at least one original chimney with diagonal shafts. A panelled ground-floor room at the north end of the east range has a stone fireplace with a four-centred head and an arcaded overmantel of carved oak.

A small timber-framed chapel, probably built in the 17th century, was in existence until c. 1846. It stood north of the rear wing and was connected to it by passages both at ground-floor and gallery level. The site is now marked by a cross set in a low brick wall. The chapel had close studding to its upper story and the timbering of the connecting passage was diagonal.[34] A wooden bell turret was taken down in 1789.[35] A description published in 1846[36] records south and west galleries internally, the latter supported on twisted pillars, and a tesselated floor. Axe-dressed and moulded stones at the base of the low yard wall near the chapel site may be of medieval origin. A long two-story stable range of brick with stone dressings lies north of the house. It dates from the early 17th century and has been little altered. The brick walls to the forecourt are thought to be the work of Peter Giffard early in the 18th century.[37] After the sale of the property in 1919 the house was altered and very thoroughly restored.[38] Many of the doors, windows, dormers, and chimneys are of this date.

In March 1710, when the greater part of the house

was leased to William Webb of Hamstall Ridware (Offlow hundred), certain rooms were retained by Catherine, widow of John Giffard, for her own use, and these included 'the chapel and all rooms, paths, and passages thereto belonging, the necessary house at the end of the gallery, the writing house, the use of one of the fireplaces in the kitchen, the water there and free passage through the same'.[39] She was also to have the use of various domestic offices and out-buildings, the 'fishpool or pond lately made . . . the canals and stews at the bottom of the garden, the pond between the court and barns, half the pigeons in the dovecot . . . also the best court and best garden'.[40]

Brewood Hall is said to have been the seat of William son of Roger Fowke temp. Edward IV.[41] It then descended with the Fowke share of the manor of Engleton[42] until 1930 when Major R. F. P. Monckton sold it to Mr. C. O. Langley,[43] steward of Brewood manor and deputy-steward of the deanery manor.[44] Mr. Langley was living at the Hall in 1956.[45] It was occupied in 1666 by Mary widow of Thomas Fowke.[46] Thomas Plimley was living there as tenant in 1743.[47] The Hon. Edward Monckton intended the Hall to be used as a jointure house by his widow who, however, remained at Somerford until her death in 1834.[48] The Hall then seems to have been occupied variously by tenants and members of the Monckton family until at least 1924.[49]

The present house, which lies on the eastern outskirts of the town, was built late in the 17th century. It appears to follow the layout of an earlier, probably medieval, plan consisting of a central hall block with gabled cross-wings projecting to the east. It is built of brick and has two stories and attics. The projecting wings on the symmetrical east front carry stone tablets below the first-floor windows, that on the north wing bearing a Hussey–Fowke achievement of arms. The other tablet is blank. Blocked lunette windows are visible on the much-altered back elevation. Internally the central hall has a stone bolection-moulded fireplace of the late 17th century, and the main staircase has twisted balusters and square newels. A ground-floor room in the north wing contains 17th-century panelling. While in the occupation of the Misses Monckton in the later 19th century, the house was considerably altered; plate-glass windows with cement quoins were inserted and a conservatory built between the front wings.[50] Topiary work in the garden, admired in 1686,[51] also disappeared at this time. Service

[26] Notes and Coll., Brewood, 60–61, 100–1; E 134, East. 35 Chas. II, no. 1; E 134, Trin. 35 Chas. II, no. 2; E 134, Mich. 9 Wm. III, no. 19; Giffard Papers at Chillington, bdles. 11, 13–15, 21–23, 26–29.
[27] S.H.C. N.S. v. 192.
[28] C.P. 25(2)/1062 6 Geo. I Hil.; W.S.L. 159/33; C.P. 43/812, rot. 417; C.P. 43/962, rot. 386; Tithe Maps and Appt., Brewood (copy in W.S.L.).
[29] Ex inf. Mr. T. A. W. Giffard (1956).
[30] Ex inf. Mr. Giffard.
[31] Tithe Maps and Appt., Brewood (copy in W.S.L.).
[32] S.H.C. v (1), 163.
[33] Giffard Papers at Chillington, bdle. 19.
[34] W.S.L., Staffs. Views, ii, pp. 139 (b, c. 1800), 140 (b, 1837), 140, (c, c. 1846). See plate facing p. 34, for reproduction of 1837 view. The 1846 view suggests that shortly before its demolition the chapel may have been altered by the insertion of lancet windows. Staffs Views, ii, p. 139 (a), is incorrectly indentified as Blackladies in S.H.C. 1942–3, 31.
[35] S.H.C. 1939, 219.

[36] Ibid., citing F. P. Palmer, Wanderings of a Pen and Pencil (1846).
[37] G. P. Mander, Brewood Forest (Wolverhampton Arch. Soc. 1936), 3. [38] Ibid.
[39] Giffard Papers at Chillington, bdle. 19.
[40] Ibid.
[41] Hicks Smith, Brewood, 32–33.
[42] Ibid.; see p. 31.
[43] Ex inf. Maj. R. F. P. Monckton (1956).
[44] Kelly's Dir. Staffs. (1928; 1940), sub Wolverhampton: Public Officers.
[45] Ex inf. Maj. R. F. P. Monckton.
[46] S.H.C. 1927, 55.
[47] Hicks Smith, Brewood, 33. [48] Ibid.
[49] Ibid.; White, Dir. Staffs. (1834; 1851); P.O. Dir. Staffs. (1872; 1876); Kelly's Dir. Staffs. (1880 and later edns. to 1924); W.S.L., D. 1813, bdles. 28, 37; W.S.L., Sale Catalogue B/1/4.
[50] Hicks Smith, Brewood, 33; ex inf. Mrs. M. E. Wakefield, Brewood (1957).
[51] Plot, Staffs. (1686), 380–1.

quarters have been added at the north-west corner of the house, and the front porch is modern. Garden walls and gate piers date from the late 17th century. Several of the outbuildings, including a timber-framed barn with long straight braces to the lower panels, are also of 17th-century date.

A messuage called 'Coldhome' in Kiddemore Green within the manor of Brewood was conveyed in 1660 by Thomas Harris to his son Thomas and Thomas's wife Elizabeth.[52] Father and son were alive in 1666,[53] but the widow of Thomas the younger and Thomas Harris, presumably the father, was living there in 1672.[54] By 1729 Coldhome was held of the manor of Brewood by a John James, as it had been earlier by his father.[55] The name Coldham is now attached to some cottages at the junction of the roads from Chillington and Boscobel (Salop.).

Land called 'Longbryche' adjoined the land in Hatton granted by the bishop in 1540 to John Fowke.[56] The land and a house recently built on it, called The Long Birch, were held by Roger Fowke (d. c. 1649), who shortly before his death assigned part of the estate to the use of his three unmarried daughters.[57] What was described as 'the capital messuage called Long Birch' was occupied in 1664 by James Greene and his mother,[58] and c. 1677 was sold by one Fowler of Salt (St. Mary's parish, Stafford, Pirehill hundred) to Walter Giffard.[59] Described c. 1680 as 'a good house',[60] it was used as a dower house by Mary Giffard of Chillington after the death of her husband Thomas in 1718.[61] She died in 1753, and the house was leased to the Vicars Apostolic of the Midland District from c. 1756 until 1804.[62] After 1804 the house seems to have been leased from the Giffards as a farm.[63] As most of the house collapsed when restoration was attempted in 1874, the foundations were blown up,[64] and in 1878 the present farmhouse was built.[65] It was sold in 1919 by W. T. C. Giffard to a Mr. Southern of Lower Penn (Seisdon hundred), who had sold it by 1939 to Mr. W. N. Meanley, the owner in 1956.[66]

The old house at Long Birch appears to have been of three distinct dates.[67] The entrance range was a tall block of mid-17th-century character containing two stories and attics. The symmetrical front had three curvilinear gables to the parapet, mullioned and transomed windows and a pilaster treatment. The central two-story porch had a round-headed entrance and a hipped roof. Behind this range was an even taller block with stone mullioned windows and massive chimneys, probably of late-16th-century

date. At the extreme rear were timber-framed gabled wings with overhanging upper stories which may have been of medieval origin.

Pearce Hay, an estate of 51 acres c. 1841, was then owned by Thomas Vaughton[68] having formerly belonged to a family called Pitt.[69] Vaughton sold it in 1843 to T. W. Giffard,[70] and the farm called Pearce Hay was owned in 1956 by Mr. T. A. W. Giffard.[71] By 1940 it was over 150 acres in size.[72] The farmhouse is a building of the early 17th century and retains exposed timber-framing on its south side. There is a three-story addition of c. 1835.

Land at Woolley ('Wulveley') near Hyde was granted in 1273 by Peter de Wulveley to his son, also Peter.[73] In 1661 Peter Giffard of Chillington leased 'his capital messuage or tenement called Woolley' to his son John Giffard of Blackladies for 21 years.[74] In c. 1841 Woolley farm was owned by T. W. Giffard and in the tenure of William Icke.[75] It was owned in 1956 by Mr. T. A. W. Giffard.[76] The north block dates from the late 17th century and has a large central stack. The south block carries the date 1824 and the initials T.L.

AGRICULTURE. The bishop's manor of Brewood was being farmed on the three-field system by 1367.[77] Open fields named Shurgreave Hill Field, Hargreave Field, Eachells (or Nechells) Field and Burgage Field in the manor of Brewood, Quarry Field and Church Field which seem to have been shared by the bishop's manor and the deanery manor, and Cross Field, Mill Field, Street Field, and Butts Field in the vill of Horsebrook within the bishop's manor were being inclosed piecemeal from at least 1696.[78] By 1800 there seems to have been no open-field arable remaining in the manor.[79]

By 1724 'waste ground called Bishop's Wood' within the bishop's manor of Brewood was common pasture for the tenants of the manor[80] and in 1834 was still an open common attached to the manor covering 44 acres and with several cottages built on encroachments.[81] It was inclosed under an agreement of 1844 between the Bishop of Lichfield as lord of the manor and T. W. Giffard as lessee.[82]

There were three open fields in the manor of Coven in 1596, Broadmeadow Field, Fulmore Field, and 'Rycrofte'.[83] Broadmeadow Field seems still to have been an open field in 1657.[84] In 1855 55 acres on Slade Heath to the east of Coven village and on Coven Heath in Bushbury (Seisdon hundred) were inclosed under an Act of 1850.[85]

[52] W.S.L., Brewood Ct. R. 1653/4–93, 30 Apr. 1660.
[53] S.H.C. 1927, 56, 59.
[54] W.S.L., Brewood Ct. R. 1653/4–93, 4 Mar. 1671/2.
[55] Ibid. 1726–31, 7 Apr. 1729.
[56] C 1/1243, no. 4.
[57] C 5/365, no. 35.   [58] Ibid.
[59] S.H.C. 1919, 241.   [60] Ibid.
[61] Hicks Smith, Brewood, 49.
[62] Ibid. 22, 49–51; Archbishop's House, Birmingham, Ecclesiastical Diary 1803–33, sub. 1804.
[63] White, Dir. Staffs. (1834; 1851); Tithe Maps and Appt., Brewood (copy in W.S.L.); 'Mara', Ancient Brewood, 46.
[64] 'Mara', Ancient Brewood, 46.
[65] Plans, &c., of this date at Chillington.
[66] Ex inf. Mr. T. A. W. Giffard (1956).
[67] Veall, Old Houses in Wolverhampton and the Neighbourhood, pl. 19; W.S.L., Staffs. Views, ii, pp. 136 (b, 1838), 139 (a, c. 1800, here incorrectly identified as Blackladies). See plate facing p. 34, for the view of 1838.
[68] Tithe Maps and Appt., Brewood (copy in W.S.L.).

[69] Hicks Smith, Brewood, 39.
[70] Ibid.
[71] Ex inf. Mr. T. A. W. Giffard.
[72] Kelly's Dir. Staffs. (1940).
[73] S.H.C. 1911, 28–29.
[74] Giffard Papers at Chillington, bdle. 10.
[75] Tithe Maps and Appt., Brewood (copy in W.S.L.); White, Dir. Staffs. (1834).
[76] Ex inf. Mr. T. A. W. Giffard (1956).
[77] H. L. Gray, English Field Systems (1915), 497.
[78] W.S.L., Brewood Ct. R., 1653/4–1799, passim.
[79] S.H.C. 1931, 80.
[80] W.S.L., D. 1766/35, Survey of Brewood manor 1724, p. 10.
[81] White, Dir. Staffs. (1834); Tithe Maps and Appt., Brewood (copy in W.S.L.).
[82] Church Comm. MS. 123780; White, Dir. Staffs. (1851).
[83] S.H.C. 1928, 118.   [84] Ibid. 122, 123.
[85] Ibid. 1941, 19. For open fields at Chillington c. 1300 see Glos. R.O., D. 340a/T 208.

MILLS. The grant of Blackladies to Thomas Giffard in 1539 included a water-mill 'within the site'[86] which was held by Humphrey Giffard in 1613[87] and by Walter Giffard in 1632.[88]

Sir John Giffard's estate in Chillington and La Hyde in 1297 included a water-mill.[89] A later Sir John had a water-mill at Chillington in 1556,[90] and there was still a mill here in 1723.[91]

In 1318 Ralph de Coven granted to John de Aldenham the homage and services of Walron the miller and his son John and a share in the old water-mill in Coven near Brewood Park with the site of the mill, fishponds, and appurtenances at a quit-rent for fourteen years and thereafter at a rent of 20s.[92] In 1322 Ralph confirmed the grant of what was then described as a third part of the mill.[93] John de Aldenham and his son were accused by the bishop in 1337 of having diverted the Saredon Brook and the Coven Brook to the use of this mill, thereby impeding the flow of water to the bishop's mill,[94] probably that at Somerford. This mill in Coven may have occupied the site of the water-mill which was attached to Aspley by 1704,[95] was described in 1757 as situated on a 'brook running . . . to Somerford mill',[96] and is probably to be identified with Standeford mill on the Saredon Brook mentioned in 1760.[97] In 1834 Standeford mill was occupied by William Shenstone,[98] and his executors owned it c. 1841 when the tenant was John Austin.[99] The ownership subsequently passed to the Yeomans family, who sold it in 1930 to Evelyn, widow of Francis Monckton of Stretton Hall, and in 1956 the building was owned by Major R. F. P. Monckton.[1] The mill was used as a grist mill until c. 1912 and continued to grind horse fodder until 1939.[2] It is an 18th-century brick building with additions to the mill-house of c. 1840.[3] In 1933 the house was damaged by fire and was partly rebuilt.[4] In 1956 the house and buildings were unoccupied.

An estate in Bushbury (Seisdon hundred) and Coven which included a water-mill was conveyed in 1614 by Sir Walter Leveson, mesne lord of Coven manor, to Francis Toncke and his wife,[5] and a mill within the manor of Coven and Brinsford (in Bushbury) was occupied by Walter Clarke in 1657.[6]

By at least 1775 the Brewood parish boundary ran just to the north of Coven mill[7] which was thus situated in Bushbury, and the remains of the mill are at Old Mill Farm, Bushbury. The centre part of the mill-house, built partly of stone, may date from the 17th century. The mill is a small derelict brick building dating from the early 18th century. The pool has been filled.

One of the two mills in Brewood held by the bishop in 1086[8] and 1291[9] was probably situated at Engleton. In 1467 the bishop leased a water-mill here for ten years at a rent of 53s. 4d. to Robert Knightley.[10] In 1538 the bishop granted the lease to Roger Fowke for 40 years at a rent of 4 marks.[11] Engleton mill was owned in 1643 by Peter Giffard and occupied by Francis Lun at a rent of £2 10s.[12] The ownership descended in the Giffard family until 1864 when the mill was sold to the Moncktons,[13] and the tenancy was held by the Mellow family between at least 1754 and 1876.[14] The mill went out of use c. 1896[15] and the derelict building was owned in 1956 by Major R. F. P. Monckton.[16] It is a brick building of the late 17th century in which earlier timbers have been reused. The east wall against the former wheel site has lower courses of dressed sandstone. The adjacent 18th-century brick dwelling is also derelict. Building stone on the site in 1956 was brought from the former Teddesley Hall for a proposed restoration.[17]

A mill descended with Hyde manor from at least 1477[18] and was owned c. 1841 by T. W. Giffard, being then in the tenure of Joseph Bill.[19] It continued in use until the Second World War,[20] and the pool, owned by Mr. T. A. W. Giffard, was well stocked with trout in 1956.[21] The three-storied brick mill and dwelling-house, forming an L-shaped block, were built early in the 19th century. In 1956 the machinery was still intact, there being two millstones, supplied from Kidderminster (Worcs.),[22] and a large metal wheel of the overshot type.

There was a windmill between Hyde mill and the road from Brewood to Kiddemore Green by 1775,[23] and in 1778 Thomas Plimley leased it with the water-mill at Hyde to Edward Kent for ten years.[24]

The second of the two mills in Brewood held

[86] L. & P. Hen. VIII, xiv (1), p. 159.
[87] S.H.C. N.S. v. 140. [88] Ibid. 162.
[89] S.H.C. 1911, 241–2.
[90] C 142/110, no. 143.
[91] Brewood Par. Reg., from transcript in W.S.L., iv, 15 Apr. 1723, baptism of John son of John Smith of Chillington mill.
[92] W.S.L., S. MS. 350A/40, f. 40a; S.H.C. 1928, 113.
[93] W.S.L., S. MS. 350A/40, f. 41a: S.H.C. 1928, 114.
[94] S.H.C. xi. 78–79.
[95] C.P. 25(2)/965, 3 Anne Trin.
[96] W.S.L., Brewood Ct. R. 1753–63, 4 July 1757.
[97] Brewood Par. Reg., from transcript in W.S.L., iv, 29 Oct. 1760.
[98] White, Dir. Staffs. (1834).
[99] Tithe Maps and Appt., Brewood (copy in W.S.L.).
[1] Ex inf. Maj. R. F. P. Monckton. The Yeomans family were farming in Coven between at least 1876 and 1896: P.O. Dir. Staffs. (1876); Kelly's Dir. Staffs. (1880; 1886; 1892; 1896).
[2] Ex inf. Mr. E. T. Cowern (1957), formerly miller.
[3] Ex inf. Mr. Cowern.
[4] Ex inf. Mr. Cowern.
[5] S.H.C. N.S. iv. 64.
[6] S.H.C. 1928, 123.
[7] Yates, Map of Staffs. (1799), based on a survey made between 1769 and 1775; Tithe Maps and Appt., Brewood (copy in W.S.L.).

[8] V.C.H. Staffs. iv. 41, no. 66.
[9] Tax. Eccl. (Rec. Com.), 250.
[10] W.S.L., S. MS. 335 (1), m. 17. A Thomas Knightley had a mill pool in Brewood in 1456: S.H.C. N.S. iii. 220.
[11] W.S.L., S. MS. 201 (1), p. 368.
[12] S.R.O., D. 260/M, box 25, bdle. k, Staffs. Royalists' Estates 1643–5.
[13] Tithe Maps and Appt., Brewood (copy in W.S.L.); Notes and Coll., Brewood, 102; W.S.L., D. 1813, bdle. 22.
[14] Brewood Par. Reg., from transcript in W.S.L., iv, 20 Oct. 1754; White, Dir. Staffs. (1834; 1851); P.O. Dir. Staffs. (1854 and later edns. to 1876).
[15] Local inf.; Kelly's Dir. Staffs. (1896), which shows it still in use.
[16] Ex inf. Maj. R. F. P. Monckton.
[17] Local inf.
[18] S.H.C. 1910, 158, 165, 169, 173; C.P. 25(2)/724, 21–22 Chas. II Hil.; Yates, Map of Staffs. (1799); W.S.L., C.B. Brewood, Giffard Abstract of Title to The Hyde 1732–79, mm. 1, 11, 14.
[19] Tithe Maps and Appt., Brewood (copy in W.S.L.); White, Dir. Staffs. (1834).
[20] Ex inf. Mr. W. Smith (1957), formerly miller.
[21] Ex inf. Mr. T. A. W. Giffard (1956).
[22] Ex inf. Mr. W. Smith.
[23] Yates, Map of Staffs. (1799).
[24] W.S.L., C.B. Brewood, Abstract of Title to The Hyde, m. 14.

by the bishop in 1086[25] was probably situated at Somerford. The grant to Richard de Somerford between *c.* 1120 and 1126 included the right to build a mill.[26] A mill rebuilt by the bishop before 1288 and in use in 1291 seems to have been at Somerford.[27] In 1337 the bishop complained that John de Aldenham had diverted the Saredon Brook by a trench to Coven mill, thus reducing the output of the mill in Brewood (probably Somerford mill), which working day and night could as a result produce only 6 qr. of 'each kind of corn' instead of thirty.[28] Somerford mill was leased by the bishop as a fulling-mill before 1473, probably to John Somerford who by then had rebuilt it.[29] It was in use as a corn-mill by 1620, and in 1623 Francis Somerford was complaining that its working was hampered, presumably by diversion of the water, by the new forge a short distance up the Penk.[30] The mill continued to descend with the manor as a grain-mill[31] and was owned by Edward Monckton *c.* 1841 when the tenant was Joseph Brewster.[32] It was in use until at least 1884.[33] Somerford Mill Farm at Catchem's End incorporates the former mill building in its northern half. The working floor was carried on a brick arcade, and the present low kitchen block housed the wheel. There are 18th-century leaded lights in the side walls, and the roof contains reused tie-beams. The living quarters adjacent to the mill date from the earlier 18th century and contain a stair of this period. Heavy main beams suggest an earlier structure rebuilt. The mill pool to the south is overgrown.

A mill situated on the Penk by Somerford Hall and driven by a turbine was used in 1956 for grinding cattle food and sawing timber.

CHURCHES. The church of Brewood served the whole of the ancient parish until the 19th century when district chapelries centred on Bishop's Wood and Coven were formed, in 1852 and 1858 respectively.[34]

There was a priest in Brewood in 1086.[35] The church had been appropriated to a prebendal stall in Lichfield cathedral for some time before *c.* 1176 when the bishop conferred this prebend of Brewood on the newly reconstituted deanery of Lichfield.[36] In or before 1275 a vicarage was ordained and endowed with the whole of the altar dues, the principal mortuary dues and tithes of lambs and wool except from the dean's demesne in Brewood.[37] The vicar was to pay to the dean an annual pension of 10 marks.[38] The advowson remained with the

deans of Lichfield[39] as prebendaries of Brewood until 1868[40] when, on the death of Dean Howard, it passed to the bishop[41] who still holds it.[42]

In 1305 William de Pecco, then vicar, acquired from John de Horsebrok, one of the vicars choral of Lichfield, a parcel of land in Brewood contiguous to the vicarage manse on the west in exchange for a 'parcel of the curtilage of the vicarage next to the steps (*schalera*) of the churchyard, which adjoins his messuage on the north and is fenced off from it'.[43] Because the bakehouse (*furnus*) of the Vicar of Brewood was on John de Horsebrok's land, William and his successors were to pay an annual rent of 3*d.* for it.[44] In 1318 this same William de Pecco reached agreement with the Abbess and nuns of Blackladies, Brewood, that he and his successors should receive tithes of wool and lambs from flocks of other persons folded on the nunnery's lands in Brewood.[45] The vicarage was assessed at £6 17*s.* 8*d.* in 1535.[46] In 1604 the vicar, described as 'no preacher, a notable swearer and drunkard', had an income of 100 marks.[47] The living was valued at £20 in 1646 when the Committee for Plundered Ministers granted the vicar £50 from the sequestrated possessions of the Dean of Lichfield, adding £8 from the rents of Blackladies and Whiteladies (in Boscobel, Salop.), sequestrated from John and Peter Giffard, farmers of these lands under the dean.[48] In 1650 the vicar had no glebe and paid the dean 3*d.* rent for the vicarage house, but he enjoyed small tithes and Easter offerings worth £20 with an augmentation consisting of the tithes of Chillington and 'the whole rent of Brewood'.[49] The augmentation seems to have been altered to £23 17*s.* 4*d.* from the impropriate tithes in 1654, with the tithes of Chillington added in 1657, the total augmentation being given as £39 a year in 1658 and 1659.[50] The vicarage received a grant from Queen Anne's Bounty at some time between 1718 and 1728.[51] The incumbent benefits under the Alport Charity on condition of attending an annual service in Cannock parish church on the Feast of St. Barnabas (11 June), preaching a sermon at this service in annual rotation with seven other beneficiaries, and residing in his benefice for at least ten months in the year.[52]

A Robert Papagy, probably at the end of the 13th century, gave two selions in 'Whete Croft' as an endowment for a mass on Sundays in Brewood church for the repose of his soul.[53] This may have been the Priest's Service which was found in 1552 or 1553 to be endowed with messuages, cottages, and lands in Brewood bringing in rents variously given as £5 or

[25] *V.C.H. Staffs.* iv. 41, no. 66.
[26] *S.H.C.* ii (1), 178.
[27] Ibid. vi (1), 177, 188; *Tax. Eccl.* (Rec. Com.), 250.
[28] *S.H.C.* xi. 78–79.
[29] W.S.L., S. MS. 335 (1), m. 17.
[30] C 1/Jas. I, C/22/51; see p. 20.
[31] C.P. 25(2)/797, 1 Jas. II Trin.; C.P. 43/763, rot. 19, 20.
[32] Tithe Maps and Appt., Brewood (copy in W.S.L.).
[33] White, *Dir. Staffs.* (1851); *P.O. Dir. Staffs.* (1854 and later edns. to 1876); *Kelly's Dir. Staffs.* (1880; 1884).
[34] *Lond. Gaz.* 1852, p. 66; ibid. 1858, p. 3134.
[35] *V.C.H. Staffs.* iv. 41, no. 66.
[36] *S.H.C.* 1924, no. 497.
[37] Ibid., no. 394.
[38] Ibid.
[39] Lich. Dioc. Regy., Bp.'s Reg. i, ff. 15*b* (1304), 90*a* (1319); *S.H.C.* n.s. x (2), 110, 114 (1362, 1376); *Valor Eccl.* (Rec. Com.) iii. 102; P.R.O., Inst. Bks.

[40] *Clergy List* (1864), ii. 33. The advowson was leased to the trustees of the late Hon. Edward Monckton in 1832 by Dean Woodhouse and in 1835 by Dean Howard: Ch. Comm. MSS. 126189, 126190.
[41] Hicks Smith, *Brewood*, 6.
[42] *Lich. Dioc. Dir.* (1955–6).
[43] *S.H.C.* 1924, nos. 295, 296.
[44] Ibid., nos. 295, 296.
[45] Ibid., no. 297.
[46] *Valor Eccl.* (Rec. Com.), iii. 102. The vicar was Henry Fleming, whose servant was accused, after his death, of robbing him of money and jewels: C 1/1351, nos. 25–29.
[47] *S.H.C.* 1915, 39.
[48] Ibid.
[49] Lichfield D. and C. MS. Bk. lv, ff. 12*a*, 31*a*.
[50] *S.H.C.* 1915, 39.
[51] C. Hodgson, *Queen Anne's Bounty* (1826), 134.
[52] See p. 64.
[53] W.S.L., S. MS. 201 (1), p. 356.

£6 which had been enjoyed by a stipendiary priest for four years past.[54] An 18th-century house in Dean Street is still called the Chantry.[55]

The large parish church of *ST. MARY AND ST. CHAD* consists of aisled nave, chancel, and west tower. The building dates from the early 13th century but has undergone so many reconstructions that it is impossible to trace its evolution with certainty. The tower was added early in the 16th century. Alterations took place in the 18th century and again in 1878–80, when it was thoroughly restored by G. E. Street. The chancel contains four altar tombs of members of the Giffard family.

added and probably larger windows inserted.[56] It is most probable that the transverse gables of both aisles disappeared at this period. Traces of weather marks on the end walls of the north aisle suggest that at one stage it was covered by a continuous roof with end gables. Carved corbels, projecting into the aisles, still exist at each end of both nave arcades. These now have no function, but they may at one time have formed part of a series supporting aisle roofs of the longitudinal gabled type. This arrangement would still necessitate comparatively low nave arcades. The final raising of the arches probably took place in the 16th century. The walls above them were rebuilt,

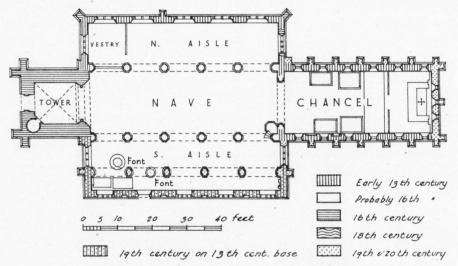

Early 13th century
Probably 16th "
16th century
18th century
19th century on 13th cent. base
19th & 20th century

0 5 10 20 30 40 feet

PLAN OF ST. MARY'S AND ST. CHAD'S CHURCH

The chancel, except for the rebuilt east wall, dates from the earlier 13th century and remains structurally little altered. There are six lancet windows in each of the north and south walls. In the north wall is a blocked doorway which formerly led to a stone-built vestry, possibly an addition of the 14th century.

The nave has wide aisles and a lofty arcade of five bays, the arches supported on tall octagonal piers. Thirteenth-century masonry at the base of the aisle walls suggests that the early plan was similar to the present one. Both internally and externally the north wall shows clear signs that the aisle was originally roofed under a series of five transverse gables. The south aisle, 3 ft. wider than the north, probably had a similar roof but the evidence here has been destroyed. This curious arrangement may have been determined by the unusual width of the aisles. The arches of the 13th-century arcade, in order to be covered by these small gabled roofs, would necessarily be very much lower than the present ones. From the existence of early masonry above the chancel arch it seems probable that the nave was always as lofty as it now is. This large expanse of walling above the early arcade suggests that a clerestory was part of the original design.

The north aisle was altered in the 14th or early 15th century when the walls were raised, buttresses

and all earlier work, except the end corbels, disappeared in the process. The great height of the arcade would now necessitate lean-to roofs to the aisles. A mid-19th-century writer suggests that the transverse gables remained until the 18th century,[57] but no such arrangement could survive the raising of the arcade to its present height. These gables must therefore have disappeared in the 16th century if not considerably earlier.

The west tower with its tall octagonal stone spire probably dates from the early 16th century. It has double buttresses at the angles, corner pinnacles, and an embattled parapet. The belfry stage has a two-light opening on each face. The west doorway has a four-centred arch, and there is a Perpendicular window above it. The tower arch has been recut but rises to the same height as the nave arcade.

In 1521 Dean Collingwood left £2 to the church for building a porch.[58] This was probably the south porch which survived until the late 18th century. Accounts of repairs to both south and north porches in 1665 indicate that the former was of wood with a shingled roof and the latter of stone and tiles.[59] Shingles for the repair of the south aisle roof appear as a constant item during the 17th century.[60]

At some time during the 18th century the east wall of the chancel was rebuilt in brick, and a

[54] *S.H.C.* 1915, 38.

[55] See p. 23.

[56] Gregory King (*c.* 1680) records a shield of arms in the east window of the south aisle, Giffard impaling Blount; Robert Giffard married Isabella Blount *c.* 1420: *S.H.C.* 1919, 238.

[57] *Notes and Coll., Brewood*, 13. The frontispiece, a conjectural drawing of the church as it might have appeared in 1700, is incorrect.

[58] *S.H.C.* vi (2), 92.

[59] *Notes and Coll., Brewood*, 90.

[60] Ibid. 13.

Venetian window,[61] described a century later as 'resembling that of a modern Italian villa',[62] was inserted. Galleries were also built in both aisles, at the west end, and across the chancel arch.[63] In 1775 it was resolved at a vestry meeting to take the whole roof off the church and replace it with one of single pitch.[64] This proposal was opposed, but a year later John Smith of Wolverhampton, builder, reported that 'a one-pitch roof will be much the cheapest'.

parish. A new font was provided, the old one being removed to a garden at Coven. Various memorial tablets are said to have been covered over or destroyed.

A thorough restoration at a cost of £6,600 took place between 1878 and 1880 under the direction of G. E. Street.[69] The east wall of the chancel was rebuilt in stone and given three graded lancets. Buttresses, dripstones, and a basement course were

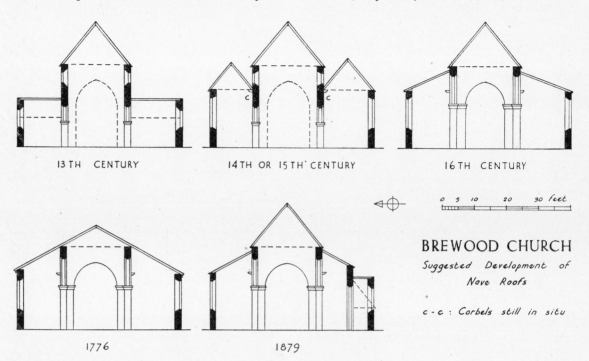

13TH CENTURY   14TH OR 15TH CENTURY   16TH CENTURY

0 5 10 20 30 feet

BREWOOD CHURCH
Suggested Development of Nave Roofs

c - c : Corbels still in situ

1776   1879

Later drawings of the church show that, at least on the south side, a single roof over both nave and aisle was adopted.[65] In 1777 the vestry ordered the north and south doors to be stopped up and the entrance made at the west door. Presumably the porches were demolished at the same time. An opening near the west end of the south chancel wall with its 'monstrous door'[66] and porch may have been of this date. New metal windows with simplified tracery were ordered for the nave. One such window remains at the east end of the north aisle.

In 1815 a faculty was granted for alterations to the galleries. A new west gallery to accommodate an organ by England was to be erected. Seats were to be allotted to former seat-holders and the remainder sold by auction.[67] Drastic alterations to the fittings took place between 1827 and 1830.[68] The church was repewed, two square family pews being provided at the north-west corner of the nave. The east gallery was demolished and the north and south galleries were rebuilt. A carved chancel screen and choir stalls were broken up and dispersed about the

added externally to the chancel, and the north vestry was demolished. The upper part of the south aisle was entirely rebuilt. Street evidently wished to revert to the early arrangement of transverse gables but owing to the much greater height of the nave arcade he could not reconstruct the aisle in its original 13th-century form. He therefore inserted a second pier arcade half-way across the aisle, its arches low enough to be covered by the gabled roofs. These roofs extend over the outer aisle only, and the wall above the new arcade is pierced by clerestory windows. In general Street adopted a 13th-century style and in several places was careful to reuse original stones in the walling. The whole church was reroofed and refloored, plaster ceilings disappeared, the galleries were cleared away, the tower arch was opened up, and the box pews were replaced by rush-seated chairs. The royal arms of Queen Anne were removed from above the chancel arch to the base of the tower. The pulpit dates from 1879[70] and the choir stalls date from 1887.[71]

The tower was restored in 1890, but soon after-

[61] W.S.L., Staffs. Views, ii, p. 131 (1842); drawing in church (1845).
[62] Notes and Coll., Brewood, 11.
[63] Hicks Smith, Brewood (1864), 5.
[64] Notes and Coll., Brewood, 97–98. This and the following details are quoted from vestry minutes.
[65] W.S.L., Staffs. Views, ii, p. 131; drawing in church; see plate facing p. 25.
[66] Notes and Coll., Brewood, 13.
[67] Lich. Dioc. Regy., Dean's Ct. Act Bk. 1813–42, pp. 30 (faculty, 4 July 1815), 34–37; White, Dir. Staffs. (1851).

[68] Notes and Coll., Brewood (1858 edn.), with MS. notes by Hicks Smith (in W.S.L. copy), 13–15; Hicks Smith, Additions to Notes and Coll., Brewood (1864), 5, 28. An interior view at this period hangs in the church. For an earlier record of monuments (1663) see W.S.L., S. MS. 252, 50.
[69] Lich. Dioc. Ch. Cal. (1880), 77; Street's plans in parish chest.
[70] Inscription in situ.
[71] Lich. Dioc. Ch. Cal. (1888), 150.

wards the spire was struck by lightning,[72] an event which occurred again in 1925.[73] In 1902 the chairs, being worn out, were replaced by oak pews.[74] A restoration of the chancel, undertaken by the Ecclesiastical Commissioners in 1904, included the removal of a partition which formed a vestry behind the altar. The chancel was thus restored to its full length. Floor levels were altered and iron railings removed from the Giffard tombs.[75] In 1911 a new stone reredos designed by W. D. Caroë and carved by N. Hitch was installed, and a vestry was screened off at the west end of the north aisle.[76] The old organ, which had been partially reconstructed in 1887,[77] was replaced by a new instrument by Binns. Stone tracery of 14th-century character was inserted in the north aisle windows in 1927 in memory of various parishioners.[78] At about this time the old circular font bowl, probably of late-16th-century date,[79] was restored to the church. In 1952 the organ was rebuilt and enlarged at a cost of over £1,500.[80]

Stained glass in the east windows was inserted in 1879 in memory of the Revd. Jeremiah Smith (d. 1854).[81] Other windows commemorate Charlotte Simpson (d. 1875); Rebecca Smith (d. 1879); James Hicks Smith (d. 1881); Maria Smith (d. 1884); Charles and Sarah Docker (d. 1893 and 1887); Mariana Wrottesley (d. 1892); Eliza Vile (d. 1894); the Revd. Edward Wrottesley (d. 1901); Sophia Briscoe (d. 1901); Mary Anne Hicks Smith (d. 1911); Frederick J. Keeling (d. 1911); Charlotte Armstrong (d. 1912), the Revd. Charles Dunkley, vicar 1907–27 (inserted 1937).[82]

The oldest of the altar tombs in the chancel[83] bears the figures of Sir John Giffard (d. 1556) and his two wives Jane (Hoord) and Elizabeth (Greysley), the latter the widow of Sir John Montgomery. It is of carved alabaster and is thought to be an early work by the Royleys of Burton. The base has twisted baluster shafts, and the panels contain the figures of a son and three daughters, together with thirteen children in swaddling clothes and the arms of Sir John Giffard and his wives. A second tomb, thought to be by the same sculptor, bears the figure of Sir Thomas Giffard (d. 1560), between his two wives, Dorothy (Montgomery) and Ursula (Throckmorton). The base has seven sons, the eldest in armour, six daughters and four children in swaddling clothes. It bears the arms of Giffard, Giffard impaling Montgomery and Giffard impaling Throckmorton. A third tomb with effigies of John Giffard (d. 1615) and Joyce (Leveson), his wife (d. 1608), has an arcaded base bearing the figures of eight sons, five of them in armour, and six daughters. The fourth

tomb has a plain arcaded base and carries the recumbent figures of Walter Giffard (d. 1632) and Philippa (White), his wife (d. 1636). In the south aisle is an incised alabaster floor slab, discovered at the restoration of the church in 1879. It bears the figures of Richard Lane (d. 1517) and Anne his wife together with four sons and seven daughters.[84]

A tablet to Joan Leveson (d. 1572), who married (1) William Skeffington, (2) William Fowke, and (3) Edward Giffard, is said to have been removed in 1772. It was found at Four Ashes in 1863 and restored to the church.[85] At the west end of the south aisle, removed from one of the piers of the nave, is an alabaster wall monument with two tiers of kneeling figures: below, Edward Moreton (d. 1630), his wife (d. 1633), three sons, three daughters and a child in swaddling clothes; above, Matthew Moreton (d. 1669), his wife (d. 1672), a son, six daughters, and a child in swaddling clothes. This monument is said to have been restored by the Earl of Ducie shortly before 1851.[86] A floor-slab nearby commemorates Edward Moreton (d. 1687). Fowke tablets in the south aisle include inscriptions to Thomas Fowke (d. 1652), Phineas Fowke (d. 1710), and members of the Holland family, 1715–40. Other tablets in the church commemorate Jane Viscountess Galway (d. 1788); the Rt. Revd. Charles Berington, Roman Catholic Vicar Apostolic of the Midland District (d. 1798); John Parrot (d. 1802); John Turner (d. 1824) and his wife; the Hon. Edward Monckton (d. 1832), his widow (d. 1834), and their issue, 1814–78; Mary Countess of Cork and Orrery (d. 1840); the Revd. A. B. Haden, vicar (d. 1863) and his wife; the Revd. William Rushton (d. 1875) and the Revd. Henry Kempson (d. 1881), both of Brewood Grammar School; William Parke (d. 1876), in whose memory the church restoration was begun in 1878; the Revd. Richard Wall (d. 1899), formerly headmaster of the grammar school.

In 1957 the plate included a silver-gilt chalice and paten cover, 1634; a silver-gilt paten, 1705; a silver paten, 1718; two Sheffield plate chalices, one of which is gilt inside the bowl, 1833; seven alms plates of pewter; a flagon with lid of old Sheffield plate, 1832, given by A. B. Haden, vicar.[87]

In 1553 there were four bells with a sanctus bell and three sacring bells.[88] A bell added in 1638[89] was no longer there by 1889 when there was a ring of seven.[90] There are now eight bells recast from the old bells with the old marks reproduced, all 1896, J. Taylor & Co.,[91] the bequest of Charles Docker.[92]

The registers date from 1562. Those from 1562 to 1649 have been printed.[93]

[72] Lich. Dioc. Mag. (1894), 29; C. Dunkley, Notes on Brewood Church (1934), 13.
[73] Lich. Dioc. Mag. (1902), 181.
[74] Ibid. (1904), 179.
[75] Ex inf. the vicar (1957); see plate facing p. 8.
[76] Dunkley, Notes on Brewood Church, 5; Lich. Dioc. Regy., Dean's Ct. Bk. 1907–14, p. 201, faculty, 17 May 1910.
[77] Lich. Dioc. Ch. Cal. (1888), 150.
[78] Lich. Dioc. Regy., Dean's Ct. Act Bk. 1924–33, pp. 229, 290, faculties, 12 Jan. and 15 Nov. 1927.
[79] Trans. Birmingham Arch. Soc. lxviii. 22.
[80] Ex inf. Mr. T. A. W. Giffard (1956).
[81] Lich. Dioc. Ch. Cal. (1880), 77.
[82] Lich. Dioc. Regy., Dean's Ct. Act Bk. 1934–8, p. 379, faculty, 27 July 1937.
[83] See plate facing p. 8. For full descriptions see Trans. Birmingham Arch. Soc. lxx. 17, 21, pl. 10; ibid. lxxi, pp.

14–15, pl. 5, pp. 22–23, pl. 9.
[84] S.H.C. 1910, 163. Brewood Par. Reg. (Staffs. Par. Reg. Soc.), introd., wrongly attributes the slab to John (d. 1576) and Margaret Lane.
[85] Hicks Smith, Additions to Notes and Coll., Brewood, 30.
[86] White, Dir. Staffs. (1851); Trans. Birm. Arch. Soc. lxxi. 23–24.
[87] Ex inf. the Vicar of Brewood (1957).
[88] S.H.C. 1915, 17.
[89] Hicks Smith, Brewood, 10.
[90] C. Lynam, Church Bells of Staffs. 5, with plates.
[91] A. E. Garbett, 'Church Bells of Staffs.' (Trans. Old Stafford Soc. 1953–4), 12.
[92] Lich. Dioc. Regy., Consist. Ct. Act Bk. 1891–9, p. 264, faculty, 21 Jan. 1896; Lich. Dioc. Mag. (1895), 104, 138, 209; ibid. (1896), 72, 148.
[93] Staffs. Par. Reg. Soc. (1906).

A vicarage house stood on the west side of the churchyard until 1864 when it was demolished and the road built over the site.[94] It was a gabled building apparently of 17th- or very early-18th-century date.[95] The foundations of an earlier and smaller house were found on the site at the time of demolition.[96] The vicarage was considered 'unfit for residence' between 1804 and 1807 when the incumbent was living either in Lichfield or in his own house in the parish.[97] It was occupied by a curate in 1851.[98] In 1833 the Revd. A. B. Haden built Deansfield for his own occupation on the eastern outskirts of the town.[99] This is a large square red-brick house with extensive grounds and stabling. In 1860 he built and occupied Elmsley, a smaller house of similar type about a quarter of a mile nearer the church. After his death in 1863 the old house west of the churchyard was demolished and Elmsley was bought as a vicarage by the Revd. E. J. Wrottesley.[1] It was still occupied by the incumbent in 1957.

The church of *ST. JOHN THE BAPTIST*, Bishop's Wood, was opened in 1850 and consecrated in 1851.[2] The vicarage, a perpetual curacy until 1868, is in the gift of the Vicar of Brewood.[3] A building of local red sandstone, it was designed by G. T. Robinson[4] in the Early English style and is cruciform with a shallow chancel, a north vestry, and a south porch which terminates in a square tower with a spire. The windows are lancets, graded at the east end and in the transepts. The trusses of the open roof form an elaborate intersection at the crossing. The oak pulpit and choir seats were installed in memory of Maria Jane Garland (d. 1894).[5] The organ, which occupies the south transept, replaced the original instrument in 1902 and was given by subscription to commemorate the 50th anniversary of the church.[6] Stained-glass windows have been inserted in memory of the Revd. John Buckham, vicar (d. 1868); Elizabeth Evans, Frances Evans and Sir Thomas Evans Bt., inserted 1895; the Revd. Thomas B. Garland, vicar 1888–1907; and Mary Archer (d. 1911). Mural tablets commemorate Howard T. Spencer (d. 1914) and the Revd. Marshall S. Walker, vicar (d. 1946).

In 1957 the plate included a silver chalice, 1850; a silver paten; a silver and glass flagon; and an electro-plated paten on foot.[7] There is one bell, 1858, C. & G. Mears.[8] The register dates from 1852.

The vicarage house, which with the school and schoolhouse lies east of the church, is of approximately the same date as the church.

The church of *ST. PAUL*, Coven, built largely at the expense of George Monckton, was consecrated in 1857.[9] The living, a vicarage by 1885, is in the gift of the Vicar of Brewood.[10] The church was designed by E. Banks of Wolverhampton[11] and is late-13th-century in style. It is cruciform in plan with an octagonal turret at the south-west angle. The stonework has a rustic finish externally and the windows are cusped lancets or have Geometrical tracery. Stained glass in the east window was inserted in 1857 to commemorate George Monckton's contribution to the church.[12] The brass lectern dates from 1871.[13] The organ formerly occupied the west gallery but was moved in 1926 to the south transept when a vestry was formed below the gallery.[14] Mural tablets commemorate I. G. Monckton (d. 1899) and G. Roper (d. 1902), vicars; Howard Rushton, organist and choirmaster (d. 1928); Rachel Edwards (d. 1928).

In 1957 the plate included a flagon, two chalices and a paten, electro-plated, all given by Thomas Hartley, and another paten.[15] There is one bell, 1857, C. & G. Mears.[16] The register dates from 1857. The vicarage lies immediately east of the church.

ROMAN CATHOLICISM. John Giffard was before the Privy Council for recusancy in 1575,[17] and the fact that the Giffards for the most part remained Roman Catholic until 1861[18] doubtless explains why there has always been a large number of Catholics in Brewood. In 1604 there were 'very many recusants' here,[19] and the figure was given as 74 in 1641[20] and 399 in 1780.[21] Until the mid-19th century most of the tenants of the Giffards were Catholics.[22]

The chapel at Chillington was regularly used for baptisms and marriages from at least 1721,[23] and about this time the altar plate there included a gold chalice and paten, six silver candlesticks, a silver crucifix, and a silver ciborium.[24] The chapel at Longbirch was used for public worship from at least 1779 and had its own priest-in-charge.[25] The chapel at Chillington was demolished *c.* 1786 while the Hall was being enlarged, but by 1791 the chapel at Blackladies had been opened for public worship under

[94] Hicks Smith, *Brewood*, 12–13.
[95] Drawing in church.
[96] Hicks Smith, *Brewood*, 12–13.
[97] Lich. Dioc. Regy., Non-residence Licences, i, ii.
[98] White, *Dir. Staffs.* (1851).
[99] Hicks Smith, *Brewood*, 12–13.
[1] C. Dunkley, *Brewood Grammar School* (1936), 46.
[2] Lich. Dioc. Regy., Bp.'s Reg. Bk. O[A], 22 Apr. 1846, 24 July 1847, 31 May 1851; Hicks Smith, *Brewood*, 69, citing *The Guardian*, 18 June 1851.
[3] *Lich. Dioc. Ch. Cal.* (1857; 1862, where it is first called a perpetual curacy; 1869); *Lich. Dioc. Dir.* (1955–6).
[4] *Notes and Coll., Brewood*, supplement pp. 4–5.
[5] Inscription in church.
[6] *Lich. Dioc. Mag.* (1902), 221.
[7] Ex inf. the Vicar of Brewood (1957).
[8] Lynam, *Church Bells of Staffs.* 4; ex inf. the Vicar of Brewood (1957).
[9] Hicks Smith, *Brewood*, 70, citing *The Guardian*, 11 Feb. 1857.
[10] *Lich. Dioc. Ch. Cal.* (1858; 1885); *Lich. Dioc. Dir.* (1955–6).
[11] *Notes and Coll., Brewood*, supplement pp. 6–7.
[12] Ibid.
[13] *Lich. Dioc. Ch. Cal.* (1872), 89.
[14] Lich. Dioc. Regy., Consist. Ct. Act Bk. 1924–30, p. 188, faculty, 21 June 1926.
[15] Ex inf. the Vicar of Coven (1957).
[16] Lynam, *Church Bells of Staffs.* 4.
[17] *Acts of P.C.* 1575–7, 46–47; but he then promised to conform and when unable to attend the parish church to be present with his family at the Common Prayer in the chapel at Chillington.
[18] *S.H.C.* n.s. v. 127–88 *passim*; Hicks Smith, *Brewood*, 52.
[19] *S.H.C.* 1915, 385.
[20] E 179/179/315, m. 1*d.*
[21] H.L., Main Papers, Return of Papists 1780.
[22] Pitt *Staffs.* 254; White, *Dir. Staffs.* (1834; 1851).
[23] Reg. of baptisms, confirmations, and marriages performed at Chillington chapel and its dependencies, 1721–70. The register is now at Archbishop's House, Birmingham, W.
[24] E. E. Estcourt and J. O. Payne, *English Catholic Nonjurors of 1715*, 349.
[25] Hicks Smith, *Brewood*, 51; S.R.O., Q/SO, Trans. 1791.

the priest from Chillington.[26] The Longbirch chapel was enlarged after the departure of the vicar apostolic in 1804 by the inclusion of the vicar's sitting-room,[27] while by 1834 the Blackladies chapel was served by two priests.[28] Both chapels were closed in 1844 when the church of St. Mary was opened.[29] In 1851 it was certified that the church was always filled to its capacity of c. 400 at the 10 a.m. Sunday mass and was usually about two-thirds full at the afternoon service.[30] The average attendance at Sunday mass in 1956 was 250.[31]

The Roman Catholic parish benefits from the following bequests: £400 from A. Plant in 1901 and £900 from the Revd. Walter Groom in 1912, which with various bequests made before 1899 were producing £80 in 1956; £500 from Miss A. Plant in 1916, producing £18 in 1956; £270 from Miss B. Howell in 1922, producing £11 in 1956; £100 from Teresa Moreton in 1933, producing £3 in 1956; £1,250 from Mrs. M. Hubball in 1951, producing £43 in 1956; and £1,000 from Mrs. M. J. McIntyre in 1956, producing £45.[32]

The convent of the Immaculate Conception, occupying the building earlier used as the union workhouse, was opened in 1920 by the Dominican sisters, who later also opened the convent school there.[33]

The church of *ST. MARY*, built 1843–4, was designed by A. W. N. Pugin (1812–52), who also gave three stained-glass windows.[34] The stone is local, the masonry being coursed rubble, and the style of the church is of the late 13th century. The building consists of an aisled nave of five bays, chancel, north vestry, south porch, and a west tower with a small broach spire. Internally there are pointed nave arcades and an open roof. The chancel screen and the crucifix in the south aisle, both of painted wood, are of the original date. The church was redecorated in 1887 when the stone altar was placed in the Lady Chapel.[35] The wooden image of the Virgin and Child on this altar was brought after 1846 from the chapel at Blackladies.[36] A stone pillar stoup of 12th-century character outside the south porch is said to have come from Whiteladies (Boscobel, Salop.).[37] Stained glass in the west window was inserted as a memorial of the First World War. Near it are mounted the sword and medals of Major E. Vaughan. Other windows commemorate Frances and Mary Magrane; the Vaughans of Blackladies (1924); George and Elizabeth Evans (1926); William and Mary Yates (1926); Anne

McDonnell (1940). In the chancel are two floor slabs bearing figures in priest's robes. These are in memory of Robert Richmond, first rector (d. 1844), and William Richmond (d. 1848), his nephew and successor. North-east of the church a rectangular stone building is now used as a church hall. The priest's house and the school, both of brick and of approximately the same date as the church, lie to the north-west.

PROTESTANT NONCONFORMITY. In 1736 the house of Joseph Mountford in Crateford in Brewood was licensed for use by Protestant Dissenters.[38] George Whitefield's preachers visited Brewood in 1745.[39] George Burder, who later became a prominent Congregational minister, when preaching in a barn there in 1777, was interrupted by a mob who banged on the doors and threw missiles.[40] No Congregational cause was established until the beginning of the 19th century. John Simpson, who resigned his office as parish clerk in 1800, then had a cottage certified for nonconformist worship, and in 1803 a small chapel was opened in Sandy Lane, the whole cost of which had been defrayed by James Neale of London, husband of Simpson's sister.[41] Brewood became a centre for the mission work of Hackney College students during vacations c. 1806.[42] The chapel there was enlarged in 1825[43] and rebuilt in 1842, with 275 free sittings and 100 others.[44] By 1940 the chapel was no longer in use as a place of worship and was sold in 1950.[45] It is an impressive red-brick building with round-headed windows and is fitted with galleries. The tall front gable has stepped sides and a segmental head.

Houses in Brewood were certified for dissenters' meetings, possibly Methodist, in 1800 (Joseph Underhill),[46] 1822 (Humphrey Webb),[47] 1824 (Thomas Leek),[48] 1826 (John Beaumont),[49] 1840 (Richard Lakeham),[50] and 1851 (Edward Blakemore).[51] The first Wesleyan Methodist chapel in the parish was erected at Coven in 1828.[52] This was replaced in 1839 by the present chapel in Lawn Lane, Coven.[53] A new Sunday school building was added in 1924, and in 1940 the chapel had seating for 120.[54] The chapel is a rectangular brick building with round-headed windows and a later porch. In 1868 a Wesleyan chapel was built in School Road, Brewood, and in 1940 seated 120.[55] It is a small brick building.

In March 1831 the house of William and George Holland was certified as a meeting-house.[56] This

[26] J. Kirk, *Biographies of the English Catholics 1700–1800*, 49; Hicks Smith, *Brewood*, 44, 51; S.R.O., Q/SO, Trans. 1791; see p. 37.
[27] Hicks Smith, *Brewood*, 50; see p. 38.
[28] White, *Dir. Staffs.* (1834).
[29] Hicks Smith, *Brewood*, 45, 50.
[30] H.O. 129/15/378.
[31] Ex inf. the parish priest (1956).
[32] Ex inf. the Treasurer of the Roman Catholic Archdiocese of Birmingham (1957). The dates are those when the legacies were notified or paid to the treasurer.
[33] Ex inf. the sisters (1956); see p. 19.
[34] White, *Dir. Staffs.* (1851); *Notes and Coll.*, Brewood, stray notes.
[35] *Kelly's Dir. Staffs.* (1932).
[36] *S.H.C.* 1939, 219, citing F. P. Palmer, *Wanderings of a Pen and Pencil* (1846).   [37] Local inf.
[38] S.R.O., Q/SM/1, Mich. 1736.
[39] Tyerman, *Life of Whitefield* (1876), ii. 112.
[40] H. F. Burder, *Memoirs of G. Burder* (1833), 22 sqq.; *V.C.H. Staffs.* iv. 133.

[41] Matthews, *Cong. Churches of Staffs.* 178; *Evangelical Magazine* (1803), 271; S.R.O., Q/SB, Ep. 1803; W.S.L., S. 603.
[42] Matthews, *Cong. Churches of Staffs.* 177.
[43] *Ev. Mag.* (1825), 387.
[44] H.O. 129/15/378.
[45] Staffs. Cong. Union Records; Charity Com. files.
[46] S.R.O., Q/SB, Ep. 1800.
[47] Lich. Dioc. Regy., Bp's Reg. Bk. G, 239.
[48] Ibid. 541.
[49] Ibid. H, 55.
[50] Ibid. L, 16.
[51] Ibid. O, 368.
[52] Ibid. G, 639; White, *Dir. Staffs.* (1834), 481.
[53] Date stone in gable.
[54] *Methodist Church Buildings, 1940* (1946), 263; ex inf. the Superintendent Minister (1954).
[55] Date stone *in situ*; *Methodist Ch. Bldgs.*, 263; ex inf. the Superintendent Minister.
[56] Lich. Dioc. Regy., Bp's. Beg. Bk. I, 170.

was undoubtedly for Primitive Methodists since William Holland, a plate-lock maker, was manager of the Primitive Methodist meeting in 1851, then held in part of a dwelling-house in Shop Lane.[57] The congregation was small at this time.[58] A Primitive Methodist chapel was built in Pendryl Avenue in 1858,[59] with seating for 80,[60] but was closed c. 1895.[61] The building was subsequently used as a carpenter's shop but had been demolished by 1956.[62]

A branch of the Salvation Army in Brewood had been closed by 1895.[63]

PRIMARY SCHOOLS. Abraham Barwicke was a schoolmaster in Brewood in 1641.[64] The charity school said to have existed there in 1724[65] may have been the 'charity school' for Somerford liberty at which thirteen poor girls were being educated and clothed by the Misses Monckton in 1834.[66] In 1851 18 girls were said to be taught and clothed in this Somerford school,[67] and 'Miss Monckton's' school still existed in 1854.[68]

A scheme for a National school in Brewood seems to have been started in 1816,[69] and by 1818 subscriptions had already been raised toward the projected building of a room for the 'daily instruction' of 350 children, in expectation of further annual subscriptions and donations from district or diocesan funds.[70] By 1834 about 140 children were being educated in this National school by subscription,[71] and the numbers in 1851 were about 60 boys and 50 girls, under a master and mistress.[72] The school received an annual parliamentary grant from 1858, and the original building in the Market Place was replaced in 1860 by the present school and school-house,[73] of which the Monckton family bore half of the cost.[74] This included a department for infants.[75] In 1870, on the death of the widow of the Revd. Henry Kempson, formerly headmaster of Brewood Grammar School, the schools inherited a bequest of £2,000 stock under his will (proved 1857), half the interest to be applied to the infant school.[76] The provisions of the will, including attendance of master, mistress, and children at such services as might be appointed on saints' days in Brewood church, and

the attendance of the children to be catechized on one Sunday in every month if the vicar or curate should institute such a practice, were embodied in a Scheme of the Charity Commissioners of 1871.[77] The average attendance c. 1884 was 140 girls and boys and 60 infants.[78] In 1894 attendance averaged 154[79] and in 1910 35 infants and 122 older children.[80] By 1905 the income from the £2,000 endowment was £50 which by Order of the Charity Commissioners that year was wholly assigned to the general purposes of the school.[81] In 1907 and 1923 the accumulated balance of the trust fund was assigned for improvements to the building.[82] The school, now called Brewood Church of England Voluntary Primary School (Mixed and Infants), became aided in 1955,[83] when it had an average attendance of 292.[84]

The building of 1818 consists of a long single story of brick situated near the south end of the Market Place. The present school building, that of 1859 and 1860, lies immediately to the south and includes a master's house.

By 1834 there was a Roman Catholic School attached to the Blackladies chapel where 33 boys and girls were educated at the expense of Mr. Evans of Boscobel (Salop.),[85] a charge which was met in 1851 by Miss Evans.[86] A school for Roman Catholic boys and girls, said to have been built in 1844,[87] seems to have been in the charge of a lay mistress from at least 1854 to 1916[88] although in 1860 and 1868 it was said to be under the superintendence of the Sisters of St. Paul.[89] It was said in 1884 to hold 80 children, with an average attendance of 72.[90] By 1894 the average attendance was 63,[91] with 60 in 1900 and 69 in 1912 and 1916.[92] In 1919 a Dominican sister was appointed headmistress of this school, by then St. Mary's primary school, and began duty the next year.[93] Since this time there has always been at least one Dominican sister in the school, generally two, and sometimes three, though the appointment of nuns is not obligatory.[94] The school managers are chosen partly by the Local Government Authority and partly by the trustees of the premises, which include a teacher's house, and have full responsibility for the school including appointment of teachers.[95] It is now known

[57] H.O. 129/15/378; William Holland then lived in Stafford Street.
[58] Ibid.
[59] Hicks Smith, Brewood, 35.
[60] Kelly's Dir. Staffs. (1892).
[61] Ex inf. Mrs. M. E. Wakefield (1957).
[62] Ex inf. Mrs. Wakefield.
[63] Ex inf. Mrs. Wakefield.
[64] Brewood Par. Reg. (Staffs. Par. Reg. Soc.), 117.
[65] M. G. Jones, Charity School Movement (1938), App. 4.
[66] White, Dir. Staffs. (1834).
[67] Ibid. (1851); Fanney Eldershaw, schoolmistress, was among the Somerford residents.
[68] The mistress being Mrs. Ann Eldershaw: P.O. Dir. Staffs. (1854).
[69] Hicks Smith, Brewood, 34.
[70] Digest of Parochial Returns to Sel. Cttee. on Educ. of Poor, 1818, H.C. 244, p. 855 (1819), ix (2).
[71] White, Dir. Staffs. (1834).
[72] Ibid. (1851).
[73] Rep. of Educ. Cttee. of Council, 1858 [2510], H.C. (1859, Sess. 1) xxi (1); P.O. Dir. Staffs. (1860).
[74] P.O. Dir. Staffs. (1876). The old building was used as a Working Men's Institute by 1874: Hicks Smith, Brewood, 34.
[75] P.O. Dir. Staffs. (1868).
[76] Staffs. Endowed Charities Elem. Educ. [Cd. 2724], pp. 25-26, H.C. (1906), xc.

[77] Ibid.
[78] Kelly's Dir. Staffs. (1884).
[79] Return of Schools, 1893 [C. 7529], pp. 540-1, H.C. (1894), lxv. Of the total income of £332 1s. 5d., £60 came from endowments and £75 8s. 7d. from voluntary contributions in the year 1891-2.
[80] Staffs. Educ. Cttee. List of Schools, 1910.
[81] Staffs. Endowed Charities Elem. Educ. 26.
[82] Staffs. Educ. Cttee. Mins. Feb. 1907; ibid. July 1923.
[83] Staffs. Educ. Cttee. List of Schools, 1951, corrected to 1955; ex inf. Staffs. C.C. Education Dept. (1956).
[84] Lich. Dioc. Dir. (1955-6).
[85] White, Dir. Staffs. (1834).
[86] Ibid. (1851).
[87] Kelly's Dir. Staffs. (1892).
[88] P.O. Dir. Staffs. (1854; 1868); Kelly's Dir. Staffs. (1892; 1916).
[89] P.O. Dir. Staffs. (1860; 1868). These were the Sisters of Charity of St. Paul of Chartres, from Selly Park, Birmingham: ex inf. the parish priest, Brewood (1956).
[90] Kelly's Dir. Staffs. (1884).
[91] Return of Schools, 1893, 540-1.
[92] Kelly's Dir. Staffs. (1900; 1912; 1916).
[93] Ex inf. the Sisters of the Convent of the Immaculate Conception, Brewood.
[94] Ex inf. the parish priest (1956).
[95] Ex inf. the parish priest.

as St. Mary's Roman Catholic Voluntary Primary School (Mixed and Infants).[96]

The school for 'Protestant' children, said to have been maintained in a cottage at Park Pales by Miss Evans of Boscobel,[97] may have been the forerunner of the National school at Bishop's Wood projected in 1851[98] and built in 1855 to take 71 children, the average attendance c. 1884 being 54 boys and girls[99] and 49 c. 1894.[1] The attendances in 1910 were 20 infants and 37 older children.[2] It was enlarged in 1912 to take 100 children,[3] but had fallen into serious disrepair by 1933.[4] It came under the control of the County Council in 1951,[5] and is now Bishop's Wood Church of England Voluntary Primary (Controlled) School (Junior Mixed and Infants).[6] The original school building has been extended and has lancet windows with diagonal glazing.

There was a National school in Coven by 1854,[7] held probably in the room used for divine service under the bishop's licence for some years before 1857 when St. Paul's Church was consecrated.[8] The building was presumably used after 1857 exclusively as a school, and this received an annual parliamentary grant from 1858.[9] In 1884 it had an average attendance of 110[10] and in 1894 127.[11] Attendances in 1900 averaged 111[12] but by 1910 had risen to 150,[13] and in 1937 were about 130.[14] The school became controlled in 1951[15] and is now known as Brewood, Coven Church of England (Controlled) School (Mixed and Infants).[16]

CHARITIES FOR THE POOR. The Revd. Francis Collie, or 'Collick', Vicar of Bushbury (Seisdon hundred), settled, probably by deed of 1625, a rent-charge of 33s. 4d. on a house and land at Essington (Bushbury parish) for doles of 12d. each to 30 poor of Brewood every Good Friday, 8d. to the minister of Brewood for announcing the forthcoming distribution on the previous Sunday, 8d. to the clerk for ringing the great bell from 7 to 8 a.m. on Good Friday morning, and 12d. each to the churchwardens for distributing the money.[17] The rent-charge had risen to £10 by 1820 when the money was part of the general fund distributed to the poor of Brewood parish in doles of between 1s. and 4s. on Good Friday and St. Thomas's Day.[18] By 1889 the common fund was distributed in coals and money, £10 of the total income being assigned to Bishop's Wood ecclesiastical district and £10 to Coven district.[19] In 1956-7 the total income was £10 11s. which was added to the distributions in February and December (see below).[20]

For some time before the Civil War the poor of Brewood received a benefaction on Good Friday from a rent-charge on land in Coven, bought with £40 given by Thomas Smith of Blackladies and £20 from the sons and sons-in-law of Richard South of Chillington.[21] Because the tenant had ceased to pay this rent-charge during the war, the land was sold for £40, which, with £20 given by will of William Smith of 'Sondford' and £10 given by Jane Lane, widow, of The Hyde, was used in 1659 to buy land in Brinsford (in Bushbury, Seisdon hundred) to produce a rent-charge of £3 10s. a year.[22] By 1820 this income was part of the general fund distributed to the poor.[23] By 1861 the rent from the Brinsford land was £12 with a further £1 from a garden at Penkridge given by the L.N.W.R. as compensation for damage done to the Brinsford land.[24] Part of the estate was sold in 1944 and the proceeds invested.[25] In 1956-7 the income was still added to the twice-yearly distributions, the rent then being £7.[26]

Bequests to the poor of Brewood of £20 and £10 were made by William (d. 1653) and John (d. 1665) respectively, sons of Thomas Fowke of Brewood, together with the interest on £20 given in their lifetime by Mrs. Mary Skrymsher, eldest daughter of Thomas, were assigned in 1670 for doles at Christmas and Midsummer.[27] Henry Fowke (d. 1681) left by will £50, the interest to be distributed among the poor of Brewood town, 'Kerrimore Lane' and Park Lane, on the Feast of St. James (25 July), after the deduction of 1s. to the clerk of the church for ringing the bell for an hour, 6s. 8d. to the vicar for a sermon on that day, and 1s. to whoever should distribute the dole.[28] In 1683 the £100 given by these four benefactors was laid out in the purchase of land called Dealf Hayes, in Bloxwich (in the Foreign of Walsall), which by 1820 was leased for £12 12s. a year, with £1 11s. 6d. as compensation for land taken c. 1799 under the Wyrley and Essington Canal Act.[29] The whole income was by 1820 added to the general fund distributed to the poor, although 6s. 8d. was paid to the vicar until 1804.[30] About 1869 Dealf Hayes and the Canal Company's payment were sold, and the income in 1889 was £17 11s. 1d. interest on stock.[31] The income was added to the general distributions in 1956-7.[32]

Thomas Fowke (d. 1692) gave £50, the income to

[96] Staffs. Educ. Cttee. *List of Schools, 1951*, corrected to 1955.
[97] 'Mara', *Ancient Brewood*, 79-80.
[98] Hicks Smith, *Brewood*, 69, citing *The Guardian*, 18 June 1851; the Misses Evans made a grant of £70 a year for the new church of St. John the Evangelist at Bishop's Wood in 1851-70.
[99] *Kelly's Dir. Staffs.* (1884).
[1] *Return of Schools, 1893*, 540-1.
[2] Staffs. Educ. Cttee. *List of Schools, 1910*.
[3] *Kelly's Dir. Staffs.* (1916).
[4] Staffs. Educ. Cttee. Mins. 23 Sept. 1933.
[5] Ibid. Oct. 1950.
[6] Staffs. Educ. Cttee. *List of Schools, 1951*, corrected to 1955.
[7] *P.O. Dir. Staffs.* (1854).
[8] With 70 seats in a west gallery for the school children: Hicks Smith, *Brewood*, 70-72.
[9] *Rep. of Educ. Cttee. of Council, 1858*, 636.
[10] *Kelly's Dir. Staffs.* (1884; 1892).
[11] *Return of Schools, 1893*, 540-1.
[12] *Kelly's Dir. Staffs.* (1900).
[13] Staffs. Educ. Cttee. *List of Schools, 1910*.
[14] Staffs. Educ. Cttee. Mins. 29 May 1937.
[15] Ibid. 20 Nov. 1950.
[16] Staffs. Educ. Cttee. *List of Schools, 1951*, corrected to 1955.
[17] *Abstract of Returns of Charitable Donations, 1786-8*, H.C. 433, pp. 1118-19 (1816), xvi (2); *5th Rep. Com. Char.* H.C. 159, p. 560 (1821), xii. An equal sum was paid to the poor of Bushbury from this property: *5th Rep Com. Char.* 571.
[18] *5th Rep. Com. Char.* 560-1, 564.
[19] Charity Com. files.
[20] Ex inf. the clerk to the Brewood parish council (1957).
[21] *5th Rep. Com. Char.* 561.
[22] Ibid.   [23] Ibid. 564.
[24] Hicks Smith, *Brewood*, 67.
[25] Charity Com. files.
[26] Ex inf. the clerk to the parish council.
[27] *5th Rep. Com. Char.* 561-2.   [28] Ibid. 562.
[29] Ibid. In 1786 the rent was £6 for the poor: *Abstract, 1786-8*, ii. 1118-19.
[30] *5th Rep. Com. Char.* 562, 564.
[31] Charity Com. files.
[32] Ex inf. the clerk to the parish council.

be distributed among the poor of Brewood, Kerri-more Lane, and Park Lane on 24 June after the vicar had been paid 6s. 8d. for a sermon and 8d. for giving notice of the dole and the clerk 1s. for ringing the great bell.[33] The money was on loan at interest in 1716 but by 1786 had been laid out in land in Great Wyrley (in Cannock) for which a rent of £1 6s. 8d was received.[34] By 1820, when the rent was £10, the whole income was part of the general fund distributed to the poor of the parish, although 6s. 8d. had been paid to the vicar until 1804.[35] The income was added to the general distributions in 1956–7.[36]

Richard Brookes at some date before 1786 devised a rent of 8s. charged on a field in Coven for the poor of Brewood, Coven, and Standeford.[37] This was still paid in 1956–7 when it was added to the general distributions.[38]

Thomas Salt, probably after 1786, gave a rent of 10s. charged on his croft in Brewood, to be distributed among the poor on St. Thomas's Day.[39] As the land forms part of the site of the Roman Catholic church in Brewood, the rent is paid by the priest and in 1956–7 was added to the general distributions.[40]

William Woolrich, or Woolridge, by will dated 1774, left three annuities of 10s., 5s., and 5s. from Bowling Alley Piece in Coven, to be distributed by the occupant of the land among the poor of Brewood, Coven, and Standeford townships not receiving parish relief.[41] By 1820 1s. each was given at Christmas to 10 poor of Brewood, 5 of Coven, and 5 of Standeford.[42] The income seems still to have been added to the general distributions in 1956–7.[43]

Lawrence Grove (d. 1685) left £10, the interest to be distributed on Good Friday among 20 of the poorest widows and others of the poorest inhabitants of the parish at 6d. a head.[44] By 1786 the money was vested in the parish officers who allowed 10s. interest upon it, as they did also on sums of £10 each given by Joseph Phipps of Somerford, and Richard Higley of London (will dated 1725), for doles on St. Thomas's Day.[45] The income by 1820 formed part of the general fund distributed to the poor.[46] What was described in 1786 as a rent-charge of £1 12s. a year, vested in the parish officers under the will of a Mr. Gilbert,[47] and in 1797 as a dole of £1 12s. from land in Coven, was probably the 4 per cent.

interest on £40 payable during her lifetime by Mrs. Cotton under the will of her brother Henry Sherratt, dated 1789.[48] After her death the estate at Coven was freed of the incumbrance and sold, and from the proceeds £40 was assigned to the minister and churchwardens of Brewood, who by 1820 were still receiving 40s. as interest on this from her executors and were distributing it with other doles on St. Thomas's Day.[49] The capital seems to have been lent subsequently to the guardians of the poor (see below). Thomas Slater, by will dated 1804 left £100 (reduced by legacy duty to £90) in trust to provide bread for the poor on St. Thomas's Day.[50] The parish officers to whom this was paid used it in 1817 towards the repair and enlargement of the workhouse and by 1820 were paying £4 10s. interest, which was added to the general fund distributed to the poor of the parish.[51] Joseph Smith of Brewood Forge by will proved in 1837 left £100, the profits to be distributed among the 'industrious' poor on St. Thomas's Day.[52] The money was put towards the building of the work-house and subsequently added to the rent paid by the guardians.[53] By 1852 the income from all these charities was represented by a payment from the guardians of the poor to the general fund.[54] James Smith, by will proved 1856, left £50 to provide bread and fuel for the poor of Brewood, and by 1889 this formed part of what was called the Workhouse Charity consisting of payments to the common fund from the overseers of the poor in respect of the charities of Joseph and James Smith and probably of Henry Sharratt also.[55] The workhouse was sold for £900 in 1878, and the proceeds were invested.[56] The total income from the Workhouse Charity and the charities of Grove, Phipps, Higley, and Slater in 1889 was £28 1s. 9d. interest on £936 5s. 7d. stock.[57] All these charities were still added to the general distributions in 1956–7.[58]

In 1956–7 the total charity income was £96 5s. 8d. which was distributed to widows, old-age pensioners, and other deserving cases, normally in sums of 10s., in February and December.[59]

Joseph Careless of Water Eaton (in Penkridge) was reputed to have given to the poor, by 1740, a close called the Poor's Butt in Butts Field.[60] A rent of 10s. was paid by 1786,[61] and by 1820 the owner of the whole field was distributing doles of 1s. to 10 poor of the parish.[62] It seems to have lapsed by 1889.[63]

[33] 5th Rep. Com. Char. 562.
[34] Ibid.; Abstract, 1786–8, ii. 1118–19.
[35] 5th Rep. Com. Char. 562.
[36] Ex inf. the clerk to the parish council.
[37] Ibid. 563; Abstract, 1786–8, ii. 1118–19.
[38] Ex inf. the clerk to the parish council.
[39] 5th Rep. Com. Char. 563. It is noted in the Abstract of 1786.
[40] Ex inf. the parish priest; ex inf. the clerk to the parish council.
[41] Abstract, 1786–8, ii. 1118–19; 5th Rep. Com. Char. 564.
[42] 5th Rep. Com. Char. 564.
[43] Ex inf. the clerk to the parish council. It was still paid in 1938: Charity Com. files.
[44] 5th Rep. Com. Char. 562–3.
[45] Ibid. 562–3, 564; Abstract, 1786–8, ii. 1118–19.
[46] 5th Rep. Com. Char. 564.
[47] Abstract, 1786–8, ii. 1118–19.

[48] 5th Rep. Com. Char. 563.
[49] Ibid. 563, 564.
[50] Ibid. 563.
[51] Ibid. 563, 564.
[52] Charity Com. files.
[53] Ibid.; see p. 19.
[54] Charity Com. files, citing the Vestry Minute Bk., Mar. 1852.
[55] Charity Com. files.
[56] Ibid.; see p. 19.
[57] Charity Com. files.
[58] Ex inf. the clerk to the parish council.
[59] Ex inf. the clerk to the parish council.
[60] 5th Rep. Com. Char. 564.
[61] Abstract, 1786–8, ii. 1118–19.
[62] 5th Rep. Com. Char. 564.
[63] It is not mentioned in a survey of 1889 in the Charity Com. files.

CANNOCK

THE ancient parish of Cannock consisted of the townships of Cannock (including Hednesford, Leacroft, and Cannock Wood), Huntington, and Great Wyrley. The greater part of the parish lay in Cannock constablewick with which the present Urban District of Cannock is roughly coextensive. The history of Huntington and of Great Wyrley will follow that of the area now in this Urban District. The account of recusancy in the three townships will be given under Cannock.

The Urban District is situated to the south and south-west of Cannock Chase, the ground sloping from 801 ft. at Castle Ring Camp near the hamlet of Cannock Wood in the north-east to 365 ft. at Wedges Mill in the south-west. The boundary on the south and south-east is formed by the Wyrley Brook, the Wash Brook, and the Newlands Brook. The soil is light, with a subsoil of gravel and clay, the geological formation being Bunter around Cannock itself and Coal Measures to the east.[1] The area is highly industrialized, mining being the chief industry, and the main centres of population are the towns of Cannock and Hednesford. There are, however, several farms around Leacroft and Cannock Wood. Under the Staffordshire Review Order of 1934 the hamlet of Hazel Slade, then in Brereton (in Rugeley), and a portion of the parish of Norton Canes (in Offlow hundred) were added to the Urban District, part of which was transferred to Norton Canes. The area of the Urban District was thereby increased from 7,965 acres to 8,155 acres.[2] The population in 1951 was 40,917.[3]

The town of Cannock lies about a mile north of Watling Street some 300 ft. lower than Cannock Chase to the north-east. The original built-up area of Cannock lies south and west of the parish church where the roads from Penkridge, Stafford, Rugeley, Walsall, and Wolverhampton converge. This part forms the centre of the modern town and, although much altered, still contains buildings of the 16th, 17th, and 18th centuries (see below). Cannock constablewick comprised 86 households in 1666,[4] and the district was described in 1747 as having 'a delightful situation'[5] and in 1817 as 'formerly a place of great resort on account of the salubrity of Reaumore-hill well, which was a fashionable watering-place in its day'.[6] By c. 1843 there was continuous building on both sides of High Street and High Green, a short way along the east side of Stafford Road, and along the south-west side of Old Penkridge Road.[7] Mill Street was built up, particularly on its south side, but the Walsall and Wolverhampton roads were almost clear of building.[8] By 1851 Cannock was 'a large and well-built village, with about 1,100 inhabitants'.[9] In 1956 the district south-west of Cannock was still being developed as an industrial

area, and there were several factories on the east side of the Wolverhampton Road. Residential development at Moss Wood to the south-west of the town dates largely from between the two World Wars and later, and there is an estate of pre-fabricated bungalows south of Longford Road. The area to the north-west was still developing as a residential district in 1956.

Hednesford, two miles to the north-east of Cannock, developed rapidly in the second half of the 19th century, after the opening of the Uxbridge Pit, from a small hamlet providing local staging services for travellers and facilities for the training of racehorses. The Cross Keys Inn and a few cottages remain from the original hamlet which was situated at Hill Top and immediately to the south of it.[10] There are still pre-19th century buildings in Forge Street and at Littleworth. Hednesford contained 53 households in 1666,[11] and was described in 1851 as 'an enclosed hamlet on Cannock heath'; it then had a population of 304,[12] which had risen to about 800 by 1860.[13] The present town centre, with the railway station as its nucleus, dates almost entirely from between 1860 and 1880, reflecting the sharp rise in population during these twenty years. The market hall and the gasworks were built in 1872, the public rooms in 1876, and the police station in 1877.[14] The present railway station dates from 1876, replacing a building of 1859 which was burnt down.[15] The latest expansion of Hednesford has been mainly to the north-west. There are large Council housing estates, some dating from before 1939, at Pye Green and Green Heath. At Pye Green there are also prefabricated bungalows and a caravan site.

Wedges Mill is a hamlet in the south-west corner of the Urban District dating from the foundation of William Gilpin's edge-tool works in 1790; a long range of two- and three-story workmen's cottages on the east side of the road are probably of the original date.[16] The site of the mill itself lay between the canal bridge and Watling Street.[17]

In Bridgtown which lies farther east along Watling Street, the oldest surviving building is part of the edge-tool works of Cornelius Whitehouse & Sons Ltd., Walsall Road, an early-19th- century factory building of brick with round-headed metal windows. A slightly later factory of similar type, occupied in 1956 by E. W. Wynn, ironfounders, stands at the corner of Watling Street and North Street. The built-up area of Bridgtown, contained in the triangle between Watling Street and Walsall Road, dates uniformly from the last third of the 19th century. By 1876 it was already laid out for streets which were being 'rapidly built'.[18]

The hamlet of Leacroft to the south-east of Cannock town had 24 households in 1666.[19] A few

[1] Kelly's Dir. Staffs. (1940), 23, 125.
[2] Ibid. (1932); Census, 1951, Staffs.
[3] Census, 1951, Staffs.
[4] S.H.C. 1927, 72, 74.
[5] Smith, New Map of Staffs. (1747).
[6] W. Pitt, Topog. Hist. of Staffs. (1817), 262. The Rumer Hill district lies to the south-west of the town.
[7] Tithe Maps and Appt., Cannock (copy in W.S.L.); S.H.C. 1947, 12.
[8] Tithe Maps and Appt., Cannock (copy in W.S.L.).
[9] White, Dir. Staffs. (1851).
[10] Yates, Map of Staffs. (1799), based on a survey made

between 1769 and 1775; Tithe Maps and Appt., Cannock (copy in W.S.L.).
[11] S.H.C. 1927, 73–75.
[12] Pitt, Staffs. 262; White, Dir. Staffs. (1851).
[13] Staffs. Advertiser, 5 May 1860.
[14] Kelly's Dir. Staffs. (1884).
[15] Cannock Advertiser Dir. (1938), 10.
[16] Ibid.; see p. 63; see plate facing p. 77.
[17] Tithe Maps and Appt., Cannock (copy in W.S.L.).
[18] P.O. Dir. Staffs. (1876).
[19] S.H.C. 1927, 73, 74.

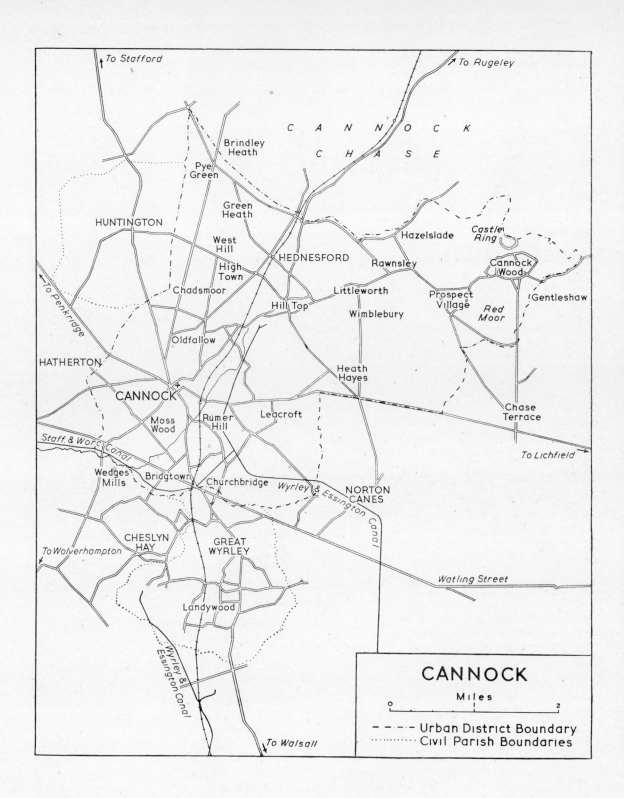

To Stafford

To Rugeley

C A N N O C K

C H A S E

Brindley
Heath

Pye
Green

Green
Heath

Hazelslade

Castle
Ring

HUNTINGTON

West
Hill

HEDNESFORD

Cannock
Wood

High
Town

Rawnsley

To Penkridge

Chadsmoor

Littleworth

Prospect
Village

Gentleshaw

Hill Top

Wimblebury

Red
Moor

Oldfallow

HATHERTON

Heath
Hayes

CANNOCK

Chase
Terrace

Moss
Wood

Rumer
Hill

Leacroft

Staff. & Worc. Canal

To Lichfield

Wedges
Mills

Bridgtown

Churchbridge

Wyrley & Essington Canal

NORTON
CANES

To Wolverhampton

CHESLYN
HAY

GREAT
WYRLEY

Watling Street

Landywood

Wyrley & Essington Canal

To Walsall

CANNOCK

Miles

0   1   2

– · – · – Urban District Boundary

· · · · · · · · Civil Parish Boundaries

scattered farms and cottages remain there. Since 1945 new houses have been built on raft foundations in this area[20] because of the danger from subsidence due to mining operations. There was an open-cast mining site to the south in 1957.[21]

Chadsmoor and High Town to the north-east of the town represent the late-19th- and 20th-century expansion of Cannock as a mining area. They now form an almost continuously built-up area joining Cannock to Hednesford. Much of West Chadsmoor consists of council and other housing dating from between the two World Wars and later.

Heath Hayes and Wimblebury to the south-east of Hednesford date largely from the twenty years between 1890 and 1910, but there are later houses on the outskirts, including a Council housing estate at Wimblebury. At Rawnsley, to the north-east of Wimblebury, are 100 houses of the terrace type built by the Cannock & Rugeley Colliery Company in 1914.[22] Prospect Village to the south-east of Rawnsley was built in its entirety c. 1926.[23] It consists of roughcast semi-detached houses standing in small gardens.

Cannock Wood, in the north-eastern corner of the Urban District, is a scattered hamlet lying on a south-eastern spur of Cannock Chase. A few cottages and farms date from before the 19th century. In 1666 it had eighteen households,[24] and in 1851 there were 'a few good farms and 275 inhabitants' with 'a large portion of the open heath, where there are a number of cottages with small plots of garden ground attached to them'.[25]

The Stafford–Walsall road runs through the town of Cannock where it is joined by the roads from Wolverhampton, Penkridge, Rugeley, and Lichfield. Watling Street crosses the south-western part of the Urban District. In the 18th century the road from Birmingham to Stafford and the north of England crossed Cannock Chase via Hednesford, where the Cross Keys Inn, built in 1746,[26] was an important posting station. Coaches travelling between London and Liverpool passed through the town of Cannock three times a week in each direction by 1818[27] and once a day by 1834, when there were also two a day in each direction between London and Manchester.[28] There were two toll-houses on Watling Street in Cannock c. 1843, one at the corner of Walkmill Lane and the other near Churchbridge, and there was another on the Stafford road a little to the north of its junction with Watling Street.[29] By 1818 letters were conveyed to Lichfield three times a week and to Walsall five

times,[30] and by 1829 Cannock lay on the route of a horse-mail travelling daily between Walsall and Penkridge.[31] There was a post-office at John Cook the tailor's by 1834 with letters coming and going to all parts via Walsall.[32]

In February 1858 Cannock station, then the terminus of the line from Walsall, was opened for passenger and goods traffic.[33] In the same year the South Staffordshire Railway began 'a well-appointed omnibus' service between Cannock and Rugeley,[34] pending the completion in the next year of the railway from Cannock to Rugeley, where it meets the main line from London to Stafford and the north-west of England.[35] There are also numerous branch lines serving the collieries. The Cannock extension of the Wyrley and Essington Canal had been constructed as far as Churchbridge by 1844[36] and to its present termination in Hednesford by 1858.[37] The Churchbridge extension of the Hatherton branch of the Staffordshire and Worcestershire Canal was built in 1860[38] to join the first canal to the north-east of Churchbridge. It was no longer in use owing to the danger of mining subsidence by 1957 when part of the eastern end was blown up to make way for the open-cast mining site.[39]

A bridge in Cannock, probably that near the mill, was rebuilt in 1281.[40] The 'bridge of Cannock near the mill' existed by 1427 when Thomas Heth of Great Wyrley bequeathed 6s. 8d. to its maintenance,[41] and the Riddings Bridge on the brook leading to the mill was mentioned in 1697.[42] The bridge at the hamlet of Wedges Mill, carrying the road from Cannock to Shareshill over the Wyrley Brook, was a wooden foot-bridge in the 17th century maintained by the parishioners of Shareshill and Cannock.[43] It was rebuilt in 1711 as a stone horse-bridge at a cost to the county of £20,[44] but the bridge there was described as new in 1830.[45]

In 1877 Cannock was divided into the three wards of Cannock, Chadsmoor, and Hednesford under a Local Board which had offices in Church Street from 1880.[47] The Urban District was established under the Local Government Act of 1894, the three new wards of Bridgtown, Heath Hayes, and Littleworth being added in 1900.[48] The main council offices have been situated at High Green in the centre of Cannock town since 1927,[49] although the offices in Church Street are still used.

Before 1834 the three townships of Cannock, Huntington, and Great Wyrley were each supporting their own poor, while the hamlets of Hednesford, Leacroft, and Cannock Wood supported theirs

[20] Local inf.
[21] See p. 63.
[22] Cannock Advertiser Dir. (1938), 11.
[23] Local inf.
[24] S.H.C. 1927, 75.
[25] White, Dir. Staffs. (1851).
[26] See p. 53.
[27] Parsons and Bradshaw, Dir. Staffs. (1818).
[28] White, Dir. Staffs. (1834).
[29] Greenwood, Map of Staffs. (1820); Tithe Maps and Appt., Cannock (copy in W.S.L.).
[30] Parsons and Bradshaw, Dir. Staffs. (1818).
[31] J. C. Tildesley, Hist. of Penkridge (1886), 73.
[32] White, Dir. Staffs. (1834).
[33] Ex inf. Public Relations Officer, London Midland Region, British Railways.
[34] Staffs. Advertiser, 24 Apr. 1858.
[35] Ibid. 1 Oct. 1859. This stretch between Cannock and Rugeley is known as the Cannock Mineral Line.
[36] W.S.L., Newspaper Cuttings box 2, unidentified

cutting dated 8 Aug. 1844 (probably Mid. Co. Herald).
[37] M. J. Wise, 'The Cannock Chase Region', Birmingham in its Regional Setting, 280.
[38] Ibid.
[39] Ex inf. Mr. L. Butler, general manager of the Staffs. & Worcs. Canal Co. until nationalization in 1947 and subsequently estate officer of the N.W. Div. of British Waterways (1956); local inf. (1957); see p. 63.
[40] Lichfield D. and C. MSS. N.5.
[41] Ibid. Chapter Act. Bk. i, f. 125a.
[42] S.R.O., D. 260/M, box II, bdle. l.
[43] S.H.C. 1934 (1), 45.
[44] Ibid. 81–82.
[45] J. Potter, List of Bridges which the Inhabitants of the County of Stafford are bound to repair (1830), 3.
[46] Kelly's Dir. Staffs. (1880).
[47] Ibid. (1884); see p. 53.
[48] Ibid. (1912); Cannock and Hednesford: Official Guide (1953), 13.
[49] Cannock Advertiser Dir. (1938), 11; see p. 53.

jointly.[50] A parish workhouse was built at Snout's Gap, Walsall Road, in 1743.[51] The workhouse on the Wolverhampton road half a mile from the centre of Cannock was built in 1872 with a capacity of 200 to replace that at Brewood as the workhouse for the Penkridge Union, which by 1880 had been renamed the Cannock Union.[52] In 1948 the workhouse became a county hostel, used partly as a hospital for the aged and partly as a home for the aged and the temporarily homeless.[53]

The village of Cannock, situated on a slight hill of gravelly soil, was often short of water in the summer until pipes were laid by the Cannock Conduit Trustees from a spring in Stringer's Meadow in Leacroft, given in 1736 by Dr. Birch to the inhabitants of Cannock.[54] The cost was met by subscriptions, the last in 1786, and also from the rents of some land within the parish inclosed in 1737,[55] and although the South Staffordshire Water Works Company was set up in 1853 the Conduit Trust continued to supply water until 1942 when through mining subsidence piping finally became impossible.[56] Under a Scheme of the Charity Commissioners of 1954 the trust's income is applied for the general benefit of the inhabitants of the ancient township or liberty of Cannock by the provision of shelters against the weather, of places of recreation and of lectures and exhibitions.[57] The income in 1955 was £276 16s. 2d. interest on stock and £22 4s. rent.[58] The tank building of the Cannock Conduit Trust, erected in 1736, stands west of the Bowling Green. It is a small hexagonal stone structure with a pyramidal roof and a ball finial.

The South Staffordshire Water Works Company's reservoir in the hills west of Rawnsley was in existence by 1880[59] but was disused by 1952.[60]

The cemetery at Oldfallow, West Chadsmoor, which has a small mortuary chapel of variegated brick, was established in 1865 on 4 acres of land granted for this purpose out of Cannock Chase by the Inclosure Commissioners.[61] In 1923 a further five acres were added.[62]

The Bowling Green, forming an island site in the centre of Cannock town, existed in 1753 when a brick wall was built round it.[63] After a long dispute over the ownership of this acre or so of land the Green was, in 1896, vested in trustees, four appointed by the Bowling Club and four by the Urban

District Council, and leased to the Club at a peppercorn rent.[64] The Trust was still in existence in 1956.[65]

By 1817 the Hednesford district was already being used for the training of race-horses,[66] as it still is,[67] and by 1834 about 100 horses were trained during a season on the Hednesford Hills.[68] In 1839 Hednesford was 'the most noted place for training available to persons in the Midland Counties'.[69] In addition to public training establishments there were two in private hands, the larger belonging to Edmund Peel who had built Hednesford Lodge (see below), at the side of Hednesford Pool in 1831 with stables for his horses.[70] He also owned one of the two studs.[71] By 1851 eleven distinguished trainers and jockeys were training some 120 horses during a season.[72] The Grand National Trophy has been won four times from the stables at Hednesford.[73]

Cannock was the scene of a skirmish in 1646 in which a troop of parliamentarian horse from Stafford repulsed a royalist force from Lichfield.[74] The Cannock Rifle Volunteers Corps was formed in 1860 and given a range on Cannock Chase by the 2nd Marquess of Anglesey.[75] In 1873 the Chase was used for part of the British Army manœuvres.[76]

Castle Ring Camp, an earthwork of the hill-fort type, situated to the north of the hamlet of Cannock Wood at the highest point on Cannock Chase (801 ft.), was bought by the Urban District Council in 1933 from the 6th Marquess of Anglesey and is scheduled as an ancient monument.[77] At Red Moor, less than a mile to the south of the camp, is the site of the Cistercian abbey of Radmore.[78]

Two pools called 'Hedne Ford Poole', situated alongside the road to Rugeley in what is now the centre of Hednesford[79] and possibly connected with local iron-working, were held of the manor of Cannock in 1595 by Gilbert Wakering[80] and were in the hands of the Marquess of Anglesey c. 1843.[81] The larger covered 27 acres in 1834,[82] but probably as a result of the floods of 1845 it had shrunk to 23 acres by 1851.[83] They have long since been built over.

Cannock town still possesses several ancient buildings. No. 79 High Street, now an ironmonger's shop, was originally a timber-framed house, probably dating from the 16th century. It has been faced with brickwork but retains a massive stone chimney at its west end and a roof truss with curved struts. There was formerly a Tudor-arched porch in the

[50] White, *Dir. Staffs.* (1834). The overseers' accounts and papers in the parish chest date from 1696.
[51] *Cannock Advertiser Dir.* (1938).
[52] *P.O. Dir. Staffs.* (1872); *Kelly's Dir. Staffs.* (1880).
[53] Ex inf. the Clerk, Cannock U.D. Council (1956).
[54] White, *Dir. Staffs.* (1851); F. W. Hackwood, *Chronicles of Cannock Chase,* 121; Pitt, *Staffs.* 261–2; Charity Com. files.
[55] Hackwood, *Chronicles of Cannock Chase,* 121; Charity Com. files.
[56] *Kelly's Dir. Staffs.* (1940); Charity Com. files.
[57] Charity Com. files.   [58] Ibid.
[59] *Kelly's Dir. Staffs.* (1880).
[60] O.S. Map 1/25,000, 43/01 (1952).
[61] *Lich. Dioc. Ch. Cal.* (1866); see p. 61.
[62] *Kelly's Dir. Staffs.* (1932).
[63] Pitt, *Staffs.* 262.
[64] Hackwood, *Chronicles of Cannock Chase,* 121; trust deed (copy in W.S.L.).
[65] Ex inf. the Clerk, Cannock U.D. Council.
[66] Pitt, *Staffs.* 262.
[67] Bob Ward's stables at Hazel Slade in 1955 produced the youngest jockey (aged 15) ever to ride in the Cesarewitch: *Express and Star,* 22 Oct. 1955.

[68] White, *Dir. Staffs.* (1834).
[69] *Sporting Mag.* June 1839, 106; see plate facing p. 63.
[70] Ibid. 107; White, *Dir. Staffs.* (1834).
[71] *Sporting Mag.* June 1839, 110.
[72] White, *Dir. Staffs.* (1851).
[73] *Cannock and Hednesford: Official Guide* (1953), 19.
[74] Hist. MSS. Com. *13th Rep.* 343–4.
[75] *Staffs. Advertiser,* 25 Aug. 1860.
[76] M. J. Wise, 'The Cannock Chase Manoeuvres of 1873' (*Army Quarterly,* lxviii), 248–56.
[77] Plaque *in situ*; *V.C.H. Staffs.* i. 336–8; ex inf. Messrs. Strutt and Parker, Lofts and Warner, Berkeley Sq., London, agents to Lord Anglesey; see plate facing p. 62.
[78] See p. 57.
[79] Hednesford Lodge, now the Anglesey Hotel, lay just to the south: Teesdale, *Map of Staffs.* (1832).
[80] Hackwood, *Chronicles of Cannock Chase,* 76; Yates, *Map of Staffs.* (1799); see pp. 59, 63.
[81] Tithe Maps and Appt., Cannock (copy in W.S.L.).
[82] White, *Dir. Staffs.* (1834).
[83] Ibid. (1851); 'The Cannock Mineral Railway', *Staffs. Advertiser,* 1 Oct. 1859.

CANNOCK: Crown Inn and Church in 1841

RUGELEY: Hagley Hall in 1814

Walhouse School, built in 1828

South doorway of the church, demolished in
1957

Plaque on the former school

CANNOCK

angle of one of the two gables facing the road.[84] A fine late-16th- or early-17th-century timber house which stood near the west end of the parish church has now disappeared. Drawings of 1836 and 1841[85] show a three-gabled front with timbering of chevron pattern on its overhanging upper story. No. 2 Walsall Road is a much altered timber-framed cottage, now a shoe shop and store rooms. The Crown Hotel is a brick house dating from c. 1700 with two gables facing the road. It formerly had mullioned and transomed windows and a central pedimented doorway over which hung the inn sign.[86] No. 10 Mill Street has an unaltered mid-18th-century brick front with a moulded eaves cornice, angle pilasters and a pedimented central doorway. The windows have brick aprons and stone key-blocks. No. 8 had at one time a similar front. No. 5 Mill Street is a tall late-18th- or early-19th-century house retaining its original garden and outbuildings. The Council House, High Green, is a dignified mid-18th-century house facing the Bowling Green. The front, faced with later stucco, has sash windows and a pedimented doorcase. The original wrought-iron gates and part of the railings are in position. The building has been used as offices by the Cannock Urban District Council since 1927.[87] There are several 18th- and early-19th-century houses on the south side of High Green, mostly much altered and with inserted shop-fronts. A Georgian house known as the Manor House which formerly stood at High Green was demolished in 1936, and modern buildings, including a cinema, occupy the site.[88] The former Local Board Offices, built in 1880, have a red-brick front with a central entrance flanked by marble shafts with carved foliage capitals.[89] The Benton Memorial Clock turret in Market Square was erected in 1935.[90]

The Anglesey Hotel, formerly Hednesford or Hedgeford Lodge, in the centre of modern Hednesford, was built in 1831 by Edmund Peel of Fazeley (in Tamworth),[91] as a summer residence and to provide stabling for racehorses. The house was unoccupied in 1851[92] and became a hotel between 1860 and 1868.[93] The white stucco front has two stepped gables with a smaller gable and a Tudor-arched portico between them. Part of the original stabling is in existence. The Cross Keys Inn, Old Hednesford, dates from 1746 and carries an original date stone on an altered stucco front. Cross Keys Farm, which lies 100 yds. farther south, is the only timber-framed building in Hednesford and probably dates from the 16th century.

At Leacroft Hill Farm an early-17th-century

timber-framed house of three bays is almost derelict. The front framing has small brick-filled panels and three gabled dormers. The farmhouse dates from 1930.[94]

The architecture of houses attached to lesser estates and of the mill is treated below under the relevant sections.

MANORS. In 1086 CANNOCK (Chenet) was assessed at one hide with appurtenances and was held by the king in demesne as part of the escheated lands of the Earldom of Mercia.[95] Some rights in the vill seem to have been among those confirmed to Bishop Walter Durdent by the Pope in 1152,[96] and any such rights were exempted from the grant made by Henry Plantagenet in 1153 to Ranulph Earl of Chester of all royal lands in Staffordshire.[97] Ranulph died at the end of that year but had meanwhile granted the vill of Cannock with all rents and appurtenances to the Cistercian abbey at Radmore.[98] This grant had been confirmed by Henry.[99] The monks were transferred to Stoneleigh (Warws.) at their own request by 1155,[1] and from at least 1169 to 1187 the vill was assessed for aids and tallages like other royal lands.[2] In 1189, when raising money for his crusade, Richard I conveyed Cannock and Rugeley to Hugh de Nonant, Bishop of Coventry and Lichfield, in free alms, together with the advowson of the church and all other rights and appurtenances, exempt from suit to the shire and hundred courts.[3] In 1191 the Pope confirmed the bishop in possession.[4] Because he conspired with John during Richard's absence, Hugh was deprived of his see, offices, and temporalities when the king returned from captivity in 1194,[5] but he was restored to favour in 1195[6] and given Cannock and his other possessions for a fine of 2,000 marks.[7] At some date between 1195 and 1198 Archbishop Hubert Walter, as primate and legate, confirmed Richard I's original grant of the vill.[8]

On Hugh de Nonant's death in March 1198, the temporalities of the see passed into the king's hands, and tallage was imposed on Cannock for the year ending Michaelmas 1198.[9] The next bishop had received the temporalities by the end of the year,[10] but by Michaelmas 1200 he had restored Cannock and Rugeley to the Crown in exchange for a rent of £10 for the two.[11] This was paid until his death in 1208,[12] after which the see was kept vacant until 1215. Meanwhile the two towns were again tallaged, with other royal manors, in 1205[13] and 1214.[14] Bishop William de Cornhill (1215–23) received £5

[84] W.S.L., Staffs. Views, iii, p. 14 (1841).
[85] Ibid., pp. 6, 9, 11, 15(b).
[86] Ibid., p. 15 (a, 1841); see plate facing p. 52. The small octagonal stone building on the right of the picture has been identified as the conduit house: S.H.C. 1942–3, 41. Its features and position, however, do not appear to confirm this identification.
[87] Cannock Advertiser Dir. (1938), 11.
[88] Ibid. 12.
[89] See p. 51.
[90] Cannock Advertiser Dir. (1938), 12.
[91] Min. of Housing and Local Govt., List of Scheduled Buildings, Cannock U.D.
[92] White, Dir. Staffs. (1851).
[93] P.O. Dir. Staffs. (1860; 1868).
[94] Local inf.
[95] V.C.H. Staffs. iv. 40, no. 26.
[96] S.H.C. 1924, no. 262.
[97] Ibid. ii (1), 221.
[98] Dugd. Mon. v. 447.

[99] Shakespeare Birthplace Trust, Leger Book of Stoneleigh Abbey, f. 8b.
[1] V.C.H. Warws. ii. 79.
[2] S.H.C. i. 56, 69, 130; ibid. ii (1), 12.
[3] Ibid. 1924, nos. 15, 22. The bishop paid a fine of 25 marks (ibid. ii (1), 4), but the Exchequer lost 61s. a year for the farm of the 2 manors (ibid. 1).
[4] Ibid. 1924, no. 264.
[5] Ibid. ii (1), 30, 33, 39.
[6] Ibid. 1924, no. 222; ibid. ii (1), 54; Roger de Hoveden, Chronica (Rolls Ser.), iii. 287.
[7] Pipe R. 1195 (P.R.S. N.S. vi), 191.
[8] S.H.C. 1924, no. 753.
[9] Ibid. ii (1), 71, 74.
[10] Ibid. 78.
[11] Ibid. 92.
[12] Ibid. 101–47 passim.
[13] Ibid. 128, 137.
[14] Ibid. 162, 164–5.

rent for the half year ending Easter 1215,[15] and although the manor, with Rugeley, was confirmed and restored to him in 1217,[16] yet from at least his last year, 1222–3, until Easter 1230, he and his successor were paid £10 from the Exchequer in return for the farm of the two manors,[17] which were once more tallaged as royal demesne in 1227.[18] In April 1230 Richard I's charter of liberties, granted to the bishop in 1189, was confirmed, and the two manors were restored to the bishop,[19] although they were tallaged for the year ending Michaelmas 1230.[20] In 1255 the bishop, as lord of Cannock and its members, was returned as holding 1 hide which was not geldable.[21] In 1259 the king granted to Bishop Roger de Meuland or Longespée (1258–95), his kinsman, free warren in all his demesne lands, including the manors of 'Kanocbury' and Rugeley.[22] The charters of 1189 were confirmed in 1290[23] and at intervals again until 1510.[24] The vills of Cannock and Rugeley were stated in 1316 to be held by the bishop as part of his liberty, with return of writs.[25]

On 28 September 1546 the Chancellor of the Court of Augmentations was ordered to 'practize and conclude' with Bishop Richard Sampson for the surrender of lands and manors, including Cannock and Rugeley, in return for benefices of equivalent value.[26] The lands were surrendered by the bishop on 29 September[27] and on 26 October were granted to Sir William Paget by letters patent,[28] confirmed by Act of Parliament the same day.[29] Sir William, created Lord Paget of Beaudesert in 1549,[30] settled his estates in 1554 on himself and his heirs male, with contingent remainder to his daughters.[31] He was succeeded in 1563 by his eldest son, Henry 2nd Lord Paget of Beaudesert.[32] Henry died in 1568, leaving an infant daughter Elizabeth[33] who became *de jure* Baroness Paget.[34] Although the estates should have descended to Henry's brother Thomas, under the settlement of 1554, Elizabeth seems to have had some rights in them until her death in 1570.[35] Thomas, her uncle, was her heir,[36] and from this time Cannock and Rugeley descended in the Paget family with the barony, of which the *caput* was at Beaudesert in Longdon (Offlow hundred),[37] until

the 6th Marquess of Anglesey (d. 1947) disposed of his property in Cannock and Rugeley in various sales after 1918.[38]

In 1298 there was a capital messuage here with a garden, together valued at 26s. 8d.[39]

From at least 1309 the courts of Cannock and Rugeley were held jointly, usually at each manor alternately.[40] A twice-yearly view of frankpledge was being held by 1274.[41] From that date until 1510 the townships there represented were Cannock-bury (or Cannock) by five frankpledges, Rugeley and Brereton by five, Great Wyrley by two, and Huntington by two.[42] From at least 1529 the vill of Cannock had only three, with one for Leacroft and one for Hednesford and Hatherton (in St. Peter's, Wolverhampton) jointly.[43] The lord's revenue from the view of frankpledge amounted to 3s. in 1274 and 1281,[44] and by at least 1424 the proceeds of the manor included 3s. called frithsilver from the view of frankpledge.[45] The same sum was paid in 1533,[46] and by 1560 it had risen to 4s.[47] Cannock was paying 1s. 6d. in frithsilver between at least 1740 and 1769, Great Wyrley 1s. and Huntington 6d.[48]

At the three-weekly courts, held by at least 1309, business included not only the usual surrenders, admittances of tenants and payments of heriots and reliefs but also the presentment of offences within the lord's woods by the forester of Cannock, the forester of Rugeley and the rider (*equitator*) and the presentment of brewing and baking against the assize of bread and ale by the ale tasters of Cannock and Rugeley respectively.[49]

At a court of survey held in 1595 defining the bounds of the manor and leet and the customs of the manor it was stated that the 'oldholders' had timber rights on the Chase and might hunt the fox, the hare, and the roe there and hawk with a sparrow-hawk.[50] These 'oldholders' owed suit only at the two great leets, while other tenants (copyholders) had to appear at the three-weekly courts or else buy their exemption at ½d. a day or 8d. a year. When an 'oldholder' died, one heriot was due for his holding, and his heir paid the equivalent of a year's chief rent when he entered upon the property. On the death

[15] *S.H.C.* 1924, 166, 168.
[16] *Pat. R.* 1216–25, 24; the sheriff was ordered to give him seisin: *Rot. Litt. Claus.* (Rec. Com.), i. 296.
[17] *S.H.C.* i. 625; ibid. ii. 109; *Cal. Lib.* 1226–40, 27–28, 64, 86, 109, 129, 149, 175.
[18] *Rot. Litt. Claus.* (Rec. Com.), ii. 184.
[19] *Close R.* 1227–31, 329; *Cal. Lib.* 1226–40, 181. The bishop's rights were upheld in 1236 (*Cal. Close* 1234–7, 324) and 1242: *S.H.C.* iv (1), 93–94; *Pipe R.* 1242 (ed. H. L. Cannon), 9.
[20] *Pipe R.* 1230 (P.R.S. N.S. iv), 236.
[21] *Rot. Hund.* (Rec. Com.), ii. 114.
[22] *S.H.C.* 1924, no. 219; *Cal. Chart. R.* 1257–1300, 18–19.
[23] *Cal. Chart. R.* 1257–1300, 347–8.
[24] W.S.L., Paget Papers (Gardner Coll.), 51 (4). Other confirmations were in 1345 (*Cal. Chart. R.* 1341–1417, 38–39), 1387, 1415, 1426 (*Cal. Pat.* 1422–9, 357–8).
[25] *Feud. Aids.* v. 17.
[26] *S.H.C.*, 1939, 132–3.   [27] Ibid. 110–11.
[28] *L. & P. Hen. VIII*, xxi (2), g. 76 (332).
[29] *S.H.C.* 1939, 133.
[30] *Complete Peerage*, x. 278. For his career see ibid. 276–80.
[31] *S.H.C.* xii (1), 194–5.
[32] C 142/137, no. 47.
[33] C 142/152, no. 150.
[34] *Complete Peerage*, x. 281.
[35] C 142/159, no. 45. The Court Rolls of Cannock and Rugeley between 23 Sept. 1567 and 4 Oct. 1570 are missing.

[36] *Complete Peerage*, x. 281.
[37] C 66/3954, mm. 19–41; *S.H.C.* xviii. 11–12; C 142/448, no. 113; C.P. 25(2)/1413, 29 Geo. III Trin.; C.P. 25(2)/1414, 41 Geo. III Trin.
[38] Ex inf. Messrs. Strutt and Parker, Lofts and Warner, Berkeley Sq., London, agents to Lord Anglesey (1956).
[39] W.S.L., D. 1734, Jeayes 2268, extent of lands of Bpric. of Cov., Lich., and Chester, 26 Edw. I.
[40] W.S.L., D. 1734, Ct. R. of Cannock and Rugeley 1309–1810; courts were also held at the unidentified 'Water Wending' in 1310 and 1355: ibid. 1309–73, mm. 2, 21. There are 18th-century court papers in W.S.L., Paget Papers (Gardner Coll.) and at Plas Newydd.
[41] Lichfield D. and C. MSS. N. 10. By 1298 Great Wyrley was paying frith fee to the lord of Cannock: ibid. Jeayes 2268, extent of lands of Bpric. of Cov., Lich., and Chester, 26 Edw. I.
[42] Ibid. Ct. R. 1309–73, m. 5, Ct. R. 1510–46.
[43] Ibid. Ct. R. 1510–46, 1546–53.
[44] Lichfield D. and C. MSS. N. 10, N. 5.
[45] W.S.L., D. 1734, Compotus R. of Bp. of Cov. and Lich., 1423–57, m. 5d.
[46] Ibid. 1532–3, m. 1.
[47] Ibid., Compotus of lands of Lord Paget, 1559–60, m. 8d.
[48] W.S.L., Paget Papers (Gardner Coll.), 9 (5), 35 (1, 7, 9).
[49] W.S.L., D. 1734, Cannock and Rugeley Ct. R. 1309–73, m. 5d.
[50] F. W. Hackwood, *Chronicles of Cannock Chase*, 76.

of a copyholder a heriot was due for each messuage, with a year's rent from the heir or two years' rent from anyone who secured the property by purchase. The heriot on each cottage was 6d., but all other heriots had to be appraised by 'the twelve men', with payment at the next audit. 'Oldholders' and copyholders might sublet their land without the lord's consent, provided he lost no rent, and they could not be impeached for committing waste on any of their lands. No cottagers might serve as jurors at the great leet so long as there were sufficient freeholders, oldholders, and copyholders to serve. When the great court was held at Rugeley, the lord gave dinner there to all the tenants from Cannock who served on the jury, and similarly for the Rugeley tenants when the great court was held at Cannock. All inhabitants might turn their cattle loose on the Chase all the year round and let them browse the hollies there in winter for a reasonable amercement.

LESSER ESTATES. A carucate of land in Cannock worth 5s. was held in 1086 by Alvric, one of the king's thegns.[51] The subsequent descent of this land is not known.

A virgate in Cannock was held of the king at some time before 1236 by Robert Trumwyn, as by his ancestors before him, possibly since the time of the Conqueror when it may have been held by Lewinus, by the service of keeping the Hay of Cheslyn within the royal forest of Cannock.[52] The overlordship had passed to Bishop Alexander Stavensby by 1236,[53] but from at least 1250[54] until at least 1575[55] this overlordship remained with the Crown. By 1250 Robert Trumwyn had been succeeded by William Trumwyn[56] who was dead by 1296.[57] The virgate, now valued at ½ mark, passed to his son William (II)[58] who was dead by 1318 and had held a messuage as well as this land.[59] The messuage, being ruinous, was worth nothing, but the virgate, consisting of 12 acres, was worth 12d.[60] William's son and heir William (III)[61] was dead by 1340 when the messuage was still ruinous and the virgate was stated to be worth only 5s., because of the sandy nature of the soil.[62] William was succeeded by his son William (IV)[63] who died in September 1349 with a son William (V) as his heir.[64] Meanwhile a messuage, garden, land, and wood in Cannock now belonging to William had been leased for ten years to a John le Carter who, towards the end of 1349, was sued by William for pulling down a chamber there and selling the timber, digging pits, and selling the stone

and clay, and cutting down and selling oak, ash, hazel, and apple-trees.[65] The messuage was still worth nothing in 1350,[66] but when William died in 1362 there was a dovecot there.[67] William (VI), his son and heir, was a minor[68] and in the same year the king granted the wardship of two parts of the child's lands, along with his marriage, to Philip de Lutteleye.[69] William was succeeded by his brother John who himself died under age in 1369, and whose heir was his sister Elizabeth, also a minor.[70] Her marriage was bought for £20 by William Strete, yeoman and butler of the king,[71] and by 1370 she was the wife of Roger Lansant.[72] She died childless in 1375, when her lands passed to her aunt Isabel, wife of William Reynald.[73] When Isabel died in 1399 she was the wife of Nicholas Ruggeley, but it was John Salwey, her son by her second husband, who succeeded her.[74]

John died in 1420, with a son Humphrey, aged only nine years, to succeed him.[75] Humphrey settled the messuage and virgate on his second son Thomas in 1486, reserving ½ acre worth 6d. out of the virgate as the inheritance of his eldest son, the lunatic Sir John.[76] Thomas succeeded in 1493[77] and at his death in 1513 left as his heir a minor, his son Thomas (II),[78] who passed into the king's wardship.[79] Sir John Salwey now seems to have secured these as well as other of Humphrey's lands, and when he died in 1518 he was holding in serjeanty a messuage and virgate in Cannock worth 12s., with three daughters to succeed him.[80] Richard Biddulph, husband of Margaret one of the coheirs, was holding a share in a messuage and other lands in Cannock at his death in 1552,[81] and shortly afterwards Thomas Salwey (II) was suing the heir Francis Biddulph, along with John Leveson of Wolverhampton who had acquired an interest in some of the Salwey lands, for detention of deeds relating to lands in Cannock and elsewhere.[82] In 1564 and 1567 Thomas again sued for his lands, including those in Cannock,[83] and it was decreed in 1568 that pending further suits the disputed inheritance should be divided among the various claimants.[84] John Leveson was said to be holding a messuage and virgate in Cannock of the queen at his death in 1575,[85] and his son and heir Thomas,[86] who in 1590 was granted two parts of a messuage and lands in Cannock by Thomas Salwey's sons Arthur and Matthew,[87] was probably holding the estate at his death in 1594.[88]

In 1310 Margery, widow of John le Olde of Leacroft, and Adam and John, sons of William Salwey, were disputing land within the manor of Cannock.[89]

[51] V.C.H. Staffs. iv. 57, no. 274.
[52] Bk. of Fees, 594; S.H.C. v (i), 167; S.H.C. N.S. x (i), 215; see p. 101.
[53] Bk. of Fees, 594.
[54] Ibid. 1186; Close R. 1251-3, 151-2; S.H.C. 1911, 407, giving the date as 1247; S.H.C. v (i), 167; Cal. Inq. p.m. iii, p. 203.
[55] C 142/175, no. 88.
[56] Bk. of Fees, 1186.
[57] Cal. Inq. p.m. iii, p. 203.
[58] Ibid.; S.H.C. 1911, 239.
[59] Cal. Inq. p.m. vi, no. 108.
[60] S.H.C. 1911, 340-1.   [61] Ibid.
[62] Cal. Inq. p.m., viii, no. 257; S.H.C. 1913, 75.
[63] Cal. Inq. p.m. viii, no. 257.
[64] Ibid. ix, no. 438.
[65] S.H.C. xii (i), 96.
[66] Ibid. 1913, 139.
[67] Cal. Inq. p.m. xi, no. 442.
[68] Ibid.
[69] Cal. Fine R. 1356-68, 233.
[70] Cal. Inq. p.m. xii, no. 421.
[71] Cal. Fine R. 1369-77, 31.
[72] Ibid. 88.
[73] Cal. Inq. p.m. xiv, no. 212.
[74] C 137/16, S.H.C. N.S. ii, pedigree facing p. 46.
[75] C 137/61; V.C.H. Worcs. iv. 342.
[76] Cal. Pat. 1485-94, 118; Cal. Inq. p.m. Hen. VII, i, pp. 360, 373; C 1/568, no. 88.
[77] Cal. Inq. p.m. Hen. VII, i, p. 373.
[78] C 142/28, no. 12.
[79] S.H.C. 1938, 89-90; ibid. 1910, 21-22.
[80] C 142/46, no. 31.
[81] C 142/96, no. 64.
[82] C 1/1383, no. 1; S.H.C. xi. 288; St. Ch. 2/26/302.
[83] S.H.C. 1938, 88-92.
[84] Ibid. 92.
[85] C 142/175, no. 88.   [86] Ibid.
[87] S.H.C. xvi. 103-4.
[88] C 142/242, no. 65.
[89] W.S.L., D. 1734, Cannock and Rugeley Ct. R. 1309-73, m. 2.

An Adam Salwey occurs in 1332[90] and 1342[91] and Richard son of Adam Salwey of Leacroft in 1360.[92] A John Salwey, who was dead by 1399, may have held land in Leacroft.[93] His son John died in 1420, leaving a son Humphrey, then aged nine,[94] who at his death in 1493 was holding land and rents in Leacroft of the bishop.[95] This land seems to have followed the same descent as his land elsewhere in Cannock[96] until at least 1594.[97]

John Birch of Leacroft, yeoman, occurs between 1586 and 1603.[98] In 1614 a settlement of land in Leacroft was made by a John Birch and his wife Elizabeth[99] and in 1624 by John Birch (of Bloxwich) and his wife Alice.[1] John Birch, attorney, of Cannock, presumably the son of John and Alice, was imprisoned by the Parliamentarians in 1643, and his estates, including lands and rents in Leacroft worth £100 annually before the Civil War, lands in Cannock called 'the Kingswood' previously worth £60, and lands in Cannock held by the courtesy of England and previously worth £50, were sequestered, having been twice plundered by the Royalists.[2] He was fined £100 in 1645, but his petition for release from sequestration in June of that year was granted in August in view of his parliamentarian sympathies.[3] This John was still living in 1663, aged 69,[4] but it was his son Edward (of the Middle Temple) aged 28 in 1663, who was assessed at fifteen hearths in Leacroft for the Hearth Tax in 1666.[5] Edward was appointed deputy to the High Steward of the honor of Tutbury in 1675,[6] and was living at Leacroft in 1694 and 1696.[7] A Dr. Birch owned the estate in 1736.[8] About 1843 a Mr. Henry Birch owned land in Leacroft, some of which was in his own hands, including a house at the junction of the roads from Lichfield and Norton by the present canal bridge.[9] Leacroft Old Hall had probably been partially demolished by 1851 when such buildings as remained were occupied by a farmer.[10] The site is now part of the Cannock and Leacroft Colliery and is the property of the National Coal Board. A long red-brick range with stone quoins, moulded cornice, and central pediment probably represents a late-17th-century stable block. At its south end a barn with a gable-end facing the road carries a date tablet of 1676. An outhouse farther north has a tablet inscribed 'Dr. W. B.' 1737. Another outhouse

with an octagonal brick base may represent the remains of a dovecot. A field south of the road was formerly known as Dovecot Meadow.[11] Later buildings on the site are occupied by the National Coal Board and part of the stable range has been converted into cottages.

Fletcher's Farm in Leacroft, held in 1641 by John Giffard of Wolverhampton,[12] and by 1645 in the tenure of Simon Breffitt at a rent of £38,[13] was sequestrated with the rest of John's estates in 1647 for his recusancy.[14] It was leased for a year in 1651 by the County Commissioners to a certain Andrew Mills[15] and sold in 1652 by the Treason Trustees to Francis Gregge of Clement's Inn.[16] Meanwhile John's son Peter claimed, in 1651, that the farm had been settled in 1641 in trust for him and his youngest sister.[17] In 1653 Anthony Dormer, by then married to Peter's sister Dorothy, claimed that the purpose of the trust had been the provision of £700 for Dorothy.[18] Dormer's claim to the estate was allowed in 1654,[19] and the lessee, Mills, was compensated in 1655 by the County Committee.[20]

John Coleman of Cannock, son of Thomas Coleman of Cannock, occurs from 1564[21], and when he died in 1596 his estates included a messuage and cottage in Hednesford, 40 acres of land and one-ninth of a meadow called Organs Meadow in Cannock, and lands held in chief elsewhere in the parish.[22] He was succeeded by his son, Walter, aged 30,[23] who with his wife Dorothy was holding a messuage and lands in Cannock at some time between 1603 and 1625.[24] Walter seems to have been succeeded by a son John whose estates in Cannock included the Old Hall,[25] but by 1646 his possessions had been sequestered because he was a papist.[26] He was dead by 1650.[27] His widow, Margaret, also a recusant, petitioned in 1652 for release from sequestration of one-third of her estate, which consisted mainly of the parish tithes, pleading the impoverishment of her six small children, and in the same year she was allowed this one-third along with her house.[28] The house of a Charles Coleman in Hednesford was stated in 1666 to have been demolished and sold.[29] A messuage or cottage with lands and appurtenances in Cannock, called 'le Old Hall' and held by copyhold tenure of the manor, was being claimed in 1703 by a Charles Coleman, as the son of another Charles

90 *S.H.C.* x (1), 119.
91 W.S.L. D. 1734, Cannock and Rugeley Ct. R. 1309–73, m. 4.
92 *S.H.C.* xiv (1), 114.
93 Burke, *Land. Gent.* (1952), 2237; C 137/15.
94 C 138/48; *V.C.H. Worcs.* iv. 342.
95 *Cal. Inq. p.m. Hen. VII,* i, no. 874.
96 C 1/108, no. 47; *S.H.C.* xi. 288; C 1/1326, nos. 44–45; *S.H.C.* xiii. 230; ibid. 1938, 88–93; ibid. xiii. 299–300; ibid. xiv (1), 204; C 142/175, no. 88; *S.H.C.* xiv (1), 207; ibid. xvi. 103–4; see p. 55.
97 C 142/242, no. 65.
98 *S.H.C.* 1929, 112; ibid. 1930, 8; ibid. 1935, 428; ibid. 1940, 7.
99 Ibid. N.S. iv. 71.
1 Ibid. N.S. x (1), 62; ibid. v (2), 43.
2 Ibid. v (2), 43; *Cal. Cttee. for Compounding,* 893; W.S.L., S. MS. 339 (transcript of Royalist Composition Papers), i, p. 333.
3 *Cal. Cttee. for Compounding,* 893.
4 *S.H.C.* v (2), 43.
5 Ibid.; ibid. 1927, 73.
6 Hist. MSS. Com. *6th Rep.* 776.
7 W.S.L. 71/6/45.
8 See p. 52.
9 Tithe Maps and Appt., Cannock (copy in W.S.L.);

White, *Dir. Staffs.* (1834).
10 White, *Dir. Staffs.* (1851).
11 Tithe Maps and Appt., Cannock (copy in W.S.L.).
12 *Cal. Cttee. for Compounding,* 2998.
13 S.R.O., D. 260/M, box 25, bdle. k, Royalist Estates 1643–5, ff. 69b–70a.
14 W.S.L., S. MS. 339 (transcript of Royalist Composition Papers), ii, p. 113.
15 *Cal. Cttee. for Compounding,* 3228.
16 Ibid. 2999.
17 Ibid. 2711.
18 Ibid. 2998–9.
19 Ibid. 2999.
20 Ibid. 3228.
21 *S.H.C.* N.S. ix. 233–4. His wife Margery occurs in 1586: *S.H.C.* xv. 168.
22 C 142/245, no. 68.
23 Ibid.
24 C 2/Jas. I, C. 16, no. 41.
25 W.S.L. 68/42 (Cannock Assessment Bk.), f. 1a.
26 *Cal. Cttee. for Compounding,* 89; *S.H.C.* 1915, 50, 390; Lichfield D. and C. MS. Bk. liv.
27 W.S.L., S. MS. 339 (transcript of Royalist Composition Papers), vi, pp. 267–8.
28 *Cal. Cttee. for Compounding,* 2929; *S.H.C.* 1915, 321.
29 *S.H.C.* 1927, 74.

Coleman and Anne, against William Wilson and his wife Margaret.[30]

Henry Plantagenet, as Duke of Normandy, granted 'Hedenedford' as pasture free from pannage dues to the local Cistercian abbey of Radmore c. 1153.[31]

A freehold in 'Edenesford' and elsewhere was held in 1352 by Roger son of Roger Trumwyn.[32] A messuage, carucate, and other lands held by Roger at his death in 1362 of the bishop[33] then passed to Katherine, sister and heir of Roger and widow of John Musard.[34] This land had passed by 1408, with the lands of the Cannock branch of the Trumwyns, to John Salwey, first husband of Iseult Washbourne, who was a relative of John Musard.[35] The estate descended with John Salwey's lands elsewhere in Cannock,[36] being held of the manor of Cannock by Thomas Leveson in 1594.[37]

Another plot of land in Hednesford, called 'le Plash', was held by Roger Trumwyn at his death in 1362 of his kinsman William Trumwyn of Cannock.[38] A field called Middle Plashes and lying to the south side of Splash Lane between Hednesford and Wimblebury was owned by the Revd. Richard Levett c. 1843.[39]

King Stephen gave land at 'Radmore' (now Red Moor) near the present hamlet of Cannock Wood to two hermits, who with others founded the Cistercian abbey there in 1141.[40] The monks had exchanged Radmore for land at Stoneleigh (Warws.) by June 1155,[41] and by Michaelmas Radmore was in the hands of the king,[42] who was there during 1155.[43] The 'king's houses at Cannock', for the upkeep of which 35s. 5d. a year was allowed between 1156 and 1161[44] and 6s. 8d. from 1162 to at least 1215 while the canons of Lanthony Secunda (Glos.) were custodians,[45] may possibly be identified with the 'king's houses and hays' at Radmore where building or repair work was carried out in about 1159.[46] The king continued to hold the houses at Cannock after the manor had been granted to the see of Lichfield in 1189[47] until at least 1215[48] but by 1230 they seem to have passed out of his hands.[49] They may be connected with the large rectangular moat, now dry, with an outer bank which still exists at Courtbanks Covert near the abbey site.[50]

'All the land of Redemore' was held by Henry de Audley in about 1228[51] and at some time after 1245 land in 'Rugemor' was held of Bishop Roger de Weseham by Henry's son James de Audley who undertook not to introduce any monks there without the bishop's permission.[52] James granted his land in 'Redemor', with buildings and woodland, to the bishop in about 1250,[53] and the estate seems then to have descended with the manor of Cannock until 1937 when it was sold with the abbey site by the 6th Marquess of Anglesey (d. 1947) to Mr. Daniel Clewley.[54]

A plot of waste in Cannock Chase called 'Le Newehaye' was leased, with two other parcels of waste, in 1348 by the bishop to Sir Richard de Stafford and his wife Isabel, with the confirmation of the dean and chapter.[55] By 1355, when the bishop confirmed the lease, the hay was surrounded by a double ditch and hedge.[56] As the 'pasture called Newhay' it was later leased to John Stanley who was dead by 1528 when his daughter Elizabeth, with her husband John Hercy, and Walter Moile or Moyle, husband of the other daughter Isabel, reconveyed their respective moieties to Bishop Geoffrey Blythe.[57] A lease for 21 years of all coal mines 'taken or found but not yet worked' in 'Newheye' and 'Redmore', near Beaudesert Park, and formerly part of Cannock Forest, was given by the queen in 1589 to Gilbert Wakering, with licence to dig and make pits.[58]

A house at Chestall (or Cheshall) to the east of Castle Ring seems to have been held by Simon de Rugeley of Hawkesyard (in Armitage parish, Offlow hundred) in 1333 and by James de Rugeley in 1370.[59] A descendant, Francis Rugeley, son and heir of either Humphrey or Antony Rugeley of Chestall, sold the house to Richard Hussey of Albrighton Hussey (Salop.) in 1562.[60] Hussey sold it to a Barlow of Derbyshire and he to a Lawrence Wright, who probably held it in about 1600 when Sir Edward Littleton of Pillaton (in Penkridge parish) also had a house there.[61] Chestall was mentioned in 1595 as one of the bounds of the manor of Cannock,[62] and Chestall Hall in Cannock Wood occurs c. 1640.[63] By the end of the 18th century the farmhouse called Chestall was owned by the Earl of Uxbridge (d. 1812)[64] and between at least 1834 and 1892 was occupied by members of the Darling family, land (and later mineral) agents to the Marquess of Anglesey.[65] John

[30] E 134/Hil. 3 and 4 Anne, no. 18.
[31] Dugd. Mon. v. 447.
[32] S.H.C. xii (1), 109.
[33] Cal. Inq. p.m. xi, no. 443*.   [34] Ibid.
[35] S.H.C. xvi. 64, 66–67; V.C.H. Worcs. iii. 471; S.H.C. N.S. ii, genealogical table facing p. 46; see p. 55.
[36] C 138/48; V.C.H. Worcs. iv. 342; Cal. Close 1419–22, 95–96; Cal. Fine R. 1422–30, 206; C 142/28, no. 12; C 142/46, no. 31; L. & P. Hen. VIII, xvi, g. 947 (39); S.H.C. xiii. 230; ibid. 1938, 88–93; ibid. xiii. 299–300; ibid. xiv (1), 204, 207; ibid. xvi. 103–4.
[37] C 142/242, no. 65.
[38] Cal. Inq. p.m. xi, no. 443*.
[39] Tithe Maps and Appt., Cannock (copy in W.S.L.).
[40] V.C.H. Warws. ii. 78–79; Dugd. Mon. v. 447.
[41] Dugd. Mon. v. 447.
[42] S.H.C. i. 17.
[43] R. W. Eyton, Itin. of Henry II, 6; Dugd. Mon. iv. 111, no. 3.
[44] S.H.C. i. 20, 23, 24, 27, 29, 32.
[45] Ibid. 35; ibid. ii (1), 166.
[46] Ibid. i. 27. £8 was spent on work on the king's fishpond in Cannock in 1163: ibid. 37.
[47] Ibid. ii (1), 1.
[48] Ibid. 166.
[49] Pipe R. 1230 (P.R.S. N.S. iv), 232.

[50] V.C.H. Staffs. i. 359.
[51] S.H.C. xii (1), 274.
[52] Ibid. 1924, no. 316.
[53] Ibid. no. 320.
[54] Ex inf. Messrs. Strutt and Parker, Lofts and Warner, Berkeley Sq., London, agents to Lord Anglesey.
[55] S.H.C. 1939, 75–76 (bounds given).
[56] Ibid. 76–77.
[57] Ibid. 77–78; ibid. xi. 268.
[58] Ibid. 1939, 112. There was mining near New Hayes on the site of the present Cannock Wood Colliery in 1775 and 1820: Yates, Map of Staffs. (1799), based on a survey made between 1769 and 1775; Greenwood, Map of Staffs. (1820).
[59] Erdeswick, Staffs. ed. Harwood (1844), 241; Shaw, Staffs. i. 222. Both place it in Longdon parish, Offlow hundred.
[60] Erdeswick, 241; Topographer and Genealogist, i. 489 490.
[61] Erdeswick, 241.
[62] Hackwood, Chronicles of Cannock Chase, 76.
[63] W.S.L. 64/42, f. 12a.
[64] Shaw, Staffs. i. 222.
[65] White, Dir. Staffs. (1834; 1851); P.O. Dir. Staffs. (1854, and later edns. to 1876); Kelly's Dir. Staffs. (1880; 1884; 1892).

Reid Walker was the tenant in 1896 and 1900[66] and Arthur Chetwynd in 1912 and 1916.[67] In 1938 it was sold by the 6th Marquess to Charles Wootten,[68] whose widow had put it up for sale by 1956.[69] The house, which has an 18th-century farmhouse as its core, was much enlarged in the middle of the 19th century and is now a red-brick mansion with stone dressings in the Tudor style. There are extensive gardens, stabling, and outbuildings.

The rectory of Cannock belonged to a prebend in Penkridge collegiate church by the late 12th century.[70] In 1189, however, the king granted the *ecclesia* of Cannock to the Bishop of Coventry and Lichfield[71] who by 1192 had given it to the canons of Lichfield, subject to an annual payment of 4s. to the canons of Penkridge.[72] The bishop subsequently allowed the Penkridge prebendary or his lessee to hold the rectorial estate of the canons at a rent of 4s.[73] In 1207 the Dean of Penkridge, after some dispute, conceded the right of appointing the chaplain to the canons of Lichfield who in turn granted to Penkridge the mortuaries of Cannock and an annual payment of one mark.[74]

Despite the speedy renewal of the dispute,[75] the rectory seems to have remained with Lichfield[76] until *c.* 1274 when the church of Penkridge had re-established its claim and the Dean and Chapter of Lichfield complained to the Pope, demanding half the mortuaries.[77] In 1290 the king confirmed the grant of 1189.[78] In 1313, however, the Crown took the opportunity of a vacancy in the deanery of Penkridge to present a royal clerk to what was then called the prebend of Cannock in Penkridge church.[79] The Dean and Chapter of Lichfield withheld the mark due each year to the canons of Penkridge[80] and apparently ejected the royal nominee from 'some of his prebendal possessions' until the sheriff intervened on the king's orders and prevented the dean and chapter from collecting tithes in Cannock.[81] The king, however, in 1315 allowed the dean and chapter to have the tithes until their complaint should be heard in the king's court.[82] The canons of Penkridge continued to exercise their right to burials and mortuaries until the Dean and Chapter of Lichfield had a graveyard at Cannock secretly consecrated by the Bishop of St. Asaph in 1330 and started conducting burials there and taking the mortuaries.[83] Three canons of Penkridge challenged their action, and the dean and chapter had them imprisoned in

Stafford gaol.[84] When the king once more appointed a royal clerk to the prebend and chapel of Cannock in 1337 during a vacancy in the deanery of Penkridge,[85] the Dean and Chapter of Lichfield sued in Chancery for a revocation of the grant[86] and meanwhile made their own appointment to the chapel.[87] In 1345 the king confirmed the grant of 1189 to the bishop and the bishop's grant to the canons of Lichfield.[88] Despite these renewed disputes the Dean and Chapter of Lichfield seem to have enjoyed uninterrupted possession of the tithes of Cannock from at least 1323[89] and to have retained the rectory without further dispute after 1345.[90]

The rectory was leased out by the Penkridge prebendary in the late 12th century for a rent of 4s.[91] and by the canons of Lichfield from at least 1323.[92] By 1564 the lease was held by John Coleman,[93] who in 1588 was occupying a house in Cannock called The Priest's Chamber.[94] In 1605 the rectory was demised to William Cumberford of Wednesbury (Offlow hundred) for the lives of John and Walter, sons of Walter Coleman of Cannock, and Thomas Hall of Sedgley (Seisdon hundred), at a rent of £18.[95] John Coleman seems to have lost the tithes by sequestration, as a papist and delinquent, by 1646,[96] and in 1650 two-thirds of the Coleman estate, which consisted mainly of the tithes, were granted to Richard Twigg of Stockton (Baswich parish) and Thomas Hide and Simon Brevett of Great Wyrley.[97] One-third of John Coleman's estate was restored to his widow Margaret in 1652.[98]

A tithe barn situated in a croft adjoining the church had disappeared by 1650.[99] The field was still called Tithe Barn Croft *c.* 1843.[1]

WOODS. In 1086 the king had woodland 6 leagues long by 4 wide attached to his manor of Cannock and woodland 3 leagues by 2 leagues attached to the adjoining manor of Rugeley.[2] Liberties in 'wood and plain' were given in 1189 by Richard I to the see of Lichfield along with these manors.[3] This woodland lay within the metes of the king's forest of Cannock.[4] The bishop's rights were limited until, with the confirmation of the manors to him in 1230, Bishop Alexander Stavensby (1224–38) claimed the 'covert of the forest of High Cannock', taking venison and excommunicating the king's steward or chief forester who sought to oppose him and at the same time preventing the two hereditary foresters in fee,

[66] *Kelly's Dir. Staffs.* (1896; 1900).
[67] Ibid. (1912; 1916).
[68] Ex inf. Messrs. Strutt and Parker, Lofts and Warner, Berkeley Sq., London, agents to Lord Anglesey (1956).
[69] Local inf.
[70] *S.H.C.* 1950–1, 50–51.
[71] Ibid. 51; ibid. 1924, nos. 15, 264, 753.
[72] Ibid. 1924, no. 754; and see no. 8.
[73] Ibid. 1950–1, 51.
[74] Ibid. 51–52; ibid. 1924, no. 291.
[75] Ibid. 1924, no. 291.
[76] Ibid., nos. 16, 23, 24, 140, 440; *Close R.* 1251–3, 151.
[77] Plot, *Natural Hist. Staffs.* 446, citing the lost portion of the *Liber Niger* of Dublin; *S.H.C.* 1924, nos. 289, 290.
[78] *S.H.C.* 1924, no. 17; *Plac. de Quo Warr.* (Rec. Com.), 719.
[79] *Cal. Pat.* 1313–17, 4, 10.
[80] *Cal. Inq. Misc.* ii, no. 1405.
[81] *S.H.C.* 1924, nos. 8, 9.
[82] Ibid., nos. 8, 10–14.
[83] *Cal. Inq. Misc.* ii, no. 1405.
[84] *Rot. Parl.* ii. 77.
[85] *Cal. Pat.* 1334–8, 144.
[86] *Cal. Close*, 1343–6, 577.

[87] Bodl. MS. Ashmole 794, i, f. 38b.
[88] *Cal. Close*, 1343–6, 577–8; *Cal. Chart. R.* 1341–1417, 38–39.
[89] Bodl. MS. Ashmole 794, i, ff. 5b, 11a, 24a, 26a, 52b, 59a, 109b, 122a.
[90] *Cal. Pat.* 1422–9, 357–8; W.S.L., Paget Papers (Gardner Coll.), 51 (4); *Valor Eccl.* (Rec. Com.), iii. 132; Lichfield D. and C. MS. Bk. liv; White, *Dir. Staffs.* (1851).
[91] *S.H.C.* 1950–1, 51.
[92] Bodl. MS. Ashmole 794, i, ff. 5b, 59a; *S.H.C.* 1939, 78–79; ibid. vi (2), 12.
[93] *S.H.C.* n.s. ix. 233–4.
[94] Ibid. 1915, 50.
[95] Lich. D. and C. MS. Bk. liv.
[96] *S.H.C.* 1915, 50; *Cal. Cttee. for Compounding*, 89.
[97] W.S.L., S. MS. 339 (transcript of Royalist Composition Papers), vi, pp. 267–8.
[98] *Cal. Cttee. for Compounding*, 2939.
[99] Lich. D. and C. MS. Bk. liv.
[1] Tithe Maps and Appt., Cannock (copy in W.S.L.).
[2] *V.C.H. Staffs.* iv. 40, no. 26.
[3] *S.H.C.* 1924, no. 15.
[4] Ibid. v (1), 166, where the bounds of the royal forest are given.

William Trumwyn, who held a virgate in Cannock, and Richard de Putes, who held a virgate in Rugeley by serjeanty, from presenting attachments of vert and venison in the swanimote of Cannock before the royal steward.[5] The king subsequently regained control of at least Trumwyn's bailiwick, but by 1286 it was evidently in the bishop's hands again.[6] The bishop had a park at Cannock by 1274,[7] and in 1280 2s. 3d. was paid to an 'oterhunter' and 11s. 6d. as the expenses of the hunters (*venatores*).[8] During proceedings following the forest eyre of 1286, Bishop Roger de Meuland (1258–95) claimed the same rights as his predecessors, namely to hold the woods free from all interference from the king's foresters, verderers, or other ministers and to hunt and take there at will all wild beasts which came from the king's forest.[9] In 1290, after being surrendered to the king, these same woods were restored to the bishop to be held in free alms as his free chase for ever, with permission to enclose and impark them so long as there were no deer leaps nor stretched nets to take deer outside the parks which might be made there.[10] These woods, although within the metes of the royal forest of Cannock, were to be quit of pleas of the forest, waste, assart, and regard, so that no justice of the forest should intermeddle, and any free tenants of the bishop there should have their rights in woods, lands, and holdings with common of pasture.[11] The metes and bounds of this free chase of Cannock, covering Cannock and Rugeley manors, were then set out.[12]

The chase, comprising the two bailiwicks of Trumwyn and of Puys (or Rugeley), descended with the manors of Cannock and Rugeley, passing in 1546 to Sir William Paget[13] and in 1583, after the flight of Thomas Lord Paget, to the queen.[14] The wood and timber in the manors of Cannock and Rugeley were valued at £20,000 in 1588,[15] and in the next year the queen leased the timber in Cannock 'Forest', apart from the hollies and 3,000 marked trees, to Fulke Greville for 21 years.[16] It was stated in 1595 that those appointed to mark the trees had not marked the full number while those marked were mostly inferior and that Greville, unlike Lord Paget, was failing to make coppices and leave standels for the preservation of the woodland.[17] By 1595 78 marked trees within the bailiwick of Trumwyn had been delivered by royal warrant and three without warrant, while 33 marked trees had been taken by unauthorized persons and others by Gilbert Wakering, the royal woodward there, for the repair of Beaudesert House (in Longdon, Offlow hundred),

likewise without warrant.[18] In addition 47 unmarked trees had been taken without warrant.[19] There were similar losses in the Rugeley bailiwick.[20] William Paget, later 5th baron (d. 1628), regained his father's estates in 1597[21] and subsequently confirmed Greville's lease.[22] The disafforestation of the area was lamented by Drayton in *Polyolbion* (1613 and 1622) and by Masters in his *Iter Boreale* (1675).[23] The 6th Marquess of Anglesey, with other landowners, leased land to the Forestry Commission after 1920 for the new State Forest of Cannock Chase,[24] which includes Shoal Hill and other land at Huntington and the area to the north and west of Cannock Wood. The area of woodland and heathland now known as Cannock Chase lies in the parishes of Cannock, Rugeley, Colwich (Pirehill hundred), and Baswich.

With the creation of the bishop's chase of Cannock in 1290, the former royal forest officials were replaced by those of the bishop. The chief wardenship of his free chase of Cannock as well as of the woods belonging to his barony of Haywood and Lichfield and of the parks already made or planned therein was given by Roger de Meuland (1285–95) to Roger de Aston of Haywood and Bishton in Colwich parish (Pirehill hundred).[25] Except for temporary dispossession during vacancies of the see in 1386 and 1415 when the king appointed his own nominees,[26] this office descended in the Aston family[27] and included in 1496 'the mastership of the game and rule of the Cankewodde'.[28] In 1538, to end disputes, Sir Edward Aston agreed to surrender the keepership of the woods, hays, and parks together with the perquisites, including four trees a year for firewood and one tree for repairs to his houses in Tixall (Pirehill hundred) and Haywood, in return for confirmation in the office of the mastership of the game within the chases of Cannock and Haywood and the parks of Beaudesert and Haywood.[29] As master of the game he was allowed to take two bucks in summer and two does in winter from the chases of Cannock and Haywood and a third buck and doe in Beaudesert Park after giving due warning to the bishop's keepers.[30] The fee of this office was the right to some portion of each deer killed in the woods by persons other than the bishops or their surveyors, with 100 cart loads of firewood annually for burning only in his own dwelling-places in Haywood and Tixall.[31] Sir Edward retained this office when the bishop's manors passed to the Pagets, and described either as chief custody of the chase or mastership of the game it descended in his family, his grandson Sir Edward dying seised of

[5] Ibid.
[6] Ibid. 167.
[7] Lichfield D. and C. MSS. N. 10.
[8] Lichfield D. and C. MSS. N. 5.
[9] S.H.C. v (1), 168.
[10] Ibid.; *Cal. Pat.* 1281–92, 344, 397; *Cal. Chart. R.* 1257–1300, 347, 348–9.
[11] *Cal. Chart. R.* 1257–1300, 348–9.
[12] Ibid. 349. There were frequent complaints of trespass in the bishop's free chase and the cutting down of timber there: *Cal. Pat.* 1292–1301, 375 (1297); ibid. 1321–4, 249–50, 256 (1322); Lich. Dioc. Regy., Bp.'s Reg. iii, f. 19a (c. 1322); *Cal. Pat.* 1343–5, 297, 489, 592 (1344, 1345); ibid. 1358–61, 581 (1361); *S.H.C.* xvi. 77 (1411).
[13] *L. & P. Hen. VIII*, xxi (2), g. 76 (332).
[14] *Complete Peerage*, x. 282; B.M. Lansd. MS. 56, f. 96a.
[15] B.M. Lansd. MS. 56, ff. 94a, 96a.
[16] *S.H.C.* 1931, 249–51.
[17] Hackwood, *Chronicles of Cannock Chase*, 76–77.

[18] Ibid. 77.
[19] Ibid.
[20] See pp. 158–9.
[21] *Complete Peerage*, x. 283.
[22] *S.H.C.* 1931, 249–51.
[23] White, *Dir. Staffs.* (1851).
[24] Forestry Commission: *Britain's Forests: Cannock Chase* (1950), 12.
[25] *S.H.C.* 1914, 131–3; ibid. 1924, no. 757; ibid. 1939, 80–81.
[26] *Cal. Close* 1381–5, 639; *Cal. Pat.* 1385–9, 23; ibid. 1413–16, 321.
[27] *S.H.C.* v (2), 18.
[28] T. and A. Clifford, *Tixall* (Paris, 1817), 51–54; *S.H.C.* 1939, 77.
[29] W.S.L., Hand Morgan Coll. Aston Papers: Cannock Chase.
[30] Ibid.
[31] Ibid.

it in 1597.[32] Further disputes between the Pagets as overlords and the Astons as hereditary wardens or masters were ended by a compromise in 1712 when Walter Lord Aston agreed to waive all claim to the mastership of the game and accept instead four bucks a year, an arrangement still in force in 1815.[33]

Besides the hereditary chief warden and master of the game, there were two foresters of the chase, one for Cannock who by at least 1473 was described as the forester of Trumwyn,[34] and one for Rugeley, each making their presentments at the joint courts of the two manors by at least 1342.[35] There was also the rider or ranger (*equitator*) who was similarly presenting forest offences in the manor courts by at least 1342,[36] and from at least 1424 until at least 1542 he presented an annual account of his office with the other bailiffs, collectors of rents, and farmers of the lands of the bishops and their successors, the Pagets.[37] His account in 1424 included 38s. 2d. from perquisites of court and sale of woods, loppings, and bark, and 22s. 6d. from fines.[38] Among the riders were Richard de Hampton, the king's yeoman, appointed in 1359 during a vacancy of the see,[39] James Arblaster, whose appointment was confirmed during another vacancy in 1385,[40] and, in 1415, Roger Assent, the king's 'servant', who was also given a forestership to hold while the temporalities were in the king's hands.[41] By 1423 the rider was Richard Ruggeley[42] and by 1472 John Eggerton.[43] Ralph Longford occurs in 1535 as rider and bailiff of Cannock Chase,[44] and in 1542 William Hervy accounted as rider for £17 10s. 5d. from the sale of wood and bark.[45] The bishop, probably in 1542, gave the office of rider, in tail, to a Littleton,[46] probably Sir Edward Littleton, keeper of Teddesley Hay.[47]

AGRICULTURE. By 1273 there was no demesne in Cannock manor and all the land was held by tenants.[48] It was stated in 1595 that there was no site of a manor and no demesne except the mill and Mill Meadow.[49] The assised rents amounted in 1273 to £8 13s. 8d., with new rents of 16s. 5½d.[50] and in 1424 to £11 14s. 1¼d. with ¼d. new rent from a John Bounde for a small piece of land next his demesne on the Green added to his garden out of the lord's waste.[51] In 1560 the rents from free tenants amounted

to 21s. 5½d. and those from copyhold tenants to £14 8s. 5½d.[52] Forty-one persons in Cannock paid pannage dues of 7s. 2½d. in 1350 for 38 pigs and 73 'hogs' (*hogg*), while five persons in Hednesford paid 5½d. for one pig and nine hogs.[53]

The following open fields within the manor were mentioned at various times between c. 1300 and 1640: 'Callughull' ('Calfe Hylles') Field, Greystones Field, Half Field, Hawsley Field, Newland Field, Sladeland Field, Hatherton Sich, and Sich Field.[54]

It was stated in 1794 that the best land on Cannock Chase for sheep and crops, especially barley and turnips, lay on the west and north sides and around Hednesford, the soil being light as opposed to the gravelly undrained heathland to the south and east.[55] At this time a breed of greyfaced hornless sheep native to Cannock Chase was very prolific, 'the common being now in many places perfectly whitened with them'.[56] The parish of Cannock, described as 'extensive . . . with scattered small farms', had 1,933½ acres sown in 1801, 481 acres with wheat, 549 with barley, 491 with oats, 12 with peas, 20½ with potatoes, and 280 with turnips or rape.[57] By 1819 seven freeholders and copyholders from Cannock were pasturing 369 sheep on the chase; 38 from Leacroft and Hednesford were pasturing 1,782 sheep, 28 cows, 1 ass, and 6 horses; and 43 from Cannock Wood were pasturing 789 sheep, 13 cows, 3 asses, and 2 horses.[58] The Cannock Agricultural Association was formed in 1845, with the help of Lord Hatherton, for tenant farmers living within an eight-mile radius of Cannock.[59] The land was used in 1940 mainly for oats, wheat, turnips, mangolds, and pasture.[60]

William Coleman and other men of Cannock in 1544 forcibly threw open certain pastures and meadows in Cannock inclosed by Ralph Bostock and Thomas Alport who had acquired them from Richard Biddulph.[61] Thomas Lord Paget held a conyger within the manor before his forfeiture in 1587,[62] and in 1595 Thomas Wolseley, William Chetwynd, William Hough, and Thomas Littleton held various inclosures on Cannock Chase to the detriment of the queen and the tenants of the manors of Cannock and Rugeley.[63] Piecemeal inclosure of the common fields seems to have begun by this

[32] S.H.C. 1939, 77, 78, 80–81; C 142/222, no. 43; C 142/248, no. 16.
[33] Clifford, *Tixall*, 55.
[34] W.S.L., D. 1734 Cannock and Rugeley Ct. R. 1463–83, m. 164. The office was held by a John Osborne in 1595: Hackwood, *Chronicles of Cannock Chase*, 77.
[35] W.S.L., D. 1734, Cannock and Rugeley Ct. R. 1309–73, m. 4. [36] Ibid.
[37] W.S.L., D. 1734, Compotus Rolls of Bp. of Cov. and Lich. 1423–57, 1461–71, 1466–7, 1471–81, 1508–21, 1521–2, 1524–5, 1526–7, 1532–3; ibid. Draft Compotus of Rec. Gen. of Bp. of Cov. and Lich. 1541–2, f. 2a.
[38] Ibid. Compotus R. 1423–57, m. 6d.
[39] Cal. Pat. 1358–61, 213; Cal. Close, 1354–60, 588.
[40] Cal. Pat. 1381–5, 553.
[41] Ibid. 1413–16, 321.
[42] W.S.L., D. 1734, Compotus R. of Bp. of Cov. and Lich. 1423–57, m. 5d.
[43] W.S.L., S. MS. 335 (1), m. 13.
[44] Valor Eccl. (Rec. Com.), iii. 130.
[45] W.S.L., D. 1734, Draft Compotus of Rec. Gen. of Bp. of Cov. and Lich. 1541–2, f. 2a.
[46] Hist. MSS. Com. 5th Rep. (1), 297.
[47] See p. 183.
[48] Lichfield D. and C. MSS., N. 10.
[49] Hackwood, *Chronicles of Cannock Chase*, 76.
[50] Lichfield D. and C. MSS. N. 10.
[51] W.S.L., D. 1734, Compotus R. of Bp. of Cov. and Lich. 1423–57, m. 5d.
[52] Ibid. Compotus of lands of Lord Paget 1559–60, m. 8d.
[53] Ibid. Cannock and Rugeley Ct. R. 1309–73, m. 71
[54] Ibid. *passim*; S.H.C. 1924, no. 584; ibid. 1939, 79; W.S.L., D. 1734, Cannock and Rugeley Survey (undated but probably 16th cent.), where 6 of these are mentioned; W.S.L. 64/42, ff. 2b, 3a. About 1843 there was a Great Stone Stile Field to the south-west of the centre of Cannock, and the name Calven Hill (now Calving Hill) was then found to the north-east of the town centre: Tithe Maps and Appt., Cannock (copy in W.S.L.).
[55] W. Pitt, *General View of Agric. of Staffs.* (1794), 53–54, 72. The breed was nearly extinct by 1873, chiefly because of crossing with a Shropshire breed: W. Molyneux, 'Cannock Chase', *Staffs. Advertiser*, 11 Sept. 1873.
[56] Pitt, *Agric. Staffs.* 52.
[57] R. A. Pelham, '1801 Crop Returns' (S.H.C. 1950–1), 232, table opp. p. 242.
[58] Molyneux, 'Cannock Chase', *Staffs. Advertiser*, 11 Sept. 1873.
[59] *Staffs. Advertiser*, 11 Oct. 1856.
[60] *Kelly's Dir. Staffs.* (1940).
[61] S.H.C. n.s. x (1), 133–5; ibid. 1910, 53.
[62] Hackwood, *Chronicles of Cannock Chase*, 76.
[63] Ibid. 78.

time.[64] William Lord Paget as lord of Cannock and Rugeley, having come to an agreement with his tenants in 1605, made an inclosure within the parish of Cannock which was subject to renewal in the manorial court every nine years, but in 1651 his son and heir William complained of attempts to throw this inclosure open.[65] It was stated in 1682 that temporary inclosures, usually for five years, were made on Cannock Chase for the growing of corn by the inhabitants of Cannock, as by those of Rugeley, Penkridge, Baswich, Brocton, Haywood, Colwich, Longdon, and Norton, by agreement with the lord of the manor concerned.[66] Henry Lord Paget, Earl of Uxbridge, at some time after 1735 allowed the inclosing of some 30 acres of Cannock Chase so that the rents might be used towards defraying the cost of piping Cannock's water-supply from Leacroft.[67] Hednesford, Leacroft, and Rumer Hill were described in 1817 as 'enclosed hamlets of Cannock'.[68]

Some 3,000 acres of land on Cannock Chase within the parish of Cannock were inclosed in 1868 under an Act of 1861.[69]

MILLS. The lord's mill at Cannock was leased at a rent of 3s. 4d. in 1274,[70] and in 1281 the mill, still held by a tenant, was extensively repaired.[71] In 1424 William the miller paid 73s. 4d. for the farm of the water-mill and a 'mora' called 'Mulnemore'.[72] Timber for the mill and repairs to the mill pond in this year cost the lord 14s. 1d.[73] In 1449 the bishop granted a twenty-year lease of the mill, called 'Coyngere', to John Justice, millward, and after John's death, the mill was leased in 1463, along with fish ponds and the 'Mylnemore,' to John Parker and Hugh Collins for 21 years.[74] During the year ending Michaelmas 1473 14d. had been spent on repairs to the mechanism of the mill and the river bank by it.[75]

In 1641 the water corn-mills in or near Cannock, commonly called Cannock Mills and lately held by John Coleman, were leased by William Lord Paget, then lord of the manor, to Walter Chetwynd for 21 years at an annual rent of £22.[76] Lord Paget sold the lease of what may have been the same mills to John Byrch of Stafford and Robert Sankey of Cannock in 1650,[77] but by 1659 the mills were held by Edward Rowley of Leacroft.[78] In 1697 Cannock Mill, situated on the brook leading from Ridding Bridge, was held by Rowley's grandson Henry Barton who in that year conveyed his rights in it to Edmund

Wilson of Cannock.[79] Wilson died in 1709, and his executors renewed the lease in 1710 to Thomas Barton, miller, for another thirteen years.[80] The present-day Cannock Mill also stands on the Ridings Brook, on the north side of Mill Street with the mill pool lying to the north.[81] It is a red-brick building retaining its water-wheel and was still operating on a small scale c. 1954.[82] The mill-house is a roughcast building of three stories dating from c. 1800. North-east of the mill pool there was formerly land called Windmill Bank.[83]

About 1250 James de Audeley granted the Bishop of Coventry and Lichfield a rent of 10s. a year from a mill at 'Canocbury'.[84] A water-mill in Cannock was held of the bishop by William Trumwyn at his death in 1317 or 1318[85] and descended with his lands in Cannock until at least 1639 when Thomas Leveson made a settlement of two water-mills and lands in Cannock and Wednesfield.[86] In 1448 the bishop sued John Justice, millward, for taking the corn of the bishop's men for grinding at this mill instead of at the lord's mill.[87]

The Walk Mill, situated a little to the south of Watling Street on the road to Cheslyn Hay south-west of the modern Bridgtown, was in existence in 1775.[88] In about 1843 it was owned by Jonathan Stokes, M.D.,[89] and it was advertised for auction in the following year as a water corn-mill.[90] There was a miller here in 1880.[91]

A Robert Wedge was holding Whitnall Mills in Cannock of Sir Edward Littleton of Pillaton (in Penkridge) c. 1643,[92] and in 1709 Robert Wedge, Mary his wife, and Robert their son made a settlement of grain mills and lands in Cannock and Saredon (in Shareshill).[93] What was called Wedges Mill was held of Sir Edward Littleton in 1754 by a John Olerenshaw,[94] but in 1768 and 1769[95] William Webb was paying the lord of Cannock 1s. 6d. rent for Wedges Mill.[96] In 1817 the mill was described as a water-mill 'situated on the Hedgeford river' and forming part of William Gilpin's edge-tool factory at Churchbridge about a mile to the east in the township of Great Wyrley.[97] It was owned by George Gilpin c. 1843.[98]

MARKETS AND FAIRS. In 1259 Henry III granted Bishop Roger de Weseham, his kinsman, the right to hold in his manor of Cannock a market every Tuesday and an annual fair on the vigil, feast,

[64] W.S.L., D. 1734, Cannock and Rugeley Survey (undated but probably 16th cent.)
[65] C 3/456, no. 3.
[66] E 178/Mich. 34 Chas. II, no. 10.
[67] White, Dir. Staffs. (1834). It is not clear whether the first Earl (d. 1743) or the second (d. 1769) is meant.
[68] Pitt, Staffs. 262.
[69] S.H.C. 1941, 19; S.R.O., Q/RDc 103.
[70] Lichfield D. and C. MSS. N. 10.
[71] Lichfield D. and C. MSS. N. 5.
[72] W.S.L., D. 1734, Compotus R. of Bp. of Cov. and Lich. 1423–57, m. 5d.
[73] Ibid.
[74] W.S.L., S. MS. 335 (1), m. 11d.
[75] W.S.L., S. MS. 335 (1), m. 12.
[76] S.R.O., D. 260/M/box II, bdle. 1. A John Coleman held a blademill in Cannock at his death in 1593 and was succeeded by his son William: C 142/245, no. 68.
[77] S.R.O., D. 260/M/box II, bdle. 1; C.P. 25(2)/596, 1650 Mich.
[78] S.R.O., D. 260/M/box II, bdle. 1.
[79] Ibid.
[80] Ibid.
[81] There was a mill on this site in 1775: Yates, Map of

Staffs. (1799), based on a survey 1769–75. A mill on the same site was described c. 1843 as situated in Leacroft: Tithe Maps and Appt., Cannock (copy in W.S.L.).
[82] Local inf.
[83] Tithe Maps and Appt., Cannock (copy in W.S.L.).
[84] S.H.C. 1924, no. 230.
[85] Cal. Inq. p.m. vi, p. 70.
[86] C.P. 25(2)/486, 15 Chas. I Mich.
[87] S.H.C. n.s. iii. 183.
[88] Yates, Map of Staffs. (1799).
[89] Tithe Maps and Appt. Cannock (copy in W.S.L.).
[90] W.S.L., Newspaper Cuttings, box 2, 8 Aug. 1844, unknown provenance.
[91] Kelly's Dir. Staffs. (1880).
[92] S.R.O., D. 260/M/box 25, bdle. k.
[93] C.P. 25(2)/966, 8 Anne Trin.
[94] S.R.O., D. 260/M/E.353a.
[95] W.S.L., Paget Papers (Gardner Coll.) 35 (7, 9).
[96] In 1762 Thomas Wolrich and in 1764 William Webb paid the lord of Cannock 1s. 6d. rent for an unnamed mill: ibid. 35 (1).
[97] Pitt, Staffs. i. 449; see p. 78.
[98] Tithe Maps and Appt., Cannock (copy in W.S.L.).

and morrow of St. Michael in Monte Tumba (15, 16, 17 October).[99] The right was upheld in 1293[1] and confirmed between 1387 and 1390.[2] The Tuesday market had been discontinued by 1747, but fairs were then held on 20 April, 20 August, and the second Monday after Michaelmas.[3] By 1834 cattle fairs were held on 8 May, 24 August, and 18 October, with a feast or wake on the Sunday following the last of these.[4] By 1868 markets were being held on Saturday evenings,[5] and a market-hall was built in Cannock in 1869.[6] By 1924 the fairs were no longer held, but markets were then held on Tuesday and Saturday.[7] By 1956 an additional market was held on Friday.[8]

A Saturday evening market was held at Hednesford from 1872 when the market-hall was built.[9] In 1956 the Hednesford market was open on Tuesdays and Saturdays.[10]

INDUSTRIES. There was coal mining within the manor by 1298.[11] In 1589 the queen leased for 21 years all mines and veins 'of coal "called pitt cole, stone cole, and sea cole" ' in New Hay and Red Moor near Beaudesert Park, with permission to dig pits and ditches called 'le sowghes' and to cut the necessary timber, to Gilbert Wakering,[12] who in 1595 held two coal-mines on the Chase, one of black coal and one of cannel coal.[13] Three colliers of Cannock Wood occur in 1601[14] and a collier of Hednesford in 1603,[15] and in 1688 Lord Paget granted a lease of his mines at Cannock Wood, 'Newhay', and elsewhere in the vicinity.[16] There were pits a little to the north-west of New Hayes on the site of the present Cannock Wood Colliery in 1775,[17] and a colliery here called Park Colliery was noted in 1820.[18] In 1817 William Gilpin was raising coal at the Walk Mill for use in his edge-tool factory at Churchbridge and for sale.[19] The colliery at Rumer Hill, near Leacroft, belonging to Edward John Littleton, later Lord Hatherton, was in operation in 1832,[20] but by 1858 these pits, over 70 yds. deep, had been closed.[21] Lord Hatherton also owned the Long House Colliery, of which Joseph Palmer, coalmaster, held the lease between 1848 and 1854.[22]

The Cannock Chase Colliery Company, launched in 1850 by the Marquess of Anglesey, had opened the Uxbridge Pit at Hednesford by 1852.[23] Between 1860 and 1867 this company opened pits at Chase Terrace (in Chasetown parish, Offlow hundred), Rawnsley, and Heath Hayes which were still in use in 1954.[24] It was among the first companies to build, about 1866, its own railway linking its collieries to the main line, and, in about 1886, to generate its own electricity.[25] In 1865 and 1874 the Cannock & Rugeley Collieries Company sank two shafts at the Cannock Wood Colliery.[26] In 1869 the West Cannock Collieries Company opened three pits in Hednesford.[27] During the trade boom which followed the Franco-Prussian War of 1871 there were several new undertakings in the Cannock Chase region, most of which failed.[28] Only one within Cannock itself survived in its original form, the Cannock and Leacroft Colliery[29] begun between 1874 and 1877.[30] The East Cannock Colliery at Hednesford, on which some £150,000 was spent, was sold for £20,000 to a new company which survived until nationalization in 1947.[31] The Wimblebury Pit was opened in 1872,[32] but it was nearly exhausted by 1896 when the Cannock & Rugeley Collieries Company took it over and started coal-drawing there instead of at their Valley Pit in Hednesford, opened in 1874.[33] The Mid-Cannock Colliery, started in 1873, was abandoned in 1882.[34] The Cannock & Huntington Colliery Company, which began to make sinkings at Huntington in 1877, met with serious water difficulties and, having abandoned the shafts, was dissolved in 1881.[35] During the 'Great Federation Lock-Out' of 1893 a Hednesford miner, Thomas Thomas, wrote ballads designed to win public sympathy for the strikers.[36]

The first new venture after the slump was the opening in 1894 of the Coppice, or Fair Lady, Colliery at Heath Hayes by the Coppice Colliery Company.[37] Lord Hatherton recovered one of the shafts at Huntington in 1897 and sank another, and coal-drawing started in 1904.[38] In 1954 the colliery was one of the largest in the Cannock Chase Coalfield.[39] The abandoned Mid-Cannock Colliery was taken over by Messrs. William Harrison in 1913 and reopened in the following year.[40] The West Cannock

[99] S.H.C. 1924, no. 219.
[1] Plac. de Quo Warr. (Rec. Com.), 710–11.
[2] Rot. Chart. (Rec. Com.), 192.
[3] Smith, New Map of Staffs. (1747).
[4] White, Dir. Staffs. (1834).
[5] P.O. Dir. Staffs. (1868).
[6] Ibid. (1872).
[7] Ibid. (1924).
[8] Ex inf. the Clerk, Cannock U.D. Council.
[9] P.O. Dir. Staffs. (1872); Kelly's Dir. Staffs. (1940).
[10] Ex inf. the Clerk, Cannock U.D. Council (1956).
[11] W.S.L., D. 1734, Jeayes 2268, extent of lands of Bpric. of Cov., Lich., and Chester, 26 Edw. I.
[12] S.H.C. 1939, 112.
[13] Hackwood, Chronicles of Cannock Chase, 76.
[14] S.H.C. 1935, 365.
[15] Ibid. 1940, 36.
[16] C 5/624, no. 103. Papers concerning the Pagets' coal-mines in Cannock Wood and Beaudesert, 1697–1702 and during the 18th cent., are preserved in W.S.L., D. 1734.
[17] Yates, Map of Staffs. (1799), based on a survey made between 1769 and 1775; Shaw, Staffs. i, Gen. Hist. 97. Shaw also mentions the 'fruitful coal-mines' of Cannock Chase: Staffs. i, Gen. Hist. 90.
[18] Greenwood, Map of Staffs. (1820).
[19] Pitt, Staffs. 263.
[20] S.R.O., D. 260/M/box B, bdle. i.
[21] C. M. Peel, 'Presidential Address' (Trans. Inst. Mining Engineers, cx), 330.
[22] S.R.O., D. 260/M/box G, bdle. d; White, Dir. Staffs. (1851). The Long House estate was to the west of Bridgtown, and in 1873 the colliery was leased to the Mid-Cannock Colliery Co.: S.R.O., D. 260/M/box 33, bdle. b.
[23] Trans. Inst. Mining Engineers, cx. 330, 332; M. J. Wise, 'The Cannock Chase Region', Birmingham in its Regional Setting, 279.
[24] Ex inf. the National Coal Board, Cannock.
[25] Trans. Inst. Mining Engineers, cx. 333. It provided the parish church with electric light: ibid.
[26] Ex inf. N.C.B., Cannock.
[27] Ibid.
[28] Trans. Inst. Mining Engineers, cx. 331.
[29] Ibid.
[30] Ex inf. N.C.B., Cannock.
[31] Trans. Inst. Mining Engineers, cx. 331.
[32] Ex inf. N.C.B., Cannock.
[33] Ibid.; Trans. Inst. Mining Engineers, cx. 331–2.
[34] Ex inf. N.C.B., Cannock; Trans. Inst. Mining Engineers, cx. 331; S.R.O., D. 260/M/E. 354, plan of the colliery between 1877 and 1881.
[35] Trans. Inst. Mining Engineers, cx. 331; Birmingham in its Regional Setting, 279.
[36] Hackwood, Chronicles of Cannock Chase, 133.
[37] Trans. Inst. Mining Engineers, cx. 331.
[38] Ibid.; Birmingham in its Regional Setting, 283; S.R.O., D. 260/M/box 35, bdle. n; ibid., box 36, bdle. d.
[39] Ex inf. N.C.B., Cannock.
[40] Trans. Inst. Mining Engineers, cx. 331.

Air view of Hednesford from the south-east, 1948. Hill Top is in the left foreground, the Roman Catholic church in the right foreground. At the centre of the photograph is the railway station, near the site of Hednesford Pool. Housing estates at Green Heath are in the background

Air view of Castle Ring from the north, 1948

CANNOCK CHASE: The first Marquess of Anglesey on his shooting pony, *c.* 1836

Hednesford Training Ground: Mr. T. W. Giffard's racehorse 'Samson', *c.* 1840

Collieries Company opened their No. 5 Pit at Hednesford in 1914.[41] Open-cast mining was begun in 1956 at a site on the north side of Watling Street to the east of Churchbridge and was being extended northwards from there in 1957.[42] The National Coal Board's office in Cannock covers the Cannock Chase area of the West Midlands Division. The County Mining College in Cannock was opened in 1928 and enlarged in 1935.[43]

The presence of slag and refuse on the western slopes of the Castle Ring Hill may indicate the site of a bloomery, while the oaks growing out of these deposits show its long disuse.[44] There was a forge at Hednesford by 1473 when William Colmore was paying the lord of Cannock 2d. new rent for its site, a parcel of waste 20 ft. square.[45] 'Blome smithes' at Risom Bridge on Cannock Chase near Beaudesert Park (in Longdon parish, Offlow hundred) were leased to William Fletcher in 1542 and still held by him in 1549.[46] Joyce Ashebye was mining ironstone in Cannock about 1553 at a place called 'Woddy Hey', selling nine loads for 33s. 4d.[47] Lord Paget received £20 as the farm of 'all le blumsmythes' in Cannock in 1560 and was working a furnace on the Chase by 1563.[48] In the year ending 24 December 1584 the Paget ironworks on Cannock Chase and in Teddesley Hay produced 164 tons 1 cwt. of iron.[49] Between at least 1692 and 1710 a forge in Cannock under the control of a partnership known as 'The Staffordshire Works' was specializing in chafery, and its output of bar iron reached 109 tons in the year ending Michaelmas 1709.[50] A plot of 'boggy ground' at the head of Green Brook Valley was leased in 1734 by the lord of Cannock for the making of two pools to John Biddulph, who before 1761 was tenant of two pools in Rugeley.[51] A forge in Cannock was still active in 1750 when the output of iron was 180 tons.[52] By 1953 there were iron-foundries in Cannock, Hednesford, and Rawnsley.[53]

Other industries in Cannock, many of which were started after 1939, include light engineering, enamelling, and the manufacture of precision instruments, brushes, electrical appliances, food preparations, and jewellery.[54] There are also clothing mills and saw-mills in the town.[55] By 1868 bricks and tiles were being manufactured at a factory on the Watling Street,[56] and by 1953 some 100,000 tiles a day were produced at the Longhouse Works on Watling Street, owned by Messrs. Henry Hawkins Ltd.[57]

William Gilpin seems to have opened an edge-tool factory at Wedges Mill in 1790, but by 1817 most of the work was done at the factory opened in 1806 at Churchbridge in Great Wyrley.[58] Industrial development was taking place to the south-west of Cannock town by 1956.

CHURCHES. There was a chapel at Cannock by the 12th century.[59] It was probably founded as a dependency of Penkridge collegiate church,[60] and by the later 12th century it was attached to a prebend in that church.[61] The right of appointing a chaplain was disputed like the rectory between the Dean and Chapter of Penkridge and the Dean and Chapter of Lichfield and was finally secured by Lichfield in 1345.[62] No vicarage was ever ordained, the benefice remaining a perpetual curacy until 1868 when it became a titular vicarage.[63] The advowson was still held by the Dean and Chapter of Lichfield in 1956.[64]

It is not known when the chapel acquired the status of a parish church. In 1293 the Bishop of Coventry and Lichfield insisted that it was a church and not a chapel,[65] and from 1330 it had its own burial ground.[66] The church was exempted from archidiaconal jurisdiction in 1255 and remained a peculiar of the dean and chapter.[67]

In 1604 the curate of Cannock was receiving a salary of £8.[68] The Committee for Plundered Ministers in 1646 granted the curate, probably Richard Bourne, an augmentation of £50 a year out of the impropriate tithe, and in 1654 Richard Bourne, described as 'former curate', was established in Cannock by the commissioners to preach the gospel at a salary of £100, which by c. 1659 had been increased by £80.[69] The incumbent in 1885 still received £1 from a rent-charge given by Henry Stone in 1686.[70] By will proved 1891 James Holford left £100, the proceeds to be divided equally between the vicar and curate of the parish church. The legacy became payable in 1905. In 1929 the income was £8.[71]

The 'service of St. Mary' at Cannock was in existence by 1421 when it was granted the contingent remainder of a messuage in Hednesford called 'Mokyntonplace', with land adjoining.[72] The Chantry of Our Lady in Cannock church was endowed by 1548 with lands, tithes, ten cows, and £1 6s. 8d. for the support of a priest who sang mass daily at the Lady Altar.[73] The chantry priest,

[41] Ex inf. N.C.B., Cannock.
[42] Local inf. (1957); see plate facing p. 76.
[43] Kelly's Dir. Staffs. (1940).
[44] W. Molyneux, 'Cannock Chase', Staffs. Advertiser, 11 Sept. 1873.
[45] W.S.L., S. MS. 335 (1), m. 11d.
[46] W.S.L., D. 1734, Compotus of lands of William Paget, 1–3 Edw. VI, m. 14d.
[47] C 1/1326, no. 40.
[48] W.S.L., D. 1734, Compotus of the lands of Lord Paget 1559–60, m. 8d.; H. R. Schubert, British Iron and Steel Industry, 179.
[49] E 122/546/16, Ironworks, 1583–5, Bk. 1. There are accounts from 1568 in W.S.L., D. 1734.
[50] B. L. C. Johnson, 'The Foley Partnership' (Ec. H.R., Ser. 2, iv), 325, 328, 336, 339.
[51] W.S.L., Paget Papers (Gardner Coll.), 35 (1). There is still a Biddulph's Pool to the south-east of Heath Hayes.
[52] E. Wyndham Hulme, 'Statistical History of the British Iron Trade 1717–50' (Newcomen Soc. 1928), 8 (from copy in W.S.L.).
[53] Cannock and Hednesford: Official Guide (1953), 25, 27, and advertisements.
[54] Ibid. 24, 27, 29, and advertisements.
[55] Ibid. 31, and advertisements.
[56] P.O. Dir. Staffs. (1868).
[57] Cannock and Hednesford: Official Guide (1953), 29.
[58] Cannock Advertiser Dir. (1938); see p. 78.
[59] S.H.C. 1950–1, 50–51.
[60] Since no vicarage was ever ordained, it is unlikely to have been an appropriated church.
[61] S.H.C. 1950–1, 50–51.
[62] See p. 58.
[63] S.H.C. 1915, 49; Lich. Dioc. Ch. Cal. (1869).
[64] Lich. Dioc. Dir. (1955–6).
[65] Plac. de Quo. Warr. (Rec. Com.), 719.
[66] Cal. Inq. Misc. ii, no. 1405.
[67] S.H.C. 1924, nos. 23, 24; ibid. 1915, 48; ibid. vi (2), 58.
[68] Ibid. 1915, 49–50.
[69] Ibid.
[70] Charity Com. files; 9th Rep. Com. Char. H.C. 258, pp. 587–8 (1823), ix.
[71] Charity Com. files.
[72] W.S.L., D. 1790/A/3/90.
[73] S.H.C. 1915, 49.

Laurence Peryn, who had been keeping a grammar school for 30 years, was allowed to continue as schoolmaster after the dissolution of the chantry at a salary of £4 14s. 5½d. a year.[74] In 1549 the chantry lands, lying in Cannock, Huntington, and Leacroft, with rents of 4s. 2d. a year in Cannock, Huntington, and Great Wyrley, were sold to John Cupper and Richard Trevour,[75] but by 1552 the lands and tithes, valued at £5, had passed to Lord Paget[76] and seem to have descended with the manor of Cannock until at least 1788.[77]

By 1548 there was a chapel dedicated to St. Margaret in the parish, possibly at Huntington.[78] It was endowed with 4d. rent, and only one mass was said there each year.[79] It possessed one little bell.[80] By 1563 the chapel was no longer in existence.[81]

Missions were established at Hednesford c. 1864,[82] Wimblebury by 1871,[83] Bridgtown and Green Heath by 1872,[84] Chadsmoor in 1874,[85] Five Ways (Heath Hayes) by 1874 (St. Chad's, closed c. 1892)[86] with a second mission here by 1885,[87] West Hill, Hednesford, by 1880 (until c. 1896),[88] Hazel Slade by 1880,[89] Brindley Heath by 1889 (until c. 1954),[90] Rawnsley Cottage by 1889,[91] Pye Green by 1894,[92] West Chadsmoor by 1947,[93] Moss Wood by 1950,[94] and in Fosters Avenue, Broadway (between Chadsmoor and Pye Green) by 1950.[95] The schoolroom at the workhouse was used for public services between c. 1880 and c. 1946.[96] The new ecclesiastical parish of St. Peter's, Hednesford, was established in 1870, the vicarage being in the gift of the Bishop of Lichfield,[97] and in 1956 included Wimblebury, Green Heath, Rawnsley, and Hazel Slade.[98]

On condition of attending an annual service in Cannock church on St. Barnabas' Day (11 June) and there preaching a sermon in rotation, the incumbents of the eight Staffordshire parishes of Abbots Bromley, Bednall, Brewood, Colwich, Lapley, Penkridge, Shareshill, and Weston upon Trent, provided they are resident for at least ten months in the year in their cures, share equally the income from the charity founded by the Revd. William Alport, of Buckinghamshire, by will dated 1720.[99] The original endowment consisted of lands in Cannock and Hednesford.[1] This land has long since been sold, and the proceeds, invested in stock, yielded £624 9s. 4d. in 1956.[2] Four of these incumbents, of Abbots Bromley, Penkridge, Shareshill, and Weston upon

Trent, with those of Bloxwich, Bradley, Castle Church, and Coppenhall, likewise on condition of their being resident in their parishes for at least ten months of the year and attending a service in Cannock church on this same day, share equally in the income of the charity founded by Miss Eleanor Alport, sister of William, by will dated 1727.[3] This charity estate consisted of a messuage and lands in Hammerwich (St. Michael's, Lichfield),[4] over 72 acres by 1847[5] and over 110 acres by 1921, when most of it was sold.[6] The income in 1956 consisted of £15 rent from two fields in Hammerwich, some 13 acres in all, and £174 16s. 6d. interest from stock.[7] These two charities were jointly administered in 1956, the Vicar of Cannock receiving 10s. 6d. for conducting the service.[8]

A sermon was preached in Cannock as late as 1823 under the terms of the Troming Charity.[9]

The church of *ST. LUKE* consists of an aisled and clerestoried nave of six bays, chancel, north vestry, south chapel, and west tower. The nave dates largely from the 14th and the tower from the 16th century. The south nave wall was rebuilt in 1752–3. Between 1878 and 1882 the nave was extended eastwards, and the present chancel and vestry were built. The south chapel was added in 1949.

The earliest masonry in the building, which occurs near the west end of the north aisle, dates from the late 12th or early 13th century. This suggests that the 13th-century church was aisled and of its present width. An almost complete rebuilding took place in the 14th century: much of the internal walling in the western part of the nave is of this date, together with the four western arches of the two arcades. The octagonal piers with scroll-moulded capitals have been rebuilt or recut, but the western responds are original. The widening of what was then the most easterly bay of the north aisle to form a chapel is also of the 14th century. There was formerly a five-light Geometrical window in the north wall of this bay[10] and the basement course externally (now restored) is also of the 14th century. The north doorway and the external buttresses to the north wall of the aisle appear to be of the same date. The tower has a 14th-century basement course and an ogee-headed doorway to the vice staircase. It is possible to reconstruct a fairly complete picture of the 14th-century church from these remaining features. An aisled nave of

[74] S.H.C. 1915, 49.
[75] Cal. Pat. 1548–9, 391–2.
[76] S.H.C. 1915, 49.
[77] C 142/448, no. 113; C.P. 43/774, rot. 510; C.P. 25(2)/1413, 28 Geo. III Hil.
[78] S.H.C. 1915, 49.
[79] Ibid.
[80] Ibid.
[81] Ibid.
[82] Lich. Dioc. Regy., Bp.'s Reg. xxxii, p. 210. This was being planned c. 1860: Staffs. Advertiser, 5 May 1860.
[83] Lich. Dioc. Ch. Cal. (1871); Lich. Dioc. Regy., Bp.'s Reg. xxxiii, p. 216.
[84] Lich. Dioc. Ch. Cal. (1872).
[85] Lich. Dioc. Mag. Aug. 1880, p. 11.
[86] Lich. Dioc. Ch. Cal. (1874; 1891); Lich. Dioc. Regy., Bp.'s Reg. xxxiii, p. 410; Kelly's Dir. Staffs. (1892).
[87] Lich. Dioc. Regy., Bp.'s Reg. xxxv, p. 52.
[88] Lich. Dioc. Ch. Cal. (1880; 1896).
[89] Ibid. (1880). For Hazel Slade's civil status see p. 152.
[90] Lich. Dioc. Ch. Cal. (1889); ex inf. the curate-in-charge, Green Heath (1956). For Brindley Heath's civil status see p. 152.
[91] Lich. Dioc. Ch. Cal. (1889); Lich. Dioc. Regy., Bp.'s Reg. xxxiii, p. 216.
[92] Lich. Dioc. Ch. Cal. (1894).
[93] Wolverhampton Express and Star, 7 Oct. 1955.
[94] Lich. Dioc. Dir. (1950–1).
[95] Ibid.
[96] Lich. Dioc. Ch. Cal. (1880); Lich. Dioc. Dir. (1946).
[97] Lond. Gaz. 1870, p. 2642; Lich. Dioc. Ch. Cal. (1869); Lich. Dioc. Dir. (1955–6).
[98] Lich. Dioc. Dir. (1955–6).
[99] Tablet in Cannock church; documents penes the Secretary of the Alport Trust (Mr. P. W. Iliff of Messrs. Gardner and Iliff, Solrs., Cannock). These include accounts dating from 1753.
[1] Documents penes the Secretary, Alport Trust.
[2] Ex inf. the Secretary (1956).
[3] Tablet in Cannock church; documents penes the Secretary of the Trust, including accounts of 1737 and from 1770 onwards.
[4] Documents penes the Secretary.
[5] Tithe Map and Appt., Hammerwich (copy in W.S.L.).
[6] Sale Catalogue, penes the Secretary, Alport Trust.
[7] Ex inf. the Secretary.
[8] Ex inf. the Secretary.
[9] See p. 74.
[10] W.S.L., Staffs. Views, iii, pp. 7, 8 (1841).

four bays had a tower at the west end and a chapel occupying the easternmost bay of the north aisle. There was no clerestory, the nave being covered by a steeply pitched roof, the line of which is still visible externally on the east face of the tower. Drawings made before the 19th-century alterations[11] show a small rectangular chancel, occupying much the same position as the two easternmost bays of the present nave and having a two-light Geometrical east window. It is known that in 1330 the Dean and Chapter of Lichfield were planning to start work on

roofs which formerly covered both nave and chancel were probably new in the 18th century and the clerestory was built or rebuilt at the same period. Writing in 1836 Edward Thomas complains that 'the original beauty of this church has been sadly disfigured by the introduction of large kitchen-like windows of the present day into the clerestory, which being also (rebuilt I suppose) of brick gives the whole a very mean appearance'.[20]

Interior drawings of 1841[21] show a flat plaster ceiling to the nave, a four-centred chancel arch, and

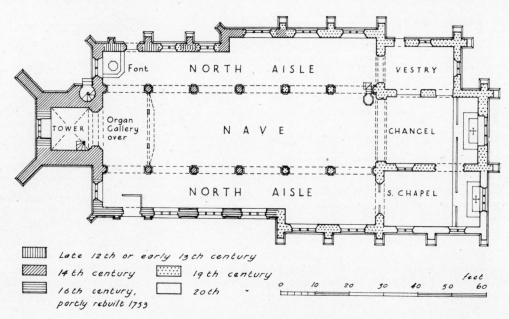

PLAN OF ST. LUKE'S CHURCH

the chancel,[12] and it is very probable that this date marks the beginning of rebuilding operations which extended to the whole church.

The tower is mainly of 16th-century masonry, refaced externally,[13] and the belfry stage with its two-light windows, Perpendicular string, and embattled parapet is of this period. It is probable that other alterations were made to the church in the 16th and 17th centuries. At one time there were large windows of very late medieval type in the north wall of the nave[14] and three existing windows on the south side may have had their origin at the same time.[15] A drawing of 1841[16] shows a vestry with a stepped gable and pinnacle on the north side of the former chancel; this was probably a 17th-century addition.

The south side of the church is said to have been rebuilt in 1753.[17] The south doorway, demolished in 1957, had a sundial above it, Tuscan pilasters, and a pediment.[18] It carried the date 1752, probably that of its insertion, but there is a tradition that it came originally from Leacroft Old Hall.[19] The hipped

galleries at the west end and over the aisles. One of these latter was approached by a stair with flat early-17th-century balusters. The nave was filled with tall box pews and there was a three-decker pulpit.

In 1849 the church was repewed and the north side restored.[22] The three most westerly windows in the north aisle and the small window above the north door were filled with heavy Geometrical tracery at this date.[23] More extensive alterations took place between 1878 and 1882[24] under the direction of N. Joyce of Stafford.[25] The nave and aisles were extended eastwards by two bays, the line of the widened chapel being continued on the north side and a similar widening introduced on the south. A new chancel was built with a combined vestry and organ chamber to the north of it. The style followed that of the 14th-century church, the piers and arches of the arcades being exactly copied and the new windows being filled with Geometrical tracery. Pointed windows replaced the 'kitchen-like' windows in the clerestory.

[11] Ibid.
[12] Bodl. MS. Ashmole 794, i, f. 37b.
[13] The date of the tower has been given as 1460: Cannock Advertiser Directory (1938). The style suggests a later date, but the evidence is obscured by much refacing.
[14] W.S.L., Staffs. Views, iii, pp. 6, 8.
[15] There is a tradition that the 3 south windows, as well as the south doorway, came from Leacroft Old Hall (see p. 56), but this is improbable.
[16] W.S.L., Staffs. Views, iii, pp. 6, 8.
[17] Pitt, Staffs. 262.

[18] See plate facing p. 53.
[19] Ex inf. Mr. F. Linford, churchwarden (1956).
[20] W.S.L., S. MS. 433 (Thomas Album 1835–7), p. 318.
[21] W.S.L., Staffs. Views, iii, pp. 7, 10.
[22] White, Dir. Staffs. (1851), 450.
[23] Photograph (1872) at Pillaton Hall, Penkridge.
[24] Lich. Dioc. Regy., Consist. Ct. Act Bk. 1875–9, p. 421, faculty, 6 Aug. 1878. It was consecrated 18 Oct. 1882: Lich. Dioc. Regy., Bp.'s Reg. Bk. 5, pp. 570–3.
[25] Kelly's Dir. Staffs. (1884).

In 1925 the north and south galleries, then considered unsafe, were cleared away,[26] and the internal plaster was removed from the walls. The south chapel, built in 1949 as a memorial to the fallen of both world wars,[27] is the full width of the south aisle and the same length as the chancel. It was designed by James Swan of Birmingham and is in a modern version of the late Decorated style. The organ was moved to a gallery at the west end of the nave in 1950[28] and the arches between the former organ chamber and the chancel were partly walled up.

Tables of charities, formerly on the west gallery, are now stored in the tower.[29]

In May 1956 a faculty was granted for the addition of a stone south porch to the church.[30]

The church formerly contained an octagonal font, probably of the 15th century, with a moulded bowl having flat shields on four of its faces.[31] The present bowl, restored and mounted on a new pedestal in memory of Jack Ball (d. 1944),[32] is similar but the shields are missing. The font's position has been moved at least twice. Near the north door is a fine ancient chest with iron bands and three locks. The altar, chancel panelling, and reading-desk date from 1932, 1936, and 1940 respectively.[33] Memorial glass was inserted in most of the windows in the late 19th and 20th centuries.

The oldest memorial in the church, commemorating Mary Warynge (d. 1613), is a wall tablet with flanking columns from which the figure, probably kneeling, was already missing in 1836.[34] A tablet to Elizabeth Bagot (d. 1638) was engraved in the early 19th century to replace an earlier one which had been plastered over in the former chancel.[35] A floor-slab now in the north aisle may be the original stone. Other wall tablets commemorate William and Eleanor Alport (d. 1721 and 1730), founders of the Alport Trust; William Finney (d. 1743) and members of his family (1746–85); Moreton Walhouse of Hatherton (d. 1796); Moreton Walhouse, his son (d. 1821); John Walhouse (d. 1835); Catharine and Ann Walhouse (d. 1836 and 1837). A tablet to Bernard Gilpin (d. 1902) was erected by his workpeople of Churchbridge and Wedges Mills; one to Napier H. Walker (d. 1916) was erected by old pupils of Walhouse National School of which he was master for 38 years. An alabaster slab engraved with a male and two female figures of the early 16th century, recorded in 1836, appears to be missing.[36]

In 1553 the church plate consisted of a silver chalice, parcel gilt with paten.[37] In 1957 it included an Elizabethan chalice; a flagon and lid, 1733, the gift of Dorothy Byrch; a dish, 1680; two dishes, 1741, the gift of Robert and Ann Fisher; a paten, 1806, the gift of William Cary; a modern chalice; a silver chalice and paten, 1956, in memory of Leonard Rowley; all of silver; a pewter flagon with lid and a pewter plate; and a ciborium.[38]

In 1553 there were three bells and one sanctus bell.[39] By 1889 there were six bells: (i) 1849; (ii–vi) 1747.[40] There are now eight bells: (i, v, vii, viii) 1923, J. Taylor and Co.; (ii) 1849, Mears; (iii, iv, vi) 1747, Bagley.[41]

The surviving registers date from 1744. The earlier registers were destroyed by fire about 1858.[42]

In the churchyard, south of the church, are the remains of a stone cross probably dating from the 13th or 14th century. It consists of a broken square shaft and a square base raised on three tall steps. The churchyard was closed for burials in 1878[43] and has been largely cleared of gravestones. An area of about 157 sq. yds. at its southernmost corner was appropriated by the Ministry of Transport in 1941 for road widening.[44]

The vicarage house, built on a site north of the churchyard in 1839 at a cost of £800,[45] is a gabled brick house with 'Tudor' details.

The church of *ST. PETER*, Hednesford, dates from 1868.[46] The site was given by the Marquess of Anglesey, and the cost of the church was about £3,000.[47] The walls are of stone, left exposed internally, and in the first instance only the nave, apsidal chancel and south transept were built. Provision was made for a tower, the tower arch being incorporated in the west nave wall. In 1904 and 1905 a north aisle in Penkridge stone and a south porch were added, the architect being T. W. Sandy of Stafford.[48] The original building has lancet windows to apse and transepts and is generally of 13th-century style. The nave and additional aisle have Perpendicular windows. The foundations were underpinned in 1937, and the walls, evidently much damaged by subsidence, were repaired. The levels in the sanctuary were altered at the same time.[49] The first organ, installed by public subscription in 1872,[50] was replaced by a new one in 1910.[51] Stained glass to the memory of Thomas Eskett was inserted in the east window in 1879.[52] The choir stalls and clergy desks date from 1924.[53] In 1957 the plate included a silver chalice given in memory of M. E. Slaney in 1924; a silver paten given in 1924; a gold chalice, 15th-century Flemish, bearing the inscription 'Maria Jesus' in knop, given by Prebendary Grier; and two

[26] Lich. Dioc. Regy., Consist. Ct. Act Bk. 1924–30, p. 100, faculty, 16 Mar. 1925.
[27] Inscription in chapel.
[28] Inscription in church.
[29] Ex inf. Mr. F. Linford.
[30] Ex inf. Mr. Linford.
[31] W.S.L., S. MS. 433, p. 318 (1836); W.S.L., Staffs. Views, iii, p. 10 (1841).
[32] Inscription in church.
[33] Lich. Dioc. Regy., Consist. Ct. Act Bk. 1930–4, p. 330, faculty, 24 Oct. 1932; ibid. 1934–8, p. 193, faculty, 13 Jan. 1936; ibid. 1938–47, p. 198, faculty, 26 Aug. 1940.
[34] W.S.L., S. MS. 433, p. 318.
[35] Ibid.
[36] Ibid.
[37] S.H.C. 1915, 48.
[38] Ex inf. the Vicar of Cannock (1957).
[39] S.H.C. 1915, 48.
[40] C. Lynam, *Church Bells of Staffs.* (1889), 7.

[41] A. E. Garbett, 'Church Bells of Staffs.' (*Trans. Old Stafford Soc.* 1953–4), 12.
[42] *Kelly's Dir. Staffs.* (1940).
[43] Lich. Dioc. Regy., Consist. Ct. Act Bk. 1938–47, pp. 273–8, faculty, 26 Sept. 1941 (which refers to the Order of 12 Feb. 1878).
[44] Ibid.
[45] White, *Dir. Staffs.* (1951).
[46] *Lich. Dioc. Ch. Cal.* (1869).
[47] *Kelly's Dir. Staffs.* (1884).
[48] Lich. Dioc. Regy., Consist. Ct. Act Bk. 1903–7, faculty, 4 July 1904.
[49] Ibid. 1934–8, p. 389, faculty, 13 Aug. 1937.
[50] *Kelly's Dir. Staffs.* (1884).
[51] Lich. Dioc. Regy., Consist. Ct. Act Bk. 1907–14, p. 182, faculty, 29 Mar. 1910.
[52] *Lich. Dioc. Ch. Cal.* (1880), 77.
[53] *Kelly's Dir. Staffs.* (1932).

patens, one gelfmetal, one electro-plated.[54] There is one small modern bell.[55] The vicarage-house to the west of the church was built in 1872.[56]

The church of *ST. PAUL* at Wimblebury dates from 1889 and 1890[57] and is of red brick with blue bands and dressings. It was originally built so that the chancel could be shut off with revolving shutters and the nave used as a day-school.[58] In 1957 the plate included an electro-plated chalice and paten and another paten.[59] There is one bell.

A school–church was opened at Bridgtown in 1874[60] and an iron church in 1876.[61] The present church of *ST. PAUL* replaced the iron church, which was becoming dilapidated, in 1899.[62] It is built of red brick with stone dressings and consists of nave, chancel, north porch, organ chamber, and vestry. There are traceried windows at the east and west ends; the other windows have mullions and round-headed lights. In 1957 the plate included a silver chalice and paten, presented in memory of Sarah Jane Barnes by her husband in 1924; an electro-plated chalice and paten; a silver private communion set (miniature); and a silver ciborium given by Mrs. A. Whitehouse in memory of her husband George A. Whitehouse (d. 1938).[63]

The church of *ST. SAVIOUR* at Green Heath was dedicated in 1888.[64] It is a plain red-brick building to which a chancel with lancet windows was added in 1901.[65] In 1957 the plate included a silver chalice and paten; a silver paten presented by the Sunday school in 1929; an electro-plated wafer cup; and a silver private communion set, given in memory of Mrs. Marland.[66] There is one bell.

A school–church was opened at Chadsmoor in 1874, and transepts and a small chancel were added in 1876.[67] The foundation stone of the present church of *ST. CHAD* was laid at Easter 1891 'in the presence of a large company of miners and their families',[68] and the church was consecrated in 1892.[69] It is built of machine-made red brick and consists of nave, chancel, south porch, vestry, and organ chamber. The windows are tall lancets, those at the east and west ends being graduated. The interior is unplastered, and one course of brickwork at sill level carries the names of subscribers to the building. The oak reredos and the lectern date from 1906.[70] Stained glass was inserted in the east window in 1908 in memory of Tabitha Benton.[71] In 1957 the plate included an electro-plated flagon, chalice, and paten, and an electro-plated ciborium.[72] There is one bell in a turret at the north-west corner of the church. The incumbent's house is east of the church.

The surviving chapel at Five Ways (Heath Hayes) was enlarged in 1891[73] and replaced by the church of *ST. JOHN THE EVANGELIST*, which was built in 1902–3[74] and consists of a nave, chancel, vestry, and porch. St. John's is of red brick with stone dressings and is similar in style to the church of St. Paul, Bridgtown (see above). The ground round the building was levelled by miners who also raised £400 in small subscriptions towards the cost.[75] In 1957 the plate included a silver flagon, 1918–19, presented as a war-memorial; a silver chalice presented in memory of Edwin Thomas Gwyther by Agnes Gwyther in 1919; a silver paten presented in 1919 by Annie Timmins in memory of her husband; and an electro-plated chalice, two patens, small chalice, and jug.[76] There is one bell.

The church of *ALL SAINTS* at Hazel Slade, built in 1884,[77] consists of nave, chancel, and north transept with a bell-cote and one bell at the west gable-end. It has pointed windows and is built of red brick with blue-brick bands. In 1957 the plate included a silver chalice and paten presented in memory of John Hall, 1910, and an electro-plated chalice and paten.[78]

The church of *ST. MARY* at Brindley Heath was dismantled in 1954.[79] The plate included one electro-plated chalice given by E. Appleyard in 1926.[80]

The church of *ST. MICHAEL AND ALL ANGELS* at Rawnsley was built in 1889[81] and is a structure of wood and corrugated iron. In 1957 the plate included a silver chalice, and two silver patens.[82] There is one bell in a bell-cote.

The church of *ST. MARK* at Pye Green is a small roughcast building with a bell in a bell-cote, and there is a hall adjoining. In 1957 the plate consisted of a chalice and paten.[83]

The small wooden church of *ST. AIDAN* in Pye Green Road, West Chadsmoor, was in use from 1947 to 1956 when it was converted into a church hall.[84] It had one bell. The present church, begun in 1955[85] on a nearby site on the opposite side of the road, was opened in 1956, the architects being Wood, Goldstraw, and Yorath of Stoke on Trent. Built of light-brown brick, the church consists of a wide nave, a shallow chancel, a south vestry, and a north porch, and has one bell.

The mission of *ST. GEORGE* in Fosters Avenue, Broadway, had been started by 1950[86] in a hut which by 1956 was used solely as a church hall, a new mission hut with one bell having been built by then. In 1957 the plate consisted of a chalice and paten.[87]

[54] Ex inf. the Vicar of Hednesford (1957).
[55] Lynam, *Church Bells of Staffs.* 15.
[56] *Kelly's Dir. Staffs.* (1932).
[57] Foundation stone, dated 3 June 1889: *Kelly's Dir. Staffs.* (1896).
[58] *Lich. Dioc. Mag.* (1889), 167.
[59] Ex inf. the Vicar of Hednesford.
[60] *Lich. Dioc. Ch. Cal.* (1875), 73.
[61] Ibid. (1877), 73; Lich. Dioc. Regy., Bp.'s Reg. xxxiii, pp. 397–8.   [62] Date on building.
[63] Ex inf. the curate-in-charge (1957).
[64] *Lich. Dioc. Ch. Cal.* (1889), 157; Lich. Dioc. Regy., Bp.'s Reg. xxxv, p. 98.
[65] *Kelly's Dir. Staffs.* (1912).
[66] Ex inf. the Vicar of Hednesford.
[67] *Lich. Dioc. Mag.* Aug. 1880, p. 11.
[68] *Lich. Dioc. Ch. Cal.* (1892), 172.
[69] Lich. Dioc. Regy., Bp.'s Reg. Bk. T, pp. 475, 485–9.
[70] Lich. Dioc. Regy., Consist. Ct. Act Bk. 1903–7, faculty, 17 Oct. 1906.

[71] Ibid. 1907–14, p. 70, faculty, 2 Apr. 1908.
[72] Ex inf. the curate-in-charge (1957).
[73] *Kelly's Dir. Staffs.* (1892).
[74] *Lich. Dioc. Mag.* June 1902, 114; ibid. May 1903, 80.
[75] Ibid. June 1902, 114; ibid. May 1903, 80.
[76] Ex inf. the curate-in-charge (1957).
[77] *Kelly's Dir. Staffs.* (1884).
[78] Ex inf. the Vicar of Hednesford.
[79] Ex inf. the curate-in-charge, Green Heath (1956). The church is first mentioned in the *Lich. Dioc. Dir.* (1950–1).
[80] Return to Archdeacon of Stafford, 1931, *penes* the Archdeacon of Stafford (1955).
[81] *Kelly's Dir. Staffs.* (1912); Lich. Dioc. Regy., Bp.'s Reg. xxxv, p. 173.
[82] Ex inf. the Vicar of Hednesford (1957).
[83] Ex inf. the Vicar of Cannock (1957).
[84] Local inf.
[85] Foundation stone.
[86] *Lich. Dioc. Dir.* (1950–1); local inf.
[87] Ex inf. the Vicar of Cannock (1957).

ROMAN CATHOLICISM. It was stated in 1604 that the 400 people of Cannock parish were 'almost all papists, as is commonly seen in the jurisdiction of the Dean and Chapter of Lichfield'.[88] Walter Coleman of Cannock, who occurs as a recusant in 1607,[89] had a Benedictine chaplain, and a Benedictine monk named Nicholas Becket died here in 1618.[90] Twenty-nine recusants in Cannock, including John Coleman, son of Walter, John's wife Margaret, and Anne and Mary Coleman, were named in 1641, along with three in Great Wyrley.[91] There were four convicted recusants, including a Charles Coleman, in Cannock c. 1667 when there were also eight in Great Wyrley and two in Huntington.[92] Only five papists in Cannock were mentioned in 1780.[93]

The immediate origin of the present mission in Cannock was the mass centre opened at Hatherton Hall, Hatherton (in St. Peter's, Wolverhampton), in 1873 and served first from the Cathedral at Birmingham, from 1874 or 1875 to 1876 by its own resident priest, and from 1876 to 1878 by a priest living at Rugeley.[94] A school–chapel dedicated to St. Mary was opened in John Street, Cannock, in 1878 with a resident priest[95] and was replaced in 1899 by the chapel of the Sacred Heart and Our Lady, Walsall Road,[96] which was in turn replaced in 1924 by the present church of St. Mary on an adjoining site.[97] The average attendance at Sunday mass there in 1956 was 615.[98]

By 1898 there was a school–chapel at Hill Top, Hednesford, dedicated to St. Joseph and St. Philomena[99] and served by the parish priest of Cannock until the appointment of a resident priest in 1907.[1] By about 1915 a site for a church and presbytery had been acquired nearby in Uxbridge Street,[2] and services were held in a hut from Christmas 1920 pending the erection of the new church.[3] Work was started in 1927, funds being raised by a worldwide appeal,[4] and mass was first said in the present church of Our Lady of Lourdes on 1 November 1933.[5] The average attendance at Sunday mass there in 1956 was 300.[6]

Between about 1902 and 1948 there was a chapel at the Union Workhouse dedicated to the Good Shepherd and served by the parish priest of Cannock.[7] There was also a mass centre, served by a visiting Polish priest, at the Polish ex-soldiers' camp at Wimblebury, open from 1947 to 1952, and mass is still said at the Polish camp at Bridgtown, opened in 1947.[8]

The Sisters of the Christian Retreat opened the present convent of the Holy Rosary at Cannock in 1898[9] and the convent of Our Lady of Lourdes at West View, Rugeley Road, Hednesford, in 1920.[10] The Hednesford community moved to Mount Pleasant, Uxbridge Street, in 1926 and, owing to mining subsidence, to York House, Anglesey Street, in 1950.[11] This latter house too was closed in 1954, and the nuns went to live in the convent at Cannock.[12] The Little Company of Mary, a nursing order, had a house in Hednesford Street between about 1913 and 1922.[13]

The church of *OUR LADY OF LOURDES* at Hednesford, the architect of which was G. B. Cox of Birmingham,[14] is a large cruciform building of stone with an entrance portico on the north side and a bell tower incorporated in the west transept. Internally the nave has narrow aisles with a series of side chapels beyond them. The pulpit, altar, and baldachino are by Bridgman of Lichfield.[15] The sculptor of the crucifix and the panels representing the Stations of the Cross was P. Lindsey Clark.[16] North of the church is a reproduction of the grotto at Lourdes. It contains an altar and is approached by a wide paved forecourt in which open-air services can be held.

PROTESTANT NONCONFORMITY. In 1648 Richard Bourne of Cannock was among the Presbyterians who signed the Testimony of the Ministers in the county of Stafford.[17] An application was made to license the house of Edward Wilson in Cannock as a Presbyterian meeting-place under the Act of Indulgence of 1672.[18] Further evidence of nonconformity occurs in 1700 when the house of John Bladen and Mary Corbett was certified as a place of worship under the Toleration Act.[19] In the summer of 1814 John Fernie the Congregational minister at Brewood started to preach at Cannock using two rooms in a dwelling house, and in October 1814 a converted building was opened as a Congregational chapel.[20] It was replaced by another built in 1824 by public subscription[21] and opened in 1825.[22] The

[88] *S.H.C.* 1915, 49.
[89] *Cal. S.P. Dom.* 1603–10, 374.
[90] H. Birt, *Obituary Notices of the English Benedictines*, 6; A. Hamilton, *Chronicle of the Augustinian Canonesses of Louvain*, i. 163. [91] E. 179/179/315, m. 2.
[92] *Cath. Rec. Soc.* vi. 302–12.
[93] H.L., Main Papers, Return of Papists, 1780.
[94] *Catholic Directory* (1874), 132; ibid. (1875), 135, 280; ibid. (1876), 135; ibid. (1877), 135, 270; ibid. (1878), 135; Bapt. Reg. at St. Mary's, dating from 1873.
[95] *Cath. Dir.* (1879).
[96] Ibid. (1900). The Bapt. Reg. (1908) gives the dedication as the Sacred Heart and the Holy Rosary. The building in which it was situated was occupied in 1956 by the Territorial Army.
[97] *Cath. Dir.* (1927); *Kelly's Dir. Staffs.* (1928).
[98] Ex inf. the parish priest, Cannock (1956).
[99] *Cath. Dir.* (1898); *Kelly's Dir. Staffs.* (1912).
[1] Ex inf. the parish priest, Hednesford (1956), citing the Hednesford Bapt. Reg.
[2] *Kelly's Dir. Staffs.* (1916); *Cath. Dir.* (1915).
[3] *Kelly's Dir. Staffs.* (1924; 1928; 1932); ex inf. the parish priest, Hednesford. The hut was used in 1956 as the parish hall.
[4] *Kelly's Dir. Staffs.* (1928); *Cannock and Hednesford: Official Guide* (1953), 19.

[5] Ex inf. the parish priest, Hednesford; the solemn opening was in June 1934.
[6] Ex inf. the parish priest.
[7] *Cath. Dir.* (1903, and later edns. to 1950); see p. 52.
[8] Ex inf. Fr. M. Bossowski, chaplain to the Polish hostel at Little Onn, Church Eaton (1956).
[9] Ex inf. the Revd. Mother Superior (1956); the building was extended in 1911 and between 1951 and 1952.
[10] Ex inf. the parish priest, Hednesford; *Cath. Dir.* (1921).
[11] Ex inf. the parish priest, Hednesford; *Cath. Dir.* (1928; 1951).
[12] Ex inf. the parish priest, Hednesford.
[13] *Cath. Dir.* (1914, and later edns. to 1922).
[14] Ex inf. the parish priest, Hednesford.
[15] Ex inf. the parish priest, Hednesford.
[16] Ex inf. the parish priest, Hednesford.
[17] *Trans. Cong. Hist. Soc.* viii. 85.
[18] Turner, *Orig. Records of Nonconformity*, i. 574.
[19] Matthews, *Cong. Churches of Staffs.* 125; S.R.O., Q/SM 1, Trans. 12 Wm. III.
[20] W.S.L., S. 603; *Evangelical Mag.* (1815), 119.
[21] White, *Dir. Staffs.* (1834); tablet *in situ*.
[22] *Evangelical Mag.* (1825), 156; Lich. Dioc. Regy., Bp.'s Reg. Bk. G, p. 582.

chapel, a red-brick building, seated 170 in 1956[23] and lies in Stafford Road.

The first Congregational chapel at Hednesford was erected in 1873 on land given by Alfred Stanley, the church originally being a branch of Wednesbury Road Church, Walsall.[24] The new chapel in Mount Street was opened in 1898 with seating accommodation for 330.[25] It is of red brick, and the former chapel which stands behind it is a smaller roughcast building.

Other Protestant meeting-houses were registered in Cannock in 1814,[26] 1816,[27] 1819,[28] and 1824,[29] probably signs of the growth of Methodism in the area. In 1842 a Wesleyan Methodist chapel was opened there.[30] In 1866[31] this chapel was replaced by Trinity Methodist chapel, a large red-brick building in Walsall Road, built by public subscription[32] and in 1940 seating 220.[33] Trinity Methodist Sunday school stands opposite the chapel.

A small Wesleyan Methodist chapel was built at Cannock Wood in 1834.[34] In 1940 the chapel seated 80 persons.[35] Situated in Chapel Lane, it is a stone building with rounded windows and a tiled roof.

A Wesleyan Methodist chapel was built in stone at Bridgtown in 1863, seating 300.[36] It was superseded by Bethel, Union Street, in 1909[37] and in 1956 was used as a day-school by the Bridgtown (Cannock) Boys' School. The red-brick Union Street chapel, built in front of this former chapel, was said in 1940 to seat 200.[38]

A Wesleyan Methodist chapel was built at Hazel Slade, in Rugeley Road, in 1876,[39] and in 1940 seated 200.[40] It is cement-faced, probably over brick.

A Wesleyan Methodist chapel was built at Wimblebury in 1870.[41] In 1940 it seated 150[42] and is of red brick with rounded windows and blue-brick dressings.

In March 1738 John Wesley preached at Hednesford on his outward and return journeys from London to Manchester; in February 1747 he again passed through the town.[43] Three Wesleyan Methodist chapels have been built in Hednesford. St. John's chapel, a roughcast building in Station Road, dates from 1873[44] and in 1940 had a seating capacity of 236.[45] The Sunday school and church

hall, of red brick, situated behind the church, were added in 1883.[46] Bradbury Lane chapel, built in 1892,[47] had a seating capacity in 1940 of 100.[48] Hill Street chapel, Old Hednesford, was built in 1890[49] and in 1940 seated 150.[50] It is a cement-rendered and roughcast building.

A Wesleyan Methodist chapel, the Williamson Memorial Mission, given by J. T. Williamson of Cannock, was built c. 1903[51] at Blackfords in Cannock Road. In 1940 it had a seating capacity of 150.[52] In March 1955 the congregation amalgamated with that at Broomhill Methodist chapel, and the old building, of corrugated iron, is now only used for women's meetings and a Sunday school.[53]

Primitive Methodism quickly gained followers in Cannock after the first visit by Hugh Bourne to the area in 1810 at the invitation of David Buxton of Cheslyn Hay. The movement had two main centres in this area, Cannock and Cannock Wood. As early as 1808 the house of Geoffrey Townsend at Cannock had been registered as a meeting-house, David Buxton being one of the witnesses of the certificate.[54] In 1810[55] the house of Samuel Craddock at Cannock Wood was also registered as a meeting-house for Primitive Methodists.[56] This was superseded by the house of John Linney at Cannock Wood in 1811.[57] Although there was serious dissension among the Primitive Methodists at Cannock Wood in 1813, John Linney's house continued as a centre of the movement for some years.[58] This meeting continued till at least 1868.[59] At Cannock the Primitive Methodists met for some time in a house in Cannock Lane[60] and also in that of William Turner, registered as a meeting-house in 1832.[61] Both these meetings had apparently lapsed by 1851.[62] Primitive Methodism in Cannock revived, however, before 1865 when a chapel was built.[63] Of red brick with rounded windows and blue-brick dressings, this stands in Mill Street. A new red-brick chapel was subsequently built by the side of it and seated 220 in 1940.[64] A Sunday school, a cement-dressed building, was added in 1924.[65]

A Primitive Methodist chapel was built at Littleworth in 1842, although it was not used exclusively as a chapel.[66] A Primitive Methodist chapel there, built in 1852 on a site given by the Marquess of

23 Staffs. Cong. Union Records.
24 Matthews, Cong. Churches of Staffs. 239–40.
25 Ibid. 242; Staffs. Cong. Union Records; tablet in situ.
26 Occupied by Charles Cotterell: Lich. Dioc. Regy., Bp.'s Reg. Bk. E, p. 383.
27 Barn occupied by Robert Green: ibid. F, p. 364.
28 House occupied by John Bradbury: ibid. F, p. 459.
29 House occupied by John Noakes: ibid. G, p. 581.
30 Ibid. L, p. 90.
31 Tablet in situ.
32 P.O. Dir. Staffs. (1868).
33 Methodist Church Buildings, 1940 (1946), 266.
34 Lich. Dioc. Regy., Bp.'s Reg. Bk. I, p. 507.
35 Meth. Church Buildings, 267.
36 Kelly's Dir. Staffs. (1892).
37 Local inf.
38 Meth. Church Buildings, 266.
39 Tablets in situ.
40 Meth. Church Buildings, 267.
41 Tablet in situ.
42 Meth. Church Buildings, 267.
43 Wesley's Journal, 21 Mar. 1738, Feb. 1746/7.
44 Tablet in situ. The foundation stone is dated 1872.
45 Meth. Church Buildings, 266–7.
46 Tablet in situ.
47 Tablet in situ.
48 Meth. Church Buildings, 266–7.
49 Tablet in situ.
50 Meth. Church Buildings, 266–7.
51 Ex inf. Mr. S. Turner.
52 Meth. Church Buildings, 267.
53 Ex inf. Methodist Supt. Minister, Cannock Circuit (1956).
54 Lich. Dioc. Regy., Bp.'s Reg. Bk. E, p. 383.
55 Ibid., p. 505.
56 The Craddock family were prominent Primitive Methodists: J. Walford, Memoirs of Hugh Bourne (1855), i. 385.
57 Lich. Dioc. Regy., Bp.'s Reg. Bk. F, p. 18; H. B. Kendall, History of Primitive Methodism, i. 169, where a photograph of the house is given.
58 Walford, Memoirs of Hugh Bourne, i. 336.
59 P.O. Dir. Staffs. (1868).
60 Walford, Memoirs of Hugh Bourne, i. 334, 366, 385; Kendall, History of Primitive Methodism, i. 169, where a photograph of the house is given.
61 Lich. Dioc. Regy., Bp.'s Reg. Bk. i, p. 171. William Turner was a prominent Primitive Methodist in the area: Kendall, History of Primitive Methodism, i. 169.
62 No return was made in the Ecclesiastical Census of that year, and they are not mentioned in White, Dir. Staffs. (1851).
63 Tablet in situ.
64 Meth. Church Buildings, 266.
65 Tablet in situ.
66 H.O. 129/15/378.

Anglesey,[67] was still in use in 1940.[68] It has since been closed and sold.[69]

In 1870 a group of Primitive Methodists started to hold services in the house of Charles Woolley of Hednesford, and in the following year a site for a chapel, in Station Road, Hednesford, was purchased for £12 17s. The chapel, named Bethesda, was opened in July 1872. By 1877 the congregation had greatly increased in numbers and a new chapel was then built, in front of the former building, at a cost of £900. An organ was added in 1879. By 1901 there was need for further accommodation, and a site for a new chapel was bought for £122. This site was never used, and since 1914 the numbers attending the chapel have decreased.[70] Bethesda chapel seated 300 in 1940.[71] It was almost closed down in 1950, but the necessary money (£600) to repair it was raised. The attendance has since improved, but the position was still critical in 1956 when money was being raised to replace the organ. The former chapel has been used as a Sunday school since 1877, a room being built over it in 1905 to meet the need for additional accommodation.[72] Both Sunday school and chapel are of brick.

A Primitive Methodist chapel was built in Bradbury Lane, Hednesford, in 1876[73] and in 1928 was replaced by a new chapel in Florence Street, Hednesford,[74] seating 200 in 1940.[75] Both buildings are of brick, and the former chapel has been used as a club for about 30 years.[76]

A Primitive Methodist chapel was built at Chadsmoor in 1876[77] and was replaced in 1911[78] by a new chapel built in front of it. The former chapel is a rough-cast building with round-headed windows and in 1956 was being used as a Sunday school and also as a day school.[79] The present chapel, of red brick with stone Gothic windows and doorways, was designed by Jeffries and Shipley.[80] In 1940 it seated 350.[81]

A Primitive Methodist chapel named Ebenezer was built at Hazel Slade in 1882.[82] A red-brick building with blue-brick dressings, it lies in Albert Road and in 1940 seated 100.[83]

A Primitive Methodist chapel was built in East Street, Bridgtown, in 1897.[84] This chapel, called Carmel, although still in use in 1940,[85] was subsequently sold and in 1956 was used as a warehouse. It is of red brick. A smaller building at the side of it, erected in 1928, was formerly used as a Sunday school and for the Ladies' Guild.[86]

Bourne Primitive Methodist chapel, situated at

Heath Hayes, was built in 1900.[87] In 1940 it seated 400.[88] It is a red-brick building and stands at the corner of Hednesford Road and Chapel Street.

A Methodist New Connexion chapel was erected at Bridgtown in 1901.[89] Becoming United Methodist after the Methodist Union of 1907 this chapel, built of red brick, stands in Park Street and in 1940 seated 494.[90] It replaced a smaller chapel, a stone-dressed building, erected in 1863[91] beside it and is now used as a Sunday school.[92] This earlier chapel replaced a former one, a red-brick building with round-headed windows and blue-brick dressings, built c. 1850 and standing behind the present chapel.

There are two former Methodist New Connexion, and subsequently United Methodist, chapels at High Town, one lying in Cannock Road and one at Broomhill. The first chapel in Cannock Road was built c. 1850[93] but was replaced by a larger chapel built in front of it in 1879.[94] The chancel of this chapel was extended in 1903 to house the organ.[95] In 1940 the chapel seated 322.[96] It is a tall rough-cast building with paired lancet windows and stone and cement dressings. It formerly had a bell which has been given to Broomhill chapel. The former chapel was used as a Sunday school after 1879 and also as a day school. In 1886 it was extended.[97] It is a small red-brick building with blue-brick dressings and is now partly plastered. The chapel at Broomhill was built in 1898.[98] It is of red brick and stands in Victoria Street. In 1940 it seated 176.[99]

A Methodist New Connexion, later United Methodist, chapel was built at Heath Hayes in 1876.[1] It stands in Wimblebury Road and in 1940 seated 200.[2] It is a cement-faced building with round-headed windows.

All the Methodist chapels in Cannock belonged to denominations which were included in the Methodist Union of 1932 and now all belong to the Methodist Church.

There is one Baptist chapel in Cannock, built at Chadsmoor, in Arthur Street, in 1905 at a cost of £1,000.[3] It replaced an earlier Baptist chapel, which stands behind it and was built in 1879.[4] This former chapel, a roughcast building with pointed windows, is used as a Sunday school and as an overflow for Chadsmoor Central Boys' School. The present chapel is of red brick with stone dressings and leaded windows. It has seating accommodation for 250.[5]

The Plymouth Brethren held a meeting as early as 1840 in Cannock; attendance on 30 March 1851 was said to number between 15 and 20 in the morn-

[67] Tablet *in situ*.
[68] *Kelly's Dir. Staffs.* (1940).
[69] *Meth. Church Buildings*, 267; ex inf. Methodist Supt. Minister, Cannock Circuit (1954).
[70] Ex inf. Mr. E. T. Purslow.
[71] *Meth. Church Buildings*, 266–7.
[72] Ex inf. Mr. E. T. Purslow.
[73] Tablet *in situ*.
[74] Tablet *in situ*; local inf.
[75] *Meth. Church Buildings*, 266–7.
[76] Local inf.
[77] Date on building.
[78] Date on building.
[79] Local inf.
[80] Tablet *in situ*.
[81] *Meth. Church Buildings*, 267.
[82] Tablet *in situ*.
[83] *Meth. Church Buildings*, 267.
[84] Tablet *in situ*.
[85] *Kelly's Dir. Staffs.* (1940).
[86] Local inf.

[87] Tablet *in situ*.
[88] *Meth. Church Buildings*, 267.
[89] Tablet *in situ*.
[90] *Meth. Church Buildings*, 266.
[91] Tablet *in situ*.
[92] Local inf.
[93] The style of the building indicates that it belongs to this period.
[94] Date on building.
[95] Ex inf. Mr. W. Berington, caretaker, son of the previous caretaker.
[96] *Meth. Church Buildings*, 267.
[97] Ex inf. Mr. W. Berington.
[98] Tablet *in situ*.
[99] *Meth. Church Buildings*, 267.
[1] Tablet *in situ*.
[2] *Meth. Church Buildings*, 267.
[3] *Kelly's Dir. Staffs.* (1912).
[4] Tablet *in situ*.
[5] *Kelly's Dir. Staffs.* (1912).

ing and between 30 and 50 in the evening.[6] The meeting survived until at least 1940.[7]

The Christadelphians have held meetings in Cannock since at least 1912.[8] By 1940 they had a hall in Price Street.[9] This is a cement-faced building.

The Salvation Army started to hold meetings in the Market Hall, Hednesford, c. 1881. The Salvation Army Barracks, a wooden building, was opened at West Hill, Hednesford, c. 1883. The Army also had a hall in Walhouse Street, Cannock, opened c. 1885. This hall, also a wooden building, was burnt down in 1951. In 1953 a large brick building, with two halls, was erected at the cost of £19,000.[10]

In 1885 a mission hall was erected for the Seamen and Boatmen's Friends' Society at Canal Basin, Hednesford, and was still used in 1940.[11] The mission has since been dissolved.[12]

A Progressive Spiritualist church in Cannock Road, Hednesford, was opened before 1932[13] and although still in use in 1940[14] has since been closed.[15]

A Pentecostal church, a concrete building standing in Hednesford Road, Heath Hayes, was built by 1942 and in 1956 was still in use.[16]

PRIMARY SCHOOLS. The chantry priest of Cannock had kept a grammar school and had taught parishioners' children for the most part freely for some 30 years before the dissolution of the chantry in 1548, when Lawrence Peryn, then priest, was ordered to continue this school at a salary of £4 14s. 5½d., corresponding to the endowment of the former Lady's Service.[17] The later history of the school is obscure.

In 1680 John Wood of Paternoster Row, London, gave a house at Cannock 'to be used by a schoolmaster for teaching children to read'.[18] For some time between 1725 and 1818 the master of this school seems to have received 24s. a year for teaching two poor boys and two poor girls under the bequest of Mary Chapman, and from 1747 to c. 1806 28s. a year for the education of three boys under the will of Dorothy Birch.[19] In 1752 John Biddulph gave in trust a meadow in Cannock called Pool Yard or Pool Yort, bought for £100, and in 1761 a piece of freehold land or garden lying at the back of the school house, for the use of the schoolmaster.[20] In 1818 the house was found to be not very suitable for its purpose.[21] The Chapman Charity was then being applied to general charitable purposes and some 40 to 60 children 'of pauper and the lowest classes' of Cannock and Cannock Wood were being educated each year by a rate, about £30 in 1817.[22] By 1823 the master received £8 a year from Pool Yard and still occupied the garden and house; attendance had dropped from some 60 under a previous master to 30.[23] The Chapman bequest was then declared sufficient for only two boys.[24] In 1864 the master of Wood's school moved to another building where he conducted a private boarding and day school for boys, with no free pupils.[25]

The vacated school-house was in the same year leased to a newly founded parochial school for infants.[26] The average attendance in 1865 was 60 and the school was then in receipt of a government grant.[27] In 1874 the endowment and house were transferred by the Charity Commissioners to the school.[28] The building was then altered and enlarged to accommodate 40 more children, making a total of 100.[29] In 1893 the average attendance was 109.[30] The school was again enlarged in 1895, the average attendance being 130 c. 1900.[31] In 1930 the Education Authority decided that the premises must be vacated immediately[32] and the school was subsequently housed in weather-board buildings off the Wolverhampton Road.[33] In 1949 it became an aided school[34] and is now known as Cannock Church of England Voluntary Primary School (Infants).

At some time between 1874 and 1888 Joseph Poynor of Cannock gave £100 to be invested for the benefit of the Infants' school, and the income in 1894 was £5.[35] The total income from endowments in 1893 was £16 14s.[36] In 1906 the amount of income of Mary Chapman's Charity to be assigned for education was fixed at three-fifths. Much of the landed endowment was sold between 1917 and 1942, and the total income in 1940 was £8 rent and £3 13s. 6d. interest on stock.[37]

The former school building on the south side of High Green is a long two-story brick range, much altered. It retains part of its original roof and chimney. A plaque on the front wall is carved with a broken pediment enclosing a mask and a scroll device. Below is the inscription 'Mr. John Wood of London, born at Cannock, founded this school 1680.'[38]

In 1828 Mrs. Walhouse of Hatherton Hall built a school, with a teacher's house, in New Penkridge Road, where she educated about 200 children at her own expense.[39] She bequeathed £800 to the school

[6] H.O. 129/15/378.
[7] Kelly's Dir. Staffs. (1940).
[8] Kelly's Dir. Staffs. (1912).
[9] Ibid. (1940).
[10] All information in this paragraph was supplied by the caretaker of the Salvation Army Barracks, Cannock (1956).
[11] Kelly's Dir. Staffs. (1940).
[12] Ex inf. Methodist Supt. Minister, Cannock Circuit (1954).
[13] Kelly's Dir. Staffs. (1932).
[14] Ibid. (1940).
[15] Ex inf. Methodist Supt. Minister, Cannock Circuit (1954).
[16] Local inf.
[17] S.H.C. 1915, 49; A. F. Leach, Schools of Medieval England (1915), 324; English Schools at the Reformation (1896), 209.
[18] 11th Rep. Com. Char. H.C. 433, pp. 514–15 (1824), xiv; White, Dir. Staffs. (1834; 1851); tablet in situ.
[19] 11th Rep. Com. Char. 513; see p. 75.
[20] 11th Rep. Com. Char. 513; S.R.O., D. 260/M/box v, bdle. a.
[21] Digest of Returns to Sel. Cttee. on Educ. of Poor (1818), H.C. 224, p. 855 (1819), ix (2).
[22] Ibid.
[23] 11th Rep. Com. Char. 515; White, Dir. Staffs. (1834).
[24] 11th Rep. Com. Char. 515.
[25] S.R.O., D. 260/M/box v, bdle. c; P.O. Dir. Staffs. (1868; 1872).
[26] S.R.O., D. 260/M/box v, bdle. c.
[27] Rep. of the Educ. Cttee. of Council 1865 [3666], H.C. (1866), xxvii.
[28] S.R.O., D. 260/M/box v, bdle. c.
[29] Ibid.
[30] Return of Schools, 1893 [C. 7529], pp. 540–1, H.C. (1894), lxv.
[31] Kelly's Dir. Staffs. (1900).
[32] Staffs. Educ. Cttee. Mins. Dec. 1930.
[33] Local inf.
[34] Ex inf. Staffs. C.C. Educ. Dept.
[35] Charity Com. files.
[36] Return of Schools, 1893, 540–1.
[37] Charity Com. files.
[38] See plate facing p. 53.
[39] White, Dir. Staffs. (1834; 1851); S.R.O., D. 260/M, box x, bdles. a–f; ibid. box. v, 6 bdles. By 1818 a Mrs. Walhouse was supporting and educating about 100 children in a Sunday school: Digest on Educ. of Poor, 1818, ii. 856–7.

by her will proved in 1843, her daughter Clara left £1,000 by will proved in 1859, and Caroline Walhouse gave another £1,000 by will proved in 1876.[40] A National school by 1851,[41] by 1854 the school was receiving an annual parliamentary grant, had certificated teachers, and included an industrial department mainly for the part-time education of boys employed in the brick-yards.[42] This department continued until at least 1860.[43] Attendances averaged 86 in 1866[44] and 171 in 1893.[45] The school was enlarged in 1898, the average attendances c. 1900 being 130 boys and 80 girls, under a master and mistress.[46] Additional classrooms were built on the opposite side of the road in 1950.[47] The old school house is now occupied by the caretaker, with Cannock Walhouse Church of England Voluntary Primary School for Boys to the south of it, and Cannock Walhouse Church of England Voluntary Primary School for Girls to the north, both schools sharing the 1950 buildings.[48]

The symmetrical stucco front has a two-story teacher's house as its central feature, dating from 1828. The classrooms, also built in 1828, lie in single-story flanking wings with gable-ends facing the road. Each gable has a pointed Gothic window and a circular window above.[49] The name of the school and the date are inscribed in contemporary lettering.

A school-church and a teacher's house were built in Bridgtown in 1874, on land given to the vicar and churchwardens of Cannock by Miss Crockett, for the poorer children of the parish.[50] The attendance in 1874 was about 90 children.[51] This National school was said in 1880 to be self-supporting, apart from a yearly grant of coal from the West Cannock Colliery Company.[52] By 1891 the school was in receipt of a parliamentary grant, the average attendance in 1892 to 1893 being 131 girls and infants.[53] It became a controlled school in 1951[54] and is known as Cannock, Bridgtown Church of England Voluntary Primary Controlled School for Girls and Infants. The school stands in Church Street, Bridgtown, to the south-east of St. Paul's Church.

A Church of England day-school was started at

Chadsmoor, Cannock, in 1874 in the nave of the church.[55] Attendance in that year averaged 110 girls and boys.[56] By 1880 it had become a National school and was said to be self-supporting, except for a yearly grant of coal from the West Cannock Colliery Company,[57] but by 1891 the boys' department was in receipt of a parliamentary grant,[58] the boys' average attendance then being 234.[59] The girls were transferred to Chadsmoor Board school opened in 1887 and the infants to Chadsmoor Infants' school opened in 1886.[60] The original building, in which the boys were accommodated, was replaced in 1934 by the present wooden building.[61] In 1951 this school became controlled,[62] and it is now Cannock Chadsmoor Church of England Voluntary Primary Controlled School for Junior Boys. It lies at the corner of Cannock Road and Church Street.

There was a church school in Hednesford by 1864.[63] A large classroom was added in 1883.[64] In 1888 it was a mixed National school under a master, and was then enlarged and again in 1892, when an infants' department was opened.[65] The average attendance was 350 children in 1900[66] and in 1912 345.[67] The school became controlled in 1954[68] and is now Cannock, Hednesford Church of England Voluntary Primary Controlled School, Junior Mixed and Infants. It stands beside St. Peter's Church, Church Hill.

The school-church at Hazel Slade was built in 1884 on a site given by the Marquess of Anglesey, for use as a day school as well as a church.[69] By 1892 it was receiving a parliamentary grant as an Infants' school, and the average attendance was 132.[70] It was still an Infants' school in 1900,[71] but by 1912 it was Mixed and Infants', with an average attendance of 110.[72] The older children were transferred c. 1920 to Rawnsley School.[73] In 1922 there were 99 on the roll,[74] and in 1924 the school was taken over by the Local Education Authority.[75] A new school was built at Hazel Slade in 1936[76] and was enlarged in 1948 by the addition of a wooden building formerly part of the Rawnsley school which was by then closed, its pupils being transferred to Hazel Slade.[77] This school is now Cannock, Hazel Slade County

[40] Charity Com. files. The £800 bequeathed by Mrs. Walhouse was the residue of £2,000, £1,200 of which had been advanced by her son, later the 1st Lord Hatherton, for the founding of the school. This fact invalidated the will, but the 1st and 2nd Lords Hatherton allowed the payment of the bequest. The 3rd Lord Hatherton seems to have transferred the money to Huntington school soon after his succession in 1888: ibid.
[41] White, Dir. Staffs. (1851).
[42] Mins. of Educ. Cttee. of Council, 1854 [1926], H.C. (1854–5), xlii; ibid. 1855 [2058], pp. 377, 380, H.C. (1856), xlvii; ibid. 1856 [2237], H.C. (1857 sess. 2), xxxiii.
[43] Rep. of Educ. Cttee. of Council, 1861 [2828], H.C. (1861), xlix.
[44] Ibid. 1866 [3882], H.C. (1867), xxii.
[45] Return of Schools, 1893 [C. 7529], pp. 540–1, H.C. (1894), lxv.
[46] Kelly's Dir. Staffs. (1900).
[47] Staffs. Educ. Cttee. Mins. 5 Feb. 1949, 21 Oct. 1950, and local inf.
[48] Ex inf. the headmistress (1956).
[49] See plate facing p. 53.
[50] Lich. Dioc. Ch. Cal. (1875), 73; Lich. Dioc. Mag. Aug. 1880, 11; P.O. Dir. Staffs. (1876); Cannock Parish Chest, document dated 2 Apr. 1878.
[51] S.R.O., D. 260/M, box v, bdle. c.
[52] Lich. Dioc. Mag. Aug. 1880, 11.
[53] Return of Schools, 1893, 540–1.
[54] Staffs. Educ. Cttee. Mins. July 1951.

[55] Lich. Dioc. Ch. Cal. (1875), 73; Lich. Dioc. Mag. Aug. 1880, 11; Kelly's Dir. Staffs. (1884).
[56] S.R.O., D. 260/M, box v, bdle. c.
[57] Lich. Dioc. Mag. Aug. 1880.
[58] Return of Schools, 1893, 540–1.
[59] Ibid. In 1894 there was a proposal to close the school, which was then £266 in debt: Lich. Dioc. Mag. (1894), 205.
[60] Ex inf. Staffs. C.C. Educ. Dept.
[61] Ibid.
[62] Staffs. Educ. Cttee. Mins. July 1951.
[63] Lich. Dioc. Regy., Bp.'s Reg. xxxii, p. 210.
[64] Lich. Dioc. Ch. Cal. (1884), 71.
[65] Ibid. (1891), 157; Kelly's Dir. Staffs. (1900).
[66] Kelly's Dir. Staffs. (1900).
[67] Ibid. (1912).
[68] Staffs. Educ. Cttee. Mins. Nov. 1954. It was then described as Hednesford St. Peter's C. of E. School.
[69] Lich. Dioc. Ch. Cal. (1884), 71; Staffs. Educ. Cttee. Rep. 30 Dec. 1922; Kelly's Dir. Staffs. (1892).
[70] Return of Schools, 1893, 548–9.
[71] Kelly's Dir. Staffs. (1900).
[72] Ibid. (1912).
[73] Staffs. Educ. Cttee. Rep. 30 Dec. 1922.
[74] Staffs. Educ. Cttee. Mins. 1 Jan. 1924.
[75] Local inf.
[76] Local inf.
[77] Local inf.

Primary School, Junior Mixed and Infants. It stands at the junction of the Brereton and Cannock Wood roads.

An Infants' school, with about 68 children on the books, was opened in 1890 in the school–church in Glover Street, Wimblebury, built in 1889.[78] It had become a mixed school by 1900, under a mistress, with average attendances then of 90[79] and in 1912 of 100.[80] The school was closed in 1940.[81]

A Roman Catholic school–chapel dedicated to St. Mary, built in Cannock in 1878,[82] had about 80 pupils in 1884.[83] It was in receipt of a parliamentary grant by 1891, and the average attendance in 1891 was 122 girls and boys.[84] The school was enlarged in 1897,[85] and after the establishment of the Convent of the Holy Rosary in 1898 the teachers were sometimes nuns,[86] Sister Mary Berchman being headmistress in 1900.[87] In 1949 it became aided and is now Cannock St. Mary's Roman Catholic Voluntary Primary School, Mixed and Infants, although in 1956 it still took children of all ages. It lies next to the Convent of the Holy Rosary, off St. John's Road, Cannock.[88]

The Roman Catholic school built at Hill Top, Hednesford, in 1898 and enlarged in 1899 had a lay mistress, assisted by the Sisters of the Convent of the Holy Rosary, Cannock, who subsequently took over the management.[89] In 1900 the average attendance was 183.[90] From 1920 to 1954 the school was run by the Sisters of the Convent of Our Lady of Lourdes, Hednesford, and since their return to Cannock, by Sisters of the Convent of the Holy Rosary.[91] In 1954 this became an aided school[92] and is now Cannock, St. Joseph's Voluntary Primary School, Mixed and Infants, although in 1956 it still took children of all ages,[93] the average attendance then being 214.[94]

A Methodist New Connexion school existed in Bridgtown, Cannock, by 1868, under a master,[95] and remained until at least 1872 when it was under a mistress.[96]

There was a Primitive Methodist school at Hednesford under a mistress, between at least 1868[97] and 1876.[98]

In 1866 a school named Cannock Chase Colliery School was in receipt of a government grant and was attended by 140 children[99] and in 1884 by 355 children.[1]

Cannock School Board was formed in 1874.[2] In 1878 a Board school was built in Walsall Road, Cannock, for boys and girls and infants, and was enlarged in 1887 and 1899, the average attendance in 1900 being 261 boys, 175 girls, and 170 infants, each department having its own head teacher.[3] This was still a Mixed and Infants' school in 1924[4] but by 1951 had been divided as Cannock, Walsall Road County Primary School for Boys and Cannock, Walsall Road County Primary School for Girls and Infants.[5]

Chadsmoor Board school for infants, to which infants from Chadsmoor Church of England school were transferred,[6] was built in 1886, the average attendance in 1900 being 363,[7] and in 1912 340.[8] This is now Cannock, Chadsmoor County Primary School for Infants, under a mistress. It stands at the corner of Cannock Road and Cecil Street.

Chadsmoor Board school for girls, to which the girls from Chadsmoor Church of England school were transferred, was built c. 1887,[9] the average attendance being 230 in 1900[10] and 340 in 1912.[11] It is now Cannock, Chadsmoor County Primary School for Junior Girls. It is housed, with the Infants' school, in buildings at the corner of Cannock Road and Cecil Street.

A Board school was built at Five Ways, Hednesford (in what is now Heath Hayes Road), in 1875 to hold 140 boys, 120 girls, and 120 infants,[12] and was in receipt of a parliamentary grant by 1882.[13] It was enlarged in 1884 for 220 boys, 200 girls, and 120 infants, the average attendances in 1892 being 219, 180, and 85 respectively.[14] It was again enlarged in 1895 for 280 boys, 240 girls, and 200 infants, the average attendances in 1900 being 250 boys, 200 girls, and 164 infants.[15] By 1912 the school was named Heath Hayes, and the average attendances were 259, 280, and 250 respectively, each department under its own head teacher.[16] In 1953 the Boys' and Girls' schools were closed because of mining subsidence[17] and in 1956 were being demolished. The Infants' school, known as Cannock, Heath Hayes County Primary School for Infants, and the caretaker's house were still in use. The boys' and girls' departments which were housed from 1953 in St. John's Church Hall, Hednesford Road, were transferred in 1956 to a new single-story prefabricated aluminium building, also in Hednesford Road.[18] They form the Cannock, Heath Hayes County Primary School for Junior Girls and Boys.

[78] Lich. Dioc. Mag. (1889), 167; Lich. Dioc. Ch. Cal. (1891), 157.
[79] Kelly's Dir. Staffs. (1900) under Hednesford.
[80] Ibid. (1912).
[81] Ex inf. Staffs. C.C. Educ. Dept.
[82] Kelly's Dir. Staffs. (1892).
[83] Ibid. (1884).
[84] Return of Schools, 1893, 540–1.
[85] Kelly's Dir. Staffs. (1912).
[86] Ex inf. the parish priest (1956).
[87] Kelly's Dir. Staffs. (1900). The headmistresses in 1884, 1892, 1896 were not nuns: ibid. (1884, 1892, 1896).
[88] Staffs. Educ. Cttee. Mins. Nov. 1949; ex inf. the parish priest, Cannock (1956).
[89] Kelly's Dir. Staffs. (1900; 1912).
[90] Ibid. (1900).
[91] Ex inf. the parish priest, Hednesford (1956).
[92] Staffs. Educ. Cttee. Mins. July, 1954.
[93] Ex inf. the parish priest, Cannock.
[94] Ex inf. the parish priest, Hednesford.
[95] P.O. Dir. Staffs. (1868).
[96] Ibid. (1872).
[97] Ibid. (1868).

[98] Ibid. (1876).
[99] Rep. of Educ. Cttee. of Council, 1866 [3882], H.C. (1867), xxii.
[1] Rep. of Educ. Cttee. of Council, 1884 [C. 4483–I], H.C. (1884–5), xxiii.
[2] Lond. Gaz. 1874, p. 2146.
[3] Kelly's Dir. Staffs. (1880; 1900).
[4] Ibid. (1924).
[5] Staffs. Educ. Cttee. List of Schools, 1951, corrected to 1955.
[6] Ex inf. Staffs. C.C. Educ. Dept.
[7] Kelly's Dir. Staffs. (1900).
[8] Ibid. (1912).
[9] Ex inf. Staffs. C.C. Educ. Dept.
[10] Kelly's Dir. Staffs. (1900).
[11] Ibid. (1912).
[12] Ibid. (1884), under Hednesford.
[13] Rep. of Educ. Cttee. of Council, 1882 [C. 3706–I], H.C. (1883), xxv.
[14] Kelly's Dir. Staffs. (1892).
[15] Ibid. (1900).
[16] Ibid. (1912), under Cannock.
[17] Local inf.   [18] Local inf

Board schools were built at West Hill, Hednesford, in 1876 for 350 boys, 226 girls, and 150 infants, each department with its own head teacher.[19] They were in receipt of a parliamentary grant by 1882.[20] The average attendances were 320, 220, and 150 respectively in 1884[21] and 336, 289, and 173 in 1912.[22] What is now the Cannock, West Hill County Primary School for Junior Boys is housed in a building enlarged in 1881.[23] The building housing Cannock, West Hill County Primary School for Junior Girls is dated 1883.[24] In 1956 Cannock, West Hill County Primary School for Infants was housed in a wooden building.

A mixed Board school opened at Rawnsley, in Cannock Wood Road, in 1877 for 200 children[25] and enlarged in 1895 for 251 children, had an average attendance in 1912 of 238.[26] The building was again enlarged in 1903.[27] In 1924 it was said to be overcrowded,[28] and the children were transferred to Hazel Slade County Primary School, Junior Mixed and Infants (see above). The Local Education Authority acquired the freehold of this old Rawnsley Council School building[29] which in 1956 was being demolished,[30] although the schoolmaster's house was still occupied.

A public elementary school for 300 children was built at Bridgtown, Cannock, in 1927.[31] This later formed two schools, Cannock Bridgtown County Primary School for Girls and Infants and Cannock Bridgtown County Primary School for Boys.[32]

Cannock, West Chadsmoor County Primary School, Junior Mixed and Infants was opened in 1932.[33] There were 554 names on the roll in January 1956.[34] The infants were transferred to a new school in 1956.[35] This building, designed by Wood, Kendrick & Williams of Birmingham,[36] is faced with aluminium and is a good example of contemporary school architecture.

Cannock, Station Road County Primary School for Infants was built in 1903 for 212 children, average attendance in 1912 being 164.[37]

Nurseries, originally built as day nurseries during the Second World War, at Cannock (Hall Court Crescent), Chadsmoor, and Hednesford were taken over as education nurseries in 1955–6.[38]

CHARITIES FOR THE POOR. William Alport of Great Wyrley, by deed of 1567, gave a rent of 10s. charged on Coal Pit (or Coldpit) Field there to be distributed equally among fifteen poor and infirm of Cannock and fifteen of Great Wyrley on Good

Friday.[39] By 1823 the 5s. due to Cannock was distributed with the following six charities on 1 January in doles varying between 2s. and 10s.,[40] and by 1956 the charity formed part of the general distribution to the poor on St. Luke's Day (18 October).[41]

Henry Smythe, by deed dated 1614, gave an annuity of £5 from lands in Cannock to provide 2s. worth of bread each Sunday for 24 poor of the parish, but by 1823 the money was used to give twelve poor, mainly widows regularly attending church, two penny loaves each.[42] The £5 was still paid in 1956 when it formed part of the general distribution.[43]

William Goldsmith, by will dated 1703, gave a rent of 40s. charged on land in Great Wyrley to be distributed among 20 poor of Cannock and 20 of Great Wyrley on St. Thomas's Day (21 December).[44] By 1823 the 20s. due to Cannock had been added to the general distribution on 1 January,[45] and in 1956 the money formed part of the general distribution.[46]

At some time before 1720 John Troming (or Trumwyn) left land in Cannock out of the profits of which 6s. 8d. was to be paid to the incumbent for a sermon on 1 January and the rest distributed after the sermon to such poor of Cannock, Hednesford, and Leacroft as attended divine service regularly.[47] The rent seems to have been £1 11s. 8d. by 1786,[48] but c. 1822 the land was let for £10 10s.[49] By 1823 the income was added to the distribution on 1 January, except for the 6s. 8d. still paid to the incumbent.[50] The rent from part of the land ceased to be paid from 1856, and in 1876 permission was given for the sale of this part for £153 15s.[51] In 1955 or early 1956 further land was sold for £387 17s. 1d.,[52] and the total income from the charity in 1956 was £29 2s. 4d. which formed part of the distribution on 18 October.[53] By 1720 three pews in the new gallery in the church had been bought with the proceeds from a sale of timber off the land with a view to letting them and adding the rents to the distribution, but by 1823 they were occupied by poor from the workhouse.[54]

Elizabeth Pinson at some date before 1786 gave £10, the income to be distributed in bread to the poor of the parish each Good Friday.[55] The interest was 10s. in 1786,[56] but before 1823 the charity had been lost through the bankruptcy of the trustee.[57] It was subsequently recovered, and by 1929 was yielding 11s.[58] which in 1956 formed part of the distribution on 18 October.[59]

John Perrot of Cannock (d. c. 1807) left £20 for

[19] Kelly's Dir. Staffs. (1884).
[20] Rep. of Educ. Cttee. of Council, 1882 [C. 3706–I], H.C. (1883), xxv.
[21] Kelly's Dir. Staffs. (1884).
[22] Ibid. (1912).
[23] Tablet in situ.
[24] Tablet in situ.
[25] Kelly's Dir. Staffs. (1892); tablet in situ.
[26] Kelly's Dir. Staffs. (1912).
[27] Tablet in situ.
[28] Staffs. Educ. Cttee. Mins. Oct. 1924.
[29] Ibid. June 1948.
[30] Local inf.
[31] Staffs. Educ. Cttee. Mins. Feb. 1927.
[32] Staffs. Educ. Cttee. List of Schools, 1951, corrected to 1955.
[33] Ex inf. Staffs. C.C. Educ. Dept.
[34] Ibid.   [35] Ibid.   [36] Ibid.
[37] Kelly's Dir. Staffs. (1912).
[38] Ex inf. Staffs. C.C. Educ. Dept.
[39] 11th Rep. Com. Char. H.C. 436, p. 511 (1824), xiv.

[40] Ibid. 513–14.
[41] Ex inf. Mr. F. Linford, churchwarden (1956).
[42] 11th Rep. Com. Char. 514.
[43] Ex inf. Mr. Linford.
[44] 11th Rep. Com. Char. 511–12.
[45] Ibid. 513–14.
[46] Ex inf. Mr. Linford.
[47] 11th Rep. Com. Char. 512.
[48] Abstract of Returns of Charitable Donations, 1786–8, H.C. 511, pp. 1118–19 (1816), xvi (2).
[49] 11th Rep. Com. Char. 512.
[50] Ibid. 512, 513–14.
[51] Char. Com. files.
[52] Ibid.
[53] Ex inf. Mr. Linford.
[54] 11th Rep. Com. Char. 512.
[55] Ibid. 516.
[56] Abstract, 1786–8, ii. 1118–19.
[57] 11th Rep. Com. Char. 516.
[58] Char. Com. files.
[59] Ex inf. Mr. Linford.

the poor which with the proceeds of a sale of timber c. 1812 from Troming's land was placed in the funds.[60] The income from Perrot's Charity was 9s. in 1956 when it formed part of the general distribution.[61]

Sarah Knight of Cannock, by will proved in 1834, left a sum to be invested to produce £5 a year for distribution to the poor of the parish.[62] By 1873 the capital had been invested in £166 3s. 4d. stock and was producing £5 in 1886.[63] The interest, £4 3s. 4d. from at least 1929, formed part of the general distribution by 1956.[64]

John Wilson and his son William in 1623 gave a rent of 10s. charged on land in Great Wyrley for distribution on Christmas Day among ten of the poorest from Cannock and ten from Great Wyrley.[65] By 1823 the charity was added to the distribution on 1 January,[66] but it was decided c. 1887 not to enforce payment of the 5s. due to Cannock, collection of which had ceased some years before.[67]

Mary Chapman (d. by 1725) in her will directed the sale of some of her lands in Cannock and the distribution of the proceeds among the most needy poor of Cannock on Christmas Day.[68] Her executors seem to have applied the proceeds to securing a rent-charge of 40s. on the land, 16s. of which was then used for distribution among the poor of the town on Christmas Day and 24s. for sending two poor boys and two poor girls to school to learn English and the Catechism.[69] By 1823 the master of

the free school was refusing to educate more than two boys for 24s., and all or part of the sum was being added to the 16s. and the whole distributed with the other charities on 1 January.[70] The charity was still paid in 1886[71] but seems to have lapsed by 1956.[72]

Dorothy Birch, by will dated 1747, gave £40, the interest to be spent on twelve penny loaves on the first Sunday of the month for twelve of the poorest most regularly present at the sacrament and the remainder in a distribution on 10 August to such poor of Cannock who could not work or in sending poor children to school or in apprenticing them.[73] Until 1806 12s. a year was spent on bread, and £1 8s. was paid to the schoolmaster of Cannock for the education of three boys, but after that date payment of the interest stopped.[74]

Elizabeth Ball of Castle Bromwich (Warws.), by will proved in 1770, gave the interest on £100 to be shared among the poor of Cannock Wood and seven neighbouring townships a week before Christmas, and in 1821 14s. was divided between Cannock Wood and Gentleshaw (Offlow hundred) for the purchase of bread.[75] This charity has since lapsed.[76]

Ann Davis, widow, at some time before 1786, left a rent of 5s. charged on lands in Norton (presumably Norton Canes, Offlow hundred), for distribution to the poor of Leacroft on Christmas Day,[77] and this was still paid in 1886.[78] It had lapsed by 1956.[79]

HUNTINGTON

HUNTINGTON, a civil parish within Cannock Rural District and formerly a township and constablewick within the ancient parish of Cannock, lies on either side of the Stafford–Walsall road to the north of the town of Cannock. The ground slopes from over 700 ft. on Cannock Chase in the north-east to some 400 ft. in the south-west, while Shoal Hill in the south rises to 656 ft. Much of the land is now agricultural or held by the Forestry Commission, but the chief occupation is mining. There were 46 households within the constablewick in 1666,[1] and the population was 114 in 1801, 195 in 1891, 351 in 1901,[2] 922 in 1921,[3] and 1,816 in 1931,[4] the sharp increase being due to the development of the Littleton Colliery here after 1897.[5] By 1951 the population had fallen to 1,587.[6] The area is 1,303 acres.[7]

Huntington Farm dates from the 18th century, and a few cottages at the north end of Huntington were part of the original hamlet. Most of the terrace

houses, in pairs and groups of four, date from the rapid expansion of the mining village in the early 20th century. The pumping station of the South Staffordshire Waterworks, dating from between 1876[8] and 1880,[9] is an impressive tall red-brick building with detail similar to that used on the former Local Board Offices in Cannock.[10] At the north end of the built-up area there are two police-houses and a post-1945 council housing estate. The pit-head baths were built between 1939 and 1941.[11]

MANOR. The 'Estendone' where Richard the forester held 1 hide of waste in 1086[12] may possibly be identified with HUNTINGTON where by 1198 Henry de Brok, lord of Pillaton (in Penkridge), was holding a carucate of land of the king by some service in the forest of Cannock and a rent of 2 marks.[13] It is possible that Henry's predecessors in Huntington were Alfred de Huntedon and Alfred's

60 11th Rep. Com. Char. 512–13, 513–14.
61 Ex inf. Mr. Linford.
62 Char. Com. files.
63 Ibid.
64 Ex inf. Mr. Linford.
65 11th Rep. Com. Char. 511.
66 Ibid. 513–14.
67 Char. Com. files.
68 11th Rep. Com. Char. 513.
69 Ibid.
70 Ibid. 513–14.
71 Char. Com. files.
72 Ex inf. Mr. Linford.
73 11th Rep. Com. Char. 515.
74 Ibid. 515–16.
75 7th Rep. Com. Char. H.C. 129, pp. 353, 354, 355 (1822), x.
76 Ex inf. Mr. Linford.

77 11th Rep. Com. Char. 514.
78 Char. Com. files.
79 Ex inf. Mr. Linford.
1 S.H.C. 1927, 18–19.
2 V.C.H. Staffs. i. 320.
3 Kelly's Dir. Staffs. (1924).
4 Census, 1951, Staffs.
5 See p. 62.
6 Census, 1951, Staffs.
7 Ibid.
8 Pipes were being laid at this date: P.O. Dir. Staffs. (1876).
9 The station had been built by 1880: Kelly's Dir. Staffs. (1880).
10 See p. 53.
11 Ex inf. the National Coal Board, Cannock.
12 V.C.H. Staffs. iv. 56, no. 273.
13 S.H.C. 1923, 24–31; Bk. of Fees, 7.

brother Brun, father-in-law to Henry, both of whom had held Pillaton before Henry succeeded to it.[14] Henry was still living in 1205[15] but seems to have been succeeded by his son Robert by 1214.[16] In 1236 Robert de Brok was holding the vill of Huntington of Bishop Alexander Stavensby;[17] but by 1250 the king had regained the overlordship since in that year Robert's son and heir Robert was fined for the alienation during his father's lifetime of part of the land in Huntington held by the service of keeping the hay of Teddesley.[18] The alienation was confirmed, Robert continuing to pay the fine annually and performing the service for the remaining land.[19] Robert de Brok was still living in 1254,[20] but was dead by 1264,[21] when his kinsman, Walter de Elmedon, did homage for the bailiwick of Teddesley.[22] In 1272 he was holding the vill of Huntington by the service of keeping this bailiwick.[23] In 1294 Walter's brother,[24] Stephen de Elmedon, successfully sued him for a messuage and a virgate of land in Huntington with other lands and rent there,[25] and in 1300 Stephen was holding the vill of the king.[26] At his death in 1302 his lands in Huntington passed with the serjeanty to his son William,[27] who died at some time after 1342 and was succeeded by his son William de 'Pylatenhale'.[28] This younger William died in 1349,[29] and the issues of Huntington and the bailiwick of Teddesley Hay were held until 1363 by Sir Hugh de Wrottesley,[30] to whom they had been granted during the minority of the heirs by the king in 1349.[31] One coheir, John, son of William's sister Margaret, of full age and more in 1363, then succeeded to a moiety of Huntington, but William, son of the other sister Joan, was then aged only fifteen,[32] and Hugh de Wrottesley still had an interest in Huntington in 1366.[33] William succeeded to his half share in 1370[34] and held the whole from 1382 after the death of his cousin John.[35] Huntington then descended with Pillaton,[36] some 25 acres here being sold by the 3rd Lord Hatherton in 1920 and a further 152 acres by the 5th Lord Hatherton in 1947.[37]

The tenement was described as a messuage and a 'carucate' of land in 1363[38] and 1370.[39] By 1502 the messuage was in ruins and worth nothing, while the 'virgate' was assessed at 6s. 8d.,[40] a valuation which was given again in 1529[41] and also in 1559 when the virgate was called 'Romeshurst'.[42] Huntington was described as a manor in 1573.[43]

Courts were held at Huntington by 1285.[44] Huntington was within the leet of Cannock by 1341, being represented by two frankpledges,[45] and it was paying 6d. in frithsilver to the lord of Cannock in at least 1740, 1762, and 1764.[46] It was still within the leet in 1805.[47] The free tenants of Sir Edward Littleton in Huntington were paying the lord of Cannock 6d. on each messuage for common in 'Cannock woods' by 1595.[48]

Attached to the vill of Huntington, itself still within the Teddesley Hay division of Cannock Forest in 1300,[49] was woodland which was formerly part of the royal forest of Cannock and for which Robert de Brok in 1262 paid a fine of ½ mark to the forest justices.[50] Robert's successor Walter de Elmedon paid a similar fine in 1271[51] and 1286.[52] Four inclosures made by Walter's tenants at Huntington and presented by the reguardors of Cannock Forest in 1286 were of 2 acres, 1 acre, ½ acre, and 1 acre, each being surrounded by a ditch and a 'dead' hedge.[53]

There were two common fields in Huntington in 1654, Pitch Field and Lightwood Field, and possibly a third, Birchin Field.[54] These had been inclosed by 1754.[55]

The inhabitants of Huntington still enjoyed common rights in Teddesley Hay in 1718.[56] They paid 11s. rent for other common rights to the lord of Cannock in 1740[57] and 10s. 6d. in 1778.[58] Huntington Common and Huntington Heath were inclosed in 1827 under an Act of 1814.[59]

CHURCH. The site of a former chapel exists west of Huntington Farm[60] but has been obliterated by colliery workings. The chapel may have been the

[14] S.H.C. 1928, 164; ibid. viii (1), 152; ibid. v (1), 42.
[15] Ibid. ii (1), 127.
[16] Rot. Fin. (Rec. Com.), 543–4.
[17] Bk. of Fees, 594.
[18] Bk. of Fees, 1185–6, 1245–6; S.H.C. 1911, 407, giving the date as 1247.
[19] Bk. of Fees, 1246; S.H.C. iv (1), 209.
[20] Rot. Hund. (Rec. Com.), ii. 115.
[21] Cal. Inq. p.m. (Rec. Com.), i, p. 26.
[22] Ex. e Rot. Fin. (Rec. Com.), ii. 409.
[23] S.H.C. iv (1), 209.
[24] Ibid. 1938, 243.
[25] Ibid. vii (1), 9.
[26] Ibid. v (1), 177.
[27] Cal. Inq. p.m. iv, no. 71; S.H.C. 1911, 271–2; Cal. Fine R. 1272–1307, 453.
[28] S.H.C. 1928, 151–2; Cat. Anct. D. ii, C 2524; Cal. Inq. p.m. xi, no. 468.
[29] Cal. Inq. p.m. xi, no. 468.
[30] Ibid.
[31] Cal. Pat. 1348–50, 396. A similar grant made by the king in 1354 to his yeoman, John de Swynnerton, seems to have been ineffective: ibid. 1354–8, 35; S.H.C. xiii. 4.
[32] Cal. Inq. p.m. xi, no. 468.
[33] S.H.C. xiii. 56–57.
[34] Cal. Close, 1369–74, 137; S.H.C. xiii. 149–50.
[35] Cal. Fine R. 1377–83, 331.
[36] C 136/93; C 139/137; C 140/45; C 142/320, no. 71; C.P. 25(2)/596, 1654 Trin.; C.P. 43/506, rot. 98; White, Dir. Staffs. (1851); see p. 119.
[37] Ex inf. the Teddesley and Hatherton Estate Office.
[38] Cal. Inq. p.m. xi, no. 468.

[39] Cal. Close, 1369–74, 137.
[40] Cal. Inq. p.m. Hen. VII, ii, no. 537.
[41] C 142/50, no. 67.
[42] C 142/124, no. 78.
[43] C.P. 25(2)/260, 15 Eliz. I East.
[44] S.R.O., D. 260/M/box 19, bdle. a, Huntington Ct. Papers. The series is very incomplete, papers surviving for 13 Edw. I, 14 and 39 Edw. III, 7 Hen. VI (rental), 13 and 17 Edw. IV; rather more have survived from the reign of Henry VII to that of Charles I inclusive, and the series finishes with 2 papers for 1708 and 1765. There are also records of courts held in 1518 and 1520 in box 5, bdle. a.
[45] W.S.L., D. 1734, Ct. R. of Cannock and Rugeley 1309–73, 1463–83, 1510–46, 1546–53.
[46] W.S.L., Paget Papers (Gardner Coll.), 9 (5), 35 (1).
[47] W.S.L. 112/25/41, perambulation of the manor of Cannock, 1805.
[48] F. W. Hackwood, Chronicles of Cannock Chase, 76.
[49] S.H.C. v (1), 177.
[50] Ibid. 137.
[51] Ibid. 154.
[52] Ibid. 175.
[53] Ibid. 169, 170.
[54] S.R.O., D. 260/M/box 3, bdle. e, deed of Mar. 1653/4.
[55] S.R.O., D. 260/M/E. 353 (a, b), map 2.
[56] W.S.L., D. 1790/A/12/26.
[57] W.S.L., Paget Papers (Gardner Coll.), 9 (5).
[58] Ibid. 9 (15A).
[59] Penkridge Inclosure Act, 54 Geo. III, c. 50 (priv. act); S.R.O., Q/RDc 22; White, Dir. Staffs. (1834).
[60] O.S. Map. 1/25,000, 33/91 (1952).

View from Littleton Colliery, Huntington, looking south-west towards Watling Street

Opencast mining site at Churchbridge, 1957

CANNOCK

View north-eastwards over Cannock from Lodge Hill, Cheslyn Hay

Workmen's dwellings at Wedges Mill, built *c.* 1795

chapel of St. Margaret within Cannock parish mentioned in 1548.[61]

Licence was given in 1871 for the holding of divine service in the schoolroom at Huntington.[62] The church of *ST. THOMAS*, built in 1872 and enlarged in 1879,[63] consists of an aisled nave, chancel, and transepts. The walls are of stone rubble with blue-brick dressings, and the windows of the transepts and chancel have plate tracery. It is within the parish of St. Luke, Cannock, and held by a curate-in-charge.[64] In 1957 the plate consisted of a silver chalice and paten.[65]

NONCONFORMITY. In 1818 the house of Mrs. Wright in Huntington was registered as a meeting-house for Protestant dissenters.[66] A small Wesleyan chapel was built there in 1847.[67] The building was not used exclusively as a chapel in 1851,[68] and the meetings probably lapsed soon afterwards.[69]

A Primitive Methodist chapel was erected at Huntington in 1925 and in 1940 seated 218.[70] It is built of red brick and lies in Stafford Road.

PRIMARY SCHOOLS. In 1871 a Church of England day school, founded at the expense of Lord Hatherton, was opened in the school-church erected by him at Huntington in that year and enlarged in 1879.[71] The attendance in 1874 had averaged 40 boys and girls[72] and c. 1892 was 60 children, under a mistress.[73] A separate school building opposite the church was erected by the 3rd Lord Hatherton in 1898.[74] By 1916 this building was overcrowded, with 96 children in the schoolroom, 33 in the classroom, and 40 in the infants' room, and Lord Hatherton agreed to extend it.[75] In 1919 he decided that he could not carry out the enlargement[76] but in 1925 and 1926 added two classrooms each for 40 children.[77] Meanwhile a public elementary school was opened in 1921 on a site north of the church bought from Lord Hatherton,[78] and this building also was enlarged in 1926.[79]

In 1928 because of overcrowding at both schools it was proposed to rent the Church Institute as a schoolroom.[80] By this date the public elementary school had been confined to infants.[81] In 1931 attendance at the church school was 260 and at the council infants' school, 188.[82] In 1934 the church school was transferred to the Local Education Authority and amalgamated with the Infants' school.[83] Under the 1944 Education Act the buildings of the former church school are used for a County Secondary Modern school, and the Junior and Infants' school, now known as Huntington County Primary School, Junior Mixed and Infants, is housed in the public elementary school buildings next to the church.

The 1898 block used by the present Secondary Modern school is a white stucco building with leaded windows and stone dressings and has flanking wings in the same style, added in 1925 and 1926.

CHARITIES FOR THE POOR. At some time before 1786 Hugh Gratley left £5, the interest whereon (5s.) was to be distributed to the poor of Huntington. By 1823 the 5s. was issuing from land in Huntington formerly belonging to Gratley.[84] John Staley by will dated 1690 gave £20, and his mother Ann Staley added another £10, the whole being laid out in that year in land in Huntington to produce a rent of 20s. which was to be distributed to the poor of the township.[85] Frances Stubbs by will of unknown date gave £10 which by 1786 was producing interest of 8s. but by 1824 seems to have been laid out in a meadow in Huntington called Widows Meadow charged with a rent of 8s.[86] An unknown donor at some time before 1786 gave a rent charge of 20s. from land in Hatherton.[87] By 1823 all these four charities were distributed at Christmas to poor widows of Huntington and other poor there with large families, in sums of 7s. or under, the largest doles going to those who tried to avoid becoming a charge on the parish.[88] The total income was still £2 13s. in 1949,[89] but the charities seem to have lapsed by 1956.[90]

GREAT WYRLEY

THE civil parish of Great Wyrley, formerly a township and constablewick within the ancient parish of Cannock, lies mainly south of Watling Street except where the Wash Brook, the joint boundary of Cannock and Great Wyrley, crosses and recrosses the road for about a mile. It includes the district of Churchbridge which takes its name from the bridge carrying Watling Street over the Wash Brook, a county responsibility by 1830 when it was described as new.[1] The boundary with Cheslyn Hay on the north-west was readjusted under the Staffordshire Review Order of 1934. Little Wyrley (in the parish of Norton Canes, Offlow hundred), lies to the east, and Essington and Hilton (in St. Peter's,

[61] See p. 64.
[62] Lich. Dioc. Regy., Bp.'s Reg. xxxiii, p. 187.
[63] *Kelly's Dir. Staffs.* (1940).
[64] *Lich. Dioc. Dir.* (1955–6).
[65] Ex inf. the curate-in-charge, Huntington (1957).
[66] Lich. Dioc. Regy., Bp.'s Reg. Bk. F, p. 511.
[67] White, *Dir. Staffs.* (1851).
[68] H.O. 129/15/378.
[69] It is not mentioned in *P.O. Dir. Staffs.* (1854; 1860).
[70] *Meth. Church Buildings, 1940* (1946).
[71] *Lich. Dioc. Ch. Cal.* (1872), 89; *Lich. Dioc. Mag.* Aug. 1880, pp. 10–11; *Kelly's Dir. Staffs.* (1884).
[72] S.R.O., D. 260/M/box v, bdle. c.
[73] *Kelly's Dir. Staffs.* (1892).
[74] Ex inf. Staffs. C.C. Educ. Dept.
[75] Staffs. Educ. Cttee. Mins. Mar. 1916.
[76] Ibid. Oct. 1919.
[77] Ibid. Jan. 1925, Apr. 1926.
[78] Ibid. Sept. 1921.

[79] Ibid. Apr. 1926.
[80] Ibid. 1928.
[81] Ibid.
[82] Ibid. Apr. 1931.
[83] Ibid. Sept. 1934.
[84] *Abstract of Returns of Charitable Donations, 1786–8,* H.C. 511, pp. 1118–19 (1816), xvi (2); *11th Rep. Com. Char.* H.C. 436, p. 516 (1824), xiv.
[85] *11th Rep. Com. Char.* 516.
[86] Ibid. 516–17; *Abstract, 1786–8*, ii. 1118–19.
[87] *11th Rep. Com. Char.* 517; *Abstract, 1786–8*, ii. 1118–19.
[88] *11th Rep. Com. Char.* 517.
[89] Charity Com. files.
[90] Ex inf. Mr. F. Linford, churchwarden of Cannock (1956).
[1] J. Potter, *List of Bridges which the Inhabitants of the County of Stafford are bound to repair* (1830), 3.

Wolverhampton, Seisdon hundred) to the south-west. The height of the ground varies between about 400 and 500 ft. The soil is light loam,[2] but much of the surface is coarse grassland, of uneven levels, consisting of the overgrown deposits from old disused collieries. The farms lie for the most part to the north-east, along the south and east borders and in Landywood, a hamlet in the southern part of the parish. The main road between Cannock and Walsall runs north to south through the parish, and there were two toll bars here by 1832.[3] The Rugeley, Cannock, and Walsall branch of the former L. & N.W. railway has a station a little over a quarter of mile north-west from the village. A branch of the Wyrley and Essington Canal terminates in the west of the parish at some of the disused pits of the former Great Wyrley Colliery and was itself no longer in use in 1956. There were 75 households within the constablewick of Great Wyrley in 1666,[4] and the population of the township was 227 in 1801.[5] By 1811, out of 82 families living in 82 houses there, 51 were employed in agriculture and 31 in trade, manufactures, or handicrafts.[6] By 1900 there were in Great Wyrley 'a few well-built residences and farmhouses, with a number of cottages',[7] but in 1951 the civil parish had 4,287 inhabitants and covered 1,644 acres.[8]

There was a camp for Polish ex-soldiers in Landywood from 1947 to 1951, with a mass centre served by a visiting Polish chaplain.[9]

Part of Cheslyn Common belonged from time immemorial to the freeholders and copyholders of Great Wyrley.[10] In 1668 some of this area was inclosed by agreement,[11] and the rents from the land inclosed were vested in the overseers of the poor of Great Wyrley.[12] In 1797, following the Act of 1792, the open and common fields, common meadows, and waste land of Cheslyn Common were inclosed, and to defray the cost of inclosing the area belonging to Great Wyrley, described as the Wyrley Side of Cheslyn Common and the Old Falls, part of the Old Falls was sold in 1793.[13]

Coal and ironstone mines in Great Wyrley were being worked by 1642.[14] In 1809 Moreton Walhouse of Hatherton leased a coal-mine in Great Wyrley for ten years to William Gilpin[15] who by 1817 had an edge-tool factory at Churchbridge (see below). Several pits were being worked by 1817,[16] although in 1831 only 87 persons from Great Wyrley, Cheslyn Hay, Cannock Wood, and Hednesford were engaged in mining.[17] By 1860 the Wyrley New Colliery Company[18] and by 1862 the Hatherton Colliery[19] were in operation, and the Wyrley Cannock Colliery

Company, which had started before 1872, was working some seven or eight shafts before it closed down in 1882.[20] The Great Wyrley Colliery Company was in operation between at least 1872 and 1924,[21] and the South Cannock Colliery Company was working at Landywood in 1876.[22] In 1896 Messrs. W. Harrison opened a large pit known as Wyrley No. 3 which was still in use in 1956[23] when there was also open-cast mining in operation on both sides of Landywood Lane.

Some of the factory buildings now occupied by Messrs. Wm. Gilpin Senr. & Co. (Tools) Ltd. at Churchbridge were erected in 1806 by William Gilpin (d. 1835), and edge tools were being manufactured here by 1817.[24] Industrial cottages immediately to the south also date from his time. Discarded grinding stones form the foundations of a building near the bridge. A tall stack erected soon after Gilpin's death and forming a local landmark was demolished in 1933.[25] Until recently the Churchbridge works housed a steam-engine made by James Watt.[26]

There was a steam mill near the north end of Walsall Road c. 1843, owned by Thomas and Edward Hick and held by John Hall.[27]

At Moat Farm two sides of a rectangular moat are still in existence, indicating the site of a medieval house. The farmhouse is a T-shaped brick building dating from c. 1700; an outhouse carries a keystone inscribed with the name Thos. Lycett[28] and the date 1758. Wyrley Hall, about 400 yds. farther west, is a stucco building dating from the early 19th century. The almost continuous buildings on both sides of Walsall Road are largely late 19th- or 20th-century in date. At the corner of Norton Lane are some earlier buildings, one of which was formerly a smithy. An outbuilding there, probably of the 17th century, is a timber-framed structure with brick panels. White House Farm, on the opposite side of the road and in 1956 in process of demolition, is a brick building with a date stone of 1711, bearing the initials T F c. In Norton Lane and in the east of the parish generally the farm buildings are derelict.

There are several isolated buildings in the western half of the parish dating from before the 19th century. Landywood Farm incorporates two bays of a timber-framed house, probably of the 16th century. The walls are of close studding, now covered externally with brickwork and plaster. At the south gable-end a massive chimney has an original stone base. Internally there are indications of an open truss between the bays at first-floor level. This has chamfered timbers and curved braces. Later addi-

[2] Kelly's Dir. Staffs. (1940).
[3] Teesdale, Map of Staffs. (1832); Tithe Maps and Appt., Cannock (copy in W.S.L.). Greenwood, Map of Staffs. (1820), shows only one toll bar.
[4] S.H.C. 1927, 19–21.
[5] V.C.H. Staffs. i. 320.
[6] Pitt, Staffs. 263.
[7] Kelly's Dir. Staffs. (1900).
[8] Census, 1951, Staffs.
[9] Ex inf. Fr. M. Bossowski, chaplain to the Polish hostel at Little Onn, Church Eaton (1956).
[10] S.R.O., Q/RDc 10, containing copy of act.
[11] S.H.C. 1931, 73–74.
[12] S.R.O., Q/RDc 10.
[13] Act for dividing and inclosing Cheslyn Hay, 32 Geo. III, c. 55 (priv. act); S.R.O., Q/RDc 10.
[14] C 3/425, no. 119: Thos. Foley v. Thos. Green and others.
[15] S.R.O., D. 260/M/box A (i), bdle. g.
[16] Pitt, Staffs. 263.

[17] M. J. Wise, 'The Cannock Chase Region', Birmingham and its Regional Setting, 281.
[18] P.O. Dir. Staffs. (1860) sub Cannock.
[19] S.R.O., D. 260/M/E. 188.
[20] P.O. Dir. Staffs. (1872); C. M. Peel, 'Presidential Address' (Trans. Inst. Mining Engineers, cx), 322.
[21] P.O. Dir. Staffs. (1872); Kelly's Dir. Staffs. (1924).
[22] P.O. Dir. Staffs. (1876).
[23] Trans. Inst. Mining Engineers, cx. 332; ex inf. National Coal Board, Cannock.
[24] Pitt, Staffs. 448–9; Cannock Advertiser Dir. (1938); Cannock Chase Courier, 23 Jan. 1953, which states that the buildings were at first used as an iron and steel works, the edge-tool factory being then at Wedge Mill, in Cannock: see p. 63.
[25] Cannock Chase Courier, 23 Jan. 1953.
[26] Ibid.
[27] Tithe Maps and Appt., Cannock (copy in W.S.L.).
[28] A Joseph Lycett owned and occupied Moat Farm c. 1843: ibid.; White, Dir. Staffs. (1834; 1851).

tions to the house include a single-story kitchen with an open roof, probably of the 17th century, and brick wings to the north and west. Part of one of the outbuildings is timber-framed. In Dunduck Lane a row of three cottages has some exposed timber-framing, but the range has been largely rebuilt or refaced with brickwork. Fishers Farm is a late-17th-century brick house with diagonal shafts to the gable-end chimney. Here, as in the case of most of the old buildings in the parish, the brickwork has been strengthened against subsidence with iron tie-rods.

There are council housing estates at Hilton Lane and between Bentons Lane and Wharwell Lane, the latter including prefabricated houses. In Landy-wood Lane and at Moat Farm and Wyrley Hall are small caravan sites.

The Secondary school in Station Road was built in 1939. The Working Mens' Institute in Walsall Road, used for a time as an extension of the elementary school,[29] is a building of variegated brick dating from 1870.[30] Harrison's Club, built c. 1900 in Wharwell Lane by the colliery owners, is now the property of the National Coal Board.[31]

MANOR. The overlordship of *GREAT WYRLEY* remained with the Crown apparently from before the Conquest[32] until at least 1487,[33] but by 1542 it had passed to the Bishop of Coventry and Lichfield, of whom the manor was then held by fealty and a rent of 4s.[34] The manor continued to be held of the lord of Cannock at this rent until at least 1842.[35]

Before the Conquest land in Great Wyrley seems to have been already attached to the office of keeper of the royal forest of Cannock, held then and in 1086 by Richard le Venur (or the forester).[36] The land then descended with the office and Richard's estate in Chesterton (Warws.) to his daughter Margery, wife of William Croc,[37] and, by 1130, to their son Walter Croc.[38] Walter seems to have been succeeded by William Croc, who was either his son[39] or his brother[40] and who, having granted all his rights in Wyrley to Radmore Abbey, became a monk there c. 1150.[41] By 1155 the monks had abandoned Rad-more for Stoneleigh (Warws.).[42] The custody of the forest seems to have been in the sheriff's hands from at least 1164 to 1174,[43] but the land at Great Wyrley

may have passed to William Croc's son William who was fined for a forest offence in 1170[44] and subsequently hanged.[45] The king gave his lands, with his sister Margery in marriage, to Robert de Brok[46] who by 1175 was forester of Cannock.[47] He was dead by 1194 and was succeeded by a Peter de Brok who became a monk[48] so that in 1195 the lands and forestership passed to Hugh de Loges, husband of Robert de Brok's daughter Margery.[49] In 1198 Hugh was found to be holding a carucate and a half of land in Wyrley by the service of keeping the forest of Cannock.[50] He was still living in 1215.[51] His wife Margery seems to have survived him,[52] but by 1224 their son Hugh had succeeded her.[53] In about 1246 this younger Hugh was imprisoned and deprived of office and lands for poaching venison within the forest,[54] but, on payment of a fine, his lands, including Great Wyrley, were restored to him, though for life only and without the forestership.[55] Before his death in 1268 Hugh had become feeble-minded and unable to manage his own affairs,[56] and by 1265 his son Richard, either in his own right or as his father's guardian, was holding some land in Great Wyrley which he then forfeited for his part against the king in the Barons' Wars.[57] He was taken back into the king's peace early in 1266[58] but did not redeem all his forfeited lands until after Michaelmas 1272.[59] In 1275 Richard, deeply in debt, was licensed to let his lands at farm,[60] but by the beginning of 1277 his manor of Wyrley was in the king's hands for his default against William de la More.[61] William had possession of the manor from at least 1279[62] until early in 1293 when Richard recovered seisin.[63] He died at the end of 1293, holding what was described as the hamlet of Great Wyrley of the king by serjeanty, and was succeeded by his son Richard.[64] When this Richard died in 1300, he held in Great Wyrley of the king by grand serjeanty 4 acres of meadow worth 1s. an acre, rents from land, messuages and cottages of 11 free tenants (30s. 1½d.) and 21 customary tenants (37s. 11¾d.), and proceeds of the two great courts attended by free tenants and of the three-weekly courts for the customary tenants, valued at 20s., in all £4 12s. 1¼d.[65]

Richard's heir was his daughter Elizabeth, aged four,[66] but his lands in Great Wyrley were assigned in dower to his widow Elizabeth[67] who in 1320, with

[29] See p. 82.
[30] Inscription *in situ*.
[31] Local inf.
[32] *S.H.C.* iv (1), 179–80.
[33] *Cal. Inq. p.m. Hen. VII*, i, no. 310.
[34] C 142/67, no. 85. Already in 1298 the lord of Great Wyrley held 4 virgates there of the bishop as lord of Cannock for 4s.: W.S.L., D. 1734, Jeayes 2268, extent of lands of Bpric. of Cov., Lich., and Chester, 26 Edw. I.
[35] Hackwood, *Chronicles of Cannock Chase*, 76; W.S.L., Paget Papers (Gardner Coll.), 35 (1, 9); *S.H.C.* 1947, 7.
[36] *S.H.C.* iv (1), 179–80.
[37] *Bk. of Fees*, 1275–7; *V.C.H. Warws.* v. 42.
[38] *V.C.H. Warws.* v. 42; *S.H.C.* N.S. x (1), 193.
[39] *S.H.C.* N.S. x (1), 194.
[40] *V.C.H. Warws.* v. 42.
[41] Dugd. *Mon.* v. 443; *S.H.C.* N.S. x (1), 194. Henry Duke of Normandy had about this time granted the monks land in Great Wyrley 'for tillage and pasture': Dugd. *Mon.* v. 443.
[42] *V.C.H. Warws.* ii. 79; *S.H.C.* i. 17, 18–19.
[43] *S.H.C.* i. 43, 71.
[44] Ibid. 61.
[45] *V.C.H. Warws.* v. 42; *S.H.C.* N.S. x (1), 194.
[46] *Bk. of Fees*, 1277.
[47] *S.H.C.* i. 72.

[48] Ibid. ii (1), 32, 95.
[49] Ibid. 45.
[50] *Bk. of Fees*, 7.
[51] *Rot. Litt. Pat.* (Rec. Com.), i. 144.
[52] *Plac. de Quo Warr.* (Rec. Com.), 707–8.
[53] *S.H.C.* iv (1), 28; *Bk of Fees*, 594.
[54] *S.H.C.* iv (1), 179–80; *Bk. of Fees*, 1394; *Close R.* 1242–7, 511; *Cal. Inq. p.m.* iii, no. 136.
[55] *Plac. de Quo Warr.* (Rec. Com.), 707–8; *V.C.H. Warws.* v. 42.
[56] *Cal. Pat.* 1266–72, 101; *S.H.C.* N.S. x (1), 200.
[57] *Close R.* 1264–8, 128; *Cal. Pat.* 1258–66, 538; *S.H.C.* vi (1), 57.
[58] *Cal. Pat.* 1258–66, 560.
[59] Ibid. 1266–72, 262, 610; *S.H.C.* iv (1), 179–80; *Close R.* 1264–8, 128; *S.H.C.* vi (1), 57.
[60] *Cal. Pat.* 1272–81, 102.
[61] *Cal. Close*, 1272–9, 412.
[62] *S.H.C.* vi (1), 94.
[63] Ibid. v (1), 163; ibid. vi (1), 211–12, 242.
[64] *Cal. Inq. p.m.* iii, no. 136; *S.H.C.* 1911, 221.
[65] *Cal. Inq. p.m.* iii, no. 593; *S.H.C.* 1911, 260–2.
[66] *Cal. Inq. p.m.* iii, no. 593.
[67] *Cal. Close* 1296–1302, 363–4; they were valued at £3 13s. 9¼d.

John de Saundrestede, her second husband, was holding 100s. rent in Great Wyrley.[68] When she died in 1337 she was said to be holding 60s. 10d. in rents there by the service of giving a barbed arrow to the king whenever he passed through Great Wyrley on his way to hunt in Wales.[69] Her heir was John de Warrewyk or de Loges, the son of her daughter Elizabeth and Nicholas de Warrewyk.[70] In 1342 John was found to be holding by petty serjeanty, giving one barbed arrow whenever the king came to hunt in Cheslyn Hay.[71] An inquiry in 1343, when John was licensed to entail Great Wyrley on his son and daughter-in-law John and Isabel, showed that there was no manor-house or capital messuage, no dovecot, orchard, mill, or demesne land there, but that the rents from free and customary tenants were worth 66s. 8d. a year and the perquisites of courts 3s. 4d.[72] The younger John seems to have died without issue before his father who was succeeded in 1349 by a daughter Eleanor, wife of John de Peyto.[73] The lands, tenements, and rents in Great Wyrley had then fallen in value from 100s. to 60s. because of the pestilence and the poverty of the tenants.[74]

When Sir John de Peyto died in 1396 he was holding a messuage and a virgate in Great Wyrley.[75] His son and heir William[76] settled the manor in 1406 on himself for life, with remainder to his son, William Peyto the younger,[77] and was dead by 1408 when the custody of his lands and heir William was given to John de Knightley the younger.[78] William was presumably of age in 1415 when he and his prospective wife Elizabeth, daughter of Robert Fraunceys, were jointly enfeoffed of the manor.[79] Sir William was taken prisoner at Dieppe in 1443.[80] He and his wife, here named Katherine, having in 1446 mortgaged their manors including Wyrley,[81] in 1449 obtained the king's licence for such mortgages so as to raise William's 'intolerable ransom'.[82] In 1451 and 1453 Great Wyrley was mortgaged to Drew Barentyn and others.[83] In 1454 Sir William and Katherine conveyed it to their son John and his wife Eleanor, daughter of Robert Montfeld, with reversion to themselves.[84] John died in 1487, holding the manor, then worth £7, of the king in chief as $\frac{1}{15}$ knight's fee.[85] John's son Edward died on 14 September within a month of his father's death, without having entered upon the inheritance, and left a son John, a minor.[86] In 1527 John settled Great Wyrley on himself and his wife Margaret[87] and died in 1542, when the manor was said to be worth £11 a year.[88] Margaret held a life interest in it, but in 1544 her son John Peyto conveyed his reversionary interest to James Leveson of Wolverhampton and Lilleshall (Salop.), a merchant of the staple.[89] James was succeeded by his son Sir Richard Leveson, who died in 1560,[90] and was succeeded by his son Walter.[91] Walter was succeeded in 1602 by his son Richard,[92] who became Vice-Admiral of England in 1604 and died in 1605 without lawful issue,[93] survived by his wife Margaret, daughter of Charles Howard, Earl of Nottingham and Lord High Admiral (d. 1624).[94] His lands passed to Sir John Leveson of Halling (Kent),[95] whose son Sir Richard succeeded soon after November 1615[96] and died childless in 1661.[97] The lands passed, through Sir Richard's niece Frances, wife of Sir Thomas Gower, to their son, Sir Thomas Leveson-Gower,[98] and then in 1689 to his uncle, Sir William Leveson-Gower,[99] whose son John, later Baron Gower, succeeded in 1691.[1] He died in 1709 and his great-grandson George Granville, created Duke of Sutherland in 1833,[2] was holding the manor in 1834.[3] The 5th Duke held it in 1927.[4]

A customary court for the manor of Great Wyrley was being held by 1300.[5] Its records survive from at least 1721 until the 20th century, with extinguishments of manorial rights down to 1934.[6]

Great Wyrley paid 3s. a year in frithsilver to the lord of Cannock by 1298.[7] By 1341 it was sending two frankpledges to the leet court of Cannock[8] and remained within the leet until at least 1805.[9] The manor was paying frithsilver of 1s. to the lord of Cannock between at least 1762 and 1769.[10]

In 1284 'the wood of Great Wyrley', having passed out of the hands of Richard de Loges, presumably with the manor, was held by William de More.[11]

[68] *Cal. Inq. a.q.d.* (Rec. Com.), 264. The place-name is wrongly transcribed in *S.H.C.* 1911, 345–6.
[69] *Cal. Inq. p.m.* viii, no. 105. John de Saundrestede survived until 1352: ibid. x, p. 92; *V.C.H. Warws.* v. 42.
[70] *S.H.C.* xii (1), 28; *V.C.H. Warws.* v. 42.
[71] *S.H.C.* 1913, 94–95.
[72] Ibid. 95–96; *Cal. Pat.* 1343–5, 10; *S.H.C.* xii (1), 24; ibid. xi. 155.
[73] *Cal. Inq. p.m.* ix, no. 369; *Cal. Fine R.* 1347–56, 181.
[74] *Cal. Inq. p.m.* ix, no. 369; *S.H.C.* 1913, 136–7.
[75] C 136/89.
[76] Ibid.
[77] *Cal. Pat.* 1405–8, 241.
[78] *Cal. Fine R.* 1405–13, 128; *Cal. Pat.* 1408–13, 42.
[79] *Cal. Pat.* 1413–16, 324.
[80] *V.C.H. Warws.* v. 43; *Cal. Pat.* 1446–52, 257.
[81] With Chesterton and Sowe (Warws.): *Dugd. Soc.* xviii, no. 2625.
[82] *Cal. Pat.* 1446–52, 257.
[83] Ibid. 501; *S.H.C.* xi. 248.
[84] *Cal. Pat.* 1452–61, 159. Sir John died in 1464: *Cal. Fine R.* 1461–71, 127.
[85] *Cal. Inq. p.m. Hen. VII*, i, no. 310.
[86] Ibid. no. 292.
[87] *S.H.C.* xi. 266. It was extended at 20 a. of land, 120 a. of pasture, 20 a. of meadow, 40 a. of wood, and £7 18s. 1½d. rent.
[88] C 142/67, no. 85.
[89] *S.H.C.* xi. 286; Shaw, *Staffs.* ii. 169.
[90] *S.H.C.* 1912, 34A; ibid. 1917–18, 404; Shaw, *Staffs.* ii. 169.

[91] *S.H.C.* 1917–18, 404.
[92] C 142/283, no. 90; Shaw, *Staffs.* ii. 169.
[93] *D.N.B.*; G. P. Mander, *Wolverhampton Antiquary*, i. 368–76.
[94] Shaw, *Staffs.* ii. 186.
[95] *Wolverhampton Antiquary*, i. 370.
[96] Ibid. 373.
[97] Shaw, *Staffs.* ii. 186.
[98] Ibid. 169; Burke, *Peerage* (1931), 2273. *Complete Peerage*, v. 486, note b, states that Frances' uncle was called Sir William and that Sir Thomas Leveson-Gower was grandson to Frances whom it describes, as does Burke, *Peerage* (1931), 2273, as daughter and not granddaughter of Sir John Leveson of Halling.
[99] Burke, *Peerage* (1931), 2273.
[1] *Complete Peerage*, vi. 36.
[2] Ibid., 37, xii (1) 535–6.
[3] White, *Dir. Staffs.* (1834).
[4] Ex inf. Trentham Estate Office, which is unable to state whether the duke still holds such manorial rights as exist (1956).
[5] *S.H.C.* 1911, 261.
[6] W.S.L., Great Wyrley Ct. Bks. 1721–1934.
[7] W.S.L., D. 1734, extent of Bpric. of Cov., Lich., and Chester, 26 Edw. I.
[8] W.S.L., D. 1734, Cannock and Rugeley Ct. Rolls, 1309–73.
[9] Ibid. 1546–53; Hackwood, *Chronicles of Cannock Chase*, 76; W.S.L. 112/25/41, ff. 5a–19a.
[10] W.S.L., Paget Papers (Gardner Coll.), 35 (1, 9).
[11] *S.H.C.* vi (1), 154.

Both Richard and William were presented before the forest justices in 1286 for making new destruction of the woods at Wyrley,[12] the vill being within the forest of Cannock.[13]

MILL. A mill in Wyrley was granted to the abbey of Radmore by Henry Duke of Normandy in about 1153.[14] Ralph the Miller, of Wyrley, occurs in 1283[15] but there was no mill here in 1343.[16] Brown's Mill, apparently in Great Wyrley, is mentioned in 1837.[17] In 1834 and 1851 there was a corn-miller at Church-bridge,[18] and there was still a miller in the parish in 1880.[19]

CHURCH. A church was built and consecrated as a chapel of ease to Cannock in 1845,[20] and in the following year Great Wyrley was joined to Cheslyn Hay to form the district chapelry of Great Wyrley.[21] The perpetual curacy, a titular vicarage since 1868,[22] is in the gift of the Vicar of Cannock.[23]

The parish church of *ST. MARK* is a stone building in the Early English style dating from 1845. It consists of nave, chancel, aisle, porch, and combined vestry and organ chamber. There are graded lancets at the east end, a window with plate tracery at the west end, and single lancets elsewhere. On the east gable of the nave is a bell-cote containing one bell. Electric lighting was installed in 1928[24] and a new reredos in 1939.[25] The Lady Chapel at the east end of the aisle and the vestry screen date from 1945.[26] In 1956 a stone pulpit was provided, and alterations, including new choir stalls, were still being made to the chancel.

With two exceptions the churchyard was cleared of gravestones c. 1950.[27] The present cemetery, opened in 1897,[28] is approached from Station Street, Cheslyn Hay, and has a small mortuary chapel.

The vicarage stands to the south-west of St. Mark's Church.

In 1957 the plate included a silver-gilt flagon, 1844; a silver-gilt chalice and paten, 1844; and a silver paten, 1920.[29] The church has one bell.[30]

NONCONFORMITY. In 1787 Thomas Poynor's house in Great Wyrley was certified as a meeting-place for Independents[31] but no permanent place of worship was erected. In 1822 the house of Joseph Ault was certified as a Dissenter's meeting house.[32]

The first Wesleyan Methodist chapel was built in Holly Lane, Upper Landywood, in 1846, and had 100 sittings.[33] In 1858 a new chapel, seating 200, was built adjacent to it. This was a rectangular brick building with round-headed windows and a gabled porch.[34] The old chapel was used as a Wesleyan day school until a new one was built adjoining the chapel in 1867.[35] After the day school was discontinued the old chapel was used as a Sunday school. By 1923 the buildings had become dilapidated, partly owing to the colliery workings, and by 1919 the Sunday school had been closed.[36] A new chapel on the corner of Shaw's Lane and the main Walsall road, Lower Landywood, was built in 1925 at a cost of £2,500.[37] It is a large red-brick building with a stone Perpendicular-style window above a single-story entrance block. In the meantime the old chapel had fallen into ruins which were finally obliterated by reconstruction of the ground after mining operations.[38]

In 1815 the house of Thomas Reeves was certified as a meeting-house[39] for Primitive Methodists.[40] The chapel in Streets Lane, Upper Landywood, dates from 1906.[41] It is a red-brick building with a half-timbered gable and a small porch. Another congregation of Primitive Methodists, after meeting at various houses, used a small chapel (now converted into a house) at Newtown, Essington.[42] In 1920 a wooden hut was erected in Jacobs Hall Lane, Landywood. In 1927[43] a new chapel was built on the same site with its frontage to the main Walsall road. It consists of a chapel, vestry, and south porch and is built of rustic bricks with stone Perpendicular-style windows.

PRIMARY SCHOOLS. The National school at Great Wyrley was built in 1849 near the churchyard and was attended by about 100 children.[44] It was supported by Lord Hatherton and other subscribers[45] and, by 1880 at least, partly by small weekly payments from the pupils.[46] In 1860 the school first received a government grant.[47] The average attendance in 1866 was 82,[48] and in 1871 66 boys and 52 girls.[49] It had been closed by 1884,[50] and in 1956 was being used as a parish hall. It is a single-story building with lighter brick diaper ornament, leaded windows, and a gabled porch. The steeply-pitched roof has a central bell-cote and a timbered gable. The former teacher's house adjoining it is of similar style and materials.

[12] Ibid. v (1), 175.
[13] Ibid. 177.
[14] Dugd. *Mon.* v. 447; see pp. 57, 79.
[15] *S.H.C.* vi (1), 131.
[16] Ibid. 1913, 96.
[17] *Staffs. Advertiser*, 5 Aug. 1837.
[18] White, *Dir. Staffs.* (1834; 1851).
[19] *Kelly's Dir. Staffs.* (1880).
[20] Lich. Dioc. Regy., Bp.'s Reg. Bk. N, pp. 267–82.
[21] *Lond. Gaz.* 3 Nov. 1846, p. 3836; see p. 102 for the mission of St. Peter.
[22] *Lich. Dioc.Ch. Cal.* (1869).
[23] Lich. Dioc. Regy., Bp.'s Reg. Bk. N, pp. 272–81; *Lich. Dioc. Dir.* (1955–6).
[24] Lich. Dioc. Regy., Consist. Ct. Act Bk. 1924–30, p. 330, faculty, 7 June 1928.
[25] Ibid. 1938–47, p. 90, faculty, 11 Apr. 1939.
[26] Ibid., p. 381, 31 Oct. 1945.
[27] Local inf.
[28] *Kelly's Dir. Staffs.* (1900).
[29] Ex inf. the Vicar of Great Wyrley (1957).
[30] Ex inf. the vicar.; C. Lynam, *Church Bells of Staffs.* 38.
[31] Matthews, *Cong. Churches of Staffs.* 127; S.R.O. Q/SB, Ep. 1787.

[32] Lich. Dioc. Regy., Bp.'s Reg. Bk. G, p. 337.
[33] H.O. 129/15/378.
[34] Thomas Sambrook, *Short History of Wesleyan Methodism at Wyrley* (1925, priv. print.), illustration p. 3.
[35] Ibid. 28.
[36] Ibid. 35.
[37] Ibid. 9.
[38] Local inf.
[39] Lich. Dioc. Regy., Bp.'s Reg. Bk. F, p. 230.
[40] J. Walford, *Hugh Bourne* (1855), i. 364.
[41] *Kelly's Dir. Staffs.* (1912).
[42] Ex inf. Mr. W. Parsons, Secretary to the Trustees.
[43] Trustees' Minute Book (from 1917), *penes* Mr. Parsons.
[44] White, *Dir. Staffs.* (1851).
[45] Ibid.
[46] *P.O. Dir. Staffs.* (1860).
[47] *Rep. of Educ. Cttee. of Council, 1860* [2828], H.C. (1861), xlix.
[48] *Rep. of Educ. Cttee. of Council, 1866* [C. 3882], H.C. (1867), xxii.
[49] *Returns relating to Elem. Educ.* H.C. 201, pp. 364–5 (1871), xxii.
[50] *Kelly's Dir. Staffs.* (1884).

A Board school (mixed) was built in 1882, the average attendance then being 160.[51] It was enlarged in 1906.[52] By 1910 the premises were unsatisfactory and the school managers were instructed to reduce numbers by excluding children from other districts.[53] In 1930 attendance averaged 249 boys, girls, and infants.[54] Owing to overcrowding, temporary premises were hired in 1938 in Great Wyrley Working Men's Institute.[55] The school is now Great Wyrley County Primary School.[56]

A Wesleyan school connected with the chapel at Landywood was built there in 1867 (or 1868),[57] and by 1880 was staffed by both a master and a mistress.[58] In 1884, however, it was described as a Sunday school.[59]

A council school was opened in 1908 at Landywood, with six classes for 350 children.[60] In 1930 the average attendance was 322.[61] This is now Great Wyrley, Landywood County Primary School for Boys and Girls and Infants.[62]

CHARITIES FOR THE POOR. Humphrey Short of Great Wyrley at some date before 1786 gave a rent charge of 10s. on a close there to be distributed at Christmas to the poorest inhabitants of Great Wyrley who were not in receipt of parish relief.[63] At some time before 1786 Ann Greenshill gave 5s. and Alice Greenshill 13s. (both charged on land in Shenstone parish), to be distributed in bread every alternate Sunday to six poor widows or poorest inhabitants of Great Wyrley.[64] By 1823 these charities, along with those of Alport, Wilson, and Goldsmith, were distributed to the poor of Great Wyrley generally on the first Friday in January, in sums varying from 3s. to 1s. 6d.[65] They were no longer paid in 1956.[66]

CASTLE CHURCH

CASTLE CHURCH has been a separate parish from at least 1546.[1] The ancient parish was roughly square in shape and mainly lay immediately south, south-east, and south-west of Stafford. Its boundary followed the course of the River Sow from a point 2 miles north-west of Stafford eastward to the confluence of the Sow and the Penk, except for a triangle of land north of the Sow comprising part of Lammascote and of Littleworth. The boundary then ran south for 6 miles along the course of the Penk, then slightly north-east in an uneven line to the base of Willowmore Hill (Bradley parish) 6½ miles away, due north for 5½ miles, and then due west for 2 miles turning north again to meet the Sow.[2] A detached strip of Coppenhall between Thorneyfields Lane and Burton Manor had become part of Castle Church by 1881.[3] The parish is mainly flat but rises in the south-west to about 450 ft. The Rising Brook rises in the south of the parish and crosses it in a north-easterly direction, joining the Spittal Brook which flows across the north-east of the ancient parish to join the Sow. Three main roads cross the ancient parish: the road to Newport in a south-westerly direction; the road to Lichfield, 'the king's highway' of the Middle Ages, later turnpiked from Radford Bridge,[4] in a south-easterly direction through Forebridge; and the road to Wolverhampton in a southerly direction through Forebridge. All three roads now converge on the borough of Stafford near the Green Bridge.

The ancient parish, which was divided into two constablewicks by 1666,[5] consisted of the vills of Castle, i.e. the area surrounding the castle of the Stafford barony, which lies in the north-west of the ancient parish with the church half a mile south-east of it; Forebridge lying south-east of and adjacent to the borough of Stafford; Rowley in the centre of the parish; Burton lying a mile north of the southern boundary of the parish; Rickerscote in the south-east of the parish; Silkmore in the east of the parish; and the hamlet of Hyde Lea on the southern boundary of the parish. Risingbrook, an area of very modern development, lies slightly south-east of Rowley. The parish had a population in 1801 of 563[6] and an area in 1831 of 3,777 acres.[7]

By the Parliamentary and Municipal Reform Acts of 1832 and 1835 an area in the north of the parish, the present Castletown and Forebridge, was taken into the borough. The new boundary in the north-west of the parish ran from the windmill at Broad Eye, Castletown, to the stile at the end of the footpath from Newport Road to Penkridge Road, then south to where the Rising Brook turns east, then along the brook to the junction with Spittal Brook, and finally to the Sow.[8] This change left the parish with an area of 3,460 acres in 1851.[9] In 1876 the triangle of land north of the River Sow and now part of Lammascote and Littleworth was taken into the borough.[10] In 1917 a larger area, roughly an intake a mile deep along the north-east boundary and comprising the area up Newport Road almost to the castle and including the church and vicarage, Rowley Park, Risingbrook, and Silkmore, was absorbed by the borough. Thus, speaking approximately, the

[51] Kelly's Dir. Staffs. (1884).
[52] Ibid. (1912).
[53] Staffs. Educ. Cttee. Mins., 22 Oct. 1910.
[54] Ibid. May 1930.
[55] Ibid. Jan. 1938.
[56] Staffs. Educ. Cttee., List of Schools, 1951.
[57] P.O. Dir. Staffs. (1860); Kelly's Dir. Staffs. (1892).
[58] Kelly's Dir. Staffs. (1880).
[59] Ibid. (1884).
[60] Staffs. Educ. Cttee. Mins., 25 Apr. 1908.
[61] Ibid. 21 May 1930.
[62] Staffs. Educ. Cttee., List of Schools, 1951.
[63] Abstract of Returns of Charitable Donations, 1786–8, H.C. 511, pp. 1120–1 (1816), xvi (2); 11th Rep. Com. Char. H.C. 436, p. 517 (1824), xiv.
[64] 11th Rep. Com. Char. 517; Abstract, ii. 1120–1.

[65] 11th Rep. Com. Char. 517; see pp. 74, 75.
[66] Ex inf. the Vicar of Great Wyrley (1956).
[1] E 301/40/16.
[2] Tithe Maps and Appt., Castle Church (copy in W.S.L.).
[3] O.S. Map 6″, Staffs. xliv, N.W. (1895, surveyed 1878–81).
[4] S.R.O., Q/RDc 15a.
[5] S.H.C. 1927, 38–39.
[6] V.C.H. Staffs. i. 320.
[7] Census, 1831, Staffs.
[8] White, Dir. Staffs. (1851); Boundary Commissioners' Rep. iii (1) (1832), Stafford.
[9] Census, 1851, Staffs.
[10] Map showing extensions of the borough: Borough Hall, Stafford.

north-east corner of the ancient parish was cut out.[11] A further intake into the borough in 1934 included Burton Manor and Rickerscote so that only two long tongues of land stretching north and east from Willowmore Hill, the south-west corner of the ancient parish, remained in the civil parish of Castle Church.[12] The area of the parish in 1951 was 1,704 acres and the population 580.[13]

The name Forebridge was given by 1288 to land immediately south of the bridge crossing the Sow into Stafford.[14] By 1327 Forebridge formed a separate vill and had nine inhabitants who were taxed for the twentieth.[15] The Green in Forebridge is mentioned in 1304[16] and most of the population of the parish was settled here in 1403, though eight cottages had been burnt and not rebuilt.[17] The Hospital of St. John, the Hospital of St. Leonard, and the house of Austin Friars were all situated in Forebridge. As early as 1295 the Hospital of St. John, which probably stood with its chapel at the junction of the present White Lion Street and Lichfield Road,[18] had tenements attached to it for the use of the poor.[19] It was claimed in 1535 by Henry Lord Stafford that the chapel there, founded by his ancestors, had been allowed to fall into decay and that the surrounding houses, once intended for poor people, were inhabited by 'unthrifty persons of evil living'.[20] Whether or not these statements were justified, it is certain that by 1543 the estate of the Master of St. John's, in Forebridge, included thirteen tenements, most consisting of house, garden, and croft.[21] By 1542 the church of the Austin Friars, which is thought to have lain south-west of the Green, had been demolished.[22] Six cottages on the Green were occupied by Lord Stafford's tenants-at-will c. 1519.[23] The pinfold 'upon the top of the Green' figured in a dispute between tenants of the barony between about 1539 and 1542.[24] In 1543 there were 32 tenements, most with garden and croft adjoining, in Forebridge around the Green and, standing upon the middle of the Green, 2 messuages, of which seven tenements had been made, and a cottage.[25] One of the houses, with garden and orchard, belonged to Billington chapel (Bradley parish).[26] During the Civil War, in 1642, the inhabitants of the Green were ordered by the Parliamentary Committee at Stafford to pull down buildings within musket shot of the town walls, being warned that those who neglected to do so would be left to shift for themselves, whereas those who submitted would receive full satisfaction for any damage and would be provided for elsewhere.[27] In 1680 the greater part

of the population of the parish still lived at Forebridge or Stafford Green, where there were between 30 and 40 houses.[28] The Green, the area covering the triangle now formed by the Lichfield and Wolverhampton roads and White Lion Street, was built up on all sides and in the centre c. 1840.[29] Farther east along the Lichfield road there were several large residential properties including Forebridge Villa, now St. Joseph's Convent, and the house now known as The Old Hough.[30] Green Hall on the north side of the Lichfield road stood alone and had considerable grounds.[31] Two well-designed terraces on the Wolverhampton road date from c. 1830. About 1840 this road was built up on its east side for a mile south of the Green, and Garden Street which runs off the Wolverhampton road just south of the Green had houses on both sides.[32] The further development of this area after its absorption by Stafford borough in 1835 is reserved for treatment with the history of the borough in another volume.

At or near the Green several 18th-century houses and cottages have survived, but, apart from the White Lion Inn,[33] there appear to be few, if any, earlier buildings. The remains of Forebridge lock-up, probably dating from the early 18th century, adjoin the west end of the White Lion at the corner of White Lion Street and Lichfield Road. This is a small square stone structure, roofed with stone slates and with a brick vault internally.

The vill of Castle with Marsh had eight inhabitants in 1327 who were taxed for the twentieth.[34] Several farms lay in the 'Castle' region, the northeast of the parish, in 1788: Highfields, Castle Farm, Eldershiers, Hill Farm, Burley Fields Farm, and Silvester's Farm.[35] About 1840 there were only five houses on the Newport road, The Hollies, opposite Rowley Avenue and the oldest residential property on the road, The Hawthorns, on the south side of the road ¼ mile south-west of The Hollies, Deans Hill on the north side ¼ mile farther on, a cottage slightly to the west, in 1851 kept as a beerhouse, and Castle Farm opposite the church.[36] About 1½ mile of this road as far as The Hawthorns was included in Stafford borough in 1835 (see above), under which its further development will be treated in another volume. On the remaining stretch of the Newport road three large houses had been built immediately south of Deans Hill by 1877.[37] By 1900 a further four houses had been built south-west of these[38] and c. 1906 another was added, Upmeads, designed by Edgar Wood. At this period it was considered remarkable for its flat roof and was described

[11] Ibid.
[12] Ibid.
[13] *Census*, 1951, Staffs.
[14] *S.H.C.* vi (1), 179.
[15] Ibid. 244.
[16] W.S.L., D. 1721/1/1, f. 131a.
[17] W.S.L., D. 1721/1/8, pp. 143, 151.
[18] See p. 91.
[19] *S.H.C.* iii (1), 299.
[20] *L. & P. Hen. VIII*, viii, p. 130.
[21] W.S.L., D. 1721/1/9, 1st nos. ff. 182a–183b.
[22] On land occupied in the 19th cent. by Eley's Brewery (A. L. P. Roxburgh, *Stafford* (1948), 60) and in 1957 part of the works of Burgess (Wholesale) Ltd. In 1542 20 loads of stone from the demolished church, which probably dated from soon after its foundation in 1343, were sold to the church of Bradley: W.S.L., D. 1721/1/12, p. 12. It is possible that this was the source of the fine 14th-cent. arcade now in Bradley church: *V.C.H. Staffs.* iv. 88.
[23] W.S.L., D. 1721/1/9, 1st nos. ff. 182a–183b.

[24] *S.H.C.* n.s. x (1), 153–6.
[25] W.S.L., D. 1721/1/9, 1st nos. ff. 193a–196b.
[26] Ibid.
[27] *S.H.C.* 4th ser. i. 35.
[28] *S.H.C.* 1919, 237.
[29] Tithe Maps and Appt., Castle Church (copy in W.S.L.).
[30] See p. 98.
[31] See pp. 90–91.
[32] Tithe Maps and Appt., Castle Church (copy in W.S.L.).
[33] See p. 91.
[34] *S.H.C.* vii (1), 244.
[35] B.M. Eg. MS. 2872, ff. 45 sqq.
[36] Tithe Maps and Appt., Castle Church (copy in W.S.L.); White, *Dir. Staffs.* (1851). The cottage is now known as Hampstead Cottage.
[37] Map of Stafford borough 1877 in W.S.L.
[38] O.S. Map 6" Staffs. xxxvii, N.W. (1900).

as 'fortress-like' and 'boxy'.[39] Castle House, in 1957 offices of the Staffordshire County Council, which stands opposite the church, was built c. 1870 and is an impressive brick mansion. In 1917 this area as far as the church was taken into Stafford borough (see above) and its further development is reserved for treatment in another volume.

Smaller houses in the Newport road and Thorny-fields Lane, still outside the borough boundary, were built between the two world wars. There has been further building of detached houses west of St. Mary's Church since 1950. Except for these, however, this area was still open country in 1957. Billington Farm, beyond the built-up area, has a date tablet of 1739 bearing the Stafford Knot. The house was refronted in the 19th century. A rebuilt brick barn fronting the road has a truss incorporating two crucks.

Rowley formed a separate vill by at least 1452,[40] the Hall being the principal building there. Rowley Park, part of the grounds of Rowley Hall[41] lying west of the Wolverhampton road, was bought before 1868 by the Staffs. Land, Building, and Investment Co. Ltd., for building villa residences around a triangular plot which was to be laid out as ornamental pleasure grounds.[42] By 1900 about 40 substantial houses had been built in this area, the most compact building being along the east end of Crescent Road.[43] Apart from an incomplete terrace in Lawn Road dating from c. 1870 there is no uniformity in the size or style of the villas in Rowley Park. The grounds of the original houses have in many cases been divided into smaller plots, so that the estate now contains houses of all sizes and periods.

In 1680 there were two little houses at Rising-brook.[44] By c. 1840 there were still only a few cottages there[45] and in 1924, seven years after the area was absorbed by Stafford borough, there were only the Royal Oak Inn and one or two houses.[46] The recent development of this area is reserved for treatment under Stafford borough in another volume.

In 1327 the joint vills of Burton and Rickerscote had nine inhabitants who were taxed for the twentieth.[47] In Burton and Rickerscote constable-wick in 1666, 30 inhabitants were assessed for 39 hearths and 15 were exempt.[48] In 1680 there were 12 or 14 houses at Rickerscote and 12 or 14 also at Burton and Hyde Lea as well as 3 large estates.[49] There was a group of houses forming a considerable hamlet on either side of the road leading from Ricker-scote House to the Plough Inn by 1840.[50] West of Rickerscote House there is a post-1945 housing estate.

In 1818 the western part of the parish to Moss Pit Bank and the Wolverhampton road was said to be 'thinly interspersed with handsome mansions'.[51] There were about half a dozen cottages in the area

of Burton Manor c. 1840 and a few cottages at Moss Pit and along Burton Bank.[52] By 1924 there had been some more building at Moss Pit and along Burton Bank.[53] North of the junction of Burton Bank and the Wolverhampton road is a post-1945 housing estate joining up with the Rickerscote estate. In 1950 there were still only a few cottages around Burton Manor itself.

The general effect of the expansion of Rowley, Risingbrook, Rickerscote, and Moss Pit is that the area east of the Wolverhampton road was completely built up by 1950 as far as Moss Pit, nearly three miles from the centre of Stafford, and the area west as far as the junction with the road to Coppenhall, nearly two miles south of the centre of Stafford; and the area between the two roads leading from the Wolver-hampton road to Rickerscote has also been built up for about half a mile.

Hyde Lea Common was ringed by small encroach-ments by 1788[54] and by c. 1840 there were a few cottages there, several of which, dating from the late 18th and the early 19th centuries, still survive.[55] A school was built there in 1863.[56] By 1881 there were two public houses there, the Crown Inn and the Dun Cow Inn, but by 1900 only one, 'The Crown,' and by 1924 there was also a post office.[57] Consider-able building of residential property has taken place there between the two world wars and since 1950.

Industrial and housing development has taken place also in Silkmore and along the stretch of the Lichfield road not taken into the borough in 1835. This has occurred mainly since 1917 when the area went into the borough and is reserved for treatment in another volume. The development of the triangle of land in the north-east of the ancient parish, on the north of the Sow taken into the borough in 1876, and of Castletown is reserved for like treatment.

There were several saline springs at Rickerscote in 1811[58] and a salt well still existed there in 1956.

CASTLE. The castle of the Stafford barony is not mentioned in Domesday Book, but the existence of the remains of what was undoubtedly a motte and bailey castle[59] and references to the existence of a chapel 'within the castle' from the time of the Conquest[60] make it probable that the first fortifica-tion of the Stafford family, on the hill south-west of Stafford, was built soon after the Conquest. In 1347 Ralph de Stafford made an agreement with John de Burcestre, mason, for the building of a castle upon 'la moete',[61] presumably the first stone castle there. In 1348 Ralph was given licence to crenellate his 'dwelling place of Stafford' and make a castle of it.[62] He was still paying workmen's wages in 1368.[63] In July 1392, four days after the death of Thomas Earl of Stafford, the king appointed his

39 Country Life, 12 Nov. 1910.
40 W.S.L., D. 1721/1/8, ff. 336a, 338a, 341a.
41 See pp. 89–90.
42 P.O. Dir. Staffs. (1868).
43 O.S. Map 6″, Staffs. xxxvii, N.W. (1900).
44 S.H.C. 1919, 237.
45 Tithe Maps and Appt., Castle Church (copy in W.S.L.).
46 O.S. Map 6″ Staffs. xliv, N.W. (1924).
47 S.H.C. vii (1), 246.
48 Ibid. 1927, 38–39.
49 Ibid. 1919, 237.
50 Tithe Maps and Appt., Castle Church (copy in W.S.L.).
51 Parson and Bradshaw, Dir. Staffs. (1818), p. ccxxiv.

52 Tithe Maps and Appt., Castle Church (copy in W.S.L.).
53 O.S. Map 6″ Staffs. xliv, N.W. (1924).
54 B.M. Eg. MS. 2872, ff. 54b–56a.
55 Tithe Maps and Appt., Castle Church (copy in W.S.L.) 56 See p. 98.
57 O.S. Map 6″ Staffs. xliv, N.W. (1890); ibid. (1900); ibid. (1924).
58 W. Pitt, Staffs. (1817), 267–8.
59 S.H.C. viii (2), 16–17; V.C.H. Staffs. i. 355.
60 See p. 95.
61 W.S.L., D. 1721/1/11, p. 207; L. F. Salzman, Building in England to 1540 (1952), 438–9.
62 Cal. Pat. 1348–50, 13.
63 W.S.L., D. 1721/1/8, pp. 55–58.

own esquire William de Walsall as constable or keeper of this castle, as well as surveyor of the park, provided the offices were still vacant.[64] After the forfeiture and attainder of Edward Stafford, Duke of Buckingham (d. 1521), when the castle escheated to the Crown, it was described as standing 'upon so goodly an height that all the country may be seen 20 or 30 miles about. And one way a man may see to the king's lordship of Caurs [i.e. Caus] in Wales 30 miles from thence, and another way to the king's honor of Tutbury.'[65] In spite of the many faults in the lead-covered roof, and in the floors and in the pointing of the battlements, 'this little castle and the members about it . . . standing pleasantly nigh much game for hunting . . . should be right pleasant for the king when it shall please his grace to make his progress into those parts in grease-time'.[66]

In 1522 the king appointed Edward Littleton of Pillaton (in Penkridge), then usher of the chamber, as constable and doorward of Stafford castle.[67] Littleton still held these offices at Michaelmas 1533,[68] though the castle and manor had been restored to Henry Lord Stafford and Ursula, his wife, in 1531.[69] Letters of Henry Lord Stafford were dated from the castle in 1532[70] but he left the neighbourhood in 1537, leasing to William Staunford (or Stanford) what was described as the manor place of the castle of Stafford, with demesne lands, stock, grain, and implements of husbandry.[71] Whether Stanford occupied the castle itself is uncertain but his name is appended to a room by room inventory of goods and furnishings left behind by Lord Stafford.[72] Lord Stafford had returned by at least 1546 and was living in the castle until 1553 and in 1561.[73] His eldest surviving son, Henry, died there in 1566.[74] In 1574 this same Edward Lord Stafford, with Lords Dudley and Paget, issued from the castle returns for musters for Staffordshire.[75] A Council, not apparently attended by Lord Stafford, was held at the castle in 1575.[76] On 27 July 1603 he wrote to the Earl of Shrewsbury from his 'rotten castle of Stafford'.[77] His son and heir, Edward (d. 1625), who was buried in Castle Church,[78] had leased what seems to have been the actual castle with the Little Park and land called 'the Lawnd' in 1607 for 21 years at £5 rent to John Cradock.[79] It was this Edward's widow, Isabel, 'the ould Lady Stafford' who had 'betaken herself to the castle' to defend it in the absence of her grand-daughter's husband, William Howard, Viscount Stafford, and who refused entry in 1643 to the parliamentary forces; whereupon they set fire to 'some of the poore out houses' in order 'to trye whether these would awake their spirites to any relentinge, but all in vaine . . .'.[80] The defenders shot some men and horses, 'which did much enrage and provoke the rest to a fierce revenge, and to practice those extremities which consumed . . . almost all the dwelling houses and out houses to the ground'. The defenders still held out for the king[81] but on 22 December 1643 the Parliamentary Committee at Stafford ordered the demolition of the castle.[82]

The stone castle built by Ralph de Stafford between 1347 and c. 1368 was rectangular in plan, measuring about 120 by 50 ft., with an octagonal tower at each of the corners and a fifth tower in the centre of the north side.[83] Ralph's agreement with John de Burcestre, mason, for building a castle on 'la moete' specified that the walls were to be 7 ft. thick at the base and that the towers were to be 10 ft. higher than the main body of the building.[84] In 1524 the castle was described as 'little and without courts . . . all uniforme, and of one fashion with two towers at each end and another in the middle . . . three chambers in each tower, each with a draught and a chimney'.[85] An inventory of the contents of the building made in 1537[86] gives an idea of the accommodation and fittings at that period. The great hall, fitted with a screen ('spere'), had windows facing north and south. It was probably on an upper floor, having a 'nether hall' beneath it. The great chamber, or solar, had at least one window facing west. It was hung with 'old arras' and furnished with forms and stools bearing the Stafford Knot. Its 'great window', partly sealed with English wainscot, was glazed with 30 panes, ten of them casements. Mention of a 'little chamber' under this window suggests that it was in the form of a projecting bay. The principal chambers, apart from those of 'my lord' and 'my lady', included those of John Russell, Lord Henry, and Lord Neville. A series of nurseries was connected by a staircase 'to my lady's chamber'; another stair led from the lord's chamber into the garden. The chapel had doors leading to the great court, to the garden, and to Lord Henry's chamber. It had eight glazed windows and appears to have consisted of a nave and chancel, the latter panelled and fitted with seats. There was also a 'little chapel'. The usual domestic rooms and buildings included a 'styllyng house' in the garden. Also in the garden was a panelled 'suppyng place' having a window and being furnished with a table. Among the outbuildings were barns, stables, and a millhouse. One of the stables was assigned to the water-carrier. A very deep well, slightly north-east of the castle and said to date from the time of Henry IV,[87] is now covered over.

The demolition of the castle in 1643 did not include the foundations or the bases of the towers. A fragment of walling was also standing when Sir William Jerningham succeeded c. 1788.[88] He intended at first to strengthen this but eventually had

[64] Cal. Pat. 1391–6, 124; Complete Peerage, xii (1), 180.
[65] E 36/150, f. 58a, printed in S.H.C. viii (2), 107.
[66] Ibid., f. 58b, printed in S.H.C. viii (2), 108.
[67] And also as parker and bailiff of the lordship of Forebridge: L. & P. Hen. VIII, iii (2), g. 2016 (22).
[68] W.S.L., Stafford Barony Mins. Accts. 24–25 Hen. VIII.
[69] L. & P. Hen. VIII, v, g. 364(29).
[70] Ibid. no. 1608.
[71] W.S.L., D. 1810, ff. 117b–18b.
[72] Ibid., ff. 120a–8a.
[73] W.S.L., D. 1721/1/11 passim; Cal. S.P. Dom. 1547–80, 180.
[74] St. Mary's Stafford Par. Reg. (Staffs. Par. Reg. Soc.), 16.
[75] Cal. S.P. Dom. 1547–80, 487.
[76] Acts of P.C. 1575–7, 12.
[77] J. L. Cherry, Stafford in Olden Times (1890), 30.
[78] Complete Peerage, xii (1), 186; Castle Church Par. Reg. (Staffs. Par. Reg. Soc.), i. 42.
[79] W.S.L., D. 1721/1/3, f. 5a.
[80] Shaw, Staffs. i, General History, 55.   [81] Ibid.
[82] S.H.C. 4th ser. i. 21.
[83] See plate facing p. 86.
[84] W.S.L., D. 1721/1/11, p. 207; a transcript is given by Salzman, Building in England to 1540, 438–9.
[85] S.H.C. viii (2), 107 n.
[86] W.S.L., D. 1810, ff. 120a–8a.
[87] S.H.C. viii (2), 83.
[88] See plate facing p. 86.

the whole site cleared and the plan exposed. His son, Sir George William Jerningham, started to rebuild on the old foundations, the work being designed and supervised by his brother Edward.[89] The scheme was never completed but by 15 October 1817 Edward Jerningham was occupying a suite of rooms at the west end, flanked by two towers, and was visited there by the antiquary, William Hamper.[90] The stone came from a quarry at Tixall (Pirehill hundred).[91] The design of the building was 'after the style of Edward III'[92] and is an early example of a castle rebuilt in the Gothic taste. The rebuilt portion consists of two octagonal towers with machicolated and embattled parapets. Between them a screen wall is enriched with arcaded panels and behind this the living rooms rise to three stories. There is evidence that the highest story and a small stair turret were later additions. The extra weight of these together with the insufficient abutment to the wide three-centred arch over the west window has contributed to the instability of the building.[93] The eastern half of the site consists only of the original foundations. During the Second World War parts of the castle, already in a decayed state, were used by the Home Guard.[94] The trees surrounding it were felled in 1949,[95] making the building a more prominent landmark in the surrounding countryside. In 1950 the mound was replanted with mixed deciduous trees and conifers and in the same year the structure was declared unsafe, the resident caretakers left, and visitors were prohibited.[96] In 1951 reports submitted by the County Planning Officer and by the Old Stafford Society in association with the Georgian Group gave details of the structural condition of the building and made recommendations for its repair and future use.[97] By 1957, partly as a result of wilful damage and the theft of lead from the roofs, the structure had further deteriorated.

Several mounds and depressions within half a mile of the castle mound may represent part of its outer defences. These include a ditch, partly wet, in the grounds of Castle House. Castle Bank, east of Thornyfields Lane, appears to be in the direct line of the principal approach from the south. An unusually wide rectangular moat, now dry, lies on the north side of the Newport road, about 1,000 yds. south-west of the castle.[98]

MANORS. The hill on which the ruins of Stafford castle now stand, with the land sloping down to the River Sow, can probably be identified as Robert de Stafford's 'Monetvile', assessed in 1086 at one hide, and held of him by Walter and Ansger.[99] Earl Edwin had held this land before the Conquest,[1] and with Bradley and its members, and Rickerscote, 'Monetvile' completed a compact 20-hide estate, known at least until 1293 as the Liberty of Bradley.[2] By 1208 the vill here was named Castle (Castell).[3] From at least 1290 a manor, eventually known as STAFFORD manor or FOREBRIDGE,[4] but also called the Castle near Stafford (1290),[5] the Castle of Stafford (1293),[6] and Castle manor (1399),[7] has existed here. It has been held by the barons of Stafford until the present day except for certain periods of alienation.

In 1297, when about to go overseas on the king's service, Edmund de Stafford was given licence to lease his manor of Stafford for eight years.[8] In 1298 and 1303 he settled it on himself and his wife Margaret.[9] Edmund died in 1308 and his widow, who subsequently married Sir Thomas de Pipe,[10] was still regarded as Baroness of Stafford[11] until her son Ralph's coming of age in 1322.[12]

Edmund Earl of Stafford was killed at the battle of Shrewsbury (21 July 1403), leaving an infant son.[13] The Castle manor was among the two-thirds of his possessions granted in 1404 to Henry IV's second queen, Joan, as part of her dower.[14] It was presumably forfeited by her between c. 1419 and 1422 on her deprivation for witchcraft,[15] since early in 1422 Anne Countess of Stafford, widow of Earl Edmund, was suing her for leave to present, by default, to the Hospital of St. Leonard, which was appurtenant to the castle and demesne of Stafford.[16] In February 1423 Edmund's son, Humphrey, though still a few months under the age of 21, was given livery of the whole of his inheritance, with issues from August 1422.[17] On his death in 1460 Anne Duchess of Buckingham and his half-brother, Thomas Bourchier, Archbishop of Canterbury, his executors, were given the custody of all the late duke's castles, honors, manors, lands, knight's fees, and advowsons in England until the coming of age of his infant grandson and heir, Henry.[18] For these they paid an annual farm to the Crown[19] until 1464 when the grant was revoked and Anne alone was given custody of the lands, surrendering the custody of the heir to the king.[20] Anne Duchess of Buckingham had married Walter Blount, Lord Mountjoy, by 25 November 1467[21] and they jointly controlled the

[89] T. A. Clifford, *Parish of Tixall* (Paris, 1817), 46 n.
[90] *S.H.C.* viii (2), 118–19, citing letter of Wm. Hamper of 24 Dec. 1817.
[91] Ibid. 119 n.
[92] Ibid. 118 n.
[93] *Trans. Old Stafford Soc.* 1951–2, 11.
[94] Inf. from Mr. S. Horne, Old Stafford Soc.
[95] Inf. from Mr. H. Venables, timber merchant of Stafford.
[96] Inf. from Mr. Venables.
[97] *Trans. Old Stafford Soc.* 1951–2, 10–14.
[98] *V.C.H. Staffs.* i. 360.
[99] *V.C.H. Staffs.* iv. 53, no. 223; Eyton, *Domesday Studies Staffs.* 35–36; *S.H.C.* viii (2), 14–20.
[1] *V.C.H. Staffs.* iv. 53, no. 223.
[2] *S.H.C.* vi (1), 258–9.
[3] Ibid. iii (1), 172–3.
[4] C.P. 43/395, rot. 179.
[5] *S.H.C.* 1911, 198–9; *Cal. Inq. p.m.* ii, no. 790.
[6] *S.H.C.* vi (1), 258–9.
[7] C 136/107.
[8] *Cal. Pat.* 1292–1301, 288.

[9] Along with other demesne manors: ibid. 372; *S.H.C.* 1911, 58–59.
[10] *Complete Peerage*, xii (1), 173.
[11] *Cal. Inq. p.m.* v, nos. 56 (p. 42), 330.
[12] Ibid. vi, no. 354.
[13] *Complete Peerage*, xii (1), 181.
[14] *Cal. Close*, 1402–5, 237; *Cal. Pat.* 1401–5, 347–9.
[15] *D.N.B.*
[16] *S.H.C.* xvii. 40–41.
[17] *Cal. Pat.* 1422–9, 75; *Complete Peerage*, xii (1), 181.
[18] C 139/180, no. 59; *Cal. Fine R.* 1452–61, 284; *D.N.B.* (Bourchier).
[19] £379 14s. 4½d. with increment of 5s. 8d. from 1461 (*Cal. Fine R.* 1461–71, 11–12) and £261 12s. 6¾d. with 6s. 8d. increment, from 1462: ibid. 62.
[20] *Cal. Pat.* 1461–7, 298. Henry Duke of Buckingham, had a 'brother' Humphrey living 1464 and 1465: ibid. 324, 463. Henry's mother Margaret, styled Countess of Stafford, who after her husband Humphrey Stafford's death in 1455, married Richard Darell, was apparently *non compos mentis* in 1466: *S.H.C.* n.s. iv. 141; *Complete Peerage*, ii. 389. [21] *Cal. Pat.* 1467–77, 69.

Church and Castle Mound, *c.* 1800

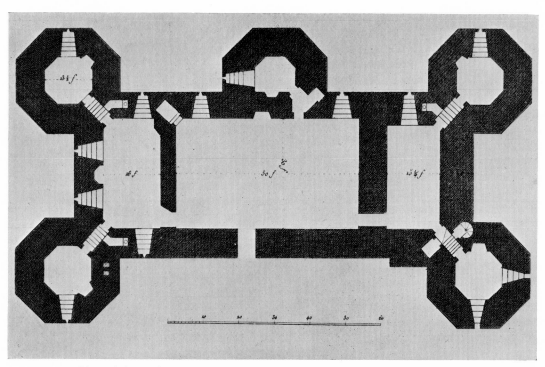

Plan of the 14th-century castle, measured before the restoration of *c.* 1815

CASTLE CHURCH

Cuttlestone Bridge, Penkridge

CASTLE CHURCH: air view of Forebridge, 1937, from the south-west. On the left of the picture the Newport road joins the Wolverhampton and Lichfield roads just short of Green Bridge, near the top left-hand corner. Beyond it is Greengate Street, Stafford. The line of trees marks the course of the Sow, which formed the northern boundary of Castle Church parish. On the right facing the Lichfield road is Green Hall. The site of the Austin Friars is at the centre of the picture young Henry Stafford's English lands from at least 1470.[22] Henry Duke of Buckingham was given licence to enter upon his inherited possessions here and elsewhere in England, Wales, the Marches, and Calais, as from Michaelmas 1472,[23] although he was not of full age until 1475.[24] His mother's lands returned to him after her death in 1480.[25] After the attainder and beheading of Henry Duke of Buckingham in 1483,[26] the stewardship of his Staffordshire lordships and lands was granted by the Crown in 1484 to Thomas Wortley, one of the knights of the body.[27] With the accession of Henry VII, Edward Duke of Buckingham, son of Henry, was restored to his father's honours,[28] and in 1498, though not of full age, was given special livery of his possessions in England and elsewhere.[29] His demesne lands of Stafford manor were usually leased as in 1486–7.[30]

The Stafford barony lands with other honors and lordships again escheated to the Crown when Edward Stafford, Duke of Buckingham and Earl of Stafford, was attainted and beheaded in 1521.[31] Stafford manor was not among the manors restored in 1522 to the former duke's son, Henry Stafford, and his wife Ursula.[32] It was not until 1531 that Stafford manor (though not the knight's fees and court leet attached to it and to Forebridge) was granted to them in tail, subject to sundry reversions and an annual rent to the Crown.[33] In 1547 Henry was restored in blood as Baron Stafford.[34] In 1554, in consequence of his good services to Queen Mary in the rebellion of the Duke of Northumberland and otherwise, Henry and Ursula's lands were confirmed to them to be held by the same rents and services as before the attainder of the late Duke of Buckingham.[35]

Ursula survived both her husband (d. 1563) and her son, Henry Baron Stafford (d. 1566), and it was only after her death in 1570 that her son Edward Baron Stafford (d. 1603) succeeded to the castle and manor of Stafford and its dependencies.[36] He died at Stafford castle in 1603, leaving the castle and manor of Stafford with its appurtenances as his only demesnes in the county.[37] His son Edward Stafford died here in 1625, his heir being an infant grandson Henry,[38] who was placed in the wardship of Thomas Howard, Earl of Arundel, the Earl Marshal.[39] On Henry Stafford's death in 1637 still under age, the heir to his lands was his sister Mary, wife of William Howard K.B.,[40] second son of the Earl Marshal.[41] The heir to the barony, Roger Stafford, son of

Richard, youngest son of Henry Baron Stafford (1547–63), surrendered his claim to the king in 1639 and died c. 1640, when the barony (created 1547) became extinct as did the direct male line of the Stafford family.[42] On 11 November 1640, however, William Howard, already Baron Stafford, was created Viscount Stafford.[43] Stafford manor and Forebridge, sequestrated with other of Viscount Stafford's estates for recusancy, were discharged in 1649,[44] but he was attainted and executed in 1680 for complicity in the Popish Plot.[45] The manor, with the castle, was assured in 1681 to his widow.[46] She and her son, Henry Howard (cr. Earl of Stafford in 1688) were found to have conveyed these by 1680 to Cardinal Howard and others in trust for the College or Society *de Propaganda Fide* in Rome, for the celebration of 4,000 masses a year for 51 years for the soul of the late viscount, and, thereafter, for beginning the process for his canonization.[47] The premises were seized into the king's hands as a result, and a warrant was authorized in 1694 for the grant of the property (called Stafford castle) to Charles Duke of Bolton.[48] The effect of this grant is not clear, since Henry Howard's lands surveyed in 1698, while he was in France with James II, included the manor, then called Forebridge, with the 'site of the old castle called Stafford castle' and a messuage called The Lodge, with about 100 acres in Castle Church parish and meadow lands there.[49] These were settled in 1720 on his nephew and heir, William Earl of Stafford (d. 1734).[50] By 1788 this estate had passed to Sir William Jerningham Bt.[51] grandson of Mary, sister of John Paul, Earl Stafford (d. 1767).[52]

Lord Stafford in 1956 owned considerable property in this part of the parish, including Hill and Burley Fields farms and the Castle Wood.[53]

In 1299 ½ carucate in Bradley without a messuage, rent of mills in Stafford borough, fixed rents from various manors, rents of cummin and pepper and of six arrows, and annual rents of frithfee and wake-fee were owed to the Castle manor.[54] In 1403 and subsequently these rents were accounted for apart from the manor and were known as Stafford Rents.[55] Assised rents and rents for a term at the will of the lord then came from the vill of Castle, the Green in Forebridge, Rowley, the Lees, and Burton as well as from Bradley, Apeton, Billington, Littywood, Longnor, and The Reule (all in Bradley), Coppenhall,

[22] *Cal. Fine R.* 1461–71, 265, 282.
[23] *Cal. Pat.* 1467–77, 367.
[24] Ibid. 507–8.
[25] Ibid. 1476–85, 217.
[26] *Complete Peerage*, ii. 389–90.
[27] *Cal. Pat.* 1476–85, 437.
[28] *Complete Peerage*, ii. 390.
[29] *Cal. Pat.* 1494–1509, 13.
[30] W.S.L., D. 1721/1/8, pp. 13–14.
[31] *Complete Peerage*, ii. 390–1; E 150/1028, no. 3.
[32] W.S.L., Stafford Barony Valor, 1522; S.C. 11/1018.
[33] *L. & P. Hen. VIII*, v, g. 364 (29). A list of freeholders in sundry Staffs. townships was drawn up in 1531–2 (W.S.L.; D. 1721/1/8, pp. 91–99), and the Ministers' Accounts for the lands of Henry and Ursula in Staffs., Salop., and Ches. 1532–3, give field names of demesne lands of Stafford manor: W.S.L., Stafford Barony Mins. Accts. 24–25 Hen. VIII.
[34] *Complete Peerage*, xii (1), 183. His Letter Book, 37 Hen. VIII to 1 Mary, is now in the William Salt Library, Stafford (D. 1721/1/10).
[35] *Cal. Pat.* 1553–4, 483.
[36] C 142/154, no. 91.

[37] C 142/284, no. 23. He had sold other Staffordshire manors in 1574, 1581, 1583, and 1589: *S.H.C.* xiv. 116; ibid. xv. 133, 145, 195.
[38] C 142/419, no. 72.
[39] *Cal. S.P. Dom.* 1625–6, 94, 133, 161, 555.
[40] C 142/565, no. 201.
[41] *Complete Peerage*, xii (1), 188–9.
[42] Ibid. 187–8.
[43] Ibid. 188–90.
[44] *Cal. Cttee. for Compounding*, 2083–6.
[45] *Complete Peerage*, xii (1), 191.
[46] C 66/3225, m. 2.
[47] *Complete Peerage*, xii (1), 192, and n.
[48] *Cal. Treas. Bks.* 1693–6, 591.
[49] E 178/6821, mm. 1–8.
[50] W.S.L. 119/40; C.P. 43/549, rot. 36; *Complete Peerage*, xii (1), 193–4.
[51] B.M. Eg. MS. 2872, ff. 45a–60a.
[52] *Complete Peerage*, xii (1), 195–6.
[53] Ex inf. Lord Stafford's Estate Office, Swynnerton.
[54] *S.H.C.* 1911, 198–9.
[55] W.S.L., D. 1721/1/8, pp. 143–58.

Dunston, Stretton, and Levedale (all in Penkridge), and from land in the parishes of Seighford and Stone and the extra-parochial area of Tillington near Stafford.[56] Along with these rents there were the proceeds of leases of the fisheries at Broad Eye (Brode) and 'Le Smalemede', of the capital messuages of Bradley and Rowley and of demesne lands there, and also of tenements and mills in the town of Stafford,[57] on the other side of the river. The proceeds of sale of small rents, including hay from Woollaston and Alstone in Bradley, hens from Levedale, six barbed arrows from Butterhill in Coppenhall, were 8s. 11d. in all.[58] An annual rent or custom of frithfee, wakefee, and 'kelghe' were paid by the vills of Bradley, Longnor, Apeton, Woollaston, Alstone, Brough and Reule, Barton, Shredicote, Billington, Mitton in Penkridge, Burton and Rickerscote, Stafford Castle, 'Mersshe', and Rowley.[59]

This group of vills and other tenements forming Stafford Rents varied from time to time, as by the inclusion of lands of Ralph Basset, lord of Drayton, inherited after 1390 by the earls of Stafford;[60] or by the tenements in Stafford town in the lord's hands after the death of Roger Bradshawe.[61] Some of these properties were still in Lord Stafford's possession in 1937.[62]

In 1293 assize of bread and beer was claimed for the Liberty of Bradley attached to the castle.[63] By 1387 the name, and possibly the location, of the court leet, as well as of the three-weekly court, for what were still then described as the members of Bradley had been changed from Castle manor to Castleforebridge.[64] Profits of the courts, beyond the fees of the steward and other ministers, were then valued at 30s. a year.[65] By 1404 these were reckoned at 40s.[66] and in 1440 what was then described as the Liberty of Forebridge was worth £4 11s. 11d. a year beyond the bailiff's fee of 40s. and other allowances.[67] The townships presenting at the view of frankpledge in 1472 and 1473 and also from 1499 to 1503 were Tillington (near Stafford), Alstone, Brough and Reule, Billington, Longnor, Barton and Apeton, Woollaston and Shredicote, and Bradley (all then in Bradley parish), with Burton, Rickerscote, and Forebridge (subsequently in Castle Church parish).[68] The Liberty and leet of Forebridge were valued in 1521 at £4 16s. 2d.[69] The bailiff's fee was 60s. 8d. by 1522[70] when this office was given by the king to Edward Littleton after the fall of the Duke of Buckingham.[71] In 1524 Henry Lord Stafford gave

the office to Thomas Barbour at fee and wages of 60s. 8d. from lands and tenements in Forebridge.[72] On 19 October 1532 courts were held at Stafford castle,[73] where, it is said, they continued to be held,[74] although the view of frankpledge was at Forebridge in 1570.[75] From at least 1625 to 1631 courts were again held at Forebridge, when the High Steward of the leet and manor was Sir Walter Chetwynd of Ingestre (Pirehill hundred) and of Grendon (Warws.), and the under-steward Thomas Worswick,[76] Mayor of Stafford, in 1622.[77] The townships included in the leet were still the same as in 1472.[78]

In 1801 the leet of Forebridge was said to include the whole of the parish of Castle Church, and also Coppenhall and Mitton in Penkridge and all the townships then in Bradley parish, thus excluding Alstone, one of the earlier members of Bradley, then in Haughton parish.[79]

The berewick of *BURTON*, a member of Bradley manor in 1086, was then assessed at 2½ hides.[80] The overlordship descended with the barony of Stafford until at least 1697.[81]

In 1242 the heirs of Roger the tailor (*cissor*) were holding ½ fee in 'Borton' of Robert de Stafford,[82] but in 1279 William le Teyllur of Burton, otherwise William son of Roger le Tayllur, declared he was holding nothing by inheritance from his father in Burton.[83] By 1247 or 1248 Julia widow of William le 'Plumer' (? Palmer) was claiming one-third of 3½ acres of land and one-third of a nook of pasture in Burton as dower.[84] Roger le Palmer of Burton by Stafford and William le Palmer of the same occur as witnesses to a grant of land in Burton in 1283,[85] and Richard le Palmer and William occur there in 1310.[86] In 1444 Simon Palmer was holding the manor of Burton by military service, paying no money rent but doing suit at the Earl of Stafford's court every three weeks.[87] In 1452 he paid 5s. 6d. rent for ½ messuage and 1 virgate of land leased to him that year,[88] but no manor is mentioned, and this may be the ½ messuage and virgate for which Peter Robyns paid 5s. 6d. rent as a tenant at will of Lord Stafford in 1488.[89]

An estate in Burton is said to have been held by 1432 or 1433 by Robert Whitgreave, and to have descended through another Robert[90] who is said to have died in 1448 or 1449.[91] His son Humphrey was followed by a son Robert on whom in 1524 the capital messuage was settled, on his marriage with Margery, daughter of Thomas Staunford, Stanford,

[56] W.S.L., D. 1721/1/8, pp. 143–7.
[57] Ibid., pp. 147–9.
[58] Ibid., p. 150.
[59] Ibid., p. 151. This rent was due at the Feast of St. Peter ad Vincula (1 Aug.): C 139/180.
[60] Shaw, *Staffs.* ii. 5, 27; W.S.L., Stafford Barony Valor, 18 Hen. VI, f. 18a; *L. & P. Hen. VIII*, v, g. 364 (29).
[61] W.S.L., Stafford Barony Valor, 18 Hen. VI, f. 18a; *L. & P. Hen. VIII*, v, g. 364 (29).
[62] W.S.L. 223/38.
[63] *S.H.C.* vi (1), 258–9.
[64] C 130/47.
[65] Ibid.
[66] *Cal. Pat.* 1401–5, 347.
[67] W.S.L., Stafford Barony, Mins. Accts. 18 Hen. VI, f. 18a.
[68] D.L. 30/108, no. 1606, mm. 1, 3; W.S.L., Forebridge Ct. R. 15–18 Hen. VII.
[69] E 150/1028, no. 3; E 36/150, f. 58a.
[70] E 36/181, f. 29a.
[71] *L. & P. Hen. VIII*, ii (2), g. 2016 (22).
[72] W.S.L., D. 1721/1/1, f. 133b.

[73] W.S.L., Stafford Barony, Mins. Accts. Mich. 25 Hen. VIII, m. 6d.
[74] J. B. Frith, Notes on some Staffs. manors . . . of Lord Stafford: W.S.L. 223/38.
[75] C 142/154, no. 91.
[76] W.S.L., D. 1721/1/9, 5th nos., pp. 1–57.
[77] J. W. Bradley, *Royal Charters . . . of Stafford* (1897), 206.
[78] W.S.L., D. 1721/1/9, 5th nos., pp. 1–57.
[79] S.R.O., Q/RDc 15.
[80] *V.C.H. Staffs.* iv. 49, no. 161.
[81] C 142/565, no. 201; E 172/6821.
[82] *Bk. of Fees*, 967.
[83] *S.H.C.* vi (1), 74, 98–99.
[84] Ibid. iv (1), 111.
[85] W.S.L., D. 1721/1/1, ff. 295b–6a.
[86] *S.H.C.* x (1), 8.
[87] W.S.L., D. 1721/1/1, f. 385a.
[88] Ibid., f. 340a.
[89] Ibid., f. 246a.
[90] Erdeswick, *Staffs.* ed. Harwood (1844), 185.
[91] *S.H.C.* iii (2), 147.

or Stamford of Rowley.[92] Robert died in 1550 and was succeeded by his son Humphrey.[93] The estate descended in the Whitgreave family (along with Great Bridgeford in Seighford and Moseley Old Hall in Bushbury)[94] until the beginning of the 18th century when the elder branch of the family became extinct and the estate was sold.[95] Burton farm on which was the moat formerly surrounding the ancient seat of the family was repurchased by Francis, second son of G. T. Whitgreave, a short time before 1851.[96] Burton Hall was acquired c. 1930 as a social and sports club by the British Reinforced Concrete Co., the moat was drained and a dance hall built.[97] The bar was added in 1956.[98]

During the 17th century the estate seems to have been tenanted by the family of Riley or Ryley, John, son of John Ryley of Burton Hall, dying in 1664 and Edward Ryley of Burton in 1669.[99]

The mid-19th-century Hall, completed in 1855 from designs by E. W. Pugin,[1] is built on the ancient moated site, and is a gabled building of red brick. On the front the letter 'W' is picked out in blue bricks. The interior contains elaborate fittings in the Gothic style.

RICKERSCOTE (Ricardescote), one of the berewicks of Bradley in 1086 and assessed at 2½ hides, was held before the Conquest by Earl Edwin and after it by Robert de Stafford, whose tenant there was one Robert.[2] The overlordship descended in the Stafford barony until at least 1697.[3] In 1294 Hervey Bagot was holding an intermediate lordship here[4] which may have descended by 1310 to William Bagot.[5]

This holding has been identified as part of the ¾ fee held in 1166 of Robert de Stafford by Roger *vigilis* or Le Waite[6] who gave land there to Stone Priory[7] and whose daughter Cecily conveyed ½ virgate there some time between 1224 and 1227 to the prior and canons of Kenilworth.[8] Hugh la Weyte held ⅓ fee in Rickerscote of the barony of Stafford by 1243,[9] but nothing further is heard of this family in connexion with the vill, unless Hugh la Wayte can be identified with Hugh de Akesey (of Doxey in Seighford, Pirehill hundred) whose widow Beatrice and brother Robert de Dokeseye were disputing in 1275 and 1277 with Richard Attewell of Rickerscote concerning rights of common of pasture appurtenant to his free tenement in Rickerscote.[10]

About the middle of the 15th century what was described as the manor of Rickerscote was settled on

Avice, daughter and heir of Sir Richard Stafford, eldest son of Sir Humphrey Stafford of Hook (Dors.), with other manors including Littywood in Bradley.[11] After her death it passed to her cousin Humphrey Stafford, who died in 1461 when his heir was another cousin, Humphrey Stafford, lord of Southwick.[12] This Humphrey Stafford died in 1469, holding, of the Duke of Buckingham, ½ fee in Rickerscote for which his heirs still owed 50s. in 1471.[13] After this date the vill or manor of Rickerscote seems to have been retained in demesne as part of the barony and within the leet jurisdiction of the manor of Forebridge between at least 1472 and 1681.[14]

Sampson Barnfield, 'eldest son of Barnfield of Dunston', seems to have been the principal resident here in about 1679.[15] A house and land (51 a.) in Rickerscote were held by Roger Hinton who died c. 1685.[16] William Goldsmith, who died in 1703, also held land here as well as in Burton and Risingbrook.[17]

A fishery in Rickerscote was held of the barony in 1444 by John Alde at a rent of 3s. 4d.[18] and in 1453 by John 'de Alle'.[19] This may be the fishery held by Hugh Goldsmith from about 1520 to 1532 for which he owed 3s. 4d. in 1533.[20] He was still holding it in 1535.[21] In 1627 William Gouldsmyth was amerced at the view of frankpledge and court baron of Forebridge for not scouring his part of the River Penk.[22]

The central block and the south cross-wing of the farmhouse known as Rickerscote Hall are timber-framed and date from c. 1600. The framing at the front, exposed above first-floor level, is in the form of square panels with quadrant ornament. Elsewhere the timbering has been encased in brick. Near the north end of the central block a single chamfered post, visible internally, may indicate the position of the open truss of a two-bay medieval hall.

One hide at *SILKMORE* (Selchemore) formed one of the berewicks of Bradley in 1086 and was held by Robert de Stafford in chief.[23] It was subsequently absorbed into the Castle manor with which demesne land in Silkmore descended until at least 1788.[24]

LESSER ESTATES. By about 1403 a capital messuage in Rowley was held of Edmund Earl of Stafford by Henry Haymes, at a rent of 33s. 4d.[25] Humphrey Earl of Stafford and Duke of Buckingham (d. 1460) leased it to various tenants.[26] One of these farmers was, presumably, Thomas Fyssher who

92 C 142/94, no. 50.
93 Ibid.
94 S.H.C. v (2), 307–8.
95 White, Dir. Staffs. (1851), 455.
96 Ibid.
97 Ex inf. the caretaker (1957).
98 Ex inf. the caretaker.
99 John Ryley was buried 11 Dec. 1664: Bradley Par. Reg. (from transcript in W.S.L., p. 73). Edward Riley buried 16 Oct. 1669: ibid., p. 74.
1 C. Calvert, History of Stafford (1886), 94.
2 V.C.H. Staffs. iv. 53, no. 222.
3 E 178/6821.
4 S.H.C. vii (1), 8, 78.
5 Ibid. x (1), 8.
6 Ibid. i, 186–7. The rest of the fee was in Tysoe (Warws.).
7 Ibid. ii (1), 275; ibid. i. 187.
8 Ibid. iii (1), 230–1. She married Richard de Bereford: ibid. i. 187.
9 Bk. of Fees, 967.
10 S.H.C. vi (1), 72, 81–82.

11 C 140/3.
12 Ibid. For pedigree, see S.H.C. n.s. iv. 204–7; S.H.C. vi (1) 149–50; Wrottesley, Pedigrees from Plea Rolls, 472; W.S.L., D. 1721/1/8, ff. 30b–31a.
13 Complete Peerage, iv. 327–8 and n.; S.C. 11/604.
14 D.L. 30/108, no. 1606; W.S.L., Forebridge Ct. R. (1499–1503); C.P. 43/395, rot. 179.
15 S.H.C. 1919, 237.
16 7th Rep. Com. Char. H.C. 129, pp. 418, 419 (1822), x; 11th Rep. H.C. 433, p. 517 (1824), xiv; Survey of 1709 in Ch. W. Accts.: W.S.L. 192/25.
17 11th Rep. Com. Char. 518.
18 W.S.L., D. 1721/1/8, p. 385.
19 Ibid., p. 341.
20 W.S.L., Stafford Barony, Mins. Accts. 24–25 Hen. VIII, m. 3d.
21 W.S.L., D. 1721/1/8, p. 247.
22 W.S.L., D. 1721/1/9, 5th nos. pp. 23–24.
23 V.C.H. Staffs. iv. 49, no. 161.
24 B.M. Eg. MS. 2872, f. 56b.
25 W.S.L., D. 1721/1/1, f. 310a.
26 W.S.L., D. 1721/1/8, p. 338.

paid 39s. 8d. as a tenant-at-will for a tenement in Rowley in 1452.[27] The overlordship of this capital messuage descended with the barony until at least 1588.[28]

Robert Standford or Staunford, who had married Fisher's daughter Elizabeth[29] or Isabel,[30] paid 2d. rent as a free tenant for the capital messuage in 1486 as well as 40s. as tenant-at-will for an orchard and tenements called the farm of Rowley.[31] In 1502 or 1503 Isabel Stanford, then a widow, was engaged in a dispute concerning a messuage, land, and meadow in 'Rowley in the parish of Castle Church', held by her in demesne as of fee, with Thomas Stanford, described as of Rowley.[32] Thomas, who was Robert's third son, was M.P. for Stafford 1529–30.[33] He was dead by 1535,[34] having held land in Rowley with what was described as the capital messuage,[35] which was the subject of dispute in 1539 between his son and heir William Stanford and Henry Lord Stafford.[36] Lord Stafford claimed that this capital messuage had been restored to him in 1531 by the Crown after the forfeiture of the barony,[37] while Stanford submitted evidences of his family's holdings in Rowley from the time of Edward III to that of Henry VIII.[38] During this suit, which lasted until at least 1547,[39] a very old man deposed, in 1539, that he had lived with Robert Standford and had heard him say that the house standing above the Green of 'Rowlowe' and in the orchard was the Lord Stafford's, called the 'Halle of Rowlowe', which had by that time become a 'caulf' house.[40] Agreement had been reached between the parties by at least 1552, when William Stanford granted an annuity out of what was called the manor of Rowley to his half-brother Roger.[41] In 1562 William settled this so-called manor on his son Edward and Edward's wife Jane, with successive remainders to their sons William and Edward, and, dying in 1570 seised of the manor and a messuage and 120 acres in Rowley, was succeeded by his grandson, William, then under age.[42] William succeeded also to the manor of Packington in Weeford and to land in Handsworth (both in Offlow hundred).[43] William Stanford, described as of Packington, was living in 1583.[44]

The next link in the descent is not clear, but in 1588 Edward Lord Stafford conveyed Rowley manor to Edward Rowley and William Brett.[45] They may have been trustees for the purpose of transferring the manor to another branch of the Stanford family since, in 1607, Sir Robert Stanford of Perry Hall died seised of it, and also of the site of the house of the former Austin Friars in Forebridge, his heir being a son Edward.[46] Sir Robert was the son of Sir William Stanford of Gray's Inn, M.P. for Stafford (1542, 1545–7) and for Newcastle under Lyme (1547–52), Justice of Common Pleas,[47] and kinsman and supporter of William Stanford of Rowley in the dispute of c. 1539.[48] In 1610 Edward Stanford joined with his wife Mary in a conveyance of the manor of Rowley (and also of the site of the Austin friary) to Richard Berington[49] who had married Edward's sister Anne,[50] and who died in 1612 holding manor and friary land in chief, by knight service.[51] Richard Berington was succeeded by a minor son John,[52] who is said to have been holding the manor in 1660.[53] 'Mr. Berrington' was living at Rowley Hall in 1679 or 1680.[54] In 1721 a John Berington made a conveyance of the manor to Thomas Hitchecocke.[55]

The present Rowley Hall was built c. 1817 by William Keen,[56] and George Keen was the occupant in 1851.[57] Part of the Rowley Hall Estate, some 120 acres, was sold before 1868 for building development.[58] By 1896 only 50 acres of park and farm were attached to the Hall.[59] The hall, a two-story mansion of stone ashlar with a semicircular Ionic porch, is now (1957) a Home Office Remand Home for girls. It was described soon after its erection c. 1817 as an 'elegant house'.[60]

By 1452 one of the principal tenants-at-will in Forebridge was John Barbor or Barbour.[61] By 1486 or 1487 Humphrey Barbour, his son, was the principal free tenant there,[62] as was Humphrey's son Robert in 1518.[63] Robert, who was given the office of bailiff of the Liberty of Forebridge in 1524,[64] died in 1531 as lord of Flashbrook in Adbaston (Pirehill hundred) and holding what was described as a capital messuage in Forebridge and Rowley, in

[27] W.S.L., D. 1721/1/8, p. 338.
[28] S.H.C. xv. 187.
[29] W.S.L., D. 1721/1/1, f. 311a.
[30] C 1/498, no. 24.
[31] W.S.L., D. 1721/1/8, p. 21. In 1488 Robert acquired other land in Rowley on 10 years' lease: W.S.L., D. 1721/1/1, f. 319a.
[32] C 1/271, no. 69.
[33] C 1/498, no. 23; S.H.C. 1917–18, 302; ibid. iii (2), 135–6. In 1519 Thomas Stanford was paying 33s. 4d. rent as a tenant-at-will in Forebridge for a barn with a pasture called Newhay, formerly held by Robert Stanford: W.S.L., D. 1721/18, p. 111.
[34] W.S.L., Stafford Barony Rental, 26 Hen. VIII, f. 5a.
[35] W.S.L., D. 1721/1/1, f. 320a.
[36] Ibid. ff. 310a–12b; S.H.C. iii (2), 136.
[37] C 1/1265, no. 57.
[38] W.S.L., D. 1721/1/1, ff. 311a–12b.
[39] C 1/1265, no. 57. Many other disputes were carried to the king's court: C 1/1329, nos. 10–11; C 1/1404, nos. 16–17; C 1/1505, nos. 55–56; C 3/146, no. 51.
[40] W.S.L., D. 1721/1/1, ff. 311a–12b.
[41] C 142/162, no. 139; S.H.C. iii (2), 136.
[42] C 142/162, no. 139. William was aged 19 in 1571, and inherited also 2 messuages, a cottage and 50 a. in Forebridge, and 2 messuages, a cottage and 80 a. in Burton and Rickerscote.
[43] Shaw, Staffs. ii. 26. William was said to have married a daughter of Oliver Briggs: C 3/160, no. 44.
[44] S.H.C. iii (2), 137.

[45] Ibid. xv. 187.
[46] C 142/299, no. 125.
[47] Shaw, Staffs. ii. 26, 109; S.H.C. iii (2), 133. There is some confusion in the biography as set out in S.H.C. 1917–18, 311.
[48] W.S.L., D. 1721/1/1, ff. 310a sqq. Field names are here given.
[49] S.H.C. iii (2), 137; ibid. n.s. iii. 44.
[50] S.H.C. v (2), 280.
[51] C 142/331, no. 139. He was buried at Castle Church, 17 Feb. 1611/12: Castle Church Par. Reg. (Staffs. Par. Reg. Soc.), i. 38.
[52] C 142/331, no. 139. A John Berrington senior of Rowley was buried at Castle Church, 28 Apr. 1649: Castle Church Par. Reg. i. 83.
[53] Erdeswick, Staffs. (1844), 448 n.
[54] S.H.C. 1919, 237.
[55] C.P. 25(2)/1062, 7 Geo. I Hil.
[56] Pitt, Staffs. 269; White, Dir. Staffs. (1834), 144.
[57] White, Dir. Staffs. (1851), 343.
[58] P.O. Dir. Staffs. (1868), p. 646; see p. 84.
[59] Kelly's Dir. Staffs. (1896).
[60] Parson and Bradshaw, Dir. Staffs. (1818), p. ccxxix.
[61] He paid 33s. 4d. rent for a barn with pasture called Newhay and 16s. 8d. for another barn and pasture called Tromyneslond: W.S.L., D. 1721/1/8, p. 339. Thomas Staunford held Newhay in 1519: see above.
[62] W.S.L., D. 1721/1/8, p. 22; S.H.C. v (2), 29: ibid. 1914, 73.
[63] W.S.L., D. 1721/1/8, p. 112.
[64] W.S.L., D. 1721/1/1, f. 133b.

which his widow, Joyce, daughter of Lewis Eyton, continued to live.[65] His heir was his son John[66] whose holding in Forebridge in 1543 was the most considerable among the lay tenants and included a house (tenanted by one Ralph Dickens) with croft and leasow of 7 acres and other named crofts, meadows, and pastures.[67] This was apparently sold c. 1600 to a family called Leigh, of London, who sold it c. 1615 to the Drakeford family.[68] In 1732 the house, Green Hall, and the estate were owned by Richard Drakeford.[69] In 1809 Edward Drakeford sold part of the estate, a messuage and tenement called Silvercroft, to Benjamin Rogers who built the house called Forebridge Villa (since 1907 St. Joseph's Convent) there.[70] Green Hall was bought in 1922 by the County Council from W. E. Pickering and used for a time as the preparatory section of the Girls' High School. Since 1949 it has been occupied by the Architect's Dept. of the County Council Education Committee.[71]

Gregory King records c. 1680 that shields of arms of the Drakefords and others were set in the windows of Green Hall.[72] In 1732 the house appears to have had a three-gabled front and a large barn near the road.[73] It was rebuilt c. 1825 when it was given an impressive stucco façade of seven bays.[74] The highest row of windows is constructed in the roof parapet and has no rooms behind it; possibly there was an intention to build another story at some future date. The iron gate and overthrow were formerly in the stable yard, now demolished.

In 1208 one Hugh son of Ralph conveyed to Eudes Prior of the Hospital of St. John, Stafford, 40 acres of land in Castle.[75] After the dissolution of the free chapel or hospital in 1547[76] its lands here and elsewhere were granted by the Crown in 1550 to the burgesses of Stafford for the endowment of a free grammar school.[77] At some date between 1551 and 1553, one William Tully, to whom the farm of these lands had been leased by the prior or keeper of the hospital in 1536 or 1537, and some of the tenants here asserted their right to withhold their rents on the grounds that the hospital was founded for relief of the poor[78] and as such was not subject to the statute of dissolution. The burgesses seem to have proved their claim by showing that, for as long as they could remember, this free chapel or hospital had not maintained or relieved any poor.[79] In 1588, however, the queen granted to Edward Wymarke of London what was described as the free chapel of St. John the Baptist in Forebridge, with all lands and tenements, to hold by fealty and at a rent of 2s. 6d. a year.[80] A similar grant was made to William Tipper and Robert Dawe in 1592 at a rent of 3s. 4d. and the same service.[81] By about 1607 some possessions

of the late hospital were in the hands of George Cradock, who at his death in 1611 held the chapel, with a messuage called St. John's House, four cottages, and a pasture called St. John's Birch, all in chief in socage.[82] His heir was his son, Matthew Craddock,[83] who by 1612 or 1613 was owing £5 9s. annual rent to the school of Stafford for what was described as the great house adjoining St. John's Chapel in Forebridge (in the occupation of a tenant), with three cottages, and for land called Stychfields.[84] At his death in 1636 Matthew Cradock held 'a chapel called St. John's Chapel in Forebridge' which passed to his son George.[85]

The hospital and chapel are thought to have stood at the junction of Lichfield Road and White Lion Street on the site now occupied by the White Lion Inn.[86] The hospital is known to have existed in 1208. Its seal depicts a cruciform building with 13th-century features[87] and may possibly perpetuate an approximate image of the chapel as it was when the matrix was struck. The west part of the White Lion Inn, now used as a clubroom, is built of stone and may represent the remains of the chapel. At the rear a single pilaster buttress and part of a window-opening are visible and some masonry is exposed in the lower part of the gable end. Elsewhere the walls are covered with roughcast but there are indications of further buttresses. The exposed masonry suggests considerable rebuilding in the 16th or 17th century and a stone wall in the yard to the south is probably of the same date, although containing earlier material reused. The eastern part of the inn consists of a timber-framed two-story house of the late 16th or early 17th century with a gabled wing, probably originally a porch, projecting towards the street.

By 1486 or 1487 a free tenement within Forebridge, namely Edmondsfurlong in Radford (Ratford), was held by the Rector of 'Spittell',[88] otherwise the hospital of St. Leonard.[89] This remained with the hospital, being held of the lords Stafford for a chief rent of 14d.[90] and was described in 1543 as 1 acre lying by Radford (Ratford) Bridge, called Edmondesfurlong,[91] or otherwise as one 'place' of land.[92] At this date the other free tenements of the parson of the Spital in Forebridge included one 'flat' called Pakkefurlong in the Greenfield, two distinct acres in the same field, one of them abutting upon the pit, and also a croft adjoining this same field and containing about 8 acres.[93] Besides this share of the arable he had two pastures, one of about 14 acres and the other of about 6 acres, lying near the Spital chapel, with two days' math of meadow.[94] In 1550 this pasture land lying beside the 'free chapel of St. Leonard' with the parcel of meadow and also 9 acres in the Greenfield, all formerly held by the

65 C 142/52, no. 45.
66 The elder son, Humphrey, predeceased his father: ibid.; W.S.L., D. 1721/1/8, p. 93.
67 W.S.L., D. 1721/1/9, 1st nos. ff. 179a–179b.
68 S.H.C. viii (2), 125.
69 W.S.L. 12/30.
70 Deeds penes St. Joseph's Convent, Stafford; see p. 98.
71 Ex inf. Staffs. C.C. Education Architect's Dept.
72 S.H.C. viii (2), 125.
73 W.S.L. 12/30.
74 See plate facing p. 87.
75 S.H.C. iii (1), 172–3.
76 Under the Act of 1 Edw. VI, c. 14.
77 Cal. Pat. 1550–3, 21.
78 C 1/1268, nos. 58–62.
79 C 1/1268, no. 63.

80 C 66/1311, mm. 2–27.
81 C 66/1382 mm. 21–38.
82 C 142/337, no. 83.
83 Ibid.
84 C. G. Gilmore, King Edward VI School, Stafford (1953), 131.
85 C 142/478, no. 70.
86 Roxburgh, Stafford, 60–61.
87 Ibid. 60 (plate).
88 W.S.L., D. 1721/1/8, p. 22.
89 S.H.C. xvii. 40–41.
90 W.S.L., Stafford Barony, Mins. Accts. Mich. 24–25 Hen. VIII, m. 2; W.S.L., D. 1721/1/8, p. 236.
91 W.S.L., D. 1721/1/9, 1st nos. f. 181a.
92 Ibid., f. 186a.
93 Ibid., f. 186b.
94 Ibid.

hospital, were granted by Edward VI to his grammar school at Stafford.[95] The barony retained some rights, for in 1588 14d. was due from the executors of 'Mr. Sutton' in chief rent for the 'Spittle lands'.[96] By 1633 the chamberlains of Stafford were paying a rent to Mistress Stafford's bailiff for these lands.[97]

The land in the vill of Forebridge given by Ralph Lord Stafford in 1343 for the foundation of a house of Austin Friars[98] with later endowments[99] appears to have lain in the region still known as the Green, since in the survey of the barony's tenements here in 1543 the late friars' churchyard, standing 'uppon the myddes of the Greene', was named as a boundary to a tenant's holding.[1] In 1544 lands and such buildings as remained of the former Austin Friars were granted in fee by Henry VIII to Edward Stanford (or Staunford) and included a croft called Friars' Orchard, pasture called the Friars' Field, and also the site of the late Austin Friars, with a croft and churchyard.[2] Edward Stanford remained in possession of these lands until in 1554 Queen Mary granted in fee to Thomas Reeve and Giles Isham the site of the late house of Austin Friars in Forebridge by Stafford with all buildings, lands, &c. within the precinct, and a croft of land called 'le freers orchard' belonging to the house.[3] Reeve and Isham, it is said, then sold their rights in the Friars' Orchard to Lord Stafford, who attempted to eject Edward Stanford.[4] In 1562, however, Stanford settled the site of the house, the 'circuit', and other appurtenances on his wife Jane with successive remainders to their two sons William and Edward. He died at Rowley in 1568, holding the property in chief as $\frac{1}{100}$ knight's fee, his heir being his son William, still under age.[5] In 1578 or 1579 William Stanford (who had inherited Rowley and other manors from his grandfather in 1570)[6] conveyed the site to Thomas Repingdon and others presumably for a settlement[7] since Sir Robert Stanford of Rowley at his death in 1607 was found to be holding the site and precincts of the late friary, with the graveyard, some 2½ acres, of the king in chief as $\frac{1}{100}$ fee.[8] His heir was his son Edward,[9] who conveyed the site of the friary with Rowley in 1610 to Richard Berington.[10]

A messuage called Rising Brook ('Risom Brook') was held at his death in 1570 by William Stanford of Rowley, along with 42 acres of land, all in socage, of Lord Stafford.[11] By will of 1663 Simon Fowler left a messuage, land, and tenements there to his wife Ann, for life, and then to his daughter Margaret Backhouse, widow.[12] There were two little houses

there c. 1680.[13] By 1778 the owner of Rising Brook House was a Mr. Moore,[14] and c. 1824 an estate of about 35 acres there was owned by John Moore of The Toft in Penkridge.[15]

Land called Lee or La Lee, now in Castle Church but then within the manor or territory of Billington in Bradley, was frequently conveyed during the 13th century by or to members of the family of Caverswall, and between c. 1260 and 1270 Richard de Lee, Thomas son of Richard de la Leye, and Nicholas son of Thomas de la Leye are all found conveying their rights in ½ virgate in Billington to Roger de Caverswall.[16] At what may have been a slightly later date, a house and garden with lands variously described as the fields of 'Leg' or in 'Le Leye within the manor of Billington' were conveyed to William de Caverswall by John de Weohaliz (or John son of John de Wethales), or Adam son of John.[17] In 1562 Henry Lord Stafford and his wife Ursula granted a lease for lives of one-half of Lees Farm to Thomas Backhouse (or Chamberlain), his wife Margaret, and his son John.[18] It may have been this John Chamberlain or Backhouse, described as of the Lees Farm, who with his wife Anne and son John received a lease for their lives of one-half of the farm in 1589, at a rent of £3 1s. 8d.[19] Meanwhile, what was presumably the other half was leased for their three lives, in 1588 at a similar rent, to George Backhouse or Chamberlain, his wife Margaret, and his son Francis.[20] On 1 July 1608 this George Chamberlain assigned his rights to John Stanley of Alstone (then in Bradley),[21] but on 14 July Lord Stafford made a further lease of a moiety to George and Margaret and a son John.[22]

In 1695 William Barnesley of the Inner Temple and others, as trustees, leased Lees House, then described as in Castle Church parish, to Humphrey Goldsmith for a term still running in 1701 when they made a conveyance of it in moieties to Thomas Salt of Beffcote and John Lees of Cowley (both in Gnosall).[23] In 1711 one-half of one of these moieties was conveyed by John Lees the elder of Cowley to Thomas Salt of Beffcote with an equivalent share of barns and other appurtenances (the tenant then being one Vincent Payne), to the use of John the elder for life, with reversion to John Lees the younger.[24] Thomas Salt of Stafford and Thomas Lees of Cowley, yeomen, in 1753 made a lease for 21 years to William Jennings, apparently already tenant there, of what was described as The White House or Lees House, at rents of £20 a year to each of them, with 6s. 8d. chief rent to the king or his

[95] *Cal. Pat.* 1550–3, 21–22.
[96] W.S.L., D. 1721/1/9, 3rd nos. f. 108a.
[97] W.S.L., S. MS. 459, ff. 100a–101a (transcript of Stafford Chamberlains' accts.).
[98] *Cal. Papal Pet.* i. 27; *Cal. Papal Reg.* iii. 137.
[99] *Cat. Anct. D.* ii, B 3631, B 3635.
[1] W.S.L., D. 1721/1/9, 1st nos., f. 196b. The buildings were sold in 1538 to James Leveson and others: *L. & P. Hen. VIII*, xiii (2), p. 254.
[2] *L. & P. Hen. VIII*, xix (1), g. 1035 (156). The tenants of these holdings were, respectively, Robert Dorrington, William Staunford, and Thomas Pictoo. Other 'superfluous edifices and buildings' within the precinct of the friars were sold in 1538 to James Leveson of Wolverhampton and others: F. A. Hibbert, *Dissolution of the Monasteries* (1910), 249–51 (transcript of inventory).
[3] *Cal. Pat.* 1553–4, 471–2. The tenants were, respectively, Thomas Pictoo and Robert Dorrington.
[4] Sta. Cha. 4/38. Lord Stafford's attorneys to receive seisin were Robert Sutton his chaplain and Thomas

Chedleton, 'vicar of the parish church of Stafford'. The end of the dispute does not appear.
[5] C 142/162, no. 148.　[6] Ibid., no. 139.
[7] *S.H.C.* xvii. 224.
[8] C 142/299, no. 125.　[9] Ibid.
[10] *S.H.C.* iii (2), 132; ibid. N.S. iii. 44.
[11] C 142/162, no. 139.
[12] *11th Rep. Com. Char.* H.C. 433, pp. 520–1 (1824), xiv.
[13] *S.H.C.* 1919, 237.
[14] W.S.L. 192/25.
[15] Ibid. It had been held 'by his grandfather before him'.
[16] W.S.L., D. 1721/1/1, ff. 85–87 (Billington Deeds).
[17] Ibid., ff. 299b–307b, *passim*; *S.H.C.* xii (1), 70.
[18] W.S.L., D. 1721/1/9, 3rd nos. f. 91a.
[19] W.S.L., D. 1721/1/3, 23.
[20] Ibid. 26.
[21] Ibid. 27, 124.
[22] Ibid. 25.
[23] W.S.L. 64/5/46.
[24] W.S.L. 64/8/46.

assigns and 4d. a year for right of way over the Lees Grounds.[25] All timber and mineral rights were reserved to the lessors.[26] Mrs. Worswick, mother of Thomas Worswick lived at Lees Farm c. 1780.[27] By about 1840 the owner of Lees Farm was Samuel Wright, his tenant being Sampson Byrd, while what was then named The White House was still owned by Lord Stafford (tenant, James Eldershaw).[28] In 1921 Leese Farm covered over 229 acres lying in the parishes of Castle Church, Bradley, and Coppenhall.[29] The farmhouse appears to have been rebuilt early in the 19th century.

Hugh de Dokesey (or Doxey) was a tenant of the barony of Stafford in Silkmore early in the 13th century, and his widow, Alice, was seeking custody of his lands in 1230.[30] In 1255 another Hugh de Doxey conveyed two crofts in Silkmore to Walter, master of the hospital of St. Lazarus, Radford, half the land to be held in free alms for ever by his successors.[31] A later master, William de Madeley, exchanged a piece of marsh (mora) here for land in Forebridge with his overlords, Margaret Lady Stafford and her second husband Sir Thomas de Pipe, who conveyed it in 1320 to Richard son of Thomas Wenlock of Stafford, together with another piece of marsh in the same place.[32] Richard also held at this time a piece of marsh of Margaret de Doxey and Thomas de Halghton or Haughton (her husband).[33] Thomas de Halughton (or Haughton) and his wife Margaret still held demesne land in Silkmore in 1335, when they were granted free warren there.[34]

The prior and canons of St. Thomas's, Stafford, acquired some holding here in or after 1383.[35] Land in Silkmore, formerly held by the church of St. Mary, Stafford, for the endowment of Jesus Mass, was given by the Crown in 1563 or 1564 to William Forster.[36]

In 1572 Thomas Knevett conveyed to Matthew and William Cradock and Matthew's heirs lands and tenements in Silkmore, then described as in the parish of Castle, near Stafford, with a free fishery in the Penk,[37] presumably adjoining. A few months later, in 1573, William Cradock and his wife Timothea made over their interest to Matthew.[38] In 1575 Matthew Cradock and his wife Elizabeth conveyed two barns and land there to Edmund Cooper.[39] In 1578 this same Matthew and Elizabeth, together with Elizabeth Cradock, widow, and Francis and

William Cradock, conveyed to Anthony Colclough and his wife Clara this free fishery, and also a messuage with a toft, dovecote, a garden, and land here.[40] Sir Anthony Colclough died in Ireland soon after 1585 or 1586 and the manor or reputed manor of Silkmore then remained with his widow as tenant in demesne as of freehold for life.[41] On her remarriage in about 1587 it was held in her right by her second husband, Sir Thomas Williams, clerk of the cheque and muster master of Ireland.[42] The land was leased to tenants during Anthony's lifetime, and until at least 1590.[43] Anthony and Clara had two or more sons.[44] In 1621 Sir Thomas Colclough and Adam conveyed a messuage, toft, garden, and dovecot in Silkmore, with a free fishery, to Richard Drakeford,[45] and a Richard Drakeford still held land in Silkmore alongside the Penk in 1732.[46]

Thomas Backhouse or Chamberlain was holding land in Silkmore by 1629,[47] and in 1650 George Chamberlain or Backhouse and his wife Margery conveyed a fishery and land there to John Doody,[48] probably by way of settlement, since meadows in Silkmore, formerly held by Thomas Backhouse, were owned by William Goldsmith at the time of his death in 1703.[49] Goldsmith held also a capital messuage of Silkmore (in which he lived) and a so-called manor or 'royalty' and land there, which he left for their lives to Margaret Wetton (described as his servant) and her daughter Mary, with the fee simple, after their deaths, to his kinsman Benjamin Parker.[50] In 1704 Benjamin made a conveyance to Margaret Wetton[51] who was possibly dead by 1720 when Edward Parker and Mary conveyed the manor and a fishery 'in the waters of the Penk ditch' to Thomas Parker,[52] probably by way of settlement, since they were again dealing by fine with the manor of 1741.[53] In 1751 Mary Parker, then a widow, suffered a recovery of the manor and fishery[54] and on her death in 1787 the estate passed to a John Parker.[55] By 1763 the manor was held by Abraham Hoskins of Shenstone Park and his wife Sarah, and another Abraham and Sarah, of Burton.[56] An Abraham and Sarah Hoskins conveyed it in 1770 to Coote Molesworth and Luke Currie, whether in trust or as a sale does not appear.[57] In 1788 Sir George Chetwynd and his wife Jane made a conveyance to Thomas Mottershaw,[58] who was dead by 1834 when his successor as tenant or owner of Silkmore House was Thomas Hartshorn.[59]

25 W.S.L. 64/18/46.
26 Ibid.
27 S.H.C. 1919, 237.
28 Tithe Maps and Appt., Castle Church (copy in W.S.L.).
29 W.S.L., Sale Cat., C/3/3.
30 Close R. 1227–31, 393.
31 S.H.C. iv (1), 246–7.
32 W.S.L., D. 1721/1/1, f. 131b, no. 5.
33 Ibid.
34 Cal. Chart. R. 1327–41, 328.
35 Cal. Pat. 1381–5, 297.
36 C 66/999.
37 S.H.C. xiii. 289.
38 Ibid. 292.
39 Ibid. xiv (1), 176–7. Cooper died in 1585 holding lands called Silkmore alias Sylkesmore, 'in Haughton', and leaving a young son John: C 142/298, no. 49.
40 S.H.C. xiv (1), 195–6. Matthew Cradock, merchant of the staple, gave his age as 70 years in 1590: Req. 2/96, no. 27, m. 4. Elizabeth was presumably widow of George Cradock whose will was proved at Stafford, 10 Mar. 1577/8: S.H.C. 1926, 34–36.

41 Req. 2/96, no. 27, m. 11.
42 Ibid., m. 12; Req. 2/96, no. 57.
43 Req. 2/96, no. 27, mm. 2, 34 sqq.; Req. 2/96, no. 57.
44 Req. 2/96, no. 27, m. 3; Req. 2/96, no. 57.
45 S.H.C. n.s. vii. 234.
46 W.S.L. 12/30.
47 When he settled a rent-charge on Broad Meadow alias Silkmore Meadow for charity: 11th Rep. Com. Char. 517.
48 C.P. (2)/596, 1650 East.
49 11th Rep. Com. Char. 518; W.S.L. 192/25.
50 W.S.L. 192/25.
51 C.P. 25(2)/965, 5 Anne Mich.
52 C.P. 25(2)/1062, 7 Geo. I Mich.
53 C.P. 25(2)/1412, 15 Geo. II Hil.
54 C.P. 43/673 rot. 217. An Edward Parker was buried at Castle Church, 23 Sept. 1750: Castle Church Par. Reg. (Staffs. Par. Reg. Soc.), i. 107.
55 W.S.L. 192/25. Mary was buried 17 Jan. 1788: Par. Reg. i. 139.
56 C.P. 43/721, rot. 216.
57 C.P. 25(2)/1411, 10 Geo. II East.
58 C.P. 25(2)/1413, 28 Geo. III East.
59 White, Dir. Staffs. (1834).

Silkmore Hall has a symmetrical late-18th-century front with three-light sash windows, some semi-circular in shape. It consists of a central block of three stories with lower flanking wings. The garden front, stair-case hall, and other features date from c. 1825. The house is now (1957) divided into flats.

AGRICULTURE. Castle Church, because it is so low-lying, has always contained marshland and been subject to flooding by the rivers Sow and Penk in the north and east of the parish. In 1224 one Master Robert de Fyleby was ordered to lower, at his own cost, a stank or dam he had raised in Forebridge, whereby 10 acres of meadow and 10 acres of pasture had been submerged.[60] In 1372 Lord Stafford had a stew called 'Spitelpol' in Forebridge.[61] By 1387 it was grown over with rushes[62] and in 1399 was a marsh.[63] This had presumably dried out by 1404 when the herbage of Spittal Pool occurs.[64] There was a pool at Broad Eye in 1299 then used as a fishpond.[65] There is evidence that Silkmore was marshland in the early 14th century, when Richard son of Thomas Wenlock was given leave to make a stank on land there.[66] No systematic draining of the marshland was undertaken, however, until the 19th century. An act for draining and inclosing Forebridge was passed in 1800[67] and under the award made in 1851 a network of drains running into the Sow was constructed and the Sow itself straightened and deepened to take the increased volume of water. The main drains constructed were the Broad-Eye–Pans–Forebridge Drain and the Rickerscote Drain. The first ran through Broad Meadow to the Green and then parallel to the old course of the Sow to join the Sow just before its confluence with the Penk. This drain was crossed by the Spittal Brook, which was embanked to form a drainage ditch until it joined the old course of the Sow, and by a drain across Spittal Meadows called Hough Drain which joined Forebridge Drain just before it went into the Sow. Dove Meadow Drain was constructed in a west–east direction to join Hough Drain. A large number of small cross-drains from Forebridge Drain ran into the old course of the Sow. Rickerscote Drain was constructed parallel to the Penk and was joined by the Pothooks Brook and by Silkmoor Drain.[68] In 1884, under the Tillington Drainage Act, Broad-Eye was made an outfall area for Tillington and the Broad-Eye–Pans Drain was widened and deepened and joined by the Tillington Outfall Drain and smaller drains.[69] All these drains still form the drainage system for this land with the result that there are good water meadows by the Penk which can be used as cattle pasture most of the year while the land drained by the Sow which has not been taken up by housing, though of poorer quality, is also used as cattle pasture. The land is still liable to occasional flooding in the winter.

Inclosure of land in Castle Church started at an early date. In 1372 Lord Stafford had an inclosed pasture in Forebridge and a park, presumably also inclosed.[70] In 1396–7 demesne lands of the Castle manor were inclosed within a bank and thorn hedge 186 perches long. An area called Smallmead, also demesne, was inclosed at this date by a bank and hedge 124 perches long.[71] There was also a park 'of the Hyde' by this date .[72] In 1399 and in 1404 the demesne lands of the Castle manor still included the inclosed pasture in Forebridge and a pasture called 'Thevesdych'.[73] In 1460 the demesne of the manor included a several pasture containing three fields, Great Hyde Field, Castle Field, and 'Maynardsgreve' Field, and a pasture called the Hough.[74]

Land called Forebridge waste, lying between the houses in Forebridge and the parish church, was inclosed by Lord Stafford about 1512.[75] In 1555 some of the inhabitants of Forebridge broke through the hedge surrounding it, alleging that it obstructed their way to their parish church and to market, though, in defence, it was stated that at the time of the inclosure Lord Stafford had left sufficient common for the tenants and also land for a highway adjoining.[76]

The only common field surviving in Forebridge in 1543 was the Green Field, lying between the road from Stafford to Radford Bridge and the Wolverhampton road.[77] By this date the holdings in the field appear to have been consolidated into compact blocks of land, some of which had their own names.[78] There were numerous crofts and inclosed pastures in Forebridge at this date and one common meadow, Poole Meadow.[79]

By 1851 about 120 acres of land remained uninclosed in Castle Church comprising the Green Field and the Green Common, both in Forebridge, Benty Dole Meadow by the Penk, a small amount of land in Lammascote, north of the Sow, Hyde Lea Common and Adgetts Common and Pen Peck Common, both at Rickerscote.[80] All this land was then inclosed, 5 acres on the Lichfield road being allotted to the parishioners of Castle Church which were thenceforth known as the Green Common.[81] This was used by the parishioners of Castle Church as grazing land until the First World War under regulations drawn up in 1801 for the administration of the old Green Common which laid down that each householder who was a parishioner might turn in one gelding or mare, or one milking cow, or two two-year-old stirks or yearlings from 'Old Mayday' to 'Old Michaelmas day', three weeks in and three weeks out, but any number of cattle between 'Old Michaelmas day' and 'Old Candlemas day', such householders paying each 5s. a year and informing the pinner of the kind of cattle they meant to lay on the common.[82] The charge had risen by 1851 to 10s.

[60] S.H.C. vi (1), 299.
[61] Cal. Inq. p.m. xiii, p. 188.
[62] C 136/47.
[63] C 136/107.
[64] W.S.L., D. 1721/1/8, pp. 197–200.
[65] S.H.C. 1911, 198–9.
[66] W.S.L., D. 1721/1/1, f. 131b, no. 5.
[67] Forebridge Drainage and Inclosure Act, 40 Geo. III, c. 58 (priv. act).
[68] S.R.O., Q/RDc 15a.
[69] Ibid. 15b.
[70] Cal. Inq. p.m. xiii, p. 188.

[71] W.S.L., Stafford Manor Bailiffs' Acct. 20–21 Ric. II.
[72] Ibid.
[73] C 136/107.
[74] C 139/180.
[75] Sta. Cha. 4/2/31, m. 6.
[76] Ibid. mm. 1–5.
[77] W.S.L., D. 1721/1/9, 1st nos. ff. 177a–91b.
[78] Ibid.   [79] Ibid.
[80] S.R.O., Q/RDc 15a.
[81] Ibid.
[82] W.S.L., D. 1786, Green Common Minute Book and Treasurer's Account Bk. 1803–1924.

a cow and 12s. a horse.[83] Under the Defence of the Realm Act it was used for allotments from 1917. Despite the lapse of the powers of this Act in 1923 and a warning from the Ministry of Agriculture and Fisheries in 1929 that since that date the allotment-holders had been encroachers and trespassers,[84] it continued until 1957 to be held as allotments but was then in process of being sold to the English Electric Co. Ltd.[85] Meetings of commoners were still held in 1956.

An interesting example of agrarian practice in the mid-18th century occurs in a lease of Lees Farm in 1753. The lessee was forbidden to plough or keep in tillage any of the arable for above four crops together and must then let all land thus tilled lie four years before it was broken up again or otherwise converted into tillage; he must not sow above 1 acre in any one year with flax seed; he must not sell any of the hay, fodder, or straw that should grow there but must consume this with beasts and cattle and spread dung in a husbandlike manner, leaving the last winter's 'mink' on some convenient place for the lessors.[86] The lessors agreed to repair the house and to make an allowance of 40s. in any one year for each of the nine pieces of arable marled in turn 'in a good husbandlike manner', i.e. '200 tumbrell loads to an acre', until the whole farm should be once marled over.[87]

The soil of the parish was described as an excellent marly loam in 1811.[88] The major part of the farming land, however, is now used as pasture for cattle.

CHURCHES. The church of St. Mary 'in the castle of Stafford' is first specifically mentioned in 1252.[89] It was then stated that this church had existed from the time of the Conquest and that its advowson had belonged to the royal free chapel of St. Mary, Stafford, until it was given in the reign of Henry II by Robert de Stafford (II) to Stone Priory.[90] Robert's grant of his chapel of Stafford had included, however, the tithes, churches, and other property belonging to it.[91] In 1253 it was decided that the king should recover seisin of this chapel[92] and in 1255 he granted it to the Dean of St. Mary's, Stafford, to confer as if it were a prebend.[93] In 1548 it was stated that all sacraments and rites, except burial, were administered in this church as in a parish church, burial being at St. Mary's Church, Stafford.[94] By 1573 it had acquired the right of burial.[95] It was

served by a salaried priest after 1548 at £8 a year, being described in 1563 as a church with cure but without institution.[96] In 1742 it was a perpetual curacy[97] and after 1868 was styled a vicarage under the Act of that year.[98]

The church of St. Mary, Stafford, appears to have retained the right to nominate the priest of St. Mary's, Castle Church, after the recovery of the advowson in 1255 from Stone Priory, and in 1548, this right lay with the dean and certain prebendaries.[99] The right of nomination may have passed in 1550 with the suppressed deanery to Henry Lord Stafford.[1]

Lord Stafford was named as patron in 1742.[2] In 1754 nomination was by the king 'by lapse'[3] and in 1795 by the king as patron in full right.[4] The nomination remained with the Crown until at least 1853[5] and from 1892 the bishop has collated to the benefice.[6]

From at least 1742 and until 1898 the dedication was to St. Lawrence;[7] since 1899 it has again been to St. Mary.[8]

In 1535 the spiritualities of 'the church below Stafford castle', then still held by the Dean of the Collegiate Church of St. Mary, Stafford, were valued at £10 9s. 2d.[9] After the suppression of the college, the possessions of the deanery were given by the Crown to Henry Lord Stafford in 1550.[10] In 1551 tithes in Castle parish were conveyed, with the deanery, to John Maynard, citizen and mercer of London.[11] After Maynard's death in 1557 these tithes, with the deanery, seem to have passed to two of his three daughters, Frances, who married Walter Robardes (of Cranbrook, Kent), and Elizabeth, wife of John Sparry.[12] In 1556 John Sparry alienated a ninth of the property to Edward Lord Stafford.[13] Meanwhile in 1563 Frances and Walter had conveyed seven-ninths to William Crompton, citizen and mercer of London,[14] who held eight-ninths of the tithes at his death in 1567.[15] His son, William Crompton, though holding some tithes in the parish at his death in 1604[16] conveyed those of the former deanery to Thomas Blackborne, who died in 1607, leaving two young daughters, Frances and Magdalene.[17] By 1638 the glebe lands and tithe seem to have been held by Dorothy Lady Stafford and nine others.[18] In the terrier of 1845 the repair of the chancel was stated to be the responsibility of Lord Stafford, who, however, disputed his liability.[19]

[83] Ibid.
[84] Ibid.
[85] Local inf.
[86] W.S.L. 64/18/46.
[87] Ibid.
[88] Pitt, Staffs. 267–8.
[89] S.H.C. iv (1), 113.
[90] Ibid.
[91] Ibid. ii (1), 210–11.
[92] Ibid. iv (1), 113; ibid. vi (1), 14, 238.
[93] Close R. 1254–6, 149.
[94] E 301/54/2.
[95] Castle Church Par. Reg. (Staffs. Par. Reg. Soc.), i. 27.
[96] S.H.C. 1915, 235. Though often in arrears this salary was paid by the Exchequer until 1658 (ibid. 238; Cal. S. P. Dom. 1654, 179; ibid. 1655–6, 99; ibid. 1656–7, 175; ibid. 1658–9, 72), and later by the Commissioners of Woods and Forests, then by the Paymaster General, and by 1884 by the Ecclesiastical Commissioners: Castle Church Terrier, 1884 (copy), penes the vicar.
[97] Ecton, Thesaurus (1742), 115.
[98] Lich. Dioc. Ch. Cal. (1868; 1869); Lich. Dioc. Dir. (1957).
[99] E 301/54/2.

[1] Cal. Pat. 1550–3, 18.
[2] Ecton, Thesaurus, 115. The living was then valued at £9 6s. 8d. clear.
[3] Lich. Dioc. Regy., Bp.'s Reg. xxi, p. 42.
[4] Ibid. xxvi, p. 126, when the perpetual curate to whom licence was given was also Rector of St. Mary's, Stafford: Parson and Bradshaw, Dir. Staffs. (1818), p. ccxxx.
[5] Lich. Dioc. Regy., Bp.'s Reg. xxxi, pp. 111, 301, 310.
[6] Ibid. xxxv, pp. 256, 366; Lich. Dioc. Dir. (1957).
[7] Ecton, Thesaurus (1742), 115; Lich. Dioc. Ch. Cal. (1898).
[8] Lich. Dioc. Ch. Cal. (1899).
[9] Valor Eccl. (Rec. Com.), iii. 117.
[10] Cal. Pat. 1550–3, 18.
[11] Ibid. 66–67.
[12] Cal. Pat. 1560–3, 399–400, 601; C 142/312, no. 155.
[13] C 142/312, no. 155.
[14] Cal. Pat. 1560–3, 601.
[15] C 142/145, no. 24.
[16] Ibid.; C 142/283, no. 107.
[17] C 142/299, no. 159.
[18] C 3/394, no. 59.
[19] Terrier, 1884 (copy), penes the vicar.

The incumbent, on condition of being resident in his benefice for at least ten months in the year, has since 1727 received an eighth of the yearly income of the Eleanor Alport Charity if he attends an annual service in Cannock church on the festival of St. Barnabas (11 June) or on the following day if the festival happens on a Sunday.[20]

A sermon is still (1956) preached on the Sunday after St. Andrew's Day under the terms of the Backhouse Charity.[21] A rent of 20s. a year for a lecture-sermon, charged on land and buildings at Butterhill in Coppenhall by William Goldsmith in 1703, was still paid in 1823[22] but has since lapsed.

Elizabeth Jane Busby, by will proved 1935, devised a house to the parishes of Castle Church and Bradley. The property was sold soon afterwards and the proceeds, £1,111 13s. 8d., were invested. One-half of the income is still (1957) used for general parish purposes in Castle Church, and the other half is paid to the Vicar of Bradley as augmentation of his stipend.[23]

The church of ST. MARY stands about 500 yards south-east of the castle mound. It was rebuilt except for the tower in 1845 and enlarged in 1898. It now consists of nave, chancel, north aisle, vestry, south porch, and west tower. In 1817 the building was described as 'an ancient edifice composed of brick on the one side, and stone whitewashed on the other, with a stone tower'.[24] The brickwork was probably a partial rebuilding of the south wall of 18th-century date. The north wall of the nave, which was then unaisled, was clearly of 12th-century origin and contained a round-headed window and doorway.[25] The chancel arch, smaller than the present one, was also said to be Norman.[26] The chancel had at least one lancet window[27] and probably dated from the 13th century. The tower, which still stands, is mainly of 15th-century date and has angle buttresses and a Perpendicular west window of which the tracery has been renewed. The hoodmould of this window terminates in carved shields, now much worn, one of which is said to have borne the Stafford chevron impaling the Neville saltire. If these arms commemorate the marriage of Humphrey Stafford (later Duke of Buckingham) with Anne Neville c. 1424[28] they would suggest a date for the building of the tower. The upper stage, which has two-light windows under triangular dripstones and an embattled parapet, was probably rebuilt in the 17th century. A date for this rebuilding may be indicated by an incised sundial of 1624 on the south side of the tower.

In 1844 it was decided in view of the poor condition of the foundations to take down and rebuild the chancel and the north wall of the nave. The architects were G. G. (later Sir Gilbert) Scott and Moffatt.[29] The Norman style of the nave and the Early English

style of the chancel were probably suggested by features of the existing church and some of the 12th- and 13th-century stones were reused. The plan followed the existing one with the addition of a north vestry. The external walls of the nave have pilaster buttresses and a corbel table at eaves level. The round-headed windows have shafts to the external jambs and deep splays internally. The south porch and the chancel arch are decorated with chevron mouldings and other Norman ornament. There are three graded lancets to the east wall of the chancel and the sill and splays of the easternmost window in the south wall form the sedilia. At the rebuilding the old fittings, which probably dated from the 18th century, were removed, the new arrangement giving 42 extra seats.[30] The lych-gate dates from 1846.[31]

In 1898 a north aisle was added to the nave in memory of the Revd. Edward Allen and his son William, between them vicars of the parish from 1853 to 1894.[32] The plans, which were prepared by John Oldrid Scott, provided for a new north vestry and organ chamber at the east end of the aisle,[33] but this part of the work was not carried out until 1912.[34] The Norman style was adopted for the aisle, the nave arcade of four bays having round arches supported on circular piers. The new north wall appears to be a reconstruction of Gilbert Scott's work. Shortly before these alterations two carved stones were dug up in the churchyard, one of which is said to have crumbled away.[35] The other was built into the west wall of the new aisle. It is slightly tapered and measures approximately 5 ft. 7 in. by 1 ft. 6 in. The face is carved in flat relief, being divided into triangular panels by a beaded moulding. The panels are filled with conventionalized foliage. The stone is probably a coffin lid dating from the second half of the 12th century.[36]

The font of Norman design with a square bowl and circular shafts was installed c. 1845. The former 18th-century font was of the simple pillar type.[37] In 1931 a carved screen in memory of the Revd. Melville Scott (vicar 1894–1924) was placed at the east end of the aisle.[38] The tower screen bears the date 1956.

On the west wall of the nave two slate tablets from the old church give details of the Chamberlain and Goldsmith charities.[39] Other tablets from the former church commemorate William Haddersich (d. 1809) and his wife and daughter; Mary (d. 1817), wife of Joseph Boulton, and their children; and Isabella Morris (d. 1821) and her daughter Rebecca Rogers (d. 1828). There are later tablets to members of the Haddersich family of Rickerscote (1825–46); the Revd. Robert Anzelark, vicar (d. 1845); Richard Bagnall (killed 1916); Guy Edwin Bostock (killed 1916); Vincent, Guy, and Ronald Bloor (killed in the First World War).

---

[20] Terrier, 1884; see p. 64.
[21] See p. 99.
[22] 11th Rep. Com. Char. H.C. 433, p. 518 (1824), xiv.
[23] Ex inf. the Lichfield Dioc. Trust.
[24] Pitt, Staffs. 269.
[25] Nightingale, Staffs. (1820), 903; W.S.L., Staffs. Views, iii, p. 33 (a, 1837).
[26] J. S. Horne, Castle Church, 5–6.
[27] W.S.L., Staffs. Views, iii, p. 32 (a, c. 1800); see plate facing p. 86.
[28] S.H.C. viii (2), 87–88; Complete Peerage, ii. 387.
[29] Lich. Dioc. Regy., Consist. Ct. Act Bk. 1841–6, p. 332, faculty, 18 June 1844.

[30] Ibid.
[31] Inscription in situ.
[32] Tablet in aisle.
[33] Lich. Dioc. Regy., Consist. Ct. Act Bk. 1891–9, p. 335, faculty, 18 Mar. 1897.
[34] Horne, Castle Church, 7.
[35] Trans. N. Staffs. Field Club, xxxviii. 162.
[36] Mr. Lawrence Stone has suggested that it belongs to the period 1160–80.
[37] W.S.L., Staffs. Views, iii, p. 37 (1845).
[38] Horne, Castle Church, 13.
[39] See p. 99.

The plate includes (1956) a silver-gilt flagon and lid, chalice, and paten, all of 1849; a silver wafer box, given in memory of Melville Hey Scott.[40]

In 1553 there were three bells and one sanctus bell.[41] In 1889 there were only two, one dated 1711.[42] There are now three bells: (i, ii) 1902, recast, C. Carr; (iii) 1902, C. Carr.[43]

The registers date from 1567 and those from 1567 to 1821 have been printed.[44]

The vicarage is a gabled brick building with Tudor chimneys standing north-west of St. Mary's Church. It dates from 1848.[45]

Another chapel, that of St. Nicholas 'within the castle', is first definitely recorded in 1292 when it was described as a free chapel,[46] although it had probably been founded much earlier as a dependent chapel of 'St. Mary's within the castle' (later St. Mary's, Castle Church) and as such had been included between c. 1138 and 1147 in the grant by Robert de Stafford (II) of that chapel and its dependent chapels to Stone Priory.[47] There is no further evidence of dependence upon St. Mary's. In 1546 it was stated that St. Nicholas's chapel had cure of souls in the castle and its precincts,[48] in 1548 that it had been founded for a priest to minister all sacraments and sacramentals except burials to the inhabitants of Stafford castle and those dwelling within the park as a parish church[49] and in 1614 that it had not been a parish church or a member of any parish church.[50] The chapel appears to have been in use until 1548, when such chapels were dissolved, and again in the reign of Queen Mary.[51]

Although the king in 1292 as guardian of the land and heir of Nicholas de Stafford (d. c. 1287) nominated a priest to this chapel of St. Nicholas,[52] the prior and convent of Stone maintained their right to it under the terms of Robert de Stafford (II)'s grant and made their own nomination, probably early in 1293.[53] They appear to have kept the right of nomination until 1336 when the prior and convent of Kenilworth, mother-house of Stone, reserved it to themselves.[54] By 1370, however, the right of nomination seems to have returned to Ralph Earl of Stafford[55] and it descended with the barony until the chapel ceased to be used.[56]

The chapel is described elsewhere.[57]

Mission churches were opened in Forebridge (St. Paul's) and in Castletown (St. Thomas's) after these areas were taken into Stafford borough. Their history is reserved for treatment in another volume.

A mission church was opened at Rickerscote in 1877 for the convenience of the parishioners of St. Paul's, Forebridge, who were at some distance from their parish church. Rickerscote has been a Conventional District since 1954.[58]

The mission church in School Lane, Rickerscote, is a brick building with a small chancel at one end and a school-room, separated from the body of the church by folding doors, at the other. It was still in use for weekly services in 1957, pending the completion of the new church of *ST. PETER* at Rickerscote, the foundations of which were laid in 1956. A wooden church hall stands beside the mission church.

The plate included (1956) a silver chalice, paten, and wafer box, and a glass and silver flagon.[59]

ROMAN CATHOLICISM. There is a tradition that the Revd. Thomas Barnaby, who was in charge of the Roman Catholic mission in Stafford borough at the time of his death in 1783, used to say mass in the garret of a house on the Green in Forebridge.[60] His successor in the Stafford mission, the Revd. John Corne, who arrived in 1784,[61] at first had a house and chapel in Tipping Street within the borough but was granted the lease of land in Forebridge, once part of the Austin Friars' estates, by the Beringtons of Winslow (Herefs.) formerly of Rowley Hall.[62] On this site Corne built a chapel which was dedicated to St. Augustine and opened in 1791, along with a house for the priest.[63] The chapel was enlarged early in the 19th century (see below), and the present church of St. Austin was opened in 1862 on a site immediately adjoining the old chapel, which was then converted into a school.[64] The church was consecrated in 1911.[65] The parish hall to the south of the church was opened in 1955.

Most, if not all, the holders of the Stafford barony since the Reformation have been Roman Catholics and have done much to encourage Roman Catholicism in and near Stafford.[66] There were said to be 'many' recusants in Castle Church parish in 1604,[67] and ten in Forebridge were mentioned c. 1667.[68] In 1780 there were stated to be 53 papists in Castle Church.[69] The attendance at mass at St. Austin's on Sunday, 30 March 1851, was 250,[70] and in 1956 the average attendance at Sunday mass was 1,150.[71]

The mission benefits from various small bequests and gifts made before 1899 for the general upkeep of the parish and for masses.[72] The income in 1956 was £17.[73]

[40] Ex inf. the Vicar of Castle Church (1957).
[41] *S.H.C.* 1915, 235.
[42] C. Lynam, *Church Bells of Staffs.* 7.
[43] A. E. Garbett, 'Church Bells of Staffs.' (*Trans. Old Stafford Soc.* 1953-4), 8.
[44] Staffs. Par. Reg. Soc. 2 vols. 1903.
[45] Horne, *Castle Church*, 7.
[46] *Cal. Pat.* 1281-92, 495.
[47] *S.H.C.* ii (1), 210-11; ibid. vi (1), 13; *Cal. Pat.* 1281-92, 495.
[48] E 301/40/40.
[49] *S.H.C.* 1915, 237.
[50] E 134/12 Jas. I, H. 11, m. 7.   [51] Ibid.
[52] *Cal. Pat.* 1281-92, 495.
[53] *S.H.C.* vi (1), 13; *Cal. Pat.* 1334-8, 308-9.
[54] *Cal. Pat.* 1334-8, 308-9.
[55] *S.H.C.* n.s. x (2), 136.
[56] C 136/47. It was still returned among the possessions of Lord Stafford in 1638: C 142/485, no. 201.
[57] See p. 85.
[58] *Lich. Dioc. Ch. Cal.* (1878), p. 74; Lich. Dioc. Regy., Bp.'s Reg. xxxv, p. 407.

[59] Ex inf. the vicar (1956).
[60] J. Gillow, *St. Thomas's Priory*, 90.
[61] Ibid. 91.
[62] Ibid. 96-98; see p. 90.
[63] Gillow, *St. Thomas's Priory*, 98-100; H.O. 129/15/367. The area of the site c. 1840 was 2 r. 17 p.: Tithe Appt. and Map 3, Castle Church (copy in W.S.L.).
[64] Gillow, *St. Thomas's Priory*, 120, 123-8. The registers date from 1804.
[65] Ex inf. the parish priest, St. Austin's (1956).
[66] *Complete Peerage*, xii (i), 'Stafford'; Gillow, *St. Thomas's Priory*, index *sub* Stafford; see p. 87.
[67] *S.H.C.* 1915, 387.
[68] *Cath. Rec. Soc.* vi. 302-12.
[69] H.L., Main Papers, Return of Papists 1780; there were said to be 67 within the borough of Stafford.
[70] H.O. 129/15/367.
[71] Ex inf. the parish priest.
[72] Ex inf. the Treasurer of the Archdiocese of Birmingham (1957).
[73] Ex inf. the Treasurer.

Early in the 19th century the chapel of 1791 was transformed into a church in the Gothic style, in which the original building formed one of the transepts.[74] Edward Jerningham, an amateur architect and brother of Sir George Jerningham, was responsible for the work.[75] Fifteenth-century glass imported from Belgium and oak stalls for the sanctuary were given by the Jerninghams.[76] In 1861–2 the new church, designed by E. W. Pugin,[77] was built and consists of an aisled and clerestoried nave of four bays and an apsidal chancel. The entrance lobby at the south-east corner was originally planned to form the base of a tower[78] but this was never completed and it now carries a wooden turret containing one bell. The building is of red brick with blue-brick ornament and stone dressings. The window above the gallery has decorated tracery and contains the 15th-century stained glass from the former church.

A presbytery built at the same time as the former chapel is still in use and is a tall three-story brick house with a symmetrical front and a pedimented doorcase.

St. Joseph's Convent in Lichfield Road was opened by the Sisters of St. Joseph of Cluny from Lichfield in 1907, with a girls' private school attached.[79] The convent also has a guest house for women.[80] The convent incorporates a stucco house, formerly known as Forebridge Villa, which was built by Benjamin Rogers between 1809 and 1816.[81] In its original form the villa was a fine example of a style not well represented in the district. The low-pitched roof has deep eaves supported on brackets and the road front has an Ionic porch with an enriched pediment. In the centre of the south-east elevation, which faces a garden laid out at the same period, is a splayed recess with niches in the ground-floor reveals. The iron balcony and the French windows show the influence of the Greek Revival and there is similar ornament internally. A semicircular bow to the principal reception room was later incorporated in a conservatory. Additions at the back of the house date from the later 19th century. Extensions to the convent include a large brick range facing the road, designed by Sandy and Norris of Stafford in 1931.[82] There were further additions in 1951.[83] The garden contains several features built up from medieval stonework, mostly window tracery, said to have come from St. Mary's Church, Stafford, at the time of its restoration in 1842.[84] South of the house the original octagonal parapet of St. Mary's tower has been set up to form part of a

formal garden. The parapet is pierced and embattled and probably dates from the 15th century.

PROTESTANT NONCONFORMITY. Of the 180 inhabitants of Castle Church returned under the religious census of 1676, two were stated to be non-conformists.[85] A house in the occupation of Edward Smith was registered as a meeting-house in 1822,[86] and a house and premises on the Green, in the occupation of 'Mr. Hollyock', was registered in 1840.[87]

A Wesleyan Methodist church at Acton Gate, at the southern extremity of the parish, was opened in 1880 as a chapel and Sunday school.[88] It is a rectangular red-brick building with blue-brick dressing and pointed windows.

Other nonconformist chapels have been opened in areas absorbed by Stafford borough and are reserved for treatment under the borough in another volume.

PRIMARY SCHOOLS. Only one of the schools built in what was the ancient parish of Castle Church still remains outside the boundary of the modern borough of Stafford. This is Hyde Lea school, built as a National school in 1863 to take 60 children.[89] It had an attendance of about 53 in 1893.[90] On 17 July 1950 it became 'controlled'[91] and it is now Castle Church, Hyde Lea Church of England (Controlled) Voluntary Primary School for Infants, under a mistress.[92] The average attendance in 1955 was 24.[93] The original building is still in use.

Dame Dorothy Bridgeman, by will dated 1694, left £200 to purchase rent-charges, three-tenths of which were to be applied to educate poor children of the township of Forebridge in Castle Church parish.[94] She died in 1697[95] but it was only in 1726, after a charity decree had been promulgated that an accrued sum of £147 was laid out in the purchase of two parcels of land in the uninclosed Green Field in Forebridge. Of this about 7 acres were conveyed to school trustees in 1741.[96] Under the Forebridge Inclosure Act of 1800 an allotment of about 5 acres in the Green Field was made in lieu of these two parcels of land, and in 1804 this was leased for 21 years, at rents of £12 for the first four and £15 for the subsequent seventeen years.[97] This rent was paid to a mistress who taught, free, all the poor children of Forebridge hamlet above five years old who applied, to read and spell, and the girls to sew. She seems to have been allowed to charge 3d. a week for children under five.[98] The numbers in this school

[74] Roxburgh, *Stafford*, 120.
[75] Ibid.   [76] Ibid.
[77] Ibid. 120–1.
[78] Ibid. 120.
[79] Ex inf. the Mother Superior (1956). The site was purchased in 1905.
[80] Ex inf. the Mother Superior.
[81] Deeds at the convent.
[82] Ex inf. the Mother Superior.
[83] Ex inf. the Mother Superior.
[84] W.S.L. 242/30: S. A. Cutlack, St. Mary's Church, Stafford, 19, 25, 27–28 and plates.
[85] W.S.L., S. MS. 33: Compton Census.
[86] Lich. Dioc. Regy., Bp.'s Reg. Bk. G (28 Feb.).
[87] Ibid. Bk. L (21 Sept.).
[88] Ex inf. the Superintendent Minister, Stafford (1956).
[89] P.O. Dir. Staffs. (1868); Kelly's Dir. Staffs. (1884).
[90] Return of Schools, 1893 [C. 7529], pp. 540–1, H.C. (1894), lxv.

[91] Ex inf. C.C. Educ. Dept.
[92] Staffs. Educ. Cttee. *List of Schools, 1951*, revised to 1955.
[93] *Lich. Dioc. Dir.* (1955–6).
[94] *Staffs. Endowed Charities, Elem. Educ.* [Cd. 2729], p. 112, H.C. (1905). The rest of the £200 was bequeathed in two-tenth shares each for schools at Brocton (in Baswich), Pelsall (in Wolverhampton), and Seighford (Pirehill hundred), and one-tenth for the minster of Pelsall: ibid. 13, 99, 103.
[95] She was the second wife and widow of Sir Orlando Bridgeman of Weston under Lizard and formerly widow of George Cradock of Caverswall castle and Castle Church: S.H.C. n.s. ii. 248, 249, and pedigree facing p. 238.
[96] *11th Rep. Com. Char.* H.C. 433, p. 519 (1824), xiv; *Staffs. Endowed Char.* 112–13.
[97] *11th Rep. Com. Char.* 520.
[98] Ibid.

are said almost to have doubled between about 1800 and 1818, when there were 50. There was still no free schooling for the children living elsewhere in the parish.[99]

By 1825 the original £15 lease fell in,[1] and the trustees built a new school-house, with dwelling-house and garden for the master or mistress, upon part of the trust land, funds being raised partly from the National Society, partly from the Lichfield Diocesan Society, and partly from subscriptions.[2] The poor children of Forebridge were still to be taught free, but the school was opened also to all the poor children of the rest of Castle Church, who seem to have paid 1d. a week, the girls (possibly those of Forebridge only) being provided with cloaks and bonnets by the trustees.[3] By 1834 it appears to have been affiliated to the National Society.[4]

In 1876 the school was rebuilt[5] by which date an Infants' School founded in 1831[6] and still existing separately as late as 1854[7] had been attached to it.[8] The accommodation by 1893 was for 477 children with average attendances of about 336.[9] By 1905 the rents from the Bridgeman Charity lands were £44 17s. of which about £42 was applied towards the support of the school.[10] The buildings were altered in 1906.[11] By 1951 it was called St. Paul's Church of England School and then became 'controlled'.[12] The average attendance in 1955 was 150[13] and the school is now Stafford, Forebridge Church of England (Controlled) School (Junior Mixed and Infants).[14]

There was a National school at Rickerscote from about 1876 for about 60 children[15] which was used from at least 1878 to 1946 both as a school and for Sunday services in connexion with St. Paul's Church.[16] The accommodation in 1892 was for 71 children and the attendance 49, and the school was receiving an annual government grant.[17] This school was held in the mission church, a separate classroom being included at one end of the building. The day school was closed in August 1946 and the few remaining children then attended Rising Brook Primary School.[18]

Other schools built to serve areas of Castle Church after their absorption by Stafford borough are reserved for treatment in another volume.

CHARITIES FOR THE POOR. Thomas Backhouse or Chamberlain by deed of 1629 gave a rent of £2 charged on land in Silkmore of which £1 13s. 4d. was to be distributed each year among the poor of Castle Church parish and 6s. 8d. paid to the minister for a sermon on the Sunday after St. Andrew's Day (30 November).[19] The poor received doles of 1s. or 6d. each until 1800 when the distribution was changed to shilling and sixpenny loaves on 24 December.[20] The sermon is still (1956) preached and the 6s. 8d. paid to the vicar.[21]

William Goldsmith of Silkmore by will proved 1703 gave a rent of £10 charged on land in Silkmore for distribution in bread each Sunday to the poor of the parish.[22] By 1823 the money was used to provide 48 penny loaves each week at the rate of two or three for each person, the balance of 8s. a year being covered by allowances in place of the 'vantage bread' (the thirteenth loaf in each baker's dozen).[23] This left a surplus of 9s. 4d. which was added to the Christmas distributions made under the charities of Backhouse and Hinton[24] (see below).

William Goldsmith also charged his land in Burton, Rickerscote, and Risingbrook, subject to the life interests of his servant Margaret Wetton and her daughter Mary, with a rent of £10 a year to provide clothing for four poor widows of the parish.[25] Any residue was to be applied towards the apprenticing of poor boys.[26] The first payment of £10 was made in 1788 when clothing for four poor widows was bought at a cost of £8 5s. 10½d.[27] Premiums for apprentices were also paid regularly from 1789 to at least 1803.[28] From then until 1822 the money was used entirely for widows' clothing, but in 1823 £5 was paid for an apprenticeship and £5 8s. 4d. was spent on clothing for thirteen poor widows.[29]

By an Order of the Charity Commissioners in 1860, such of the above three benefactions as affected the poor were reallotted between the parish of Castle Church proper and the District of St. Paul's, Forebridge, in the proportion of £4 12s. to the former and £17 1s. 4d. to the latter.[30] All three charities are still (1956) used for the benefit of poor persons.[31]

Roger Hinton by will dated 1685 left land in Rickerscote to the poor of Burton and Rickerscote and a fixed charge of 15s. on other lands in Rickerscote to the poor of Stafford Green (otherwise Forebridge).[32] As his house and lands in Rickerscote had been charged with fixed payments to four other parishes, it was settled in 1692, following a decree in Chancery of 1688, that the poor of Rickerscote and Burton should receive a fixed sum of £2 10s. a year.[33] In December 1788 19 poor shared the Burton and Rickerscote charity at the rate of 2s. 6d. each and 18 the Forebridge charity; in 1791, 17 and 15

[99] *Digest of Returns to Sel. Cttee. on Educ. of Poor,* H.C. 224, p. 856 (1819), ix (2).
[1] *11th Rep. Com. Char.* 520.
[2] *Staffs. Endowed Char.* 113.
[3] Ibid.; White, *Dir. Staffs.* (1834).
[4] White, *Dir. Staffs.* (1834).
[5] *Kelly's Dir. Staffs.* (1896).
[6] It was founded by Philip Seckerson and his wife and c. 1834 occupied a 'neat rustic cottage' near the National school: White, *Dir. Staffs.* (1834).
[7] *P.O. Dir. Staffs.* (1854).
[8] *Kelly's Dir. Staffs.* (1896).
[9] *Return of Schools, 1893,* 548–9.
[10] *Staffs. Endowed Char.* 113.
[11] *Kelly's Dir. Staffs.* (1912).
[12] Ex inf. C.C. Educ. Dept.
[13] *Lich. Dioc. Dir.* (1955–6).
[14] Staffs. Educ. Cttee. *List of Schools, 1951,* revised to 1955.
[15] *P.O. Dir. Staffs.* (1876); *Kelly's Dir. Staffs.* (1884).
[16] *Kelly's Dir. Staffs.* (1884; 1924).

[17] *Return of Schools, 1893,* 540–1.
[18] Ex inf. C.C. Educ. Dept.
[19] *11th Rep. Com. Char.* 517.
[20] Ibid.; W.S.L. 192/25.
[21] Ex inf. the Vicar of Castle Church (1957).
[22] *11th Rep. Com. Char.* 518; W.S.L. 192/25. The land included that already charged under Backhouse's Charity.
[23] *11th Rep. Com. Char.* 519.
[24] Ibid.
[25] Ibid.
[26] Ibid.
[27] W.S.L. 192/25.
[28] Ibid.
[29] Ibid. Some of the apprenticeship indentures are among the Castle Church parish documents: W.S.L. 215–89/25.
[30] Copy of Terrier, 1884, *penes* the Vicar of Castle Church.
[31] Ex inf. the vicar (1956).
[32] *7th Rep. Com. Char.* H.C. 129, p. 418 (1822), x.
[33] W.S.L. 192/25; the allocations were later modified.

respectively.[34] Following the Forebridge Inclosure Act of 1800, and reallotments and sales of lands resulting from this, the rents paid to these two charities were increased, and in 1805 for the two together were £11 19s. 6d. rising in 1820 to £17 17s. 6d.[35] The two charities became amalgamated in course of time, and for some years before 1821 had been distributed in bread on Christmas Eve among the poor of the whole of Castle Church parish, along with Backhouse's and part of Goldsmith's Charities[36] (see above). Of the money due at Christmas 1821, £6 was given in shoes to children of poor persons in the parish, as an inducement to them to attend the Sunday school; £6 7s. was distributed in bread; 12s. was paid for coals for a poor woman; and 8s. was allowed to one of the poor tenants for arrears of rent, leaving a balance of £12 10s. 11d. for the following year.[37] During the winter of 1822–3 £29 15s. 2d. was distributed in coals, shoes, clothes, and money, still throughout the parish, but the parish officers were then informed that £6 4s. should have been applied exclusively to the poor of Burton and Rickerscote.[38]

By a Scheme of the Charity Commissioners of 1909 part of the income (then £15 16s. 9d.) was assigned to Burton and Rickerscote, while 15s. a year plus one-fifth of the residue of the income after deduction of four other fixed payments was assigned to the parish of St. Paul, Forebridge.[39] The income was to be applied in the form of subscriptions to hospitals and the provision of nurses or other care for the sick poor or of outfits for young persons entering upon a trade or occupation or into service.[40] In 1955 £18 19s. 10d. was paid to the Burton and Rickerscote trustees and £22 9s. 3d. to the Forebridge trustees.[41]

Simon Fowler, by will dated 1663, gave a rent of 40s. to the poor of Forebridge, charged during the lifetime of his wife Ann on an estate in The Reule (then in Gnosall, now in Bradley) and after Ann's death on an estate in Risingbrook.[42] The money was still assigned to the Forebridge poor in 1786,[43] and c. 1810 it was distributed among poor women there.[44] Payment then ceased and was never revived.[45]

A Mr. Thorley (d. probably 1723), bequeathed £40 to the poor of Castle Church, and in 1778 £1 12s. interest on it was paid to the churchwardens by a Mrs. Lander.[46] Although the charity was still in existence in 1786,[47] all traces of it had been lost by 1823.[48]

Another charity for the poor of Forebridge, described in 1786 as 10s. a year interest on money vested in the corporation of Stafford,[49] may have been represented by the annual distribution by 1823 of 6s. or so in the form of pound parcels of 'plums' at Christmas among the inhabitants of some fifteen or sixteen old houses in Forebridge liberty, which had established a prescriptive right to receive them.[50] This charity subsequently lapsed.

Lucy Emma Johnson of Rickerscote by will proved 1917 gave £175 to be invested and the interest paid to the Rickerscote Clothing Club.[51] In 1939 the income was £6 9s. 6d., but when the club ceased in 1946 the capital, under the terms of the will, was returned to the residuary estate.[52] In 1954, however, the sum of £100 accumulated dividends was paid to the priest-in-charge of St. Peter's, Rickerscote, for the purchase of clothing for the poor of Rickerscote.[53]

CHESLYN HAY

THE civil parish of Cheslyn Hay, formerly an extra-parochial liberty, lies two miles south of Cannock, and shares with it a boundary formed by the Wyrley Brook. To the east and north-east it is bounded by the neighbouring civil parish of Great Wyrley, the boundary between them having been adjusted under the Staffordshire Review Order of 1934 'to follow a more satisfactory line'. The soil is light, with a subsoil of gravel and sand. In 1940, when the land was held by many freeholders, the chief crops were wheat, barley, oats, and turnips.[1] The farm land is situated to the west and north-west of the village which lies mainly along the south-eastern boundary of the parish. There were ten persons chargeable for the hearth tax here in 1666.[2] Before the inclosure

of 1797 Cheslyn Common had attracted numerous squatters who lived in mud huts there, but the opening of the mines in the district 'brought some respectable inhabitants to the place who established a plan for relieving the poor and . . . erected a Methodist chapel and Sunday school'. Thus by 1834 the liberty of Cheslyn Hay was 'nearly as civilized as its neighbours'.[3] The village, formerly known as Wyrley Bank, was in 1834 inhabited mainly by colliers and ling-besom makers, and then consisted of many cottages 'from the clay-built shed to the most convenient dwelling'.[4] The population was 443 in 1801, 2,560 in 1901,[5] and 3,130 in 1951.[6] The area is 823 acres.[7]

Thomas Leveson in 1636 secured the right to

[34] W.S.L. 192/25; the allocations were later modified.
[35] 7th Rep. Com. Char. 420, 423.
[36] 11th Rep. Com. Char. 518.
[37] Ibid.
[38] Ibid.
[39] The other fixed payments were for the poor of Lichfield, Wolverhampton, Walsall, and Stafford.
[40] Charity Com. Scheme, sealed 16 Feb. 1909.
[41] Charity Com. files.
[42] 11th Rep. Com. Char. 520–1.
[43] Abstract of Returns of Charitable Donations, 1786–8, H.C. 511, pp. 1118–19 (1816), xvi (2).
[44] 11th Rep. Com. Char. 521.
[45] Ibid.
[46] W.S.L. 192/25. 'Lander' is wrongly spelt 'Sander' in 11th Rep. Com. Char. 519.
[47] Abstract, 1786–8, ii. 1118–19.

[48] 11th Rep. Com. Char. 519. 'Mr. Thorley's land' in Rickerscote occurs in a survey of 1709 (W.S.L. 192/25); a William Thorley of Burton died in 1723: Castle Church Par. Reg. (Staffs. Par. Reg. Soc.), i. 52.
[49] Abstract, 1786–8, ii. 1118–19.
[50] 11th Rep. Com. Char. 521.
[51] Charity Com. files.
[52] Ibid.
[53] Ibid.
[1] Kelly's Dir. Staffs. (1940).
[2] S.H.C. 1927, 71.
[3] White, Dir. Staffs. (1834).
[4] Ibid.; Tithe Maps and Appt., Cannock (copy in W.S.L.).
[5] V.C.H. Staffs. i. 320.
[6] Census, 1951, Staffs.
[7] Ibid.

work the coal and lead mines in Cheslyn Hay and to use a road through the Hay and Cannock Forest.[8] In 1640 he granted to Andrew Giffard a rent charge of £48 on the coal- and iron-mines here for twelve years as the settlement of a debt.[9] In 1834 there was one colliery in Cheslyn Hay,[10] but in 1851 Edward Sayers, coalmaster, was working the Oldfalls and the Coppice collieries.[11] The New Colliery owned by Frederick Gilpin was in operation by 1868,[12] and by 1872 there were still the Old Coppice Colliery, worked by Joseph Hawkins, coalmaster, and the Oldfalls Colliery, owned by Bagnall & Sons Ltd.[13] A new shaft was sunk in 1877 at the Old Coppice Colliery,[14] apparently the only survivor of these three collieries in 1880,[15] and a further shaft was sunk c. 1920.[16] The output of the colliery in 1954 was only 180,000 tons a year owing to the complex geological structure.[17] The Nook and Wyrley Colliery, a smaller undertaking, was in operation from 1874 until 1949.[18] The other main industry since at least 1868 has been the manufacture of bricks and tiles.[19]

Thomas Leveson's attempt to inclose Cheslyn Hay during Henry VIII's reign was forcibly opposed by those with common rights there,[20] but 600 acres were inclosed by an agreement of 1668 between Robert Leveson and the freeholders and copyholders of Great and Little Saredon (in Shareshill) and Great Wyrley.[21] A further 311 acres of Cheslyn Common were inclosed in 1797 following the Act of 1792, 55 acres being sold along with the allotments on Old Falls in Great Wyrley to defray expenses.[22]

The original nucleus of the village appears to have been near the east junction of High Street and Low Street. In both these streets and in Cross Street are a few buildings dating from before the middle of the 19th century. The Red Lion Inn, a low brick house now plastered externally, is probably of the late 17th century. Many of the houses elsewhere were built in the early years of the 20th century. The fire station in Station Street, presented by Thomas A. Hawkins in 1908,[23] was sold in 1952 after a re-organization of the fire service[24] and in 1956 was being used as a garage. There is a council housing estate near the west junction of High Street and Low Street. A decontamination centre, standing west of the recreation ground, dates from the Second World War and was converted into a community centre

c. 1950.[25] Two police houses were built in Station Street c. 1949.[26] The architecture of the Lodge Farm is treated below.

THE HAY. *CHESLYN HAY*, a division of the royal forest of Cannock, had passed by 1236 from the king to Bishop Alexander Stavensby (1224–38), who annexed it with other parts of the forest to the manors of Cannock and Rugeley[27] restored to him in 1230.[28] The king had recovered it by 1250 and retained the lordship until 1550.[29] The keepership of the Hay was farmed for 1 mark a year in 1236 by Robert Trumwyn who held the office like his ancestors before him, possibly since the reign of the Conqueror.[30] It descended with lands in Cannock, held by this service of keeping Cheslyn Hay, until at least 1590[31] and remained in the Leveson family until at least 1621.[32] The annual value of the Hay was given as 100s. in 1293[33] but as only 13s. 4d. in 1318.[34]

The king granted Cheslyn Hay to John Dudley, Earl of Warwick, and his heirs in 1550.[35] His widow held it from 1554 until her death in 1555,[36] and in 1563 it was part of the possessions of their son Ambrose Dudley,[37] who had been restored in blood in 1558 and in 1561 given some of his father's titles.[38] In 1563 Ambrose granted timber from the Hay, and in 1569 land there, to John Leveson[39] who had an interest in the keepership (see above).[40] John's son Thomas, who succeeded him in 1575,[41] held free warren in the Hay in 1593[42] and held both Hay and keepership at his death in 1594.[43] His son and heir Walter[44] was holding the Hay, with free warren there, at his death in 1621 when he was succeeded by his son Thomas.[45] A royalist colonel, Thomas died an exile in France,[46] and Cheslyn Hay, although sequestered along with his other possessions and sold by the Treason Trustees in 1652 to John Baker and Edward Stephens,[47] was held by Thomas's son, Robert, by 1655[48] and was still in his hands in 1680.[49] Robert was succeeded by his daughter Sarah, wife of Charles Fowler of Pendeford (in Tettenhall, Seisdon hundred),[50] who was described as lord of Cheslyn Hay in 1711[51] and whose granddaughter Sarah, coheir of his son Richard, married John Lane of King's Bromley (Offlow hundred).[52] The Lodge Farm mentioned in 1817[53] was owned by J. N. Lane of King's Bromley in 1834 and 1851,

8 C.P. 25(2)/485, 11 Chas. II Hil.; C 3/425, no. 19.
9 Cal. Cttee. for Compounding, 1868.
10 White, Dir. Staffs. (1834).
11 Ibid. (1851).
12 P.O. Dir. Staffs. (1868).
13 Ibid. (1872).
14 Ex inf. the National Coal Board, Cannock.
15 Kelly's Dir. Staffs. (1880).
16 Ex inf. N.C.B., Cannock.
17 Ex inf. N.C.B.
18 Ex inf. N.C.B.
19 P.O. Dir. Staffs. (1868); Kelly's Dir. Staffs. (1940).
20 Sta. Cha. 2/26/302.
21 S.H.C. 1931, 73–74.
22 Ibid. 93; S.R.O., Q/RDc 10.
23 Inscription in situ.
24 Charity Com. files; the income from the proceeds was to be used for the benefit of the inhabitants of Cheslyn Hay under a scheme of 1950.
25 Ex inf. Mr. P. Hudson, Cheslyn Hay.
26 Station Street is a continuation of High Street and was presumably renamed after the coming of the railway.
27 Bk. of Fees, 594; S.H.C. v (1), 167.
28 Close R. 1227–31, 399.
29 Bk. of Fees, 1186; S.H.C. v (1), 167, 176–7; Cal. Pat. 1549–51, 364–5.

30 Bk. of Fees, 594; S.H.C. v (1), 167; ibid. N.S. x (1). 215.
31 S.H.C. xvi. 103–4; see p. 55.
32 C 142/390, no. 148.
33 S.H.C. vi (1), 270.
34 Ibid. 1911, 341.
35 Cal. Pat. 1549–51, 364–5.
36 Ibid. 1553–4, 129; Complete Peerage, ix. 726.
37 Cal. Pat. 1560–3, 478.
38 Complete Peerage, viii. 68.
39 Cal. Pat. 1560–3, 478; G. P. Mander, Wolverhampton Antiquary, i. 177; S.H.C. xiii. 273.
40 S.H.C. 1938, 88–93.
41 C 142/175, no. 88.
42 S.H.C. 1930, 365.
43 C 142/242, no. 65.   44 Ibid.
45 C 142/390, no. 148.
46 Shaw, Staffs. ii. 168.
47 Cal. Cttee. for Compounding, 2485–6.
48 C.P. 25(2)/596, 1654–5 Hil.
49 C.P. 25(2)/726, 32 Chas. II Trin.
50 Shaw, Staffs. ii. 169.
51 S.R.O., Gamekeepers' Deputations.
52 Shaw, Staffs. ii. 203; H. M. Lane, Lane of Bentley Hall (1910), 25–26.
53 Pitt, Staffs. 263.

when it occupied much of Cheslyn Hay.[54] The farm-house is of brick, dating from c. 1800 and, with the farm, is now the property of the National Coal Board.

CHURCH. Cheslyn Hay was joined to Great Wyrley in 1846 to form the new ecclesiastical parish of St. Mark.[55] The mission chapel of St. Peter in Pinfold Lane was opened c. 1950[56] in the former National school buildings.[57] One of the two cemeteries in the parish of St. Mark[58] is situated in Cheslyn Hay between Pinfold Lane and the Wolverhampton road and has a small mortuary chapel.

ROMAN CATHOLICISM. By 1907 the Cheslyn Hay and Wyrley Mission Station, served from Cannock, had been opened in Cheslyn Hay.[59] Known as St. George's Mission Hall by 1908, it continued in use until at least 1912.[60]

PROTESTANT NONCONFORMITY. Methodism in this parish owes its origin to the opening of neighbouring coal-mines which drew to the village of Wyrley Bank (now Cheslyn Hay) 'respectable inhabitants' who in about 1788 built a chapel and Sunday school,[61] later belonging to the Methodist New Connexion.[62] The chapel was rebuilt on the old site in 1819 and in 1851 seated 250.[63] This chapel, now called Salem, was rebuilt in the High Street in 1855 and enlarged in 1898; in 1940 it seated 460.[64] A library of about 2,000 volumes was opened in connexion with this chapel in February 1924.[65]

A small brick building in Station Street with an almost illegible inscription above the door is probably the chapel and Sunday school dating from 1819. It is now used as part of a carpenter's shop. Salem Chapel is a large building with an imposing front of 1898, having two semicircular turrets and a scrolled parapet. The body of the building and the cast-iron railings date from 1855. The Sunday school, built in 1889,[66] stands immediately to the east.

In 1851 there was a smaller Methodist New Connexion preaching place near Wedges Mills, closely connected with the Wyrley Bank chapel, James Lawson being secretary to the trustees of both. This had been converted into a chapel in 1845, and seated 90 people, but by 1851 the congregation was small.[67] It had ceased to exist by 1872.[68]

Primitive Methodism was introduced into this area by David Buxton who, having come under the

influence of Hugh Bourne at Ramsor (in Ellastone, Totmonslow hundred), invited him to Wyrley. Bourne first came there in July 1810[69] and in succeeding years preached frequently in the neighbourhood.[70] Eventually, in 1848, a Primitive Methodist chapel was established at Wyrley Bank.[71] There were then 100 sittings, 70 of them free.[72] The present chapel, named Mount Zion and built in 1880,[73] lies in Cross Street and in 1940 seated 250.[74] It has a rough-cast front with pointed windows.

SCHOOLS. A British and Foreign Society school was set up in Cheslyn Hay before 1839 and received a Treasury grant of £100 a year.[75] In June 1840 it was transferred to new buildings.[76] It was still in existence in 1884 when it was receiving a parliamentary grant[77] but cannot be traced after this date. In 1880 it was run by a master.[78] Attendance in 1871 was about 74 boys and girls.[79]

Already by 1818 the Methodists had a Sunday school in Cheslyn Hay in which an average of 100 children were taught and which was supported solely by an annual sermon.[80] This was still a Sunday school in 1851,[81] but by 1868 this Methodist New Connexion school seems to have become a day school and was taught by a master.[82] It was again described as a Sunday school in 1884.[83]

The Primitive Methodists were said to have a school here for children of both sexes, supported by voluntary contributions and school pence, by 1876 and until at least 1880.[84]

A National school was opened in Cheslyn Hay in 1875 on a site in Pinfold Lane given in 1871 by Lord Hatherton.[85] It was in receipt of a parliamentary grant by 1882 when attendance averaged 101 pupils.[86] The school had been closed by 1892.[87]

In 1882 a board school was founded in Cheslyn Hay for 250 children,[88] and was enlarged in 1895.[89] Attendance in 1883, when the school was also in receipt of an annual parliamentary grant, averaged 209 pupils.[90] In 1909 the old National school buildings were leased to the Local Education Authority and were subsequently used as an extension of the council school to take 126 boys, attendance at the school in 1910 averaging 422 older children and 166 infants.[91] In 1925 they were found to have developed a serious crack, and in 1930 it was decided to vacate them immediately.[92] The boys' and

[54] White, Dir. Staffs. (1834; 1851).
[55] See p. 81.
[56] Local inf.; Lich. Dioc. Dir. (1955-6).
[57] See below.
[58] See p. 81.
[59] Catholic Dir. (1908).
[60] Ibid. (1909-13).
[61] White, Dir. Staffs. (1834). The registers date from 1789: List of Nonconformist Registers, prefaced to Armitage Par. Reg. (Staffs. Par. Reg. Soc.), 16.
[62] H.O. 129/15/378.
[63] Ibid.; White, Dir. Staffs. (1834).
[64] Methodist Church Buildings, 1940 (1946), 266; Kelly's Dir. Staffs. (1900; 1940).
[65] Kelly's Dir. Staffs. (1928).
[66] Inscription in situ.
[67] H.O. 129/15/378.
[68] Noted in 1868 but not in 1872: P.O. Dir. Staffs. (1868; 1872).
[69] J. Walford, Memoirs of Hugh Bourne (1855), i. 282-3.
[70] Ibid. i. 335, 343, 385; ii. 9.
[71] White, Dir. Staffs. (1851).
[72] Ibid.
[73] Kelly's Dir. Staffs. (1892; 1940).
[74] Meth. Church Bldgs. 264.

[75] Mins. of Educ. Cttee. of Council, 1854 [1926], H.C. (1854-5), xlii.   [76] Ibid.
[77] Ibid. 1884 [C. 4483-I], H.C. (1884-5), xxiii.
[78] Kelly's Dir. Staffs. (1880). It is here distinguished from both the Methodist New Connexion school and the Primitive Methodist school.
[79] Returns relating to Elem. Educ. H.C. 201 (1871), lv.
[80] Digest of Returns to Sel. Cttee. on Education of Poor, H.C. 224, p. 856 (1819), ix (2).
[81] White, Dir. Staffs. (1851).
[82] P.O. Dir. Staffs. (1868).
[83] Kelly's Dir. Staffs. (1884).
[84] P.O. Dir. Staffs. (1876); Kelly's Dir. Staffs. (1880).
[85] Kelly's Dir. Staffs. (1884); Lich. Dioc. Ch. Cal. (1875), 78.
[86] Rep. of Educ. Cttee. of Council, 1882 [C. 3706-I], H.C. (1883), xxv.
[87] Kelly's Dir. Staffs. (1892).
[88] Ibid. (1884).   [89] Ibid. (1912).
[90] Rep. of Educ. Cttee. of Council, 1883 [C. 4091-I], H.C. (1884), xxiv.
[91] Staffs. Educ. Cttee. Mins., 24 Apr. 1909, 22 Oct. 1910.
[92] Ibid. 24 Oct. 1925, 20 Dec. 1930. Between c. 1930 and 1942 they were used as a boys' club and are now (1956) the mission church of St. Peter.

girls' departments were amalgamated from January 1931 under the headmaster.[93] The schools have been reorganized as Cheslyn Hay County Primary School for junior boys and girls and infants.[94] They stand on a site adjoining the old National school buildings with their frontage facing Hatherton Street.

A school for educationally sub-normal boys and girls, the William Baxter School, has been maintained since 1951 by the Staffordshire Education Committee[95] in the buildings formerly occupied by the Isolation Hospital.

· PENKRIDGE

THE ancient parish of Penkridge consisted of the four townships of Penkridge, Coppenhall, Dunston, and Stretton. Penkridge township, covering nearly three-quarters of the parish in 1834, was roughly coextensive with the present civil parish of Penkridge. The history of Coppenhall and Dunston will follow that of the area now contained in the civil parish; the history of Stretton is treated in the volume dealing with Cuttlestone West.

The present parish of Penkridge includes the hamlets of Levedale, Longridge, Drayton, Whiston, Bickford, Congreve, Mitton, Pillaton, Lyne Hill, and Otherton and the village of Gailey. It is crossed by the River Penk, which forms the south-western and north-eastern boundaries, and by several small streams. The ground lies mostly between 275 and 400 ft., and the soil is light loam in the east of the parish and strong in the west, the subsoil being red sandstone in some places and gravel and clay in others, while the geological strata are Keuper to the west and Bunter to the east.[1] Under the Staffordshire Review Order of 1934 the civil parish was extended to include Kinvaston, previously a separate civil parish, and parts of Acton Trussell and Bednall and Lapley parishes, while at the same time parts of Penkridge were added to Acton Trussell and Bednall, Lapley, and Dunston. The area was increased as a result from 10,783 acres to its present 10,809 acres.[2] The population in 1951 was 2,195.[3]

In 1834 Penkridge township was divided into the four constablewicks of Penkridge, Levedale, Pillaton, and Whiston, each responsible for the upkeep of its own roads.[4] The town of Penkridge was described at the end of the 16th century as 'at present . . . only a small village, famous for a horse-fair'.[5] The constablewick of Penkridge contained 212 households in 1666,[6] and by 1834 the town was composed of several short streets and a large market-place.[7] The widening of the main Stafford–Wolverhampton road between 1932 and 1934[8] drastically altered the west side of the town. In the early 19th century the thoroughfare was so narrow that coachmen were said to have found the manipulation of a

four-in-hand more difficult in Penkridge than at any other place between London and Liverpool.[9] On the east side of the stretch known as Clay Street 20 or 30 houses were destroyed, several of them ancient. These are now replaced by a row of modern buildings. Landmarks on the west side of High Street, including the little square known as Stone Cross and the partly timber-framed[10] George and Fox Inn, also disappeared. A map of 1754[11] shows the base and shaft of the Cross still standing near the junction of High Street and Pinfold Lane; the pinfold itself is shown east of the Old Deanery. At this time there was no road connecting Pinfold Lane with Church Lane, and Church Lane itself was built up on both sides. A roughly triangular group of buildings stood on the present open site at Crown Bridge with a narrow lane and a small bridge to the south of them.[12] On the north side the open stream was crossed by a ford. The St. Michael's Road area, probably developed after the coming of the railway, has middle-class houses in good gardens dating from the middle and late 19th century. The area to the east of the town between the Penk and the Cannock road, still known as the Marsh, was mentioned as common grazing land in 1598[13] and was inhabited by at least 1614.[14] The common was inclosed in 1827 under an Act of 1814.[15] The area was used by troops during the Second World War,[16] and the new housing estate there, started before the war, has since been extended. There are modern houses and bungalows along the main road both north and south of Penkridge town.

The constablewick of Levedale contained nine households in 1666.[17] There were 18 or 20 yeomen's houses in Levedale itself in 1680 and four houses, none of which was a gentleman's residence, in Longridge.[18] By 1834 the constablewick included the present hamlets of Drayton, Longridge, and Preston.[19] Drayton in 1666 had formed with Dunston a constablewick in which there were 49 households, 15 of them too poor to pay hearth tax,[20] and in Drayton itself there were 9 or 10 houses in 1680, none of them a gentleman's residence.[21]

[93] Ibid. Apr. 1931.
[94] Staffs. Educ. Cttee., *List of Schools, 1951*, revised to 1955.
[95] Ex inf. Staffs. C.C. Educ. Dept. (1956).
[1] *Kelly's Dir. Staffs.* (1940).
[2] Ibid. (1932); *Census*, 1951, Staffs.
[3] *Census*, 1951, Staffs.
[4] White, *Dir. Staffs.* (1851).
[5] Camden, *Britannia* (1695), 530.
[6] *S.H.C.* 1927, 31–34.
[7] White, *Dir. Staffs.* (1934).
[8] Ex inf. Staffs. C.C. Roads and Bridges Dept.
[9] J. C. Tildesley, *Penkridge*, 73.
[10] Ibid. 15.
[11] S.R.O., D. 260/M/E. 353 (a), map 5, part of which is reproduced below, facing p. 104.

[12] Probably the lane shown in W.S.L., Staffs. Views, viii, p. 30 (1836).
[13] S.R.O., D. 260/M/box 12, bdle. a, Penkridge Ct. Bk. 1598–1654, f. 18a.
[14] *Penkridge Par. Reg.* (Staffs. Par. Reg. Soc.), 128.
[15] S.R.O., Q/RDc 22.
[16] Mass was said at the camp during the Second World War, either by commissioned chaplains or the parish priest of Cannock as officiating chaplain: ex inf. the Very Revd. J. B. Hickson, V.F., formerly parish priest of Cannock and in 1956 at Sutton Coldfield, Warws.
[17] *S.H.C.* 1927, 30–31.
[18] Ibid. 1919, 219.
[19] White, *Dir. Staffs.* (1834).
[20] *S.H.C.* 1927, 28–29.
[21] Ibid. 1919, 219.

Preston had 4 houses in 1680, with several 'good yeomen' residing there but no 'gentlemen'.[22]

Whiston and Bickford formed one constablewick in 1666 when there were 15 households in Whiston and 8 in Bickford, besides 5 others in the constablewick too poor to be chargeable for the hearth tax.[23] There were 12 or 14 houses in Whiston in 1680 and 5 or 6 yeomen's houses in Bickford.[24] By 1834 the constablewick of Whiston included the hamlets of Bickford, Congreve, and Mitton.[25] Congreve had contained 6 or 7 houses in 1680.[26] Mitton, with Longnor in Bradley parish, in 1666 formed a constablewick in which there were 9 households.[27] Mitton itself contained 6 or 7 yeomen's houses in 1680[28] and 3 farmhouses and 2 cottages in 1834.[29]

Pillaton constablewick contained 14 households in 1666,[30] and there were 14 or 15 houses in the hamlet of Pillaton in 1680, in addition to the Hall,[31] but only 2 farms in 1834.[32] In 1955 the buildings of a former airfield to the south-west of the Hall were being used as stores by the County Council Agricultural Executive Committee. Pillaton constablewick in 1834 included the hamlets of Wolgarston, Otherton, Rodbaston, Water Eaton, and Gailey.[33] Wolgarston contained 12 houses in 1680, none a gentleman's residence.[34] Otherton and Rodbaston formed a single constablewick in 1666 containing 10 households, 5 of them too poor to be chargeable for hearth tax.[35] Otherton was said to contain 3 houses in 1680, and one good house in Rodbaston was noted then.[36] By 1834 there were 5 farms and a few cottages in Otherton.[37] There was a small Roman settlement on Watling Street in what is now Water Eaton about 1½ mile east of Stretton Bridge.[38] By 1666 the Water Eaton portion of Stretton and Water Eaton constablewick contained 17 households, 9 of them too poor to be chargeable for hearth tax.[39] The hamlet contained 5 houses in 1680, all occupied by freeholders.[40] In about 1841 Water Eaton consisted of 778 acres of 'old inclosed land', including what is now Gailey, in addition to 626 acres of 'new inclosed land' on Calf Heath.[41]

Gailey Hay formed, with Teddesley Hay, a division of the Forest of Cannock which before 1300 included the vills of Penkridge and Wolgarston, Pillaton, Otherton, Rodbaston, and Water Eaton, and also Calf Heath,[42] and it was in the parish of Penkridge by 1252.[43] By 1834 Gailey seems to have been an alternative name for the hamlet of Spread Eagle,[44] which had consisted by 1775 of a few houses around the crossroads formed by Watling Street and the Stafford–Wolverhampton road[45] and was still part of Water Eaton in 1851.[46] The road widening at Gailey crossroads in 1929 and 1937, besides absorbing parts of Gailey churchyard, involved the demolition of the Spread Eagle Inn at the north-west corner of the crossing,[47] but a new inn has replaced it. There are five post-1945 council houses in the cul-de-sac near Croft Farm.

The Stafford–Wolverhampton road runs from north to south across the parish, and Watling Street crosses the southern portion from east to west. In 1754 a road which has now largely disappeared led from Lyne Hill to Hatherton, running south of Pillaton Hall.[48] The old road from Penkridge to Pillaton Green then ran in a straight line south of the present road, cutting off the corner by Quarry Heath, and existing field boundaries follow the line of the old road at the Pillaton end.[49] The road running north of Quarry Heath towards Cannock Chase was not in existence.[50] Much of the Stafford–Wolverhampton road in the parish was widened between 1929 and 1937, and the work included the building of the dual-carriageway south of Penkridge town and the construction in 1937 of the roundabout where the road crosses Watling Street at Gailey.[51] In 1754 a cross stood at the junction of the Stafford–Wolverhampton road and the lane leading to Lower Drayton.[52] Coaches travelling between London and Manchester, Birmingham and Manchester, and Birmingham and Liverpool passed through Penkridge daily in each direction by 1818.[53] A daily horse-mail was established in 1829 to run between Walsall and Penkridge via Bloxwich and Cannock.[54] There was formerly a toll gate on the Wolverhampton road north of the turning to Rodbaston where 'Mile Houses' now stand.[55] The timber-framed house in Cannock Road east of the canal bridge is known as 'Tollgate Cottage'. An early 19th-century brick toll house stands on the road to Cannock at the eastern extremity of the parish. It is octagonal in form, the hipped slate roof terminating in an octagonal chimney.

Cuttlestone Bridge,[56] which carries the road from Penkridge to Congreve over the Penk, was mentioned at some time between about 1225 and 1259 as 'pons de Cuthuluestan'[57] and occurs again in 1261.[58] Its upkeep was the responsibility of the hundred

[22] S.H.C. 1919, 219.
[23] Ibid. 1927, 60–61.
[24] Ibid. 1919, 219.
[25] White, Dir. Staffs. (1834).
[26] S.H.C. 1919, 219.
[27] Ibid. 1927, 39.
[28] Ibid. 1919, 219.
[29] White, Dir. Staffs. (1834).
[30] S.H.C. 1927, 23.
[31] Ibid. 1919, 219; see pp. 119–20.
[32] White, Dir. Staffs. (1834).
[33] Ibid.
[34] S.H.C. 1919, 219.
[35] Ibid. 1927, 38. [36] Ibid. 1919, 219.
[37] White, Dir. Staffs. (1834).
[38] Trans. Birmingham Arch. Soc. lxix. 51, 52.
[39] S.H.C. 1927, 61–62.
[40] Ibid. 1919, 219.
[41] Tithe Maps and Appt., Penkridge (copy in W.S.L.).
[42] S.H.C. vi (1), 166, 177. Penkridge, Wolgarston, and Otherton lay within Cannock Forest by 1166: ibid. 1923, 293–6. Calf Heath, mentioned in 994 (ibid. 1916, 108), was still within the Forest in 1311: ibid. 1911, 311.

[43] Close R. 1251–3, 128.
[44] White, Dir. Staffs. (1834).
[45] Yates, Map of Staffs. (1799), based on a survey made 1769–75.
[46] Lich. Dioc. Regy., Bp.'s Reg. Bk. O(A) 1847–53, pp. 374, 381.
[47] There was a Spread Eagle Inn on this corner in 1849: ibid. pp. 374–5.
[48] S.R.O., D. 260/M/E. 353 (a, b).
[49] Ibid.
[50] Ibid.
[51] Ex inf. Staffs. C.C. Surveyor's Dept.; original docs. penes Staffs. County Council; Lich. Dioc. Regy., Consist. Ct. Act Bk. 1924–30, pp. 445–8; ibid. 1934–8, pp. 339–43.
[52] S.R.O., D. 260/M/E. 353 (a), map 17; see plate opposite.
[53] Parsons and Bradshaw, Dir. Staffs. (1818).
[54] Tildesley, Penkridge, 73.
[55] S.R.O., D. 260/M/E. 353 (a, b), map 16.
[56] See plate facing p. 87.
[57] S.R.O., D. 260/M/box 3, bdle. i.
[58] S.H.C. 1950–1, 48.

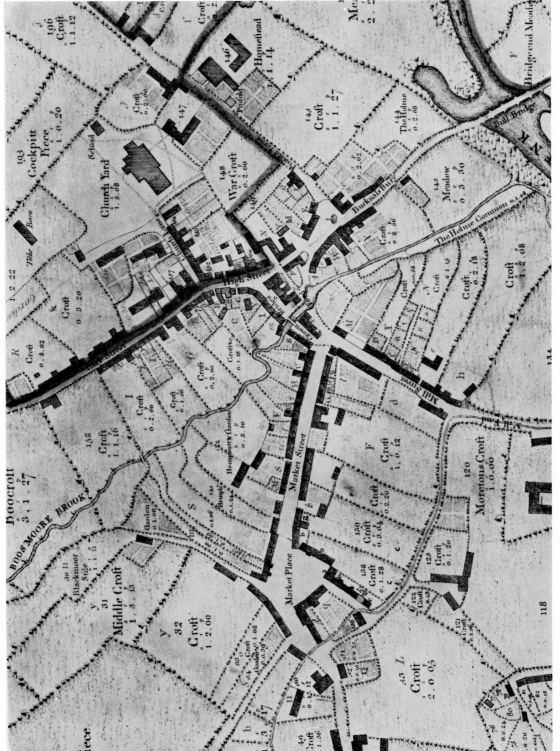

PENKRIDGE: Plan of 1754

Church and Bull Bridge, *c.* 1800

Pillaton Hall, *c.* 1800

PENKRIDGE

in the 17th century[59] and of the county by 1830 when it was described as old but in good repair.[60] It is built of stone ashlar and consists of five segmental arches, the piers between them resting on splayed cutwaters. It may date from the 17th or 18th century but has been widened at least once and altered and repaired at various times. Bull Bridge, which carries the Stafford–Wolverhampton road over the Penk, occurs as 'Bolde brugge' in 1376,[61] and although it was the hundred's responsibility in the 17th century,[62] it was repaired in 1711 at a cost of £25 raised in the county.[63] In 1763 it had neither posts nor rails[64] and was rebuilt in 1796.[65] It was widened in 1822,[66] and in 1824 £64 5s. 3d. was spent on removing 'buildings at Bull Bridge'.[67] The present bridge is of stone ashlar and has five graduated arches with rusticated voussoirs. The stone parapets are curved at the ends and terminate in small octagonal piers. Crown Bridge which used to carry the Cannock road over the Boosmore Brook, to the east of the junction of the present Market Street and Mill Street, seems to have been the hundred's responsibility in the 17th century[68] and the county's by 1830 when it was described as new.[69] It has since been built over. Mitton Bridge, presumably that which now carries the road from Bradley over the Church Eaton Brook, was described as new in 1830 when it was the county's responsibility.[70]

The Staffordshire and Worcestershire Canal, opened in 1772,[71] had a wharf at Penkridge by 1831[72] where by 1834 boats were calling several times daily to take goods to all parts,[73] while the wharf on the same canal at Gailey seems to have been in use since the opening of the canal.[74] By 1955 these two wharves were little used except by pleasure craft.[75] There are fifteen canal bridges in the parish. All are small humped bridges of red brick except that carrying Watling Street near Gailey Wharf which in its present widened form dates from 1952.[76] The older bridges are all numbered and named on small oval cast-iron tablets. The lock-keeper's house by Penkridge Bridge was built or adapted in the late 18th century and has round-headed windows with Gothic glazing. At Gailey the canal basin and former coal wharf lie on the south side of Watling Street. Opposite the wharf is the former toll-clerk's house, now enlarged. Nearer the bridge are two cottages

with round-headed Gothic windows. One of these, in the shape of a circular tower, was the lock-keeper's cottage within living memory.[77]

The Grand Junction Railway was opened in 1837, with two trains daily to both Stafford and Wolverhampton stopping at Penkridge and Spread Eagle (later called Gailey) by 1838.[78] The railway viaduct, which spans the Levedale Road and the River Penk, is faced with rusticated stone and has seven segmental arches, each 30 ft. in span and 37 ft. high, springing from battered piers. It dates from 1837 and is considered a fine early work of Thomas Brassey (1805–70), the railway engineer.[79] Penkridge station lies a little to the south-west of the centre of the town. Gailey station, just south of Watling Street, was closed in 1951.[80] To the south of Penkridge station the main line is joined by a branch line which runs from the Littleton Colliery in Huntington (Cannock parish) and has sidings on the canal south of Otherton.

During the early 17th century maintenance of a beacon near Congreve, probably situated on Beacon Hill a mile and a half south-west of the town of Penkridge, was the responsibility of the hundred.[81]

There are several instances of burgage tenure in the town of Penkridge between c. 1290 and 1471.[82]

The townships of Penkridge, Coppenhall, Dunston, and Stretton were each supporting their own poor by 1834.[83] Before the establishment of the Penkridge Union, with its workhouse first at Brewood and then at Cannock, the parish workhouse stood on the north side of Cannock Road, formerly Husbandman Street, opposite Reynolds Cottage.[84] The building was used as cottages in the last half of the 19th century but has recently been demolished.[85] The site is occupied by modern houses.

The gasworks were built by a limited liability company in 1872 and taken over by the Stafford Corporation in 1902.[86] A sewage scheme was installed in 1931.[87]

A Free Reading Room was established in the Market Square by Lady Hatherton in 1881.[88] The present room was built in Market Street by the Revd. the Hon. Cecil J. Littleton in 1885 for 'working men of good character on payment of a nominal subscription' and was at once 'largely patronized by the class for whose especial benefit it was designed.'[89] Although partly occupied as a

[59] Ibid. 1934 (1), 45.
[60] J. Potter, *List of Bridges which the inhabitants of the County of Stafford are bound to repair* (1830), 3.
[61] W.S.L., D. 1790/A/6/2; *S.H.C.* 1950–1, 25 n. 66.
[62] *S.H.C.* 1934 (1), 45. Orders were given for its repair in 1726 at the expense of the hundred and in 1727 at the expense of the county: S.R.O., Q/SM, Ep. 1726, T. 1727.
[63] *S.H.C.* 1934(1), 80, 82.
[64] Ibid. 30.
[65] Ibid. 88, 89. For a view of c. 1800 see plate opposite.
[66] S.R.O., Q/Fa.
[67] Ibid. July 1824.
[68] *S.H.C.* 1934 (1), 45, map facing p. 144; S.R.O. D. 260M/E. 353 (a), map 5.
[69] Potter, *List of Bridges*, 3; see plate facing p. 104.
[70] Potter, *List of Bridges*, 3.
[71] *S.H.C.* 1934 (1), 111.
[72] Tildesley, *Penkridge*, 38.
[73] White, *Dir. Staffs.* (1834).
[74] Pitt, *Staffs.* 257; White, *Dir. Staffs.* (1834; 1851).
[75] Ex inf. Mr. L. Butler, until 1955 Estate Officer of the North-Western Division of British Waterways.
[76] Local inf.
[77] Local inf.

[78] Tildesley, *Penkridge*, 37, 38. There were 6 daily in each direction stopping at Penkridge by 1851: White, *Dir. Staffs.* (1851).
[79] Tildesley, *Penkridge*, 73; *D.N.B.*
[80] Ex inf. Public Relations Office, London Midland Region, British Railways.
[81] S.R.O., Q.S.O., ii, f. 123a.
[82] *S.H.C.* 1931, 237, 242, 244, 245–6; C 136/10 (12); W.S.L., D. 1790/A/6/2; Glos. R.O., D. 340a/T 207/4. In 1392 a moiety of a burgage was the subject of an action in what was called the court of the vill: *S.H.C.* 1931, 244. In 1350 Penkridge was among the towns of England, including also Lichfield, Stafford, Newcastle, Burton, and Wolverhampton, whose mayors and bailiffs were ordered to provide men for the king's service: ibid. viii (1), 93.
[83] White, *Dir. Staffs.* (1834).
[84] S.R.O., D. 260/M/E. 353 (a, b), map 5; a note of 1806 reads 'now a workhouse'.
[85] Local inf.
[86] *Kelly's Dir. Staffs.* (1924).
[87] Ibid. (1932).
[88] Tildesley, *Penkridge*, 86.
[89] Ibid. *Kelly's Dir. Staffs.* (1892), states that it was erected by public subscription at a cost of £200.

billiards and snooker club, its use as a reading-room had ceased for some years before its opening as a church hall in 1957.[90]

The police station at the junction of Bellbrook and Cannock Road is a small classical building of red brick with stone windows and a moulded cornice. Part of it formerly housed the Savings Bank and may date from the bank's establishment in 1819.[91] An inscription on the frieze, dated 1858, probably refers to the building's enlargement and conversion into a police station. The brick lock-up, containing two cells, and the wooden stocks stand on the opposite side of Bellbrook. In 1954 three police houses were built south of the town on the east side of the Wolverhampton road, and there is a single house of this date at Gailey roundabout.

The Peace Memorial Hall in Pinfold Lane dates from 1926. It is a single-story brick and roughcast building with a half-timbered porch. A bowling green lies immediately to the south.

A Provident Clothing Society was started in Penkridge in 1831[92] and was still in existence in 1928.[93]

There was horse-racing at Penkridge after the fair on Midsummer Day by 1680,[94] and in 1696 £1 was spent on 'staking for the plate at Penkridge' on behalf of the Duke of Rutland.[95] There was a three-quarter mile race-course to the east of Preston Hill where September races were held by about 1825 and were still being held in 1834.[96]

Elizabeth I passed through Penkridge in 1575.[97] Royalist troops quartered here were worsted in a small skirmish in May 1645.[98] Richard Hurd (1720–1808), Bishop of Coventry and Lichfield (1774–81) and of Worcester (1781–1810), was born at Congreve, the son of John Hurd, a wealthy farmer there, and was educated at Brewood Grammar School.[99] He was appointed preceptor to the Prince of Wales and the Duke of York in 1776 and declined the Archbishopric of Canterbury in 1783.[1]

About 1590 Edward Littleton was said to be willing to build a furnace if he could secure 'any vent and utterance for sowes'.[2] There was an iron foundry at Penkridge by 1635,[3] and by 1754 there was a pool called Ironmonger Pool to the east of Pillaton Hall,[4] while to the south-east of what is now Preston Hill Farm there was a pool with two fields called Far Sough Piece and New Sough Piece.[5] The former Hazel Mill, in Pillaton, seems at some period

to have been connected with iron-working.[6] Although by 1817 iron was still the town's chief manufacture, its extent was by then 'inconsiderable'.[7] The mill downstream from Bull Bridge was in temporary use as a rolling-mill between 1827 and 1832.[8] There was a forge at Congreve, probably on the site of the former mill, by 1717, and its output then and in 1750 was 120 tons.[9] It continued in use until at least 1832[10] but was untenanted c. 1841.[11]

Quarry Heath to the east of Penkridge town occurs as common land in 1598,[12] but the area was inhabited by at least 1635,[13] the heath being inclosed in 1827 under the Act of 1814.[14] There were 'stonepits' at Quarry Heath, in the Wolgarston–Wood Bank area, and to the south-east of the town in 1754.[15] Lord Hatherton owned quarries at Wolgarston, Wood Bank, and Quarry Heath by 1862,[16] and the stone used in the 19th-century restoration of Lichfield Cathedral is thought to have come from Penkridge.[17] The firm of Ingram was quarrying at Wood Bank and Quarry Heath between at least 1892 and 1912,[18] while the firm of Walker was working at Quarry Heath between at least 1924 and 1940.[19] All these quarries were abandoned by 1955, those at Quarry Heath being then used by squatters as a caravan site, while those at Wood Bank were being used as a rubbish tip by the Cannock R.D.C. Yew Tree Cottages and several other mid-19th-century buildings in the area have walls of small coursed rubble, probably surplus material left when larger blocks were quarried.

West of Calf Heath Bridge and adjoining the Midland Tar Distillery (Brewood parish) is the United Lamp Black Ltd. Carbon Works, opened during the Second World War.[20] Immediately to the south is the Four Ashes Sand and Gravel Quarry.

Church Farm in Pinfold Lane and a cottage in Bellbrook are the only domestic buildings of certain medieval date in the town itself. Church Farm is T-shaped in plan, having a long two-story range parallel to the road and a tall brick wing at its east end. The former, which was faced with brickwork in the 18th century, contains in the centre a former single-story hall enclosed at both ends by tall cruck trusses. Weathering on the outer face of the west truss and a mullioned window below the collar-beam indicate that this was formerly the west end of the building. The brick outhouse with heavy roof timbers which now lies beyond it may represent a

[90] Ex inf. the Vicar of Penkridge (1955); *Staffs. Advertiser and Chronicle*, 2 May 1957.
[91] Tildesley, *Penkridge*, 84.
[92] Ibid. 86; White, *Dir. Staffs.* (1851).
[93] *Kelly's Dir. Staffs.* (1928). It was no longer noted in 1932: ibid. (1932).
[94] *S.H.C.* 1919, 219.
[95] Hist. MSS. Com. *Rutland, IV*, 556.
[96] White, *Dir. Staffs.* (1834); Teesdale, *Map of Staffs.* (1832).
[97] *Penkridge Par. Reg.* 74.
[98] Tildesley, *Penkridge*, 18 n.
[99] *D.N.B.*
[1] Ibid.
[2] Hist. MSS. Com. *Middleton*, 495.
[3] C.P. 25(2)/485, 11 Chas. I Mich.
[4] S.R.O., D. 260/M/E. 353 (a), map 3.
[5] Ibid. map. 8.
[6] There was still much furnace clinker on the site of the mill in 1956, and Tildesley, *Penkridge*, 71, mentions that there was a rolling mill in this area at Bangley. For the site see p. 128.
[7] Pitt, *Staffs.* 256.
[8] S.R.O., Q/RDc 22a; Teesdale, *Map of Staffs.* (1832).

[9] E. Wyndham Hulme, 'Statistical History of the British Iron Trade, 1717–50' (*Newcomen Soc.* 1928), 8 (copy in W.S.L.); *Penkridge Par. Reg.* 311.
[10] *Penkridge Par. Reg.* 319; Yates, *Map of Staffs.* (1799), based on a survey made between 1769 and 1775; S.R.O., Q/RDc 22a; Teesdale, *Map of Staffs.* (1832). It was stated in 1817 that the forge had been held by an ironmaster named Barker, father of the Miss Barker of Congreve who wrote a novel called 'A Welch Story': Pitt, *Staffs.* 258. A Thomas Barker, junior, occurs in 1777: S.R.O., D. 260/M/box 16, bdle. a.
[11] Tithe Maps and Appt., Penkridge (copy in W.S.L.), no. 2798; it was owned by the lord of Congreve.
[12] S.R.O., D. 260/M/box 16, bdle. a, Penkridge Ct. Bk. 1598–1654, f. 15a.
[13] *Penkridge Par. Reg.* 57. There was a family living at 'the Quarry Pit' by 1630: ibid. 53.
[14] S.R.O., Q/RDc 22a.
[15] S.R.O., D. 260/M/E. 353 (a), maps 4, 5.
[16] Ibid. E. 188, Lord Hatherton's Mines Rental, 1862.
[17] *Kelly's Dir. Staffs.* (1892).
[18] Ibid. (1892; 1896; 1912).
[19] Ibid. (1924; 1928; 1932; 1940).
[20] Ex inf. the Clerk, Cannock Rural District Council.

17th-century malthouse. Within, the hall roof has smoke-blackened purlins and curved wind-braces. A rough upper floor and a chimney are insertions, probably of the 17th century. The long bay lying east of the hall has a 16th-century stone fireplace and chamfered ceiling beams. It may represent a much-altered bay of the medieval house. The brick cross-wing dates from *c.* 1680 and has a contemporary staircase, possibly brought from elsewhere, in its south-west angle. The house in Bellbrook probably dates from the later 15th century and retains most of its original framing. The front or north wall has close-set studding; at the back the studs are widely spaced. The gable-ends have been largely rebuilt in brick. Evidence in the roof space shows that the house had three distinct divisions: the centre was a single-story open hall and has heavily smoke-blackened roof timbers, the flanking trusses having cambered tie-beams below which are large curved braces. The east bay, always of two stories, has externally a shallow 16th-century oriel window to light the solar. The west bay, also probably two-storied, had a cross-passage, blocked in the 17th century by a chimney. An earlier chimney, inserted in the hall bay, joins it in the roof space.

There are many timber-framed houses in the town dating from the 16th and early 17th centuries; in most cases the walls were refaced or rebuilt in brick from *c.* 1700 onwards. The Old Deanery in Pinfold Lane is exceptional in being partly of stone, possibly reused material from demolished buildings connected with the college. It consists of a stone central block of 16th- or early-17th-century date flanked by two timber cross-wings which are slightly earlier. The two-storied central block may have replaced an earlier timber-framed hall. It has a massive contemporary stone chimney with brick stacks above the roof line. An original stone doorway in the north wall has deeply splayed jambs. The doorway on the south side has a four-centred head and the stone-mullioned windows are original. The loft space was designed for use as attics and has cambered collars to give headroom. The timber-framed east wing has a stone plinth and may be slightly later than the west wing, which is now enclosed by 18th-century brickwork. Church Cottages, lying north of the churchyard, formerly comprised a single timber-framed house of three or more bays, possibly of early-16th-century origin. An altered open truss near the north end indicates the position of the single-story hall. A cross passage, blocked by a later chimney, is incorporated in the two-story south bay.

The White Hart Inn on the east side of High Street is a three-storied timber-framed building dating from *c.* 1600. The front, which has three small gables, shows a different decorative use of framing to each story. The ground floor is close-studded, the first floor has a herringbone pattern and on the top floor the gables have small square panels with quarter-round fillings. At first-floor level is a slight projection supported on small shaped brackets. A carriageway originally penetrated the central bay but this feature has now been moved to the south bay, replacing a mullioned and transomed window on small supporting brackets.[21] Similar windows,

all restored, still exist on the first floor and there are restored four-light windows in the gables. The rear of the building has modern alterations and additions.

In Market Street a house known as 'Two Steps' was formerly the Blacksmith's Arms Inn. In its present form it dates from the later 16th century but contains in an altered central bay some evidence of a single-story hall. The sides of the carriageway piercing the south-east bay and the wall facing the street have exposed timbers. The adjoining cottage may originally have formed part of the building and one of its walls, exposed in the carriageway, has an original carved door-head pegged between uprights near ground level. A house on the opposite side of the street has a front elevation of mid-19th-century brick but remains timber-framed at the rear. It dates probably from *c.* 1600 and consists of a central block with two cross-wings. Near the centre are remains of what may have been a medieval cruck truss.

On three sides of School Square, formerly the Market Place, are timber-framed buildings probably dating from before 1600. Corner Cottage, at the junction of the square with New Road, has a small two-storied wing which probably represents the solar wing adjoining an original hall, now rebuilt. A carved stone, perhaps a fireplace lintel, has been built into a chimneypiece and is now dated 1680. The houses on the north-east and south sides of the square have been brick-faced. On the south side the building recently named the Manor House[22] has modern oriels with lead glazing. It has original timbers internally and a separate brick wing of the late 17th century.

Bowcroft Cottages in New Road is a restored timber-framed range of three bays of which the east bay is the oldest. There are indications internally that the structure was originally single-storied. In Cannock Road Reynolds Cottage is a three-bayed timber house probably dating from the late 16th century with a contemporary chimney in the central bay. The row of timber-framed cottages west of Haling Grove was originally one long house, possibly of the early 16th century, with a hall bay and a cross-passage. Facing the road is the early stout timber-framing, now brick-filled. Other timber-framed houses in the town which appear to date from the 16th and early 17th centuries include three cottages in Mill Street, one at Mill End, a two-bay house in the Marsh and Old Tollgate Cottage in the Cannock road.

Wyre Hall in the Cannock road is a stone and brick house dating in part from the early 17th century. The west half of the road front is of this date, the lowest story being of stone ashlar. The present doorway occupies a window site, the earlier door jambs and lintel being visible a few feet farther west. The upper stories are of brick with stone mullioned windows and stone quoins. The east wing was altered and additions were made to the house in the 19th century. Most of the house fronts in Mill Street date from the 18th and early 19th centuries but at its junction with Bellbrook is a brick house dated 1673. Ivy House[23] in Church Lane has a symmetrical brick front with stone key-blocks to the windows and a moulded stone cornice. It is dated

[21] W.S.L., Staffs. Views, viii, pp. 26 (1837), 27 (1836).
[22] No evidence has been found to connect this house with any of the Penkridge manors.
[23] Occupied by the vicar before 1832 (Tildesley, *Penk-*

ridge, 38). In 1834 it was a boarding school: White, *Dir. Staffs.* (1834). Later in the 19th cent. it became the doctor's house: *Kelly's Dir. Staffs.* (1884, and later edns. to 1940).

1741. Rock House, standing back from New Road in a large garden, is a red-brick house with a Tuscan porch of the late 18th century probably built by a member of the Croydon family.[24] The Littleton Arms at the corner of Church Lane is a tall early-19th-century building of colour-washed brick. It replaced an earlier inn of the same name. Its principal front has sash windows and a central doorway approached by a double flight of steps. Haling Grove or Haling Dene, now the offices of the Cannock R.D.C., stands on the south side of the Cannock road and dates from c. 1840. A row of cottages was demolished to clear the site. It is a mansion with an Ionic porch, a three-story central block, and two-story flanking wings.

In general many of the red-brick frontages in the town date from the mid-19th century[25] when much rebuilding was done on the Hatherton estate.

In Levedale a largely rebuilt cottage known as 'Salen' has a medieval cruck truss forming the central partition between its two bays. The upper part of a similar truss is visible internally at the east gable end. The roof has heavy purlins and inverted curved wind-braces. The west bay contains a wide fireplace having a heavily moulded 16th-century lintel which spans the room. The central partition contains early wattle and daub filling. The brickwork of the side walls probably dates from c. 1700, and there have been later additions to the house.

The Swan Inn, Whiston, is a timber-framed house of 16th-century origin, later faced with brickwork. A bay has been demolished at its west end. The central bay, which retains a wide fireplace and a moulded ceiling beam, was probably the hall with its cross-passage to the west. On one gable-end is a stone dated 1711, with initials T.H·A.; this may represent the date of the brickwork facing. At Bickford there are two timber-framed cottages partly rebuilt in brick which date from the 16th or early 17th century. The bailiff's cottage on the Whiston–Bickford road is much altered but is probably of the 16th century. There is some original framing and a large early chimney at its east end. A fireplace at the west end is dated 1697 with initials G.I.M. A barn east of the house is partly timber-framed.

In Otherton the ruined buildings known as Otherton Cottages comprised originally a single timber-framed house of four bays, dating probably from the beginning of the 16th century. The south bays have close-studding to the side walls with heavy braces and original early window spaces. The southernmost bay, always of two stories, retains curved wind-braces to the roof and most of its original upper floor. A small central bay with a later-inserted floor has a wide fireplace with stone jambs and an embattled wooden lintel. The north bay of the house was rebuilt in the early or mid-17th century, the older roof being retained. The ground-floor walls are of stone ashlar, those above being of brick with stone quoins. The stone mullioned windows are of two and four lights, and there are oval lights in the side walls of the upper room. A lean-to of similar date on the north side of the house has been partly destroyed by the addition of a small 18th-century brick wing. The building, which was subsequently divided into cottages, had been abandoned by 1955 and stands isolated in the fields without road access. In 1754 it was still a 'homestead'.[26]

At Lyne Hill, a brick and stone rubble cottage with dormer windows, of 17th-century origin, is said to be the only thatched house left in the parish. The west bay is open to the roof and was probably built and always used as an outhouse.

Near the site of Hazel Mill is a much-altered timber-framed cottage which may date from the 16th century. A 17th-century stone cottage at Quarry Heath has had an upper story added in brickwork. Longford House, 200 yds. south of Longford Bridge, is a two-story brick house with stone dressings. It is dated 1706 and has alterations of 1872.

About 300 yds. south of the old road from Penkridge to Pillaton Green is a moated site (possibly that of Hussey Hall), its position marked by depressions in a ploughed field.

A cottage at Gailey on the Wolverhampton road near Marsh Farm is partly timber-framed and probably dates from the early 17th century. Pool Farm and Plough Farm are 17th-century brick houses on the north side of Watling Street. The former has a timber-framed barn at the rear and was raised one story at a later date. Plough Farm was formerly the Plough Inn.[27] Gailey Farm and Eaton House, south of Watling Street, are 18th-century brick houses, the former having a good pedimented doorcase.

Such manor-houses as still exist are described under their respective manors.

MANORS. *PENKRIDGE*, held before the Conquest by King Edward, was still a royal manor in 1086 when it was assessed at ½ hide.[28] To it belonged six members, namely Wolgarston ('Tuhgarestone'), Drayton, Congreve, and Dunston, and also Cowley and Beffcote (both in Gnosall), together assessed at 6½ hides.[29] By at least 1156 and until 1172 Walter Hose, or Hussey, held land in Penkridge of the king worth £8 a year.[30] In 1173 Penkridge was apparently restored to the Crown for from that year until 1206 it was tallaged as royal demesne,[31] but in 1207 land here, described as the manor, was restored to Hugh Hose, son of Walter, for a fine of 200 marks and two palfreys to the king and 2 marks and a horse worth 20 marks to the queen, to hold by service of 1 knight's fee and payment of £10 a year.[32] Hugh, however, was in the king's wardship from 1209 to 1214[33] and in 1215 conveyed the manor with the dependent vills of Congreve, Wolgarston, Cowley, Beffcote, and Little Onn (in Church Eaton) to Henry of London, Archbishop of Dublin (1213–28),[34] and formerly Archdeacon of Stafford.[35] Some intermediate lordship appears to have remained with the

[24] A Richard Croydon was in occupation in 1818 (Parsons and Bradshaw, *Dir. Staffs.* (1818)) and in 1834: White, *Dir. Staffs.* (1834).
[25] Tithe Maps and Appt., Penkridge (copy in W.S.L.).
[26] Ibid.; S.R.O., D. 260/M/E. 353 (a, b), map 3.
[27] Ex inf. the owner (1955).
[28] *V.C.H. Staffs.* iv. 38, no. 8.
[29] Ibid.

[30] *S.H.C.* i. 20, 65.
[31] Ibid. i. 69, 140; ibid. ii (1), 3, 137.
[32] Ibid. ii (1), 141, 143, 147–8, 151; *Rot. de Ob. et Fin.* (Rec. Com.), 403.
[33] *S.H.C.* ii (1), 153, 156, 157, 158, 160: *Bk. of Fees*, 143.
[34] *Rot. Chart.* (Rec. Com.), 218.
[35] Le Neve, *Fasti* (1854), i. 571.

Hussey family, for it was claimed for John Hussey in 1300,[36] Thomas Hussey in 1462,[37] and John Hussey in 1503.[38]

Before his death in 1228, and probably by 1225, the Archbishop of Dublin had granted two-thirds of the manor to his nephew Andrew le Blund,[39] who in 1236 was holding this part of the king by service of 1 knight's fee[40] and in 1259 was sued by a later archbishop, Fulk (1256–71), for land in Penkridge as the right of the church of Dublin.[41] Andrew died in 1259, apparently not of sound mind, leaving a widow Ellen who was given custody of his lands and heir.[42] Their son Hugh had succeeded by 1271[43] and was said in 1285 to be holding two-thirds of the manor of Penkridge, worth £20, of the king by homage and service of two armed horsemen, one of them with a caparisoned horse, for 40 days at his own expense whenever the king went with an army to Wales.[44] In 1293 Hugh claimed the rights of infangthief and gallows in Penkridge[45] and in 1305 was granted free warren there.[46] By 1315 Hugh had settled Penkridge on Margery, or Margaret, widow of his son Hugh, and her son Hugh[47] but before July 1316 made another settlement, retaining Penkridge for himself.[48] Hugh and his wife Nichola were alive in 1318,[49] but in 1328 his grandson Hugh succeeded.[50] In 1350 Nichola, then the wife of John de Alveton, conveyed to Hugh her rights in one-third of the manor which she held in dower.[51] This Sir Hugh was succeeded in 1361 by his son John.[52]

In 1363 John Blount conveyed the manor to John de Beverley,[53] against whom Sir Hugh's widow Joyce recovered one-third as her dower in 1366.[54] By 1367 John de Beverley had settled the manor on himself and his wife Amice.[55] John was granted free warren on all the demesne lands belonging to the manor of Penkridge both within and without the royal forest of Cannock in 1368,[56] and in 1372 he was given view of frankpledge with infangthief and outfangthief and waif and stray in the manor and its fees and members, namely Wolgarston, Drayton, Congreve, Dunston, Cowley, Beffcote, and Little Onn, for a rent of 5s.[57] John de Beverley died in 1380, and his widow Amice then held the manor in chief by knight service until her death in 1416.[58]

In 1414 Amice leased the manor to Sir Humphrey Stafford of Hook (Dors.) for five years at a rent of 24 marks, Sir Humphrey undertaking to repair the weirs, walls, 'haies', inclosures, and all the buildings of the tenants-at-will.[59] In 1415 one of Amice's grandsons and coheirs, Robert Langford, conveyed the reversion of his half of the manor to Sir Humphrey, his wife Elizabeth, and their issue,[60] and in June 1416, a few months before Amice died, her other grandson and coheir Walter Dauntsey conveyed the reversion of his half to Sir William Haukeford (or Hankeford) and his heirs.[61] These two grants were confirmed by the king in 1417.[62] When Sir William Haukeford died in 1424 his trustees did fealty for his moiety, and he was succeeded by his grandson Richard.[63] The later descent of this half of the manor is obscure. The other moiety was settled by Sir Humphrey Stafford on himself and his heirs in 1427[64] and was soon afterwards conveyed by him to his son John and daughter-in-law Anne with Littywood (in Bradley.)[65] John was dead by January 1428 and was succeeded by his infant son Humphrey,[66] who in 1457 was described as lord of Penkridge[67] and was holding what may have been the whole manor at his death in 1461.[68]

Penkridge then descended with Littywood in Bradley[69] until 1519 when Robert, 2nd Lord Willoughby de Broke, who had mortgaged Penkridge to Edmund Dudley for five years in 1507[70] and to Edward Greville of Milcote (Warws.) in 1518,[71] mortgaged it to George Monoux, citizen and alderman of London, reserving to himself a rent of £5 and the fair of Penkridge.[72] Robert died in 1521,[73] and this rent was divided in 1535 or 1536 with his other Staffordshire possessions, including Littywood, between his two surviving granddaughters and co-heirs, Elizabeth, wife of Fulke Greville, and Blanche, wife of Francis Dautrey.[74] In 1542, after the death of Blanche, what was described as the manor of Penkridge was conveyed to Elizabeth and Fulke by Sir Anthony Willoughby,[75] presumably the brother of Robert Lord Willoughby de Broke (d. 1521).[76] Meanwhile, Monoux had foreclosed on the mortgage and in 1539 granted the manor to Sir John Dudley who, as the heir of Edmund Dudley, the mortgagee

[36] S.H.C. v (1), 177.
[37] C 146/3.
[38] Cal. Inq. p.m. Hen. VII, ii, no. 638.
[39] S.H.C. vi (1), 218–19; ibid. iv (1), 36; Pipe R. 1230 (P.R.S. N.S. iv), 58–59.
[40] Bk. of Fees, 593.
[41] S.H.C. iv (1), 139.
[42] Cal. Pat. 1258–66, 35; S.H.C. iv (1), 139.
[43] S.H.C. vi (1), 50.
[44] Feud. Aids, v. 2.
[45] Plac. de Quo Warr. (Rec. Com.), 714.
[46] Cal. Chart. R. 1300–26, 59.
[47] S.H.C. 1911, 325; C 143/102, no. 6; S.H.C. xiii. 11. Margery's husband was dead by 5 Feb. 1315: Cat. Anct. D. iii, C 2938.
[48] C 143/115, no. 5.
[49] S.H.C. x (1), 26.
[50] Cal. Close 1327-30, 296; S.H.C. xiii. 11.
[51] S.H.C. xi. 164.
[52] Cal. Inq. p.m. xi, no. 12.
[53] S.H.C. xiv (1), 111; Cal. Pat. 1361-4, 491–2. John de Beverley was described as the king's yeoman in 1366 (Cal. Pat. 1364-7, 256), and as the king's esquire in 1368: Cal. Chart. R. 1341–1417, 212.
[54] S.H.C. xiii. 56.
[55] Cal. Pat. 1367-70, 34. In 1376 Thomas, another son of Sir Hugh le Blount, released his rights in the manor to John, Amice, and their heirs: Cal. Close, 1374-7, 367.
[56] Cal. Chart. R. 1341-1417, 212.

[57] Ibid. 222-3.
[58] Cal. Close 1377-81, 418; C 138/21. By 1381 she was the wife of Robert Bardolf (C 145/224) and by 1402 once more a widow: Feud. Aids, v. 18.
[59] S.H.C. 1931, 248-9.
[60] Ibid. xi. 222. Robert was the son of Anne, daughter of John de Beverley and Amice: C 138/21.
[61] S.H.C. xi. 225. Walter was the son of Elizabeth, daughter of John and Amice: C 138/21.
[62] Cal. Pat. 1416-22, 61, 110.
[63] C 139/12.
[64] S.H.C. xi. 229.
[65] Cal. Pat. 1422-9, 486; C 139/34.
[66] C 139/34.
[67] S.H.C. N.S. iv. 99.
[68] C 140/3.
[69] C 140/41; S.H.C. N.S. iv. 204-7; Cal. Close, 1485-1500, 21; Cal. Inq. p.m. Hen. VII, ii, no. 638; V.C.H. Staffs. iv. 79.
[70] W.S.L., S. MS. 249, ff. 131b–136a.
[71] Ibid., ff. 125b–126a.
[72] Ibid., f. 124a.
[73] C 142/41, no. 18.
[74] 'Act concerning the partition of lands between the heirs of Lord Broke', 27 Hen. VIII, c. 44: Stat. Realm iii. 605-7.
[75] C.P. 40/1073, rot. 5d; Complete Peerage (orig. edn.), viii. 150.
[76] W.S.L., S. MS. 249, f. 131b.

of 1507, had earlier claimed the manor against Monoux, and to Edmund Sutton.[77] In 1550 Dudley, then Earl of Warwick and later Duke of Northumberland, settled it on his son John Viscount Lisle (d. 1554) and John's wife Anne, daughter of Edward Seymour, Duke of Somerset and Lord Protector until 1550.[78] The younger John Dudley died without issue in 1554 as Earl of Warwick,[79] and his widow, who married Sir Edward Unton of Wadley (Berks.) in 1555,[80] retained a life interest in Penkridge.[81] She became insane in 1566, and on her husband's death in 1582 the queen granted to Fulke Greville, the son of Elizabeth and Fulke, the reversion of the manor which lay with the Crown as part of the estates forfeited by the Duke of Northumberland in 1553.[82] The custody of Anne's person and lands during her lifetime was given to her younger son Henry Unton in 1583.[83]

The manor passed to Fulke Greville and his heirs in 1590,[84] and in 1606 he was succeeded by his son Fulke, the poet, created Baron Brooke of Beauchamp's Court (Warws.) in 1621,[85] who in 1626 or 1627 settled half the manor of Penkridge as jointure on Lady Katherine Russell who married his cousin Robert Greville.[86] In 1628 he settled the whole manor on Robert and, dying unmarried later in the same year, was succeeded by him.[87] Robert Lord Brooke was killed by a musket ball while directing the siege of Lichfield Cathedral in 1643.[88] The manor then descended with the barony of Brooke[89] until 1749 when Francis Greville, Lord Brooke and Earl of Warwick (d. 1773), conveyed it to Sir Edward Littleton of Teddesley Park,[90] to whose ancestor it had been leased in 1583 by Henry Unton.[91] In 1812 Sir Edward was succeeded by his great-nephew, Edward John Walhouse, who took the name of Littleton and was raised to the peerage as Baron Hatherton in 1835.[92] The 4th Lord Hatherton still held manorial rights in Penkridge in 1940,[93] but his son, the present Lord Hatherton, sold over 1,520 acres there in 1953.[94]

The view of frankpledge within the manor of Penkridge and its fees and members, namely Wolgarston, Drayton, Congreve, and Dunston, with Cowley and Beffcote (in Gnosall), and Little Onn (in Church Eaton), was granted to John de Beverley and his heirs for 5s. a year in 1372.[95] By at least April 1540 the townships included were Penkridge, Coton and Cowley presenting jointly, Little Onn

and Beffcote presenting jointly, and Congreve.[96] Penkridge vill then presented by four frankpledges,[97] and by at least 1576 Coton and Cowley were presenting by three, Little Onn and Beffcote by five, Dunston and Drayton by five, and Congreve by four.[98] By 1611 the three sets of joint townships were presenting by four pledges each, as was Penkridge, while Congreve sent five.[99] An incomplete series of records of this court leet survives from 1539 to 1695.[1] Incomplete series of records of the court baron of Penkridge for 1398 and from 1539 to 1695 also survive.[2]

When Andrew le Blund sued John, chaplain of Penkridge, in 1250 for taking fish from his free fishery of Penkridge, John's defence was that it was a public fishery.[3] The lord of Penkridge was stated in 1598 to have all fishing rights within the manor and a moiety of them outside the manor between Swanford Down and Acton Bridge,[4] but his rights in a mile of the Penk were disputed by the lords of Congreve between at least 1633 and 1698.[5] When Sir Edward Littleton bought the manor of Penkridge in 1749 he asserted his rights in the river against the lord of Congreve[6] and was holding a free fishery in the Penk in 1763.[7] He again asserted his rights in the river in 1775, as did Lord Hatherton in 1838 and 1840.[8]

One third part of Penkridge manor, later to become the *DEANERY MANOR*, was retained by Henry of London, Archbishop of Dublin, when he alienated the rest of the manor to his nephew Andrew at some time between 1215 and 1228.[9] In 1256 Fulk de Saundford, soon after his accession to the Archbishopric of Dublin and before his appointment as Dean of Penkridge, mortgaged his land in Penkridge.[10] The offices of archbishop and dean were united in perpetuity in 1259,[11] and in 1293 this third of the manor of Penkridge, valued along with the advowson of the church at 70 marks a year, was held by the archbishop.[12] At this time the dean and chapter of the college were claiming view of frankpledge, fines for infraction of the assize of bread and beer, and infangthief within their manor of Penkridge.[13] Archbishop Richard Feringes (1299–1306) leased 90 acres of arable, 17 acres of meadow and 53 acres of pasture and moorland in Penkridge to Robert de Shireburne, without royal licence, at an annual rent of 61s. 4d.[14] The land was seized by Edward I, presumably on the archbishop's death,

[77] B.M. Cott. MS. Titus B ii, f. 190a; *L. & P. Hen. VIII*, xiv, p. 157; C 1/498, no. 19. When Lord Broke's lands were partitioned, Dudley's rights in the manor and fair of Penkridge were respected: *Stat. Realm* iii. 605–7.
[78] C 142/196, no. 45; *Complete Peerage*, ix. 722–6; ibid. (orig. edn.), viii. 64.
[79] C 142/196, no. 45; *Complete Peerage* (orig. edn.), viii. 64.
[80] C 142/196, no. 45.
[81] B.M. Cott. MS. Titus B ii, f. 190a.
[82] Ibid.; C 142/196, no. 45.
[83] C 142/196, no. 45; *S.H.C.* 1928, 166.
[84] Hist. MSS. Com. *12th Rep. App. I*, 40; C 66/1361, mm. 14, 15.
[85] *Complete Peerage*, ii. 331–2.
[86] C 142/501, no. 63; *Complete Peerage*, ii. 333.
[87] C 142/501, no. 63; *Complete Peerage*, ii. 332–3.
[88] *Complete Peerage*, ii. 333; Harwood, *Lichfield* (1806), 20–22.
[89] *Complete Peerage*, ii. 334–5; C.P. 43/534, rot. 314.
[90] S.R.O., D 260/M/box 6, bdle. b; *Complete Peerage*, ii. 335.
[91] *S.H.C.* 1928, 166.
[92] *Complete Peerage*, vi. 394–5.

[93] *Kelly's Dir. Staffs.* (1940).
[94] Ex inf. the Teddesley and Hatherton Estate Office, Penkridge.
[95] *Cal. Chart. R.* 1341–1417, 222.
[96] S.R.O., D. 260/M/box 12, bdle. a.
[97] Ibid.
[98] Ibid.
[99] Ibid. box 16, bdle. b.
[1] Ibid. box 12, bdle. a; ibid. box B, bdle. a.
[2] Ibid. box 12, bdle. a; ibid. box B, bdle. a.
[3] *S.H.C.* iv (1), 120.
[4] S.R.O., D. 260/M/box 16, bdle. a, Ct. Bk. 1598–1654, f. 13a.
[5] Ibid., box 16, bdle. c.
[6] Ibid., box 16, bdle. a.
[7] C.P. 43/587, rot. 232.
[8] S.R.O., D. 260/M/box a, bdle. b.
[9] *S.H.C.* vi (1), 218–19; ibid. iv (1), 36.
[10] Ibid. 1950–1, 17.
[11] Ibid. 1950–1, 14–15.
[12] Ibid. vi (1), 259.
[13] Ibid. 242.
[14] *Cal. Pat.* 1307–13, 595; *S.H.C.* 1950–1, 18.

and remained in the hands of the Crown until 1313.[15] From this time until the dissolution of the college in 1547 the overlordship presumably descended with the deanery. At some time between 1528 and 1534 the value of the dean's prebend in the church of Penkridge was given as 26s. 8d.,[16] consisting in 1535 of 20s. from land and 6s. 8d. from waif and stray.[17] In 1543 the dean granted to Edward Littleton the farm of the site of the college with the house and a croft, of two fields or closes in Penkridge, of arable, of a pasture there, of the perquisites of the view of frankpledge and the deanery court, and of all other lands and tenements belonging to the deanery in Penkridge, for 80 years.[18]

In 1548 these lands, along with the site of the dissolved college 'or mansion house of the priests of that college', all still leased to Edward Littleton, were granted by the Crown with all other possessions of the deanery to John Dudley, Earl of Warwick.[19] Dudley's lands were forfeited to the Crown in 1553,[20] and in 1557 the house and the adjoining croft, now said to be of 1½ acre, were granted to William Rigges of Stragglethorpe (Lincs.) and William Buckberte.[21] The lease was then still held by Edward Littleton,[22] and at his death in 1558 he held what was described as the reversion of the house and half the croft.[23] When his son and heir Sir Edward died in 1574, this capital messuage was in his hands and known as College House.[24] The college with all its rights, members, lands, tithes, and appurtenances was granted by the Crown in 1581 to Edmund Downynge and Peter Aysheton,[25] who sold it in 1583 to John Morley and Thomas Crompton.[26] In 1585 the site of the college, with lands and tithes, was settled on Edward Littleton by John Morley, Elizabeth his wife, and Thomas Crompton.[27] What was described as the liberty of the deanery in 1598, and as the deanery manor of Penkridge by at least 1722, descended in the Littleton family with the manor of Pillaton[28] until at least 1827.[29] The great tithes remained in the family until at least 1862.[30] The 3rd Lord Hatherton sold over 360 acres of the deanery estate in 1919.[31]

The manor was surveyed in 1566,[32] 1587,[33] 1598,[34] 1658,[35] and 1722.[36] Various records of the courts leet and baron exist for the years 1565 to 1737.[37] The bounds of the deanery leet were given at the survey of 1598.[38]

The mansion house of the resident canons appears to have survived until at least the end of the 16th century.[39] It may have been identical with an 'old house called Deanery Hall, long the seat of the Chambley family' which was demolished in 1850.[40] If so it probably formed part of a row of buildings on the north side of Church Lane,[41] all of which have now disappeared. Church Cottages, formerly a single house, may date from the early 16th century and Church Farm is in part medieval. It is possible that these buildings had some connexion with the college. The house in Pinfold Lane, now known as the Old Deanery, contains no medieval work and was probably built after the dissolution of the college. Deanery Farm, demolished in 1937,[42] was not a building of great antiquity.

Before the Conquest Alric, a free man, held 3 virgates in BICKFORD of the king, and he held the same land as a king's thegn in 1086, when it was described as land for one plough.[43] By 1274 Bickford was held along with Whiston of Burton Abbey as 1½ hide,[44] and the overlordship seems to have descended with that of Whiston, apparently passing in 1546 to the Pagets who held it until at least 1633.[45]

In 1251 and 1253 Alexander de Bickford and Hawise his wife were suing Robert de Whiston, Henry de Bardmerscote (or 'Bermundeston') and Ismannia his wife, and Reynold and Richard de Bickford for land in Bickford.[46] Robert de Whiston claimed in 1253 to be holding two parts of 2 virgates there, while Henry de Bardmerscote and Ismannia claimed the third part as her dower,[47] and in 1255 Robert secured against Alexander and Hawise his claim to 2½ virgates there.[48] By 1255 Bickford and Whiston were held as one estate by a Robert de Whiston.[49] Robert 'lord of Whiston' in 1311 conveyed to his daughter Cecily rents and services from a tenement in the vill of Bickford,[50] and in 1334 Rose and Adam de Shareshill were given land in Bickford, Whiston, and Saredon (in Shareshill) as Rose's dower.[51] Bickford then appears to have been absorbed into Whiston until 1556 when as the manor of Bickford it passed with Whiston to Sir Thomas

[15] Cal. Pat. 1307–13, 595. Feringes was followed in 1307 by Richard de Havering who was never consecrated and resigned in 1310. John de Leche was archbishop from 1311 to 1313.
[16] S.H.C. 1950–1, 24.
[17] Valor Eccl. (Rec. Com.), iii. 99.
[18] E 315/68, p. 386.
[19] Cal. Pat. 1548–9, 30.
[20] Complete Peerage, ix. 725–6.
[21] Cal. Pat. 1557–8, 215–16.
[22] Ibid. 216.
[23] C 142/124, no. 178.
[24] C 142/172, no. 119.
[25] C 66/1198, m. 18.
[26] S.R.O., D. 260/M/box 7, bdle. i.
[27] S.H.C. xv. 167.
[28] S.R.O., D 260/M/box 16, bdle. a, Ct. Bk. of the manor of Penkridge 1598–1654, f. 14a; C 142/320, no. 71; Cal. Cttee. for Compounding, 2082; C.P. 43/286, rot. 169; C.P. 43/506, rot. 98; S.R.O., D. 260/M/box 4, bdle. d; S.R.O., Gamekprs.' Deps.; see p. 119.
[29] S.R.O., Q/RDc 22.
[30] S.R.O., D. 260/M/E. 25.
[31] Ex inf. the Teddesley and Hatherton Estate Office, Penkridge.
[32] W.S.L., D. 1798, box 20.
[33] S.R.O., D. 260/M/box 4, bdle. d.
[34] Ibid. box 16, bdle. a, ff. 10a–11a.
[35] Ibid. box 17, bdle. c.
[36] Ibid. box 4, bdle. d.
[37] Ibid. box 12, bdle. i; ibid. box 4, bdle. d; ibid. box 17, bdle. e; ibid. box 16, bdle. b; W.S.L., D. 1798, bdle. 20.
[38] S.R.O., D. 260/M/box 16, bdle. b, Ct. Bk. of the manor of Penkridge 1598–1654, ff. 10a–11a.
[39] E 315/68, p. 386.
[40] White, Dir. Staffs. (1851) 466–7.
[41] S.R.O., D. 260/M/E. 353 (a, b), map 5 (1754), giving 'House, Barn, and Garden, late Chamleys'.
[42] Ex inf. Staffs. C.C. Estate Agent.
[43] V.C.H. Staffs. iv. 57, no. 273. With 2 other thegns, Chenvin of Codsall and Udi of Saredon, he contributed to a rent of 12s. payable to the Sheriff: ibid.; Eyton, Domesday Studies, Staffs. 73.
[44] Rot. Hund. (Rec. Com.), ii. 114.
[45] S.H.C. 1937, 187–9; L. & P. Hen. VIII, xxi (1), pp. 76–77; C 142/110, no. 143; C 142/127, no. 45; C 142/500, no. 41.
[46] S.H.C. iv (1), 123, 128.
[47] Ibid. 128.
[48] Ibid. 246–7.
[49] Rot. Hund. (Rec. Com.), ii. 114.
[50] W.S.L., S. MS. 350A/40, f. 16a.
[51] S.H.C. xi. 47, 50.

Giffard on the death of his father Sir John.[52] It descended with Whiston and Chillington (in Brewood) in the Giffard family until at least 1823.[53] In 1834 and 1851 the land in Bickford was owned by T. W. Giffard.[54]

In 1086 *CONGREVE*, a member of the royal manor of Penkridge, was assessed at 1 hide.[55] It descended as a member of Penkridge until at least 1372,[56] and by 1814 the manor of Congreve was held of the manor of Penkridge by a rent of £1 1s.[57]

Four virgates in Congreve had passed by November 1227 from Alditha de Congreve to Andrew de Sandon and a mill there from Alditha to John de Teveray, although Alditha was survived by three nieces, daughters of her sister Alice.[58] In 1236 two of the nieces, Edith de Congreve and Iseult, laid claim to part of the land and mill against John de Teveray and his wife Alice.[59] Robert Teveray, described as of Congreve, held a free tenement here in 1271[60] and was dead by 1302 when his widow Juliana held in dower one-third of what was described as the manor.[61] The remaining two-thirds had passed to Robert's son John, who had granted them to his brother William Teveray and William's wife Idonea.[62] William died childless, but in 1302 John Teveray's heir Adam, son of Richard Collins of Rugeley, conveyed his rights in the whole manor to Idonea, by then married to Matthew son of William de Hales, and her heirs.[63]

By 1323 the rights of all claimants of the manor, including Idonea and Matthew, Juliana, John son of Robert Teveray and Adam Collins, had been conveyed to Simon de Dumbleton, clerk, and his wife Eleanor.[64] Simon, in 1326 described as of Congreve,[65] had been succeeded by 1344 by his son Roger de Congreve,[66] who was followed by his brother Geoffrey.[67] By his will of 1403 Geoffrey de Congreve left his possessions to Agnes his wife, Robert his son, and Agnes, Robert's wife, after the payment of 13s. for prayers for his soul.[68] Robert was still living in 1433[69] but was dead by October 1438 when the king ordered the restoration of the manor to Richard his son and heir.[70] Richard, who made a settlement of at least the capital messuage of the manor in 1460 or 1461[71] and was still living in 1477,[72]

was followed by his son Ralph who was alive in 1537.[73] His son John having predeceased him, Ralph was succeeded by a grandson Francis, who occurs in 1578[74] and 1591.[75] The next heir was Francis's son Thomas, who occurs in 1594 as the husband of Elizabeth, daughter of Roger and Margaret Fowke of Gunstone (in Brewood),[76] and was still living in 1607.[77] He at some time demised the capital messuage or 'mannor place' called Congreve Hall to his son Thomas for seven years.[78] Another son, Francis, had succeeded his father by 1620,[79] and after some dispute he secured the Hall from his brother in 1622 in return for an annuity.[80] The Hall was at that time occupied by a John Bryan, Francis being described, like his father and grandfather, as of Stretton.[81] Francis died in 1629 and was succeeded by his son Richard,[82] who was still alive in 1680.[83] Richard was succeeded by his son John,[84] who had been resident at Congreve in 1680[85] and whose son John (II), with his son John (III), made a settlement of the manor in 1725.[86] A John Congreve died in 1729[87] and it was John (II)'s youngest son, the Revd. Richard Congreve, who became head of the family, dying in 1782.[88] His heir was his elder son William, who made a settlement of the manor in 1798[89] and owned most of the land in Congreve c. 1841.[90] William died without issue and was succeeded by his brother Richard, who was holding the manor by 1851 and died in 1857.[91] His heir was his son William Walter who died in 1864 and whose son and heir William Congreve of Congreve and of Burton Hall (Ches.) died in 1902.[92] His son and heir, General Sir Walter Norris Congreve, a V.C. of the Boer War, of Congreve and Chartley Castle, (in Stowe parish, Pirehill hundred), died in 1927, and his elder surviving son and heir, Sir Geoffrey Cecil Congreve, a V.C. of the First World War, who died in action in 1941, was succeeded by his brother, Major John Congreve, who in 1956 still owned Congreve Manor (c. 4 a.) and Congreve Manor Farm (c. 200 a.).[93]

The Manor House is a red-brick building standing above the road on its west side. It incorporates an early-18th-century farmhouse and has flanking wings in a later-18th-century style which were added

[52] C 142/110, no. 143.
[53] C 142/127, no. 45; C 142/337, no. 113; C 142/500, no. 41; C.P. 43/812, rot. 417; C.P. 43/962, rot. 386; Whiston and Bickford: record of Ct. Baron and Ct. of Survey, 1725, among Giffard Papers at Chillington, Brewood; see p. 82.
[54] White, *Dir. Staffs.* (1834, 1851).
[55] *V.C.H. Staffs.* iv. 38, no. 8.
[56] *Rot. Chart.* (Rec. Com.), 218; *S.H.C.* iv (1), 50, 232–3; *Close R. 1234–7*, 377; *Cal. Chart. R. 1341–1417*, 222.
[57] Penkridge Inclosure Act, 54 Geo. III, c. 50 (priv. act).
[58] *S.H.C.* iv (1), 48.
[59] Ibid. 232–3; *Close R. 1234–7*, 377.
[60] *S.H.C.* vi (1), 50.
[61] W.S.L., S. MS. 350A/40, f. 80a.
[62] Ibid.; W.S.L., S. MS. 201 (1), p. 434.
[63] W.S.L., S. MS. 350A/40, f. 80a.
[64] W.S.L., S. MS. 201 (1), p. 434; W.S.L., S. MS. 350A/40, ff. 80a–81a; *S.H.C.* 1911, 82–83, 88–89.
[65] W.S.L., S. MS. 350A/40, f. 81a.
[66] Ibid., f. 82a.
[67] W.S.L., S. MS. 47 (8), Congreve Papers (Pedigrees).
[68] W.S.L., S. MS. 350A/40, ff. 78a–79a. In 1380–1 Geoffrey's wife was a Katherine: *S.H.C.* xvii. 192.
[69] W.S.L., S. MS. 350A/40, f. 79a.
[70] Ibid., f. 82a.
[71] Ibid., f. 12a.
[72] W.S.L., S. MS 47 (8).

[73] Ibid. Ralph had succeeded his father in Stretton by 1521: E 36/150.
[74] W.S.L., S. MS. 47 (8); *S.H.C.* v (2), 92; W.S.L. 3/49, Will of Hugh Pinson.
[75] *S.H.C.* xvi. 122.
[76] W.S.L., S. MS. 47 (8); *S.H.C.* v (2), 93; ibid. xvii (1), 8.
[77] W.S.L., S. D. Pearson 1601.
[78] W.S.L., S. D. Thorpe 397.
[79] *S.H.C.* n.s. vii. 214; C 2/Jas. I, C. 22, no. 88.
[80] W.S.L., S. D. Thorpe 397.
[81] W.S.L. 3/49; W.S.L., S. D. Pearson 1601.
[82] W.S.L., S. MS. 47 (8); C 142/456, no. 72. William Congreve the dramatist (1670–1729) was the son of Richard's second son, William: *S.H.C.* v (2), 94; *D.N.B.*
[83] *S.H.C.* 1919, 219.
[84] Burke, *Peerage* (1931), 601.
[85] *S.H.C.* 1919, 219.
[86] C.P. 25(2)/1063, 11 Geo. I Trin.; Burke, *Peerage* (1931), 601.
[87] Stretton Parish Register, from transcript in W.S.L.
[88] Burke, *Peerage* (1931), 601.
[89] Ibid.; C.P. 43/860, rot. 347.
[90] Tithe Maps and Appt., Penkridge (copy in W.S.L.).
[91] White, *Dir. Staffs.* (1851); Burke, *Peerage* (1931), 601.
[92] Burke, *Peerage* (1931), 601.
[93] Ibid. 601–2; local inf. Major Congreve has not accepted succession to the baronetcy (1956).

c. 1930. It has since been converted into flats, the tenants being the Midland Tar Distillery of Four Ashes, Brewood.[94] The Manor Farm, on the east side of the road near the river, is a late-17th- or early-18th-century brick farmhouse.

The part of Beacon Hill Common that lay within the manor of Congreve was inclosed in 1827 under the Act of 1814.[95]

Although in 1598 the lord of Penkridge was said to have all fishing rights in the Penk within the manor of Penkridge,[96] the lords of Congreve were claiming a fishery in a mile of the river between at least 1633 and 1698.[97] When, moreover, Sir Edward Littleton bought the manor of Penkridge in 1749, he asserted his right to fish in the Penk from Jeverns Croft down to Cuttlestone Bridge against the lord of Congreve.[98]

The prebend of Congreve in the collegiate church of Penkridge was valued at £2 13s. 4d. in 1291.[99] In 1535 it consisted of the site of the *PREBENDAL MANOR* and its lands, worth 5s., assised rents of 5s. and great and small tithe averaging 46s. 8d.[1] Synodals of 3s. were due every three years to the Dean of Penkridge.[2] From 1537 the last prebendary was granting three-yearly leases of the prebend,[3] which in 1548 was held jointly by William Fyncheley, John and William Bourne, and William Mountford at a rent of £4 4s.[4] At the dissolution of Penkridge college the prebend presumably descended with the rest of the collegiate possessions, and in 1585 it passed to Edward Littleton[5] who had already been granted a 21-year lease of it in 1577 or 1578.[6] It then descended in the Littleton family with Pillaton[7] until at least 1709.[8] In 1919 the 3rd Lord Hatherton sold Congreve House and some 146 acres in Congreve,[9] an estate which may formerly have been prebendal property.

Congreve House lies some 250 yds. north-east of Congreve Manor House and has a separate farmhouse and farm buildings immediately to the south-west. It is a square red-brick house dating from *c.* 1800 with a frontage added late in the 19th century. A stone dated 1673 with the initials 'I.B.' has been reset in one of the chimneys.

In 1086 *DRAYTON* was a member of the royal manor of Penkridge and consisted of one hide which was waste.[10] By 1194 the vill was in the possession of Hervey, husband of Millicent the sister and heir of Robert de Stafford,[11] and in 1211 Millicent, then a widow, sued for ⅓ virgate in Drayton as dower.[12]

The overlordship descended in the Stafford barony until at least 1460.[13]

William de Stafford, a younger son of Hervey Bagot and Millicent, seems to have held an intermediate lordship after his father's death,[14] and this was said to be in the hands of his heirs in 1460.[15]

In 1194 Hervey Bagot, with the assent of Millicent, granted the vill of Drayton to the priory of St. Thomas, near Stafford, for a rent of ½ mark a year and a gift of 35 marks towards the fine which he owed the king for the barony of Stafford.[16] Richard de Stretton, who was disputing Hervey Bagot's right to Drayton, quitclaimed to the canons such rights as might be adjudged to him,[17] and William de Stafford, with the assent of his brother Hervey and his mother Millicent, subsequently confirmed his father's grant.[18] Edward I granted the prior and convent the right of free warren in all their demesne lands in Drayton and elsewhere in 1284.[19] By 1291 the prior and canons were holding 1½ carucate in Drayton worth £1 a year, £1 5s. 2d. in rents, and profits from stock of £1 1s. a year,[20] and by 1535 the priory's annual income from what was then called the manor of Drayton was £9 4s. 8d., consisting of 26s. from demesne lands, £5 18s. 2d. in rents, 6d. from the courts, and 40s. from the mill.[21]

In 1539, after the dissolution of St. Thomas's Priory, the manor was granted to Roland Lee, Bishop of Coventry and Lichfield,[22] who in 1540 settled the reversion on a Thomas Fowler.[23] When the bishop died in 1543, Thomas having predeceased him, the manor seems to have passed to the bishop's nephew, Brian Fowler, who died seised of it in 1587.[24] It then descended with the Fowlers' estate in Baswich eventually passing to George John Earl Spencer[25] (d. 1834), who sold it in 1790 to George Molineux, a merchant of Wolverhampton.[26] Molineux sold it in 1790 to Sir Edward Littleton of Teddesley Park,[27] whose heir, created Lord Hatherton in 1835,[28] held it in 1851.[29] The 3rd Lord Hatherton (d. 1930) sold some 368 acres in Lower Drayton and some 312 acres in Upper Drayton in 1919.[30]

The farmhouse known as Drayton Manor dates from the early 19th century, and the site is not ancient.

GAILEY (Gageleage) had been granted to Burton Abbey by Wulfric Spot by 1004,[31] but during the reign of the Confessor it was held by Bodin, a free man.[32] By 1086 Gailey (Gragelie), assessed at one

94 Ex inf. present tenant (1956).
95 S.R.O., Q/RDc 22.
96 S.R.O., D. 260/M/box 16, bdle. a, Ct. Bk. 1598–1654, f. 12a.
97 Ibid. bdle. c.   98 Ibid. bdle. a.
99 *Tax. Eccl.* (Rec. Com.), 242.
1 *Valor Eccl.* (Rec. Com.), iii. 106.   2 Ibid.
3 *S.H.C.* 1950–1, 36 n. 98.
4 Ibid. 37.
5 *S.H.C.* xv. 167; see p. 111.
6 C 66/1173, m. 24.
7 C.P. 25(2)/184, 1 Chas. I Hil.; C 142/456, no. 76; C.P. 25(2)/596, 1654 Trins; C.P. 25(2)/725, 28 Chas. II Mich.; see p. 119.
8 C.P. 43/506, rot. 98.
9 Ex inf. the Teddesley and Hatherton Estate Office, Penkridge.
10 *V.C.H. Staffs.* iv. 38, no. 8.
11 *S.H.C.* ii (1), 263, 265; *Complete Peerage*, xii (1), 170.
12 *S.H.C.* iii (1), 151–2.
13 *Bk. of Fees*, 543; *Complete Peerage*, xii (1), 171; C 139/180.

14 *S.H.C.* viii (1), 160–1.
15 C 139/180.
16 *S.H.C.* ii (1), 263, 265.
17 Ibid. viii (1), 161.
18 Ibid. 160–1.
19 Ibid. 136.
20 *Tax. Eccl.* (Rec. Com.), 253.
21 *Valor Eccl.* (Rec. Com.), iii. 110.
22 *L. & P. Hen. VIII*, xiv (2), p. 156.
23 C 142/69, no. 119.
24 C 142/216, no. 21; *S.H.C.* v (2), 135.
25 S.R.O., D. 260/M/box 12, bdles. c, d; ibid. box 16, bdle. a, Penkridge Ct. Bk. 1598–1654, f. 10a; W.S.L., Hand Morgan Coll., Aston Papers.
26 S.R.O., D. 260/M/box 12, bdle. d.
27 Ibid.
28 *Complete Peerage*, vi. 394–5.
29 White, *Dir. Staffs.* (1851).
30 Ex inf. the Teddesley and Hatherton Estate Office.
31 *S.H.C.* 1916, 14, 117.
32 *V.C.H. Staffs.* iv. 53, no. 214.

hide and worth 2s., was parcel of the lands of Robert de Stafford and held by Hervey.[33] At some time between 1158 and 1165 Rennerius, son of Edricht of Wolseley, having been granted the land of Gailey by Robert de Stafford (II) in fee and inheritance, gave it along with its woodland to the nuns of Blithbury (in Mavesyn Ridware, Offlow hundred).[34] Gailey appears to have passed from the nuns of Blithbury to the nuns of Black Ladies, Brewood, and before 1189 to have been taken into the king's hands.[35] In 1200 King John gave land in Broom (Worcs.) to Black Ladies as compensation,[36] and by 1247 this land of Gailey formed a hay in the royal forest of Cannock.[37]

In 1550 the king granted Gailey Hay to John Dudley, Earl of Warwick,[38] and in 1554 it was given to his widow for life.[39] She died in 1555,[40] and the Hay seems subsequently to have passed to her son, Ambrose Dudley.[41] Some interest in the Hay, apparently the keepership of the herbage and pannage, was granted by the Crown to Lord Stafford in 1558.[42] In 1561 one twenty-fifth part of Gailey Hay, with lands, woods, rents, and other appurtenances, held by knight service of the queen by Sir Edward Littleton of Pillaton and Edward James, was leased by them to William Fowke, who in 1580 conveyed it to Richard Mylles with reversion to Sir Edward Littleton and Edward James.[43] Mylles died in possession of it between 1591 and 1607.[44] In 1567 Lord Stafford granted the herbage and pannage of the Hay to twenty persons, including Sir Edward Littleton, Edward James, Thomas and John Webbe, John Eginton the elder and younger, John and Thomas Fletcher, William Lynehill, Richard Walhouse, William Henney, William Fowke, Humphrey Norton, John Swancott, and William Cartwright.[45] Land in Gailey Hay was conveyed to Sir Edward Littleton and Edward James by Ambrose Dudley in 1569,[46] and in 1589 Henry, son and heir of William Cartwright, conveyed one twenty-fifth part of lands in Gailey and elsewhere to Edward James.[47] John Fletcher of Lyne Hill, Humphrey Norton, and Thomas Webbe died in 1604, each holding one twenty-fifth part of the Hay, and were succeeded by their respective children, John Fletcher, Elizabeth Norton, and John Webbe.[48] In 1610 eleven persons, including a William and John Henney, John Swancote, Elizabeth Norton, Edward Webbe, and William Lynhill, settled eleven twenty-fifths of land in Gailey Hay on Walter Walhouse,[49] on whom in

the same year his father William settled a further twenty-fifth part, formerly held by Richard Walhouse, William's father.[50] Walter succeeded his father in 1615[51] and died in possession of a twenty-fifth part in 1633.[52] The Sir Edward Littleton who died in 1610 was said to be holding the Hay of the king at that time,[53] while Edward James was holding six twenty-fifths when he died in 1613 with a son Edward succeeding him.[54] In 1619 John Eginton died in possession of a twenty-fifth part of 'a certain great waste called Galey Hay' and was succeeded by his son John.[55] Edward James of Kinvaston was lord of nine parts by 1663,[56] and in 1674 Humphrey Giffard of Water Eaton, a grandson of a Thomas Fletcher of Water Eaton,[57] with his wife Dorothy made a settlement of a twenty-fifth part.[58] In 1693 or 1694 a Thomas Linton and others were dealing by fine with a twenty-fifth part.[59] A Thomas Lionell, otherwise Lynell, held a twenty-fifth in 1763.[60]

About 1775 11 of the twenty-five parts were apparently held by Moreton Walhouse, 3 by Robert James of Kinvaston, 2 by the Revd. Jonas Slaney of Rodbaston, 1 by the four Misses Stubbs of Water Eaton, the descendants of Humphrey Giffard, 1 by Robert Crocket, 1 by James Perry of Lyne Hill, 1 by Mary Yates which was sold in about 1786 to Edward Monckton, and 5 respectively by George Lynell of Stourbridge, Simon Glover, John Bourne, John Collins, and John Birch.[61] These last 5 parts were subsequently sold to Sir Edward Littleton,[62] who was named as lord of the manor in 1778.[63] In 1789 Thomas Devey Wightwick and Lucy conveyed a quarter of two elevenths of the manor to Joshua Ledsam,[64] and in 1791 William Lionel Holmes and Margaret conveyed what was described as the manor of Gailey to Sir Edward Littleton.[65] In 1820 William Brearley, his wife Mary, and other members of his family held an eleventh part of the manor.[66] Edward John Littleton was said to be lord of the manor in 1834[67] and as Lord Hatherton still held it in 1851.[68] In 1919 the 3rd Lord Hatherton sold over 250 acres in Gailey including the Spread Eagle Inn.[69]

No house with the name of Gailey Hall has existed within living memory.[70]

In 1086 Robert de Stafford was lord of 3 hides in *LEVEDALE* worth 10s.[71] These 3 hides probably correspond with the $\frac{2}{3}$ knight's fee held of Robert de Stafford (II) in 1166.[72] Levedale was held of the barony of Stafford as 1 knight's fee from at least

[33] V.C.H. Staffs. iv. 53, no. 214.
[34] S.H.C. ii (1), 244–5.
[35] Rot. Chart (Rec. Com.), 80.
[36] Ibid.
[37] Rot. Hund. (Rec. Com.), ii. 115, where Hugh de 'Boygis', the royal forester who lost his office, should read Hugh de Loges: S.H.C. iv (1), 179–80; Close R. 1242–7, 511; Bk. of Fees, 1394.
[38] Cal. Pat. 1549–51, 364–5.
[39] Ibid. 1553–4, 129.
[40] Complete Peerage, ix. 726.
[41] C 142/353, no. 91; S.H.C. xiii. 274.
[42] Cal. Pat. 1557–8, 254; ibid. 1560–3, 291–2.
[43] C 142/299, no. 127.
[44] Ibid.
[45] S.H.C. xiii. 266–7.
[46] Ibid. 274.
[47] Ibid. xv. 189.
[48] C 142/284, no. 21; C 142/409, nos. 48, 49.
[49] S.H.C. n.s. iii. 36.
[50] C 142/353, no. 91.
[51] Ibid.

[52] C 142/497, no. 158.
[53] C 142/320, no. 71.
[54] C 142/338, no. 88.
[55] C 142/373, no. 24.
[56] S.R.O., D. 260/M/box 9, bdle. g.
[57] S.H.C. n.s. v. 200.
[58] C.P. 25(2)/725, 26 Chas. II Trin.
[59] C.P. 25(2)/873, 5 Wm. and Mary Hil.
[60] C.P. 43/720, rot. 199.
[61] S.R.O., D. 260/M/box 9, bdle. g; C.P. 43/767, rot. 272–84; M.P.L. 66; S.H.C. n.s. v. 174, 200.
[62] S.R.O., D. 260/M/box 9, bdle. g.
[63] S.R.O., Gamekprs.' Deps.
[64] C.P. 25(2)/1413, 29 Geo. III Mich.
[65] C.P. 25(2)/1413, 31 Geo. III East.
[66] C.P. 43/947, rot. 156.
[67] White, Dir. Staffs. (1834).
[68] Ibid. (1851).
[69] Ex inf. the Teddesley and Hatherton Estate Office.
[70] Local inf.
[71] V.C.H. Staffs. iv. 53, no. 221.
[72] S.H.C. i. 163–5.

1236[73] until at least 1460[74] and by a rent of 1s. 2d. between at least 1727 and 1756.[75]

The tenants of the 3 hides in 1086 were Brien and Drew.[76] Brien's heir was his son Ralph, whose son Robert seems to have held the mesne lordship of $\frac{2}{3}$ knight's fee in Levedale in 1166.[77] In 1272 and 1285 Robert de Standon, a descendant of Robert, was holding Levedale of the Stafford barony,[78] and in 1316 Vivian de Standon was lord.[79] This Standon mesne lordship was still said to be held by the heirs of Robert de Standon in 1558[80] and 1610.[81]

Three free men were holding the 3 hides of Brien and Drew in 1086.[82] In 1166 Engenulf de Gresley seems to have been holding $\frac{2}{3}$ knight's fee in Levedale of Robert fitz Ralph,[83] and in 1199 Henry de Verdon, who had married Hawise, one of Engenulf's three daughters and coheirs,[84] was claiming a virgate here in his wife's right.[85] In the same year Robert de Sugenhall and Parnel, another sister, made a conveyance of 4 bovates in Levedale.[86] A Henry de Verdon was holding a fee in Levedale with other coparceners in 1242 or 1243,[87] and in 1255 Henry de Verdon and Richard de Kilkenny were described as lords of Levedale, holding there 3 hides which contributed 3s. to the sheriff's aid, 3s. to the view of frankpledge, and 12d. to the hundred.[88] In 1272 Robert de Standon as mesne lord was suing Amice, widow of Henry de Verdon, for the wardship and marriage of Henry's son and heir Henry,[89] who was holding the vill as coparcener with Roger de Pywelesdon and Henry de Caverswall in 1285.[90]

In 1294 Joan, widow of William de Caverswall, and William de Doune were suing Henry de Caverswall of Levedale, who may have been Joan's son, for taking fish from their free fishery at Levedale and 'Doune'.[91] A Henry de Caverswall was holding the knight's fee in Levedale in 1303,[92] and in 1329 Roger de Caverswall, described as of Levedale, was suing Margaret, Henry's widow, for waste in the houses held in dower of his inheritance there.[93] By 1374 lands and tenements there had descended to one Agnes, then wife of Walter de Stafford, described as of Levedale,[94] and William and Agnes made a settlement of 3 messuages, 2 carucates, meadow,

and rent in Levedale and Stafford in 1373.[95] A John Stafford died in 1420 holding a messuage, a carucate, and meadow in Levedale directly of Humphrey Earl of Stafford and was succeeded by his son John, a minor.[96] Levedale appears to have descended eventually to Sir William Stafford of Bishop's Frome (Herefs.), whose daughter and heir Margaret, as widow of Sir George de Vere, settled the reversion in 1537 on her elder daughter Elizabeth and son-in-law Sir Anthony Wingfield.[97] Sir Anthony, with his son and heir apparent John Wingfield, conveyed the manors of Levedale and Longridge in 1542 to Edward Littleton,[98] who as Sir Edward died seised of them in 1558.[99] Meanwhile, in 1552, on the death of Sir Anthony, his eldest surviving son Robert Wingfield suffered a recovery of the manor[1] but in 1561 conveyed his rights in it to Sir Edward Littleton, son and heir of the first Sir Edward,[2] as did Charles, Richard, Anthony, and Henry Wingfield, Robert's brothers.[3] This Sir Edward, who made a settlement of the manor in 1573,[4] died holding it in 1574,[5] and his son and heir Edward held it at his death in 1610.[6] The manor then descended in the Littleton family with Pillaton[7] until at least 1851 when the 1st Lord Hatherton was described as its lord and the owner of the soil.[8] The 3rd Lord Hatherton sold over 500 acres in Levedale in 1919.[9]

The capital messuage called the Hall House was occupied by Thomas Warde in 1654.[10] In 1754, as Levedale Hall, it was tenanted by Edward Bartlem,[11] and c. 1841, as the Old Hall, by Richard Bartlem.[12] It is no longer standing.

Certain lands in Levedale appear to have remained with the overlords between at least 1368 and 1720 when rents were paid by tenants there to the barony of Stafford.[13]

A messuage, virgate, and nook of land in *LONG-RIDGE* were settled in 1272 by Robert son of William de Longrug on Rose, daughter of Richard the miller and probably mother of Robert, with successive remainders to her sons Robert, Richard, Thomas, Nicholas, and her daughter Juliana.[14] Richard de Teveray, Canon of Penkridge, was sued by Thomas de Longrugge in 1276 for disseising him

[73] *Bk. of Fees*, 543.
[74] C 139/180. This was the amount paid to Lord Stafford by tenants in Levedale by 1698: E 178/6821.
[75] S.R.O., D. 260/M/box 8, bdle. d.
[76] *V.C.H. Staffs.* iv. 53, no. 221.
[77] *S.H.C.* i. 163–5.
[78] Ibid. iv (1), 204; *Feud. Aids*, v. 1; *V.C.H. Warws.* v. 155; *Close R.* 1247–51, 271–2.
[79] *Feud. Aids*, v. 16; *V.C.H. Warws.* v. 155.
[80] C 142/124, no. 178.
[81] C 142/320, no. 71.
[82] *V.C.H. Staffs.* iv. 53, no. 221.
[83] *S.H.C.* i. 163, 165.
[84] Ibid. v (1), 13; the other sisters were Denise, who married Stephen de Wiverston (Worston), and Parnell, who married Robert de Sogunhul (Sugnall).
[85] Ibid. iii (1), 51–52.
[86] Ibid. 168–9.
[87] *Bk. of Fees*, 967, 974.
[88] *Rot. Hund.* (Rec. Com.), ii. 114.
[89] *S.H.C.* iv (1), 204.
[90] *Feud. Aids*, v. 1.
[91] *S.H.C.* vii (1), 18; ibid. vi (1), 217. The fishing was presumably in the tributary of the Church Eaton Brook separating Levedale from Down House in Bradley.
[92] *Cal. Chan. R. Var.* 1277–1326, 96.
[93] *S.H.C.* ix. 8.
[94] Ibid. xiii. 117.
[95] Ibid. xi. 195.

[96] C 138/45.
[97] *S.H.C.* 1931, 223; C 54/406, no. 29; *Complete Peerage*, x. 244; *Hunts. Visitation*, Camden Soc. o.s. xliii. 126. Yet in 1533 'Lord Vere' was said to owe suit at the barony manor of Forebridge for one half of the manor and Leonard Harcourt for the other half: W.S.L. Stafford Barony, Mins. Accts. 24–25 Hen. VIII, m. 5d.
[98] *S.H.C.* xi. 285; C.P. 40/1115, m. 9d; *Hunts. Visitation*, 126 (where John Wingfield is given as the second son).
[99] C 142/124, no. 178.
[1] C.P. 40/1152, rot. 613d; C 142/124, no. 178.
[2] *S.H.C.* xvii. 210–11.
[3] Ibid. 211; S.R.O., D. 260/M/box 8, bdle. d; *Hunts. Visitation*, 127; *S.H.C.* 1931, 224.
[4] C.P. 25(2)/260, 15 Eliz. I East.
[5] C 142/172, no. 119.
[6] C 142/320, no. 71.
[7] C 142/456, no. 26; C.P. 25(2)/596, 1654 Trin.; C.P. 43/506, rot. 98; S.R.O., D. 260/M/box 8, bdle. d; C.P. 43/719, rot. 232; see p. 119.
[8] White, *Dir. Staffs.* (1851).
[9] Ex inf. the Teddesley and Hatherton Estate Office.
[10] S.R.O., D. 260/M/box 3, bdle. e, a deed of 1653/4.
[11] Ibid. E. 353 (a, b), map. 9.
[12] Tithe Maps and Appt., Penkridge (copy in W.S.L.).
[13] W.S.L., D. 1721/1/8, p. 57; E 178/6821; W.S.L. 119/40. In 1534 or 1535 the rent of 14d. was called frith fee: W.S.L., Stafford Barony Rental 26 Hen. VIII, f. 12a.
[14] *S.H.C.* iv (1), 254–5.

of common of pasture in 10 acres in Longridge,[15] and in 1308 Master Richard de Teveray (presumably this same Richard), his wife Ann, and his son Richard, with Robert de Colton, were accused of disseising John Colling and his wife Rose of 10 acres here.[16] In 1406 Simon Pykstoke and his wife Alice conveyed lands in Longridge to Ralph Stafford,[17] and in 1420 John Stafford died holding lands in Longridge of the Dean of Penkridge as of the college.[18] In 1558 and 1574 the manor of Longridge was said to be held of the rectory or prebend of Coppenhall.[19] John Stafford was succeeded by his son John, a minor, and Longridge appears to have descended with Levedale (see above) to Margaret, daughter and heir of Sir William Stafford of Bishop's Frome (Herefs.), who in 1537, as the widow of Sir George de Vere, settled the reversion of the manors of Longridge and Levedale on her elder daughter Elizabeth and son-in-law Sir Anthony Wingfield.[20] Longridge continued to descend with Levedale,[21] and c. 1841 the land there was owned by Lord Hatherton.[22] In 1919 the 3rd Lord Hatherton sold some 340 acres there.[23]

A lordship over land and tenements in LYNE HILL (Linhull) was held in 1237 by Hugh de Loges,[24] lord of Otherton, and in 1284 by Andrew le Blund,[25] lord of Penkridge. Edward Littleton was apparently claiming some rights there in 1558,[26] and land at Lyne Hill within the deanery manor of Penkridge was held by a later Edward Littleton in 1585.[27] The hamlet of Lyne Hill was stated to be within the manor of Penkridge in 1598,[28] but Lyne Hill was described as a manor held by the Littletons in 1629,[29] 1642,[30] and 1654.[31]

Richard de Linhill was holding land there of Hugh de Loges in 1237,[32] and a Richard son of William Edrich of 'Loynhull' occurs in 1271.[33] Adam, son of Roger de Lynhull, was claiming a messuage and ½ virgate there in 1308,[34] while a William Lynehull and his wife Alice occur in 1467.[35] At some time between 1551 and 1553 and again in 1558 a messuage and land there, previously held by Thomas Lynell,

were claimed by his son William.[36] Edward Lynehill of Lyne Hill occurs between 1586 and 1602,[37] and his house there was mentioned in 1598.[38] A Thomas Lynell and his wife Anne occur in 1618,[39] and a Thomas Lynell of 'Lynell' died in 1655.[40] Another Thomas Lynehill of Lyne Hill occurs in 1657[41] and is probably the Thomas Lynell who was chargeable for tax on two hearths in Penkridge in 1666,[42] and the Thomas Linehill, 'a rich yeoman', who occupied one of the two houses in the hamlet in 1680.[43] A Thomas Lynehill of Lyne Hill died in 1708.[44]

John Fletcher of Lyne Hill, who occurs from 1596[45] and whose house there was mentioned in 1598,[46] died at Lyne Hill in 1604 seised of a messuage and lands there, with a minor son, John, as his heir.[47] It was probably this John Fletcher who died between 1659 and 1662, leaving a son John as his heir.[48] This son is probably the John Fletcher who had five hearths in Penkridge chargeable for tax in 1666[49] and who died in 1678.[50] A John Fletcher occupied the second of the two houses in Lyne Hill in 1680[51] and died in the following year, 'the last of the Fletchers of Lynell'.[52]

In 1834 and 1851 Lyne Hill was described as a farm situated a mile south of Penkridge.[53]

Two hides in MITTON formed a berewick of Robert de Stafford's manor of Bradley in 1086.[54] By 1166 Mitton appears to have formed part of the knight's fees held of the barony of Stafford by Robert fitz Ralph of Standon.[55] Fitz Ralph's intermediate lordship apparently descended to Vivian de Standon who by 1250 had devised his rights to Thomas and Walter his sons.[56] Nothing more is heard of this mesne lordship. The overlordship descended with the barony of Stafford until at least 1720,[57] and Lord Stafford still had some rights in the manor in 1851.[58]

It seems probable that the ⅔ knight's fee held of Robert fitz Ralph in 1166 by Ivo de Mutton was this land in Mitton.[59] Ivo de Mutton was succeeded by a son Ralph and Ralph by a son Adam[60] who held land there[61] and whose son Ralph de Mutton (II) was

[15] S.H.C. vi (1), 79.
[16] Ibid. ix (1), 16.
[17] Ibid. xi (1), 216.   [18] C 138/45.
[19] C 142/124, no. 178; C 142/172, no. 119.
[20] C 138/45; S.H.C. 1931, 223; C 54/406, no. 29; Complete Peerage, x. 244; Hunts. Visitation (Camden Soc. o.s. xliii), 126.
[21] S.H.C. xi. 285; C.P. 40/1115, m. 9d; C 142/124, no. 178; C.P. 40/1152, rot. 613; S.H.C. xvii. 210–11; C.P. 25(2)/260, 15 Eliz. I East.; C 142/172, no. 119; C.P. 25(2)/596, 1654 Trin.; C.P. 43/676, rot. 321; see p. 115. It was described in 1610 as the manor or farm of Longridge held of the rectory or prebend of Longridge: C 142/320, no. 71. A messuage described as Long Bridge Farm, in the tenure of William Smart, was said to be parcel of the Deanery Manor in 1654: S.R.O., D 260/M/box 3, bdle. e, deed dated Mar. 1653/4.
[22] Tithe Maps and Appt., Penkridge (copy in W.S.L.).
[23] Ex inf. the Teddesley and Hatherton Estate Office, Penkridge.
[24] Close R. 1234–7, 525.
[25] S.H.C. iv (1), 240–1.
[26] C 1/1507, no. 46.
[27] S.H.C. xv. 167.
[28] S.R.O., D. 260/M/box 16, bdle. a, Ct. Bk. 1598–1654, f. 17a.
[29] C 142/456, no. 76.
[30] C.P. 25(2)/486, 18 Chas. I Mich.
[31] C.P. 25(2)/596, 1654 Trin.
[32] Close R. 1234–7, 525.
[33] S.H.C. v (1), 150.
[34] Ibid. ix (1), 16.
[35] Ibid. 1928, 146.
[36] C 1/1307, nos. 62–64; C 1/1507, no. 46.
[37] S.H.C. 1929, 61, 327; ibid. 1935, 468.
[38] S.R.O., D. 260/M/box 16, bdle. a, Ct. Bk. 1598–1654, f. 2a.
[39] S.H.C. n.s. vi (1), 43.
[40] Penkridge Par. Reg. (Staffs. Par. Reg. Soc.), 254.
[41] S.R.O., D. 260/M/box A [i], bdle. x.
[42] S.H.C. 1927, 33.
[43] Ibid. 1919, 219.
[44] Penkridge Par. Reg. 294.
[45] S.H.C. 1932, 203; ibid. 1935, 59, 468. A John Fletcher, late of 'Lynehille', occurs in 1475: ibid. n.s. vi (1), 93.
[46] S.R.O., D. 260/M/box 16, bdle. a, Ct. Bk. 1598–1654, f. 2a.
[47] C 142/284, no. 21.
[48] D. 260/M/box 7, bdle. l, Inquisition into Penkridge Charities, Jan. 1661/2.
[49] S.H.C. 1927, 33.
[50] Penkridge Par. Reg. 268.
[51] S.H.C. 1919, 219.
[52] Penkridge Par. Reg. 270.
[53] White, Dir. Staffs. (1834; 1851).
[54] V.C.H. Staffs. iv. 49, no. 161.
[55] S.H.C. i. 163.
[56] Close R. 1247–51, 271–2.
[57] Bk. of Fees, 543, 966; C 136/47; C 139/180; E 36/150, f. 59a; W.S.L. 119/40.
[58] White, Dir. Staffs. (1851).
[59] S.H.C. i. 163.
[60] Ibid. xii (1), 245–6.
[61] Close R. 1247–51, 271–2.

dead by 1241 leaving an infant daughter Isabel.[62] The custody of Mitton was still in the hands of Thomas and Walter, sons of Vivian de Standon, in 1250,[63] but by 1257 Isabel seems to have been in possession and already married to Philip de Chetwynd.[64] Philip was dead by 1284,[65] and in 1290 Isabel and her second husband, Roger de Thornton, were suing Eve *de albo monasterio*, her sons William and Alan, and Roger de Pullesdon, lessees of Mitton, for cutting down trees and taking fish from the stew and for other waste there.[66] In 1291, after Isabel's death, her son Philip de Chetwynd (II), granted a life interest in what was then called the manor of Mitton and in Brereton (in Rugeley) to Roger de Thornton,[67] who was dead by 1297.[68] Philip (II) and his wife Isabel made a settlement of the manor in 1305,[69] and by 1308 Philip (II) was dead, leaving a son Philip de Chetwynd (III), a minor.[70] Isabel was described as lady of the manor in 1316,[71] but in 1317 Philip (III) was granted free warren there.[72] Mitton then descended in the family of the Chetwynds of Ingestre, with The Reule in Bradley until 1735,[73] and with Brereton in Rugeley until at least 1828 when the manor was held by Charles Chetwynd, Earl Talbot (d. 1849).[74] In *c.* 1841 the earl held most of the land here, which was at that date divided into three farms of roughly equal area.[75]

The house now known as Mitton Manor is a mid-19th-century red-brick house with stone dressings. It has two front gables with ornamental barge-boards and a central gabled porch.

A messuage and virgate in Mitton were held in 1411 by Richard Mercer of Mitton as a freehold tenement.[76] At some time between 1504 and 1518 John Mercer, and at some time between 1518 and 1529 John's daughters, were suing a Richard Mercer for detention of deeds relating to messuages and lands in Mitton and elsewhere that had belonged to Roger Mercer, John's grandfather.[77] A John Mercer conveyed 2 messuages and lands in Mitton to a Thomas Pycto in 1554,[78] and in 1599 a Francis Pictoe and his wife Elizabeth made a settlement of two messuages and lands there.[79]

Mitton was within the leet of Forebridge in Castle Church between at least 1472 and 1801, and presented jointly with Longnor (in Bradley) by at least 1499.[80] The township paid 20d. a year in frith

fee, wake fee, and kelth from at least 1402,[81] and 20s., then described as rent, was still being paid in 1698[82] and probably in 1720 also.[83]

By 1391 the Earl of Stafford had free warren here.[84]

Land in 'the More near Penkridge' was held of the church of Penkridge, probably at some time during the 13th century, by an Omiat de More, whose son Adam subsequently granted it with the marriage of his sister Edith to Humfrey de More to hold of the church for 2s. a year.[85] Anne, daughter of Stephen de More, granted all the land held by her father 'in the moor and without' to Alfred de More to hold of the church for 2s. a year, probably *c.* 1300.[86] The Dean and Chapter of Penkridge were claiming view of frankpledge, assize of bread and beer, and infangthief in 'More' by 1293,[87] and in 1298 the king gave the Archbishop of Dublin, as Dean of Penkridge, to hold in free alms a messuage and virgate in Penkridge, formerly held by William de la More[88] who had been hanged for felony in 1293.[89] In 1312 the Archbishop of Dublin was proceeding against persons who during the recent voidance in the archbishopric had damaged the fishpond in what was described as his manor of *LA MORE* by Penkridge.[90] A similar charge was brought against John de la More in 1345 concerning a close at La More and fishponds there.[91]

Land in the manor of Moor Hall was parcel of the lands shared by the canons resident and the sacristan of Penkridge by 1547.[92] The hamlet of Moor Hall in the manor of Penkridge occurs in 1598 when there was also mention of Moor Hall House and Moor Hall Wood.[93] In 1680 Moor Hall was described as an old farm owned by the Littletons,[94] and in 1752 as a manor owned by Sir Edward Littleton.[95] Moor Hall Farm occurs in 1820, situated to the west of Pillaton,[96] and *c.* 1841 Moor Hall, with a garden, was owned by Lord Hatherton and leased to John Cooke.[97] Lands nearby, called Moor Hall Piece and Big Moor Hall Close, were also owned by Lord Hatherton and leased to various tenants.[98]

In 1754 the house known as Moor Hall stood on the site of the present Moor Hall Cottages.[99] These cottages date from the middle of the 19th century. They were owned in 1956 by Lord Hatherton.[1]

Before the Conquest Ailric, a free man, was holding a hide in *OTHERTON*.[2] By 1086 this hide,

[62] *S.H.C.* iv (1), 119; ibid. xii (1), 246–9.
[63] *Close R.* 1247–51, 271–2.
[64] Uncalendared entry on Pat. R. 41 Hen. III (C 66/71), m. 13d, from W.S.L., S. MS. 332 (1), p. 230.
[65] *S.H.C.* vi (1), 136.
[66] Ibid. 196.
[67] Ibid. 202; ibid. 1911, 46–47.
[68] Ibid. vii (1), 41.
[69] Ibid. 1911, 64–65.
[70] Ibid. ix (1), 4, 5.
[71] *Feud. Aids*, v. 16.
[72] *Cal. Chart. R.* 1300–26, 367.
[73] *S.H.C.* xii (1), 299, 300; C 130/91; C 130/260; *S.H.C.* xii (1), 305–6, 308–9, 310–11; ibid. N.S. iii. 177–8; ibid. xii (1), 323–4; *Cal. Close*, 1447–54, 513; *S.H.C.* xii, (1) 332, 335; C 142/106, no. 67: C.P. 25(2)/724, 22 Chas. II Mich.; *V.C.H. Staffs.* iv. 82–83.
[74] C.P. 43/678, rot. 370; C.P. 43/869, rot. 441; C.P. 43/981, rot. 386; see p. 155.
[75] Tithe Maps and Appt., Penkridge (copy in W.S.L.).
[76] *S.H.C.* xv. 125.
[77] C 1/340, no. 19; C 1/521, no. 37.
[78] *S.H.C.* xii (1), 217.
[79] Ibid. xvi. 187.

[80] D.L. 30/108/1606; W.S.L., Forebridge Manor Ct. R. 1499–1503, mm. 2, 6; S.R.O., Q/RDc 15.
[81] W.S.L., D. 1721/1/8, p. 151.
[82] E 178/6821, m. 6.
[83] W.S.L. 119/40.
[84] *S.H.C.* xv. 41.
[85] *S.H.C.* 1928, 150.
[86] Ibid. 151.   [87] Ibid. vii (1), 5–6.
[88] *Cal. Pat.* 1292–1301, 336; *Cal. Close* 1296–1302, 152; *S.H.C.* vi (1), 246.
[89] *Cal. Inq. Misc.* i, no. 167; *Cal. Close* 1288–96, 354–5.
[90] *Cal. Pat.* 1307–13, 545.
[91] *S.H.C.* xiv (1), 62.
[92] Ibid. 1950–1, 41.
[93] S.R.O., D. 260/M/box 16, bdle. a, Ct. Bk. 1598–1654, ff. 2a, 17a.
[94] *S.H.C.* 1919, 219.
[95] C.P. 43/676, rot. 321.
[96] Greenwood, *Map of Staffs.* (1820).
[97] Tithe Maps and Appt., Penkridge (copy in W.S.L.).
[98] Ibid.
[99] S.R.O., D. 260/M/E. 353(a), map 3.
[1] Ex inf. Teddesley and Hatherton Estate Office.
[2] *V.C.H. Staffs.* iv. 53, no. 215.

valued at 3s., was parcel of the lands of Robert de Stafford[3] and probably represents the ¼ fee which was held in 1166 of Robert de Stafford by William fitz Walter.[4] The overlordship remained in the Stafford barony until at least 1284.[5]

In 1086 Clodoan held Otherton of Robert de Stafford.[6] The William fitz Walter who held ¼ knight's fee of Robert de Stafford in 1166[7] was probably the William who was lord of Otherton in 1167.[8] By 1237 Otherton was held by Hugh de Loges,[9] lord of Great Wyrley (in Cannock). This intermediate lordship was held by Hugh's son Richard in 1285[10] and by Richard's son, also Richard, in 1300,[11] but by 1350 it was in the hands of Sir Robert de Haughton as lord of Rodbaston.[12] Between at least 1397 and 1610 a lordship over Otherton seems to have remained with the lords of Rodbaston.[13]

By 1255 Adam de Otherton was the tenant in occupation of Otherton, which was still assessed at a hide, which was geldable, and owed 12d. to the sheriff's aid, 12d. to the view of frankpledge, and 4d. to the hundred.[14] Adam occurs again in 1271[15] and though still alive in 1300[16] was dead by 1308, leaving a widow Alice and a son and heir John.[17] In 1336 John gave his son William a rent of 40 marks from his lands and tenements in Otherton,[18] and he was dead by 1338, leaving a widow Andrea; his son William was dead by 1350.[19] The lord of Rodbaston then granted to William's widow Joan the custody of William's son John, with that of John's sister Amice, if John should die under age.[20] William de Engleton and his wife Avice seem to have been holding Otherton by 1375 when Joan, the widow of William de Otherton, sued them for one-third of a messuage, a carucate, and 26s. rent in Otherton, with meadow, pasture, and wood there, as her dower.[21] William was certainly lord in 1378[22] and died seised of what was described as the manor in 1397.[23] It passed to his daughter Joan, wife of John de Wynnesbury,[24] and the descent followed that of Pillaton[25] until at least 1851 when Lord Hatherton, who owned most of the land here c. 1841, was lord of the manor.[26]

Otherton was valued at £4 in 1529[27] and £8 17s. 9d. in 1558.[28] By 1657 there were eight freeholders holding of the lord of the manor and eight tenants holding for years, for lives, or at the lord's pleasure.[29] A John Webb held 'an ancient messuage' in Otherton in 1657.[30] He was probably the John Webbe who was taxable on two hearths in 1666[31] and was living here in 1680,[32] dying in 1682.[33] A Robert Stevenson was taxable on three hearths in the constablewick of Otherton and Rodbaston in 1666,[34] and in 1680 a John Stephenson was living in Otherton.[35]

The ruined building now known as Otherton Cottages[36] has an early-16th-century origin. The present Otherton farmhouse was not in existence in 1754[37] and probably dates from c. 1800.

Richard Littleton held a fishery here in 1484.[38]

Land in 'Bedintun', granted in 993 by King Ethelred to Wulfric Spot[39] and by Wulfric to Burton Abbey by 1004,[40] was assessed in 1086 at ½ hide.[41] It was worth 13s. before the Conquest and 7s. 4d. in 1086.[42] This ½ hide probably corresponds with the ½ hide in 'Bedintona' and 'Pilatehala' mentioned between 1100 and 1113.[43] In 1114 or 1115 'Bedintona' was waste while 'Pilatehala' was inhabited,[44] and nothing further is heard of 'Bedintona' after 1135 at the latest.[45] In 1185 the Pope confirmed Burton Abbey in its possession of PILLATON[46] which was still assessed at ½ hide in 1274.[47] The overlordship of Pillaton still belonged to the abbey in 1535,[48] but after the Dissolution it passed into the hands of the king who granted it in 1546 to Sir William Paget,[49] in whose family the overlordship remained until at least 1769.[50]

By 1113 a certain Edwin was holding the ½ hide in 'Bedintona' and Pillaton of Burton Abbey at a rent of 20s.,[51] but by 1115 he was holding Pillaton for six hours' labour and Beddington for only 4s. as it was waste, although it would have rendered five hours' labour if inhabited.[52] Abbot Geoffrey granted 'Bedintona' and Pillaton to Edwin of 'Pilatehala' at some time between 1114 and 1135 to hold as his father had held them, for life, at a rent of 20s.[53] Edwin was to entertain the abbot when he went to

³ V.C.H. Staffs. iv. 53, no. 215.
⁴ S.H.C. i. 185.
⁵ Bk. of Fees, 543, 967, 974; Rot. Hund. (Rec. Com.), ii. 114; Feud. Aids, v. 1.
⁶ V.C.H. Staffs. iv. 53, no. 215. Robert de Cludewan of Lyne Hill was holding land at Otherton in 1251: S.H.C. iv (1), 244–5.
⁷ S.H.C. i. 185.   ⁸ Ibid. 48, 51.
⁹ Close R. 1234–7, 525.
¹⁰ Feud. Aids, v. 1; Cal. Pat. 1266–72, 101.
¹¹ S.H.C. v (1), 177; Cal. Inq. p.m. iii, no. 137.
¹² S.H.C. 1928, 144.
¹³ C 137/47; C 139/137; C 142/50, no. 67; C 142/124, no. 178; C 142/172, no. 119; C 142/320, no. 71.
¹⁴ Rot. Hund. (Rec. Com.), ii. 114; the lords of Otherton were given as Robert Cocus and Elias de Otherton. Adam seems to have been Elias's son: S.H.C. vi (1), 55.
¹⁵ S.H.C. v (1), 150, 152.
¹⁶ Ibid. 177.
¹⁷ Ibid. ix (1), 3, 6.
¹⁸ Ibid. 1928, 144.
¹⁹ Ibid. xi. 84; ibid. 1928, 144.
²⁰ Ibid. 1928, 144.
²¹ Ibid. xiii. 125. 'Avice' was evidently 'Amice', sister of John de Otherton: ibid. 1928, 144–5.
²² Ibid. 1928, 144–5.
²³ C 136/93.   ²⁴ Ibid.
²⁵ C 139/137; C 142/320, no. 71; C 142/456, no. 76; C.P. 25(2)/596, 1654 Trin.; C.P. 43/520, rot. 72; see p. 119.
²⁶ Tithe Maps and Appt., Penkridge (copy in W.S.L.); White, Dir. Staffs. (1851).

²⁷ C 142/50, no. 67.
²⁸ C 142/124, no. 178.
²⁹ S.R.O., D. 260/M/box A [i], bdle. f. court baron, court of recognition, and court of survey of Sir Edward Littleton, Oct. 1657.
³⁰ Ibid.
³¹ S.H.C. 1927, 38.
³² Ibid. 1919, 219.
³³ Penkridge Par. Reg. 271.
³⁴ S.H.C. 1927, 38.
³⁵ Ibid. 1919, 219.
³⁶ See p. 108.
³⁷ S.R.O., D. 260/M/E. 353 (a), map 3.
³⁸ S.H.C. n.s. vi (1), 153.
³⁹ W.S.L. 84/3/41.
⁴⁰ S.H.C. 1916, 14, 117.
⁴¹ V.C.H. Staffs. iv. 44, no. 97.
⁴² Ibid.
⁴³ S.H.C. v (1), 22.
⁴⁴ Ibid. 28.
⁴⁵ Ibid. 35.
⁴⁶ Ibid. 15.
⁴⁷ Rot. Hund. (Rec. Com.), ii. 115.
⁴⁸ Valor Eccl. (Rec. Com.), iii. 147.
⁴⁹ S.H.C. 1937, 187–9; L. & P. Hen. VIII, xxi (1), pp. 76–77.
⁵⁰ C 142/320, no. 71; W.S.L., Paget Papers (Gardner Coll.), 35 (1, 9); Complete Peerage, x, 'Paget'.
⁵¹ S.H.C. v (1), 22.
⁵² Ibid. 28.
⁵³ Ibid. 35.

those parts and give him fitting help when he asked for an aid from the land.[54] Abbot Richard granted Pillaton in fee farm to one William for 10s., service of his body, entertainment of the abbot and the monks when they came on the church's business, and a 'galga' for the making of meed.[55] William of Pillaton occurs between 1159 and 1175,[56] but by 1175 Abbot Bernard had granted Pillaton to one Alfred[57] who was probably the Alfred de Huntedon who held it before 1188 and was succeeded by his brother Brun.[58] Between 1182 and 1188 Abbot Richard granted the land to Henry de Broc at a rent of 16s., along with Brun's lands and forest office and Brun's daughter in marriage.[59] Henry de Broc was still living in 1205,[60] but by 1214 had been succeeded by Robert de Brok[61] who was alive in 1237.[62] Robert's son Robert (II) was holding Pillaton in 1255[63] and was dead by 1264.[64] His kinsman Walter de Elmedon succeeded[65] and in 1293 conveyed some rights in a messuage, a carucate, 20 acres of wood, and 20s. rent in Pillaton to his brother Stephen de Elmedon,[66] who died in 1302 holding of Walter a messuage and 80 acres of land there, worth 1 mark a year.[67] Stephen's son and heir William subsequently appeared as lord of Pillaton and granted what was described as the manor of Pillaton to William son of William de Wrottesley.[68] Stephen's widow Juliana with Reynold de Charnes, her husband, unsuccessfully sued William son of William de Wrottesley in 1304 for ⅓ messuage, a carucate, 20 acres of wood, and 20s. rent in Pillaton as her dower.[69]

In 1310 William de Wrottesley conveyed to William de Elmedon and Rose his wife a messuage, a carucate, 10 acres of meadow, 40s. rent, and a mill in Pillaton,[70] and William de Elmedon settled the manor on his son William and this son's wife Joan in 1342.[71] This younger William died in 1349 holding the manor for 16s. and two appearances at the abbot's court each year.[72] William's coheirs were John de Kenilworth and William de Engleton, sons of his sisters Margaret and Joan and both minors, but the manor remained with his wife Joan,[73] who was still alive in 1378.[74] In 1382 John, by then named 'de Pilatenhale', died, and his share of the manor passed

to his cousin William,[75] who died in 1397 holding the whole manor at a rent of 13s. 4d. and was succeeded by his daughter Joan, wife of John de Wynnesbury.[76] She died in 1450 and was followed by her son Hamlet Wynnesbury[77] whose son William succeeded in 1473.[78] William died in 1502 when the manor, held by a rent of 16s. was valued at 30s.[79] His heir was his daughter Alice, wife of Richard Littleton,[80] and when she died in 1529, the manor, still held by a rent of 16s. was valued at 100s.[81]

Alice was succeeded by her son Edward Littleton,[82] who, as Sir Edward, died at Pillaton in 1558 when the manor was still held for a rent of 16s. but was valued at £15 3s. 9d.[83] His son and heir, another Sir Edward, died in 1574 and was succeeded by his son Edward,[84] who was followed in 1610 by his son, also Edward.[85] This Edward's son, again Edward, was created a baronet in 1627 and succeeded his father in 1629.[86] His estates had been sequestered by September 1646,[87] but in 1650 his relative Fisher Littleton of Teddesley Lodge compounded for them.[88] They were released from sequestration in 1653,[89] and in 1654 Pillaton was in the hands of Sir Edward's son Edward.[90] The manor remained in the family until at least 1851,[91] although the seat was moved from Pillaton to Teddesley Park after the death in 1742 of Sir Edward the 3rd baronet.[92] Sir Edward, the 4th baronet, still a minor in 1749,[93] was succeeded in 1812 by his great-nephew Edward John Walhouse of Hatherton (in St. Peter's, Wolverhampton), who took the name of Littleton and was created Baron Hatherton in 1835.[94] He owned nearly all the land here c. 1841,[95] and the estate was still held in 1955 by the present Lord Hatherton.[96]

An incomplete series of records of the courts leet and baron for the manor of Pillaton survives from 1353 to 1749.[97]

The remaining buildings at Pillaton Hall, dating from the 16th century, are surrounded by a large moat, partly rectangular and partly oval,[98] which has been drained since c. 1860.[99] The existence and size of the moat are proof that an important house on the same site preceded the present one. The remains consist of a gatehouse range with the restored chapel of St. Modwena at its eastern end. This range, which

[54] Ibid.
[55] Ibid. 37.
[56] Ibid. 1937, 16.
[57] Ibid. v (1), 40.
[58] Ibid. 42.
[59] Ibid.; ibid. vi (1), 101 ibid. 1928, 164; Cal. Inq. p.m. iv, no. 217.
[60] S.H.C. ii (1), 127.
[61] Rot. de Ob. et Fin. (Rec. Com.), 543–4.
[62] Rot. Hund. (Rec. Com.), ii. 115.
[63] Ibid.
[64] Cal. Inq. p.m. (Rec. Com.), i, p. 26; Ex. e Rot. Fin. (Rec. Com.), ii. 409.
[65] Ex. e Rot. Fin. (Rec. Com.), ii. 409; S.H.C. vi (1), 279, 280.
[66] S.H.C. 1911, 48–49; ibid. 1938, 243.
[67] Cal. Inq. p.m. iv, no. 71; S.H.C. 1911, 271–2.
[68] W.S.L., S. MS. 350A/40, f. 84a.
[69] S.H.C. vii (1), 115, 118, 139.
[70] Ibid. 1911, 74–75.
[71] Ibid. 1928, 151–2.
[72] Cal. Inq. p.m. xi, no. 468.
[73] Ibid.
[74] S.H.C. xiii. 149–50.
[75] Cal. Fine R. 1377–83, 331. William was born and baptized at Penkridge in 1348: Cal. Inq. p.m. xiii, no. 63.
[76] C 136/93.
[77] C 139/137.

[78] C 140/45.
[79] Cal. Inq. p.m. Hen. VII, ii, no. 537.
[80] Ibid.
[81] C 142/50, no. 67.
[82] Ibid.
[83] C 142/124, no. 178.
[84] Ibid.; C 142/172, no. 119.
[85] C 142/320, no. 71.
[86] Burke, Peerage (1931), 1198; C 142/456, no. 76.
[87] S.H.C. 1915, 209.
[88] Cal. Cttee. for Compounding, 2081–2.
[89] Ibid. 2082.
[90] C 25(2)/596, 1654 Trin.
[91] Burke, Peerage (1931), 1197–8; C.P. 25(2)/725, 28 Chas. II Mich.; C.P. 43/674, rot. 321; White, Dir. Staffs. (1851).
[92] Burke, Peerage (1931), 1197–8; Pitt, Staffs. 256–7. His widow was living at Pillaton Hall in 1754: S.R.O., D. 260/M/E. 353 (a, b), map 3.
[93] S.R.O., D. 260/M/box 5, bdle. a, Pillaton Ct. R. 1745, 1749. He was 84 when he died in May 1812: Tildesley, Penkridge, 46. For a portrait of 1756 see plate facing p. 132.
[94] Complete Peerage, vi. 394.
[95] Tithe Maps and Appt., Penkridge (copy in W.S.L.).
[96] Ex inf. the Teddesley and Hatherton Estate Office.
[97] S.R.O., D. 260/M/box 5, bdle. a, Pillaton Ct. R.
[98] V.C.H. Staffs. i. 365.
[99] Inf. from caretaker.

is approached by a bridge over the moat, represents the north side of what was originally a square courtyard plan. Only a single free-standing chimney and fragments of walling survive from the other ranges. The rebuilding of the house by the Littletons was probably begun during the earlier 16th century: internally a newel stair and a framed partition appear to be of this date, while some of the external features are more typical of the late 16th century. The gatehouse range is of two stories, the central block rising to three stories and having four angle turrets to its upper half. The turrets have diaper ornament and below them are projecting buttresses of V section. The gatehouse arches are of stone with four-centred heads. The upper part of the block was rebuilt in 1706,[1] the stone cornice and tall windows being of this date. Most of the other windows in the range are of 16th-century design and have been restored. An isolated chimney-stack, which stands near the west end of the gatehouse block, originally formed part of the west range and evidently belonged to the kitchen. It has a very wide fireplace with baking ovens, and above the moulded lintel two relieving arches and the weathering of the former roof are visible. The remains of clustered stacks terminate the chimney. The base of what was probably the fireplace of the great hall survives on the south side of the courtyard and, near the north end of the former east range, part of another chimney projects from the external wall. In its complete form the house contained 25 hearths.[2] East of the moat is a garden wall of 16th- or early-17th-century brickwork and north of the house an early-18th-century barn survives.

By 1754 Pillaton was still intact and was occupied by a Lady Littleton.[3] A visitor in 1786, however, reported that only a farmer lived there, that the chapel was ruinous and that demolition was imminent. At this period the great hall still contained stained-glass windows portraying biblical subjects, the signs of the Zodiac, and scenes representing the seasons of the year. There was also a large fireplace and much carved panelling.[4] In a kitchen window, thought formerly to have been in the chapel, was a representation of St. Modwena, flanked by smaller kneeling figures.[5] Thirteen years later three sides of the courtyard had been demolished, but eight tall chimneys were left standing.[6] Several of these had disappeared by 1841 when John Buckler made extensive drawings of the remains.[7] Between 1884 and 1888 Lord Hatherton restored the gatehouse

range and largely rebuilt the chapel.[8] The latter is still used regularly for services,[9] and the house is occupied by a caretaker.

PRESTON is mentioned *c.* 1215.[10] Half a virgate there was held at some time before 1261 by a woman called Avice for a rent of 2*s.* paid to Nicholas Pinel.[11] Avice later granted the land to Richard and John, Canons of Penkridge, who were to maintain her in possession for life.[12] Richard and John subsequently granted the land to William Adleinere for 40*s.*[13] It appears that by 1261 tithe from the land belonged to the prebend of Penkridge.[14] By 1548 land at Preston worth 12*d.* and in the tenure of Thomas Preston belonged to one of the two resident canons of Penkridge, while one of the three closes of land shared among the vicars choral, the resident canons, and the sacrista of the college was Preston Close.[15] Land in Preston seems to have been in the hands of Edward Littleton by 1585[16] and the hamlet of Preston was stated to be within Penkridge manor in 1598.[17] Edward Littleton's land here passed at his death in 1610 to his son Edward,[18] who was holding what was described as the manor or farm of Preston at his death in 1629.[19] The manor descended in the Littleton family with Pillaton[20] until at least 1837[21] and was described in 1851 as a liberty belonging to Lord Hatherton.[22] Two farms, Preston Vale and Preston Hill, which occur in 1820[23] and 1832,[24] were held of Lord Hatherton *c.* 1841 by William Brune and A. F. Lewis respectively.[25] Both were sold by the 3rd Lord Hatherton in 1919 to their respective tenants[26] and in 1955 still existed as farms, Preston Vale being occupied by Mr. L. T. J. Griffin.[27] Preston Vale is a red-brick farmhouse, the west front of which dates from the late 17th century. Among the farm buildings is a former steam-mill, now operated by electricity. Preston Hill is shown as a project on a map of 1754[28] and the site is not ancient.

Before the Conquest Alli, a free man, was holding 3 hides in *RODBASTON* (Redbaldestone) which by 1086 were part of the lands of Richard the Forester.[29] The land seems to have descended with Great Wyrley in Cannock,[30] passing by 1195 to Hugh de Loges.[31] In this year Hugh had a house here,[32] and his 1 carucate of land in Rodbaston, held by a serjeanty in Cannock Forest (presumably the chief forestership), was assessed at 10*s.* a year in 1198.[33] Rodbaston was described as a manor in 1199.[34] The manor then followed the same descent as Great Wyrley until 1290,[35] and in 1255 was held

[1] Dated rainwater heads with initials E.L. and S.L.
[2] *S.H.C.* 1927, 23.
[3] S.R.O., D. 260/M/E. 353 (a, b), map 3.
[4] *Gent. Mag.* lix (2) (1789), 1078–9.
[5] Ibid., pl. iii.
[6] W.S.L., Staffs. Views, viii, p. 39 (1799); see plate facing p. 105.
[7] W.S.L., Staffs. Views, viii, pp. 37, 38, 40–47.
[8] Tablet in chapel, &c.   [9] See p. 131.
[10] Hist. MSS. Com. *Middleton*, 57.
[11] *S.H.C.* 1950–1, 47.   [12] Ibid. 47–48.
[13] Ibid. 48.   [14] Ibid.
[15] Ibid. 41–42, the other 2 being Cadsey and Longridge closes.
[16] *S.H.C.* xv. 167.
[17] S.R.O., D. 260/M/box 16, bdle. a, Ct. Bk. 1598–1654, f. 17*a*.
[18] C 142/320, no. 71.
[19] C 142/456, no. 76.
[20] C.P. 25(2)/596, 1654 Trin.; C.P. 43/506, rot. 98; S.R.O., D. 260/M/box 17, bdle. c; White, *Dir. Staffs.* (1834); see p. 119.

[21] S.R.O., D. 260/M/box 28, bdle. a.
[22] White, *Dir. Staffs.* (1851).
[23] Greenwood, *Map of Staffs.* (1820).
[24] Teesdale, *Map of Staffs.* (1832).
[25] Tithe Maps and Appt., Penkridge (copy in W.S.L.).
[26] Ex inf. the Teddesley and Hatherton Estate Office. The area of Preston Hill was then 387 a. and that of Preston Vale 285 a.
[27] Ex inf. Miss Griffin (1955).
[28] S.R.O., D. 260/M/E. 353 (a), map 8.
[29] *V.C.H. Staffs.* iv. 56, no. 262.
[30] See p. 79.
[31] *S.H.C.* ii (1), 45, 51. It was not, however, alienated like Great Wyrley to Radmore Abbey.
[32] Ibid. Hugh's 'castrum' at Rodbaston was mentioned in 1215: *Rot. Litt. Pat.* (Rec. Com.), 144.
[33] *Bk. of Fees*, 7.
[34] *S.H.C.* iii (1), 45.
[35] *Bk. of Fees*, 594; *S.H.C.* 1911, 127–8; *Cal. Close* 1264–8, 128; *S.H.C.* iv (1), 179; *Cal. Close* 1268–72, 432; *S.H.C.* vi (1), 57; *Rot. Hund.* (Rec. Com.), ii. 115; *S.H.C.* vi (1), 169, 195; see p. 79.

as 1½ curucate, quit of suit at county and hundred courts, by the service of keeping Cannock Forest.[36]

Richard de Loges's son Richard was holding the manor jointly with his wife Elizabeth in 1290,[37] and on his death in 1300 the annual value of the manor was given as 12d. from the capital messuage and garden, 26s. 8d. from 80 acres of arable in demesne, 4s. from 4 acres of meadow, 40d. from a water-mill, and 20s. 6d. from rents.[38] The manor remained with Richard's widow Elizabeth who, with her second husband John de Saundrestede, in 1322 granted the reversion after their deaths to John de Weston of Weston under Lizard.[39] Elizabeth died in 1337[40] and her husband in 1353 when he was described as John de Saundrestede of Rodbaston.[41] Nothing further is heard of a Weston claim, and although John de Loges, grandson of Elizabeth, quitclaimed his rights in the manor to Ralph de Stafford in 1344[42] and Sir Robert de Haughton was described as lord of Rodbaston in 1350,[43] the manor passed to Eleanor, daughter of John de Loges,[44] presumably on the death of John de Saundrestede. Eleanor, with her husband John de Peyto, had granted it by 1372 to John de Beverley and his wife Amice.[45]

The manor then followed the descent of Penkridge[46] until 1518, when Sir Robert Willoughby, 2nd Lord Willoughby de Broke (d. 1521), having made a settlement of it in 1516,[47] mortgaged it with Penkridge to Sir Edward Greville.[48] When Robert died in 1521 his heirs were the three daughters of his son Edward, who had predeceased him.[49] One of these, Elizabeth, became the ward of Sir Edward Greville in 1522 and subsequently married his second son Fulke.[50] Following an Act of Parliament of 1535 or 1536, Rodbaston, with Robert's other Staffordshire manors, was divided between his two surviving granddaughters, Elizabeth, wife of Fulke Greville, and Blanche, wife of Francis Dautrey.[51] In 1542, after the death of Blanche, the whole manor was conveyed to Elizabeth and Fulke by Sir Anthony Willoughby,[52] presumably the brother of Robert, 2nd Lord Willoughby de Broke,[53] and probably trustee. Elizabeth survived her husband and died in 1563, with her son Sir Fulke succeeding her.[54] He

was followed in 1606 by his son Sir Fulke, the poet, created Baron Brooke of Beauchamp's Court in 1621.[55] At his death in 1628 the manor passed to his sister Margaret, wife of Sir Richard Verney, who then became in her own right de jure Baroness Willoughby de Broke.[56] She was succeeded in 1631 by her son Sir Greville Verney,[57] and the manor then descended with the barony of Willoughby de Broke (in abeyance from 1521 to 1694)[58] until at least 1851.[59] Lord Willoughby de Broke owned 307 acres c. 1841[60] in Rodbaston which were leased to James Turner who was still the tenant in 1851.[61]

Members of the family of Eginton occur as tenants in either Rodbaston or Otherton in 1380,[62] and Sampson Eginton held the lease of the site of the manor, called the Mott Place, at his death c. 1556.[63] John Eginton, father and son, were mentioned in 1567[64] and a John was holding land here in 1589[65] and 1614.[66] In 1619 a John Eginton succeeded his father John in a messuage here[67] and is probably the John who occurs with his wife Sarah and son John in 1630.[68] John Eginton was taxable on eight hearths in the constablewick of Otherton and Rodbaston in 1666,[69] and 'Mr. Eginton' was holding inclosures in Rodbaston in 1673[70] and 1674.[71] Mr. John Eginton was living in the one 'good house' in Rodbaston in 1680.[72] Land here was leased in 1720 by the lord of the manor to John Eginton 'the younger' of Rodbaston, for the lives of his wife Lucy and sons John and Theophilus,[73] and John Eginton 'the younger' was holding land here of the lord of the manor in 1724.[74] A John Eginton 'of Robaston' died in 1729 at Shenstone (Offlow hundred) where he had lately gone to live.[75] A Jeremiah Eginton was dealing by fine in 1768 with what was described as the manor of Rodbaston.[76]

The site of the early capital messuage, represented by a mound surrounded by a large rectangular moat[77] lies over a mile south of Penkridge and about 500 yds. east of the Wolverhampton road. By 1690 the manor-house, presumably the Eginton house, was the only house in Rodbaston and was situated 500 yds. to the south-east of this, on or near the site of the present Stables Farm.[78] It seems to have had a

[36] Rot. Hund. (Rec. Com.), ii. 115.
[37] S.H.C. vi (1), 195, 200, 205–7.
[38] Cal. Inq. p.m. iii, no. 593; S.H.C. 1911, 262.
[39] S.H.C. 1911, 96–97, 345–6; ibid. ix (1), 85, 128; ibid. N.S. ii. 36.
[40] Cal. Inq. p.m. viii, no. 105.
[41] Ibid. x, no. 102.
[42] S.H.C. xii (1), 28.
[43] Ibid. 1928, 144.
[44] Ibid. xi. 183.
[45] Cal. Pat. 1370–4, 183; S.H.C. xi. 183.
[46] Cal. Close 1377–81, 418; S.H.C. 1931, 248–9; ibid. xi. 222, 225–6; C 138/21; C 139/12; C 139/34; C 140/3; see p. 109.
[47] S.H.C. xii (1), 182.
[48] W.S.L., S. MS. 249, ff. 125b–126a, 136b.
[49] C 142/41, no. 18.
[50] V.C.H. Warws. iii. 16; Burke, Peerage (1931), 2420.
[51] 'Act concerning the partition of lands between the heirs of Lord Brooke', 27 Hen. VIII, c. 44: Stat. Realm, iii. 605–7.
[52] C.P. 40/1117, m. 5d.
[53] W.S.L., S. MS. 249, f. 131b.
[54] C 142/143, no. 2; Complete Peerage (orig. edn.), viii. 151, where the date of Elizabeth's death is wrongly given as 1560.
[55] Complete Peerage, ii. 332.
[56] Wards 7/49, no. 213; Complete Peerage (orig. edn.), viii. 151.

[57] C 142/514, no. 55.
[58] Complete Peerage (orig. edn.), viii. 151–3; E 134, East. 26 Chas. II, no. 5; W.S.L., D. 1553/28, 36, 48–50, 55 (e), 57.
[59] White, Dir. Staffs. (1851).
[60] Tithe Maps and Appt., Penkridge (copy in W.S.L.).
[61] White, Dir. Staffs. (1851).
[62] S.H.C. xvii. 191.
[63] B.M. Eg. MS. 3008, f. 46a, Rodbaston Ct. R. 1556.
[64] S.H.C. xiii. 266–7.
[65] Ibid. xv. 193.
[66] C 142/347, no. 21.
[67] C 142/373, no. 24.
[68] W.S.L., D. 1553/103(a).
[69] S.H.C. 1927, 38.
[70] W.S.L., D. 1553/102.
[71] E 134, East. 26 Chas. II, no. 5.
[72] S.H.C. 1919, 219.
[73] W.S.L., D. 1553/99.
[74] Ibid. 100.
[75] Penkridge Par. Reg. (Staffs. Par. Reg. Soc.), 312, 313. He was there described as 'an ingenious magistrate, a good neighbour, and a generous worthy gentleman'.
[76] C.P. 25(2)/1411, 8 Geo. III Trin. A Jeremiah, son of Mr. John Egginton, was baptized at Penkridge 29 May 1697: Penkridge Par. Reg. 217.
[77] V.C.H. Staffs. i. 365; Tithe Maps and Appt., Penkridge (copy in W.S.L.), where it is called the Roundabout.
[78] S.R.O., D. 260/M/E. 353 (a), maps 16 (1690), 3 (1754).

private chapel,[79] but this and the house have now disappeared.

In 1834 William Holland owned what was then called Rodbaston Hall, together with land that *c.* 1841 amounted to over 180 acres.[80] Dr. Charles Holland was owner by 1851,[81] but in 1852 the Hall was sold to Thomas Shaw Hellier.[82] The Hall, grounds, and farm were sold in 1871 to Henry Ward, whose widow Jane remained there until her death about 1915, the Hall and some 583 acres being offered for sale in November of that year.[83] In 1919 the Staffordshire County Council bought Rodbaston Hall, the Hall farm, and the Grange and in 1921 opened the Staffordshire Farm Institute there.[84]

Rodbaston Hall lies about 500 yds. south of Stables Farm. Although a house was in existence there by at least 1841,[85] the present mansion may date from some years later. The Hall was described in 1860 as 'a neat modern mansion, seated on a pleasant eminence and commanding views of the surrounding country', and containing 'a choice selection of paintings, the productions of eminent artists'.[86] It now stands in a well-timbered garden and is a tall square brick house with a classical porch. Later additions include those of 1955 for the Farm Institute. The existing farm buildings lie mainly to the west.

Stables Farm and the adjoining cottages date from the mid-19th century and have picturesque Tudor features.

The lord of the manor held view of frankpledge for Rodbaston in at least 1554, 1556, and 1559,[87] and records of the court baron survive for at least 1547, 1554 or 1555, 1556,[88] 1607, and 1608.[89]

Before the Conquest Ordmer, a free man, held one hide in *WATER EATON* (Etone), which by 1086 was parcel of the lands of Robert de Stafford and was then assessed at 8s.[90] The overlordship descended in the Stafford barony until at least 1460.[91]

Hervey was holding the hide in Water Eaton of Robert de Stafford in 1086.[92] Hervey de Stretton held ½ knight's fee in Water Eaton in 1166,[93] and his grandson Richard de Stretton held ¼ fee there in

1243.[94] In 1263 the lordship was said to be held jointly by Richard and the Dean of Wolverhampton,[95] and Richard's son Richard was described in 1285 as lord of ⅓ fee here, said to be held directly of the king.[96] Thomas Champion, lord of Stretton, was also lord of Water Eaton in 1345,[97] and in 1428 Robert Congreve, lord of Stretton, held ¼ fee here, apparently of the king.[98] This intermediate lordship seems to have remained with the lords of Stretton until at least 1633[99] and possibly until 1725.[1]

In 1166 Adam of 'Ectone' was holding ½ knight's fee of Hervey de Stretton,[2] and an Adam de Etona occurs at some time between 1176 and 1184.[3] Adam de Beysin of Water Eaton, presumably his son, occurs in 1228[4] and was holding Water Eaton of Richard de Stretton as ¼ fee in 1243.[5] He died in 1243 or 1244 leaving a minor son Robert, as his heir.[6] The manor then followed the same descent as Longnor in Bradley until at least 1300,[7] being valued at 5s. in 1263.[8] In 1305, however, Walter de Beysin was complaining that for at least 40 years past, since the death of his great-grandfather Adam, land there had been annexed, during successive minorities, to the king's hay of Gailey,[9] and at his death in 1310 Walter was holding in Water Eaton only 40s. rent.[10] His son and heir Thomas,[11] who in 1315 petitioned Parliament for an inquiry into the lands in Water Eaton absorbed into Gailey,[12] was described as lord in 1316[13] but apparently held nothing there at his death in 1318.[14] He was succeeded by his brother Walter[15] who at his death in 1345 was holding rent worth 40s. and two mills in Water Eaton but no demesne land, woods, pastures, or meadows there.[16] When Walter's son and heir[17] John died in 1360, he held 60s. rent in Water Eaton jointly with his wife Anne,[18] who held 2 carucates of land, 12 acres of meadow, and 5 marks' rent in the manor as her dower until her death in 1402.[19]

The manor continued to descend with Longnor in Bradley from 1360[20] until at least 1538 when it was in the hands of Thomas Aston and his wife Bridget.[21] It was still held by Bridget in 1552,[22] but by 1560 she had been succeeded by her son John[23] who was still living in 1572[24] but by 1595 seems to have been

[79] There is mention of a chapel wall and chapel yard *c.* 1673: W.S.L., D. 1553/102 (E. 10). Chapel yard occurs as a field name in Rodbaston *c.* 1841; Tithe Maps and Appt., Penkridge (copy in W.S.L.).
[80] White, *Dir. Staffs.* (1851).
[81] Ibid.
[82] W.S.L., Sale Catalogue, E/2/7.
[83] Ibid.; *P.O. Dir. Staffs.* (1872); *Kelly's Dir. Staffs.* (1912; 1916); Lich. Dioc. Regy., Consist. Ct. Act Bk. 1914–20, p. 34, faculty, 5 Mar. 1915.
[84] *Staffs. Advertiser*, 15 Oct. 1921; *Kelly's Dir. Staffs.* (1940); ex inf. Staffs. C.C. Estate Agent.
[85] Tithe Maps and Appt., Penkridge (copy in W.S.L.).
[86] *P.O. Dir. Staffs.* (1860).
[87] B.M. Eg. MS. 3008, ff. 48*a*–50*a*; B.M. Eg. R. 2102.
[88] B.M. Eg. MS. 3008, f. 46*a*.
[89] B.M. Eg. MS. 3005, ff. 48*a*, 52*a*.
[90] *V.C.H. Staffs.* iv. 53, no. 213.
[91] *S.H.C.* i. 170, 171; C 136/47; C 137/20; C 139/180.
[92] *V.C.H. Staffs.* iv. 53, no. 213.
[93] *S.H.C.* i. 170, 171.
[94] *Bk. of Fees*, 967.
[95] *Cal. Inq. p.m.* i, no. 557; *S.H.C.* 1911, 135–6.
[96] *Feud. Aids*, v. 2.
[97] *Cal. Inq. p.m.* viii, no. 507.
[98] *Feud. Aids*, v. 22.
[99] C 139/153; C 60/525, rot. 39.
[1] C.P. 25(2)/597, 1659 Hil.; C.P. 25(2)/1063, 11 Geo. I Trin.

[2] *S.H.C.* i. 170, 171.
[3] Ibid. iii (1), 204–5.
[4] *Close R.* 1227–31, 18; *V.C.H. Staffs.* iv. 80.
[5] *Bk. of Fees*, 967.
[6] *Cal. Inq. p.m.* i, no. 557; *S.H.C.* 1911, 135–6.
[7] *Cal. Inq. p.m.* i, no. 557; *S.H.C.* 1911, 135–6; *Cal. Geneal.* i. 364; *Feud. Aids*, v. 2; *S.H.C.* v (1), 173, 177; *V.C.H. Staffs.* iv. 80.
[8] *S.H.C.* 1911, 135–6.
[9] *Cal. Inq. Misc.* i, no. 2416; *S.H.C.* iv (2), 106.
[10] *Cal. Inq. p.m.* v, no. 222; *S.H.C.* 1911, 302.
[11] *Cal. Inq. p.m.* v, no. 222.
[12] *S.H.C.* iv (2), 106.
[13] *Feud. Aids*, v. 16.
[14] *Cal. Inq. p.m.* vi, no. 168; *S.H.C.* 1911, 341–2.
[15] *Cal. Inq. p.m.* vi, no. 168.
[16] Ibid. viii, no. 507.
[17] Ibid.
[18] Ibid. x, no. 633.
[19] *S.H.C.* xi. 207–8; *Cal. Close* 1399–1402; C 137/31.
[20] *Cal. Close*, 1360–4, 68; *S.H.C.* xi. 190; ibid. xiv (1), 139–40; ibid. xiii. 149, 171–2; ibid. xi. 205–6, 207–8; C 138/32; C 138/39; C 139/153; *Cal. Inq. p.m.* Hen. VII, iii, no. 76; *V.C.H. Staffs.* iv. 81.
[21] *S.H.C.* xii (1), 185–6.
[22] Ibid. N.S. ix. 19–20.
[23] Ibid.
[24] Ibid. xvii. 220.

followed by Thomas Aston.[25] Sir Thomas Aston made a settlement of the manor in 1604.[26] By 1674 the manor had been divided into seven parts, four of which were held by Humphrey Giffard and his wife Dorothy, daughter of Thomas Fletcher of Water Eaton,[27] and two by John Stubbs, husband of Humphrey's daughter and coheir Jane.[28] Humphrey was living here in 1680.[29] A Richard Aston was dealing by fine with one-seventh of the manor in 1755,[30] and in 1781 Jonas Slaney and Mary conveyed a quarter of two-sevenths to Benjamin Crutchley and Henry Whateley.[31] In 1782 Martha Stubbs, presumably a descendant of John Stubbs of Water Eaton and Jane, conveyed another quarter of two-sevenths to Benjamin Crutchley,[32] while James Rann and Elizabeth conveyed a similar portion to Joshua Ledsam and John Moore, also in 1782.[33] James Rann, Martha Stubbs, spinster, and Thomas Devey Wightwick were described as lords of the manor in 1784.[34] Benjamin Crutchley and Jane conveyed a half of one-seventh of the manor and Calf Heath in 1788 to Edward Monckton,[35] and in the same year Thomas Devey Wightwick and Lucy conveyed to Joshua Ledsam a quarter of five-sevenths of the manor.[36] In 1790 Margaret and Mary Aston were dealing by fine with what was called the manor,[37] but the Hon. Edward Monckton was described as lord of the manor from 1786 to 1793.[38] Joseph Brearley also was named as lord between 1791 and 1793.[39] In 1820 William Brierley, or Brearley, and his wife Mary, with Louisa, Mary, Jane, and Emma Brierley, suffered a recovery of five-sevenths of the manor.[40] In 1821 William Aston and Mary conveyed to Edward Monckton such rights as they had in the manor.[41] William Brierley of Edgbaston (Warws.) was described as lord of the manor in 1834 and with Edward Monckton of Somerford owned most of the land.[42] Brierley was dead by 1838, and his land in Water Eaton was then bought by Edward Monckton.[43]

In 1552 Bridget Aston leased the lordship of the manor for 21 years to Thomas Litler who leased 2 messuages here to Sir Edward Littleton.[44] On Sir Edward's death in 1558 his son and executor Edward refused to pay the 2 heriots then claimed by John Aston as son and heir of Bridget.[45]

To the west of the group of buildings at Water Eaton are traces of a moat. The farmhouse and Vernon Cottage date from the earlier 18th century, but a timbered barn of four bays is probably of the 17th century.

WHISTON, granted by Wulfric Spot to Burton Abbey by 1004,[46] was assessed at one hide in 1086[47] and 1114 or 1115[48] and was valued in 1086 at 4s.[49] At some time not later than 1143 King Stephen confirmed the Abbot of Burton's rights in Whiston.[50] The overlordship remained with Burton Abbey until the Dissolution[51] when it passed to the king, who in 1546 sold it to Sir William Paget.[52] It then descended in the Paget family until at least 1769.[53]

In 1086 a certain Nauuen was holding the hide in Whiston of the abbey.[54] At some time between 1100 and 1113, as 'Navenus', he was paying a rent of 10s. for it[55] and again in 1114 or 1115 as 'Nablus'.[56] Alexander de Bickford and his wife Hawise were suing Henry de Bardmerscote (or Bermundeston) and his wife Ismannia in 1251 for land in Whiston,[57] and in 1255 Alexander and Hawise surrendered all claim to 3½ virgates and 30 acres here to Robert de Whiston.[58] In this year Robert was paying the Abbot of Burton 10s. rent for Whiston and Bickford, which were jointly assessed at 1½ hide, not geldable, and contributed 18d. to the sheriff's aid, 18d. to the view of frankpledge, and 6d. to the hundred.[59] A Robert de Whiston occurs in 1285[60] and was still alive in 1291.[61] He was dead by 1293[62] and his heir seems to have been another Robert, who occurs in 1300.[63] In 1313 a Robert de Whiston settled the reversion of the manor of Whiston after his death on John de Whiston the younger,[64] probably his son,[65] but was still lord in 1316.[66] John seems to have succeeded in 1323 or 1324[67] but was dead by 1333 when his widow Rose and her second husband Adam de Shareshill sued John's young son John for land in Whiston as Rose's dower.[68] This they recovered in 1334 against John[69] but not against William le Franklin of Whiston, Alice his wife and John his son, who claimed to be occupying the land by grant of John de Whiston the elder.[70] The younger John de Whiston served as a knight at Creçy in 1346 and Calais in 1347,[71] and in 1358 his messuage and lands in Whiston were valued at 10s. a year.[72] Sir John was dead by July 1359,[73] leaving a son and heir Nicholas

[25] C 142/310, no. 55; S.H.C. xvi. 175.
[26] S.H.C. xviii (1), 38.
[27] C.P. 25(2)/725, 26 Chas. II Trin.
[28] Ibid.; C.P. 43/366, rot. 41; S.H.C. N.S. v. 174, 200.
[29] S.H.C. 1919, 219.
[30] C.P. 34/193 (pt. 2), p. 140.
[31] C.P. 25(2)/1413, 21 Geo. III Mich.
[32] C.P. 25(2)/1413, 22 Geo. III Trin.   [33] Ibid.
[34] S.R.O., Gamekprs.' Deps.
[35] C.P. 25(2)/1413, 28 Geo. III Hil.
[36] C.P. 25(2)/1413, 29 Geo. III Mich.
[37] C.P. 25(2)/1413, 31 Geo. III Mich.
[38] S.R.O., Gamekprs.' Deps.
[39] Ibid.
[40] C.P. 43/947, rot. 156.
[41] C.P. 25(2)/1519, 1 and 2 Geo. IV Hil.
[42] White, Dir. Staffs. (1834).
[43] W.S.L., D. 1813, bdles. 45, 46.
[44] S.H.C. N.S. ix. 19–20.
[45] Ibid.; C 142/124, no. 178.
[46] S.H.C. 1916, 4, 117.
[47] V.C.H. Staffs. iv. 44, no. 96.
[48] S.H.C. v (1), 28.
[49] V.C.H., Staffs. iv. 44, no. 96.
[50] S.H.C. v (1), 11–12.
[51] Rot. Hund. (Rec. Com.), ii. 114; Feud. Aids, v. 1; S.H.C. xiv. 140–1.

[52] S.H.C. 1937, 187–9; L. & P. Hen. VIII, xxi (1), 76–77.
[53] C 142/110, no. 143; C 142/127, no. 45; C 142/500, no. 41; Complete Peerage, x. 276–84; W.S.L., Paget Papers (Gardner Coll.), 35 (1, 9).
[54] V.C.H. Staffs. iv. 44, no. 96.
[55] S.H.C. v (1), 22.
[56] Ibid. 28.
[57] Ibid. iv (1), 123, 128.
[58] Ibid. 246–7.
[59] Rot. Hund. (Rec. Com.), ii. 114. The Christian name Robert seems to have been used in four successive generations of the Whiston family: S.H.C. 1928, 160.
[60] Feud. Aids, v. 1.
[61] S.H.C. 1928, 160.
[62] Ibid. vi (1), 238.
[63] Ibid. v (1), 178.
[64] Ibid. 1911, 82–83.
[65] W.S.L., S. MS. 350A/40, f. 10a.
[66] Feud. Aids, v. 17.
[67] W.S.L., S. MS. 350A/40, f. 8a.
[68] S.H.C. xi. 47.
[69] Ibid. 50.
[70] Ibid. 46, 54.
[71] Ibid. N.S. ii. 53.
[72] S.H.C. xiii. 33.
[73] W.S.L., S. MS. 350A/40, f. 8a.

who was dead by 1362.[74] Sir John's widow Elizabeth, a daughter of Sir John de Weston of Weston under Lizard, married, as her second husband, Adam de Peshale.[75] Nicholas's heir was Agnes, sister of Sir John de Whiston and wife of Edmund Giffard of Chillington in Brewood,[76] and from 1366 until at least 1376 Edmund and Adam de Peshale were disputing possession of the manor, the Abbot of Burton intervening as overlord.[77] It appears that Edmund and Agnes conceded a life interest in the manor to Adam,[78] who c. 1376 demised it for a term of years to a Walter Pryde, clerk.[79] On Edmund Giffard's death in 1377[80] his son John Giffard disseised Walter Pryde[81] and was still disputing Adam's claim to the manor in 1379.[82] Whiston does not appear among the lands held by Sir Adam de Peshale at his death in 1419.[83] Robert Giffard, grandson of John,[84] made a settlement of the manor in 1472,[85] from which date it descended with Chillington in Brewood[86] until at least 1861, the estate being sold at some time between then and 1877 by W. P. Giffard.[87]

The annual value of the manor in 1370 was £7 16s. 8d. comprising £4 13s. 4d. from the demesne lands, 6s. 8d. from the three fish ponds, 30s. from assised rents, and 30s. from a water-mill.[88] The manor was valued with Bickford at £10 in 1557[89] and at £10 4s. 4d. in 1560 and 1633.[90] The bounds of the manor were given at a survey made in 1725.[91]

Whiston Hall was held c. 1644 by Richard Adams and William Bayley, tenants apparently of Peter, John, and Francis Giffard.[92] In 1666 a John Dudley was answering for the tax on 5 hearths there.[93] The Hall was owned by Thomas William Giffard c. 1841 and occupied along with 259 acres by John Draycott.[94] Whiston Hall is square in plan and of three distinct periods. A timber-framed wing of two stories with a large central stack forms the north side and dates from the late 16th century. Attic rooms, divided by queen-post trusses, are part of the original structure. There is a contemporary window, now blocked, in the north wall. To the south is a late-17th-century brick range with a central doorway on the west front and some original lead-glazed windows of the mullioned and transomed type. This range has a contemporary chimney and a staircase

with turned balusters. Completing the square plan to the east is a 19th-century addition.

LESSER ESTATES. Lands in Penkridge called 'le Heyhouse' were part of the possessions of Penkridge College at the time of the Dissolution in 1547 and had been assigned for the support of the two resident canons, being leased to Edward Harte at a rent of 2s.[95] By 1585 the messuage called the Hay House with lands in Penkridge, Levedale, and Dunston had passed to Roger Fowke of Brewood as son and heir of William Fowke and in that year was sold by him to Edward Littleton for £280.[96] Edward was holding it at his death in 1610 when it was described as the farm of 'Heyhouse juxta Longridge'.[97] It descended in the Littleton family with Pillaton[98] until its sale in 1919 to Mrs. E. Basset.[99] It was described as a house and farm in 1680[1] and c. 1841 was in the tenure of John Critchley the younger.[2] The tall redbrick farmhouse was reconstructed early in the 19th century, but the stone plinth indicates that an earlier house of approximately the same size stood on the site. In 1956 a rectangular moat extending round three sides of the house was filled in. A small cottage about 200 yds. farther east is partly timber-framed.

In 1086 nine clerks held a hide in Penkridge of the king.[3] The subsequent descent of this land is obscure, unless it may be assumed to have formed the endowment of the prebend of Penkridge in Penkridge College.[4]

This prebend was held by Roger 'the archdeacon' (probably Roger Archdeacon of Shropshire c. 1121–80) and was in the king's hands from at least 1183 until 1189.[5] It is probably to be identified with the prebend of La More, held at some time during the 12th century by William, son of Edwin a priest of Wolverhampton, and at William's instance subsequently conferred by the Dean and Chapter of Penkridge on his son Hugh.[6] Elias de Bristol, Dean of Penkridge from 1199 to c. 1226, appointed as next prebendary Robert de Caverswall,[7] who in 1227 sued Adam son of Maud for 5½ acres and a messuage in Penkridge as appurtenant to his prebend but was found to have alienated them to Maud's mother to be held as a lay fee at a rent of 6d.[8] In 1291 the prebend of Penkridge was valued at £4,[9] and it

[74] S.H.C. xiii. 20.   [75] Ibid.
[76] Ibid. xiii. 148.
[77] Ibid. 1937, 141; ibid. xiii. 79, 148; ibid. xiv. 140–1.
[78] Ibid. xiii. 148.
[79] Ibid. 203.
[80] Ibid. N.S. v. 105.
[81] Ibid. xiii. 203.
[82] Ibid. 148, 155, 157.
[83] Ibid. N.S. ii. 95; C 138/41.
[84] S.H.C. N.S. v. 105–9.
[85] S.H.C. xi. 240.
[86] C 142/110, no. 143; C 142/127, no. 45; C 142/337, no. 113; C 142/500, no. 41; W.S.L. 159/33; C.P. 43/812, rot. 417; C.P. 43/962, rot. 386; Tithe Maps and Appt., Penkridge (copy in W.S.L.); White, Dir. Staffs. (1851); Whiston and Bickford Ct. Papers (1611–1725) among Giffard Papers at Chillington, Brewood; Whiston Estate Map (18th cent.) in the Chillington Estate Office.
[87] Ex inf. Mr. T. A. W. Giffard (1956); Burke, Land. Gent. (1952), 975. W. P. Giffard sold his estate at High Onn in Church Eaton in 1863: V.C.H. Staffs. iv. 94.
[88] S.H.C. xiii. 79.
[89] C 142/110, no. 143.
[90] C 142/127, no. 45; C 142/500, no. 41.
[91] Whiston Ct. Papers among Giffard Papers at Chillington, Brewood.
[92] S.R.O., D. 260/M/box 25, bdle. k, list of Royalists'

Estates, ff. 34b, 46b–47a. A 'Mr Gyfforde' apparently living at Whiston, contributed to the repair of Penkridge church in 1630: ibid., box 7, bdle. i, a copy of the Levy Book.
[93] S.H.C. 1927, 60. John Giffard, gentleman, was living at Whiston in 1680, presumably at the Hall: ibid. 1919, 219.
[94] Tithe Maps and Appt., Penkridge (copy in W.S.L.).
[95] S.H.C. 1950–1, 41.
[96] Ibid. 1928, 149; ibid. xv. 165.
[97] C 142/320, no. 71.
[98] C.P. 25(2)/484, 1 Chas. I Hil.; C.P. 25(2)/486, 18 Chas. I Mich.; C.P. 25(2)/596, 1654 Trin.; C.P. 25(2)/725, 28 Chas. II; C.P. 43/506, rot. 98; Tithe Maps and Appt., Penkridge (copy in W.S.L.); see p. 119.
[99] Ex inf. the Teddesley and Hatherton Estate Office, Penkridge.
[1] S.H.C. 1919, 219.
[2] Tithe Maps and Appt., Penkridge (copy in W.S.L.).
[3] V.C.H. Staffs. iv. 45, no. 115.
[4] S.H.C. 1950–1, 19.
[5] Ibid. i. 109, 140; Le Neve, Fasti, i. 573.
[6] S.H.C. 1950–1, 49.
[7] Ibid. 49–50. Robert was the son of a priest: ibid. vi(1), 31.
[8] Ibid. iv (1), 49–50.
[9] Tax. Eccl. (Rec. Com.), 242.

was still so named in 1365 when Robert de Sulgrave, a pluralist, was holding it.[10] In 1535, the prebend was valued at £9 6s. 8d., having a manse with lands worth 20s., assised rents of 13s. 4d. a year, great and small tithes averaging £5 10s., Easter offerings averaging 30s. and oblations averaging 20s.[11] Synodals of 6s. 8d. were due to the Dean of Penkridge every third year.[12] The prebend was leased to Sir Edward Littleton for 21 years in 1547,[13] and in 1548 he paid the royal bailiff of the dissolved college £9 6s. 8d. rent for it.[14] The prebend then presumably descended with the rest of the collegiate property,[15] and in 1585 it was granted to Edward, grandson of Sir Edward Littleton[16] and holder of a 21-year lease of the prebend since 1577 or 1578.[17] The prebend then descended in the Littleton family with Pillaton[18] until at least 1709.[19] The estate in Penkridge sold by the 5th Lord Hatherton in 1953[20] may have included former prebendal land.

The prebend of Longridge in Penkridge college was valued at £2 in 1291.[21] In 1535 the prebend consisted of tithe of grain worth 16s. and was the only prebend in the church of Penkridge that did not owe synodals to the dean.[22] It seems to have been leased about this time to a William Cresswell.[23] From 1540 the lease was granted by terms of three years to Edward Avery[24] who in 1548 was paying a rent of £2 4s. 3d. to the royal bailiff of the dissolved college.[25] The prebend then presumably descended with the rest of the collegiate property,[26] and in 1585 it passed to Edward Littleton[27] to whom the Crown had already granted a 21-year lease in 1577 or 1578.[28] The prebend remained in the Littleton family[29] until at least 1709,[30] and part of the estate in Longridge owned by the 1st Lord Hatherton c. 1841[31] and sold by his grandson in 1919[32] may have been former prebendal land.

Wolgarston (Tuhgarestone) was assessed in 1086 at one hide[33] and remained a distinct member of Penkridge manor until at least 1372.[34] It seems to have been completely merged into the manor by at least 1523 when Beatrice Hussey was holding lands and tenements, described as in Penkridge and Wolgarston, of the lord of Penkridge.[35] Her son and heir William Hussey of Coleshill (Warws.) made a settlement in 1531 of such lands and tenements in Penkridge and Wolgarston as he held of the manor of Penkridge,[36] and on his death in 1532 he held, besides Hussey's Hall, two estates in Penkridge.[37]

One of these, described as in Wolgarston, consisted of a messuage, land, and a water-mill with a pond and a croft, all worth 40s. and in the tenure or occupation of Edward Littleton; the other, described as in Penkridge and Wolgarston and valued at 30s., consisted of 2 messuages, a water-mill, five cottages, and land.[38] William's heirs were his four daughters, Alice, of age and then wife of Robert Boteler, and Anna, Dorothy, and Winifred Hussey, all under age.[39] In 1544 the three younger daughters, with their respective husbands, conveyed to Edward Littleton their three portions of two messuages, five cottages, half a water-mill and land in Penkridge, Wolgarston, and elsewhere in the parish.[40] At the same time they conveyed to him the reversion of their three parts of the one messuage, with its appurtenances, which their mother Beatrice was holding for her life.[41] When Edward Littleton died in 1558 his estates included twelve messuages, six cottages, a water-mill, land, wood, and heath in Penkridge and Wolgarston, held of the manor of Penkridge and valued at £11 2s. 3d.[42] When his grandson Sir Edward died in 1610 he was holding a messuage and a water-mill in Wolgarston.[43] By c. 1841 the main farm buildings, with the land attached, were occupied by William Taylor as tenant of Lord Hatherton who owned all the land in Wolgarston.[44] The 'stock and grain farm known as Wolgarston', some 325 acres in extent, was sold to the tenant by the 5th Lord Hatherton in 1947.[45] The farmhouse is a tall square brick building, partly cement rendered, dating from the late 18th or early 19th century.

Three virgates of land in Penkridge were claimed in 1199 by William de Mora as heir of his father Robert.[46] Henry, son of a John de la More, occurs in 1381[47] and by 1405 had been succeeded by a son John.[48] This John's widow Anne died in 1435 holding a messuage in Penkridge of the king and was succeeded by her son Thomas More.[49] Thomas died in 1480 leaving two daughters, Eleanor, wife of Thomas Forster, and Beatrice, wife of William Hussey,[50] and in 1486 or 1487 Thomas's last surviving trustee conveyed a messuage in Penkridge and lands in Wolverhampton and Chillington (in Brewood) to Thomas Forster and Eleanor and a messuage and lands in Penkridge to William Hussey and Beatrice.[51] The descent of the share of Thomas Forster and Eleanor is obscure, but in 1522 Beatrice, by then a widow, died in possession of a messuage in

[10] S.H.C. 1950–1, 24.
[11] Valor Eccl. (Rec. Com.), iii. 106; S.H.C. 1915, 209.
[12] Valor Eccl. (Rec. Com.), iii. 106.
[13] S.H.C. 1950–1, 36 n. 98.
[14] Ibid. 36.
[15] See p. 111.
[16] S.H.C. xv. 167.
[17] C 66/1173, m. 24.
[18] C.P. 25(2)/484, 1 Chas. I Hil.; C 142/456, no. 76; C.P. 25(2)/486, 18 Chas. I Mich.; C.P. 25(2)/596, 1654 Trin.; C.P. 25(2)/725, 28 Chas. II Mich.; see p. 119.
[19] C.P. 43/506, rot. 98.
[20] Ex inf. the Teddesley and Hatherton Estate Office, Penkridge.
[21] Tax. Eccl. (Rec. Com.), 242.
[22] Valor Eccl. (Rec. Com.), iii. 106.
[23] Req. 2/4/284.
[24] S.H.C. 1950–1, 36 n. 98.
[25] Ibid. 37.
[26] See p. 111.
[27] S.H.C. xv. 167.
[28] C 66/1173, m. 24.
[29] C 142/456, no. 76; C.P. 25(2)/596, 1654 Trin.; C.P. 25(2)/725, 28 Chas. II Mich.; see p. 119.

[30] C.P. 43/506, rot. 98.
[31] Tithe Maps and Appt., Penkridge (copy in W.S.L.).
[32] Ex inf. the Teddesley and Hatherton Estate Office, Penkridge.
[33] V.C.H. Staffs. iv. 38, no. 8.
[34] S.H.C. i. 48, 50; Rot. Chart. (Rec. Com.), 218; S.H.C. v (1), 177; Cal. Chart. R. 1341–1417, 222–3.
[35] C 142/40, no. 120.
[36] Ibid.; S.H.C. 1928, 148–9.
[37] C 142/54, no. 51.
[38] Ibid.   [39] Ibid.
[40] S.H.C. xi. 286–7.
[41] Ibid.
[42] C 142/124, no. 178.
[43] C 142/320, no. 71.
[44] Tithe Maps and Appt., Penkridge (copy in W.S.L.).
[45] W.S.L., Sale Cat. B/2/10, 93–94; ex inf. the Teddesley and Hatherton Estate Office, Penkridge.
[46] S.H.C. iii (1), 57–58.
[47] Ibid. xvii. 183; ibid. xv. 117.
[48] Ibid. xv. 117.
[49] C 139/73; S.H.C. 1928, 147–8; ibid. n.s. iv. 193, 198.
[50] C 140/76; S.H.C. n.s. vii. 277–8.
[51] W.S.L., S. MS. 350A/40, f. 83a.

Penkridge called Hussey's Hall which was held of the king and worth 30s. a year.[52] Her son William died in 1532, leaving four daughters,[53] the three youngest of whom apparently granted their shares of Hussey's Hall to Edward Littleton of Pillaton in 1544.[54] When Edward died in 1558 he was holding this messuage with the lands and appurtenances, valued at 20s., of the queen by service of $\frac{1}{100}$ knight's fee.[55] The messuage then descended with Pillaton until at least 1610.[56]

Land at Bitham, formerly held by Thomas Lynell, was being claimed with land at Lyne Hill by his son William at some time between 1551 and 1553.[57] In 1583 a Richard Mylles made a settlement of land there[58] which he was holding when he died at some time between 1591 and 1607.[59] 'Bythom' was described as a hamlet within the manor of Penkridge in 1598,[60] and in 1680 there was said to be a farmhouse at Bitham occupied by a Mr. Thorley, a freeholder.[61] Bitham then lay to the south-east of the town of Penkridge, a little to the north of Otherton,[62] and c. 1841 the name survived in three fields, called Near, Mid, and Far Bitham.[63]

AGRICULTURE. The common fields within the manor of Penkridge between 1548 and 1598 seem to have been Clay Field, Prince Field, 'Manstonshill', Mill Field, Wood Field, and 'Lowtherne' Field,[64] all of which are still found in 1654 with 'Lantern' presumably as an alternative form of 'Lowtherne' and with the addition of 'Fyland', Old Field, and 'Whotcroft'.[65] All had been inclosed by 1754.[66] Stretton Meadow and Hay Meadow seem still to have been held in common in 1548[67] and 'Overwoolgaston', 'Netherwoolgaston', and Stretton Meadows in 1654.[68] What was called Hay Meadow in 1754 lay on the right bank of the Penk, between Cuttlestone and Bull bridges, with Holmford Meadow across the river, below Bull Bridge.[69] In 1718 an agreement was secured by the inhabitants of the neighbouring townships of Acton Trussell, Bednall, and Huntington that the tenants of Penkridge, Wolgarston, Drayton, and Lynehill should plough and sow only that part of Teddesley Hay called Penkridge Field.[70]

By 1543 inclosure of fields was taking place within the deanery manor of Penkridge, when two fields or closes in Penkridge called 'Heyfelde' and 'Kylnfeld' occur.[71] Open fields still existed at this date, there being mention of Longfurlong and 'Cleyfeld super Heyfurlong'.[72] Clay Field and Hogstones Field may have been common fields in 1654,[73] but these had been inclosed by 1754.[74] An inclosed meadow called 'More Orciarde' is mentioned in 1543,[75] but in 1654 there were still common meadows within the deanery manor[76] which had, however, been inclosed by 1754.[77]

'The field of Preston' was mentioned in 1261,[78] and Preston Field seems to have been a common field in 1558, probably within either Penkridge manor or Penkridge deanery manor.[79]

There seem still to have been common fields in Drayton in 1587,[80] but they had been inclosed by 1779.[81]

An agreement was made in 1662 between the lords of Gailey Hay and the freeholders and commoners there for the cultivation of the common of Gailey Hay for 5 years.[82] The commoners were to pay a seventh part of the corn grown to the lords, who were to erect and maintain a fence round the common while it was under cultivation.[83]

'Wollefordelfeld' seems to have been a common field in Levedale in 1294.[84] Clay Field occurs in 1548,[85] and by 1654 there were at least three common fields in the manor, namely 'Helsmatch', 'Priest Moore', and 'Clayless' fields,[86] all of which had been inclosed by 1754.[87]

Tenants of the lord of Otherton had been making assarts within the bounds of Cannock Forest before 1286.[88] The common fields of Otherton, including 'Waterbrooke' Field, Middle Field, and Yondermore (otherwise Rendermore) Field, were inclosed in 1617 by agreement between the owners and occupiers.[89]

Tenants of the lord of Pillaton also had been making assarts within the bounds of Cannock Forest before 1286.[90] A field in Pillaton called 'Crofthull' which is mentioned at some time between 1342 and 1349 seems to have been a common field,[91] but by 1754 there were no common fields in Pillaton.[92]

Low Field within the manor of Rodbaston was a common field in 1554.[93] It was recorded in 1674 that two common fields, 'Overhighfield' and 'Netherfield', in which part of Rodbaston lay, had been inclosed beyond living memory, at which time the first had been divided into 'Aspeheathe', Highfield, and Hamptonway, and the second into Overgallows, Nethergallows, Crane Pit Leasow (otherwise Campe Pit or Oxe Leasow), Hambreeth or Hembreeth, and Ballbyrch.[94]

[52] C 142/40, no. 120; S.H.C. 1928, 148–9.
[53] C 142/54, no. 51.
[54] S.H.C. xi. 286–7; L. & P. Hen. VIII, xvi, p. 404.
[55] C 142/124, no. 178.
[56] C 142/172, no. 119; C 142/320, no. 71; see p. 119.
[57] C 1/1307, nos. 62–64.
[58] S.H.C. xv. 150.
[59] C 142/299, no. 127.
[60] S.R.O., D. 260/M/box 16, bdle. a.
[61] S.H.C. 1919, 219.
[62] Plot, Map of Staffs. (1682).
[63] Tithe Maps and Appt., Penkridge (copy in W.S.L.).
[64] S.H.C. 1915, 40, 42; S.R.O., D. 260/M/box 7, bdle. c; ibid. box 16, bdle. a.
[65] S.R.O., D. 260/M/box 3, bdle. e, deed of 1653/4.
[66] Ibid. 353 (a, b), maps 4, 5.
[67] S.H.C. 1950–1, 42.
[68] S.R.O., D. 260/M/box 3, bdle. e, deed of 1653/4.
[69] Ibid. E. 353 (a, b), maps 5, 7.
[70] W.S.L., D. 1790. Penkridge Field lay in the south-west corner of Teddesley Hay: S.R.O., D. 260/M/E. 353 (a, b), map 10.
[71] S.R.O., D. 260/M/E. 315/68, p. 386.
[72] Ibid.
[73] Ibid. box 3, bdle e, a deed of 1653/4.
[74] Ibid. E. 363 (a, b), map 5.
[75] Ibid. E. 315/68, p. 386.
[76] Ibid. box 3, bdle. e, a deed of 1653/4.
[77] Ibid. E. 363 (a, b), map 5.
[78] S.H.C. 1950–1, 48.
[79] S.R.O., D. 260/M/box 7, bdle. c.
[80] Ibid. box 4, bdle. d.
[81] Ibid. E. 353 (a), map 17.
[82] Ibid. box 9, bdle. g.   [83] Ibid.
[84] Ibid., box 8 bdle. d. What seem to have been holdings in common fields were conveyed c. 1215 by Geoffrey son of John de Levedale to William son of Stephen de Levedale: Hist. MSS. Com. Middleton, 57.
[85] S.H.C. 1950–1, 42.
[86] S.R.O., D. 260/M/box 3, bdle. e, deed of 1653/4.
[87] Ibid. E. 353 (a, b), map 9.
[88] S.H.C. v (1), 171.
[89] Ibid. 1931, 244–5.
[90] Ibid. v (1), 170.
[91] Ibid. 1928, 153.
[92] S.R.O., D. 260/M/E. 353 (a), map 3.
[93] B.M. Eg. MS. 3008, f. 46a.
[94] E 134, East. 26 Chas. II, no. 5.

Congreve Field within the manor of Water Eaton seems to have been a common field in 1589.[95]

Tenants and inhabitants of the township of Penkridge, of the hamlets of Wolgarston, Preston, Bitham, Lyne Hill, and Moor Hall within Penkridge manor and of the manor of Drayton had common rights for all cattle in Teddesley Hay, with 'stray common' thence into 'Cannock Wood'.[96] They also had common on Penkridge Heath adjoining Dunston and Drayton, with 'stray common' thence into the common fields of Dunston and Drayton, sharing these rights on intercommoning with the tenants of Dunston.[97] They had further common rights on The Marsh, Quarry Heath, Broad Moor, 'Williford', Bowes Moor, Hazel Mill Green, Wood Brook, Little Home, and 'Lomfordes' Brook.[98] All these rights were shared by the tenants of the deanery manor also.[99] The tenants of Congreve had common in their own fields and on the part of Whiston Common that lay within Penkridge manor; the tenants of Whiston had common on their side of Whiston Common and in their own fields.[1]

In 1775 the 600 or so acres of common or waste land known as Gailey Common, lying on the north side of the Watling Street to the south-east of Rodbaston within the manor or lordship of Gailey, were inclosed under an Act of 1773.[2] One-seventh of the common was assigned to the owners of the manorial rights.[3] The remaining six sevenths were divided proportionately among the landowners of the townships of Hatherton (in St. Peter's, Wolverhampton), Otherton, Rodbaston, Water Eaton, and Kinvaston (in St. Peter's, Wolverhampton), who were entitled to common in Gailey, and, so divided, these six sevenths became part and parcel of the particular township and parish to which they were assigned.[4]

Some 626 acres of common land and waste within the manor of Water Eaton and situated on Calf Heath were inclosed in 1813 under an Act of 1799 and passed mainly to Edward Monckton.[5]

Penkridge Heath, lying to the east of Longridge within Penkridge manor and the deanery manor, Hay meadow and other common land within Penkridge manor, common land within the deanery manor, Lyne Hill Green, common land in Otherton and Pillaton and common land in Drayton were inclosed in 1827 under an Act of 1814.[6] In Drayton certain lanes were stopped up at this date and allotted as small plots of land.[7]

When the manor of Penkridge passed back into the king's hands in 1172 it was restocked with sixteen oxen and a cow (50s. 8d.), sixteen pigs (12s. 6d.),

oats seed (16s.), and a draught animal (3s.).[8] In 1801 the ancient parish (excluding Coppenhall) contained 2,481 acres, 1,173 sown with wheat, 395 with barley, 375 with oats, 10 with potatoes, 100 with peas, 320 with beans, and 108 with turnips or rape.[9] The present parish, still agricultural, continues to grow grains, roots, and pulses and also has some sheep farms.[10] Some dairy and stock-farming is also carried on in the parish.[11]

By 1860 Rodbaston Hall farm, then the property of Thomas Shaw Hellier, was devoted to dairy-farming and stock-farming and steam machinery was being used while the outbuildings and labourers' cottages were 'replete with conveniences rarely met with'.[12] In 1871 it was described as a model farm.[13] In 1919 Rodbaston Hall, the Hall Farm, and the Grange were bought by the County Council which in 1921 opened the Staffordshire Farm Institute there; there were 30 students in 1940.[14] The farm then covered 315 acres, one-third of which was arable land.[15]

In 1919 the County Council acquired 242 acres of the Stables farm and the Old farm, Rodbaston, and established 13 smallholdings there, adapting the 2 existing houses and building 11 new ones.[16] In 1933 it established 5 smallholdings each with its own house on 160 acres in Levedale adding a further 28 acres in 1935.[17] These are spaced out along the roads from Penkridge to Levedale and Coppenhall. A further 4 smallholdings were established on the 14 acres of Preston Barns in 1935, using the existing house and building 3 new ones, and in 1937 9 new homesteads and 3 cottage holdings were set up on the 351 acres of the Deanery farm, the farmhouse being demolished.[18]

MILLS. In 1086 there was a mill attached to Penkridge manor valued at 5s.[19] Two mills here were repaired in 1172 at a cost of 20s.,[20] and 'broc' mill, apparently within the manor, was mentioned at some time between about 1225 and 1259.[21] By 1598 three water-mills called Penkridge Mills had been leased by the lord of the manor to a James Southall.[22] Robert Lord Brooke granted the mill of Penkridge in 1626 or 1627, as part of her jointure, to Lady Katherine Russell who married Robert, his cousin and heir, and this latter Robert was holding the mill at his death in 1643.[23] His son Francis was suing a Richard Tomlinson and his wife Ellen for suit and service belonging to the ancient mills of the manor in 1658,[24] and Francis's brother and heir held two mills in Penkridge in 1662.[25] By 1754 there was a

[95] S.H.C. 1929, 347.
[96] S.R.O., D. 260/M/box 16, bdle. a, Ct. Bk. 1598–1654, f. 17a.
[97] Ibid., ff. 17a–18a.
[98] Ibid., f. 18a.
[99] Ibid.
[1] Ibid.
[2] 'Act for dividing and inclosing . . . Gailey Common', 13 Geo. III, c. 100 (priv. act); C.P. 43/767, rot. 272–84; M.P.L. 66; Yates, Map of Staffs. (1799).
[3] Gailey Inclosure Act, 13 Geo. III, c. 100 (priv. act).
[4] Ibid.
[5] 'Act for dividing and inclosing the commons and waste lands within the manor of Water Eaton', 39 Geo. III, c. 73 (priv. act); S.R.O. Q/RDc 56; Tithe Maps and Appt., Penkridge (copy in W.S.L.).
[6] S.R.O., Q/RDc 22.
[7] Ibid.
[8] S.H.C. i. 65, 66.
[9] S.H.C. 1950–1, table facing p. 242.

[10] Official Guide to Penkridge (1949), 3, 6.
[11] Personal inf.
[12] P.O. Dir. Staffs. (1860); W.S.L., Sale Catalogue E/2/7.
[13] W.S.L., Sale Catalogue E/2/7.
[14] Staffs. Advertiser, 15 Oct. 1921; Kelly's Dir. Staffs. (1940); ex inf. Staffs. C.C. Estate Agent.
[15] Kelly's Dir. Staffs. (1940).
[16] Ex inf. Staffs. C.C. Estate Agent.
[17] Ex inf. County Estate Agent.
[18] Ex inf. County Estate Agent.
[19] V.C.H. Staffs. iv. 38, no. 8.
[20] S.H.C. i. 65.
[21] S.R.O., D. 260/M/box 3, bdle. i.
[22] Ibid., box 16, bdle. a, Penkridge Ct. Bk. 1598–1654, f. 19a.
[23] C 142/501, no. 63; Complete Peerage, ii. 332–3.
[24] E 134, East. 1658, no. 10; Complete Peerage, ii. 334.
[25] C.P. 43/223, rot. 119.

mill to the east of Bull Bridge on the site of the present mill.[26] Estimates for rebuilding Penkridge Mill were submitted in 1764.[27] It was in use as a rolling-mill between at least 1827 and 1832[28] but seems to have been a corn-mill from at least 1834.[29] It was sold by the 4th Lord Hatherton in 1938,[30] the owner in 1956 being Mr. Bottomley. Penkridge Mill is a three-story brick building of the late 18th century. The undershot wheel was removed in 1939, and the mill pool was filled in during the Second World War with waste soil from the army camp in The Marsh. By 1956 electrical plant had replaced the older gear.[31] The Mill House, about 100 yds. to the south, is a small double-fronted brick house dating from c. 1830. It has a trellis porch and ornamental glazing to the casement windows.

A mill in Penkridge, held by John de la More in 1293,[32] was granted with his other lands there to the Archbishop of Dublin in 1298.[33] In 1342 the archbishop granted to Thomas More of Penkridge a pond called 'Mooremille Poole' by 'Millehull' in the fee of Penkridge to hold of the dean and chapter of Penkridge for 1d. a year.[34]

Between at least 1775 and 1820 there was a windmill in Penkridge situated to the east of the road to Water Eaton shortly before it passes Cuttlestone Bridge.[35]

A mill in Congreve had passed by 1227 from Alditha de Congreve to John de Teveray,[36] and in 1236 Edith, one of Alditha's nieces, sued John and his wife Alice for a quarter of it.[37] One Richard 'ad molendinum de Congreve' occurs in 1260.[38] Congreve Mill was leased with the Hall by Thomas Congreve to his son Thomas at some time before 1620 and secured by Francis Congreve in 1622.[39] Richard Congreve held two water corn-mills in the manor in 1660.[40] South-west of Manor Farm farmyard a diversion of the river indicates a mill site. The building now occupying the site was at one time a blacksmith's shop.[41]

Hervey Bagot's grant of Drayton manor to St. Thomas's Priory in 1194 included the mill of Drayton, with suit of mill, maintenance of the mill pool, and haulage of the mill-stone.[42] The mill was worth £1 a year in 1291[43] and 40s. in 1535.[44] About 1643 the tenant was paying Walter Fowler £3 for the mill and 10s. for the mill-house,[45] but by 1754 the mill no longer existed.[46] A small brick bridge over the Penk at Lower Drayton, where there was formerly a ford

and a track leading to Teddesley, probably marks its site.[47] A partly timber-framed building nearby has exposed close studding and is of late-16th-century origin. This and the cottage adjoining it may have formed part of the mill-house.

There was a water-mill in Mitton in 1417 or 1418, part of which was then assigned as dower to Thomasine, widow of Richard Chetwynd.[48] The mill of Mitton occurs again c. 1489.[49] Depressions in the field north-west of Mitton Bridge suggest that this was the site of the former mill pool.

A mill in Pillaton is mentioned c. 1280.[50] Juliana, widow of Stephen de Elmedon, and her husband Reynold de Charnes were claiming a share in a water-mill here, apparently situated on the boundary between Pillaton and Huntington (in Cannock), in 1304 when a third part of it was held by Robert, son of Adam Acton, of William de Elmedon for a rent of 5s.[51] A mill in Pillaton was included in the grant made in 1310 by William son of William de Wrottesley to William de Elmedon,[52] who himself settled a mill called 'le Haselnemulne' with the manor of Pillaton on his son William and daughter-in-law Joan in 1342.[53] The 'Hasyll' Mill occurs in 1598, when there was also mention of 'Hasill' Mill Pool on the boundary between Penkridge and Teddesley Hay.[54] There has been no building in existence since at least 1754,[55] but the pool was in the hands of the lord of Pillaton c. 1841.[56] The site of Hazel Mill lies north of Quarry Heath about 200 yds. south-east of Bangley Park, and the position of the pool and causeway can still be seen.

A water-mill in Rodbaston, worth 40d. a year, was held by Richard de Loges in 1300.[57]

In 1086 there was a mill at Water Eaton valued at 3s.[58] The water-mill there in 1310 was worth 13s. 4d. a year,[59] and when Walter Beysin died in 1345 he was holding, in addition to the water-mill, a fulling-mill which was worth only 8s. because of its dilapidated state.[60]

There was a water-mill in Whiston in 1370 valued at 30s. a year.[61] In 1652 a mill situated on the Whiston Brook within the manor was held by Stephen Cotton at a rent of £1,[62] and a mill there, owned by T. W. Giffard c. 1841,[63] remained in operation until shortly before the Second World War.[64] The building, of red brick, is partly two and partly three stories in height and probably dates from the later 18th century.

[26] S.R.O., D. 260/M/E. 353 (a), map 5.
[27] W.S.L., Hand Morgan Coll., Littleton Papers.
[28] S.R.O., Q/RDc 22; Teesdale, Map of Staffs. (1832).
[29] White, Dir. Staffs. (1834; 1851).
[30] Ex inf. the Teddesley and Hatherton Estate Office, Penkridge.
[31] Ex inf. Mr. Bottomley, present owner (1956).
[32] S.H.C. vi (1), 246.
[33] Cal. Pat. 1292–1301, 336.
[34] S.H.C. 1928, 147.
[35] Yates, Map of Staffs. (1799), based on a survey made between 1769 and 1775; Greenwood, Map of Staffs. (1820).
[36] S.H.C. iv (1), 48.
[37] Ibid. 232–3.
[38] W.S.L., S. MS. 350A/40, f. 82a.
[39] W.S.L., S.D. Thorpe 397.
[40] S.R.O., D. 260/M/box 16, bdle. a.
[41] Local inf. For the forge here see p. 106.
[42] S.H.C. ii (1), 263.
[43] Tax. Eccl. (Rec. Com.), 253.
[44] Valor Eccl. (Rec. Com.), iii. 110.
[45] S.R.O., D. 260/M/box 25, bdle. k, list of Royalists' Estates 1643–5, ff. 36b–37a.

[46] S.R.O., D. 260/M/E. 353 (a), map 17.
[47] The mill was situated 'half a mile above Dunston' in 1533, when the lord of Drayton was paying rent to Lord Stafford for the water-course to it: W.S.L., Stafford Barony Mins. Accts. 1532–3, m. 11d.
[48] S.H.C. xii (1), 308–9.
[49] W.S.L., D. 1721/1/8, p. 229.
[50] S.H.C. 1931, 243.
[51] Ibid. vii (1), 121.
[52] Ibid. 1911, 74–75.
[53] Ibid. 1928, 151–2.
[54] S.R.O., D. 260/M/box 16, bdle. a, Penkridge Ct. Bk. 1598–1654, ff. 4a, 35a.
[55] S.R.O., D. 260/M/E. 353 (a, b), map 4; see p. 106.
[56] Tithe Maps and Appt., Penkridge (copy in W.S.L.).
[57] Cal. Inq. p.m. iii, no. 593; S.H.C. 1911, 262.
[58] V.C.H. Staffs. iv. 53, no. 213.
[59] Cal. Inq. p.m. v, no. 222; S.H.C. 1911, 302.
[60] Cal. Inq. p.m. viii, no. 507; S.H.C. 1913, 110.
[61] S.H.C. xiii. 79.
[62] Giffard Papers at Chillington Hall, Brewood, Survey of High Onn and Whiston 1652 (among Ct. Papers).
[63] Tithe Maps and Appt., Penkridge (copy in W.S.L.).
[64] Local inf.

There are remains of two large mill pools south-east of Wolgarston. Two water-mills were held by William Hussey in 1532, one of them, a walk or fulling-mill, being situated in Wolgarston and in the tenure of Edward Littleton, and the other being part of Hussey's estate in Penkridge and Wolgarston.[65] The tithes of Wolgarston mill were being farmed by Sir Edward Littleton in 1548 for 6d. a year,[66] and his estate in Penkridge and Wolgarston included a water-mill at his death in 1558.[67] His grandson was holding the mill when he died in 1610.[68] A John Boyden was holding a corn-mill in Wolgarston as tenant of Edward John Littleton in 1834,[69] and by 1851 the mill was held by Henry Wood of Wolgarston, farmer, bone crusher, and manure manufacturer.[70] It had become a grist mill again before its final disuse c. 1912.[71] It was sold with Wolgarston Farm in 1947 by Lord Hatherton[72] and by 1956 was derelict, most of the gear having been dismantled.[73] The mill, which is built against a stone dam surmounted by a causeway, is a long red-brick building on a stone base and is partly of two and partly of three stories. It appears to be of the 18th and 19th centuries, but some of the masonry may be older.

MARKETS AND FAIRS. A market every Thursday within the manor of Penkridge was granted to Andrew le Blund by the king in 1244.[74] The right was upheld by Andrew's son Hugh in 1293[75] and confirmed to John de Beverley in 1364.[76] In 1381 it was found that Robert Bardolf, husband of Amice the widow of John de Beverley, was holding a market in Penkridge as Hugh Blount had done before him, without the king's licence and to the injury of the burgesses of Stafford.[77] Amice died in 1416 seised of the market[78] which then descended with the manor until at least 1521,[79] both having been mortgaged to George Monoux in 1519.[80] By 1584 Penkridge was described as 'no market town',[81] but Sir Fulke Greville was granted a market there in 1617.[82] This was evidently held on Tuesday; it had been discon-

tinued by 1680[83] but had been resumed by 1747.[84] Market day was still Tuesday in 1817.[85] In 1834, however, this market was said to have been long obsolete although the spacious market-place was still in existence.[86] By 1868 a cattle-market was held on each alternate Monday[87] and by 1924 every Monday.[88] This stock market was still held in 1940,[89] and by 1955 a general market was held on Monday.

A fair in the vill of Penkridge was granted with the manor by Hugh Hose to the Archbishop of Dublin in 1215.[90] A fair on 28 and 29 September and the three days following was granted to Hugh le Blund by the king in 1278,[91] and in 1293 Hugh claimed the fair as annexed to the manor time out of mind.[92] The grant was confirmed to Hugh and his heirs in 1312[93] and to John de Beverley in 1364,[94] and the fair descended with the manor until at least 1617.[95] It was held from 26 September to 2 October by 1598,[96] and in 1617 the king granted that it should be held from 23 to 30 September.[97] By 1674 there was confusion over the starting date,[98] but by 1680 it was held from 23 to 29 September.[99] The date was fixed in 1756, apparently after further confusion, for the first Monday and Tuesday in September.[1]

Three additional fairs were granted to the lord of the manor in 1617,[2] and by 1680 these were held on May Day, Midsummer Day, and 28 October.[3] By 1817 there were only two fairs at Penkridge, held on 30 April and 10 October,[4] but by 1834 a fair on 2 September had been added.[5] All three were still held in 1912,[6] but had been discontinued by 1924.[7]

By 1522 horses were being dealt in at the fair.[8] By 1598 they were the sole merchandise,[9] and Penkridge was described about this time as 'a small village famous for a horse fair'.[10] The two fairs were stated in 1817 to be among the best in England for saddle and draught horses.[11] By 1834 all three fairs were devoted to cattle as well as horses.[12] The horse fairs seem to have been held in the area of The Marsh to the east of the town by 1754,[13] and the name Horse Fair still attaches to land there.

It was stated in 1598 that the court of pie powder

[65] C 142/54, no. 51.
[66] S.H.C. 1950–1, 43.
[67] C 142/124, no. 178.
[68] C 142/320, no. 71.
[69] White, Dir. Staffs. (1834); Tithe Maps and Appt., Penkridge (copy in W.S.L.).
[70] White, Dir. Staffs. (1851). Wood occurs as a farmer in Wolgarston in 1860: P.O. Dir. Staffs. (1860).
[71] Local inf.
[72] W.S.L., Sale Catalogue B/2/10, p. 94.
[73] Local inf.
[74] Cal. Chart. R. 1226–57, 228.
[75] Plac. de Quo Warr. (Rec. Com.), 714; S.H.C. vi (1), 246.
[76] Cal. Chart. R. 1341–1417, 189.
[77] C 145/224; C 138/21.
[78] C 138/21.
[79] S.H.C. xi. 225–6; Cal. Close 1422–9, 110–11; S.H.C. xi. 229; C 142/41, no. 18; see p. 109.
[80] W.S.L., S. MS. 249, f. 124a.
[81] S.H.C. 1929, 266.
[82] C 66/2143, no. 6.
[83] S.H.C. 1919, 219.
[84] Smith, New Map of Staffs. (1747).
[85] Pitt, Staffs. i. 256.
[86] White, Dir. Staffs. (1834). A tenement in the market place is mentioned in 1441: S.H.C. n.s. iii. 159.
[87] P.O. Dir. Staffs. (1868).
[88] Kelly's Dir. Staffs. (1924).
[89] Ibid. (1940).
[90] Rot. Chart. (Rec. Com.), 218.
[91] Hist. MSS. Com. 5th Rep. i. 295.

[92] S.H.C. vi (1), 246.
[93] Cal. Chart. R. 1300–26, 195.
[94] Ibid. 1341–1417, 189.
[95] C 138/21; S.H.C. xi. 225–6; Cal. Close, 1422–9, 110–11; S.H.C. xi. 229; W.S.L., S. MS. 249, ff. 124a, 125b–126a, 131b; C 142/41, no. 18; Stat. Realm, iii. 605–7; C 142/196, no. 45; S.R.O., D. 260/M/box 16, bdle. a, Ct. Bk. 1598–1654, ff. 13a–14a; C 66/2143, rot. 6.
[96] S.R.O., D. 260/M/box 16, bdle. a, Ct. Bk. 1598–1654, ff. 13a–14a.
[97] C 66/2143, no. 6.
[98] Cal. S.P. Dom. 1673–5, 340; Tildesley, Penkridge, 67–68.
[99] S.H.C. 1919, 219.
[1] Tildesley, Penkridge, 70; Smith, New Map of Staffs. (1747).
[2] C 66/2143, no. 6.
[3] S.H.C. 1919, 219.
[4] Pitt, Staffs. 256.
[5] White, Dir. Staffs. (1834).
[6] Kelly's Dir. Staffs. (1912).   [7] Ibid. (1924).
[8] Hist. MSS. Com. Middleton, 347, 361, 368.
[9] S.R.O., D. 260/M/box 16, bdle. a, Ct. Bk. 1598–1654, ff. 13a–14a. There are toll books of the horse fair for 1558, 1579, and 1640 in B.M. Eg. MS. 3008, ff. 2a–22a.
[10] Camden, Britannia, 530.
[11] Pitt, Staffs. 256.
[12] White, Dir. Staffs. (1834).
[13] S.R.O., D. 260/M/E. 353 (a), map 5, showing 'Big Horse Fair' and 'Little Horse Fair' in this area; Tithe Maps and Appt., Penkridge (copy in W.S.L.), showing two pieces of land here called Horse Fair c. 1841.

held during the Michaelmas fair determined all actions under 40s. and exercised jurisdiction over waif and stray, felons' goods, toll, 'picage', stallage, and other incidents belonging to the fair within the manor of Penkridge and also the deanery liberty.[14] The lord had the use of all commons and grounds adjoining the place where the fair was held during fair time.[15]

In 1373 or 1374 Geoffrey de Congreve, lord of Congreve, granted to a Thomas Mountfort a messuage in Congreve, to hold for 12s. a year with the duty of supervising the fairs of Penkridge.[16]

CHURCHES. The church of Penkridge was reputedly founded by King Eadred (946–55)[17] and was certainly in existence c. 1006.[18] King Stephen gave it in 1136 to the bishop and churches of Coventry and Lichfield subject to the life interest of Jordan, a clerk of Roger de Fécamp,[19] but it had returned to the Crown by 1182 when it was a collegiate church with a dean and prebendaries.[20] The deanery was held from 1215 by the archbishops of Dublin,[21] and the parish was served presumably by the prebendaries of the church or by their vicars choral. The college was dissolved in 1547,[22] but its peculiar jurisdiction over the parish survived until the 19th century.[23]

In 1548, after the dissolution of the college, a vicar and an assistant priest were appointed to serve the cure by the Chantry Commissioners,[24] and the advowson seems to have remained with the Crown until it was granted in 1581 to Edmund Downynge and Peter Aysheton.[25] These seem to have granted it in 1583 to John Morley and Thomas Crompton[26] who with John's wife Elizabeth conveyed it in 1585 to Edward Littleton.[27] The advowson has since descended in the Littleton family with Pillaton manor, the present patron being Lord Hatherton.[28] The living seems to have been a perpetual curacy by the 18th century[29] and has been styled a titular vicarage since 1868.[30]

In 1548 the first Vicar of Penkridge, Thomas Bolt, formerly prebendary of Blurton in St. Mary's, Stafford, and the first assistant minister, William Graunger, formerly vicar-choral of the last prebendary of Penkridge, were appointed at salaries of £16 and £8 respectively, paid out of the Court of Augmentations.[31] There were still two clerks or ministers here between 1600 and 1604[32] and between 1634 and 1643.[33] In 1646 the Committee for Plundered Mini-

sters increased the salary of £24 paid to Nathaniel Hinde, vicar from at least 1636, by a grant of £50 a year out of the impropriate rectory, and in 1652 the Committee raised his salary to £100 a year out of the tithes of Hilton and Featherstone (in St. Peter's, Wolverhampton).[34] The incumbent still benefits under the charities of William and Eleanor Alport on condition of attending an annual service in Cannock parish church on the Feast of St. Barnabas (11 June), preaching a sermon at this service in annual rotation with seven other beneficiaries and residing in his benefice for at least ten months a year.[35] The Misses R. A. and S. E. Warner (d. 1936) devised land and a house in trust to be used as a residence for the assistant curate or the income thereof to be used to augment his stipend or to be applied for the spiritual or bodily welfare of Anglican members of Penkridge parish.[36] The property was sold in 1937, and the profits were invested in £359 11s. 2d. stock, the interest still being applied to the original aims of the charity.[37]

By 1321 there were two chantries in the church, the King's chantry and the chantry of the Blessed Virgin Mary, each served by one priest.[38] The two priests were among the prebendaries of Penkridge in 1365,[39] and in 1380 these 'prebendaries' of St. Mary and the King, by custom resident and supporting the burdens of hospitality in the church, were each receiving 10½d. a week from the common rents of the college.[40] As this was then inadequate to support the burdens as hitherto, it was ordered that the resident priests should each receive 3½d. a week more from the common fund, and the king confirmed this in 1387.[41] In 1533 Thomas Webbe occurs as resident canon, paying tax of 5s. 4d., and he remained at Penkridge with a salary of £6 11s. 2¼d. until 1548.[42] William Yates occurs as the other resident canon between 1535 and 1548 with a salary of £6 16s. 4¼d. and in 1548 a pension of £6.[43] The canons lived in a house which was worth 2s. a year by 1546.[44]

By 1548 there was a Morrow Mass priest in the church appointed by the inhabitants of Penkridge and endowed with 3s. 4d. rent from a cottage in Whiston.[45]

By 1552 there was a Trinity Guild in the church, endowed with a messuage and lands in Whiston leased to John Butler for 7s. and with 15 kine and £20.[46] The Trinity priest had a salary of 8 marks paid from the profits on the cattle.[47]

Also by 1552 the organ player in Penkridge church

[14] S.R.O., D. 260/M/box 16, bdle. a, Ct. Bk. 1598–1654, f. 14a.
[15] Ibid.
[16] W.S.L., S. MS. 350A/40, f. 82a.
[17] Dorothy Styles, 'Early History of Penkridge Church' (S.H.C. 1950–1, 3 n.1).
[18] S.H.C. 1916, 119, 120.
[19] Ibid. 1924, nos. 262, 452, 593.
[20] W.S.L. 84/6/41; S.H.C. vi (1), 23; ibid. i. 107. The exact position of the 9 clerks who held land in Penkridge of the king in 1086 is not clear: see p. 124.
[21] S.H.C. 1950–1, 10–11, 14.
[22] Ibid. 36.
[23] Ibid. 43–45; ibid. 1915, 203; White, Dir. Staffs. (1834); W.S.L., C.B. Penkridge.
[24] S.H.C. 1915, 205, 209, 406.
[25] Cal. Pat. 1548–9, 30; C 66/1198, m. 18.
[26] S.R.O., D. 260/M/box 7, bdle. i, a list, apparently written by Sir Edward Littleton (d. 1812), of the post-Reformation grants of Penkridge college.
[27] S.H.C. xv. 167.
[28] C 142/520, no. 71; C 142/455, no. 76; C.P. 25(2)/596,

1654 Trin.; C.P. 43/676, rot. 321; White, Dir. Staffs. (1834); Lich. Dioc. Dir. (1955–6); see p. 119.
[29] Note in par. reg., from transcript in W.S.L., C.B. Penkridge; Pitt, Staffs. 256; White, Dir. Staffs. (1834; 1851).
[30] Lich. Dioc. Ch. Cal. (1869); Lich. Dioc. Dir. (1955–6).
[31] S.H.C. 1915, 205, 209, 406.
[32] Penkridge Par. Reg. (Staffs. Par. Reg. Soc.), 24, 27, 82.
[33] Ibid. 55, 58, 61, 62, 64, 67, 68, 93, 94, 140, 146.
[34] S.H.C. 1915, 210; Penkridge Par. Reg. 94.
[35] See p. 64.
[36] Charity Com. files.
[37] Ex inf. Lichfield Dioc. Trust (1956).
[38] S.H.C. 1950–1, 52 n.134.
[39] Ibid. 24.
[40] Cal. Pat. 1385–9, 367.
[41] Ibid.
[42] S.H.C. 1915, 204, 209; ibid. 1950–1, 38.
[43] Ibid. 1915, 204, 209; ibid. 1950–1, 38.
[44] Ibid. 202.
[45] Ibid. 205.
[46] Ibid. 206.
[47] Ibid.

was supported from lands in the parish of Brewood leased to John Bickford for 4 marks.[48] These may be identical with the lands in Chillington (in Brewood) given by Richard Littleton for the support of the Penkridge organ player, as well as for obits and lamps in the church, and granted by the Crown in 1562 to Cecily Pickerell, widow.[49]

Before the Dissolution the church of Penkridge served a large area and had four prebendal chapels at Coppenhall, Dunston, Stretton, and Shareshill. A fifth, at Pillaton, occurs only in 1272.[50] The church at Shareshill secured parochial status soon after the Dissolution,[51] but those at Coppenhall, Dunston, and Stretton remained dependent on Penkridge until the 19th century.[52]

The church of *ST. MICHAEL* is a fine building of local red sandstone standing to the west of the village. It has a total length of 142 ft. and consists of an aisled chancel, aisled nave, west tower, south porch, and north-west vestry. The existing building was begun early in the 13th century and was completed on approximately its present plan by *c.* 1300. There are no traces of the earlier church. The porch and tower were in the first instance 14th-century additions. In the 16th century the tower was raised, clerestories were added and new windows inserted, so that the exterior is now almost entirely of Perpendicular character. The church has a fine set of 16th- and early-17th-century monuments.

The aisled chancel of four bays was built during

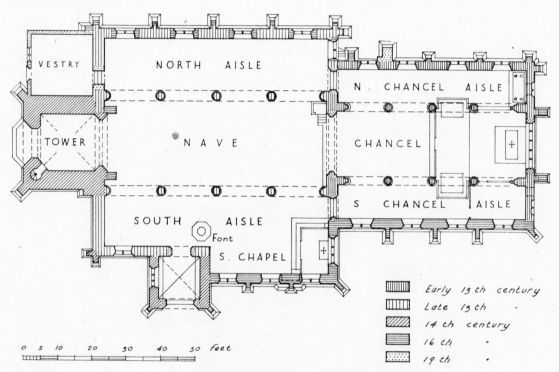

PLAN OF ST. MICHAEL'S CHURCH

There was a dependent chapel at Levedale, dedicated apparently to St. Laurence and endowed with a meadow in Bradley, in 1552 and 1553, but it was no longer in use in 1563.[53] There seems also to have been a chapel at Bickford in 1553.[54] There was a chapel at Preston, apparently 200 yds. south-east of the present Preston Vale Farm,[55] before 1732, by which year it had been converted into a small house.[56] In the 19th century missions were established at Whiston (1880)[57] and Levedale (*c.* 1881)[58] and in the former oratory chapel at Pillaton Hall (1888).[59] A chapel of ease was opened at Gailey in 1850[60] and the consolidated chapelry of Gailey-with-Hatherton attached to it in 1869,[61] the patronage being in the hands of Lord Hatherton and trustees.[62]

the earlier 13th century. Masonry of this date occurs in the north and east walls and in the spandrels above the arcades. The piers of the arcades are circular with moulded capitals and 'water-holding' bases. The abaci are undercut and have an unusual subsidiary roll moulding.[63] Each eastern respond consists of a cluster of shafts, three engaged and two detached, the capitals of the latter being carved with foliage reminiscent of 12th-century 'water-leaf' ornament. The pointed arches have heavy filleted rolls and on their inner faces are hood-moulds ending in headstops. Here as elsewhere the stonework was largely recut in the 19th century. The original chancel had no clerestory, a single gabled roof of steep pitch being carried down over the aisles; the

[48] Ibid.
[49] *Cal. Pat.* 1560–3, 257.
[50] *S.H.C.* 1924, nos. 763, 764.
[51] See p. 179.
[52] See *V.C.H. Staffs.* iv. 167–8.
[53] *S.H.C.* 1915, 207.
[54] Ibid. 206.
[55] Local inf.
[56] Perambulation 1732, in Penkridge Par. Reg. 1735–90, f. 1*b*; Tildesley, *Penkridge*, 30.

[57] Tildesley, *Penkridge*, 86; *Kelly's Dir. Staffs.* (1912); *Lich. Dioc. Dir.* (1955–6).
[58] *Kelly's Dir. Staffs.* (1884; 1912); *Lich. Dioc. Dir.* (1955–6).
[59] See pp. 119, 120, 134.
[60] White, *Dir. Staffs.* (1851).
[61] *Lond. Gaz.* 1869, pp. 7056–8.
[62] *Lich. Dioc. Dir.* (1955–6).
[63] Lynam suggests that the mouldings show Irish influence: *Trans. N. Staffs. Field Club* (1891), 45.

13th-century roof line, visible above the chancel arch and on the east wall, shows that the external aisle walls were about a third of their present height. The outline of a single pointed lancet can be seen internally at the east end of the north aisle and its sill is retained externally. No other 13th-century window survives.

The nave of the earlier church was probably in use during the rebuilding of the chancel, but on its completion *c.* 1250 the reconstruction of the nave began. The four-bay arcades follow the same pattern but the water-holding bases have been replaced by a double-roll moulding, a clear indication of the later date. The aisles are wider than those of the chancel, probably because room was required for altars to stand beside the arches connecting with the chancel aisles. The extra widening of the south aisle is not of this period. The overall width of nave and aisles did not allow of a single gabled roof; the aisles had separate pent roofs, the lines of which can still be traced, and the external walls could therefore be higher than those of the chancel.

In the 14th century a single-story porch was added; the stoup inside its east wall has a typical ogee head. The lowest stage of the tower is of the same period. The arch mouldings of the west door-way are continued without a break down the jambs, and there is a scroll drip-stone above it. Also in the 14th century the chancel was altered to give additional height and better lighting. The aisle walls were raised to two-thirds of their present height, bringing them into line with those of the nave. The roof pitch was flattened and buttresses, still preserved on the north side, were added externally. A large five-light window with flowing tracery was inserted in the east wall, and an arcaded reredos, now destroyed, was probably of the same date.[64]

Alterations on a large scale were made during the 16th century, some at least after the dissolution of the college in 1547 and the destruction which accompanied it. Early in the century many of the Staffordshire towers were rebuilt to a uniform pattern, but among them the Penkridge tower is outstanding for its handsome proportions. On the west face the middle stage has a very large Perpendicular window and there are four windows of similar style to the belfry stage. The embattled parapet has angle and median pinnacles; below the parapet an ornamental band is carved with shields in square frames, a departure from the more usual lozenge design. There are also individual shields above the belfry windows. The widening of the south nave aisle at its east end to form a chapel is probably the earliest of the 16th-century alterations to the body of the church. On the south side a recessed table tomb is an integral part of the wall and forms a projection externally. The tomb, which is covered by a cusped arch, bears an alabaster slab on which are incised the figures of Richard Littleton[65] (d. 1518) and his wife Alice, formerly Wynnesbury (d. 1529). The fact that other family monuments were originally

near at hand[66] suggests that the chapel was built at about this date and used by the Littletons while the church was still collegiate. The new walls were made about half as high again as the original nave walls and have external buttresses and an embattled parapet with pinnacles. On the south side are three tall windows with central transoms and pointed heads. The curious geometrical tracery may have been suggested by the 13th-century windows which these replaced. The large east window formerly contained Perpendicular tracery similar to that in the tower windows.[67] The chapel appears to have served as a prototype for a general remodelling of the nave, the walls being raised and new windows inserted. At the same time a room was added above the porch so that the high parapet line became continuous externally. A clerestory, consisting of a pair of square-headed two-light windows to each bay, was built above the arcades.

Alterations on the same lines, probably dating from 1578 and later, were made to the chancel. An inscription of this date together with the name of James Riddings, vicar, appears outside the priest's door. The south wall, which includes this door, was refaced or rebuilt. The existing north wall was raised in height and on its external face masonry of three dates can now be distinguished: the lowest third is of the 13th and the middle third of the 14th century, while the 16th-century walling occurs above the 14th-century buttresses. In general the alterations to the chancel are inferior to those of the nave. The tall pointed windows have less elaborate tracery, and the clerestory windows are not paired. Externally the east walls of the two chancel aisles have blind square-headed windows of Perpendicular type, but there is no sign that these ever penetrated the walls. A single window of the same design, in this case glazed, occurs on the north side of the nave, possibly replacing a north doorway. The original church contained several altars, one of which was dedicated to St. John the Baptist by 1403[68] and some of which were destroyed at the dissolution of the college. The eastern respond of the south chancel arcade is pierced to accommodate a double piscina, one to serve the high altar and the other an altar in the south aisle. The stonework has been renewed, but a fragment of original moulding survives on the north face. A small doorway through the east wall of the aisle was probably inserted late in the 16th century after the subsidiary altar had been removed. The doorway is now blocked with modern masonry. Traces of piscinae or credence tables can be seen in the other aisles, and the priest's doorway has a holy-water stoup on its eastern jamb.

A buttress at the corner of the south chapel is dated 1677, probably indicating repairs to the stonework. In 1799 over £250 was spent on the church.[69] The building was restored and re-seated in 1831[70] when a new gallery in the north aisle, together with existing galleries at the west end, brought the total number of sittings to 1,200. During

[64] R. Garner, *Nat. History of County of Stafford* (1844), 135.

[65] Gregory King gives Richard Westcott, a possible explanation being that Richard's grandfather changed his name from Westcott to Littleton: *S.H.C.* 1919, 217. For a full description see S. A. Jeavons, 'Monumental Effigies of Staffs.' (*Trans. Birm. Arch. Soc.* lxix), no. 9. The monument is reproduced by A. Oliver, *Incised Effigies*, pl. 25. For a drawing of *c.* 1838 see plate facing p. 133.

[66] *S.H.C.* 1919, 215–17.

[67] W.S.L., Staffs. Views, viii, pp. 13 (b), 20, 21. The first of these is reproduced facing p. 133. The tracery was probably altered when memorial glass was inserted in 1864.

[68] W.S.L., S. MS. 350A/40, ff. 78a–79a.

[69] Tildesley, *Penkridge*, 30.

[70] White, *Dir. Staffs.* (1834), 503; Tildesley, *Penkridge*, 37; and see plate facing p. 133.

Thomas Giffard the Younger, c. 1784, aged about 20

Sir Edward Littleton in 1765, aged 28

PENKRIDGE: the interior of the church in 1832

Alabaster tomb-slab of Richard Littleton
(d. 1518) and his wife Alice (d. 1529)

Tile found in Brewood churchyard in 1908, thought
to be of the 13th century and to depict Judas Iscariot
throwing away the pieces of silver

this restoration the alabaster monuments were recut and probably moved to their present positions. The vestry at the north-west corner of the church, built of stone and in the Tudor style, may also be of this period. Mid-19th-century drawings and photographs of the interior[71] show a flat plaster ceiling to the nave, box pews, a three-decker pulpit, and an arcaded reredos. The west end was then dominated by galleries and by a large organ placed in the blocked arch of the tower. In 1881 the church was very thoroughly restored by J. A. Chatwin[72] of Birmingham. The nave floor was lowered and the chancel arch, originally of the same height as the arcades, was raised 8 ft. The impressive proportions of the interior owe much to these alterations. New pews were installed, all the galleries were removed, the tower arch was opened up, and the organ was moved to its present position north of the chancel. The nave was given an elaborate new roof of late medieval design, its carved devices illustrating the history of the church and of the Littleton family. Six oak angels, which had survived from the corbels of the 16th-century roof,[73] were incorporated. A dilapidated staircase giving access to the room over the porch was cleared away. The porch itself and the arches connecting nave and chancel aisles were altered and restored. While work was in progress several inscribed floor-slabs and a Littleton vault were discovered. The marble pavement of the sanctuary, incorporating a memorial slab to the 2nd Lord Hatherton (d. 1888) dates from 1888 and the stone pulpit from 1890.[74] In 1948 the east end of the south nave aisle was reinstated as a chapel to commemorate those who died in both world wars.[75]

The octagonal font dates from 1668. It has a reeded base and the bowl is carved with various devices including the initials 'C.R.' After a period of disuse the stonework was recut in 1864 and the font restored to the church.[76] Eight late-15th-century misericords survive from the collegiate church,[77] and some original carving is preserved in front of the choir stalls and in the screens behind them. The wrought-iron gates which form the chancel screen are dated 1778 and are of Dutch origin. They were obtained by the Hon. William Littleton from a Dutch settler in South Africa.[78]

There is now no ancient glass in the church. In 1680 Gregory King[79] records several shields of arms, including those of England and France in the east window and those of Congreve, Fitzherbert, and Willoughby de Broke elsewhere. The east window now contains memorial glass to the 1st Lord

Hatherton (d. 1863).[80] Other windows commemorate members of the Littleton, Croydon, and Keeling families (1864–1931).[81]

An incised alabaster floor slab, now in the south chancel aisle, bears the figures of William Wynnesbury and his wife with the small figure of their daughter between them. William Wynnesbury died in 1502, but the date inscribed is not clear and has been variously interpreted.[82] This slab was formerly near the tomb of Richard Littleton in the south chapel.[83] Also at one time in the south chapel[84] but now in the chancel is a fine alabaster monument bearing effigies of Sir Edward Littleton (d. 1558) and his two wives Helen (Swynnerton) and Isabel (Wood). On the north side of the chancel is a somewhat similar tomb with effigies of Sir Edward Littleton (d. 1574) and his wife Alice (Cockayne). Both these monuments are thought to be the work of the Royleys of Burton.[85] Against the east wall of the north chancel aisle is an elaborate two-tier monument,[86] the lower stage bearing the effigies of Sir Edward Littleton (d. 1610) and his wife Margaret (Devereux),[87] the upper those of their son, also Sir Edward (d. 1629), and his wife Mary (Fisher). This monument was formerly against the north wall of the aisle[88] where additional spacing between two of the windows suggests that it was already contemplated when the wall was altered. An incised alabaster slab has been mounted on the aisle wall: it shows the kneeling figures of a Littleton family in mid-17th-century dress. At the east end of the south chancel aisle, now the vicar's vestry, is a marble wall monument with a carved sarcophagus commemorating Sir Edward Littleton (d. 1742). Elsewhere are wall tablets to Alexander Ward (1729), Thomas Perry, curate (1743), John Eginton (1752), John Herbert (1769), and to several vicars of the parish. There are also tablets to members of the Littleton family dated 1888, 1897, 1917, 1923, and 1930. In the south nave aisle is a tablet to Commander Sir Geoffrey C. Congreve, killed in 1941. The east wall of the churchyard incorporates a carved stone obelisk, designed by Sir Charles Nicholson as a memorial of the First World War.[89]

In 1956 the plate included two silver chalices, one set with four mother-of-pearl medallions; three silver patens, one dated 1802 and one set with four amethysts, given by Herbert Mansfield Whitehead, 1911; a silver flagon and lid, given by the parishioners in memory of J. Bolders (d. 1914); and a wood and silver wafer box.[90]

In 1553 there were four bells and a sanctus bell.[91] The five bells here at the time of the church

[71] W.S.L., Staffs. Views, viii, pp. 11, 23, 25; photographs in church.
[72] Tildesley, *Penkridge*, 39–46.
[73] W.S.L., Staffs. Views, viii, p. 11.
[74] *Kelly's Dir. Staffs.* (1940).
[75] O. Law, *Hist. of the Parish Ch. Penkridge* (1949), 11.
[76] An earlier inscription is shown in W.S.L., Staffs. Views, viii, p. 10 (b). Another view (p. 10 (a), 1831) describes the font as in the vicarage garden.
[77] *Trans. Birm. Arch. Soc.* lxvii. 51–52. This account gives only 6.
[78] *Trans. N. Staffs. Field Club.* xxxviii. 186.
[79] *S.H.C.* 1919, 217–18.
[80] *Kelly's Dir. Staffs.* (1884).
[81] Inscriptions *in situ*; Lich. Dioc. Regy., Consist. Ct. Act Bk. 1907–14, p. 230, faculty, 7 Nov. 1910; ibid. p. 434, 23 Sept. 1913; Consist. Ct. Act Bk. 1934–8, faculty, 17 July 1937.
[82] *S.H.C.* 1919, 216. For illustrations see Oliver,

Incised Effigies, pl. 26, and W.S.L., Staffs. Views, viii, p. 14.
[83] *S.H.C.* 1919, 216.
[84] Ibid. 215.
[85] For description see S. A. Jeavons, 'Monumental Effigies of Staffs.' (*Trans. Birm. Arch. Soc.* lxx), nos. 87–89 and 109–10, pl. 6 (b) and 12 (a).
[86] *Trans. Birm. Arch. Soc.* lxxi. 12–13, pl. 2.
[87] The arms of Littleton impaling Devereux were formerly on the lower monument: *S.H.C.* 1919, 214.
[88] Ibid.
[89] *Kelly's Dir. Staffs.* (1940).
[90] Ex inf. the Vicar of Penkridge (1957).
[91] *S.H.C.* 1915, 203. Another bell had been sold with the consent of the parishioners and the proceeds applied in pulling down the altars and 'defacing' the church; in buying and painting 37 yds. of cloth to go over the rood loft; in painting the table at the high altar with scriptures; in glazing the windows; in hiring a young man to teach in the writing school; in a gift to 3 lame persons: ibid.

restoration in 1831 were sold and replaced by a new peal of eight, by W. and J. Taylor of Oxford.[92] This peal was rehung in an iron frame by Taylor, in 1894, and again rehung, with ball bearings, by J. Taylor, in 1953.[93]

The registers of marriages and burials start in 1572 and those of baptisms in 1575. Those from 1572 to 1735 have been printed.[94]

Over £60 was spent on a house and garden occupied by Thomas Perry, the incumbent, in 1728.[95] At a later date the vicars lived at Ivy House,[96] a Georgian building in Church Lane which still stands. In 1804 and 1814 it was stated that there was no parsonage house in the parish.[97] In 1831 E. J. Littleton (Lord Hatherton in 1835) gave £8, Colonel Walhouse £100, the Revd. J. C. Stafford, the vicar, £20, and the Governors of Queen Anne's Bounty £200, the whole being spent on the building of a vicarage house on an acre of land given by Mr. Littleton, who also gave 3,300 bricks for a stable and other buildings.[98] A further £50, paid as compensation by the railway company before 1851 for laying the railway between the vicarage house and the church, was used to make improvements to the house.[99]

The house, about 300 yds. south-west of the church, is approached from the churchyard by a tunnel passing under the railway. It is a dignified square stucco house, with a low-pitched slate roof and wide eaves. The north-east corner in the same style is a later addition.[1]

In 1754 a large tithe barn was still standing about 150 yds. south of the church.[2]

The small chapel of *ST. MODWENA* occupies the east end of the existing range of buildings at Pillaton Hall. Before the greater part of the Hall was demolished in the 18th century it formed the north-east corner of the quadrangular plan, abutting on the moat on two sides. The present building dates from the earlier 16th century, being contemporary with the rebuilding of the Hall at that period. After the removal of the Littleton family to Teddesley it became ruinous,[3] but during the 19th century it was converted into a cottage by the insertion of an upper floor.[4] In 1888 it was thoroughly restored and reinstated for use as a chapel.[5]

The building is of stone and is rectangular on plan with a gallery at the west end. It has a four-light window in the east wall and a three-light window at the east end of the north wall. Both have central transoms and internal four-centred arches. Farther west in the north wall are two three-light windows, one above and one below gallery level. A doorway in the west wall gives access to the gallery from the existing north range of buildings. The south wall, part of which formerly abutted on the demolished east range, has two doorways, one on the

ground floor and the other at gallery level. The former is the original entrance to the chapel from the courtyard and has a stoup outside it. The upper doorway is approached by a carved oak stair dating from 1888. Farther east in this wall are two oblique squints, one above the other, giving a view of the altar from former ground- and first-floor rooms in the east range. Internally in the south wall is a pointed niche, probably representing an original piscina. The gallery, incorporating original oak panels, was reconstructed in 1888, and the present low-pitched roof is of the same date. The stone font forms a projection in the middle of the west wall, its faces carved with trefoil-headed panels. Seventeenth-century balusters have been used for altar rails, and the sanctuary is paved with old tiles. The stone altar is modern. Stained glass in the windows dates from the 19th century.[6] The representation of St. Modwena in the large north window was suggested by pictorial glass which still survived at Pillaton Hall in 1789[7] but has now disappeared. Mounted on the south wall is a curious wooden figure, traditionally said to represent King Herod, wearing a crown and large gauntlets. The face is grotesquely carved and has projecting teeth. The figure, which may date from the 13th or early 14th century, was found hidden at Pillaton and remained for many years at Teddesley Hall.[8]

In 1956 the plate included a silver-gilt chalice and paten, copies of those, dated 1525, found in the walls of Pillaton Hall in the reign of George II. Round the bottom of the chalice stand is inscribed 'Sancta Maria ora pro nobis', and round the rim, 'Pater de celis Deus miserere nobis'. Round the rim of the paten is inscribed 'Sancta Trinitas unus Deus miserere nobis'. There are also wine and water cruets of crystal and silver.[9]

CHRISTCHURCH, Gailey, dating from 1850, is built of stone rubble in the Early English style and consists of nave, shallow transepts, chancel, and north vestry. In the nave the stone is left exposed, and there is a steeply pitched open roof. The windows are single and grouped lancets. In 1876 the chancel was extended, the north vestry built, and a small south vestry converted into an organ chamber, the cost being defrayed by Mr. and Mrs. Henry Ward of Rodbaston Hall.[10] There are stained-glass windows and memorial tablets to members of the Ward family and others.

The widening of the cross-roads at Gailey in 1929 caused the removal of 153 sq. yds. from the churchyard.[11] The war memorial was moved and new walls and fences erected. A further 280 sq. yds. was taken in 1937.[12]

In 1956 the plate included a silver-gilt chalice and paten, given in 1915 by Anne, Caroline, Mabel, and Margaret Ward, in memory of their mother, Jane

[92] Tildesley, *Penkridge*, 37, 38–39; C. Lynam, *Church Bells of Staffs.* 22.
[93] A. E. Garbett, 'Church Bells of Staffs.' (*Trans. Old Stafford Soc.* 1953–4), 14; *Lich. Dioc. Mag.* (1895), 196.
[94] Staffs. Par. Reg. Soc. 1945–6.
[95] Note in Par. Reg.: Tildesley, *Penkridge*, 31.
[96] Tildesley, *Penkridge*, 38.
[97] Lich. Dioc. Regy., Non-residence Licences.
[98] Tildesley, *Penkridge*, 81.
[99] White, *Dir. Staffs.* (1851).
[1] W.S.L., Staffs. Views, viii, p. 29 (1841).
[2] S.R.O. D. 260/M/E. 353 (a), map 5; see plate facing p. 104.
[3] *Gent. Mag.* lix (1789), 1078.

[4] The joist holes are still visible. For illustrations of the chapel in 1841, see W.S.L., Staffs. Views, viii, pp. 38, 40, 45.
[5] Inscription in chapel; *Lich. Dioc. Ch. Cal.* (1889).
[6] *Trans. N. Staffs. Field Club*, lxii. 88.
[7] *Gent. Mag.* lix (1789), 1078, pl. iii.
[8] *Trans. N. Staffs. Field Club*, xxxviii. 186.
[9] Ex inf. the Vicar of Penkridge.
[10] Lich. Dioc. Regy., Consist. Ct. Act Bk. 1875–9, p. 37, faculty, 7 Dec. 1875; *Kelly's Dir. Staffs.* (1884).
[11] Lich. Dioc. Regy., Consist. Ct. Act Bk. 1924–30, pp. 445–8, faculty, 17 Sept. 1929.
[12] Ibid. 1934–8, pp. 339–43, faculty, 4 Mar. 1937.

Ward of Rodbaston Hall; a silver ciborium, 1946; a Sheffield plate paten on foot; and two wine and water cruets.[13] There is one bell.[14] The register dates from 1870.

The vicarage house dating from 1870–1 is at Hatherton (in St. Peter's, Wolverhampton).

The mission church at Whiston is of red brick and consists of nave, small chancel, and south porch. It has pointed windows and a bell-cote above the west gable. In 1956 the plate included a silver chalice and paten.[15]

The mission church at Levedale stands on the east side of the road and is a small weather-boarded building with leaded windows. In 1956 the plate included a silver chalice and silver paten, formerly the property of the late Revd. J. H. Kenysson, Vicar of Penkridge, who presented them to Levedale church.[16]

NONCONFORMITY. William Vincent who was summoned before the Consistory court of Lichfield in 1668 for teaching without licence may have been a dissenter.[17] John Wesley preached in the parish in November 1745 when travelling from Macclesfield to Wednesbury (Seisdon hundred).[18] In 1777 the house of William Robinson[19] and in 1817 the house of John Yates were registered as meeting-houses.[20] A Wesleyan Methodist chapel was opened in 1828[21] and is a plain red-brick building standing in New Road. A new stone chapel with Gothic windows was built on to this in 1934[22] with a frontage on the newly widened Clay Street.

In October 1811 Hugh Bourne, the leader of the Primitive Methodists, after preaching for the first time at Penkridge, noted that 'it would be difficult to raise a work here though it might be done'.[23] In March 1813 he was again at Penkridge and noted, 'The people are going on well and can hold meetings themselves and I think John Cheadle will be a preacher.'[24] A regular Primitive Methodist preaching place had already been established at Whiston by 1812[25] and by 1834 a chapel had been opened there.[26] No regular Primitive Methodist preaching place was established at Penkridge, however, until about 1849.[27] The Penkridge meeting continued until at least 1892[28] and Whiston chapel until at least 1896.[29] Both have since been closed. The latter is a small brick building, adjoining a cottage opposite Ivy

Farm and in 1956 was partly derelict and used as an outhouse.

A meeting-house of the Christian Brethren was erected in 1846.[30] The Brethren continued to meet in Penkridge until at least 1896.[31]

In 1851 there was an Independent chapel at Gailey Wharf, opened in 1844.[32] This chapel has since disappeared.

PRIMARY SCHOOLS. At some date before May 1553 the salary of a young man to teach in the writing school at Penkridge had been raised from part of the proceeds of the sale of a church bell.[33] This school, which was possibly held in the room over the south porch of the church,[34] appears to have had a continuous existence until at least 1668.[35] In 1695 a charity school, planned in 1693 by Edward Littleton, Edward James, John Eginton, and others,[36] was built in the churchyard due west of the church.[37] Its aim was to teach poor children to read and to instruct them in Anglican doctrine.[38] By 1730 this school was decaying through the death and falling off of subscribers.[39] It was agreed, however, that it should be continued with the purpose of clothing and instructing 12 boys in reading, writing, and accounts and 8 girls in these subjects and in knitting and sewing.[40] For this the master and mistress should receive £8 a year.[41]

Apparently the earliest endowment, apart from subscriptions, was a rent-charge of 10s. on land in Penkridge left by Thomas Stevens by his will dated 1730.[42] Francis Sherratt (d. Dec. 1773),[43] by will dated 1732, left land in Penkridge to Sir Edward Littleton of Pillaton in trust 'to provide a schoolmaster in Penkridge to teach eight poor boys, born in Penkridge, in reading the bible and writing'.[44] Of these, four were to be elected by the churchwardens and four by Sir Edward Littleton and his heirs; they were normally to stay for four years, and each was to be provided with a blue 'bonnet'.[45] Further endowments were £50 by will of Sir Edward Littleton, invested in 1742 and yielding £1 14s. 6d. dividend;[46] 10s. rent-charge (on land in Wheaton Aston) left by will of John Smart (d. 1751);[47] a sum of £44 10s. from an unspecified source, on which by at least 1753 or 1754 interest of £2 4s. 6d. was due to be paid through the Littleton trustee of the time,[48] and £500 in stock left by Thomas Clarke by will

[13] These were to replace vessels stolen from the church: ibid. 1914–20, p. 34, faculty, 5 Mar. 1915.
[14] Lynam, *Church Bells of Staffs.* 12.
[15] Ex inf. the Vicar of Penkridge.
[16] Ex inf. the vicar.
[17] A. G. Matthews, *Cong. Churches of Staffs.* 56.
[18] *Wesley's Journal*, 9 Nov. 1745.
[19] S.R.O., Q/SM, 3, East. 1777.
[20] Lich. Dioc. Regy., Bp.'s Reg. Bk. F, p. 458.
[21] H.O. 129/15/378; Lich. Dioc. Regy., Bp.'s Reg. Bk. H, p. 415; Charity Com. files.
[22] Local inf.
[23] Walford, *Memoirs of Hugh Bourne*, i. 343.
[24] Ibid. i. 365.
[25] Ibid. i. 349.
[26] White, *Dir. Staffs.* (1834). It may be this chapel, and not the Wesleyan Methodist chapel at Penkridge, that was registered in 1828: Lich. Dioc. Regy., Bp.'s Reg. Bk. H, 415; H.O. 129/15/378.
[27] H.O. 129/15/378.
[28] *Kelly's Dir. Staffs.* (1892).
[29] Ibid. (1896).
[30] H.O. 129/15/378. Thomas Timby, of 'Luddle', Penkridge, was deacon.
[31] *Kelly's Dir. Staffs.* (1896).

[32] H.O. 129/15/378. Benjamin Bishop of Gailey Wharf was manager. It was described as a moveable chapel.
[33] *S.H.C.* 1915, 203.
[34] Tildesley, *Penkridge*, 35.
[35] *Penkridge Par. Reg.* (Staffs. Par. Reg. Soc.), 120; Lich. Dioc. Regy., Visitation Call Bk. 1616; Matthews, *Cong. Churches of Staffs.* 56.
[36] S.R.O., D. 260/M/box 7, bdle. j.
[37] Ibid. E. 353 (a), map 5, reproduced facing p. 104.; Tildesley, *Penkridge*, 51; *11th Rep. Com. Char.* H.C. 436, p. 523 (1824), xiv.
[38] S.R.O., D. 260/M/box 7, bdle. j.
[39] Ibid.
[40] Ibid.
[41] Ibid.
[42] *11th Rep. Com. Char.* 523. He was buried 23 July 1720: *Penkridge Par. Reg.* 315.
[43] Buried 23 Oct.: *Penkridge Par. Reg.* 316.
[44] Ibid. 320; will dated 20 Mar. 1731/2: S.R.O., D. 260/M/box 7, bdle. j; *11th Rep. Com. Char.* 523.
[45] *11th Rep. Com. Char.* 523.
[46] Ibid.
[47] Ibid. 521; *Abstract of Returns of Charitable Donations, 1786–8*, H.C. 511, pp. 1118–19 (1816), xvi (2).
[48] *11th Rep. Com. Char.* 523.

dated 1799, and transferred to Littleton in trust in 1804.[49]

Already by about 1730 part of the revenues had been paid to a schoolmistress for teaching the girls, and in 1806 the trustees decided that she should receive one-fifth of the interest on Clarke's legacy.[50] By 1824 the annual income from endowments was £36 3s. of which the master received £5 8s. from rents, four-fifths of Clarke's interest and all the interest on money benefactions, while the mistress had £2 16s. and the rest of the interest from the Clarke bequest.[51] The remaining endowments were used for the upkeep of the buildings and the provision of books and of blue caps for the boys, though no further clothing had been provided since 1821, owing to the falling-off in subscriptions.[52] The master was then teaching reading, writing, and arithmetic free to 12 boys, aged 7 to 11, and English, grammar, and geography to the 'advanced' ones; the mistress taught reading, knitting, and sewing free, to 8 girls who, like the boys, came at the age of 7 and stayed four years.[53] The master also took 'a great number' of paying pupils, some of them boarders.[54]

Meanwhile by 1818 Edward Littleton had built and endowed another school in Penkridge, providing a house for master and mistress and a salary of £100, the school to be opened in 1819 on Dr. Bell's plan.[55] The charity school seems to have continued for some little time longer in the old buildings in the churchyard but these were pulled down in 1831 and pupils and endowments were transferred to this new National school in the Market Place, now School Square.[56] By 1834 the school was educating about 260 children, some of whom were also clothed by Lord Hatherton and from the charity funds.[57] At this date there seem to have been a master and a mistress,[58] and the whole school continued to be free until 1854 when, because of the proposed enlargement of the building and appointment of assistant teachers, fees amounting to 2d. or 4d. a week or 6s. a quarter were charged for each child and the school received an annual parliamentary grant.[59] Lord Hatherton, although the Trust required him, so he said, to instruct 8 boys free and provide them with blue bonnets, now proposed to admit 12 boys and 12 girls free, and provide them respectively with caps and bonnets.[60] By 1855 two assistants teachers for the boys had been appointed.[61]

In 1858 the number of pupils averaged 126 boys and 106 girls; in October 1867 there were 114 boys, 92 girls, and 100 infants on the books.[62] In this latter year there were said to be 12 free pupils,[63] and the endowment was £36 a year.[64] Average attendance in 1892 was 120 boys, 140 girls, and 70 infants.[65] By 1951 the boys' and girls' departments were organized as separate schools, Penkridge Voluntary Primary Schools, Church of England, for Boys and Girls.[66] In 1954 they became aided[67] and in 1955 had average attendances of 143 and 135 respectively. The schools still cater for senior children.[68]

In 1930 the trust land left by Francis Sherratt was sold for £100.[69] The total income from all endowments in 1953 was £27 7s. 2d.[70]

For the 1818 school building the architect, Joseph Potter, submitted both classical and Gothic designs,[71] the latter, probably, being the one accepted. The existing schoolhouse is of the same date and has a symmetrical red-brick front with pointed casements and a Gothic fanlight to the central doorway. The old school building was replaced in 1889[72] by the present long single-story range. It has stone window-frames and two gabled porches. The east porch has carving in the gable and a tablet commemorating the erection of the building by public subscription in memory of the 2nd Lord Hatherton. There have been later alterations and additions.

A council school, a long red-brick range dated 1909 which lies east of the National school and faces Bellbrook, was opened in 1910 to take 150 infants.[73] Attendance in 1937 numbered 51.[74] The school still caters only for infants and is designated Penkridge County Primary School.[75]

By 1860 there was a parochial school for boys and girls in Gailey supported by voluntary contributions and small weekly payments by scholars.[76] By 1862 there were 62 children attending the school, and the master, who received a salary of £35 as well as the 'school pence' amounting to £18 8s. 1d., had a house provided.[77] This may have been the origin of the National school, dated 1865, and enlarged in 1881, average attendance in 1892 being 75.[78] The school was largely rebuilt in 1894 at a cost of £325, for 110 children, and by 1912 the average attendance was 96, under a schoolmistress.[79] In 1904 it was scheduled by the Board of Education as overcrowded and was reorganized to take only junior pupils.[80] In

[49] 11th Rep. Com. Char. 524. By 1823 this was represented by £525 stock, producing £21 per annum: S.R.O., D. 260/M/box 7, bdle. j.
[50] 11th Rep. Com. Char. 523.
[51] Ibid. 524.
[52] Ibid. The clothing provided in 1784 included suits for 6 boys and petticoats for 4 girls: Tildesley, Penkridge, 51.
[53] 11th Rep. Com. Char. 524.
[54] Ibid. And having resigned the mastership he still kept an academy in the High Street: Tildesley, Penkridge, 52; White, Dir. Staffs. (1834).
[55] Digest of Returns to Sel. Cttee. on Educ. of Poor, H.C. 224 (1819), ix (2).
[56] Tildesley, Penkridge, 52–53; White, Dir. Staffs. (1834).
[57] White, Dir. Staffs. (1834).
[58] Ibid.
[59] S.R.O., D. 260/M/box 7, bdle. j; Mins. of Educ. Cttee. of Council, 1854 [1926], p. 219, H.C. (1854), xlii.
[60] S.R.O., D. 260/M/box 7, bdle. j; ibid. box x, bdle. d.
[61] Ibid. box 7, bdle. j, Statement of Expenditure.
[62] Ibid. box x, bdle. d.
[63] Schools Enquiry Com. [3966], H.C. (1867–8), xxviii (12).
[64] Rep. of Educ. Cttee. of Council [3882], H.C. (1867), cxxii.
[65] Kelly's Dir. Staffs. (1892).
[66] Staffs. Educ. Cttee. List of Schools, 1951.
[67] Ex inf. the Staffs. C.C. Educ. Dept.
[68] Lichfield Dioc. Dir. (1955–6).
[69] Charity Com. files.
[70] Ibid.
[71] S.R.O., D. 260/M/E. 399, 400.
[72] Inscription in situ.
[73] Staffs. Educ. Cttee. Mins., 25 July 1908, Jan. 1910; Kelly's Dir. Staffs. (1912).
[74] Staffs. Educ. Cttee. Mins., 26 June 1937.
[75] Ex inf. Staffs. C.C. Educ. Dept.
[76] P.O. Dir. Staffs. (1860).
[77] S.R.O., D. 260/M/box x, bdle. e. Lord Hatherton gave £5 of the £18 10s. raised by subscription, and a collection at Gailey church brought in £10 1s. 1½d. Children were drawn from Calf Heath, Spread Eagle, Rodbaston and Rodbaston Lock, Micklewood, Gravelly Way, and Fullmoor ('Fomer'), and from Crateford and Somerford in Brewood parish, as well as from Gailey and Gailey Lea.
[78] Kelly's Dir. Staffs. (1892).
[79] Ibid. (1912).
[80] Staffs. Educ. Cttee. Mins., 20 Aug. 1904.

1937 there were 41 pupils.[81] In 1956 it was still 'transitionally assisted' and was Gailey Voluntary Primary Church of England School for Junior Boys and Girls and Infants,[82] and average attendance in 1955 was 70, under a mistress.[83] The school stands immediately east of the church.

By 1818 there were three dame schools in Penkridge, taking 110 children.[84]

A Wesleyan day-school was opened in the parish in 1846.[85]

A school-church at Levedale, which was used for a day-school, was built in 1881, average attendances c. 1884 being 25 boys and girls and 65 infants.[86] The land was given by Lord Hatherton who paid for the building.[87] This was still existing as a school-church down to 1900[88] but by 1912 was described as a mission church.[89]

A similar school at Whiston is said to have been built in 1880 on land leased to the Vicar of Penkridge by Captain Congreve.[90] It was for 30 children and the average attendance c. 1884 was 25.[91] It still existed in this form until at least 1900[92] but by 1912 was solely a mission church.[93]

CHARITIES FOR THE POOR. Edward Littleton (d. 1705), bequeathed to the poor of Penkridge £40 which was producing £2 a year in 1786.[94]

John Smart (d. 1751), besides his bequest to the charity school,[95] left a rent-charge of 10s. on his house and land in Wheaton Aston (Lapley parish) to the poor of Penkridge.[96] The income had risen to £1 by 1939.[97]

Thomas Stevens, by will dated 1730, left, in addition to his educational bequest,[98] a rent of 10s. charged on his barns and lands in Clay Street, Penkridge, to the poor of the parish.[99] By 1823 this and Smart's Charity were distributed to the poorest persons on St. Thomas's Day (21 Dec.).[1] In 1930 the rent-charge was redeemed since the property was due to be demolished under the road-widening scheme, and the proceeds were invested in £20 stock.[2]

Elizabeth Rudge, by will dated 1804 with a codicil of 1805, left £50 to be invested and the income distributed among the most deserving poor women of Penkridge township every Christmas Eve.[3] The money was invested in stock in 1818, and by 1823 the income was £1 14s., distributed among the poorest old women at the rate of 2s. 6d. each.[4]

Mary Reynolds bequeathed £50, and her sister,

Elizabeth Potts, by will dated 1818, left a similar sum, directing that the interest on both amounts should be distributed among poor persons of Penkridge on Candlemas Day (2 February) in the parish church.[5] In 1821 the money was invested in stock which by 1882 was producing an income of £3 0s. 6d.[6]

Mary Shawe's Charity, founded before 1873,[7] consisted by 1935 of £107 18s. 3d. stock producing an income of £2 13s. 8d. which was distributed among 12 poor widows on St. Thomas's Day.[8]

Ann Price, by will proved in 1868, left £100 to be invested and the interest distributed on 1 March among poor widows of Penkridge.[9]

Under a Scheme of 1939 these seven charities are applied to the poor of the whole civil parish as constituted before 1934.[10] The income, apart from that of the Price Charity, which is exclusively for poor widows, may be used for grants to hospitals and provident societies, aid to the sick, grants of relief in kind, and temporary financial assistance in emergencies.[11] The total income in 1955 was £12 4s., which was distributed in kind.[12]

Sir Stephen Slaney, by deed of 1622, gave £40 for the poor and for the marriage of poor maids in Penkridge, and the sum was used to secure a rent-charge of £3 on a messuage and lands in the parish.[13] A rent of £2 10s. was being collected by 1743 from William Byrch, owner of the estate, but payments then lapsed, although an attempt was made in 1756 to recover the money.[14] When Miles Moor, part of the endowment, was subsequently bought by Sir Edward Littleton (d. 1812), the heir of William Byrch gave him an indemnity against this charge.[15] In 1823 the Charity Commissioners decided against any attempt at its recovery.[16]

Gifts of money to the use of the poor consisting of £10 from Henry and Joan Duncalfe in 1624, the interest to be distributed upon Good Friday, £5 from John Langford in 1626, £10 from Margaret Littleton (d. 1627), £10 from Thomas Malkin by will of 1628, £40 from Sir Edward Littleton (d. 1629), £20 from William Littleton in 1652, a rent-charge of 20s. on land in Penkridge left by Robert Phillips by will of 1656, £10 from John Tonke by will c. 1657, £5 from Elizabeth Aston at an unspecified date, £6 from Randulph Thorley in 1628 for loans to young tradesmen of Penkridge for three years at a time, and £20 from Mary Littleton c. 1642 for poor widows of the parish, were all still effective in 1662, although some of the money was found to

[81] Ibid. 29 May 1937.
[82] Ex inf. Staffs. C.C. Educ. Dept. The term 'transitionally assisted' means that its status under the 1944 Education Act has not yet been determined.
[83] Lichfield Dioc. Dir. (1955–6).
[84] Digest of Returns to Sel. Cttee. on Educ. of Poor, H.C. 224, pp. 864, 875 (1819), ix (2).
[85] Rep. Wesleyan Educ. Cttee. (1847).
[86] Kelly's Dir. Staffs. (1884).
[87] Tildesley, Penkridge, 86.
[88] Kelly's Dir. Staffs. (1896; 1900).
[89] Ibid. (1912); Lichfield Dioc. Dir. (1955–6).
[90] Tildesley, Penkridge, 86.
[91] Kelly's Dir. Staffs. (1884).
[92] Ibid. (1900).
[93] Ibid. (1912); Lichfield Dioc. Dir. (1955–6).
[94] Abstract, 1786–8, 1118–19; Tildesley, Penkridge, 75.
[95] See p. 135.
[96] 11th Rep. Com. Char. 521.
[97] Charity Commissioners' Scheme, 28 Nov. 1939.
[98] See p. 135.
[99] 11th Rep. Com. Char. 522.

[1] Ibid.
[2] Charity Com. files.
[3] Tildesley, Penkridge, 76.
[4] Ibid. 76–77; 11th Rep. Com. Char. 522.
[5] Tildesley, Penkridge, 77.
[6] Ibid.
[7] The Revd. J. A. Fell (d. 1873) was a trustee; Charity Com. files.
[8] Charity Com. files.
[9] Ibid.
[10] Charity Commissioners' Scheme, 28 Nov. 1939; see p. 103.
[11] Scheme, 1939.
[12] Charity Com. files.
[13] S.R.O., D. 260/M/box 7, bdle. k; 11th Rep. Com. Char. 522; Tildesley, Penkridge, 77.
[14] S.R.O., D. 260/M/box 7, bdle. k; 11th Rep. Com. Char. 522.
[15] S.R.O., D. 260/M/box 7, bdle. l; 11th Rep. Com. Char. 522.
[16] 11th Rep. Com. Char. 522.

have been lent without adequate security.[17] All seem to have lapsed by 1823.[18] The interest on £10 given by Margaret Bott, at an unknown date, for the poor, had ceased to be paid by 1643.[19]

Thomas Whitby of Dunston, by will dated 1650, left £17 2s. 9d. to Ann Webb of Otherton, who settled it in 1666 on trustees to the use of the poor,[20] but payment seems to have been stopped by 1786.[21] Alexander Wood (or Ward) (d. 1729),[22] left £40, the interest to be distributed on St. Thomas's Day to the poor of the parish who most frequented the prayers of the Church and the Sacrament.[23] Thomas Houghton (or Haughton) of Mitton, at an unknown date, left £10, the interest to be paid on St. Thomas's Day to such poor of Penkridge as his trustees thought deserving.[24] The Widow Ingram, also at an unknown date, left £20 for ever to the poor of Penkridge.[25] These four charities seem likewise to have lapsed by 1823.[26]

Ann Littleton (d. 1728)[27] bequeathed the interest on £50 to the poor, to be paid each Candlemas Day by the heir of the Littletons of Pillaton.[28] The income was £2 10s. in 1786,[29] but in 1824 this was recognized as having been merged in the general benefactions of the Littleton family and to be no longer a specific charge.[30]

Thomas Clarke of London, by will dated 1799, left, in addition to his educational charity,[31] £10 a year 'long annuities' to be distributed on St. Thomas's and Candlemas Days by the incumbent and churchwardens among the poor of the town not already receiving alms or relief out of the rates.[32] This annuity was distributed until at least 1823.[33]

Other bequests, apparently of temporary duration, were made to the poor between 1599 and 1750.[34]

Almshouses in New Road were built in 1866 by the Dowager Lady Hatherton as a memorial to her husband.[35] They consisted of five tenements for superannuated labourers from the Teddesley estate.[36] They form a red-brick range of single-story dwellings with a higher central block. The houses have gabled porches with ornamental barge-boards.

COPPENHALL

COPPENHALL, a civil parish formerly part of the ancient parish of Penkridge, is bounded on the east by the Pothooks Brook. The centre of the village lies at 416 ft., the ground rising from under 275 ft. in the east of the parish to over 475 ft. in the west. The soil is stiff loam, with a subsoil of clay and gravel.[1] The parish is still mainly agricultural. A detached strip of Coppenhall, running northwards along the east side of Thornyfields Lane, was added to Castle Church between c. 1849 and 1878.[2] The area of the parish is 907 acres.[3]

About 1558 the inhabitants of Coppenhall including the hamlet of Butterhill ('Butterall') numbered over 120.[4] In the constablewick of Coppenhall and Butterhill there were fourteen households chargeable for hearth tax in 1666 and five too poor to be taxable.[5] Coppenhall contained 10 or 12 houses in 1680 and Butterhill 4, there being no gentleman's residence in either,[6] and in 1811 there was a population of 92 with 16 houses.[7] The population of the civil parish in 1951 was 113.[8]

Coppenhall had 332 acres under cultivation in 1801,

152 acres being sown with wheat, 19 with barley, 67 with oats, 3 with potatoes, 81 with beans, and 10 with turnips or rape.[9] Four farmers with a blacksmith were named in 1834,[10] and in about 1849 there were three farms of over 100 acres, one of them being of nearly 300 acres, with several of less than 100 acres.[11] In 1940 there were four farms, two of them over 150 acres.[12]

On low-lying ground at Coppenhall Gorse is a large moated site.[13] The area enclosed is about 100 yds. in diameter and is approximately oval. Beyond the moat is an outer bank and to the east is a further incomplete system of banks, roughly rectangular in shape. Most of the moat is dry but there are indications of an inlet to the north-west, leading from a field formerly known as The Springs.[14] Surrounding the site the names of eleven fields incorporate the word 'park',[15] indicating the existence of an important early dwelling. A detailed examination of the site and excavations undertaken in 1951 suggest that the period of its occupation was during the earlier 14th century.[16]

[17] S.R.O., D. 260/M/box 7, bdle. k; ibid. bdle. l, Inq. of Jan. 1661/2; *Penkridge Par. Reg.* (Staffs. Par. Reg. Soc.), 135.
[18] None is mentioned in *11th Rep. Com. Char.*, and they are probably to be included among the *Report*'s 'lost charities'.
[19] S.R.O., D. 260/M/box 7, bdle. k, list of Penkridge Charities 1661.
[20] Ibid.
[21] It is not mentioned in the *Abstract, 1786–8*, 1118–19.
[22] *Penkridge Par. Reg.* 314.
[23] Tildesley, *Penkridge*, 76; *Abstract, 1786–8*, 1118–19.
[24] Tildesley, *Penkridge*, 79; *Abstract, 1786–8*, 1118–19.
[25] Tildesley, *Penkridge*, 79. A 'Widow Ingram of Penck' died in 1663 (*Penkridge Par. Reg.* 260), but other widows of that name occur between 1667 and 1711: ibid. 263, 271, 289, 297.
[26] There is no mention of them in *11th Rep. Com. Char.*
[27] *Penkridge Par. Reg.* 294.
[28] *11th Rep. Com. Char.* 523.
[29] *Abstract, 1786–8*, 1118–19.
[30] *11th Rep. Com. Char.* 523; S.R.O., D. 260/M/box 7, bdle. l, Inq. of Jan. 1661/2; *Penkridge Par Reg.* 135.
[31] See pp. 135–6.
[32] *11th Rep. Com. Char.* 523; Tildesley, *Penkridge*, 75.
[33] *11th Rep. Com. Char.* 523.

[34] *Penkridge Par. Reg.* 116, 118; Tildesley, *Penkridge*, 86.
[35] Tildesley, *Penkridge*, 85.
[36] Ibid.
[1] *Kelly's Dir. Staffs.* (1940).
[2] Tithe Maps and Appt., Penkridge (copy in W.S.L.); O.S. Map 6", xliv. NW. (1895, surveyed 1878–81).
[3] *Census*, 1951, Staffs.
[4] *S.H.C.* n.s. ix. 7. There seems also to have been a hamlet of Hyde in the Middle Ages: see pp. 139–40, 142.
[5] *S.H.C.* 1927, 45.
[6] Ibid. 1919, 219.
[7] Pitt, *Staffs.* i. 261.
[8] *Census*, 1951, Staffs.
[9] R. A. Pelham, '1801 crop returns for Staffs.' (*S.H.C.* 1950–1), table opp. p. 242.
[10] White, *Dir. Staffs.* (1834).
[11] Tithe Maps and Appt., Penkridge (copy in W.S.L.).
[12] *Kelly's Dir. Staffs.* (1940).
[13] *V.C.H. Staffs.* i. 362 (with plan); Tithe Maps and Appt., Penkridge (copy in W.S.L.), no. 77. There was a fox covert at Coppenhall Gorse in 1900: O.S. Map 1/2,500, xliv, 2 (1902).
[14] Tithe Maps and Appt., Penkridge (copy in W.S.L.).
[15] Ibid.
[16] *Trans. Old Stafford Soc.* (1951–2), 15–23.

Coppenhall Hall is a much-altered farmhouse, built mainly of brick. The west end of the front range is timber-framed and consists of two bays and part of a third. The roof and attic story appear to date from the 16th century, but it is possible that the lower part of the framing is older. The front gables are later additions and the east end of the range has been rebuilt. There is also a mid-19th-century brick addition at the rear. Two carved oak bosses, probably of 15th-century date, have been reset in the present hall. They consist of grotesque faces framed in foliage and with stems issuing from their mouths. Depressions to the north and west of the house may represent the remains of a moat. The buildings of Church Farm, the other large farm in the village, are not ancient. Doxeywood Cottage in Thornyfields Lane is a small timber-framed structure of two bays, probably having at one time a third bay to the south. The front and the north gable end have exposed framing of the late 16th or early 17th century. On the west side of the road to Hyde Lea is the former smithy, which ceased working soon after 1950. Chase View is a mansion of yellow brick, built c. 1865 on a commanding site as a residence for Henry Woodhouse, engineer to the L. & N.W. Railway at Stafford.[17] It has been used as offices by the English Electric Co. since c. 1942.[18] Since the First World War the residential outskirts of Stafford have spread along the west side of the road from Hyde Lea and there are several modern detached houses to the south-east of the village.

MANOR. *COPPENHALL* (Copehale), which had been held, T.R.E., by three freemen, was held in 1086 as a hide by Bueret from Robert de Stafford.[19] The overlordship descended in the barony of Stafford until at least 1524.[20] Lord Stafford was still described as lord of the manor in 1884,[21] and payments from Coppenhall were included among Stafford Rents from at least 1368 until at least 1720.[22] Land there remained in the Stafford family until at least 1892.[23]

Bueret, the tenant in 1086[24] seems to have been followed before 1166 by an Ulpher de Coppenhall.[25] Coppenhall seems to have formed the $\frac{2}{3}$ fee held in demesne by Geoffrey de Coppenhall in 1166.[26] Robert fitz Geoffrey had succeeded before 1222.[27] A Robert de Coppenhall held a small or mortain fee here in 1242[28] and this or another Robert 'de Coppenhall' or 'de Botarhale' was released, before 1255, by Robert de Stafford from his service due for $\frac{1}{2}$ fee.[29]

Ulpher had granted half his demesne lands in Coppenhall, with woodland there, probably before 1166, to a William Bagot.[30] The land has been identified with The Hyde, and this William Bagot, described as of The Hyde, was succeeded, by 1182, by a son William (II)[31] who was holding $\frac{1}{2}$ knight's fee in Coppenhall of Robert fitz Geoffrey in 1222 and 1227.[32] He had married one of the three daughters and coheirs of Robert fitz Odo of Loxley (Warws.), through whom he acquired Patshull (Seisdon hundred).[33] By 1236 he had been succeeded by his son Robert, and he, by 1248 or 1249, by his son William (III), when his widow Ascira was claiming dower in rents in The Hyde and Coppenhall.[34] Following the surrender of the intermediate lordship by Robert de Coppenhall, William (III) was described as lord of Coppenhall in 1255.[35] It was presumably this same William (III) on whom a manor of Hyde was settled, for life, by a Richard Bagot in 1276, with successive remainders to his sons William, Robert, and Edmund.[36] In 1279 Richard recovered possession[37] but in 1285 William (III) was holding the manor of The Hyde as 1 knight's fee.[38] In 1303 a grant of free warren in his demesne lands in The Hyde was made to William Bagot (IV),[39] and in 1305 the manor of The Hyde was settled on William and his wife Eleanor.[40] William (IV) was described as lord of Coppenhall in 1316[41] but at some date between 1308 and c. 1324 (when he died, leaving no issue), he conveyed this manor of The Hyde to Ralph Lord Stafford.[42] Eleanor, by then wife of John de Ferrers, lord of Chartley, conveyed her life interest in the manor to the same Ralph de Stafford in 1326.[43]

In 1327 The Hyde was settled in fee tail on Ralph de Stafford and his wife Katherine, to hold in chief.[44] Meanwhile, William Bagot's heir seems to have been Sir Ralph Bagot,[45] probably his brother, whose daughter Joan, in 1359, conveyed all her rights in the manor to Ralph, by then Earl of Stafford.[46] In 1378 Hugh Earl of Stafford conveyed The Hyde and all his lands in Coppenhall to Richard and Nicholas de Stafford and four others,[47] presumably by way of a settlement since the manor of Hyde was held by the barony in 1397.[48] In 1403, on the death of Edmund Earl of Stafford, his heir being an infant, the king granted to the queen two-thirds of a carucate of demesne land in two-thirds of the manor, with 4 acres meadowland, two stews, and two-thirds of the park of Hyde (in Castle Church).[49] This grant was confirmed in 1404.[50]

[17] *P.O. Dir. Staffs.* (1868).
[18] Ex inf. the English Electric Co. (1956).
[19] *V.C.H. Staffs.* iv. 53, no. 218.
[20] *Red Bk. Exch.* (Rolls Ser.), 267; *S.H.C.* i. 150, 181–2; *Bk. of Fees*, 543; C 142/41, no. 18.
[21] *Kelly's Dir. Staffs.* (1884).
[22] W.S.L., D. 1721/1/8, p. 56; W.S.L. 119/40; see pp. 87–88.
[23] B.M. Eg. MS. 2872, ff. 45*a*–60*a*; *Kelly's Dir. Staffs.* (1892). About 1849 about 69 a. were held of them by tenants: Tithe Maps and Appt., Penkridge (copy in W.S.L.).
[24] *V.C.H. Staffs.* iv. 53, no. 218.
[25] *S.H.C.* n.s. xi. 122; *S.H.C.* ii (1), 211.
[26] *Red Bk. Exch.* 267; *S.H.C.* i. 150, 181–2.
[27] *S.H.C.* iv (1), 20–21, 60. He is probably to be identified with the Robert de Coppenhall who was Dean of Penkridge in about 1180: ibid. vi (1), 23; ibid. 1950–1, 7 n.11. A Geoffrey son of Geoffrey de Coppenhall occurs around the end of the 12th cent.: ibid. vi (1), 23, and n. 7.
[28] *Bk. of Fees*, 967, 972.
[29] *S.H.C.* n.s. xi. 129; *Rot. Hund.* (Rec. Com.), ii. 114.

[30] *S.H.C.* n.s. xi. 122–3.
[31] Ibid.; W.S.L., D. 1721/1/1, f. 110*a*.
[32] *S.H.C.* iv (1), 20–21.
[33] *S.H.C.* n.s. xi. 124–5; *V.C.H. Warws.* iii. 130–1.
[34] *S.H.C.* n.s. xi. 126–8, 144; *S.H.C.* iv (1), 117–20.
[35] *Rot. Hund.* (Rec. Com.), ii. 114.
[36] *S.H.C.* 1911, 30–31.
[37] Ibid. vi (1), 141; ibid. n.s. xi. 133.
[38] *Feud. Aids*, v. 2; *S.H.C.* n.s. xi. 144.
[39] *Cal. Chart. R.* 1300–26, 37; *S.H.C.* n.s. xi. 144.
[40] *S.H.C.* 1911, 64–65. She was Eleanor of Louvaine, widow of Sir William de Douglas: ibid. n.s. xi. 138–40.
[41] *Feud. Aids*, v. 16.
[42] W.S.L., S. MS. 201 (1), p. 436; *S.H.C.* n.s. xi. 139; *Complete Peerage* xii (1), 174.
[43] W.S.L., D. 1721/1/1, f. 158*b*; *S.H.C.* n.s. xi. 139.
[44] *Cal. Pat.* 1327–30, 7; C 143/229, no. 109.
[45] Shaw, *Staffs.* ii. 280.
[46] *S.H.C.* n.s. xi. 142–3; W.S.L., D. 1721/1/1, f. 159*a*.
[47] W.S.L., D. 1721/1/1, ff. 110*b*, 159*a*.
[48] W.S.L., Stafford Manor, Bailiff's Acct. 20–21 Ric. II.
[49] *Cal. Close*, 1402–5, 238.
[50] *Cal. Pat.* 1401–5, 347.

By 1397, and until at least July 1403, rents from lands in The Hyde and Coppenhall were held of the barony by a Humphrey de Stafford.[51] Some time between 1443 and 1453 a manor of Hyde was settled on Avice or Amice, daughter and heir of Sir Richard Stafford son and heir of Sir Humphrey Stafford of Hooke (Dors.).[52] Avice, who by 1438 was married to James le Botiller or Ormond, later Earl of Wiltshire (d. 1461), died childless in 1457.[53] Her heir was her cousin, Humphrey Stafford (son of John), who died seised of The Hyde in 1461 and was succeeded by his cousin Sir Humphrey Stafford of Hooke and of Southwick (in North Bradley, Wilts.), son of William younger brother of Richard and John Stafford.[54] In 1469 he became Earl of Devon, and was beheaded.[55] Another Sir Humphrey Stafford then entered what were later described as lands and tenements in Hyde and Coppenhall, claiming them by virtue of a conveyance to his father, Humphrey son of Ralph, by Sir Humphrey Stafford of Hooke, grandfather of the Earl of Devon, but was dispossessed in 1473 by the heirs of Alice, aunt of the earl, namely Elizabeth and her husband Sir John Coleshill, Anne and her husband John Willoughby, and Thomas Strangeways, husband of the third daughter Eleanor.[56] In 1483 Sir Robert Willoughby, son of Anne, was cleared of a charge of wrongfully dispossessing Humphrey of these lands[57] and, as Lord Willoughby de Broke, in 1502 died seised of what was called the manor of Hyde-Coppenhall, worth £7 7s. 4d. and held of the Earl of Stafford by fealty.[58] His heir was his son Robert,[59] who in 1516, with his second wife Dorothy and son Edward, made a settlement of this and other manors.[60] Hyde-Coppenhall then descended with Littywood in Bradley,[61] being conveyed in 1542 by Sir Anthony Willoughby to Fulke Greville and Elizabeth.[62] In 1552 they conveyed it, for her life, to Anne Neville, a daughter of Ralph Earl of Westmorland (d. 1549), and granddaughter of Edward Stafford, Duke of Buckingham (d. 1521).[63] In 1628 Margaret, wife of Sir Richard Verney of Compton Verney (Warws.), succeeded her brother to what was called the manor of Hyde or Hyde-Coppenhall.[64] On her death in 1631 the manor was described as Hyde-Coppenhall otherwise Coppenhall,[65] and it probably then descended with the barony of Willoughby de Broke (in abeyance from 1521 to 1694). By c. 1849 the 16th Lord Willoughby de Broke (d. 1852) owned a farm of 297 acres in Coppenhall, the tenant being Samuel Wright, and

a small holding of 6 acres, the tenant being a Mr. Ansell.[66] The 18th Lord Willoughby de Broke still owned land here at the end of the century.[67]

The Cholmeley family seem to have occupied the 'farm of Coppenhall' as tenants since the early 15th century.[68] In 1547 Thomas Cholmeley, Mary his wife, and their sons Edward and Henry were granted by Sir Fulke Greville the lease for their lives of a capital messuage and land in Coppenhall at a rent of 57s. 10½d.[69] Messuages and lands in Coppenhall and Hyde were leased to Edward and Henry by Sir Fulke and his wife in 1557,[70] and in 1565 messuages and lands in Coppenhall, Hyde, and elsewhere were settled on Edward for 40 years at a rent of £5 5s. 4d.[71] Sir Fulke's son Sir Fulke in 1607 leased the capital messuage and arable land, meadow, and pasture in Coppenhall to a Henry Cholmeley for 21 years,[72] and as Lord Brooke Fulke renewed the lease in 1627.[73] Henry died later in the same year.[74] Robert, Matthew, and Edward Cholmeley made a settlement of lands in Coppenhall in 1660,[75] and land there was settled on Edward in 1663.[76]

Coppenhall Hall was bought and occupied after the First World War by Mr. James Holt, farmer.[77] He still owned it in 1956, the tenant being Mr. Sumner.[78] The building is described above.[79]

The prebend of Coppenhall in the collegiate church of Penkridge occurs by 1261[80] and was valued at £10 in 1291.[81] In 1535 the prebend, valued at £16, consisted of the site of the *PREBENDAL MANOR*, worth 20s., chief rents of 30s., tithe of grain averaging £6, other tithes and oblations averaging £6 10s., and Easter offerings, averaging 10s.[82] Synodals of 6s. 8d. were due every three years to the Dean of Penkridge.[83] A lease of the prebend was granted in 1547 to Sir Edward Littleton who the following year paid £20 rent for it to the royal bailiff of the dissolved college.[84] The prebend presumably descended with the rest of the collegiate possessions,[85] and in 1585 it passed with view of frankpledge and tithe in Coppenhall to Edward Littleton,[86] grandson of the lessee of 1547 and holder of a 21-year lease since 1577 or 1578.[87] The prebend descended in his family with Pillaton[88] until at least 1709,[89] and the 30 acres in Coppenhall owned by the 3rd Lord Hatherton c. 1849[90] may have been former prebendal land.

LESSER ESTATES. One Elias de Coppenhall (living c. 1160) made various grants of land in

[51] W.S.L., Stafford Manor, Bailiff's Acct. 20–21 Ric. II; W.S.L., D. 1721/1/8, pp. 145, 163.
[52] C 140/3. [53] *Complete Peerage*, x. 128 and note.
[54] C 140/3. [55] *Complete Peerage*, iv. 327–8.
[56] *S.H.C.* N.S. iv. 204–7; ibid. N.S. vi (1), 149–50; W.S.L., D. 1721/1/4 (Stafford Pedigrees), ff. 30b–31a.
[57] *S.H.C.* N.S. vi (1), 149–50; *Complete Peerage* (orig. edn.), viii. 150.
[58] *Cal. Inq. p.m. Hen. VII*, ii, no. 638. [59] Ibid.
[60] *S.H.C.* xii (1), 182.
[61] *V.C.H. Staffs.* iv. 79.
[62] C.P. 40/1113, m. 5d.
[63] *S.H.C.* xii (1), 193; *Complete Peerage* (orig. edn.), viii. 112.
[64] Wards 7/49/213.
[65] C 142/474, no. 55.
[66] Tithe Maps and Appt., Penkridge (copy in W.S.L.).
[67] *Kelly's Dir. Staffs.* (1900), which, like the edns. for 1892 and 1896, calls him lord of the manor, a title which earlier directories had given to Lord Stafford.
[68] C 2/Jas. I, C. 8/6c. [69] *S.H.C.* xii (1), 199.
[70] W.S.L., D. 1553/58. [71] *S.H.C.* xiii. 240.

[72] C 2/Jas. I, H. 10/13.
[73] W.S.L., D. 1553/54.
[74] *Penkridge Par. Reg.* (Staffs. Par. Reg. Soc)., 136. His son Edward occurs in 1623: C 2/Jas. I, C. 8/60.
[75] C.P. 25(2)/597, 12 Chas. II East.
[76] C.P. 25(2)/123, 14 and 15 Chas. II Hil.
[77] Local inf. [78] Local inf.
[79] See p. 139. [80] *S.H.C.* 1950–1, 47.
[81] *Tax. Eccl.* (Rec. Com.), 242.
[82] *Valor Eccl.* (Rec. Com.), iii. 99–100.
[83] Ibid. 100.
[84] *S.H.C.* 1950–1, 36 and note 98.
[85] See p. 111. The statement c. 1558 that the prebend as well as the vicarial estate passed to Edward Cholmeley (*S.H.C.* N.S. ix. 7) seems incorrect.
[86] *S.H.C.* xv. 167.
[87] C 66/1173, m. 24.
[88] C 142/455, no. 76; C.P. 25(2)/485, 8 Chas. I East.; C.P. 25(2)/486, 18 Chas. I Mich.; C.P. 25(2)/596, 1654 Trin.; C.P. 25(2)/725, 28 Chas. II Mich.; C.P. 43/490, rot. 164; see p. 119.
[89] C.P. 43/506, rot. 98. [90] See p. 141.

Coppenhall to Stone Priory (Pirehill hundred), including 2 virgates held of him by Ranulf his brother.[91] Part of this land was confirmed to the priory by a Robert de Coppenhall after some dispute.[92] Robert de Coppenhall, Dean of Penkridge c. 1180, granted to the priory the messuage in Coppenhall where his father and then he himself had lived, along with an orchard, an alder grove, and ½ virgate *in campo*,[93] while Robert son of Geoffrey de Coppenhall gave the priory 2s. out of the farm of the lands of Butterhill ('Butterales').[94] At some time after c. 1217 Hervey de Stafford confirmed the canons in their possession of land granted by Elias and of the 2s. rent from Butterhill.[95] Part of Elias's grant, the land between Hyde and 'Holedene' with meadow, was given to William Bagot (II), son of William Bagot of The Hyde, by Prior Sylvester for homage and a rent of 40d.[96]

A Henry de 'Butterhall', lord of Butterhill, occurs possibly early in the 14th century.[97] At some unknown date Margery, daughter of John le Rede of Longdon, gave to John de Pykstoke and his heirs all her rights in the whole lordship of the vill of Butterhill and Coppenhall.[98] In 1324 Philip de Pickstock acquired 2 acres in Butterhill from Richard de Wenlock,[99] and by 1403 Nicholas de Pickstock was holding tenements here of Lord Stafford by rent of six barbed arrows (worth 12d.).[1] His heirs were holding as free tenants of the barony a messuage called Butterhill (Butterhall) between at least 1452 and 1486.[2] In 1518 William Greene was paying a rent to Lord Stafford for a messuage and a carucate of land, formerly held by Nicholas Pickstock,[3] and between at least 1627 and 1631 Ralph Greene paid 12d. for what was almost certainly this same tenement at Butterhill.[4]

An estate in Butterhill of some 111 acres including Butterhill House was owned c. 1849 by Edward Moore and occupied by Richard Wright.[5] By 1868 it seems to have been owned by William Marson, who was living in Butterhill by 1872,[6] and James Cramer Marson seems to have succeeded by 1876, although he was then not resident there.[7] By 1880 the estate was owned and farmed by Mrs. Lydia Busby,[8] who was still living there in 1900.[9] Mrs. A. J. Busby was one of the chief landowners in Coppenhall in 1912 and 1916,[10] but between at least 1924

and 1932 Butterhill House was owned and occupied by T. P. Darlington.[11] Miss Darlington was living there in 1940.[12] The house subsequently passed to the present Mr. Darlington, and he sold it in 1955 to Mr. A. N. Hillier, who had converted it by 1956 into flats.[13] The present house is a mid-19th-century brick building with gabled dormers, ornamental barge-boards, and stone bay windows.[14] There is a large walled garden to the north.

An estate in Butterhill of some 30 acres including the present Butterhill Farm and the windmill (see below) was owned c. 1849 by Lord Hatherton and occupied by William Handy.[15] It seems to have been united by 1868 to the Butterhill House estate[16] with which it then descended until 1955[17] and in 1956 was still owned by Mr. Darlington.[18] The farmhouse and many of the outbuildings date from the early 19th century.

MILLS. Henry Cholmeley and his wife Francis conveyed a windmill and ½ acre of land in Coppenhall to John Giffard (or Halfepenye) in 1616.[19] This may have stood in the Windmill Field 'adjoining Hyde Lea' mentioned in 1661,[20] but by the mid-19th century the field-name alone survived.[21]

A second windmill standing on high ground some 150 yds. west of Butterhill Farm and locally said to have been the only six-sail mill in the county was in use by 1820.[22] About 1849 it was part of Lord Hatherton's estate in Coppenhall occupied by William Handy.[23] It seems to have gone out of use between 1872 and 1876,[24] but the tackle was not removed until 1912.[25] The derelict brick tower probably dates from c. 1800.

CHURCH. There was a church at Coppenhall by 1200.[26] It may have been of independent foundation and subsequently appropriated to Penkridge College[27] of which it was a dependency by 1261.[28] A vicarage had been ordained by 1291.[29] By the Reformation 'all manner of sacraments and sacramentals, as well in christening of children as others', were administered in the church[30] which was described in 1563 as a chapel of ease to Penkridge with cure.[31] The churchyard, however, was not consecrated for burials until 1870.[32] The benefice

[91] S.H.C. vi (1), 23–24; ibid. ii (1), 248.
[92] Ibid. vi (1), 24.   [93] Ibid. 23.
[94] Ibid. 24; ibid. ii (1), 275.
[95] Ibid. ii (1), 275.
[96] Ibid. vi (1), 24.
[97] W.S.L., D. 1721/1/1, f. 110b.
[98] Ibid., f. 110a.   [99] Ibid., f. 153a.
[1] W.S.L., D. 1721/1/8, p. 150.
[2] W.S.L., Stafford Barony, Mins. Accts. 24–25 Hen. VIII, m. 2 (reciting rental of 31 Hen. VI); W.S.L., D. 1721/1/8, p. 150.
[3] W.S.L., D. 1721/1/8, p. 113.
[4] W.S.L., D. 1721/1/9, 6th nos., pp. 9, 28, 48.
[5] Tithe Maps and Appt., Penkridge (copy in W.S.L.). Wright was farming in Coppenhall in 1834 and 1851: White, Dir. Staffs. (1834; 1851).
[6] P.O. Dir. Staffs. (1868; 1872).
[7] Ibid. (1876).
[8] Kelly's Dir. Staffs. (1880).
[9] Ibid. (1900).
[10] Ibid. (1912; 1916).
[11] Ibid. (1924; 1928; 1932).
[12] Ibid. (1940).
[13] Ex inf. Mrs. Hillier (1956).
[14] A field to the north of the house in about 1849 was known as 'Old House Piece': Tithe Maps and Appt., Penkridge (copy in W.S.L.).

[15] Ibid. Handy was tenant of the mill in 1834: White, Dir. Staffs. (1834).
[16] P.O. Dir. Staffs. (1868).
[17] Ibid. (1872; 1876); Kelly's Dir. Staffs. (1880, and later edns. to 1940); ex inf. Mrs. Hillier.
[18] Ex inf. Mrs. Hillier.
[19] S.H.C. n.s. vi (1), 16. Two mills were included in Lord Willoughby de Broke's estate in Coppenhall, Hyde, and Rodbaston in 1516: S.H.C. xii (1), 182.
[20] W.S.L., D. 1792, Coppenhall deed, 10 Oct. 1661; it seems to have been an open field.
[21] Tithe Maps and Appt., Penkridge (copy in W.S.L.).
[22] Greenwood, Map of Staffs. (1820).
[23] Tithe Maps and Appt., Penkridge (copy in W.S.L.), Coppenhall, no. 28.
[24] It is mentioned in P.O. Dir. Staffs. (1872) but not in that for 1876.
[25] Ex inf. Mr. G. Howell, Stafford Mill (1957).
[26] See architectural description of church.
[27] This is suggested by the fact that a vicarage was ordained and by Bagot's claim to the right of presentation.
[28] S.H.C. 1950–1, 50–51.
[29] Tax. Eccl. (Rec. Com.), 242.
[30] S.H.C. n.s. ix. 7.
[31] S.H.C. 1915, 206.
[32] Lich. Dioc. Ch. Cal. (1871), 74.

became a perpetual curacy after the Reformation,[33] and since 1892 it has been united with that of Dunston.[34]

The right of presentation to the vicarage was claimed without success against the Dean of Penkridge by Richard Bagot in 1310.[35] The Crown presented in 1342, when the chapel was said to be annexed to the prebend of Bold in Penkridge College,[36] but by the time of the Dissolution the right of presentation was held by the Prebendary of Coppenhall.[37] It then passed to the Crown[38] and presumably descended with the advowson of Penkridge church[39] with which it was granted in 1585 to Edward Littleton.[40] It descended in his family until c. 1897, its recent history being the same as that of Dunston.[41]

The vicarage was valued at 13s. 4d. in 1291.[42] In 1548 the vicar had a house and lands in Coppenhall, all tithes in Coppenhall and Butterhill and tithe of corn in the hamlet of Hyde, the total being valued at £4.[43] In the same year the vicar was ordered to continue to serve the chapel at his old salary.[44] In 1550 the glebe and vicarial tithe were granted by the Crown to John Bellowe and William Fuller[45] but by 1554 were held by John Leveson and his wife Joyce who then granted them to Edward Cholmeley.[46] About 1558 the inhabitants of Coppenhall were accusing Edward of having made no provision for a vicar so that there was then no one to serve the cure.[47] The vicarial tithes were held by the Cholmeley family until at least 1703.[48] The curate's stipend was £4 in 1604[49] and the same in 1651 when it was stated to be paid out of the fee farm of Penkridge College.[50]

A service is held in the church each Sunday under the terms of Helen Perry's gift of 1902.[51]

The church of *ST. LAWRENCE* is a small stone building consisting of a nave and chancel with a timber bell turret at the west end. It dates from c. 1200 and is of special interest as a comparatively unaltered example of a small church of this period.[52] The walls are of stone ashlar and are of exceptional thickness, the east and west walls being further thickened at the base.

The chancel was probably built shortly before 1200. In the east wall are three widely spaced lancets, the most southerly having a semicircular head externally, the others being slightly pointed. In each instance the heads are cut from a single stone. externally the jambs and heads are chamfered and there are deep internal splays. The south wall has two similar windows. The pointed chancel arch is of two orders, springing from semicircular responds

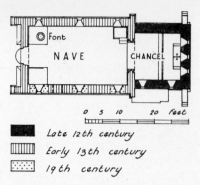

PLAN OF ST. LAWRENCE'S CHURCH

with hollowed bell capitals and square-edged abaci. The plinths are square and the base mouldings consist of two rolls, the lower one flattened. The nave probably dates from soon after 1200. In the west wall are three graded lancets with pointed heads. Externally they appear as independent lights but internally they are contained under a single arch with splayed jambs, exhibiting an early form of three-light window. Below the window the west doorway has an undercut dripstone terminating in much-decayed carved stops. The arch is pointed and carries a filletted roll-moulding which is continued down the jambs. In both north and south walls of the nave are three pointed lancets, those on the south being largely modern. Traces of a south doorway, which was already blocked before the mid-19th century,[53] are still visible between the two more westerly lancets. The buttresses abutting on the chancel arch and those at the west end of the nave are probably original; the buttresses at the east end of the chancel are later additions. At some period, possibly in the 16th century, a small wooden bell turret with a pyramidal roof was added at the west end of the nave, and in the 18th century two windows were inserted in the south nave wall.[54] The former lancets were blocked, but parts of their stonework may have survived. A thorough restoration of the church took place c. 1866 at a cost of £500.[55] Previously the interior had contained box-pews, a Georgian pulpit, turned altar rails, and a plaster ceiling.[56] At the restoration the church was reroofed, lancets were reinstated in the south nave wall, the gable-ends were rebuilt, and a circular window was inserted in the east gable. A new bell turret with a taller spire was added. Internally the Georgian fittings were removed and a stone pulpit and a circular font installed. The church contains memorial tablets to

[33] *S.H.C.* 1915, 207; ibid. N.S. ix. 7–8; White, *Dir. Staffs.* (1851). It was called a vicarage by the *Lich. Dioc. Ch. Cal.* from 1876.
[34] *Lond. Gaz.* 1892, pp. 4812–13; *Lich. Dioc. Dir.* (1955–6).
[35] *S.H.C.* ix (1), 25.
[36] *Cal. Pat.* 1340–8, 353; *S.H.C.* 1950–1, 25.
[37] *S.H.C.* N.S. ix. 6.
[38] Ibid. 7–8.
[39] See p. 130.
[40] *S.H.C.* xv. 167.
[41] C.P. 25(2)/484, 1 Chas. I Hil.; C.P. 25(2)/596, 1654 Trin.; C.P. 25(2)/725, 28 Chas. II Mich.; C.P. 43/506, rot. 98; White, *Dir. Staffs.* (1834; 1851); *Lich. Dioc. Ch. Cal.* (1898); see pp. 119, 148.
[42] *Tax. Eccl.* (Rec. Com.), 242.
[43] *S.H.C.* 1915, 206; ibid. N.S. ix. 7; *Cal. Pat.* 1549–51, 254.

[44] *S.H.C.* 1915, 206.
[45] *Cal. Pat.* 1549–51, 254.
[46] *S.H.C.* xii (1), 214.
[47] Ibid. N.S. ix. 7.
[48] C.P. 25(2)/597, 12 Chas. II East.; C.P. 25(2)/723, 14 Chas. II Hil.; C.P. 25(2)/965, 2 Anne Trin.
[49] *S.H.C.* 1915, 207, 211.
[50] Ibid. 203.
[51] See p. 148.
[52] W.S.L., S. MS. 433 (Thomas Album, c. 1835); W.S.L., Staffs. Views, iii, p. 152 (1838).
[53] W.S.L., Staffs. Views, iii, p. 152 (1842), shows the doorway unblocked with a small lancet above it, possibly John Buckler's own idea of the original arrangement.
[54] W.S.L., Staffs. Views, iii, p. 152.
[55] *Kelly's Dir. Staffs.* (1884). The date is given as 1861 in *Trans. N. Staffs. Field Club*, xlvi. 223.
[56] W.S.L., Staffs. Views, iii, p. 154 (1842).

the Revd. Evan Price (d. 1875) and his wife; also to Lillie (d. 1911), wife of Charles H. Wright.

A memorial pulpit and lectern were given in memory of Charles Mort by his widow Helen who by will proved 1917 bequeathed an annual interest of £5 for their maintenance.[57] In 1932 £20 accumulated income was used towards the cost of the heating apparatus,[58] and in 1957 the income was accumulating for use, as necessary, in the maintenance of the church.[59] The east lancets were restored in 1930, and stained glass was inserted in memory of the Revd. Charles E. Cope.[60] The oak lych-gate to the churchyard was erected in 1932 as a memorial to Charles H. and Lillie Wright.[61] The church still benefits from the gift of £100 made by Henry Woodhouse of Llandudno (Caernarvonshire) to provide an income for the upkeep of the fabric.[62]

In 1553 the plate included a silver chalice and paten and a brass censer.[63] In 1955 it included an Elizabethan silver chalice, a silver flagon, a pewter alms dish, an electro-plated alms dish, and an electro-plated paten, 1897.[64] In 1548 there were two bells,

identified in 1553 as one bell and a sanctus bell.[65] The present silver bell was cast by Clibury of Wellington in 1670.[66]

There is a register of baptisms from January 1678/9 to 1812, with nine marriages, 1684–1783, 1831, 1837.[67] The entries down to 1776 are copied mainly from the Bradley register with some from the Haughton register, but not consistently so. There is also a register of marriages from 1847 and of burials from 1871.[68]

CHARITIES FOR THE POOR. John Webb of Coppenhall, by will proved 1759, left to the poor of Coppenhall a rent of 20s. charged on land here.[69] In 1928 £2 accumulated income was paid to the church cleaner,[70] but by 1955 the charity had not been distributed for some years because no one had qualified to receive it.[71]

In about 1848 the poor of Coppenhall were stated to own Stitch Meadow here,[72] but no payment seems to have been made subsequently for lack of any record of the charity.[73]

DUNSTON

THE civil parish of Dunston, formerly part of the ancient parish of Penkridge, lies mainly to the west of the Stafford–Wolverhampton road north of Penkridge. It is bounded on the east by the Penk, and part of the northern boundary is formed by the Pothooks Brook, which enters the Penk at the north-eastern extremity of the parish, and by a tributary of the brook. The ground slopes from 375 ft. in the west to below 250 ft. at the Penk. The soil is stiff loam, the subsoil marl with sand and gravel.[1] Part of Penkridge was added to the civil parish of Dunston under the Staffordshire Review Order of 1934, increasing the area from 1,448 acres to 1,752 acres. In 1680 there were 20 houses in Dunston,[3] and in 1817 44 houses, with a population of 214.[4] The population in 1951 was 295.[5]

Dunston's marly loam soil and the meadows by the Penk were commended in 1817.[6] In 1827 100 acres of common on Dunston Heath were inclosed under an Act of 1814.[7] There were six farms and a smithy in Dunston in 1834,[8] and of seven farms of c. 1841 three were of over 100 acres.[9] In 1940 there were thirteen farms and a smithy, and five of the farms were over 150 acres, one of them then being a dairy farm.[10] In 1933 the County Council bought

103 acres in Dunston and established eight small-holdings, each with a house.[11]

On the west side of the road between Little Heath and Tofts a field which still contains pools was known in 1754 as Motes[12] and c. 1841 as Moat Bank.[13] It probably marks the site of a medieval house. It is said that an ancient house, from which the stone was carted away in the 19th century, formerly stood north of Dunston Heath near the present Yew Tree Farm.[14] Dunston Hall, rebuilt on the site of an older house by Frederick C. Perry c. 1870, is a large stuccoed mansion bearing his monogram. It has Gothic detail to the principal doorway and a central tower-like feature. Depressions in the north-east corner of the garden may indicate the presence of a former moat. The brick stable-range dates from the late 18th or early 19th century. Dunston House, lying opposite the church, is a square late-18th-century building of red brick. Alterations to the top story and elsewhere date from the late 19th century. Dunston Farm is of earlier-18th-century date. The Toft, known in the early 19th century as Old Toft,[15] was built c. 1700 and in its original form was a T-shaped brick house with a symmetrical front and a moulded stone cornice. The

[57] Charity Com. files.
[58] Ibid.
[59] Ex inf. the Vicar of Dunston-with-Coppenhall (1957).
[60] Inscription in situ; Lich. Dioc. Regy., Consist. Ct. Act Bk. 1930–4, p. 90, faculty, 29 Dec. 1930.
[61] Lich. Dioc. Regy., Consist. Ct. Act Bk. 1930–4, p. 308, faculty, 19 July 1932.
[62] Charity Com. files; ex inf. Lichfield Dioc. Trust (1957).
[63] S.H.C. 1915, 207.
[64] Ex inf. the Vicar of Dunston-with-Coppenhall (1955).
[65] S.H.C. 1915, 206, 207.
[66] C. Lynam, Church Bells of Staffs. 8 and pl. 89; A. E. Garbett, 'Church Bells of Staffs.' (Trans. Old Stafford Soc. 1953–4), 54, 20.
[67] Transcript in W.S.L.
[68] Ex inf. the Vicar of Dunston-with-Coppenhall.
[69] Abstract of Returns of Charitable Donations, 1786–8, H.C.5 11, pp. 1118–19 (1816), xvi (2); Charity Com. files.
[70] Charity Com. files.

[71] Ex inf. the Vicar of Dunston-with-Coppenhall.
[72] Tithe Maps and Appt., Penkridge (copy in W.S.L.).
[73] Charity Com. files.
[1] Kelly's Dir. Staffs. (1940).
[2] Ibid.; Census, 1951, Staffs.
[3] S.H.C. 1919, 219.
[4] Pitt, Staffs. 261.
[5] Census, 1951, Staffs.
[6] Pitt, Staffs. 261.
[7] S.R.O., Q/RDc 22; White, Dir. Staffs. (1834).
[8] White, Dir. Staffs. (1834).
[9] Tithe Maps and Appt., Penkridge (copy in W.S.L.).
[10] Kelly's Dir. Staffs. (1940).
[11] Ex inf. Staffs. C.C. Estate Agent.
[12] S.R.O., D. 260/M/E. 353 (a).
[13] Tithe Maps and Appt., Penkridge (copy in W.S.L.).
[14] Ex inf. Mr. Stanley, Little Heath.
[15] W.S.L., D. 1771, Pickstock Papers, Richard Cooke's Survey (undated, but between 1812 and 1831).

back wing has an early-19th-century extension and at the front a Georgian porch and a bay-windowed addition date from the present century. Toft Farm, formerly New Toft House,[16] appears to be an 18th-century building with later alterations.

At Little Heath part of a small thatched cottage of 17th-century origin is timber-framed and was formerly single-storied. At the south-west end a cobbler's workshop was added before the mid-19th century, and this trade was carried on for several generations by the Stanley family who still occupy the house.[17] There are few old cottages in the parish, most of those on the main road having been built or rebuilt by Frederick C. Perry of Dunston Hall.[18] The Home Farm, until 1934 in Penkridge parish, is dated 1892. There was formerly a toll-gate cottage at Acton Gate, lying in the angle between the main road and the road to Acton Trussell.[19] Immediately east of the school a small weatherboarded reading-room, dating from c. 1900, was given a brick extension after the First World War and now serves as a village hall.[20] Farther east a police house was built in 1952, and on a new service road north of the church there are six council houses, dating from 1953.[21]

The former vicarage house, which lies over half a mile south of the church, probably dates from the mid-19th century. It is a gabled house of red brick with Tudor windows. In 1902 additional service accommodation was provided at the expense of Helen Perry.[22] The house is now the property of the Cannock R.D.C. and has been converted into flats.[23] The present vicarage was built in 1951 on a plot of land immediately west of the churchyard given by the Rt. Hon. G. E. P. Thorneycroft.[24]

MANORS. In 1086 *DUNSTON*, assessed at 2 hides, was a member of the royal manor of Penkridge,[25] but by 1166 Robert de Stafford seems to have been lord of 1 knight's fee in Stretton and Dunston.[26] The Stafford lordship in 1243 included 1¼ small or mortain fee in Stretton and Dunston[27] which descended in the barony until at least 1460.[28] Dunston continued to be held of the barony by knight service until at least 1604.[29] Some land in Dunston was retained by the Staffords and held of them by freehold and leasehold tenants between at least 1331 and 1542.[30] In 1391 the Earl of Stafford had free warren in Dunston.[31]

In 1166 Hervey de Stretton was holding of Robert de Stafford, in demesne, the fee apparently situated in Stretton and Dunston.[32] Richard de Stretton, probably Hervey's great-grandson, was holding the 1¼ fee in Stretton and Dunston by 1243,[33] and in 1273 his widow Agnes was suing his son and heir Richard (II) for a third of 11 messuages and 2½ virgates in Dunston.[34] By 1285 Agnes and her then husband William de Draycote were said to be holding one-third of the vill of Richard (II),[35] but in 1296 they surrendered to him most of the lands and tenements in Dunston which they held as Agnes's dower, Richard giving them in return 16 acres in Stretton for life.[36] Richard (II)'s widow Rose was claiming dower rights in lands in Dunston in 1297,[37] but the Stretton lordship seems to have ended about this time. Their capital messuage in Dunston was mentioned at some time between 1273 and 1292.[38]

Land in Dunston called 'Edwenes brughe' formerly held by Robert Bagot was leased by Richard de Stretton, probably Richard (I), to Simon de Pickstock and Thomas his brother.[39] Thomas acquired from Richard de Stretton (II) 5 messuages in Dunston with 2 oxgangs of land, the villeins dwelling there and 4s. rent,[40] along with a further messuage and 4 acres of land here.[41] In 1285 Thomas and William de Pickstock were said to be holding two-thirds of the vill of Dunston of Richard,[42] and what may have been the other third was granted to them by Richard[43] at some time after 1286, the year in which he had received it from William de Draycote and Agnes, widow of Richard (I).[44] William and Agnes also conveyed to Thomas de Pickstock their rights in land in Dunston called 'Bagotisbryge'.[45] Thomas seems to have been succeeded before 1289 by his cousin John, the son of William de Pickstock and a minor;[46] and although his title to some of the land was disputed by a William son of William de Pickstock between 1289 and 1301,[47] John was named as lord of Dunston in 1316.[48]

John's heir was his son William Pickstock, a burgess of Stafford,[49] who was succeeded, probably by 1325, by a son Nicholas described as of Stafford in 1328 or 1329 and still living in 1339.[50] Simon son of Nicholas was lord in 1375[51] and 1379.[52] Simon's son John occurs in 1419,[53] and in 1437, as John Pickstock of Levedale, he granted his lands in Dunston to Robert Derrington of Gayton (Pirehill

---

[16] W.S.L., D. 1771, Pickstock Papers, Richard Cooke's Survey (undated, but between 1812 and 1831).

[17] Ex inf. Mr. Stanley.

[18] They bear his monogram and are dated between 1889 and 1898.

[19] Tithe Maps and Appt., Penkridge (copy in W.S.L.).

[20] Local inf.

[21] Ex inf. the Vicar of Dunston-with-Coppenhall (1956).

[22] Lich. Dioc. Regy., Consist. Ct. Act Bk. 1899–1903, p. 368, faculty, 16 May 1902.

[23] Ex inf. the vicar.   [24] Ex inf. the vicar.

[25] *V.C.H. Staffs.* iv. 38, no. 8.

[26] *Red Bk. Exch.* (Rolls Ser.), 266; *S.H.C.* i. 170.

[27] *Bk. of Fees*, 967.

[28] *Feud. Aids*, v. 3, 22; C 136/18(8); C 136/25(2); C 137/38, 39; C 139/180.

[29] W.S.L., Stafford Barony, Mins. Accts. 1532–3, m. 11d; C 142/284, no. 25.

[30] W.S.L., D. 1721/1/8, pp. 57, 80, 145.

[31] *S.H.C.* xv. 41.

[32] *Red Bk. Exch.* 266; *S.H.C.* i. 170.

[33] *Bk. of Fees*, 967.

[34] *S.H.C.* vi (1), 59.

[35] *Feud. Aids*, v. 3.

[36] W.S.L., D. 1721/1/1, 1st nos., f. 122b. The lands retained ultimately passed with lands in Stretton to William le Champion, who surrendered the lands in Dunston to Lord Stafford in 1329: W.S.L., S. MS. 350A/40, f. 69a; W.S.L., D. 1721/1/1, 1st nos., f. 123b.

[37] *S.H.C.* vii (1), 40.

[38] Ibid. viii (1), 165.

[39] W.S.L., D. 1721/1/1, 1st nos., f. 122a.

[40] W.S.L., S. MS. 201 (1), p. 432.

[41] W.S.L., D. 1721/1/1, 1st nos., f. 122b.

[42] *Feud. Aids*, v. 3.

[43] W.S.L., D. 1721/1/1, 1st nos., f. 123a.

[44] Ibid. 1st nos., f. 122b.

[45] Ibid. 1st nos., f. 122a.

[46] *S.H.C.* vi (1), 191.

[47] Ibid. vii (1), 70, 82.

[48] *Feud. Aids*, v. 17.

[49] W.S.L., S. MS. 201 (1), pp. 396–7.

[50] Ibid., p. 397; *S.H.C.* ix (1), 108, 111; W.S.L., D. 1721/1/1, 1st nos., f. 123b.

[51] *Cal. Inq. p.m.* xiv, no. 212.

[52] W.S.L. 51/46, bdle. l, no. 11.

[53] W.S.L., S. MS. 201 (1), p. 397; *S.H.C.* xvii. 36.

hundred) and Agnes his wife,[54] who in 1438 settled the reversion on their son John with remainder to a younger son George.[55] Robert was dead by 1441, but Agnes continued to hold Dunston for life.[56] John was succeeded by a son John and he by a son Hamlett, described as of Coton in 1517 or 1518.[57] In 1573 Hamlett's son John conveyed two messuages, 30 acres of land, 12 acres of meadow, and 20 acres of pasture in Dunston to his son Sampson, described as of Coton.[58] Sampson Derrington died in 1596, holding what was called the manor of Dunston, and his heir was Katherine, a minor, the daughter of his son Anthony Derrington.[59] The queen granted the wardship to Richard Masterson of Nantwich (Ches.) to whose son, Thomas, Katherine was married by 1597.[60] Katherine died in 1603 holding the manor and leaving an infant son Thomas as her heir.[61] He gained possession in 1631,[62] and he and his wife Mary conveyed the manor in 1638 to Thomas Adshed of Milwich (Pirehill hundred),[63] who sold it in 1647 or 1648 to Henry Pickstock, described as of Dunston.[64] Henry was chargeable for three hearths in Dunston in 1666[65] and was still living in 1667.[66] This estate presumably descended with the Toft estate until c. 1841 at least, when the Pickstock family's 186 acres in Dunston included Dunston House and land in the east of the parish as well as the Toft in the west.[67] Dunston House is described above.[68]

Hervey de Stafford was lord of a knight's fee in DUNSTON, Drayton, and Water Eaton by 1236,[69] while by 1243 Robert de Stafford was lord of half a small fee in Dunston and Drayton, in addition to the 1¼ small fee in Stretton and Dunston.[70] This ½ fee descended in the Stafford barony until at least 1460.[71]

By 1243 this ½ fee was held of Robert by a William de Stafford,[72] who by 1271 was claiming a third share of land in Dunston against Richard de Stretton and others.[73] Later, probably in 1281, William stated that his ancestors had held a third of the vill of the barony.[74] His land may perhaps be identified with what was called a manor of Dunston settled by 1452 on Avice, daughter and heir of Sir Richard Stafford

who had succeeded his father Sir Humphrey Stafford of Hooke (Dors.) in about 1427.[75] Avice died without children, and the manor passed to her cousin Humphrey Stafford, lord of Southwick (in North Bradley, Wilts.) in 1461.[76] This manor then descended with Littywood in Bradley[77] until at least 1634 when it passed to Sir Greville Verney.[78] His descendants continued to hold land in Dunston until at least 1896,[79] the 16th Lord Willoughby de Broke (d. 1852) owning over 114 acres c. 1841.[80] The 19th baron (d. 1923) owned some 195 acres here in 1903.[81]

In 1409 Sir Fulke Pembrugge, lord of Acton Trussell, was holding land in Dunston of Lord Stafford,[82] and in 1464 Sir William Trussell died seised of land here in 'Welesmedewe', his heir being his son Thomas.[83] Thomas Fowke, of the City of London, merchant of the staple, who acquired half Acton Trussell, also bought what was described as the manor of DUNSTON from Lord Stafford in 1577 and conveyed half of it in 1578 to John Barbour.[84] Thomas Fowke died seised of half this manor in 1586, his heir being his eldest son John, a minor.[85] In 1589 what were described as lands in Dunston were conveyed to a John Fowke, along with Acton Trussell and Bednall,[86] and in 1598 a Thomas Fowke was holding the manor jointly with John Barbour in fee simple.[87]

By 1600 Thomas Fowke had been succeeded by his son John who in 1602 sold his half of the manor to William Anson of Lincoln's Inn.[88] William's son and heir William (II), having succeeded in 1644,[89] made settlements of what was called the manor in 1658[90] and 1667[91] and conveyed it in 1681 to his son, William (III).[92] A manor of Dunston, with Acton Trussell and Bednall, was said to be held by William's grandson Thomas in 1736 and 1752; by Thomas's nephew George in 1785 and 1789; and by George's son Thomas, created Viscount Anson in 1806, in 1790, 1791, and 1792.[93] In 1818 this Thomas's son Thomas William, created Earl of Lichfield in 1831, succeeded to the manor,[94] which descended in the

[54] W.S.L. 51/46, bdle. 1, nos. 15, 16; W.S.L., S. MS. 201 (1), p. 397.
[55] W.S.L. 51/46, bdle. 1, no. 17.
[56] Ibid. no. 20.
[57] W.S.L., S. MS. 201 (1), p. 397.
[58] S.H.C. 1926, 69–70.
[59] C 142/250, no. 26; C 60/376, no. 9.
[60] Req. 2/84/47; C 142/250, no. 26.
[61] C 142/284, no. 25.
[62] C 60/520, no. 32.
[63] C.P. 25(2)/486, Chas. I Hil.; W.S.L. 51/46, bdle. 1, no. 27.
[64] W.S.L., S. MS. 201 (1), p. 397. Henry's father Thomas had been a tenant within the manor 17 years before.
[65] S.H.C. 1927, 29.
[66] W.S.L. 51/46, bdle. 2.
[67] Tithe Maps and Appt., Penkridge (copy in W.S.L.); W.S.L., D. 1771, Pickstock Papers, Richard Cooke's Survey (undated, but between 1812 and 1831; see p. 146.
[68] See p. 143.
[69] Bk. of Fees, 543.
[70] Ibid. 967.
[71] C 136/24(10); C 136/18(8); C 136/25(2); C 137/38, 39; C 139/180.
[72] Bk. of Fees, 967. As Hervey had been succeeded by Robert, his brother, it is not likely that this William is to be identified with the William de Stafford who was a younger son of Hervey: S.H.C. viii (1), 160.
[73] S.H.C. vi (1), 52. In 1272 2 messuages and 1 virgate in Dunston were conveyed to him by Robert de Weston and his wife Joan: ibid. iv (1), 252–3.

[74] Ibid. vi (1), 154.
[75] C 140/3.
[76] Ibid.
[77] C 142/501, no. 63; S.H.C. xii (1), 193; ibid. 1931, 223–4; Wards 7/49, no. 213; V.C.H. Staffs. iv. 79–80.
[78] C 142/474, no. 55.
[79] W.S.L., D. 1553/28, 36, 55 (d, g, h), 57, 101, 105; P.O. Dir. Staffs. (1868, and later edns. to 1876); Kelly's Dir. Staffs. (1880, and later edns. to 1896).
[80] Tithe Maps and Appt., Penkridge (copy in W.S.L.).
[81] W.S.L., D. 1771, Pickstock Papers, Dunston Rate Bk. (1903).
[82] C 137/73.
[83] C 140/9.
[84] W.S.L., D. 1765/28, Abstract of Title of Viscount Anson to the Manor of Dunston, m. 1.
[85] C 142/213, no. 133.
[86] S.H.C. xvi. 97.
[87] S.R.O., D. 260/M/box 16, bdle. a, Penkridge Ct. Bk. 1598–1654, f. 10a. The bounds of the manor are here given, f. 5a.
[88] W.S.L., D. 1765/28, mm. 2–3; S.H.C. 1934 (2), 36.
[89] Burke, Peerage (1949), 1221.
[90] C.P. 25(2)/597, 1658 Mich.
[91] C.P. 25(2)/724, 19 Chas. II Trin. A Mrs. Mary Anson, widow, was taxable on 8 hearths in the constablewick of Dunston and Drayton in 1666: S.H.C. 1927, 29.
[92] W.S.L., D. 1765/28, m. 6.
[93] Ibid.; S.R.O., Gamekprs.' Deps.; Burke, Peerage (1949), 1221.
[94] C.P. 43/943, rot. 351; Complete Peerage, i. 175; ibid. viii. 648.

family until at least 1880 along with much of the land in Dunston.[95]

The other half of the manor, held by John Barbour in 1598,[96] was granted by him to Hugh Whitby of Rickerscote (in Castle Church) in 1602.[97] After Hugh's death the moiety passed to his son John, who, in pursuance of a trust reposed in his father, conveyed a half of this moiety to Thomas Spokes, otherwise Whitby, of Dunston in 1612.[98] A William Whitby and others in 1641 settled this quarter of the manor with lands in Dunston on Thomas Whitby the younger,[99] whose son and heir George seems to have held half the manor in 1725.[1] Thomas son of George was succeeded in 1744 by his niece Ann Whitby, who as Ann Parker, widow, sold half the manor of Dunston to George Anson in 1788.[2]

In 1652 Thomas Whitby, to settle his debts, had leased a messuage and land in Dunston for 99 years to George Oswald of Bransford (Worcs.), but at some time between 1687 and 1692 Thomas's son George sold the messuage and lands to Thomas Pickstock, the mortgage at the same time being cleared with Elizabeth, widow of George Oswald.[3] Thomas Pickstock and others made a settlement of lands in Dunston in 1717,[4] and in 1725 Thomas made a further settlement of the messuage, by then called the Toft, with lands including the Long Toft and the Withy Flat, prior to the marriage of his daughter Elizabeth.[5] In 1732, when he was living at the Newhouse in Penkridge parish, he and his son and heir Thomas, of Dunston, appointed further trustees of the Toft, by then in the hands of tenants.[6] Ralph Pickstock, son of a Thomas Pickstock, occurs in 1756,[7] and a Ralph Pickstock of Aston (Warws.) owned the Toft in 1776 when he leased it to Henry Pickstock, probably his brother, for three years.[8] Ralph was living at the Toft in 1804 and died in 1808, his brother and nephew, both named Henry, being among his executors.[9] Ralph, son of the younger Henry,[10] was living there by 1822 when the estate consisted of the Slang Toft (about 3 a.) and the Broad Toft (about 10 a.).[11] Between at least 1851 and 1872 Thomas Pickstock, farmer, was living at the Toft,[12] while Mrs. Thomas Pickstock was farming there between at least 1876 and 1884[13] and Ralph Pickstock between at least 1892 and 1896.[14] By 1903

Ralph had sold the house and buildings to Arthur Meakin whose tenant was Joseph Eccles.[15] By 1924 the Toft was owned and occupied by B. C. Griffin, who died in 1955 and whose widow still lived there in 1956.[16] Toft Farm is described above.[17]

Thomas Anson held courts leet and baron at Dunston in at least 1792 and 1811.[18]

In 1452 the Duke of Buckingham leased the farm of a fishery in the Penk within Dunston to the lord of Acton Trussell for 12d.[19] These waters, from the cross at Swanford, apparently the boundary between Dunston and Drayton, downstream to Acton Bridge, were leased and sub-leased between about 1483 and 1543.[20] The tenant of Acton Trussell, 'one Fowke of Penkeriche', was lessee in 1533, when he also paid 5½d. for licence to divert the stream to Acton Mill.[21] Thomas Whitby granted William Anson and his heirs a fishery in the Penk from Swan Lane to Litty Meadow Ditch in 1617,[22] and Ann Parker's grant of her share of the manor of Dunston in 1788 included a fishery.[23] Thomas Pickstock and others made a settlement of a free fishery in the waters of the Penk at Dunston in 1717,[24] and a fishery here was offered for sale in 1821, probably by Ralph Pickstock.[25]

Elizabeth, daughter and heir of William Trumwyn of Cannock, was holding a messuage and land in Dunston of Simon Pickstock at her death in 1375.[26] The estate then descended with the Trumwyn family's lands in Cannock[27] and consisted of 46 acres of arable, 8 acres of meadow, and 11s. 6d. rent, worth in all 20s., in 1493, when it was said to be held of the Duke of Buckingham.[28] It was described as a manor of *DUNSTON* in 1559 and 1560 when two-thirds of the estate were sold to Francis Biddulph,[29] already holder of the third part.[30] In 1564 Francis and his wife Isabel sold the whole estate to John Cowper,[31] but the lands were divided with other disputed Trumwyn property among various claimants in 1568.[32] Thomas Salwey, one of the claimants, and Arthur and Matthew Salwey, conveyed their share to John Cowper in 1576,[33] while a further messuage and lands in Dunston were settled on John and Edmund Cowper in 1578 by Francis Pycto and his wife Elizabeth.[34] Edmund died in possession of a messuage and lands in Dunston

95 White, *Dir. Staffs.* (1834; 1851); Tithe Maps and Appt., Penkridge (copy in W.S.L.); *P.O. Dir. Staffs.* (1872; 1876); *Kelly's Dir. Staffs.* (1880). The Earl of Lichfield was still one of the chief landowners in Dunston in 1884: *Kelly's Dir. Staffs.* (1884).
96 S.R.O., D. 260/M/box 16, bdle. a, Ct. Bk. 1598–1654, f. 10a.
97 *S.H.C.* xvi, 216; ibid. 1934 (2), 36.
98 Ibid. 1934 (2), 36.
99 C.P. 25(2)/486, 17 Chas. I East.
1 W.S.L., D. 1765/28, mm. 7–8; W.S.L. 51/46, bdle. 2.
2 W.S.L., D. 1765/28, mm. 8–9.
3 W.S.L. 51/46, bdle. 2.
4 C.P. 25(2)/1061, 3 Geo. I East.
5 W.S.L. 51/46, bdle. 2. A field in Dunston called 'The Toafe' occurs in 1598: S.R.O., D. 260/M/box 16, bdle. a, Ct. Bk. 1598–1654, f. 5a.
6 W.S.L. 51/46, bdle. 2. The elder Thomas seems to have lived at Newhouse between at least 1718 and 1743: ibid.; W.S.L., D. 1771, Pickstock Papers.
7 W.S.L. 51/46, bdle. 2; the deed is fragmentary.
8 W.S.L., D. 1771, Pickstock Papers.
9 Ibid., will of Ralph Pickstock.   10 Ibid.
11 W.S.L. 51/46, bdle. 2.
12 White, *Dir. Staffs.* (1851); *P.O. Dir. Staffs.* (1860; 1868; 1872). White, *Dir. Staffs.* (1834), mentions Thomas Pickstock as a farmer in Dunston.

13 *P.O. Dir. Staffs.* (1876); *Kelly's Dir. Staffs.* (1880; 1884).
14 *Kelly's Dir. Staffs.* (1892; 1896).
15 W.S.L., D. 1771, Dunston Rate Bk. (1903).
16 Local inf.
17 See pp. 143–4.
18 W.S.L., D. 1766/28, m. 9.
19 W.S.L., D. 1721/1/8, p. 338.
20 W.S.L., Stafford Barony, Mins. Accts. 1532–3, m. 11d.
21 W.S.L., Lord Stafford's Title concerning the Waters of Dunston.
22 W.S.L., D. 1766/28, mm. 3–4.
23 Ibid. m. 9.
24 C.P. 25(2)/1061, 3 Geo. I Trin.
25 W.S.L., D. 1771, Pickstock Papers.
26 *Cal. Inq. p.m.* xiv, no. 212.
27 *S.H.C.* i. 341; ibid. N.S. ii. 74, 75; *S.H.C.* xiii. 130; *Cal. Inq. p.m. Hen. VII*, i, nos. 841, 874; *L. & P. Hen. VIII*, xvi, p. 460; *S.H.C.* xi. 288; C 142/96, no. 164; see p. 55.
28 *Cal. Inq. p.m. Hen. VII*, i, no. 874.
29 *S.H.C.* xii (1), 238; ibid. xiii. 211.
30 C 142/96, no. 64.
31 *S.H.C.* xiii. 227; ibid. 1938, 91.
32 Ibid. 1938, 92–93.
33 Ibid. xiv (1), 183.
34 Ibid. 197.

in 1585 with a son John as his heir.[35] In 1607 John Cowper made a settlement of what was called the manor of Dunston with 3 messuages, other land, and 16s. rent there.[36]

In this same year John conveyed a capital messuage called the Hall of Dunston, with land, to William Anson, reserving for life a rent of £16 10s. 8d.[37] In 1612 William Anson leased the Hall to Edward Anson for three lives, at a rent of 47s. 6d.[38]

William Critchley, who was living at Dunston between at least 1818[39] and 1851,[40] owned and occupied an estate of 137 acres here c. 1841, including a farm on the site of what is now Dunston Hall.[41] By 1852 Frederick C. Perry was living at what was called Dunston Hall and died there in 1900.[42] He was succeeded by Helen Perry who in 1900 settled the Dunston estate, then comprising 904 acres, in favour of George Benjamin Thorneycroft,[43] who was living at the Hall by 1901.[44] His grandson, the Rt. Hon. G. E. P. Thorneycroft, sold the Hall in 1951 to Mr. A. Alcock, who converted it into flats for members of his family[45] and in 1956 sold it to the English Electric Company.[46] The Home Farm with about 480 acres around Dunston was still in Mr. Thorneycroft's possession in 1956[47] but the cottages were being sold as they fell vacant.[48] Dunston Hall and the Home Farm are described above.[49]

Thomas Giffard, probably the second son of Humphrey Giffard of Water Eaton,[50] was chargeable for two hearths in the constablewick of Dunston and Drayton in 1666.[51] Amy, wife of Thomas Giffard described as of Dunston, was buried at Penkridge in 1682.[52] What was called a manor of *DUNSTON* was held by Peter Giffard of Chillington (in Brewood) before 1743.[53]

As a member of the manor of Penkridge Dunston was included in the grant made by the king in 1372 to John de Beverley of the view of frankpledge in Penkridge and its fees and members.[54] By at least 1540 the vills of Dunston and Drayton were presenting jointly at the view[55] and were represented by five frankpledges from at least 1576,[56] but only four of these were present at the view of October 1608.[57]

A survey of the manor of Penkridge in 1598 showed that tenants of Penkridge, Wolgarston, Preston, Bitham, Lynehill, and Moor Hall, of the deanery manor, and of Drayton manor had stray common from Penkridge Heath into the common fields of Dunston, while the tenants of Dunston and Drayton had common rights in Penkridge Heath.[58] Dunston, including 100 acres of Dunston Heath, was inclosed in 1827 under the Act of 1814.[59]

The prebend of Dunston in Penkridge College existed by 1261[60] and was valued at £5 6s. 8d. in 1291.[66] In 1535 the prebend consisted of the site of the *PREBENDAL MANOR* and its lands together worth 20s., assised rents of 10s. 4d., tithes averaging £3 9s. 8d., and Easter offerings averaging 20s.[62] Synodals of 6s. 8d. were due every three years to the Dean of Penkridge.[63] The tithes and oblations had been leased by 1548 to Joan Corbett for £7 4s. 8d. and the lands to Thomas Webbe and Sampson Egginton for £10 10s. 4d., both rents being paid to the royal bailiff of the dissolved college.[64] The prebend presumably descended with the rest of the collegiate possessions,[65] and in 1585 it passed with view of frankpledge and tithe in Dunston to Edward Littleton.[66] It then descended in his family with Pillaton[67] until at least 1709.[68] The 50 acres in Dunston, 45 of them on Dunston Heath, which were sold by the 3rd Lord Hatherton in 1919,[69] may have been former prebendal land.

CHURCH. The chapel of St. Leonard at Dunston existed, evidently as a dependency of Penkridge church, by 1445 when the Dean of Penkridge confirmed its dedication and granted an indulgence of 100 days to all who, confessing their sins, should visit it and make some contribution to it.[70] A similar indulgence of 40 days was ordained in 1446.[71] The chapel was then already annexed to the prebend of Dunston in Penkridge church,[72] but no vicarage seems to have been ordained.[73] The chapel, called a chapel of ease to Penkridge with cure in 1563[74] and a 'free chapel' in 1752,[75] was described in 1784 as 'a member of Penkridge church and consolidated to it.'[76] It was still within the peculiar jurisdiction

[35] C 142/298, no. 49.
[36] *S.H.C.* N.S. iii. 5.
[37] C 2/Jas. I, A. I, no. 39. In 1549 a messuage in Dunston called 'le Hall' with land there in the tenure of Joan Corbett, widow, and formerly the property of the dissolved chantry of St. Thomas Becket in St. Mary's, Stafford, was sold by the Crown to Henry Tanner and Thomas Bocher of London: *Cal. Pat.* 1548–9, 420.
[38] C 2/Jas. I, A. I, no. 39.
[39] Parsons and Bradshaw, *Dir. Staffs.* (1818).
[40] White, *Dir. Staffs.* (1834; 1851).
[41] Tithe Maps and Appt., Penkridge (copy in W.S.L.).
[42] Memorial tablet in Dunston Church.
[42] Ex inf. Messrs. Fowler, Langley, and Wright, Wolverhampton, Solrs. to the Thorneycroft Estate.
[44] *S.H.C.* N.S. iv, list of subscribers, corrected to 1 May 1901; Burke, *Land. Gent.* (1949), 2503.
[45] Ex inf. Mr. A. Alcock.
[46] Ex inf. the English Electric Co.
[47] Ex inf. Messrs. Owen Bennion and Son, Estate Agents, Eccleshall.
[48] Local inf.   [49] See pp. 143, 144.
[50] *S.H.C.* N.S. v. 173, 200.
[51] Ibid. 1927, 29.
[52] *Penkridge Par. Reg.* (Staffs. Par. Reg. Soc.), 271.
[53] W.S.L. 159/33.
[54] *Cal. Chart. R.* 1341–1417, 222.
[55] S.R.O., D. 260/M/box 12, bdle. a, Penkridge Court Papers.

[56] Ibid.; ibid. box 16, bdle. b.
[57] Ibid. box 16, bdle. b. The court papers do not specify the number of frankpledges after 1611.
[58] Ibid. box 16, bdle. a, Ct. Bk. 1598–1654, f. 16a.
[59] S.R.O., Q/RDc 22; White, *Dir. Staffs.* (1834).
[60] *S.H.C.* 1950–1, 47–48.
[61] *Tax. Eccl.* (Rec. Com.), 242.
[62] *Valor Eccl.* (Rec. Com.), iii. 106; there was no tithe of grain.
[63] Ibid.
[64] *S.H.C.* 1950–1, 36 note 98, 37, 40–41.
[65] See p. 111.
[66] *S.H.C.* xv. 167.
[67] C 142/455, no. 76; C.P. 25(2)/486, 18 Chas. I Mich.; C.P. 25(2)/596, 1654 Trin.; C.P. 25(2)/725, 28 Chas. II Mich.; C.P. 43/490, rot. 164; see p. 119.
[68] C.P. 43/506, rot. 98.
[69] Ex inf. the Teddesley and Hatherton Estate Office, Penkridge.
[70] W.S.L., S. MS. 201(1), p. 432.
[71] Ibid.
[72] Ibid.
[73] The prebendary seems to have held all the tithes in 1535: *Valor Eccl.* (Rec. Com.), iii. 106.
[74] *S.H.C.* 1915, 207.
[75] C.P. 43/676, rot. 321.
[76] W.S.L., Hand Morgan Coll., Littleton Papers (Shareshill curacy).

of Penkridge in 1834.[77] The perpetual curacy was styled a titular vicarage after 1868,[78] and the benefice was united with that of Coppenhall in 1892.[79]

The right of appointing the curate presumably lay with the prebendary of Dunston until the dissolution of Penkridge College. The presentation then probably descended with that of Penkridge,[80] but the chapel is first mentioned as held by the Littletons in 1752.[81] They retained the presentation[82] until it passed c. 1897 to F. C. Perry of Dunston Hall.[83] It was settled by Helen Perry with the rest of the estate in 1900 on G. B. Thorneycroft[84] whose grandson, the Rt. Hon. G. E. P. Thorneycroft, held it in 1956.[85] Helen Perry, by deed of 1902, augmented the vicar's stipend by £220 annual interest on £6,779 15s. 7d. stock on condition that he should hold two services at Dunston and two at Coppenhall each Sunday.[86] Since 1950 this has been modified so that the vicar holds one service in each church every Sunday.[87]

The former chapel of *ST. LEONARD* was probably of early-15th-century date, rebuilt, except for the tower, in the 18th century. Drawings of 1838 and 1841[88] show that the original tower had single-light windows to the belfry stage and a larger medieval window, then blocked, below. On its north and south faces the tower had a high double-chamfered basement course, and a Georgian doorway had been inserted in the west wall. The body of the church, rebuilt or refaced with brickwork, had round-headed 18th-century windows. In 1843 it was recorded that there were no monuments and that there was no means of reaching the belfry from the interior.[89]

Between 1876 and 1878 the chapel was demolished and a new church erected on the same site at the sole expense of Frederick C. Perry and his mother, brothers, and sisters.[90] It is a stone building in 14th-century style and consists of nave, chancel, transepts, vestry, and a spired west tower. At this period the churchyard was not consecrated. In 1887 a new churchyard, given by the family of a former parishioner,[91] was consecrated, previous burials having been at Penkridge.[92] In 1907 the vestry was added and a new organ installed.[93] The church contains memorial tablets to Thomas Perry (d. 1861), in whose memory the church was built, to his widow Mary (d. 1881), and to later members of the family.

There are memorial windows and a tablet to members of the Hand family including Charles Frederic Hand (d. 1900), also tablets to John Taylor Duce (d. 1886), Albert Pickstock (d. 1926), and three members of the Thorneycroft family (d. 1913, 1924, and 1943).

In 1553 the plate consisted of one chalice.[94] In 1955 the plate included a silver chalice, paten, and paten on foot; a pewter chalice, paten on foot, and alms dish; and an electro-plated chalice and paten given in 1861 to the Revd. E. Price by his friends.[95] There were two bells in the ancient chapel in 1553.[96] There was one bell in the new church by 1889.[97] There is now a carillon of eight tubular bells, rung from a keyboard, given by Mrs. Perry of Dunston Hall in 1890.[98]

The registers are partly included in those of Penkridge which date from 1572. Dunston has a separate register of baptisms from 1853 and of marriages from 1878 when the church was first licensed.

SCHOOL. A parochial school for boys and girls was built at Dunston in 1866 on a site given by the Earl of Lichfield, the expense of the building being met by subscription.[99] By 1871 it was run on National Society lines, and the average attendance was 15 boys and girls.[1] In 1910 the school had an average attendance of 21 infants and 42 older children.[2] By 1910 it had been enlarged.[3] In 1930 average attendance was 60[4] and in 1937 34.[5] The school became controlled in 1952.[6] It is now called Dunston Church of England Voluntary Primary Controlled School, Junior Mixed and Infants, and had an average attendance in 1955 of 32, under a mistress.[7] Older children now attend school at Penkridge or at Rising Brook (Castle Church).

The building is of red brick, the original block, which dates from 1866, having lancet windows with diagonal glazing bars.

CHARITY FOR THE POOR. Dennis Fieldhouse, probably c. 1680,[8] bequeathed to the poor of Dunstan £10 which was producing interest of 8s. a year by 1786.[9] This interest was still being paid in 1823,[10] but by 1898 all traces of the charity had been lost.[11]

[77] White, *Dir. Staffs.* (1834).
[78] *Lich. Dioc. Ch. Cal.* (1885).
[79] *Lond. Gaz.* 1892, pp. 4812–13.
[80] See p. 130.
[81] C.P. 43/676, rot. 321.
[82] White, *Dir. Staffs.* (1834; 1851); *Lich. Dioc. Ch. Cal.* (1897).
[83] *Lich. Dioc. Ch. Cal.* (1898).
[84] Ex inf. Messrs. Fowler, Langley, and Wright, Solrs., Wolverhampton.
[85] *Lich. Dioc. Dir.* (1955–6).
[86] Ex inf. the Lichfield Dioc. Trust.
[87] Ibid.; Charity Com. files.
[88] W.S.L., Staffs. Views, iv, pp. 107 (a, 1838), 108 (1841); for a reproduction of the former see plate facing p. 178.
[89] W.S.L., S. MS. 436, p. 176.
[90] Lich. Dioc. Regy., Consist. Ct. Act Bk. 1875–9, pp. 99–104, faculty, 11 Apr. 1876; memorials in church and churchyard.
[91] *Lich. Dioc. Ch. Cal.* (1888), 151.
[92] *Kelly's Dir. Staffs.* (1892).

[93] Lich. Dioc. Regy., Consist. Ct. Act Bk. 1907–14, p. 6, faculty, 27 May 1907.
[94] *S.H.C.* 1915, 207.
[95] Ex inf. the Vicar of Dunston-with-Coppenhall (1955).
[96] *S.H.C.* 1915, 207.
[97] C. Lynam, *Church Bells of Staffs.* 10.
[98] Ex inf. the vicar.
[99] *P.O. Dir. Staffs.* (1868).
[1] *Returns relating to Elem. Educ.*, H.C. 201, pp. 364–5 (1871), lv.
[2] Staffs. Educ. Cttee. Mins., 1910.
[3] *Kelly's Dir. Staffs.* (1916).
[4] Staffs. Educ. Cttee. Mins., 25 Apr. 1931.
[5] Ibid. 29 May 1937.
[6] Ibid. 2 Feb. 1952.
[7] *Lich. Dioc. Dir.* (1955–6).
[8] A Dennis Fieldhouse was buried at Penkridge in 1680: *Penkridge Par. Reg.* (Staffs. Par. Reg. Soc.), 269.
[9] *Abstract of Returns of Charitable Donations, 1786–8*, H.C. 511, pp. 1118–19 (1816), xvi (2).
[10] *11th Rep. Com. Char.* H.C. 436, p. 524 (1824), xiv.
[11] Charity Com. files.

RUGELEY

RUGELEY, now an Urban District, includes the mining village of Brereton and the hamlets of Slitting Mill and Etching Hill. The urban district with Hazel Slade and the area now known as Brindley Heath[1] formed the ancient parish. Rugeley is bounded by the Trent on the north-east and by the high ground of Cannock Chase on the west, and these natural features until recently determined the shape of settlement within the parish, most of the building being concentrated along the north-east, south-west axis of the Stafford–Lichfield road. The Rising Brook flows down from the Chase through Hagley Park and the centre of the town into the Trent. The geological strata include Bunter Pebble Beds below the unproductive Cannock Chase uplands to the west, the northern limit of the South Staffordshire Coal Measures to the south, and Keuper Marl under the productive soils to the east and south-east.[2] The area of the Urban District is 2,879 acres and of Brindley Heath, which includes much of Cannock Chase, 5,580 acres.[3]

Rugeley was described in 1747 as 'a handsome clean well-built town of exceeding pleasant and healthful situation'.[4] By 1834 it was considered 'the largest and handsomest market town in the Cuttlestone hundred'.[5] At this time it was said to consist in the main of one long street with short roads leading off it.[6] During the previous twenty years many new houses had been erected and some of the old ones rebuilt.[7] Albion Street had been formed a few years before, and Church Street was under construction, most of the houses being well built and some 'even elegant, being occupied by wealthy families and having neat lawns and pleasure grounds'.[8] The greatest expansion of the town in the second half of the 19th century took place to the south and east, although parts of the Brereton and Armitage roads were already built up by 1842.[9] The area east of Market Street, where there was once a forge,[10] contains the gas works and is largely industrial. When the Roman Catholic church was built in 1849–51[11] it was on the outskirts of the town, but a network of small streets to the south and east as far as the canal soon followed, together with a great increase of building on the Brereton and Armitage roads. The greatest alteration to the town centre took place in 1878 when the old Town Hall was demolished and Anson Street was cut to connect the Market Place with Wolseley Road.[12] The south-west end of Church Street was built up late in the 19th century. In the 20th century council housing estates

to the west and south greatly increased the area of the town. The estates at Burnt Hill and Newman Grove were built before the Second World War while Springfield Crescent, containing two-story prefabricated houses, dates from immediately after it. Attlee Crescent was laid out c. 1950. The large Pear Tree housing estate on rising ground south-west of the town was begun in 1953.

Brereton had several dwellings by 1775[13] and has been a mining area since at least the early 19th century.[14] It was described in 1834 as 'a village with several well-built houses'.[15] The Redbrook housing estate was laid out by the National Coal Board in 1953 and the St. Michael's estate is still (1957) under construction.

Etching Hill, which takes its name from a natural hill of that name (454 ft.) surmounted by a circular burial mound,[16] has developed as a purely residential district where the houses are all privately owned and as such is one of the first areas in the parish in which extensive building has taken place above the 300-ft. contour.[17] The village hall in East Butts Road was built in 1948.[18]

By 1775 there were houses at Stone House, now the hamlet of Slitting Mill.[19] The village hall, south-west of Horns Pool, was built in 1953.[20]

The hamlet of Glovers Hill lay to the south-east of Rugeley town on the Brereton road in 1834 and 1851,[21] but it was subsequently absorbed by the urban spread.

The hamlet of Hazel Slade, now in Cannock but formerly within the ancient parish of Rugeley, was non-existent in the middle of the 19th century, but a few streets of continuous terrace housing were built later, presumably in connexion with the pits near Cannock Wood opened in 1865 and 1874.[22] The front doors open directly upon the pavements and there are no gardens but only communal drying grounds at the rear of the houses. There are some later houses to the north-east and an estate of prefabricated bungalows to the south.

Rugeley lies on the main Stafford–Lichfield road which continues south to London and north to the Potteries and Manchester. By 1818 there were three coaches daily to London and Liverpool and one to Manchester from 'The Dog and Partridge', while from 'The Swan' there were coaches to London and Liverpool four days a week.[23] By 1834 there was also a coach to Birmingham six days a week.[24] A by-pass road running west of the town centre was opened in 1957 as Western Springs Road by the President of

---

[1] See p. 152.
[2] *Kelly's Dir. Staffs.* (1940); Christina W. Barker, 'An Urban Study of Rugeley' (Nott. Univ. B.A. Thesis, 1956), 23.
[3] *Census*, 1951, Staffs.
[4] White, *Dir. Staffs.* (1851).
[5] Ibid.
[6] Ibid.
[7] Ibid.
[8] Ibid.
[9] Tithe Maps and Appt., Rugeley (copy in W.S.L.).
[10] See p. 162.
[11] See p. 167.
[12] See p. 153.
[13] Yates, *Map of Staffs.* (1799), based on a survey 1769–75.

[14] See p. 161.
[15] White, *Dir. Staffs.* (1834).
[16] *V.C.H. Staffs.* i. 376. The name 'Eychilhill' occurs in 1504 among the bounds of the neighbouring manor of Wolseley: *Cal. Inq. p.m. Hen. VII*, ii, p. 540.
[17] Christina W. Barker, 'An Urban Study of Rugeley', introd. and p. 20.
[18] Date on building.
[19] Yates, *Map of Staffs.*
[20] Date on building.
[21] White, *Dir. Staffs.* (1834; 1851).
[22] It does not appear in Tithe Maps and Appt., Rugeley (copy in W.S.L.), or White, *Dir*, Staffs. (1851); see p. 62.
[23] Parson and Bradshaw, *Dir. Staffs.* (1818).
[24] White, *Dir. Staffs.* (1834).

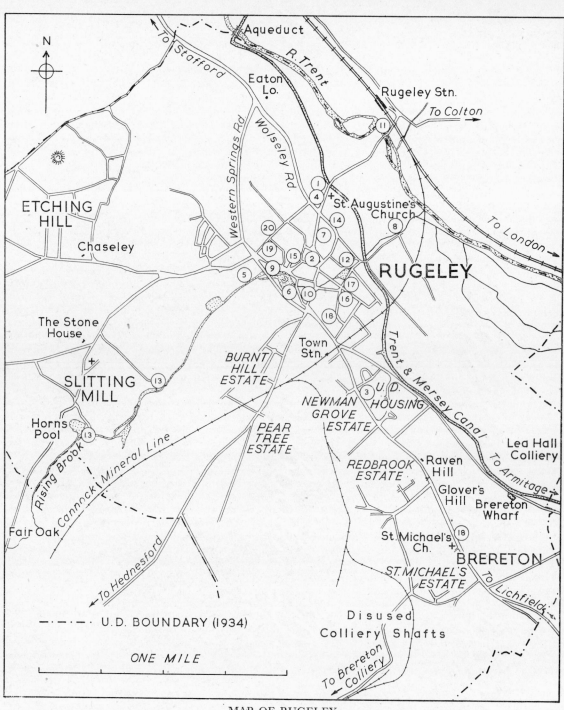

MAP OF RUGELEY

1 Rugeley Old Church
2 Town Hall
3 Rugeley District Hospital
4 Grammar School
5 Hagley Hall
6 Moat
7 Site of Old Hall Garden
8 Site of Turkeyshall Mill
9 Hagley Mill
10 Central Mills
11 Colton Mill

12 Site of Forge
13 Sites of Slitting Mills
14 Former Vicarage
15 Site of Tithe Barn
16 R.C. Church of SS. Joseph and Etheldreda
17 Heron Court Congregational Chapel
18 Wesleyan Methodist Chapel
19 Primitive Methodist Chapel
20 Former National School for Girls and site of Sarah Hopkins's almshouses

Western Springs, Illinois, with which Rugeley has ties of comradeship.[25] The railway station on the main line from London to Stafford and the north-west of England (Rugeley Trent Valley Station, situated in Colton parish, Pirehill hundred), was opened in 1847, and in 1851 there were trains in each direction four times a day, with buses leaving 'The Talbot Arms' to meet each train.[26] In 1859 the railway from Walsall was extended from Cannock to join the main line at Rugeley,[27] and this branch, known as the Cannock Mineral Line,[28] has a station (Town Station) in the south-west part of the town and another in Brindley Heath. The Trent and Mersey Canal, opened in 1777,[29] passes through Rugeley close to the Trent which it crosses on an aqueduct at Brindley's Bank north-west of the town. The aqueduct formerly had five arches and was said in 1834 to have been 'so admirably constructed by that eminent engineer Mr. Brindley' that it had 'withstood the floods of the river for more than half a century without requiring material repairs'.[30] It appears to have been rebuilt, however, in the middle of the 19th century and is now a structure of blue brick with six arches. By at least 1817 there was a wharf to the south-east of the town connected by rail to Brereton Colliery,[31] but this wharf went out of commercial use between 1940 and 1956.[32] The course of the line to the colliery can still be clearly distinguished near the Wesleyan almshouses in Brereton.

A bridge called 'Elemetebrugge' occurs in 1357.[33] A stone bridge, presumably on the site of the present Colton Bridge carrying the road that leads to the main line station and to Uttoxeter (Totmonslow hundred) and Abbots Bromley (Pirehill hundred) over the Trent, was built in 1646 at a cost of some £30 by Mr. Chetwynd (probably John Chetwynd of Rugeley), but it was broken down in the floods of 1708.[34] Colton Bridge was rebuilt in 1790[35] and is of stone ashlar with a single segmental arch. Although it was a county responsibility by at least 1830,[36] Rugeley bore one-quarter of the cost of its repair and enlargement in 1886 and 1887.[37] It was probably at this time that it was widened on the north side and the present parapets and piers were added.[38] The building of a brick bridge over the 'Town Brook' 'from the present bridge over the brook by the Anchor down to Mr. Banks's garden', that is, over the Rising Brook in Brook Square between the present Upper and Lower Brook Street, was ordered by the vestry in 1821.[39] In 1827 the vestry also ordered the building of a bridge 'over the brook near the wharf'.[40]

The inhabitants of Rugeley were unable to relieve their poor in 1598, and various other parishes were ordered by the justices in Quarter Sessions to assist them with weekly sums.[41] A workhouse was built c. 1780,[42] presumably at Etching Hill where the parish workhouse was situated by 1834 at the house now called Chaseley.[43] The salary of the governor was £25 in 1822 and was confirmed at this figure in 1831.[44] The poor of Rugeley were transferred to the Union Workhouse opened in Lichfield in 1841,[45] and in 1845 the vestry ordered the leasing to the Guardians of the Poor of the Lichfield Union of the 'very large brick and tile dwelling house . . . now unoccupied and hereto used as the workhouse for the poor of the parish'.[46] Chaseley is a large stucco house in its own grounds. It formerly had a sym-metrical late-Georgian front, but there have been many alterations and additions.

The larger of the two iron-foundries in Rugeley in 1834 had 'a gas apparatus which supplies both its own workshops and the town with its brilliant vapour'.[47] The municipal gas-works were completed in 1849, and by 1851 there were some 45 public lamps.[48] In 1843 the vestry meeting expressed its appreciation of 'the Rural Police now stationed in Rugeley' and recommended that premises in Albion Street be taken on lease by the parish officers for use by the police.[49] By 1851 there was a police station, apparently in Horse Fair, with an inspector and two men.[50] The new Town Hall opened in 1879 included a police station,[51] and the present station in Anson Street was opened in 1907.[52] In 1859 the vestry was considering the provision of a fire engine.[53] There was a 'fire engine station' in the new Town Hall,[54] and the present fire station in Taylors Lane was opened in 1936.[55] The Rugeley Home and Cottage Hospital in Church Street was founded by Mrs. Levett in 1866,[56] and the Rugeley District Hospital was opened in 1871,[57] while by 1912 the Urban District Council had a cottage small-pox hospital near Brindley Heath.[58] The sewering of the town was

[25] Staffs. Advertiser and Chronicle, 13 June 1957.
[26] White, Dir. Staffs. (1851).
[27] Staffs. Advertiser, 1 Oct. 1859.
[28] Rugeley: Official Guide (1955), 15.
[29] S.H.C. 1934 (1), 109.
[30] White, Dir. Staffs. (1834).
[31] W. Pitt, Topog. Hist. Staffs. (1817), 266; Parsons and Bradshaw, Dir. Staffs. (1818); Greenwood, Map of Staffs. (1820).
[32] Kelly's Dir. Staffs. (1940), 362, Brereton Wharves Ltd., coal and coke merchants, Town Wharf; ex inf. the Divisional Manager, British Waterways, N.W. Div. (1956).
[33] W.S.L., D. 1734, Cannock and Rugeley Ct. R. 1274–1373, m. 27.
[34] Rugeley Parish Bk. 1680–1813, cited as the Constables Bk. by W. N. Landor, Rugeley Par. Reg. (Staffs. Par. Reg. Soc.), p. xxiii (the book is no longer lost, as there stated); H. E. Chetwynd-Stapylton, Chetwynds of Ingestre, Pedigree 'Chetwynds of Rugeley and Grendon'; see p. 152.
[35] S.H.C. 1934 (1), 89.
[36] J. Potter, List of Bridges which the inhabitants of the County of Stafford are bound to repair (1830), 7, where it is returned under Pirehill hundred (i.e. in Colton parish).
[37] Staffs. Advertiser, 13 Mar. 1886; ibid. 3 Apr. 1886, for list of local subscriptions; Kelly's Dir. Staffs. (1892).
[38] W.S.L., Staffs. Views, viii, p. 106 (1842).

[39] Rugeley Vestry Order Bk. 1819–81, 1 Dec. 1820, 28 June 1821.
[40] Ibid. 19 Oct. 1827.
[41] S.H.C. 1935, 70, 78.
[42] Rugeley Parish Bk. 1680–1813, vestry minutes, 4 May 1780.
[43] White, Dir. Staffs. (1834); Tithe Maps and Appt., Rugeley (copy in W.S.L.), nos. 786–92; W.S.L., D. 1568, W. N. Landor's Bk. of Cuttings on Rugeley: Diary of Sarah Powell, 1798–1845, 3.
[44] Rugeley Vestry Order Bk. 1819–81, 30 Sept. 1822, 4 and 9 Mar. 1831.
[45] White, Dir. Staffs. (1851), 484.
[46] Rugeley Vestry Order Bk. 1819–81, 21 Oct. 1845.
[47] White, Dir. Staffs. (1834).
[48] Ibid. (1851).
[49] Rugeley Vestry Order Bk. 1819–81, 25 Mar. 1843.
[50] White, Dir. Staffs. (1851).
[51] Kelly's Dir. Staffs. (1880).
[52] Ibid. (1912).
[53] Rugeley Vestry Order Bk. 1819–81, 18 Aug. and 22 Sept. 1859.   [54] Kelly's Dir. Staffs. (1880).
[55] Ibid. (1940), where it is wrongly described as in Anson Street.
[56] Charity Com. files.
[57] Kelly's Dir. Staffs. (1880).   [58] Ibid. (1912).

undertaken by the local board set up in 1865 mainly for that purpose.[59] The South Staffordshire Water Works Company had a pumping station near Fairoak by 1880, the water being stored in Hednesford reservoir,[60] and there are now (1957) two pumping stations in Brindley Heath, one (dated 1932) on the site of the former slitting mill south-east of Hagley Farm and the other in Tudor style at Brindley Bank (dated 1905). The Rugeley Free Jubilee Library was formed in 1887 and housed in the Reading and Recreation Room, Bow Street.[61]

The ancient stone pinfold, situated apparently on the north side of Sheep Fair, was moved c. 1829 at the expense of the parish to a site on the Marlpits estate where it still stood in 1878.[62] In 1774 the vestry had ordered the conversion of part of the pinfold 'into a place of security for felons, &c., previous to their being carried before a magistrate'.[63]

A parliamentarian garrison seems to have been set up at Rugeley in 1645.[64] In 1859 a company of volunteers was enrolled.[65] The commander of the Cannock Chase manœuvres of 1873 set up his flag on Etching Hill.[66] An R.A.F. camp (R.A.F. Hednesford) in Brindley Heath was taken over in 1956 as a camp for refugee Hungarians. An army camp on Stile Cop, formerly used for prisoners of war, is now (1957) abandoned.

A maypole was set up between Sandy Lane and Horse Fair for the coronation celebrations of George III[67] and was still there in the mid-19th century.[68]

There was foot-racing on a 3-mile course at Etching Hill by 1678.[69] By 1834 horse races were generally held on a 1½-mile course at 'Hitchin Hill' on the last Thursday in September,[70] and by 1851 they were held during the first week in October.[71] September horse-racing at Rugeley was mentioned in 1854 and 1860.[72]

A fire in Rugeley on 20 May 1649 burnt down 29 houses and the tithe barn.[73] Another fire in February 1709 began at a baker's house at the west end of the town at 9 a.m. and was fanned by a strong south-west wind.[74] The amount of damage done then was assessed at £808 3s. 2d., and appeals for assistance were sent to parishes outside as well as inside the county, £340 1s. 4½d. being raised from Staffordshire alone.[75] Damage done by the 'great rain' on 15 September 1708 was assessed at £200.[76]

A local board for Rugeley was set up in 1865 under the Act of 1858.[77] The Urban District Council of Rugeley was formed in 1894, when Brereton, including Hazel Slade, Slitting Mill, and Etching Hill, was made into a separate civil parish within the Lichfield Rural District.[78] Under the Staffordshire Review Order of 1934 parts of Brereton, including Slitting Mill and Etching Hill, and parts of Armitage with Handsacre and of Longdon were added to the Urban District. Hazel Slade was added to the Urban District of Cannock, and the remainder of the former civil parish of Brereton stayed within the Lichfield Rural District as the new civil parish of Brindley Heath.[79]

The ancient parish was stated in 1646 to contain many hundred communicants,[80] and it included 219 households in 1666.[81] The population in 1801 was 2,030.[82] In 1951 the population of the Urban District was 8,525 and of Brindley Heath, including the R.A.F. camp, 5,028.[83]

Mrs. Mary Knowles (1733–1807), Quakeress, painter, and friend of Dr. Johnson, was the eldest daughter of Moses and Mary Morris of Rugeley.[84] William Palmer (1824–56), the second son of Joseph Palmer of Rugeley, timber merchant and sawyer, started practice in Rugeley as a doctor in 1846, and was hanged at Stafford in 1856 on the charge of poisoning John Parsons Cook at 'The Talbot Arms'.[85] Professor T. G. Bonney (1833–1923), the Cambridge geologist, was born at Rugeley, the eldest child of the Revd. Thomas Bonney, master of Rugeley Grammar School.[86]

The south-west end of the town contains the largest number of old buildings, and it seems probable that the fire of 1709[87] missed this area. A group of timber-framed cottages at the corner of Elmore Lane and Sandy Lane survived until shortly before the First World War.[88] Two existing houses on the south-west side of Horse Fair have timber-framing of 17th-century type. A framed building opposite, demolished in 1956, was probably more ancient.[89] Sheep Fair was evidently a built-up street at an early date. Nos. 16 and 18, formerly the White Lion Inn,[90] form an L-shaped timber-framed block dating from the late 16th or early 17th century. It retains a large central chimney with diagonal shafts. A brick house of c. 1700 opposite has original mullioned and transomed windows to the first floor. At the upper end of the street several old houses, some timber-framed, are derelict or partly demolished. A timber-framed outhouse adjoining the Vine Inn is said to

[59] Kelly's Dir. Staffs. (1880).
[60] Ibid.
[61] Kelly's Dir. Staffs. (1892, and subsequent edns. to 1928).
[62] W.S.L. 70/4/44; W.S.L., D. 1792, copy of plan dated 1829. The name Marlpits is still given to the area lying between the railway to Cannock, the line to Brereton Colliery, and the road to Lichfield.
[63] Rugeley Parish Bk. 1680–1813, f. 56a.
[64] Hist. MSS. Com. 13th Rep. App. I (1), 324.
[65] P.O. Dir. Staffs. (1868).
[66] M. J. Wise, 'The Cannock Chase Manœuvres of 1873' (Army Quarterly, lxviii, no. 2), 248–56.
[67] Handbill of 1814 penes Mr. E. C. Toye, Rugeley Grammar School.
[68] See plate facing p. 152.
[69] Lond. Gaz. 29 July–1 Aug. 1678; Hist. MSS. Com. 13th Rep. App. VI, 125.
[70] White, Dir. Staffs. (1834).
[71] Ibid. (1851).
[72] P.O. Dir. Staffs. (1854; 1860).
[73] Rugeley Par. Reg. (Staffs. Par. Reg. Soc.), 96; Lich. D. and C. MS. Bk. liv, f. 101a; Rugeley Parish Bk. 1680–1813.

[74] S.R.O., Q/SR, Trans. 1709, m. 7; Rugeley Parish Bk. f. 3b.
[75] S.R.O., Q/SR, Trans. 1709, mm. 6, 7.
[76] Rugeley Parish Bk.; Rugeley Par. Reg., p. xxiii.
[77] Kelly's Dir. Staffs. (1912).
[78] Ibid.; Rugeley: Official Guide (1955), 11; ex inf. the Clerk, Lichfield Rural District Council (1956).
[79] Ex inf. the Clerk, Lich. R.D. Council.
[80] S.H.C. 1915, p. lxxiv.
[81] Ibid. 1927, 3–18.
[82] V.C.H. Staffs. i. 320.
[83] Census, 1951, Staffs.
[84] D.N.B.
[85] Ibid.; W.S.L., D. 1548, which includes 'Life and Trial of William Palmer' (consisting of The Times Report of the Trial of William Palmer and Life and Career of William Palmer, both dated 1856) and Palmer's death-mask; R. Graves, They Hanged my Saintly Billy (1957).
[86] D.N.B. 1922–30.
[87] See above.
[88] Ex inf. Mr. Toye; see plate opposite.
[89] Min. of Housing and Local Govt., List of Scheduled Buildings (1948).
[90] Ibid.

The old church before its partial demolition, *c.* 1823

Horse Fair, in 1856, showing the maypole

RUGELEY

Market Street, 1856, showing the Talbot (later the Shrewsbury) Arms on the left, the former Town Hall in the background, and William Palmer's house, set back, on the right

Interior of the old Town Hall during the inquest on Walter Palmer, 1856

RUGELEY

have been formerly a malthouse.[91] Two late-18th-century brick houses at the corner of Bow Street and Crossley Stone form a single square block. Good symmetrical brick fronts with three-light sash windows face both streets. The doorway to Crossley Stone has fluted pilasters, an enriched frieze, and a voluted pediment. An added bay on the south side has 'Greek' detail of c. 1820. About 1842 this property included a brewery.[92]

The main street through the town consists of Lower Brook Street, Upper Brook Street, and Market Street. The first two names occur only after the middle of the 19th century before which Market Street extended as far as Brook Square.[93] Most of the houses in both streets have been rebuilt since this period. An exception is the tall gabled brick house, now Nos. 5 and 7 Lower Brook Street, which dates from the late 17th century. Nos. 17 and 19 Upper Brook Street have an imposing stucco façade with good 'Regency' detail, the only example of this type in Rugeley. The property, which was formerly occupied by a farmer, changed hands in 1825[94] and was evidently rebuilt as a shop. A much-altered building of c. 1700 stands near the Market Place on the south side of Bow Street. The south-east side of the Market Place is occupied by a property formerly the home of the Landors, which originally dated from the 17th century and had five hearths taxable in 1666.[95] The front, which was rebuilt in 1773,[96] has been covered with stucco and much altered but retains its original doorway, cornice, and enriched key-stones. Until 1878 the Town Hall stood in the centre of the Market Place.[97] It consisted of a square brick building of c. 1790[98] with an open arcade of three bays to the ground floor and a cupola on the roof. A small single-story structure to the north[99] was replaced c. 1850 by an extension of the Town Hall with 'Tudor' details. The Shrewsbury Arms Hotel in Market Street was known until at least 1810 as 'The Crown'.[1] In the early 19th century it became 'The Talbot Arms', and its name was again changed after the trial of William Palmer in 1856.[2] Parts of the structure may date from c. 1700, but the building was largely remodelled in the early 19th century, and the existing frontage is of this period. In 1834 a large Assembly Room had 'lately been built' here.[3] Palmer's house on the opposite side of the street[4] has an altered frontage but retains two gabled wings at the rear, one timber-framed and one of stone, which probably date from the 17th century. The Red Lion Inn has exposed timber-framing at the rear and an end gable wall of stone. It dates from c. 1600 and has a fragment of contemporary panelling internally. The brick front was renewed after a fire in 1950.[5] At the junction of Market Street and Wolseley Road is a timber-framed range, now plastered, known as The Sycamores. It

was formerly a single house of four bays dating from the late 16th or early 17th century. At the rear are the remains of another timber-framed range. No. 37 Wolseley Road is a detached 3-story brick house with a good symmetrical front of c. 1790. The buildings of Rugeley Grammar School at the junction of Wolseley Road and Colton Road all date from the 19th century or later. The former school, of which the first stone was laid by Richard Hollinhurst, mason, on 9 September 1707,[6] appears to have been rebuilt c. 1820 by the Revd. John Clarke who also rebuilt the master's house.[7] This second school building has also disappeared, but the house, in an altered form, is now (1957) used as offices and class-rooms. Residential property in Wolseley Road includes Eaton Lodge, a large house in its own grounds which was probably built c. 1830 by Capt. George Hamilton.[8] It had become the home of the Sneyd family by 1854[9] and is now the Eaton Lodge Hotel and Country Club.

Albion Street, east of Market Street, was constructed c. 1830[10] and contains some typical detail of that period. Beyond it the group of buildings connected with the Roman Catholic Church date from 1849 to 1851.[11] Heron Court, now St. Anthony's Convent, was built in 1851 by Joseph Whitgreave, co-founder of the church.[12] It is a tall gabled house of dark brick with stone dressings in the mid-19th-century Tudor style. At this period the buildings including the 'elegant mansion of Heron Court' were considered 'the greatest ornaments of the town'.[13]

The Town Hall, erected at the corner of the Market Place and Anson Street on the site of the Shoulder of Mutton Inn,[14] was opened in 1879.[15] The building has a tall clock tower and is of red brick with Bath stone dressings. The style is a highly ornamental version of mid-Victorian Gothic. It contains a covered market and offices on the ground floor with assembly rooms above. The mid-19th-century wing of the demolished Town Hall was reconstructed at the Anson Street end of the new building.

Brereton House has a good late-18th-century brick front with five windows to each of the upper floors and a central Roman Doric doorcase with a pediment. The forecourt is bounded by a low brick wall with a simple wrought-iron gate and stone piers in the centre. The property was owned and occupied by Elizabeth Birch c. 1842.[16]

The two houses known as Brereton Hall and Lanes End form together a very long three-story range with two projecting wings at the rear. The road front was formerly of stone, but plate-glass windows and a facing of yellow brick were added in the late 19th century. A ground-floor room at the

[91] Ex inf. the licensee.
[92] See p. 161.
[93] Ex inf. Mr. Toye.
[94] Deed penes Mr. C. R. Morris, owner.
[95] S.H.C. 1927, 10. The Landors have lived in Rugeley since at least 1589: ibid. 1934, 97–122; Rugeley Par. Reg. 17.
[96] Rugeley Parish Bk. 1680–1813.
[97] See plates opposite.
[98] White, Dir. Staffs. (1851).
[99] W.S.L., Staffs. Views, viii, pp. 105 (b), 107 (b, 1814); Tithe Maps and Appt., Rugeley (copy in W.S.L.).
[1] Ex inf. Mr. Toye.
[2] See p. 152.
[3] White, Dir. Staffs. (1834).

[4] See plate opposite.
[5] Ex inf. the licensee.
[6] Rugeley Parish Bk. 1680–1813.
[7] White, Dir. Staffs. (1851).
[8] He was occupying the house in 1834: White, Dir. Staffs. (1834).
[9] P.O. Dir. Staffs. (1854).
[10] White, Dir. Staffs. (1834).
[11] See also p. 167.
[12] White, Dir. Staffs. (1851).
[13] Ibid.
[14] Ex inf. Mr. Toye.
[15] Kelly's Dir. Staffs. (1880).
[16] Tithe Maps and Appt., Rugeley (copy in W.S.L.).

south end of Brereton Hall has moulded oak beams, probably of 17th-century date. The general structure and layout suggest that a 17th-century house had a long mill or other early industrial building of slightly later date adjoining it. The detail of the two front porches and most of the interior fittings would be consistent with a conversion into two dwelling houses c. 1800. It was already in double occupation by 1842.[17] At the rear is a stone barn with 17th-century timber-framing in the gables. A later tall brick outbuilding has been converted into a cottage. A culvert runs below this building, and there are two artificial pools in the field east of the house. In the early 20th century Lanes End is said to have been a girls' orphanage.[18]

The Cedar Tree, formerly Cedar Lodge, is an 18th-century brick house, with a central doorway flanked by two-story semicircular bays. The stucco front and the bays, which are surmounted by cast-iron balustrades, are probably additions of the early 19th century.

The Hollybush Inn at Brereton Slade is a timber-framed building with a thatched roof. It consists of three bays with a single-story wing at the back and a brick addition at the west end. The two eastern bays probably date from the 16th century, and there are indications that they were formerly of one story, open to the roof. The two-story bay to the west appears to have been added at a slightly later date.

MANORS. In 1086 *RUGELEY*, assessed at ⅕ hide, was held by the king as part of the escheated lands of the earldom of Mercia.[19] Lands in Rugeley were held of the king by Robert de Sancto Paulo in 1156 and 1157[20] but apparently not afterwards, and the vill was tallaged like other royal lands from 1173 until 1187.[21] Richard I granted it to the Bishop of Coventry and Lichfield in 1189 along with Cannock,[22] with which it henceforth descended.[23] The Marquess of Anglesey, into whose family the manor had passed in 1546,[24] disposed of all his property in Rugeley in various sales after 1918.[25]

The manor had no capital messuage in 1298,[26] and there seems to have been none before or after that date.

From at least 1309 the courts of Rugeley were held jointly with those of Cannock, usually at each manor alternately.[27] A view of frankpledge was held by 1277,[28] and Rugeley was represented jointly with Brereton by five frankpledges by 1341[29] and separately by four by 1463.[30] The lord of Rugeley's revenue from this view was 3s. 6d. by 1277[31] and 13s. in 1291.[32] Between at least 1424 and 1533 the proceeds of the manor included 3s. for frithsilver from the fixed view of frankpledge,[33] and between at least 1762 and 1769 the constable was paying 4s. 1½d. in frithsilver.[34] In 1826 the vestry of Rugeley voted an allowance of 10s. each to the constables and headboroughs for their expenses in attending the leet.[35] The constables were still elected at the October court leet in 1834.[36]

It was stated in 1595 that the bailiff of Rugeley was allowed 18d. and the Bailiff's Acre.[37]

The bounds and customs of the manor were set out with those of Cannock at the survey of 1595.[38]

By 1228 the overlordship of *BRERETON* seems to have been held by the Bishop of Coventry and Lichfield.[39] It descended with the manor of Rugeley until at least 1555.[40]

A mesne lordship of Brereton was held c. 1228 by Sir Henry de Audley[41] whose son James surrendered part of it, the land at Red Moor, to the bishop in 1250.[42] James was still mesne lord in 1254,[43] but nothing further is known of this lordship.

About 1228 Sir Henry de Audley granted his land in Brereton, except for Red Moor, to Adam de Mutton,[44] who gave 6 acres of this land soon afterwards to William de Mutton, probably his brother.[45] Sir Adam was dead before 1241, leaving a son Ralph, a minor, to succeed him, and Henry de Audley granted the custody of the lands in Brereton to Adam's widow Isabel.[46] Ralph himself was dead in 1241,[47] with an infant daughter Isabel as his heir,[48] and in 1254 his widow Agnes was claiming ⅓ carucate in Brereton as her dower against Hugh de London who called upon James de Audley to warrant his title.[49] Ralph's daughter Isabel was married, apparently by 1257, to Philip de Chetwynd,[50] who was dead by 1284.[51] By 1290 she was the wife of Roger de Thornton.[52] Her son Philip de Chetwynd (II) succeeded her in 1291[53] and in that year granted a life interest in the manor to Roger,[54] who was dead

[17] Tithe Maps and Appt., Rugeley (copy in W.S.L.).
[18] Local inf.
[19] *V.C.H. Staffs.* iv. 39, no. 23.
[20] *S.H.C.* i. 20, 23.
[21] Ibid. 69, 70, 130.
[22] Ibid. 1924, no. 15.
[23] Ibid. ii (1), 92, 128, 137, 162, 164–5; *Pat. R.* 1216–25, 24; *Close R.* 1227–31, 329; *Cal. Chart. R.* 1257–1300, 347–8; *Feud. Aids*, v. 17; *S.H.C.* 1939, 110–11, 132–3; *L. & P. Hen. VIII*, xxi (2), g. 76 (332); *Cal. S.P. Dom.* 1595–7, 468; C 142/448, no. 113; White, *Dir. Staffs.* (1851); see pp. 53–54.
[24] See p. 54.
[25] Ex inf. Messrs. Strutt & Parker, Lofts & Warner, Berkeley Sq., London, agents to Lord Anglesey (1956).
[26] W.S.L., D. 1734, extent of lands of Bpric. of Cov., Lich., and Chester, 26 Edw. I.
[27] See p. 54. Courts were also held at the unidentified 'Water Wending' in 1310 and 1355: ibid.
[28] Lichfield D. and C. MSS., N. 16.
[29] W.S.L., D. 1734, Cannock and Rugeley Ct. R. 1309–73, m. 5.
[30] Ibid. 1463–83, 1510–46, 1546–53.
[31] Lichfield D. and C. MSS., N. 16.
[32] *Tax. Eccl.* (Rec. Com.), 250.
[33] W.S.L., D. 1734, Compotus R. of Bpric. of Cov. and Lich. 1423–57, m. 5; ibid. 1532–3, m. 5d.
[34] W.S.L., Paget Papers (Gardner Coll.), 35 (1, 9).
[35] Rugeley Vestry Order Bk. 1819–81, 13 Jan. 1826.
[36] White, *Dir. Staffs.* (1834).
[37] F. W. Hackwood, *Chronicles of Cannock Chase* (1903), 79. A meadow in Rugeley called the 'Reveacre' occurs by 1424: W.S.L., D. 1734, Compotus R. of Bpric. of Cov. and Lich. 1423–57, mm. 5, 10; W.S.L. 335 (1), m. 13d.
[38] Hackwood, *Chronicles of Cannock Chase*, 77, 79; for the customs see pp. 54–55.
[39] *S.H.C.* xii (1), 274.
[40] Ibid. 1924, nos. 230, 316; ibid. xii (1), 258, 304–5; C 142/106, no. 67.
[41] *S.H.C.* xii (1), 274.
[42] Ibid. 1924, nos. 230, 316.
[43] Ibid. iv (1), 132.
[44] Ibid. xii (1), 274.
[45] Ibid.
[46] Ibid. xii (1), 246, 275–6.
[47] *Close R.* 1237–42, 418.
[48] *S.H.C.* iv (1), 119; ibid. xii (1), 246–9.
[49] Ibid. iv (1), 132.
[50] Uncalendared entry on Pat. R. 41 Hen. III (C 66/71), m. 132, 29 Mar. 1257 (from W.S.L., S. MS. 332 (1), p. 230); *S.H.C.* xii (1), 249.
[51] *S.H.C.* vi (1), 136.
[52] Ibid. 196.
[53] *Cal. Fine R.* 1272–1307, 290.
[54] *S.H.C.* vi (1), 202; ibid. 1911, 46–47.

in 1297.[55] Philip made a settlement in 1307 of a messuage, a carucate, 40 acres of wood, and 40s. rent in Brereton,[56] and was dead by 1308 when his son Philip (III), a minor, had succeeded.[57] A protracted lawsuit then began concerning the dower of Isabel, widow of Philip (II).[58] The manor then descended with Reule in Bradley[59] until at least 1735.[60]

John Viscount Chetwynd (d. 1767), was lord of Brereton in 1750,[61] and by 1780 the manor was held by his daughter Catherine, wife of John Talbot,[62] whose son John Talbot (Chetwynd-Talbot in 1786), created Viscount Ingestre and Earl Talbot in 1784, was lord in 1785.[63] His son Charles Chetwynd was holding the manor in 1800,[64] and although his right to the manor was questioned by the Marquess of Anglesey in 1818,[65] the estate remained in the family until the sale of the collieries in 1923 and of the rest of the property between then and 1951.[66]

From at least 1341 Brereton was within the leet of Cannock and Rugeley and was represented, with Rugeley, by five frankpledges at the twice-yearly view, but by 1463 Brereton presented separately by one frankpledge.[67] The lord of the manor was holding his own view of frankpledge in 1832 and 1837 along with a court baron.[68] Surveys of the manor between 1797 and 1837 show it as situated in the parishes of Rugeley, Longdon, and Armitage.[69] The respective boundaries of the manors of Brereton, Armitage, and Handsacre were in dispute by 1806.[70]

The manor of HAGLEY seems to have originated in the land in Rugeley held, probably from the time of Henry II, by the keepers of the hay of Rugeley within the forest of Cannock.[71] The overlordship was held by the lords of this woodland until at least 1762.[72]

Land in Rugeley seems to have been granted by Henry II to a William de Puys (Puteo), whose son Roger had succeeded him by 1166.[73] Roger was still living in 1176,[74] but by 1189 his younger brother Richard was holding the land, apparently 30 acres in extent, although Roger had left a son, also Richard.[75] This brother Richard was dead by 1194 and had been succeeded by another brother, Reynald.[76] In 1198, however, Reynald, as keeper of an unspecified hay within the Forest of Cannock, was holding 15 acres in Rugeley worth 3s. a year, while his nephew Richard was holding a quarter of a carucate, also by some forest service.[77] Agnes, the widow of Roger, and her

husband William de Eisse sued Richard in 1199 for dower in Roger's land, and he gave them ⅓ virgate in Rugeley called 'Hoddesley'.[78] All 30 acres had passed to Reynald's son Robert by 1225,[79] but Richard secured them in 1227, giving Robert land in Warwickshire in exchange.[80] Reynald's widow Sarah sued Richard for dower in the 30 acres in 1230, and he gave her an annuity of 7s. 6d.[81] Richard de Puys was holding a carucate in Rugeley in 1236 by the service of keeping the hay of Rugeley,[82] and this office and the appurtenant land in Rugeley had passed by 1288 to a William de Puys, who had the status of a 'valettus' and built a small house and a barn there worth 40s.[83]

William was dead by 1301, leaving a daughter Agnes, wife of William de Thomenhorn (Tamhorn), who was ousted from the land by the overlord on the grounds of illegitimacy.[84] Agnes and William, however, were reinstated in 1302.[85] William de Thomenhorn was still living in 1332,[86] but by 1347 his son, or grandson, Thomas de Thomenhorn, held 8 messuages in Rugeley with a carucate of land, meadow and pasture, 16s. rent, and a mill.[87] Thomas's heir was his son William,[88] whose wife Anne survived him and was succeeded after her death by William's brother Thomas.[89] By 1392 Thomas was holding a messuage with ½ virgate in Rugeley, and since several of his buildings there had been destroyed by fire at some time before that year, he built himself a new house (novum manerium) consisting of a hall, four chambers, a chapel, a kitchen, two barns, a stable, an oxstall, a brewery, and a gatehouse with a drawbridge, felling 100 oaks within the bishop's chase of Cannock for the purpose as part of his right to timber for building, fencing, and fuel appurtenant to his tenement in Rugeley.[90] The bishop, challenging this right, claimed that twelve oaks were sufficient for the more modest buildings of Thomas's ancestors,[91] but it was agreed in 1393 that Thomas should in future cut sufficient timber for repairs under the supervision of the bishop's officials and, as keeper of the bailiwick of Rugeley, enjoy general timber rights.[92]

Thomas and his wife Alice in 1398 or 1399 granted the reversion of what was described as the manor of Rugeley and of the lands held by the service of keeping the hay of Rugeley to Adam de Peshale of

55 Ibid. vii (1), 41.
56 Ibid. xii (1), 286–7.
57 Ibid. 287–8; ibid. ix (1), 5–6.
58 Ibid. ix (1), 5–6, 8–9, 42, 46.
59 Cal. Chart. R. 1300–26, 367; S.H.C. xii (1), 300, 305–6, 307–8, 313–14, 316, 335–6; C 142/75, no. 77; C 142/106, no. 67; C 142/236, no. 87; C 142/485, no. 189; V.C.H. Staffs. iv. 82–83.
60 S.R.O., Gamekprs.' Deps.; V.C.H. Staffs. iv. 83.
61 S.R.O., Gamekprs.' Deps.; Chetwynd-Stapylton, Chetwynds of Ingestre, Pedigree III.
62 S.R.O., Gamekprs.' Deps.; Complete Peerage, xii (1), 624.
63 S.R.O., Gamekprs.' Deps.; Complete Peerage, xii (1), 624.
64 C.P. 43/869, rot. 441.
65 W.S.L. 41/15/45.
66 P.O. Dir. Staffs. (1876); ex inf. the Estate Offices, Ingestre (1957).
67 W.S.L., D. 1734, Ct. R. of Cannock and Rugeley, 1309–73, 1463–83, 1510–46, 1546–53.
68 W.S.L. 41/17/45, 41/21/45.
69 W.S.L. 41/2/45, 41/13/45, 41/14/45, 41/19/45, 41/21/45; W.S.L., Estate Maps, Brereton (1796).
70 W.S.L. 41/11/45.
71 See pp. 158–9.
72 S.H.C. ii (1), 33; Bk. of Fees, 7, 594; S.H.C. v (1), 166–7; vii (1), 92–93; Cal. Inq. p.m. xi, p. 390; C 138/51; Cal. Inq. p.m. Hen. VII, ii, p. 222; C 142/55, no. 73; Hackwood, Chronicles of Cannock Chase, 77; W.S.L., Paget Papers (Gardner Coll.), 10 (14).
73 S.H.C. i. 43, 47.
74 Ibid. 79.
75 Ibid. iv (1), 36.
76 Ibid. ii (1), 33.
77 Bk. of Fees, 7.
78 S.H.C. iii (1), 168.
79 Ibid. iv (1), 36.
80 Ibid. 226–7.
81 Ibid. 228–9.
82 Bk. of Fees, 594.
83 S.H.C. 1911, 191; ibid. xv. 53.
84 Ibid. vii (1), 92–93.
85 Ibid. 93.
86 Ibid. x (1), 120.
87 Ibid. xi. 161.
88 Cal. Inq. p.m. xi, p. 390.
89 Ibid.; Cal. Close, 1360–4, 505.
90 S.H.C. xv. 53.
91 Ibid.
92 Ibid. 1939, 77; W.S.L., D. 1734, Paget Deeds, no. 1578.

Weston under Lizard in the event of their having no children,[93] but they were stated to be holding the 'manor' for life only in 1406 when Adam granted the reversion to his daughter Margaret and her husband Richard Mutton.[94] Sir Thomas de Thomenhorn died in 1416 or 1417, and the 'manor' and lands passed to William Mutton, the son and heir of Richard and Margaret and a minor.[95] The manor consisted in 1421 of 100 acres of arable each worth 2d. a year, 20 acres of meadow each worth 6d., 100 acres of pasture each worth 4d., 6 acres of wood worth nothing because there was no customary wood cut, and 23s. in rent.[96] William Mutton was of age in 1437[97] and was still living in 1492,[98] but in 1500 his son John died seised of 6 messuages, pasture, meadow, and four mills in 'Hagley' and Rugeley, worth £10 and held by the service of keeping the bailiwick of Rugeley.[99] John's son and heir John made settlements of what was called the manor of Hagley in 1513[1] and 1527,[2] and in 1530 he settled the reversion of his Staffordshire lands after the death of himself and his wife Constance on his grandson Edward Harpesfield (later Mitton), a minor, in the event of Edward's marrying Anne Skrymsher.[3] John seems to have mortgaged the manor in 1532, reserving a rent from it to his daughter and heir Joyce.[4] He died in 1533, when the manor, with certain cottages in Penkridge, was valued at £6 6s. 8d.[5] and Joyce seems to have been in receipt of the rent in that year.[6] Thomas Skrymsher, father of Anne, subsequently sued John's widow Constance and others for the custody of John's heir and for deeds relating to Hagley and elsewhere,[7] while Richard Weston of Brereton and others were suing for deeds relating to the manor on behalf of Joyce, apparently in 1533.[8]

By 1544 Richard Weston's son John was described as of Hagley[9] and held the manor in 1547.[10] He died in 1566,[11] and by 1571 his son Richard's right to Hagley was being disputed by Edward Harpesfield, then lord of Weston under Lizard.[12] Richard and his wife Barbara, however, held the manor in 1578,[13] and Richard was succeeded in 1613 by his son, also Richard,[14] who made a settlement of the manor in 1624.[15] This Richard was M.P. for Lichfield in 1621,

knighted in 1635, and a baron of the Exchequer from 1634 until 1645.[16] About 1643 he owned lands in Rugeley and Brereton, leased to eighteen and six tenants respectively, in addition to his demesnes.[17] He was succeeded in 1658 by his grandson Philip,[18] who sold the manor to Anne Lane in 1710.[19] By 1725 the manor was held by Warin Faulkner,[20] whose Jacobite sympathies seem to have led to the plundering of Hagley Hall in 1745.[21] He died in 1748,[22] and by 1752 the manor had passed to Assheton Curzon[23] (Baron Curzon of Penn in 1794, Viscount Curzon in 1802),[24] who is said to have spent much of the year at Hagley and to have kept hounds and race-horses there.[25] He died in 1820,[26] and by 1823 Hagley was in the hands of his younger son Robert,[27] who died in 1863.[28] Hagley was sold in 1864 to William Harrison, the local colliery owner, and in 1878 or 1879 to the 3rd Marquess of Anglesey (d. 1880).[29] The 6th Marquess (d. 1947) sold the Hall and some of the land to Mr. Cumberland Brown of Luton (Beds.) in 1927.[30] Most of this estate, with the Hall, passed to the South Staffordshire Waterworks Company in or soon after 1931, the remainder being sold for building plots.[31] The Marquess retained Hagley Farm, comprising some 146 acres until its sale in 1944 to Mr. C. J. Whieldon[32] who in 1941 or 1942 had bought the Hall and its surrounding land[33] and was still living there in 1957.

The lords of Hagley held courts baron between at least 1585 and 1728.[34]

The 14th-century capital messuage probably occupied the low-lying site to the west of Crossley Stone where a large moat encircling an island is still in existence. The present Hagley Hall stands on high ground some 300 yds. farther west, the level falling away steeply on its south side to form a cliff above the Rising Brook. Sir Richard Weston (d. 1658) is said to have built the first house, at one time known as Bank Top, on this site.[35] In 1666 his heir was taxable for fifteen hearths.[36] Towards the end of the 18th century the house was remodelled and greatly extended by Assheton Curzon,[37] who also improved the grounds, planted shrubberies, and built a high wall round the park.[38] Alterations to the east side of the house were made in the early 19th

---

[93] S.H.C. xi. 204.
[94] Ibid. 215.
[95] C 138/51.
[96] Ibid.
[97] S.H.C. N.S. ii. 118.
[98] Cal. Inq. p.m. Hen. VII, i, p. 304.
[99] Ibid. ii, pp. 221–2.
[1] S.H.C. N.S. ii. 126.
[2] S.H.C. xi. 267.
[3] Ibid. N.S. ii. 128–9.
[4] C 1/927, nos. 16–18; C 142/55, no. 73.
[5] C 142/55, no. 73.
[6] C 1/927, no. 17.
[7] C 1/887, no. 23.
[8] C 1/927, nos. 16–18; C 142/55, no. 73.
[9] C 1/1085, no. 31.
[10] S.H.C. xii (1), 199.
[11] Erdeswick, Staffs. ed. Harwood (1844), pedigree no. 2 between pp. 164 and 165.
[12] S.H.C. 1931, 201; ibid. 1938, 162–3.
[13] Ibid. xiv (1), 199.
[14] C 142/333, no. 20.
[15] S.H.C. N.S. x (1), 57–58.
[16] S.H.C. 1920 & 1922, 25–26.
[17] S.R.O., D. 260/M/box 25, bdle. k, Royalists' Estates 1643–5, ff. 128b–129b.
[18] D.N.B.; Erdeswick, Staffs. pedigree no. 2 between pp. 164 and 165; S.H.C. N.S. vii. 72, gives the date as 1656 and S.H.C. 1920 & 1922, 26, corrects this to 1652.

[19] The Landor Accounts, in the possession of the exors. of the late W. N. Landor, Esq., of Rugeley, in 1955; S.R.O., Gamekprs.' Deps.
[20] The Landor Accounts.
[21] Rugeley Par. Reg. (Staffs. Par. Reg. Soc.), p. xviii.
[22] Rugeley Par. Reg. 1721–1812, p. 103, from transcript in W.S.L.
[23] W.S.L., Paget Papers (Gardner Coll.), 10 (14).
[24] Complete Peerage, iii. 582.
[25] W. N. Landor, 'Ancient Rugeley' (Rugeley Par. Mag. Jan. 1941).
[26] Complete Peerage, iii. 583.
[27] C.P. 43/959, rot. 226.
[28] Burke, Peerage (1931), 2547.
[29] Rugeley Par. Reg., p. xviii.
[30] Ibid.
[31] Charity Com. files.
[32] Ex inf. Messrs. Strutt & Parker, Lofts & Warner, Berkeley Sq., London, agents to Lord Anglesey (1956); Beaudesert Hall Estate Sale Catalogue 1932 (copy in W.S.L.), the farm being withdrawn from this sale.
[33] Ex inf. Mr. C. J. Whieldon (1957).
[34] W.S.L. 22/1/41, 22/2/41, 22/3/41, 22/4/41, Hagley Ct. R.; Rugeley Par. Bk. 1680–1813, f. 29b.
[35] Rugeley Par. Reg., p. xvii.
[36] S.H.C. 1927, 16.
[37] White, Dir. Staffs. (1834).
[38] W. N. Landor, 'Ancient Rugeley' (Rugeley Par. Mag. Jan. 1941).

century. About 1932 the greater part of the building was demolished, leaving only the central portion which had contained the kitchen and service quarters of the 18th-century mansion.[39] Plans and drawings of the mansion before its partial demolition[40] show gabled wings at the rear which may have represented the 17th-century house. Facing south and reaching to the edge of the cliff were the principal 18th-century rooms which included an octagonal drawing-room, the base of which is still in position below ground level. Alterations to the present house by Mr. C. J. Whieldon include an entrance porch incorporating parts of stone columns brought from Abbots Bromley[41] (Pirehill hundred).

On the crown of the hill to the west is an 18th-century brick stable range, now cottages, with a domed cupola at its north gable-end. Beyond this is an ice-house sunk in the hillside consisting of a circular domed brick chamber approached by a narrow passage.[42] Two ranges of well-designed brick outbuildings dating from the 18th century lie between the Hall and Hagley Farm. In the cliff below the house are a series of rock-cut chambers which may represent an 18th-century garden feature or grotto. Alternatively, it has been suggested that the caves were cut by the colliery owner William Harrison to provide work for unemployed miners.[43] The largest of the chambers has a barrel ceiling and two flanking aisles, the arcades supported on square-cut piers. A niche and pedestal at one end has prompted the suggestion that the room contained an altar and was used as a chapel. The Rising Brook, which runs along the base of the cliff towards Hagley Mill and the former moat, falls over several low weirs and is spanned by a small late-18th-century stone bridge. This is of vermiculated masonry and has a wrought-iron balustrade with circular piers surmounted by vases. A pool at the upper end of the park was made by William Harrison.[44] Since 1930 successive building schemes have encroached on the grounds, and the old moated site is now (1957) cut off from the garden by the new by-pass road.[45]

Hagley Farmhouse was formerly of red brick with stone dressings and was probably built in the late 17th century. It is now (1957) covered with roughcast and has recently been reroofed.

LESSER ESTATES. A Philip de Rugeley succeeded in 1224 to lands in Rugeley held of the king by his father Richard.[46] An Adam de Rugeley, who occurs holding fishing rights at Rugeley in 1326,[47] paid tax here in 1327[48] and 1332[49] and was still alive in 1339.[50] A Simon de Rugeley, who also paid tax here in 1327[51] and 1332[52] and was prominent in the county as sheriff, knight of the shire, commissioner, and tax collector between 1336 and 1348,[53] was granted free warren on his demesne lands in Rugeley and elsewhere in 1337.[54] The bishop leased a fishery in the Trent within the manor to him in 1342,[55] and at his death in 1349 he held of the bishop a messuage in Rugeley with a carucate, meadow, pasture, and rent of 22s. from cottars.[56] His heir was his son Henry aged 14 and studying at Oxford.[57] A Nicholas de Rugeley of Hawkesyard (in Armitage, Offlow hundred) had inherited houses, woods, and gardens in Rugeley from a kinsman, Thomas de Rugeley, by 1412.[58] A Simon de Rugeley of Hawkesyard, who died in 1516, was holding a messuage in Rugeley of the bishop, with 27 acres of arable, an island in the Trent called 'le Holmes', and a fishery in the river.[59] His son and heir Thomas died in 1552 holding lands, tenements, and a fishery in Rugeley of Lord Paget and a messuage, lands, and tenements in Brereton of Thomas Chetwynd.[60] A Simon de Rugeley held an estate in Rugeley in 1663.[61]

The Dean and Chapter of Lichfield as rectors of Rugeley held a house there in 1276 situated across the street from that assigned to the vicar,[62] and in 1356 they were accusing the vicar, presumably as farmer of the rectory, of neglecting to repair it.[63] In 1359 they leased the estate, then called Puysland and consisting of the house and all buildings there, except the tithe barn, and 45½ acres of arable and 4 acres of meadow in Rugeley to Henry Puys, his wife Juliana, and their heirs for a rent of 16s., confirming the grant in 1363 and 1389.[64] The estate may have passed to Thomas Meverell of the Bold (in Blithfield, Pirehill hundred), son of Nicholas Meverell, before his death in 1517,[65] and his son and heir Lewis was holding it when he died in 1532.[66] It then passed to Lewis's daughter Mary,[67] who married John Chetwynd of Ingestre (Pirehill hundred).[68] John's son by his second wife, Sir Walter Chetwynd, granted the house with lands belonging to it to his brother Thomas Chetwynd of Rugeley and his heirs in 1614.[69] The estate then descended in his family, the Chetwynds of Rugeley and Grendon, being held in 1761 by Lady Raymond and by 1764 by her second husband, Lord Robert Bertie.[70] In 1768 Lord Robert conveyed what was

[39] Plans penes Mr. Whieldon.
[40] W.S.L., Staffs. Views, viii, p. 113 (1795), p. 114 (b, 1814); Sale Catalogue (Marquess of Anglesey), 1919 (copy penes Mr. Whieldon); plans penes Mr. Whieldon; for the view in 1814, see plate facing p. 52.
[41] Ex inf. Mr. Whieldon.
[42] An almost identical ice-house exists at Malvern Hall, Solihull (Birmingham): F. W. B. Yorke, 'Some Midland Ice-houses' (Trans. Birm. Arch. Soc. lxxii), 22–23, pl. 10.
[43] Ex inf. Mr. S. Horne, Old Stafford Society.
[44] Rugeley Par. Reg., p. xviii.
[45] See pp. 149–51. The building of the road has necessitated the alteration of the course of the Rising Brook here.
[46] Ex. e Rot. Fin. (Rec. Com.), i. 111.
[47] S.H.C. ix. (1), 112.
[48] Ibid. vii (1), 327.   [49] Ibid. x (1), 120.
[50] Shaw, Staffs. i. 175–6.
[51] S.H.C. vii (1), 327.
[52] Ibid. x (1), 120.
[53] Ibid. 1917–18, 69; Cal. Close, 1341–3, 506, 539; Cal. Pat. 1345–8, 319.
[54] Cal. Chart. R. 1327–41, 421.

[55] W.S.L., D. 1734, Ct. R. of Cannock and Rugeley 1309–73, m. 4.
[56] Cal. Inq. p.m. ix, p. 225.   [57] Ibid.
[58] S.H.C. xvi. 80.
[59] C 142/82, no. 93.
[60] C 142/98, no. 67.
[61] C.P. 25(2)/723, 14–15 Chas. II Hil.
[62] S.H.C. 1924, no. 89.
[63] Bodl. MS. Ashmole 794 (1), f. 93a.
[64] S.H.C. vi (2), 16; Cal. Pat. 1361–4, 378. Henry was one of three farmers in 1356 when the house was called The Old Hall: Bodl. MS. Ashmole 793 (1), f. 94a.
[65] C 142/34, no. 66.   [66] C 142/55, no. 23.
[67] Ibid.; C 142/34, no. 66.
[68] Chetwynd-Stapylton, Chetwynds of Ingestre, 149, 159.
[69] Ibid. 159 and Pedigree 'Chetwynds of Ingestre'; S.H.C. n.s. iv. 74.
[70] Lich. D. and C. MS. Bk. liv, f. 103a; W.S.L., Paget Papers (Gardner Coll.), 35 (1); Chetwynd-Stapylton, Chetwynds of Ingestre, Pedigree 'Chetwynds of Rugeley and Grendon'.

described as the 'manor' of Rugeley to Thomas Anson (Viscount Anson of 1806) of Shugborough (in Colwich, Pirehill hundred) and Orgrave (in Alrewas, Offlow hundred).[71] In 1780 'a very ancient timber-house, which once belonged to the Chetwynds, and is now the property of Mr. Anson', still stood opposite the parish church,[72] and part of the garden wall is still (1957) visible between Anson Street and Market Street.[73] Viscount Anson was succeeded in 1818 by his son Thomas William (Earl of Lichfield in 1831)[74] who was holding the 'manor' in 1829[75] and an estate of some 445 acres in and around the town c. 1842.[76] The property was all sold between 1895 and 1938.[77] Fishing rights in the Trent formed part of this estate between at least 1768[78] and 1829.[79]

Ralph Weston, whose father had been a cousin of Philip Weston of Hagley, died in 1757 at Stone House, in what is now the hamlet of Slitting Mill,[80] and his nephew Ralph (d. 1794) lived here.[81] Between 1807 and c. 1842 Stone House was owned by Thomas Pickering or his trustees.[82] In 1808 Sarah Hopkins moved here with her brother Samuel from 'The Forge' (later Fair Oak House), and she remained here until her death in 1844.[83] James Gardner, of Gardner & Sons, Solicitors, Crossley Stone, lived here between at least 1854 and 1880 and James W. Gardner between at least 1884 and 1928.[84] Shortly before the Second World War the house was converted into a country club by Cannock Chase Hotels Ltd.[85] In 1940 it was taken over by the Air Ministry and in 1957 was their No. 6 Works Area H.Q.[86] The oldest part of the house is a roughly square block at its south-east corner dating from the late 16th or early 17th century. It is of stone ashlar, built directly upon the rock, and has two stories, cellar, and attics. The south front has twin gables and retains some original stone mullioned windows and moulded window hoods. The house was remodelled early in the 18th century when a symmetrical entrance front was added on the east side. There are further additions of the early 19th century and of c. 1840.

A house and land called Raven Hill lay on the road between Rugeley and Brereton by 1775,[87] and in 1796 the estate was held of the manor of Brereton by Lord Curzon of Hagley Hall.[88] About 1842 the estate, comprising some 62 acres, was owned by Lord Curzon's son Robert and was in the tenure of James Wright.[89] During the Second World War the house was the property of the Urban District Council and in 1948 was taken over by British Electronic Products Ltd. (since 1950 the Lancashire Dynamo Electronic Products Ltd.),[90] who have erected factory buildings in the grounds. The oldest part of the house is on the south side and dates from the late 18th century. There are numerous additions, mostly of the mid-19th century.

A fishery in the Trent cum solo within the manor of Rugeley was granted by the bishop in 1339 to Robert Mauveysin, his wife, and his heirs at a rent of 3s. 2d., on condition that no mill or mill-pool should be made nor the stream diverted.[91] The stretch of river granted lay in the north-eastern corner of the manor, between 'Hemprudinge over-ende', near the wood of Anselm le Mareschal called Ashley Hay, to 'Assheleyenetherende'.[92] By 1762 a fishery in the Trent was held of the lord of Rugeley by a Mr. 'Secheverill', who was paying 3s. 2d. for it and still held it in 1764.[93]

WOODS. In 1086 the king had woodland three leagues long by two broad attached to his manor of Rugeley.[94] The lordship descended with that of the woodland of Cannock, both areas being organized together as a free chase belonging to the manors of Cannock and Rugeley from 1290.[95] Much of the new Cannock Chase State Forest lies in Brindley Heath.

In 1589, while the chase was in the queen's hands owing to the forfeiture of Thomas Lord Paget, the lease of much of the timber there was granted to Fulke Greville for 21 years, and the royal surveyor reported that there were 3,123 acres of wood within the lordship of Rugeley, each acre being worth at least £7.[96] By 1595 the wooded area was much reduced.[97] Between 1589 and 1595 the queen's steward took 180 trees from the bailiwick, and Greville, Gilbert Wakering, and others illicitly cut trees belonging to the queen.[98] Greville, unlike Lord

[71] C.P. 25(2)/1411, 8 Geo. III Trin.; *Complete Peerage*, i. 173.
[72] Pennant, *Journey from Chester to London* (1811), 128.
[73] This wall is identified by W. N. Landor, 'Ancient Rugeley' (*Rugeley Par. Mag.* Oct. 1940), who also states that the house was once called Lower Hall to distinguish it from Bank Top at Hagley.
[74] *Complete Peerage*, i. 173–4; C.P. 43/942, rot. 351.
[75] C.P. 43/984, rot. 322.
[76] Tithe Maps and Appt., Rugeley (copy in W.S.L.).
[77] Ex inf. the Earl of Lichfield's Estate Office, Eccleshall (1957).
[78] C.P. 25(2)/1411, 8 Geo. III Trin.
[79] C.P. 43/984, rot. 322. About 1842 Lord Lichfield owned part of the Trent within the parish near Colton mill: Tithe Maps and Appt., Rugeley (copy in W.S.L.).
[80] W.S.L., S. 1549/2, unident. newspaper cutting 17 Oct. 1757; Erdeswick, *Staffs.* ed. Harwood (1844), Weston pedigree between pp. 164 and 165.
[81] Erdeswick, *Staffs.* Weston pedigree.
[82] W.S.L. 47/29/45; Tithe Maps and Appt., Rugeley (copy in W.S.L.).
[83] W.S.L. 47/29/45, 47/30/45, 47/31/45, 47/32/45; W.S.L., D. 1568, W. N. Landor's Bk. of Cuttings on Rugeley: Diary of Sarah Powell, 1798–1845; Tithe Maps and Appt., Rugeley (copy in W.S.L.); documents *penes* Charity Com.
[84] *P.O. Dir. Staffs.* (1854, and later edns. to 1876); *Kelly's Dir. Staffs.* (1880, and later edns. to 1928); W.S.L., D. 1766/28, Wolverhampton Deanery Ct. R. 1919–38, p. 112.

[85] Ex inf. member of Air Ministry staff, Stone House.
[86] Ex inf. member of Air Ministry staff.
[87] Yates, *Map of Staffs.* (1799), based on survey made 1769–75; the name is there given as 'Reveing Hill'.
[88] W.S.L., Estate Maps: Brereton.
[89] Tithe Maps and Appt., Rugeley (copy in W.S.L.).
[90] Ex inf. the Company; *Staffs. Advertiser and Chronicle*, 28 Feb. 1957.
[91] Shaw, *Staffs.* i. 175–6; *S.H.C.* 1939, 115–16.
[92] Shaw, *Staffs.* i. 176; *S.H.C.* 1939, 116. 'Assheleye-netherende' lay on the north-eastern boundary of the manor in 1300: *Cal. Chart. R.* 1257–1300, 348. 'Hempe-holme' lay in that part of the manor in 1595 (Hackwood, *Chronicles of Cannock Chase*, 77), and *c.* 1843 there was a Hempholme field on the southern bank of the Trent on the Armitage side of the Rugeley–Armitage boundary: Tithe Maps and Appt., Armitage (copy in W.S.L.).
[93] W.S.L., Paget Papers (Gardner Coll.), 35 (1).
[94] *V.C.H. Staffs.* iv. 39, n. 23.
[95] *S.H.C.* 1924, no. 15; ibid. v. 166–8; *Bk. of Fees*, 594; *Cal. Pat.* 1281–92, 344, 397; *Cal. Chart. R.* 1257–1300, 347, 348–9; *L. & P. Hen. VIII*, xxxi (2), g. 76 (332); *Complete Peerage*, x. 282–3; Forestry Commission, *Britain's Forests: Cannock Chase* (1950), 12; see pp. 59–60.
[96] Hackwood, *Chronicles of Cannock Chase*, 78; *S.H.C.* 1931, 249–50.
[97] Hackwood, *Chronicles of Cannock Chase*, 78.
[98] Ibid. 77–78.

Paget before him, was making no coppices and leaving no standels while cutting the timber granted to him.[99] As a result of this destruction of the woodland the tenants of the manor were losing their customary timber and the queen was losing her pannage dues.[1] It was further stated in 1595 that the browsing of the hollies within the manor of bailiwick of Rugeley was worth at least £7 a year to the Crown but that this revenue was endangered by Greville's workmen who were felling many of the hollies, although these had been excepted from the lease.[2]

The keepership of the hay or bailiwick of Rugeley followed the same descent as the manor of Hagley, which was held in serjeanty by the keepers,[3] until 1588 when the queen granted the keepership of Rugeley Bailly to William Sneade[4] on whom William Paget, having received most of his father's estates from the Crown in 1597,[5] conferred the office of keeper of the forests in the ambulation or 'le Walke' called 'Ridgley baylywick' within the chase in 1598.[6]

The forester of Rugeley, like the forester of Cannock, made presentments at the joint courts of the two manors by at least 1342.[7]

AGRICULTURE. By 1277 there was no demesne and all the land in the manor was held by tenants.[8] In this year 8d. was spent on the lord's conyger.[9] Twenty-eight persons in the manor were paying pannage dues in 1350 for 35 pigs and 25 'hogs' (hogg'),[10] and in 1819 37 freeholders and copyholders of Rugeley and Etching Hill were pasturing 3,367 sheep on Cannock Chase.[11]

In 1801 the parish of Rugeley had 608 acres sown, 110 with wheat, 214 with barley, 166 with oats, 20 with potatoes, 95 with turnips or rape, and 3 with rye.[12] The land by the Trent and the heavier soils to the east of the town were used in 1956 mainly for pasture, while to the south and south-east the agricultural land was used mainly for arable.[13] In 1956 there were six farms within the Urban District, of an average size of 70 acres, all mixed but with a tendency in favour of dairy-farming, pigs, and poultry, but very few of the population were engaged in agriculture.[14] It was then expected that much of the agricultural land would have to be used for housing estates to accommodate the expanding population.[15]

In 1353 the manor possessed common fields called Up Field, Church Field, and Hodgley ('Hoddesleye'),[16] lying respectively to the north-west of the town, to the north-west and north, and to the south-east.[17] By the 16th century there were in addition three 'small common fields' called Redbrook Field, Ravenhill ('Revynghill') Field, and Newland Field.[18] Piecemeal inclosure seems to have begun by the 16th century,[19] and in 1755 Up Field, Church Field, and Hodgley were inclosed by agreement.[20]

In the 16th century there were eight common meadows: Oldington Mead, Mowen Mead, 'Broode' Mead, 'the mead at the Brook', Turkyshall Mead, Woodfall Mead, Fleet Mead, and Assheley Mead.[21]

In 1885 4,790 acres of common on Cannock Chase within the parish were inclosed under an Act of 1864.[22]

MILLS. In 1086 there was a mill worth 30s. attached to the manor of Rugeley.[23] In 1277 the mill was held by a tenant,[24] and was described as newly built in 1298.[25] When the bishop in 1339 granted part of the Trent within the manor to Robert Mauveysin, he stipulated that no mill or mill-pool should be constructed and that the stream should not be diverted.[26] Before 1423 there was a fulling mill in Rugeley belonging to the lord of the manor and leased by 1424 to Thomas Walker of Penkridge and John Walker of Rugeley at a rent of 20s. with an increase of 6s. 8d.[27] Repairs costing 16s. 10d. were carried out between 1470 and 1473.[28] In 1475 three oaks were taken from the bailiwick of Rugeley for further work on this mill, 15s. being paid to the carpenter, while in the same year another 5s. was paid to a labourer for repairing it in four places.[29] In the year ending Michaelmas 1533 the fulling mill, recently held by Thomas Hille for 40s., was leased to Robert Gibson of Rugeley for 53s. 4d.[30] and it was still leased at that rent in 1560.[31] Another mill in Rugeley had been leased by the lord by 1560.[32] A mill situated near the present Leathermill Lane from at least 1775[33] was held of the lord of Rugeley by members of the Brittain family from before 1803[34]

[99] Ibid. 77.
[1] Ibid. 77–78.
[2] Ibid. 77.
[3] Bk. of Fees, 7, 594; S.H.C. v. 166–7; ibid. vii (1), 92–93; Cal. Inq. p.m. xi, p. 390; S.H.C. xv. 53, 147; ibid. xi. 204, 215; C 138/51; Cal. Inq. p.m. Hen. VII, ii, pp. 221–2.
[4] W.S.L., D. 1734, Paget Deeds, no. 1592.
[5] Complete Peerage, x. 283.
[6] S.H.C. 1939, 81.
[7] W.S.L., D. 1734, Ct. R. of Cannock and Rugeley 1342.
[8] Lichfield D. and C. MSS., N. 16.
[9] Ibid.
[10] W.S.L., D. 1734, Cannock and Rugeley Ct. R. 1309–73, m. 8.
[11] W. Molyneux, 'Cannock Chase' (Staffs. Advertiser, 11 Sept. 1873).
[12] R. A. Pelham, '1801 Crop Returns' (S.H.C. 1950–1), table opp. p. 242.
[13] Christina W. Barker, 'An Urban Study of Rugeley' (Nott. Univ. B.A. Thesis), 23.
[14] Ibid.
[15] Ibid. 23–24.
[16] W.S.L., D. 1734, Cannock and Rugeley Ct. R. 1309–73, m. 16.
[17] Names on Tithe Maps and Appt., Rugeley (copy in W.S.L.); R.C. Bapt. Reg. 1836–52, title-page, where the

old Catholic School in Heron Street is described as 'apud Hodgley'.
[18] W.S.L., D. 1734, Cannock and Rugeley survey, undated but probably 16th cent. Three acres in 'Ryvynghull' were mentioned in 1424: ibid. Compotus R. of Bpric. of Cov. and Lich. 1423–57, m. 5.
[19] Ibid. Cannock and Rugeley survey.
[20] W.S.L., D. 1792.
[21] W.S.L., D. 1734, Cannock and Rugeley survey.
[22] S.H.C. 1941, 19; S.R.O., Q/RDc 105.
[23] V.C.H. Staffs. iv. 39, no. 23.
[24] Lichfield D. and C. MSS. N. 16.
[25] W.S.L., D. 1734, extent of lands of Bpric. of Cov., Lich., and Chester, 26 Edw. I.
[26] S.H.C. 1939, 115–16.
[27] W.S.L., D. 1734, Compotus R. of Bpric. of Cov. and Lich. 1423–57, m. 5.
[28] W.S.L. 335 (1), m. 14.
[29] W.S.L., D. 1734, Compotus R. of Bpric. of Cov. and Lich. 1471–81, m. 19d.
[30] Ibid. 1532–3, m. 6d.
[31] W.S.L., D. 1734, Compotus of lands of Lord Paget 1559–60, m. 8.
[32] Ibid.
[33] Yates, Map of Staffs. (1799), based on a survey 1769–75.
[34] W.S.L. 47/45 (6).

and owned by a James Brittain *c.* 1842.[35] It was still in use as Turkeyshall Mill in 1884,[36] but there is now (1957) no trace of the site.

Thomas de Thomenhorn held a mill in Rugeley in 1347,[37] and John Mitton was holding four water-mills with his lands in Hagley and Rugeley in 1500.[38] Richard Weston, lord of Hagley, inherited a walk mill in Rugeley from his father in 1566,[39] and in 1578 his possessions in Rugeley, Cannock, Brereton, and Longdon (Offlow hundred) included two water-mills and two fulling mills.[40] He still held the walk mill in 1592.[41] By 1600 there was a messuage within the manor of Hagley called 'le wyndmyll', formerly held by Erasmus Wolseley, whose son and heir Thomas owed a relief for this and other tenements within the manor.[42] Philip Weston was holding two water gristmills in Rugeley and Cannock 'Heath' by 1681[43] and a paper-mill on the Rising Brook to the east of Rugeley town between at least 1671 and 1685.[44] Assheton Curzon as lord of Hagley owed the lord of Rugeley 6*s.* rent for corn-mills and 1*s.* for the watercourse in 1762,[45] and his son owned a mill on the northern side of Hagley Park *c.* 1842.[46] A mill here seems to have descended with the rest of the Hagley estate and was owned in 1919 by the Marquess of Anglesey who then offered it for sale.[47] In 1957 Hagley Mill was owned by Messrs. Isaac Nixon & Son Ltd.[48] and was used for grinding cattle food. The building contains brickwork of the 18th century and later, the base being of stone and possibly dating from the early 17th century. The wheel, of the breast type, was formerly at the west end of the mill building. Water power was replaced by electricity in 1954–5.[49] The pool and watercourse have been filled in.

The only other mill still operating in Rugeley in 1957 was that off Bees Lane (The Central Mills, Messrs. H. T. Nock Ltd.). This may occupy the site of the ancient manorial mill, and there has been a mill here from at least the early 19th century.[50] The mill house, now used as offices, dates from this time, but the mill itself was rebuilt in 1912 when the undershot wheel was replaced by a turbine. Since 1952 electricity only has been used.

A fulling mill in Rugeley was settled on William Chetwynd in 1680,[51] and the estate in Rugeley which

passed from the Chetwynd family to William Anson in 1768 was said to include three mills by 1829.[52]

By 1469 Thomas Coton was tenant of a mill in Rugeley leased to him for 30 years by Nicholas Brokholes.[53] John Hearn's mill, dam, and floodgates in Rugeley were damaged in the floods of September 1708.[54]

Between at least 1860 and 1896 there was a steam corn-mill in Market Street owned by Messrs. Timmis & Co.[55]

MARKETS AND FAIRS. A market to be held every Thursday within the manor of Rugeley was granted to the Bishop of Coventry and Lichfield by the king in 1259,[56] and the bishop apparently upheld this right in 1293.[57] In 1382, however, he was accused of having held a market in Rugeley for twenty years without the king's licence and to the prejudice of the burgesses of Stafford who were losing 12*d.* a year as a result.[58] The charter of 1259 was confirmed at some time between 1387 and 1390.[59] Further complaints were made in 1661 that the inhabitants of Rugeley were usurping privileges in the matter of markets,[60] but the Thursday market was still being held in 1747[61] and 1851.[62] By 1868 general markets were held each Saturday as well as Thursday, with a cattle market every alternate Tuesday.[63] The Saturday market had lapsed by 1912[64] but by 1956 was again held along with the other two. There are now 26 stalls in the general market offering a wide variety of goods, and stallholders come from several neighbouring towns.[65] The cattle market had become a weekly event by 1956.[66]

The charter of 1259 included a grant of a fair to be held annually on the Vigil, Feast, and Morrow of St. Augustine of Canterbury (25–27 May),[67] and this right, too, was apparently upheld in 1293.[68] The inhabitants of Rugeley were stated in 1661 to be usurping privileges in the matter of fairs as well as markets,[69] but by 1747 Rugeley had two fairs a year, for saddle horses on 26 May and for cattle on 10 October.[70] By 1834 there were four cattle fairs a year, on 14 April, from 1 to 6 June (a large fair for colts and horses), on 21 October, and on the second Tuesday in December when Earl Talbot generally gave prizes for the best fat cattle shown.[71] By 1912

[35] Tithe Maps and Appt., Rugeley (copy in W.S.L.).
[36] *Kelly's Dir. Staffs.* (1884); *Staffs. Advertiser,* 11 Feb. 1860, where it is stated to be in Turkeyshall Lane.
[37] *S.H.C.* xi. 161.
[38] *Cal. Inq. p.m. Hen. VII,* ii, pp. 221–2.
[39] *S.H.C.* 1938, 146–7.
[40] Ibid. xiv (1), 199
[41] W.S.L. 22/2/41, Hagley Ct. R. 16 Oct. 34 Eliz. I.
[42] W.S.L. 22/3/41, Hagley Ct. R. 29 Jan. 42 Eliz. I.
[43] C.P. 25(2)/726, 34 Chas. II East.
[44] W.S.L. 22/4/41, Hagley Ct. R. 14 Oct. 23 Chas. II; J. Ogilby, *Map of London–Holyhead Road* (1675).
[45] W.S.L., Paget Papers (Gardner Coll.), 35 (1), Chief Rent R.
[46] Tithe Maps and Appt., Rugeley (copy in W.S.L.).
[47] *Sale Catalogue (Marquess of Anglesey),* 1919 (copy *penes* Mr. C. J. Whieldon, 1957).
[48] Isaac Nixon appears as a corn merchant in Albion Street in 1928 and 1932: *Kelly's Dir. Staffs.* (1928; 1932). The firm of Isaac Nixon & Son Ltd. occurs there in 1940: ibid. 1940.
[49] Ex inf. Mr. Nixon (1957).
[50] Parsons and Bradshaw, *Dir. Staffs.* (1818); White, *Dir. Staffs.* (1834; 1851). It is not clear whether the mill shown in this area on Yates, *Map of Staffs.* (1799), based on a survey 1769–75, and Greenwood, *Map of Staffs.* (1820), is Hagley Mill or a mill on this central site.

[51] C.P. 25(2)/726, 32 Chas. II Mich.
[52] C.P. 25(2)/1411, 8 Geo. III Trin.; C.P. 43/984, rot. 322.
[53] *S.H.C.* n.s. iv. 166.
[54] Rugeley Parish Bk. 1680–1813.
[55] *P.O. Dir. Staffs.* (1860); *Kelly's Dir Staffs.* (1896).
[56] *Cal. Chart. R.* 1226–57, 18–19.
[57] *S.H.C.* vi (1), 277; *Plac. de Quo Warr.* (Rec. Com.), 710–11.
[58] C 145/224, no. 13; *Cal. Pat.* 1381–5, 145.
[59] *Cal. Rot. Chart.* (Rec. Com.), 192.
[60] *Cal. S.P. Dom.* 1660–1, 561.
[61] Smith, *New Map of Staffs.* (1747).
[62] White, *Dir. Staffs.* (1851).
[63] *P.O. Dir. Staffs.* (1868).
[64] *Kelly's Dir. Staffs.* (1912).
[65] Christina W. Barker, 'An Urban Study of Rugeley' (Nott. Univ. B.A. Thesis), 10–11.
[66] Ibid. 11.
[67] *Cal. Chart. R.* 1226–57, 18–19.
[68] *S.H.C.* vi (1), 277; *Plac. de Quo Warr.* (Rec. Com.), 710–11.
[69] *Cal. S.P. Dom.* 1660–1, 561.
[70] Smith, *New Map of Staffs.* (1747). The surviving street-names Horse Fair and Sheep Fair may indicate the sites of these two fairs.
[71] White, *Dir. Staffs.* (1851).

only the June fair was still held[72] and though held in 1932,[73] had lapsed by 1940.[74]

INDUSTRIES. Rugeley's chief manufacture by 1817 was hatmaking.[75] There were some 30 journeymen hatters in the town and its neighbourhood by 1834,[76] and the manufacture was still flourishing in 1851.[77] There were brick and lime kilns in operation by 1832.[78] Rugeley possessed a large brewery at Crossley Stone and two chemical works in 1834[79] and a tan-yard and a brass foundry as well as the brewery in 1851.[80] In 1955 the industries included engineering, quarrying, tanning, colour manufacture, and the making of clothes, boots, shoes, and electrical apparatus.[81]

Brereton Colliery was in existence by at least 1814[82] and in 1834 was being worked by Earl Talbot.[83] The present drawing shaft there was sunk in 1876,[84] and although much of the coal has now (1957) been worked out, production is expected to continue for about fifteen years.[85] By 1834 the Hayes Colliery, near the Brereton Colliery, was being worked by Joseph Palmer[86] and in 1851 by the Marquess of Anglesey.[87] It was closed before 1928.[88] The Fair Oak Colliery was opened in 1871 but was closed after some years owing to water difficulties.[89] The West Cannock No. 5 Pit at Brindley Heath was opened by the West Cannock Collieries Company in 1914.[90] Boreholes were put down to the north-east of Brereton before 1848 and again in 1863, but the existence of coal in the area was not conclusively proved.[91] It had, however, been established by 1956,[92] and the National Coal Board are now (1957) preparing to open a new pit at Lea Hall Farm within the next few years.

There were iron-mines and a forge within the manor of Rugeley by 1298.[93] In 1380 there were seventeen workers in iron.[94] A piece of waste land here called 'le forgeplace' was held by John Paynter for a rent of 2d. by 1533,[95] and Thomas Chetwynd, lord of Brereton, was holding a forge here of the lord of Rugeley in 1555.[96] William Lord Paget and his son and heir Henry were given leave in 1560 by the Crown to fell any oak, beech, or ash on Cannock

Chase or in any wood in Cannock, Rugeley, and elsewhere in the county for fuel in the making of iron,[97] and the Paget ironworks on the Chase were already in operation.[98] Thomas Lord Paget's property was confiscated by the Crown in 1587,[99] and in 1589 the queen leased to Fulke Greville for 21 years at an annual rent of £211 10s. two iron-furnaces and two iron-forges on the Chase with all the waters appurtenant; all woods and trees in the Forest of Cannock, excepting 3,000 marked trees, for use as fuel in the furnaces; five workmen's cottages; and all mines or ironstone in the forest.[1] Greville undertook to pay 1d. for each load of ironstone removed and to work 'one onlie furnace' with the two forges, using the timber only for the iron-work.[2] He was mining iron-stone on the Chase at a place called Black Mine in 1595.[3] William Paget, son of Thomas Lord Paget, recovered two furnaces and two forges on the Chase along with other of his father's possessions in 1597[4] and subsequently confirmed Greville's lease.[5] A boy was killed in 'the forge whiele' in 1605.[6] Walter Chetwynd of Rugeley was granted the lease of a furnace, a forge, and a slitting mill within the parish by Lord Paget before 1646, by which year they had been sequestered with the rest of Walter's property, the lease having three years still to run.[7] There was a forge near the modern hamlet of Slitting Mill by 1682.[8] The floods in Rugeley in September 1708 damaged the dams and floodgates of Furnace Pool, Tipper's Forge Pool, and Forge Pool and the dam of Brindley's Pool.[9] The slitting mill at Rugeley, presumably near the site of this hamlet, was handling most of the output of the Staffordshire iron-works between 1692 and 1710, and in the year ending Michaelmas 1709 its output of rod iron reached 608 tons.[10] In 1746 the slitting mill and forge in Rugeley, with all ponds and pools appurtenant, lands near the forge, two workmen's houses, and coal were leased to a group of partners for 21 years at a rent of £60.[11] There was a mill, presumably this slitting mill, on the Rising Brook near the present hamlet of Slitting Mill c. 1775, with a forge about a mile upstream from the mill.[12] A piece of land in Brindley Slade was leased in 1735 for the making of a pool

[72] Kelly's Dir. Staffs. (1912).
[73] Ibid. (1932).   [74] Ibid. (1940).
[75] Pitt, Staffs. 264. There are references to felt-makers and haberdashers of hats from 1730: W.S.L. 32/7/45, 87/33, 112/31/41, 89/33, 90/33.
[76] White, Dir. Staffs. (1834).   [77] Ibid. (1851).
[78] Teesdale, Map of Staffs. (1832).
[79] White, Dir. Staffs. (1834); Tithe Maps and Appt., Rugeley (copy in W.S.L.).
[80] White, Dir. Staffs. (1851).
[81] Rugeley: Official Guide (1955), 24–26.
[82] W.S.L., Paget Papers (Gardner Coll.), 58 (8); Pitt, Staffs. 266.
[83] White, Dir. Staffs. (1834); S.R.O., Shrewsbury Coll., valuations, surveys, and maps of Brereton and Hayes Collieries, 1848–81.
[84] Ex inf. National Coal Board, Cannock.
[85] Christina W. Barker, 'An Urban Study of Rugeley' (Nott. Univ. B.A. Thesis, 1956), 24–25.
[86] White, Dir. Staffs. (1834).
[87] Ibid. (1851); S.R.O., Shrewsbury Coll., valuations, surveys, and maps of Brereton and Hayes Collieries, 1848–81.
[88] Kelly's Dir. Staffs. (1912; 1928).
[89] C. M. Peel, 'Presidential Address' (Trans. Institute of Mining Engineers, cx), 333; A. Williams, Sketches in and around Lichfield and Rugeley (1892), 303.
[90] Ex inf. N.C.B., Cannock (1956).
[91] C. M. Peel, 'Presidential Address', 333.
[92] Ex inf. N.C.B., Cannock (1956).

[93] W.S.L., D. 1734, extent of lands of Bpric. of Cov., Lich., and Chester, 26 Edw. I.
[94] S.H.C. xvii. 186–8; Rugeley Par. Reg., p. vii.
[95] W.S.L., D. 1734, Compotus R. of Bpric. of Cov. and Lich. 24–25 Hen. VIII, f. 5b.
[96] C 142/106, no. 67.
[97] Cal. Pat. 1558–60, 326.   [98] See p. 63.
[99] Complete Peerage, x. 282.
[1] Hist. MSS. Com. 12th Rep. (i), 39; S.H.C. 1931, 249–51.
[2] S.H.C. 1931, 250. In 1588 there was discussion with Lord Burghley whether Greville should pay £300 for as much wood (3,000 cords) as would make 100 tons of iron: ibid. 251; B.M. Lansd. MS. 56, no. 34.
[3] Hackwood, Chronicles of Cannock Chase, 76.
[4] Cal. S.P. Dom. 1595–7, 468; Complete Peerage, x. 281–3.
[5] S.H.C. 1939, 249–51.
[6] Rugeley Par. Reg. 33.
[7] W.S.L., S. MS. 330 (transcript of Royalist Comp. Papers), i, pp. 633–40.
[8] Plot, Map of Staffs. (1682).
[9] Rugeley Parish Bk., 1680–1813; Rugeley Par. Reg., p. xxiii.
[10] B. L. C. Johnson, 'The Foley Partnerships' (Ec. H. R. 2nd ser. iv), 325, 326.
[11] W.S.L., Paget Papers (Gardner Coll.), 35 (1); W.S.L., C.B. Rugeley: Slitting Mill.
[12] Yates, Map of Staffs. (1799), based on a survey made 1769–75.

to John Biddulph, who before 1761 was tenant of two pools called Furnace and Brindley Pools.[13] He still held the land in Brindley Slade in 1762,[14] and *c.* 1775 there was a furnace on the Rising Brook where it is joined by the stream from Brindley Valley near the road to Rugeley about a mile north of Hednesford.[15] There was also a forge in the town of Rugeley *c.* 1775[16] in the area where there are still two streets called Forge Lane and Forge Road. The furnace at Brindley Valley was still in existence in 1820.[17] There were two slitting mills in Rugeley in 1832, one near the hamlet now called Slitting Mill and the other *c.* 400 yds. south-east of Hagley Farm.[18] Rugeley had two forges and rolling mills and two iron foundries in 1834[19] and in 1851 a large sheet-iron and tin-plate mill and two foundries.[20]

CHURCHES. There was a church in Rugeley by 1189 when Richard I granted it with the manor to the Bishop of Coventry and Lichfield.[21] By 1192 the bishop had given the church to the Dean and Chapter of Lichfield, though he then reserved episcopal rights.[22] In 1255 the bishop exempted the church from archidiaconal jurisdiction, and the dean and chapter thus acquired a peculiar jurisdiction.[23] In 1338, however, they delegated their right of probate and their disciplinary powers over the parishioners to the Vicar of Rugeley.[24]

A vicarage was instituted in 1276,[25] and the advowson has remained with the dean and chapter.[26]

The rectory which by the 14th century was regularly leased out,[27] was being farmed by the vicar in 1329[28] and 1356.[29]

In 1535 the dean and chapter's annual revenue from the appropriated church was £4 2s. 8d.[30] They granted a lease of the tithes along with the advowson for £3 6s. 8d. in 1548[31] and 1554.[32] In 1637 the great tithe, the tithe barn of three bays, and the adjoining cottage were leased to Walter Littleton of Lichfield for twenty years at a rent of £3 6s. 8d.[33] The history of that part of the rectorial estate called Puysland is treated above.[34]

The vicarage was endowed in 1276 with a house, the small tithe, oblations and offerings, the tithes of pannage, mills and fisheries, mortuaries, a rent of ½ mark from land in Rugeley, and a paddock.[35] Richard de Rugeley subsequently granted the vicar

an adjoining messuage at a rent of 12d. a year[36] and another messuage, next to this, and land were given by Pain, sometime servant of the Precentor of Lichfield.[37] The vicar's annual income in tithes and offerings was £5 2s. in 1535.[38] The value of the vicarage was given as £24 in 1604 and as £40 in 1646 when the Committee for Plundered Ministers granted an augmentation of £50 a year out of the sequestered rectory.[39] The value was given as £38 a year in 1650, and the endowments then consisted of the small tithe, Easter offerings, a house lately repaired by the vicar at his own expense, a backside and croft of 3 roods, and glebe land consisting of 5 acres of arable and meadow.[40] By will proved 1844 Sarah Hopkins of Stone House left £1,000 to be invested, the profits to be applied to enlarge or rebuild Rugeley church,[41] but it was decided in 1940 to use the current income to augment the stipend of the incumbent.[42] In 1949 the income was £431 1s. 5d. from stock and rents.[43] By will proved 1939 the Revd. W. J. Stanton of Eaton Lodge left £1,000 to be invested and the income applied for the benefit of the Rugeley Assistant Clergy Fund.[44]

William de Thomenhorn's right to a private oratory with a chaplain celebrating mass there daily was confirmed to him in 1329, for two years, by the Dean and Chapter of Lichfield on condition that he surrendered the licence previously granted him by the bishop.[45] In 1356 the Vicar of Rugeley complained that he was losing offerings through the ministrations of Thomas de Thomenhorn's chaplain who, it was alleged, had taken vestments, chalices, books, bread, wine, and candles from Rugeley church to the chapel.[46] In 1360 the bishop gave a licence for an oratory for two years to Henry Puys,[47] and in 1364 a similar licence to the vicar for an oratory within the vicarage house.[48]

The Chantry of Our Lady in the parish church was endowed by 1553 with eight cottages and lands worth in all 45s. 7d. a year.[49] These were leased by the Crown in 1567 for 21 years to a Robert Hurleston at a rent of 70s. 4d., the principal tenant then being Thomas Ryve, schoolmaster.[50] It was stated in 1590 that the property had been immemorially vested in trustees with the profits used for the maintenance of a grammar school.[51]

[13] W.S.L., Paget Papers (Gardner Coll.), 35 (1), Cannock Lease Bk.
[14] Ibid.
[15] Yates, *Map of Staffs.*
[16] Ibid.
[17] Greenwood, *Map of Staffs.* (1820).
[18] Teesdale, *Map of Staffs.* (1832); Tithe Maps and Appt., Rugeley (copy in W.S.L.).
[19] White, *Dir. Staffs.* (1834); Tithe Maps and Appt., Rugeley (copy in W.S.L.), no. 443, showing the forge and pool in the present Forge Road.
[20] Ibid. (1851).
[21] *S.H.C.* 1924, nos. 15, 16, 264, 753; *Rot. Chart.* (Rec. Com.), i. 49–50.
[22] *S.H.C.* 1924, nos. 16, 25, 140, 440, 754.
[23] Ibid., nos. 23, 24; *S.H.C.* 1915, 219; ibid. vi (2), 58.
[24] Bodl. MS. Ashmole 794 (1), Chapter Act Bk. 1321–84, f. 64a.
[25] *S.H.C.* 1924, no. 89.
[26] *Lich. Dioc. Dir.* (1955–6). They granted leases of it in 1546 and 1554: *S.H.C.* vi (2), 16–17.
[27] *S.H.C.* 1924, no. 90; Bodl. MS. Ashmole 794 (1), ff. 94a, 132a, 161a.
[28] Bodl. MS. Ashmole 794 (1), f. 34a.
[29] Ibid. f. 193a.

[30] *Valor Eccl.* (Rec. Com.), iii. 132.
[31] *S.H.C.* vi (2), 16.
[32] Ibid. 16–17.
[33] Lich. D. and C. MS. Bk. liv (1), Oliverian Survey, f. 101a.
[34] See p. 157.
[35] *S.H.C.* 1924, no. 89.
[36] Ibid., no. 710.
[37] Ibid., no. 711.
[38] *Valor Eccl.* (Rec. Com.), iii. 149.
[39] *S.H.C.* 1915, 221.
[40] Lich. D. and C. MS. Bk. liv (1), f. 101a.
[41] Charity Com. files.
[42] Ibid.
[43] Ibid.
[44] Ibid.
[45] Bodl. MS. Ashmole 794 (1), f. 35b.
[46] Ibid., f. 93b.
[47] *S.H.C.* n.s. viii. 8.
[48] Ibid. 22.
[49] *S.H.C.* 1915, 220.
[50] Ibid.
[51] Ibid. Elsewhere the chantry priest had kept a grammar school before the dissolution of the chantry, e.g. at Cannock: ibid. 49.

There was a keeper of a Light of the Blessed Mary by 1448.[52]

By 1548 Agnes Weston, widow, had given 4 acres of arable and ½ acre of meadow worth 2s. 4d. a year to endow an obit in memory of Richard Weston, a lamp before the rood, and 8d. to be used for the poor; Margery Moore, Richard Fletcher, and William Truebody had each given, for a perpetual yearly obit, rents of 1s. 11d. or 1s. 9d. of which 4d. was for the poor; and Thomas Starkey, priest, had given a cow worth 12s.[53] In 1549 the lands given by Agnes Weston, then held by the vicar, were sold by the Crown to John Cupper and Richard Trevour of London.[54] In 1571 the queen granted the burgesses of Stafford an annual rent of 1s. 9d. from a messuage in Rugeley called 'The Swanne' hitherto given to an obit there.[55]

property in Rugeley, apparently three cottages, was used to pay the salary of the organist in the parish church.[65] In 1952 the cottages, by then disused, were sold to the Urban District Council for £187.[66] In 1941 A. W. Whitworth gave a piece of land in Etching Hill for a church or mission room or some other parochial object, and the plot is still (1957) held by the parish.[67] Elizabeth Poynton of Rugeley, by will proved 1949, left a house and shop for use by the parish.[68] The property was sold in 1951 for £700 which was then invested.[69]

The former parish church of *ST. AUGUSTINE* consisted of nave, chancel, north aisle, north chapel, west tower, and south porch. After the completion of the present church in 1823 the old building was partly demolished. The chancel and the adjacent north chapel, under separate gabled roofs, were left

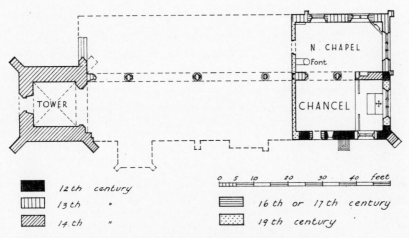

PLAN OF ST. AUGUSTINE'S (OLD) CHURCH

An assistant priest was appointed in 1325 because Henry de Barton alias de Passelewe, the first vicar, was helpless and blind.[56] In 1356 and 1357 the dean and chapter rebuked the vicar for being non-resident despite the stipulation that he must fulfil his duties personally.[57] From 1639 to 1646 the vicar, Richard Chapman, was non-resident and the church was served by a curate.[58]

Sermons were still preached in 1956 under the terms of the Chetwynd Charity.[59] The Revd. James Deakin, schoolmaster of Rugeley (d. 1727), bequeathed £10, the interest to be paid to the vicar for a sermon on Ascension Day.[60] By 1821 the £10 had been used to redeem land tax for Bamford's Charity School, and 10s. a year was then paid from this for the sermon.[61] This charity had been lost by 1890.[62] In 1826 Sarah Hopkins gave land to endow a sermon on any Sunday afternoon in the parish church.[63] The income was £15 in 1951, and in 1956 arrangements were being made to sell the land to the National Coal Board.[64] By 1838 the rent from

standing and walled up on the west side. In 1957 they were still in use for a Sunday school and occasional services. The west tower was left in position, but the nave and aisle were demolished except for the arches of the arcade.

The oldest part of the remaining structure is the chancel which dates from the late 12th century. The south wall, which has a contemporary string course and a single-light window, is of this date. The window's pointed head may be a later replacement. The 12th-century nave was probably without aisles; the eastern respond and the most easterly pier of the arcade are circular on plan and represent an early-13th-century reconstruction of the nave. The north chapel, of the same length as the chancel but slightly narrower, is an addition of the later 13th century. The east window consists of three graded lancets under a single head, and there is a flat contemporary buttress at the north-east angle. The chapel is divided from the chancel by an arcade which originally consisted of two bays. The remains of a

52 Ibid. 220.
53 Ibid.
54 *Cal. Pat.* 1548–9, 391–2, 397.
55 *Charters of the Borough of Stafford*, ed. J. W. Bradley (1897), 105. There was a tenement called The Swan within the manor before 1462: W.S.L., D. 1734, Compotus R. of Bpric. of Cov. and Lich. 1461–71, m. 5d.
56 Bodl. MS. Ashmole 794 (1), f. 11b.
57 Ibid. ff. 93a, 173a.
58 *S.H.C.* 1915, 219, editor's note in copy in W.S.L.
59 See pp. 170–1.

60 *7th Rep. Com. Char.* H.C. 129, p. 23 (1822), x.
61 Ibid.
62 Unprinted Report of 1890 in Charity Com. files.
63 Ibid.
64 Charity Com. files.
65 Ibid.
66 Ibid.
67 Ibid.; ex inf. the Lich. Dioc. Trust (1957).
68 Charity Com. files.
69 Ibid.

single-light window, part of the earlier north wall of the chancel, are visible in the spandrel between the arches. The west respond and single pier of the arcade have engaged semicircular shafts with wide fillets. The bell capitals, undercut abaci, and double-roll bases are typical of the period 1250–1300. Alterations to the chancel itself of about this time include a trefoil-headed piscina and a two-light window with original geometrical tracery. West of the piscina is a large niche with a trefoil head, presumably a single *sedile*. The walling which partially blocks the eastern arch of the arcade appears to date from the 14th century and was probably inserted to form a screen between the two altars, On the chapel side is a double piscina and an ogee-headed recess. It seems probable that the floor level of the sanctuary was formerly higher and that this recess represents another single *sedile*. At the back of the recess is an oblique shaft cut through the masonry and communicating with a small ogee-headed opening on the west face of the wall. The wall and openings have been much restored, but if this feature is original it suggests a squint enabling a server to keep both chancel and chapel altars in view. The priest's door in the south wall of the chancel has a shouldered arch and may be of post-Reformation date. Near it is a roughly built pyramidal buttress. The head of a 15th- or 16th-century two-light window has been built into the 19th-century west wall of the chancel. This window was formerly immediately west of the priest's door.[70] In the north wall of the chapel are two post-Reformation windows, and the east window of the chancel was formerly of the 'churchwarden Gothic' type, having simple interlacing tracery.[71]

Except at its east end the nave arcade dates from the late 13th century and is similar to the arcade dividing chancel and chapel. It has a pointed arch at each end with two wide semicircular arches between them. The central arches are twice the width of the others, suggesting that two piers have been removed and that the arcade originally consisted of six equal bays. No traces of nave walls exist and burials have taken place within the area of the former nave. A short length of the west wall of the aisle, which includes the jamb of a large window, projects from the north-east angle of the tower. The tower itself is of the 14th century with boldly projecting angle buttresses and a later castellated parapet. The west face has a pointed doorway of two orders above which is a two-light 14th-century window. There are two-light openings in the belfry stage and single openings with ogee heads in the stage below. Above the tall 14th-century tower arch are the weather marks of the former nave roof, the pitch of the south slope having been altered three times. The buttress at the north-east corner is corbelled out above the level of the former aisle and bears a weather mark showing that the aisle had a gabled roof.

Drawings of the church[72] before its partial demolition show that the south nave wall continued in the same line as that of the chancel. The roof was also continuous and contained four dormer windows, three near the west end probably being used to light the gallery. Just east of the tower was a large porch with a pointed arch and angle buttresses. Between this and the chancel there are traces of two tall blocked arches, suggesting that there was formerly a short projecting aisle on the south side, the arcade having four bays and corresponding with what are now the two central arches of the north arcade. The character of the inserted windows suggests that the demolition of the aisle and the walling-up of the arcade took place in the 17th century.

Under the terms of the lease of the rectory in 1637 Walter Littleton was obliged to repair the chancel 'which will now necessarily cost him 20 nobles'.[73] The north chapel, which was almost certainly the site of the altar dedicated to Our Lady before the dissolution of the chantries,[74] was still known as 'Westons' Chancel' in the 18th century.[75] The church already had a west gallery by 1718, in which year a north gallery was added.[76] During the building of the new church in 1822 it was decided at a vestry meeting to keep the tower of the old church in repair at the expense of the parish.[77] The monuments in the body of the old church were moved to the north chapel. A restoration of what was left of the church took place between 1869 and 1872.[78] In 1883 stained glass was inserted in one of the chancel windows in memory of Louisa Frances and Francis Mary Levett.[79] The building had been 'restored and beautified' in 1891 by the addition of two stained glass windows,[80] one in memory of Ralph Armishaw (d. 1890) and the other, the east chancel window, in memory of the Revd. Robert Litler. The stone tracery of 'Decorated' type in the latter was probably inserted at the same time. The carved stone font, although of 15th-century design, probably also dates from the late 19th century. There are fragments of medieval glass in the lancet window of the chancel.

Monuments in the north chapel include an incised alabaster floor slab bearing part of a female figure and an incomplete inscription dated 1400.[81] A second figure has been obliterated by wear. There is also a stone slab with brasses bearing a single figure and inscribed to John Weston (d. 1566).[82] Wall tablets of Jacobean design with coats of arms commemorate Ralph Weston (d. 1605), partly illegible, and Richard Weston (d. 1613). Across the north-east corner is a massive marble tablet with typical carved ornament of *c.* 1700 to Thomas son of William Landor (d. 1670), Walter Landor (d. 1706), and Anna Landor (d. 1716). Other tablets commemorate Philip Weston (d. 1713), Elizabeth Landor (d. 1753), Joseph Landor and Mary his wife (the latter d. 1774), Robert Cotton (d. 1793), and Susanna his wife (d.

[70] W.S.L., S. MS. 433, 230 (*c.* 1836); W.S.L., Staffs. Views, viii, pp. 95 (a, *c.* 1800), 95 (b, 1835). The views dated 1835 and 1835 are probably copies of an earlier drawing.
[71] W.S.L., S. MS. 433, 230; W.S.L., Staffs. Views, viii, p. 95 (a, b), drawing (a) showing a 14th-cent. window which may have been replaced by the 'churchwarden' window early in the 19th cent.
[72] W.S.L., S. MS. 433, 230, reproduced facing p. 152; W.S.L., Staffs. Views, viii, p. 95 (a, b).
[73] W.S.L., S. MS. 339 (transcripts of Royalist Composition Papers), iv, p. 321; see p. 157.

[74] See p. 162.
[75] *Rugeley Par. Reg.*, p. xii.   [76] Ibid., p. viii.
[77] Rugeley Vestry Order Bk. 1819–81.
[78] W. N. Landor, 'Ancient Rugeley' (*Rugeley Par. Mag.*, Sept. 1942).
[79] *Lich. Dioc. Ch. Cal.* (1884), 73–74.
[80] Ibid. (1892), 173.
[81] Copied by Edward Thomas: W.S.L., S. MS. 433, 230.
[82] Ibid.; W.S.L., Staffs. Views, viii, pp. 111 (a, b), 112, are copies of this and other Weston tablets from B.M. Harl. MS. 5816.

1810), Elizabeth Landor (d. 1814), Samuel Barnett (d. 1803), who established iron and tin works at King's Bromley (Offlow hundred), and the Revd. Edward R. Pitman (d. 1879), master of King Edward's School. Two 17th-century tablets to members of the Chetwynd family (1653–91), recorded *c.* 1836, were later removed to Grendon (Warws.).[83] In the churchyard the tomb of Elizabeth Coting (d. 1694) and of the wife of Edward Hollinhurst (d. 1696) bears an unusual slab carved with two shrouded figures.[84] Near the priest's door are the remains of a churchyard cross. Many of the stones in the churchyard wall are ancient and may represent material from the demolished church. In 1875 a new burial ground, a continuation of the old churchyard, was consecrated by the bishop.[85]

In or about 1818 it was decided that a new parish church was necessary owing to the increase in population.[86] A site east of the old church, large enough for a new burial ground, was given in 1819 by Viscount Anson.[87] The building, which is of stone in a simplified late Gothic style, was designed by C. Underwood.[88] It originally consisted of a rectangular nave of five bays with aisles and clerestory, a shallow chancel, and a tall west tower.[89] It was consecrated on 21 January 1823.[90] Internally the nave arcades have lofty shafted piers and four-centred arches, the aisles being occupied by north and south galleries. The base of the tower forms an entrance lobby, and there is a large gallery across the west end of the church. Tables of parish charities are placed below this gallery.

In 1867–8 the fittings were altered and the box pews cut down to form open seats.[91] The marble font dates from 1874.[92] By 1894 great dissatisfaction was being expressed with the building which was considered in bad structural repair as well as 'inconveniently arranged and unsuited for purposes of public worship'. In particular it was found impossible to preserve due order in the galleries and 'to prevent the young people who crowd into them at an evening Service from behaving in an irreverent and unseemly manner'.[93] The sum left by Sarah Hopkins by will proved 1844 for the improvement of the church had by this time accumulated to about £3,000.[94] After discussion of various alternative schemes,[95] it was decided to enlarge the existing church and a new chancel with north and south aisles was dedicated on 29 June 1906. The stone was

given by Lord Lichfield.[96] The work is finely executed, and the design is a scholarly example of Perpendicular architecture by Frank L. Pearson.[97] The north aisle forms a Lady Chapel, and the south aisle contains a vestry and organ loft. The west end of the church remains as it was built in 1822 but the start of a proposed new nave arcade is visible near the chancel arch. The east window of the Lady Chapel was given in memory of Fanny Louise Slade in 1906 by her sister.[98] Other stained glass windows in the chapel date from 1907 and commemorate Gilbert Woolland and Thomas and Mary Ann James.[99] The carved organ screen was given in memory of Emma O. Litler (d. 1908).[1] The reredos, carved in North Italy, and the panelling of the sanctuary were presented in 1930 by W. J. Stanton in memory of his wife.[2] Wall tablets in the church commemorate Rebecca Simpson (d. 1849), Mary and William Landor (both d. 1860), Robert W. Nuttall (d. 1904), John A. B. Burrough (d. 1918), and Robert Landor and members of his family (1914–51.)

In 1553 the plate included a silver chalice with paten, a copper cross, two pewter candlesticks, and a latten censer.[3] In 1704 Mary Chetwynd gave the church a new silver cup and a new flagon.[4] In 1957 the plate consisted of two silver-gilt chalices, two silver-gilt patens and a silver-gilt flagon, all 1855, the gift of William Bamford, and that of the old church of St. Augustine a silver chalice and paten and a silver viaticum.[5]

In 1553 there were three bells and two little bells.[6] Before 1706 there were four bells which were recast in that year by Abraham Rudhall of Gloucester into five bells, and a sixth, the treble, was added.[7] There are still six bells: (i) 1707, Abel [*sic*] Rudhall; (ii–vi) 1706, Abel [*sic*] Rudhall.[8] These were removed to the new church in 1823.[9]

The registers date from 1569. Those from 1569 to 1722 have been printed.[10]

The former vicarage house lies 150 yds. southeast of the parish church. A house which occupied this site *c.* 1800[11] had flanking gables, a central semicircular bow, and a timber-framed range of outbuildings to the south-east. It may originally have dated from the 17th century or earlier. This house survived until *c.* 1840 when it was rebuilt by the Revd. T. D. Atkinson[12] with the exception of the south wing which is early 18th century in character. The brick stable range is dated 1821. The front

[83] W.S.L., S. MS. 433, 230; W. N. Landor, 'Ancient Rugeley' (*Rugeley Par. Mag.*, Nov. 1940).
[84] W.S.L., S. MS. 433, 230.
[85] *Lich. Dioc. Ch. Cal.* (1876), 74.
[86] Lich. Dioc. Regy., Bp.'s Reg. Bk. 1819–25, pp. 403–9.
[87] Ibid.
[88] W. N. Landor, 'Ancient Rugeley' (*Rugeley Par. Mag.*, Oct. 1942).
[89] W.S.L., Staffs. Views, viii, pp. 96 (b), 99, 105.
[90] Lich. Dioc. Regy., Bp.'s Reg. Bk. 1819–25, pp. 403–9.
[91] Lich. Dioc. Regy., Consist. Ct. Act Bk. 1865–71, p. 130, faculty, 15 Oct. 1867.
[92] W. N. Landor, 'Ancient Rugeley' (*Rugeley Par. Mag.*, Nov. 1942).
[93] Lich. Dioc. Regy., Consist. Ct. Act Bk. 1891–9, pp. 273–4, faculty, 20 Apr. 1896.
[94] Ibid.
[95] *Lich. Dioc. Mag.* (1894), 53; ibid. (1898), 148; Lich. Dioc. Regy., Consist. Ct. Act Bk. 1891–9, pp. 273–4, faculty, 27 Mar. 1896; ibid. 1903–7, p. 189, faculty, 25 Apr. 1904.
[96] *Lich. Dioc. Mag.* (1906), 120.
[97] Ibid. (1905), 92–93.

[98] Ibid. (1906), 186.
[99] Lich. Dioc. Regy., Consist. Ct. Act Bk. 1903–7, p. 489, faculty, 2 Apr. 1907.
[1] Tablet in church.
[2] Tablet in sanctuary.
[3] *S.H.C.* 1915, 219.
[4] Rugeley Parish Bk. 1680–1813, f. 4a. In 1871 the vestry resolved to sell the old silver plate and buy a new silver chalice and paten, with a silver flagon also if the proceeds were sufficient: Rugeley Vestry Order Bk. 1819–81, 7 Dec. 1871.
[5] Ex inf. the Vicar of Rugeley (1957).
[6] *S.H.C.* 1915, 219.
[7] Rugeley Parish Bk. f. 1b.
[8] C. Lynam, *Church Bells of Staffs.* (1889), 24 and pl. 108; A. E. Garbett, 'Church Bells of Staffs.' (*Trans. Old Stafford Soc.* 1953–4), 18.
[9] A. Williams, *Sketches in and around Lichfield and Rugeley* (1892), 318.
[10] Staffs. Par. Reg. Soc. 1928, with MS. index in W.S.L.
[11] W.S.L., Staffs. Views, viii, p. 96, undated drawing probably by Shaw, *c.* 1800.
[12] White, *Dir. Staffs.* (1851).

garden wall is built of old stones, probably from the former church. The house ceased to be the vicarage in 1921[13] and has been used since 1951[14] as an extension of the Working Mens' Club in Bow Street. The present vicarage in Church Street, acquired in 1923,[15] dates from c. 1830.

A field at the junction of Bow Street and Taylor's Lane, known c. 1842 as Tithe Barn Croft, indicates the site of the former tithe barn.[16]

The church of *ST. MICHAEL* at Brereton was opened in 1837,[17] and in 1843 Brereton was constituted a district chapelry.[18] The living, a perpetual curacy until 1868 when it became a titular vicarage, has always been in the gift of the Vicar of Rugeley.[19] The church was built as a small cruciform stone chapel in the Early English style. It had an octagonal bell turret in the north-west angle of the crossing. The building was enlarged and much improved in 1876–8 under the direction of Sir George Gilbert Scott.[20] He extended the transepts eastwards thus giving the church, in effect, north and south aisles each of three bays. He also formed the present chancel by raising the floor level at the east end of the former nave and surrounding it with low stone screens. The sedilia and the treatment of the chancel window internally are part of this scheme. The Revd. Edward Samson, vicar, contributed £1,000 to the cost of the improvements.[21] The font, which has an arcaded bowl on a base of coloured marble, is inscribed to the memory of George Augustus Selwyn, Bishop of Lichfield (d. 1878). The reredos dates from 1883.[22] In 1887 the tower was raised in height to accommodate a clock and four additional bells.[23] The upper part was rebuilt to the original design. A carved oak porch was added outside the west door in 1891,[24] and the south-west vestry is dated 1894. The oak pulpit was given in 1895[25] and the murals in the chancel in 1897,[26] both by the Revd. Edward Samson. The east end of the north aisle was fitted up as a Lady Chapel in 1927–8.[27]

All the windows contain memorial stained glass. Among others they commemorate the Revd. J. C. Weatherall, first vicar. There are mural tablets in memory of Robert Simpson (d. 1869), and his wife and daughter; the Revd. John Holford Plant (d. 1891), missionary and former curate; Arthur L. Samson, killed in action 1915; Edward Samson, former vicar (d. 1921). The colours of two Indian regiments, presented in 1888 and 1897 by Col. J. E.

and Col. W. A. Weatherall respectively, were removed in 1956.[28] Those of the 108th Madras Infantry were given to the Royal Inniskilling Fusiliers and those of the 22nd Bombay Infantry to the museum of the Royal Military Academy at Sandhurst.[29]

The churchyard was extended in 1876 and 1894.[30] The lychgate dates from 1883.[31]

In 1957 the plate included a silver chalice; two silver patens; a silver flagon, 1836, the gift of Mrs. E. Sneyd; and a silver paten.[32] There was one bell until 1887 when four more were added.[33] All five still existed in 1957.

The vicarage is of approximately the same date as the church and is a large red-brick house lying about 400 yds. to the north-west.

The mission of St. John the Baptist was opened in 1871 at the infants' school at Stone House (now Slitting Mill).[34] The chapel now (1957) consists of part of the former school cottage and a single-story brick extension of 1871 with round-headed windows. In 1957 the plate included an electroplated chalice, paten, and flagon.[35] There is one bell, attached to the cottage chimney.

The mission chapel at Etching Hill was licensed for divine service and the sacraments in 1881.[36] It is a small corrugated-iron building in Church Lane. In 1957 the plate consisted of a silver chalice and paten, 1910, and a glass and silver flagon.[37] There is one bell.

There was a mission room in Horse Fair between c. 1875 and 1881[38] and another mission in Rugeley, dedicated to St. Mary, between c. 1880 and 1916.[39] Between 1882 and c. 1894 there was a mission chapel at Fairoak.[40]

The missions at Hazel Slade and Brindley Heath are treated under Cannock as both districts became part of the new parish of St. Peter, Hednesford, for ecclesiastical purposes in 1870.[41]

ROMAN CATHOLICISM. There were said to be 'some recusants' in Rugeley in 1604,[42] and Sir Richard Weston of Hagley Hall was returned as a papist in 1648.[43] Only nine papists in Rugeley were mentioned in 1780.[44]

By 1836 evening services were being held each Sunday in a temporary Roman Catholic church in Rugeley,[45] and mass was being said here on Sunday mornings by 1839.[46] The mission was served by the

[13] *Rugeley Par. Reg.*, p. xi.
[14] Ex inf. the caretaker (1957).
[15] Lich. Dioc. Regy., Bp.'s Reg. Bk. W, pp. 124, 125.
[16] Tithe Maps and Appt., Rugeley (copy in W.S.L.).
[17] Lich. Dioc. Regy., Bp.'s Reg. Bk. 1834–7, pp. 539–40, 541–3, 544–8.
[18] *Lond. Gaz.* 1843, p. 2987.
[19] Lich. Dioc. Regy., Bp.'s Reg. Bk. 1834–7, pp. 539–40, 541–3, 544–8; *Lich. Dioc. Ch. Cal.* (1868; 1869); *Lich. Dioc. Dir.* (1955–6).
[20] Lich. Dioc. Regy., Consist. Ct. Act Bk. 1875–9, p. 130, faculty, 22 June 1876. [21] Ibid.
[22] Ibid. 1879–91, p. 317, faculty, 12 June 1883.
[23] Ibid., p. 522, faculty, 20 Sept. 1887.
[24] *Lich. Dioc. Ch. Cal.* (1892), 172.
[25] *Lich. Dioc. Mag.* (1895), 122.
[26] Ibid. (1897), 137.
[27] Lich. Dioc. Regy., Consist. Ct. Act Bk. 1924–30, p. 230, faculty, 21 Jan. 1927; ibid., p. 344, faculty, 7 Aug. 1928.
[28] *Wolverhampton Express and Star*, 10 Dec. 1956.
[29] Ibid.
[30] *Lich. Dioc. Ch. Cal.* (1877), 73; *Lich. Dioc. Mag.* (1894), 184.

[31] Lich. Dioc. Regy., Consist. Ct. Act Bk. 1879–91, p. 317, faculty, 12 June 1883.
[32] Ex inf. the Vicar of Brereton (1957).
[33] Lynam, *Church Bells of Staffs.* 5; Lich. Dioc. Regy., Consist. Ct. Act Bk. 1879–81, p. 522, faculty, 4 Oct. 1887.
[34] Lich. Dioc. Regy., Bp.'s Reg. xxxiii, p. 188; *P.O. Dir. Staffs.* (1872); *Lich. Dioc. Ch. Cal.* (1874), where the dedication is first given as St. John the Baptist.
[35] Ex inf. the Vicar of Rugeley (1957).
[36] Lich. Dioc. Regy., Bp.'s Reg. xxxiv, p. 191. A mission here was mentioned in 1880: *Lich. Dioc. Ch. Cal.* (1880).
[37] Ex inf. the Vicar of Rugeley (1957).
[38] *Lich. Dioc. Ch. Cal.* (1875; 1881).
[39] Ibid. (1880; 1916).
[40] Ibid. (1882; 1894). [41] See p. 67.
[42] *S.H.C.* 1915, 219.
[43] Ibid. 392; ibid. N.S. vi (2), 331.
[44] H.L., Main Papers, Return of Papists 1780.
[45] R.C. Bapt. Reg. 1836–52, title-page; *Cath. Dir.* (1838). There is a local tradition that these services were held in a house in Nine-foot Row, an alley behind Albion Street: ex inf. Mr. A. W. Neal, Hon. Sec., Landor Soc., Rugeley (1956).
[46] *Cath. Dir.* (1839); Bapt. Reg. 1836–52, title-page.

priest from Tixall[47] (Pirehill hundred) until the appointment to Rugeley of a resident priest, John S. Grenside, in 1846.[48] Mass was said in the school from 1847 until at least 1849 when the building of the present church of SS. Joseph and Etheldreda was begun on ground bought by the Revd. T. L. Green of Tixall in 1842.[49] The church, which derives its dedication from the Christian names of the two principal founders, Joseph Whitgreave of Heron's Court and his sister Etheldreda, was solemnly opened in August 1851 and consecrated in June 1951.[50] By 1848, when the mission was described as 'paralysed with poverty', there were some 500 Roman Catholics in and near Rugeley.[51] The estimated number attending mass on Sunday 30 March 1851 was 350.[52] The average attendance at Sunday mass in 1955–6 was 448.[53]

The Sisters of the Christian Retreat opened St. Anthony's Convent at Heron's Nest, Heron Street, in 1901, but to accommodate members of the order who had been expelled from France the convent was moved in 1904 to Heron Court in the same street,[54] a house built opposite the Roman Catholic church in 1851 by Joseph Whitgreave.[55] Heron's Nest was retained as the residence of the nuns' chaplain until the early 1920's and was later sold.[56]

The mission benefits from the following bequests for general parish purposes: £1,700 from Canon Duckett, parish priest of Rugeley, in 1907, producing an income of £26 in 1956; £500 from Mrs. Bolton in 1927, producing £20 in 1956; and £600 from Miss M. Harris in 1945, producing £18 in 1956.[57] Canon Duckett also bequeathed £1,000 for the maintenance and repair of the church fabric, and this produced £21 in 1956.[58]

The church of SS. JOSEPH AND ETHELD-REDA, dating from 1849–51, consists of an aisled nave of six bays, chancel, north chapel, south vestry, and tall west tower. The local stone of which it is built was given by the 1st Marquess of Anglesey 'without limit or restriction'.[59] The church was designed by Charles Hanson of Clifton (Som.)[60] in a 14th-century style. An octagonal spire with flying buttresses was added to the tower in 1868.[61] Soon after 1930 a turret which had formed part of the spire was found to be decayed and was removed.[62] Further repairs to the spire were carried out in 1948.[63]

The chancel and baptistery screens are of wrought iron and the aisles contain carved stone panels representing the Stations of the Cross. A window in the Lady Chapel, which lies north of the chancel, was fitted with stained glass in memory of Joseph and Etheldreda Whitgreave after the former's death in 1885. There are two bells, 1546 and 1848.[64]

The presbytery, for which the Marquess of Anglesey also gave the stone, is a simple gabled building lying south of the church and of similar date. The former school lay beyond it and it was originally intended that the whole group should be linked by a cloister.[65]

PROTESTANT NONCONFORMITY. In 1672 William Grace, the ejected Vicar of Shenstone (Offlow hundred), was licensed as a Presbyterian teacher in the house of John Panells in Rugeley.[66] Robert Travers, the Presbyterian minister at Lichfield c. 1693–1738, occasionally visited Rugeley.[67] Regular Congregational meetings here can be traced back to c. 1794 when they were first held in Samuel Sleigh's house in Brereton Road,[68] and in 1806 the house, then occupied by his widow Catherine, was registered as a meeting-house.[69] After services had been held there for four years, the Staffordshire Association sent an itinerant minister who was to use Rugeley as a base for his work, and in 1811 services were held in a cottage in Bow Street.[70] This was soon closed against the worshippers who returned to Mrs. Sleigh's house until 1813 when Providence Chapel in Elmore Lane was opened.[71] In 1832 two rooms were added for use as Sunday schools.[72] Improvements were made to the chapel in 1861,[73] but in 1874, as the building was considered too old and inconvenient, the congregation was transferred to a new chapel adjoining the mansion called Heron Court.[74] The Sunday school was transferred to a room in Heron Court, but, as it was not possible to purchase this part,[75] the school was subsequently moved back to Elmore Lane until the opening of new schools near Heron Court in 1896.[76] Providence Chapel was then sold to help pay off the debt on the new chapel.[77] This seats 300.[78]

The former congregational chapel in Elmore Lane had a gabled brick front with a central round-headed entrance and round-headed windows to the ground

[47] Bapt. Reg. 1836–52; *Cath. Dir.* (1838–46). Catholics in Rugeley had been the concern of the priests of Tixall from at least 1806: Bellamore Bk. (bapt. reg.), at St. John the Baptist's R.C. Church, Great Haywood (Pirehill hundred).
[48] Bapt. Reg. 1836–52, *sub* 1846; *Cath. Dir.* (1847), pp. 60, 104.
[49] Bapt. Reg. 1836–52, title-page; *Cath. Dir.* (1850); White, *Dir. Staffs.* (1851); H.O. 129/15/377.
[50] *Centenary Celebrations 1851–1951, Souvenir Programme* (priv. print. Rugeley); Bapt. Reg. 1836–52, note on p. 53.
[51] *Cath. Dir.* (1848); White, *Dir. Staffs.* (1851).
[52] H.O. 129/15/377.
[53] Ex inf. the parish priest (1956).
[54] Ex inf. Sister Mary Alban, one of the founder-members of the convent.
[55] White, *Dir. Staffs.* (1851); ex inf. Mr. Neal.
[56] Ex inf. Sister Mary Alban. The French nuns had been accompanied by their chaplain.
[57] Ex inf. the treasurer of the Archdiocese of Birmingham (1957). The dates are those when the legacies were notified or paid to the treasurer.
[58] Ex inf. the treasurer.
[59] Tablet in church.
[60] White, *Dir. Staffs.* (1851).
[61] *Rugeley Mercury*, 26 Mar. 1948.

[62] Ex inf. Mr. Neal.
[63] *Rugeley Mercury*, 26 Mar. 1948.
[64] Ex inf. Mr. Neal. A ring of 8 was intended: White, *Dir. Staffs.* (1851).
[65] White, *Dir. Staffs.* (1851).
[66] *Cal. S.P. Dom.* 1672, 196, 203; Turner, *Orig. Records*, i. 507; Mathews, *Calamy Revised*, 231.
[67] A. G. Mathews, *Cong. Churches of Staffs.* 114, 256.
[68] G. Key, *Records of 100 Years of Congregationalism in Rugeley* (Birmingham, 1897), 6.
[69] Ibid. 107–8; Lich. Dioc. Regy., Bp.'s Reg. Bk. E, p. 258.
[70] Key, *Congregationalism in Rugeley*, 12; Mathews, *Cong. Churches of Staffs.* 178–9.
[71] Key, *Congregationalism in Rugeley*, 13–14, 16; *Evangelical Mag.* (1814), 154.
[72] Key, *Congregationalism in Rugeley*, 27, 54–57.
[73] Ibid. 88.
[74] It had been intended to purchase the whole mansion and use the house portion as the minister's residence (ibid. 97), but this part remained a private house until it became a convent in 1904: see above.
[75] Ibid., plate on p. 16.
[76] Ibid. 93, 95; Charity Com. files.
[77] Key, *Congregationalism in Rugeley*, 96–97.
[78] Charity Com. files.

floor and to the gallery.[79] The building was converted into a pair of cottages in 1896 and the front much altered. An original tablet inscribed 'Providence Chapel 1813' and a memorial tablet to Mrs. Mary Shawyer (d. 1816) are now (1957) in the Heron Court Schools.

Heron Court Chapel is built of the same materials as the mansion. The stone entrance porch has an Early English arcade of three bays. The school buildings lie to the west of the chapel and are of red brick.

In 1806, on the application of a group of Wesleyan Methodists, the house of Thomas Gething[80] at Brereton, was registered as a meeting-house.[81] In 1808 a house in Rugeley was registered as a meeting-house for Wesleyans.[82] In 1810 a Wesleyan chapel was opened at Brereton[83] and another, Hodgley Chapel, in Lichfield Street, Rugeley, in 1839 to hold 120.[84] In 1870 an entrance front of variegated brick was added to the Rugeley chapel, which was then enlarged[85] and in 1940 seated 240.[86] The Brereton chapel was replaced by the present building on or near the same site in 1872.[87]

Other dwellings in Rugeley were registered as meeting-houses in 1809,[88] 1828,[89] and 1837,[90] and in Brereton in 1828,[91] all possibly for Primitive Methodists. By 1868 a Primitive Methodist chapel had been built at Rugeley[92] with seating for 220.[93]

In 1708 the house of Richard Norris in Rugeley was registered as a meeting-house for Quakers.[94] There was a Quaker meeting at the Town Hall on 16 August 1810.[95] Regular Quaker meetings were held in Rugeley from 1824 to 1826[96] and from 1829 to 1870.[97] In 1851 they were being held in a building in the Market Place, erected in 1830.[98]

PRIMARY SCHOOLS. The English School, otherwise Bamford's School or the Writing School, said to have been founded because the master of the grammar school refused to instruct his pupils in English, owed its foundation to a bequest by John Bamford, cooper, of Rugeley.[99] By will dated 1734, he left the reversion of £400, on the death of his wife, the interest to be employed for instructing free in one school 16 boys of the poorest families in Rugeley in reading, writing, accounts, and the church catechism, the schoolmaster to be paid 20s. a year for each pupil.[1] Meanwhile a further £50 had been bequeathed to the poor of this parish by Mary Jenks of Sutton Coldfield (Warws.), by will dated 1750, and this added to the £400 was in 1767 laid out in the purchase of property in Colton parish (Pirehill hundred), the rents to be used for teaching 18 poor boys and any surplus in buying necessary books or apprenticing scholars.[2] A bequest of £500 for this school by John Riley, by will proved 1802, was used in 1813 to buy land and premises near the Horse Fair, Rugeley, for a schoolhouse with adjoining schoolrooms and a garden behind.[3] In 1818 there were said to be 60 children in this school, 45 of whom were taught free and 4 of whom were boarders, the master receiving £35 a year besides his house and school, from funds then arising from the £36 11s. rents.[4] The last of its masters was George Ordish, who died in 1857, and the school was then closed.[5] There were about 30 boys in the school at this time.[6] Until at least 1860 the schoolroom was made use of as a reading-room and night-school,[7] and in 1880 the buildings were sold.[8] The proceeds were invested in £127 9s. stock and the income, amounting to £3 3s. 8d., together with the rents of £28 and £11 from the property in Colton, was applied by 1905 for the support of the National schools in Rugeley and Brereton.[9]

The Prince of Wales National School was built in 1845 in Lichfield Street.[10] By will proved 1849 Rebecca Simpson left £1,125 10s., the income to be applied as necessary towards the salaries of either the master or the mistress of this school or both; towards that of a master or mistress of an infants' school for the poor of Rugeley, or towards the rent of a building for an infants' school; and for a house for a master or mistress.[11] The school was in receipt of an annual parliamentary grant by 1850,[12] in which year a further £35 was granted to the master of the National school out of the surplus income of Chetwynd's Charity.[13] Attendance in 1851 averaged 60 boys and 150 infants,[14] while in 1865 the combined average was 193 and in 1884 294.[15] The building was

[79] Staffs. Cong. Union Records.
[80] Thomas Gething witnessed the certificate of the Wesleyan Methodist chapel here in 1810: Lich. Dioc. Regy., Bp.'s Reg. Bk. E, p. 609.
[81] Ibid., p. 259.
[82] Ibid., p. 440, being the house of Samuel Cox; this certificate too was witnessed by Thomas Gething.
[83] Ibid., p. 609.   [84] H.O. 129/15/377.
[85] Tablet in situ.
[86] Meth. Church Buildings 1940 (1946), 267.
[87] Tablet in situ.
[88] S.R.O., Q/SM3, East. 1809; the building was owned by Mrs. Brittain and held by the Misses Hull.
[89] Lich. Dioc. Regy., Bp.'s Reg. Bk. H, p. 413, being the house of Richard Brodnock.
[90] Ibid. K, p. 7, being the room and premises of John Goodwin.
[91] Ibid. H, p. 61, being a building in the occupation of Elizabeth Birch.
[92] P.O. Dir. Staffs. (1868), 631.
[93] Meth. Church Buildings 1940 (1946), 267.
[94] S.R.O., Q/SM1, Epiph. 1707/8.
[95] W.S.L., D. 1568, W. N. Landor's Bk. of Cuttings on Rugeley: Diary of Sarah Powell, 1798–1845.
[96] Friends' Book of Meetings (1824), 14; ibid. (1825), 14; ibid. (1826), 14.
[97] Ibid. (1829–70).
[98] H.O. 129/15/377. The building was not used exclusively as a place of worship.

[99] Rugeley Par. Reg., p. xv.
[1] Ibid.; John 'Balmford' was buried here in 1734: Rugeley Par. Reg. 14 Feb. 1733/4, from transcript in W.S.L.; 7th Rep. Com. Char. H.C. 129, p. 285 (1822), x.
[2] 7th Rep. Com. Char. 285–7. Some of the property may have been in Colwich (Pirehill hundred).
[3] Ibid. 287–8.
[4] Digest of Returns to Sel. Cttee. on Educ. of Poor, H.C. 224, p. 265 (1819), ix (2).
[5] White, Dir. Staffs. (1834; 1851); Rugeley Par. Reg., p. xv.
[6] G. Griffiths, Free Schools . . . of Staffs. (1860), 257.
[7] Ibid.; Rugeley Par. Reg., p. xv.
[8] Staffs. Endowed Charities (Elem. Educ.) [Cd. 2729], pp. 106–7, H.C. (1906), xc; Rugeley Vestry Order Bk. 1819–81, 31 Aug. 1866.
[9] Staffs. Endowed Char. 107.
[10] White, Dir. Staffs. (1851).
[11] Staffs. Endowed Char. 103.
[12] Mins. of Educ. Cttee. of Council, 1850 [1357], p. 179, H.C. (1851), xliv.
[13] Staffs. Endowed Char. 105; see pp. 170–1. The Tithe Appt. (c. 1843) had assigned the Chetwynd Charity estate in Great Wyrley to 'The Trustees of Rugeley School'. A grant was still made in 1882: Charity Com. files.
[14] White, Dir. Staffs. (1851).
[15] Rep. of Educ. Cttee. of Council 1865 [3666], H.C. (1866), xxvii; ibid. 1884 [C. 4483–I], H.C. (1884–5), xxiii.

enlarged in 1855 and 1876.[16] In 1892, the trustees of the Prince of Wales School were authorized to sell £333 15s. 3d. stock belonging to the foundation to provide for a new infants' school (see below).[17] The Prince of Wales School, after this date only for boys, was enlarged in 1894.[18] Average attendance has remained about 250.[19] It is now Rugeley Church of England Voluntary Primary School for Junior Boys.

In 1892 an infants' school was built in Talbot Street, with funds formerly belonging to the Prince of Wales School, on a site given by the governors of the Grammar School, and the infants of the Prince of Wales School were transferred there.[20] The school was enlarged in 1898[21] and 1913.[22] Attendance in 1910 averaged 155,[23] in 1930 132,[24] and by 1956 280.[25] This is now Rugeley Church of England Voluntary Primary School for Infants.

A National school for girls was founded in 1826 by Harriet Baroness de la Zouche, wife of the Hon. Robert Curzon of Hagley Hall, in newly built premises in Church Street, Rugeley, leased for 99 years from the Trustees of Rugeley Free Grammar School.[26] Sarah Hopkins provided a house for the schoolmistress,[27] and in 1828 she conveyed a house and land in Rugeley to trustees to provide £2 a year for the schoolmistress, the balance to be given to the almswomen of her newly erected almshouses or towards the repair of the school.[28] Sixty girls were being taught in this school by 1834, paying 2d. a week each.[29] The endowment was increased by members of the Curzon family between 1841 and 1855, to provide for repairs, heating, and equipment,[30] and by £25 a year from Chetwynd's Charity in 1850.[31] The freehold reversion of the premises in Church Street was bought in 1868 from the Grammar School Trustees,[32] and the building was enlarged in 1869,[33] 1885, and 1894.[34] The school was in receipt of a parliamentary grant by 1882 when attendance averaged 147.[35] Between c. 1912 and 1930 the attendances averaged 230.[36] By 1905 the endowments, represented by £1,079 3s. 6d. stock, were producing £26 17s. a year.[37] The Curzon Charity was wound up in 1955 when the balance, £102 0s. 8d., was paid to Rugeley Church of England Schools account.[38] The school is now Rugeley Church of England Primary School for Junior Girls.

A school at Brereton for 80 children, taught on the Madras System, was built c. 1826 by the Misses Sneyd, presumably the Misses Elizabeth and Harriet (or Henrietta), who in 1834 were still contributing largely towards its support.[39] A National school for boys and infants was built in Redbrook Lane, Brereton, in 1843.[40] This and the girls' school benefited under the will of Rebecca Simpson, proved 1849,[41] and in 1850 £35 a year was allotted from Chetwynd's Charity to the master of the boys' school.[42] As National schools for girls, boys, and infants the schools received an annual parliamentary grant from 1854,[43] and in 1872 they shared an annual endowment of £162 a year.[44] In 1881 a new classroom was added to the Redbrook Lane school where both the boys' and infants' classrooms were extended in 1888.[45] In 1891 the girls' school was rebuilt by the Vicar of Brereton, the Revd. E. Samson, in memory of his brother,[46] and the average attendance in 1892 was 120.[47] The boys' and infants' schools in that year had an average attendance of 151 and shared an endowment of £124 11s. 9d.[48] By 1905 the three schools together enjoyed an income of £66 11s. 5d. from the Simpson bequest, while the girls' school also received £18 4s. from the Sneyd endowment.[49] In 1933 the boys' and infants' buildings in Redbrook Lane were found to be unsatisfactory,[50] and in 1947 it was agreed that the institution should be discontinued as soon as possible.[51] By 1951 the three schools were housed in the former girls' school building and had been reorganized as Brereton Church of England Voluntary Primary School, Junior Mixed and Infants, under a mistress.[52] Average attendance in 1955 was 105 children.[53]

Raven Hill County Primary School, Junior Mixed and Infants, was opened in 1954, with accommodation for 280 children.[54]

St. Etheldreda's Roman Catholic School was built by subscription in 1847 north-east of the presbytery.[55] It received an annual parliamentary grant from 1853.[56] Attendance averaged 99 in 1882[57] and 75 in 1893.[58] By 1892 a house was attached to

[16] Kelly's Dir. Staffs. (1884).
[17] Staffs. Endowed Char. 103.
[18] Kelly's Dir. Staffs. (1896).
[19] Staffs. Educ. Cttee. List of Schools, 1910; Kelly's Dir. Staffs. (1912); Staffs. Educ. Cttee. Mins. Nov. 1930.
[20] Lich. Dioc. Ch. Cal. (1893), 195. The date of completion is given as 1894: Staffs. Endowed Char. 103; Kelly's Dir. Staffs. (1896).
[21] Kelly's Dir. Staffs. (1912).
[22] Staffs. Educ. Cttee. Mins. 22 Feb. 1913.
[23] Staffs. Educ. Cttee. List of Schools, 1910.
[24] Staffs. Educ. Cttee. Mins. Nov. 1930.
[25] Lich. Dioc. Dir. (1955–6).
[26] Staffs. Endowed Char. 103; tablet in situ.
[27] Tablet on the present Hopkins Almshouses.
[28] Staffs. Endowed Char. 103–4.
[29] White, Dir. Staffs. (1834).
[30] Staffs. Endowed Char. 104.
[31] Charity Com. files; see pp. 170–1. A grant was still paid in 1882: Charity Com. files.
[32] Staffs. Endowed Char. 104.
[33] P.O. Dir. Staffs. (1872); Kelly's Dir. Staffs. (1880).
[34] Kelly's Dir. Staffs. (1896).
[35] Rep. of Educ. Cttee. of Council, 1882 [C. 3706–I], H.C. (1883), xxv.
[36] Kelly's Dir. Staffs. (1912); Staffs. Educ. Cttee. Mins. 20 Nov. 1930.
[37] Staffs. Endowed Char. 104.

[38] Charity Com. files.
[39] White, Dir. Staffs. (1834): Staffs. Endowed Char. 22; Tithe Maps and Appt., Rugeley (copy in W.S.L.).
[40] White, Dir. Staffs. (1851).
[41] Staffs. Endowed Char. 22–23.
[42] Ibid. 105; see pp. 170–1. The mistress of the Infants' school still received a grant from the charity in 1882: Charity Com. files.
[43] Mins. of Educ. Cttee. of Council, 1854 [1926], p. 218, H.C. (1854), xlii; ibid. 1857 [2380], p. 166 (1857–8), xlv.
[44] P.O. Dir. Staffs. (1872).
[45] Lich. Dioc. Ch. Cal. (1882), 79; ibid. (1889), 154; tablet in situ.
[46] Lich. Dioc. Ch. Cal. (1892), 172.
[47] Return of Schools, 1893 [C. 7529], pp. 548–9, H.C. (1894), lxv.
[48] Ibid.   [49] Staffs. Endowed Char. 22–23.
[50] Staffs. Educ. Cttee. Mins. Oct. 1933.
[51] Ibid. 1947.
[52] Staffs. Educ. Cttee. List of Schools, 1951.
[53] Lich. Dioc. Dir. (1955–6).
[54] Staffs. Educ. Cttee. Mins. May 1953; ex inf. Staffs. C.C. Educ. Dept.
[55] White, Dir. Staffs. (1851).
[56] Mins. of Educ. Cttee. of Council, 1853 [1787], p. 266, H.C. (1854), li.
[57] Rep. of Educ. Cttee. of Council, 1882.
[58] Return of Schools 1893 [C. 7529], H.C. (1894), lxv.

the school for the teacher.[59] The premises were condemned in 1905,[60] and in 1908 the present school, a brick building on the south-east side of the church, was completed.[61] The Sisters of the Christian Retreat were in charge by 1912.[62] It is now known as St. Joseph's Roman Catholic Voluntary Primary School, Mixed and Infants.

A Wesleyan school in Rugeley was founded in or just before 1860 to take up to 50 boys and girls.[63] This was in Lichfield Street and was under a mistress.[64] It was presumably one of the two Wesleyan schools in the parish returned in 1871,[65] but its later history is obscure.

A Wesleyan school was built in Brereton in 1838 on land bought by Miss Elizabeth Birch from the trustees of the Wesleyan Chapel, to teach the poor children of the neighbourhood; the master was always to be a member of the Wesleyan Methodist Society and the teaching along religious lines.[66] The school was endowed by Miss Birch with £1,500 to pay £50 a year salary to the master and £10 a year for stationery.[67] By 1860 the master was taking 6 paying pupils and attendance averaged 30.[68] The school was closed in 1899.[69] The site was exchanged in 1904 for a larger one, also the property of the trustees of the Wesleyan Chapel,[70] the endowment scheme was reorganized and provision was made for applying any residue of income for exhibitions at Rugeley Grammar School, or other approved institution, for boys and girls resident in Brereton who had been at least three years at a public elementary school.[71] Permission was given for the school trustees to use £1,000 out of the capital towards the building of new schools, opened in 1905.[72] In 1930 the attendance was 173.[73] In 1949 the school became controlled[74] and in 1952 was named The George Vickers Methodist Primary School, to commemorate George Vickers, schoolmaster from 1853 to 1904.[75] There were 160 on the roll of the school in 1954.[76]

Sarah Hopkins, by will proved in 1844, left £600 to provide £15 a year for a schoolmistress to teach children aged from 2 to 10, not exceeding 25 in number and living in the Cannock Chase area of Rugeley.[77] She also gave the lease of a cottage and land near the Stonehouse, in Rugeley, any profits to be used to augment the salary of the schoolmistress, who was to occupy, rent free, the schoolroom and room above it adjoining the cottage.[78] The school had been enlarged by 1871 when a mission chapel

was opened there.[79] In 1890 owing to the small endowment it was still without a certificated teacher, and in 1892 it had an average attendance of 35.[80] It had been closed by 1896.[81]

A mixed National school was built at Stonehouse in 1894, and the Sarah Hopkins legacy was transferred to it.[82] The average attendance here c. 1900 was 66.[83] By 1905 the original schoolroom with the cottage and land were let for £8 a year, and the income on the endowment of £564 14s. 2d. was £14 2s. 4d.[84] In 1919 the Local Education Authority bought the school and reopened it in 1921 as Slitting Mill Council School, Mixed and Infants.[85] Attendance in 1930 averaged 59.[86] It is now Rugeley Slitting Mill County Primary School, Junior Mixed and Infants.

A day-school for infants was opened in 1882 at Etching Hill, following the opening in 1880 of a Sunday school in the mission room there.[87] It was closed by 1892.[88]

A large mission room and schoolroom were erected in 1882 at Fair Oak Colliery, Rugeley, out of a barn and fitted up to hold 60 to 70 children at both day and Sunday schools.[89] It was a National school with an average attendance of 44 in 1884[90] and is said to have continued some time after the closing of the colliery.[91]

A council school was opened in 1926 at Brindley Village,[92] and average attendance in 1931 was 93.[93] It is now Brindley Heath, Brindley Village County Primary School, Junior Mixed and Infants.

CHARITIES FOR THE POOR. William Chetwynd of Rugeley (d. 1691)[94] bequeathed £500 to be laid out in land, the profits to provide a 3d. loaf every Sunday for each of the 20 poorest parishioners for life, 2s. for each of the same 20 poor on St. Thomas's Day (21 Dec.) 'for meat against the festival', and 2s. each on Good Friday; 40s. a year for the vicar for sermons to these poor on St. Thomas's Day and Good Friday; and the surplus to apprentice the children of poor parishioners.[95] Mary Chetwynd, William's sister and executrix, laid out this money, with a further £100 of her own, on an estate at Great Wyrley in Cannock.[96] From at least 1714 until 1812 the rent from the estate was £30.[97] In 1812 the property, which had coal under part of it, was valued at £147 6s. 5d. a year, reduced in 1815 to £110.[98] From at least 1812 until 1821 the 20 poor

59 *Kelly's Dir. Staffs.* (1892).
60 Staffs. Educ. Cttee. Mins. 24 June 1905.
61 Ibid. 8 Feb. 1909; tablet *in situ*.
62 *Kelly's Dir. Staffs.* (1912).
63 *Annual Rep. of Wesleyan Educ. Cttee.* (1860).
64 *P.O. Dir. Staffs.* (1860).
65 *Returns relating to Elem. Educ.* H.C. 201, pp. 362–3 (1871), lv.
66 Griffiths. *Free Schools . . . of Staffs.* 569; *Staffs. Endowed Char.* 24; tablet *in situ*.
67 *Staffs. Endowed Char.* 24.
68 Griffiths, *Free Schools . . . of Staffs.* 569.
69 Ex inf. the Secretary to the School Trustees (1955).
70 *Staffs. Endowed Char.* 24–25.
71 Ibid. 25.
72 Ibid.; *Kelly's Dir. Staffs.* (1912).
73 Staffs. Educ. Cttee. Mins. 22 Nov. 1930.
74 Ibid. 18 June 1949.
75 Ex inf. the Secretary to the Trustees.
76 Ibid.
77 *Staffs. Endowed Char.* 23.
78 Ibid.
79 See p. 166.
80 *Kelly's Dir. Staffs.* (1892).

81 Ibid. (1896).
82 Ibid. (1900).
83 Ibid.
84 *Staffs. Endowed Char.* 24.
85 Staffs. Educ. Cttee. Mins. 1919, 1921.
86 Ibid. 30 Nov. 1930.
87 *Lich. Dioc. Ch. Cal.* (1881), 71; ibid. (1883), 73; *Kelly's Dir. Staffs.* (1884).
88 It is not mentioned in *Kelly's Dir. Staffs.* (1892).
89 *Lich. Dioc. Ch. Cal.* (1883), 73.
90 *Rep. of Educ. Cttee. of Council, 1884* [Cd. 4483—I], H.C. (1884–5), xxxiii.
91 Ex inf. former pupil (1957); *Kelly's Dir. Staffs.* (1884); see p. 161.
92 Staffs. Educ. Cttee. Mins. 1926.
93 Ibid. 1931.
94 *Rugeley Par. Reg.* (Staffs. Par. Reg. Soc.), 166.
95 *7th Rep. Com. Char.* 282–3; Chetwynd-Stapylton, *Chetwynds of Ingestre*, 168–70.
96 *7th Rep. Com. Char.* 282–3; Chetwynd-Stapylton, op. cit. 168–70; *Abstract of Returns of Charitable Donations, 1786–8*, H.C. 511, pp. 1120–1 (1816), xvi (2).
97 *7th Rep. Com. Char.* 282.
98 Ibid. 282–3.

were each given a 6d. loaf every Sunday, this, with the £4 on St. Thomas's Day and Good Friday and the £2 for sermons, making £32 in all, but no apprentices were bound out, the surplus money being used in rebuilding the farmhouse and repairing the property at a cost of £448.[99] By 1882 £8 was paid to the Vicar of Rugeley for preaching and for arranging the distribution in Rugeley, and £4 went to the Vicar of Brereton for arranging the distribution there.[1] A scheme of 1915 ordered that only £2 was to be paid in respect of sermons and distribution and this only to the Vicar of Rugeley; that the weekly bread and the doles on St. Thomas's Day and Good Friday were to be paid to 38 named persons; and that out of the residue £17 might be used for 3d. bread doles each week and 2s. doles on Good Friday to the poor of the ancient parish, and the rest for assisting persons under 21 who were starting a trade and for general charitable purposes.[2] Much of the land in Great Wyrley seems to have been sold between 1905 and 1934.[3] In 1956 the income was about £620 interest on stock, most of which was distributed in grants for medical treatment and general assistance, and the Vicar of Rugeley still received £2 for sermons on St. Thomas's Day and Good Friday.[4]

Between at least 1850 and 1882 grants were made out of surplus income of the Chetwynd Charity to the National schools in Rugeley and Brereton,[5] and by various schemes between 1875 and 1916 grants were made to Rugeley Grammar School.[6] In 1956 the annual educational grants were £110 to the Grammar School, £40 to the Rugeley Church of England schools and £20 to the Brereton Church of England schools.[7]

A legacy of Thomas Landor of £26, to provide an annual gift of six pennyworth of bread every Sunday for six poor persons born in Rugeley, was charged by his son Walter Landor, by will dated 1703, on his own lands in Abbots (then Pagets) Bromley (Pirehill hundred), and in Gentleshaw, described as in Cannock.[8] These lands were then further charged with finding clothes for twelve poor persons and also 4d. each in bread every Sunday, the surplus to be used for apprenticing poor children.[9] The income in 1821 was £60 10s. still applied in bread, clothes, and apprenticing children, but since 1817 the amount of bread given had been doubled, while an average of seven children had been apprenticed each year since 1815 at the rate of £5 10s. each.[10] By a scheme of 1880 the maximum allowance for bread was fixed at £50; £10 was allotted to dispensaries and hospitals; and the residue was allotted for the

apprenticing of children over fifteen, or in providing Landor Exhibitions for up to five years at Rugeley Grammar School or other schools for children over ten who had attended an efficient elementary school at Rugeley for not less than three years.[11] Another scheme of 1929 authorized the trustees at their discretion to use the money assigned for apprenticing to assist poor persons under 21 years who were starting a trade, and a further scheme of 1953 authorized the use of £100 each year for the general benefit of the poor instead of for bread and hospital benefits.[12] In 1956 the income was £161 11s. interest on stock, which was distributed among twelve old people in two loaves each weekly and gifts at Christmas for clothing.[13] Money was also available for educational grants as required.[14]

Margery Sneyd, spinster, of Cannock Wood (d. 1702)[15] bequeathed £50 to provide doles on St. Thomas's Day for such of the poor of Rugeley as were communicant Anglicans.[16] This was charged by her executor, Humphrey Moore (also of Cannock Wood), on half of his land called Swinbrook Leasow in Marchington township in Draycott in the Clay (Offlow hundred), the rest of which, by his will dated 1706, he charged with a similar bequest on his own account, the total rent being £4 10s.[17] By 1821 £8 from this land and 35s. from an allotment in Hanbury (Offlow hundred) made under the Needwood Forest inclosure award were given away on St. Thomas's Day along with the charities of Whiston, Avarne, and Sutton (see below) in sums of 2s. 6d. and under to the poor, especially those not receiving parish relief.[18] The land in Hanbury was bringing in a rent of £2 in 1940, and in 1942 the land at Marchington, let for £7 14s. 8d., was bought by the War Department for £250 by compulsory purchase order.[19] The charity had lapsed by 1956, but attempts to revive it were being made in 1957.[20]

Mary Whiston, thought to have been cook to the William Chetwynd (d. 1691), bequeathed £10 for distribution to the poor on Good Friday, and Ellen Avarne, by will dated 1731, gave a further £10 to the poor.[21] Each of these bequests was producing 4s. by 1821 when the money was added to the distribution on St. Thomas's Day,[22] and the combined income in 1932 was 3s. 4d. interest on stock.[23] Attempts to revive these charities were being made in 1957.[24]

A Mary Sutton bequeathed £40 which by 1786 was producing £1 a year for the poor.[25] At some time after 1798 £30 of the capital was used to purchase the land-tax on the Chetwynd Charity estate at Great Wyrley (see above), the trustees of that estate paying in return 30s. a year to the minister and church-

[99] Ibid. 283.
[1] Charity Com. files.
[2] Ibid.
[3] Ibid.
[4] Ex inf. Mr. H. P. H. Jeffery, Clerk to the Chetwynd Charity Trustees (1957).
[5] See pp. 168, 169.
[6] Charity Com. files.
[7] Ex inf. Mr. Jeffery.
[8] 7th Rep. Com. Char. 284. A Mr. Thomas 'Launder' was buried 23 Jan. 1670/1 and a Thomas son of Mr. Thomas 'Launder' on 22 Feb. 1670/1: Rugeley Par. Reg. 130. Gentleshaw is now in Longdon (Offlow hundred).
[9] 7th Rep. Com. Char. 284.
[10] Ibid. 285.
[11] Staffs. Endowed Char. 107. This followed the resolution of the vestry meeting in 1879: Rugeley Vestry Order Bk. 1819–81, 8 Aug. 1879, 24 Jan. 1880.

[12] Charity Com. files.
[13] Ex inf. Miss D. Landor, a trustee (1957).
[14] Ex inf. Miss Landor.
[15] Rugeley Par. Reg. 191.
[16] 7th Rep. Com. Char. 288.
[17] Ibid.
[18] Ibid. 289.
[19] Charity Com. files.
[20] Ex inf. the Vicar of Rugeley (1957).
[21] Abstract 1786–8, ii. 1118–19, 1120–1; 7th Rep. Com. Char. 289. A Mrs. Averne was buried at Rugeley in 1732: Par. Reg., transcript in W.S.L.
[22] 7th Rep. Com. Char. 289.
[23] Charity Com. files.
[24] Ex inf. the vicar.
[25] Abstract, 1786–8, ii. 1118–19. A Mary Sutton was buried at Rugeley in 1672 and a Mrs. Mary Sutton in 1709: Rugeley Par. Reg. 131, 207.

wardens of Rugeley for the poor.[26] By 1821 this 30s. and 4s. interest on the remaining £10 were added to the St. Thomas's Day distribution.[27] In 1882 the 30s. was being distributed in money doles on Good Friday with part of Chetwynd's Charity (see above), while in 1929 the income from the rest of Sutton's Charity was represented by 1s. 8d. interest on £3 6s. 11d. stock.[28] The vicar was trying to revive the charity in 1957.[29]

Catherine Barber, by will proved 1842, gave £400, the interest to provide coals, clothing, and other necessaries to poor of Rugeley who were Anglican.[30] The income in 1932 was £9 14s. interest on stock.[31] Attempts to revive the charity were being made in 1957.[32]

By 1851 Joseph Godwin had bequeathed £150, the interest to be distributed on 8 November among five poor women who attended church regularly, widows of 63 and over being preferred.[33] The money was producing £3 10s. interest on stock in 1932.[34] Attempts were being made to revive the charity in 1957.[35]

Under the Rugeley Inclosure Award of 1885 land at Etching Hill was allotted to the poor of Rugeley under the name of Poor Allotment.[36] It was first let by the allotment wardens in 1888 for £4 9s. 4½d. and the rent in 1926 was £3 12s. 9d.[37] The charity was still in force in 1955.[38]

A bequest by a Mrs. Eagle for the poor of Brereton was producing by 1896 £5 16s. 8d. which was distributed on St. Thomas's Day.[39] In 1957 the income, £6 6s. 6d. was distributed to poor widows.[40]

A John Blood, probably in 1703 or 1705, bequeathed £10, the interest to be distributed to the poor on St. John's Day, but this charity had been lost by 1786.[41]

In 1826 Sarah Hopkins of the Stonehouse erected four almshouses behind the Girls' National school in Church Street, Rugeley, for four poor women,[42] and by 1834 four widows were living there and were each receiving 1s. a week.[43] Sarah Hopkins's endowment included part of the rent from a house and land in Rugeley conveyed to trustees in 1828, £18 from Johnson's tenement in Rugeley, and a bequest of £1,000.[44] Catherine Barber, presumably by the will proved 1842 (see above), left a further £100, and Rebecca Simpson, presumably by the will proved 1849 (see above), £500. Elizabeth Curzon, by will proved 1859, bequeathed £500 to the almshouses.[45] The widows were receiving 5s. a week each in 1868.[46] About 1938 the inmates were transferred to the present almshouses, also in Church Street, and the old buildings were demolished.[47] The income in 1954 was £49 10s. 8d. interest on stock and rent of £76 11s. 3d. from Johnson's tenement.[48] The alms-houses are still occupied (1957). The present brick range consists of four single-story dwellings. The stone dressings have been preserved from the former buildings and one gable bears the original tablet commemorating the erection and endowment of the almshouses by Sarah Hopkins in 1826.

H. R. Sneyd of Eaton Lodge, Rugeley, built eight cottages in Fortescue Lane (then New Lane) in 1870 for poor aged women.[49] These cottages were maintained after his death by his two daughters, the Misses Sneyd,[50] who also erected six cottages on the adjoining site in Church Street for ladies in reduced circumstances in memory of their father and mother in 1885.[51] In 1893 one of these daughters, Harriet, built six houses in Fortescue Lane for old couples chosen by herself in memory of Fanny Louisa Sneyd,[52] presumably her sister. Harriet Sneyd, by will proved 1913, gave £3,000 as endowment for the cottages in Fortescue Lane, which were to be used as almshouses for aged and infirm or needy Anglicans in Rugeley and Brereton; a further £3,000 for the six Ladies' Homes in Church Street, which were to be for Anglican women either of limited means or in any way requiring a home; and a final £3,000 for the six houses in Fortescue Lane then let at a nominal rent to aged couples but in future to be occupied free by aged Anglican couples resident in Rugeley or Brereton.[53] All three sets of almshouses are still occupied (1957). Those erected by H. R. Sneyd consist of a single-story range of red brick with blue-brick dressings. The houses in Church Street erected by the Misses Sneyd are built in two two-story blocks, one behind the other, each block containing three dwellings. They have half-timbered gables and a commemorative inscription. The six houses in Fortescue Lane form a two-story block with small gables and much ornamental brickwork.

The Walters Almshouses in Taylors Lane were erected in 1890 by J. T. Walter, in memory of his mother Elizabeth and wife Fanny, for six poor aged women.[54] These were purchased by the Revd. the Hon. Cecil J. Littleton and conveyed in 1906 to the trustees of the Girls Friendly Society as homes for its members and associates.[55] Known as the Littleton Houses of Rest,[56] they are still occupied (1957) and consist of a two-story red-brick range with blue-brick dressings, having gabled porches and diagonal glazing bars to the windows.

Thomas Birch and Miss Elizabeth Birch built six cottages in Brereton in 1824 to be let to poor persons of 50 and over.[57] Before 1851 Elizabeth bequeathed £1,500, the income to be spent on repairs and on the provision of 4s. a week to each of the occupants

[26] 7th Rep. Com. Char. 289.   [27] Ibid.
[28] Charity Com. files.
[29] Ex inf. the vicar.
[30] Charity Com. files.
[31] Ibid.
[32] Ex inf. the vicar.
[33] White, Dir. Staffs. (1851); Charity Com. files.
[34] Charity Com. files.
[35] Ex inf. the vicar.
[36] Charity Com. files.
[37] Ibid.
[38] Ex inf. Mr. G. H. Brown, Rugeley (1957).
[39] Kelly's Dir. Staffs. (1896).
[40] Ex inf. the Vicar of Brereton (1957).
[41] Abstract, 1786–8, ii. 1120–1; 7th Rep. Com. Char. 289. A John son of John Blood was buried at Rugeley in 1703 and a John Blood in 1705: Rugeley Par. Reg. 193, 195.
[42] Tablet in situ.

[43] White, Dir. Staffs. (1834).
[44] Charity Com. files; the rent was subject to the payment of £2 to the mistress of the girls' school in Church Street.
[45] Ibid.
[46] P.O. Dir. Staffs. (1868).
[47] Charity Com. files.   [48] Ibid.
[49] Tablet in situ; Kelly's Dir. Staffs. (1892).
[50] Kelly's Dir. Staffs. (1892).
[51] Tablet in situ.
[52] Tablet in situ; statement in her will (copy in Charity Com. files).
[53] Charity Com. files.
[54] Tablet in situ, which states that the building was formerly the Walters Arms [sic] House.
[55] Ibid.
[56] Ibid.
[57] Ex inf. the Steward to the Trustees (1957).

who were to attend the Wesleyan Methodist Chapel in Brereton.[58] The occupants in 1868 were poor widows.[59] These almshouses are still occupied (1957) and consist of a very plain single-story red-brick row situated in a lane opposite St. Michael's Church.

The Revd. Edward Samson, formerly Vicar of Brereton, by deed of 1904 established the four Samson Cottage Homes opposite St. Michael's as homes for needy inhabitants of Brereton and of Armitage and Pipe Ridware (Offlow hundred) and for any who might have served the donor and his heirs.[60] Church Cottage, Brereton, which was to form a fifth home, was sold in 1904 and the proceeds applied for the upkeep of the other almshouses.[61] These are still occupied (1957) and consist of a single-story range, each house having a projecting gabled bay window.

Jane Cotton by will dated 1808 left £300 to the inhabitants of Rugeley for general charitable purposes, and it was in respect of this bequest that three spinsters or widows of 60 years and over from Rugeley were included among the inmates of the almshouses in Longdon (Offlow hundred) founded in 1815 by Jane's sister Ann, while two poor boys and four poor girls from Rugeley were also admitted to the school in Longdon founded at the same time.[62] The school was closed c. 1840, but in 1890 the inmates of the almshouses still included three women from Rugeley.[63] In 1957 two widows from Rugeley were living here.[64]

SHARESHILL

SHARESHILL is a small parish lying six miles north of Wolverhampton, an equal distance south from Penkridge, and three miles south-west from Cannock. It is mainly agricultural and as yet almost untouched by the nearby industries. The main road from Wolverhampton to Cannock crosses the parish on the south-east, and the Staffordshire and Worcestershire Canal runs through the north-west corner. The only large centre of population is the village of Shareshill, closely grouped, with narrow tortuous roads and a church, a post-office, and several timber-framed houses. The ancient parish is divided into the two civil parishes of Shareshill and the Saredons (Great and Little), of 994 acres and 1,833 acres respectively.[1] The Saredons occupy the northern half of the ancient parish, which is separated from Shareshill by a small watercourse in a valley with steep descents from north and south, the boundary having been adjusted under the Staffordshire Review Order of 1934. All three townships occupy relatively high ground on a formation of water-bearing Pebble Beds, the highest point (Saredon Hill between Great and Little Saredon) reaching 500 ft., but the ground falls steadily to the west where the sub-soil is Boulder Clay and unbedded sand and gravel. The boundaries of the parish are not physically conspicuous, except for the northern boundary formed by the Saredon Brook (the 'Sare-brook' of early records) which flows due west into the Penk near Somerford, in Brewood.

There were 23 households in Shareshill constable-wick chargeable for hearth tax in 1666 and 13 too poor to be taxable.[2] In Great Saredon constablewick there were 14 chargeable and 7 too poor,[3] and in Little Saredon constablewick 15 chargeable and 7 too poor.[4] The population of Shareshill in 1801 was 200 and of the Saredons 241,[5] and in 1951 301 and 428 respectively.[6]

The tile-works belonging (1956) to Stella Tileries

Ltd. lie in the south-east of the parish and were in operation by 1940.[7]

There are remains of a medieval moated site to the north-east of Shareshill village,[8] but these are partly obliterated by the school playground. To the west of Moat House Bridge in the north-west of the parish two sides remain of a homestead moat.[9] Another homestead moat lies near Black Lees Farm.[10]

The village contains several timber-framed houses but none appears to date from before the 16th century. A cottage at the east end of Elms Lane has exposed timber-framing in large panels above a high stone plinth. It probably dates from the late 16th century and one of its bays was originally a single-story hall. An inserted floor in the hall and the easternmost bay of the cottage are of the 17th century. Two timber-framed cottages in Tarts Row, now largely faced with brickwork, date from c. 1600. Manor Farm contains in its south half a well-preserved early-17th-century house with attics and a central chimney-stack. The west wall has close-studded framing above a sandstone plinth and a door-way with a shaped head. Stone-mullioned windows, now blocked, remain in the cellar. Internally there are stop-chamfered beams and a moulded hearth lintel. A continuation of the framing north-wards suggests that the taller brick addition of c. 1750 replaced an earlier structure. The brick malt-house is dated 1761 and the 18th-century brick barn has restoration tablets inscribed 'T.S. 1855'. Home Farm is an 18th-century brick building but a wide fireplace and chamfered joists internally suggest that it is a reconstruction of an older house. The large brick barn was originally a timber-framed structure of five bays dating from the early 17th century. At Orchard Brook, an early-19th-century house, there is a low timber-framed annexe of c. 1600. There are indications that Villa Farm, an 18th- and mid-19th-century house with wide eaves, is a reconstruction of

[58] Ex inf. the steward; White, *Dir. Staffs.* (1851).
[59] *P.O. Dir Staffs.* (1868).
[60] Ex inf. the Lichfield Dioc. Trust (1957).
[61] Ex inf. the Lich. Dioc. Trust.
[62] Report of 1890 in Charity Com. files.
[63] Ibid.
[64] Ex inf. the Vicar of Longdon (1957).
[1] *Census*, 1951, Staffs.
[2] *S.H.C.* 1927, 21–22.
[3] Ibid. 23.
[4] Ibid. 24.

[5] *V.C.H. Staffs.* i. 320.
[6] *Census*, 1951, Staffs.
[7] *Kelly's Dir. Staffs.* (1940).
[8] Ex inf. the Inspectorate of Ancient Monuments, Ministry of Works (1957). *V.C.H. Staffs.* i. 346, 348, describes it as possibly Roman. There were formerly remains of a similar site to the south of the village: ibid. 192.
[9] *V.C.H. Staffs.* i. 366.
[10] See p. 177.

a timber-framed structure. Hall Farm dates in part from c. 1700. The Lodge and The Elms are early 19th-century houses in their own gardens. In March 1956 the licensing justices approved a scheme for moving the licence of the Swan Inn, a small brick building in Elms Lane, to The Elms.[11]

The corrugated iron village hall in Elms Lane was built as a Temperance Hall by Mr. A. L. Vernon of Hilton Park c. 1904.[12] Eight council houses in Elms Lane date from c. 1952.

An alteration in the course of the Cannock–Wolverhampton road in 1939[13] changed the appearance of the south end of the village and several buildings, including a public house, were demolished.

Great Saredon Hall is a brick house, the oldest part of which appears to date from c. 1700. Adjoining it is a brick outbuilding with stone dressings which is at least 100 years older. It retains stone-mullioned windows and two stone doorways with four-centred heads. Saredon Hall Cottages, immediately to the west, form a timber-framed range of three bays, probably dating from the 16th century. The most northerly bay, in which there is a moulded and embattled fireplace lintel, appears originally to have been a single-story hall.

Little Saredon Manor, formerly the Hall Farm, is a moated house of stone, brick, and timber, and is of various dates. The central timber-framed portion, largely faced externally with brickwork, probably represents a 16th-century hall. The porch at its east end has a classical stone doorway, probably of the 17th century. There are later additions at both ends of the building. The house was much restored in 1942 and later, and many of the features, such as the oak staircase and fireplaces, were brought from elsewhere. Two sides of a rectangular moat and part of a third are still in existence.

Hollybush Hall is a timber-framed house of the early or mid-17th century. Internally there is an open gable-end fireplace, chamfered ceiling beams, and an oak staircase with shaped flat balusters.

William Henry Havergal (1793–1870), the composer of sacred music and writer of books on the subject, was Vicar of Shareshill from 1860 until his death,[14] although he was absent for much of his incumbency owing to blindness and infirmity.[15] His daughter, Frances Ridley Havergal (1836–79), was a writer of hymns.[16]

MANORS. *SHARESHILL* appears in Domesday as 'Servesed' assessed at 3 hides.[17] It had been held before the Conquest by three freemen and afterwards by Robert de Stafford[18] with whose barony the overlordship descended until at least 1565.[19]

In 1086 one Hervey was holding Shareshill of Robert de Stafford[20] but at some date prior to 1166 the holder of the fee appears to have been Robert Burnell, whose sister Sybil was married to Ralph Purcell, the owner of lands in several southern counties.[21] This marriage must have established Ralph in Staffordshire, for he held ⅔ fee of Robert de Stafford in 1166.[22] Ralph was dead by 1212 when Sybil was suing a Robert Purcell for dower, and in 1213 she was granted the capital messuage of Shareshill.[23] Robert was holding a full fee in Shareshill by 1243.[24] Otewy (or Otwell) Purcell had lands in Shareshill by 1252[25] and by 1255 he was holding the fee, which was still assessed at 3 hides, geldable, and paid 3s. to the sheriff's aid, 3s. to the view of frankpledge, and 12d. to the hundred.[26] Otewy, alive in 1271,[27] was dead by 1281, when his widow Denise was claiming dower in a messuage, a carucate of land, 20 acres of wood, and 50s. rent in Shareshill.[28] The heir Otwell Purcell (II) was then a minor[29] but was of age by 1284.[30] He was named as lord in 1316[31] and was still alive in 1328.[32] By 1332 he had been succeeded by his son Thomas, who conveyed some rights in the manor in that year to Sir John de Swynnerton, lord of Hilton.[33]

In October 1334, however, Ralph de Stafford granted 1½ knight's fee in Shareshill and Coven to Sir William de Shareshill and Denise his wife together with the homage and services of Thomas Purcell,[34] licence to enfeoff having been obtained in September.[35] This transaction was in effect the interposition of a mesne lordship between Purcell and the overlord, but it was followed in 1339 by the transfer of two-thirds of the manor by Purcell to Sir William, with quitclaim of the third part held by Beatrice, widow of Otwell, in exchange for Great Tew (Oxon.).[36] Sir William de Shareshill, possibly Purcell's relative by marriage, became prominent in law and administration as chief justice of the King's Bench and certainly the most considerable judicial figure of the reign of Edward III.[37]

Sir William settled the manor in 1341 on his mother Katherine and her second husband John de Hodington for the life of Katherine,[38] but by an arrangement of 1344 the manor was settled on Sir William for life with successive remainders to Katherine and to his son William and William's wife Joan and their heirs.[39] John de Swynnerton, son of the Sir John to whom the manor had been conveyed in 1332, quitclaimed all right therein to Sir William in 1358.[40] The manor was settled on Sir William's grandson William and his wife Katherine in 1367 and the transaction confirmed in 1369 some months after Sir William's withdrawal to the Franciscan

[11] *Express and Star*, 6 Mar. 1956.
[12] Local inf.
[13] Ex inf. Staffs. C.C. Surveyor.
[14] *D.N.B.*; *Lich. Dioc. Ch. Cal.* (1870; 1871).
[15] Lich. Dioc. Regy., Reg. Non-res. Lic. 1865–70.
[16] *D.N.B.*
[17] *V.C.H. Staffs.* iv. 53, no. 219. [18] Ibid.
[19] *Red Bk. Exch.* (Rolls Ser.), 267; *Bk. of Fees*, 543; ibid. 966–7, 974; *Rot. Hund.* (Rec. Com.), ii. 114; *S.H.C.* vi (1), 119, 128–9; *Feud. Aids*, v. 1; *Cal. Chanc. R. Var.* 1277–1326, 96; *S.H.C.* xi. 138; C 136/47; C 142/143, no. 42.
[20] *V.C.H. Staffs.* iv. 53, no. 219.
[21] *S.H.C.* vi (1), 128–9; B. H. Putnam, *The Place in Legal History of Sir William Shareshull* (1950), 2.
[22] *Red Bk. Exch.* 267; *S.H.C.* i. 181.
[23] *S.H.C.* iii (1), 159, 176–7.
[24] *Bk. of Fees*, 967.
[25] *Close R.* 1251–3, 262.

[26] *Rot. Hund.* (Rec. Com.), ii. 114, the lord's name being rendered 'Estry Purcel' and the vill's 'Farnshulf'.
[27] *S.H.C.* v (1), 152.
[28] Ibid. vi (1), 119.
[29] Ibid. 119, 128–9.
[30] *Feud. Aids*, v. 1. [31] Ibid. 16.
[32] W.S.L., D. 1790/A/8/19.
[33] Ibid. no. 21; W.S.L., S. MS. 350A/40, f. 3a.
[34] *S.H.C.* xi. 138.
[35] *Cal. Pat.* 1334–8, 11.
[36] W.S.L., S. MS. 350A/40, ff. 3a–4a; W.S.L., S. MS. 201 (1), pp. 325–6; *S.H.C.* xi. 97, 147.
[37] Putnam, *Sir William Shareshull*, 3–6 et passim.
[38] W.S.L., S. MS. 201 (1), pp. 326–7; Putnam, *Sir William Shareshull*, 6 and App. I (pedigree).
[39] *S.H.C.* xi. 154.
[40] W.S.L., S. MS. 350A/40, ff. 4a–5a; *S.H.C.* xiv (1), 100–1.

house at Oxford where he died within a year.[41] His grandson having settled the manor in 1390 on himself and his second wife Margaret and their heirs, with remainder to his niece Margaret and her husband Richard Harcourt,[42] died without issue in 1400, and Harcourt entered into possession under the entail, to the exclusion of the heirs of the settlor, who were his neices Katherine, wife of Roger Wylily, Joan, wife of William Lee, and the two infant daughters of Richard Harcourt.[43] In 1406 William Lee and Joan and Roger Wylily and Katherine confirmed to Richard Harcourt and his daughter Isabel the beneficial interest in Shareshill.[44] Joan Lee seems to have recovered the manor by 1439,[45] and in 1441 or 1442 the reversion after her death was said to lie with a distant cousin, Joan, and her husband John Dynham.[46] Joan Lee leased the manor to Richard Hall in 1441 or 1442.[47] She had died without issue by 1455,[48] and Sir Robert Harcourt, great-nephew of Richard Harcourt,[49] died holding the manor of Shareshill in 1470, with a son John as his heir.[50] Robert's widow Margaret claimed dower in one-third of the manor in 1474,[51] and although John Harcourt seems to have held it in 1475,[52] Margaret was seised of the whole manor at her death in 1486, with reversion to Sir Robert Harcourt, son of John.[53] Robert's cousin Sir Simon Harcourt of Witham (Berks.) had succeeded by October 1509,[54] and the manor then descended in the Harcourt family[55] until 1604, when Sir Walter Harcourt settled the manor on John Skinner,[56] presumably an intermediary for Sir Walter Leveson of Wolverhampton, who was holding the court baron of Shareshill in December 1605.[57] Sir Walter, with Anne his wife and Thomas Leveson, presumably his brother, made a settlement of the manor in 1611[58] and was granted free warren in 'Great Shareshill' in 1618 or 1619.[59] Sir Walter died in 1621 leaving an infant son Thomas[60] who was holding the great court of Shareshill in October 1637.[61] By September 1639 the manor had passed to Sir Edward Littleton

of Pillaton,[62] in Penkridge parish, who made a settlement of it in 1642.[63] The manor then descended in the Littleton family with Pillaton,[64] the 4th Lord Hatherton being lord of the manor in 1940.[65]

The view of frankpledge attached to the lordship of the manor of Shareshill in at least 1469[66] belonged by 1527[67] and also between at least 1623 and 1630 to the lordship of Great Saredon.[68]

In 1604 the Dean and Chapter of Lichfield were holding a messuage in Shareshill, with pasture, meadow, and 40 acres in the common fields, of the manor of Shareshill at a rent of 3s.[69] The estate had been leased to Edward Bourne by 1650 when it consisted of 37 acres and was valued at £15 13s. 6d.[70] The dwelling, said to be much out of repair and possessing about an acre of ground, was worth 50s.[71] The dean and chapter owned over 60 acres in Shareshill about 1841, when the estate, most of it in the tenure of John Jackson and situated to the west of the village, included a house on the road to the south-west of the church.[72]

The manor of *GREAT SAREDON* ('Sardone'), which lay in the north of the parish and was sometimes styled 'Beresardon', appears in Domesday as one of the fees of Robert de Stafford, having been held formerly by four free thanes.[73] The overlordship descended with the Stafford barony until at least 1565.[74]

In 1086 Hervey was holding Saredon of Robert de Stafford,[75] but by 1166 it formed parcel of one of the fees held of Robert de Stafford (II) by Robert fitz Ralph, founder of the Standon family,[76] in which family a mesne lordship seems to have descended until at least 1300.[77]

A Nicholas de Sardonia was holding Great Saredon of Robert fitz Ralph in 1166 as $\frac{2}{3}$ knight's fee.[78] By 1243 the tenant in possession was Henry de Audley, holding Saredon as a whole fee,[79] and a further intermediate lordship seems to have descended in the Audley family until at least 1471.[80]

Henry de Audley's daughter Emma married

---

[41] W.S.L., S. MS. 201 (1), pp. 319–21; Shaw, *Staffs.* ii. 281; Putnam, *Sir William Shareshull*, 8. Sir William's son William had probably died shortly before this settlement: Putnam, op. cit. 8 and App. I.
[42] *S.H.C.* xi. 208; ibid. N.S. iii. 228; Putnam, op. cit., App. I.
[43] C 137/4; *S.H.C.* N.S. iii. 228; Putnam, op. cit., App. I.
[44] *S.H.C.* xi. 215–16; W.S.L., S. MS. 201 (1) p. 315.
[45] W.S.L., S. MS. 201 (1), pp. 336.
[46] Ibid., p. 317; Putnam, *Sir William Shareshull*, App. I.
[47] W.S.L., S. MS. 201 (1), p. 338.
[48] *S.H.C.* N.S. iii. 220.
[49] Ibid. iv. 272.
[50] C 140/38.
[51] *S.H.C.* N.S. iv. 197.
[52] W.S.L., S. MS. 350A/40, ff. 13a–14a.
[53] E 150/1013 (1); *Cal. Inq. p.m. Hen. VII*, i, p. 140.
[54] *S.H.C.* 1914, 205; S.R.O., D. 260/M/box 3, bdle. a, Shareshill Cr. R. 4 Oct. 1509.
[55] *S.H.C.* 1914, 205–7; D. 260/M/box 3, bdle. a; E 36/150, f. 58b.
[56] *S.H.C.* xviii (1), 44, 46.
[57] S.R.O., D. 260/M/box 3, bdle. a.
[58] *S.H.C.* N.S. iii. 67–68.
[59] C 66/2173, no. 13.
[60] C 142/390, no. 148; Shaw, *Staffs.* ii. 169 (pedigree).
[61] S.R.O., D. 260/M/box 3, bdle. a; W.S.L., S. MS. 201 (1), p. 394.
[62] S.R.O., D. 260/M/box 3, bdle. a.
[63] C.P. 25(2)/486, 18 Chas. I Mich.
[64] C.P. 25(2)/596, 1654 Trin.; *S.H.C.* 1928, 162; C.P. 25(2)/725, 28 Chas. II Mich.; C.P. 43/490, rot. 164; C.P. 43/506, rot. 98; C.P. 43/520, rot. 72; C.P. 43/676, rot. 321;

[64 cont.] S.R.O., Gamekeprs.' Deps.; White, *Dir Staffs.* (1834; 1851).
[65] *Kelly's Dir. Staffs.* (1940).
[66] S.R.O., D. 260/M/box 3, bdle. a.
[67] Ibid.
[68] S.R.O., D. 260/M/box 8, bdle. m. This collection contains an incomplete series of court rolls for Shareshill from 1469 to 1701 and for Great Saredon for 1527, 1549, and 1603 (box 3, bdle. a), and for 1623 and 1630: box 8, bdle. m. There are 2 for Little Saredon for 1469 and 1481 (box 3, bdle. a) and there is a roll of chief rents paid from the three manors in the early 18th cent.: box 8, bdle. m. Various other records of the courts leet and baron of Shareshill and the Saredons survive for the 16th and 17th cents.: W.S.L., D. 1798, bdle. 19.
[69] W.S.L., S. MS. 201 (1), p. 410.
[70] Lichfield D. and C. MS. Bk. liv (Oliverian Surveys, vol. i), f. 129a.
[71] Ibid.
[72] Tithe Maps and Appt., Shareshill (copy in W.S.L.).
[73] *V.C.H. Staffs.* vi. 53, no. 216.
[74] *Red Bk. Exch.* (Rolls Ser.), 265; *Bk. of Fees*, 543; ibid. 966–7, 974; *Rot. Hund.* (Rec. Com.), ii. 114; *Feud. Aids*, v. 3; *Cal. Chan. R. Var.* 1277–1326, 96; C 136/47; C 142/143, no. 42.
[75] *V.C.H. Staffs.* iv. 53, no. 216.
[76] *Red Bk. Exch.* 265; *S.H.C.* i. 163.
[77] *Bk. of Fees*, 974; *S.H.C.* v (1), 146, 178–9; ibid. vi (1), 121, 193; *Feud. Aids*, v. 3; *V.C.H. Warws.* v. 155.
[78] *Red Bk. Exch.* 265; *S.H.C.* i. 47, 50, 163.
[79] *Bk. of Fees*, 966–7.
[80] *S.H.C.* vi (1), 107, 121, 183, 193, *Feud. Aids*, v. 3; C 140/38.

Griffin ap Madoc, lord of Bromfield in Lower Powys,[81] who in 1244 was granted exemption from suit at hundred and county courts so long as he held the lands in Derbyshire, Staffordshire, and Cheshire which he had as Emma's dower.[82] By 1255 Griffin was holding Great Saredon, which was then assessed at 2 hides, and for eight years had performed none of the services due to the king, except the 2s. paid annually to the view of frankpledge, so that the king had lost in all 6 marks.[83] Griffin died in 1269,[84] and in 1279 Emma was being sued for what was called the manor of 'Beresardon' by a John Wymer of Stafford, as the nephew of a Nicholas le Bere who was alleged to have held the manor during the reign of Henry III.[85] Emma, the wife of William of Worcester by 1288, continued to hold the manor, apparently consisting of a messuage, a carucate, and 6 marks rent, until at least 1290.[86] William de la Pole and Gladys his wife were holding the manor of Beresardon by 1293 when John Wymer, having again sued for it, acknowledged her right.[87] William, still alive in 1303,[88] was dead by 1308,[89] but Gladys continued to hold the manor until at least 1316.[90] Griffin de la Pole, son and heir of William, was 29 years of age in 1319 when he was found entitled to restoration of his lands, held in wardship by Sir John de Cherletone,[91] and he heads the section of the tax list of 1327 dealing with Saredon.[92] As lord of Great Saredon Griffin with his son William conveyed land there to Sir William de Shareshill in 1349,[93] and in 1352 Griffin granted the manor to John Musard,[94] who three weeks later conveyed it to Sir William de Shareshill and his wife Denise.[95] Griffin's son William confirmed this conveyance the following March,[96] and although his son John began an action to recover the manor in 1370,[97] Great Saredon descended with Shareshill[98] until at least 1851 when the 1st Lord Hatherton held the manor.[99]

What was later known as LITTLE SAREDON appears in Domesday as Seresdon, assessed at a hide and held of the king by Udi, a thane of King William and the successor at Saredon of the pre-Conquest Gamel, who had owed suit to King Edward (soca

ejus fuit regis).[1] The royal manor to which Saredon was subordinate was no doubt Kinver (in Seisdon hundred),[2] since by 1182 Saredon had been given to the priory of Dudley by Osbert de Kenefare[3] and in 1253 the Crown claimed 12s. rent from Robert de Whiston in respect of land in Saredon which had been alienated from the king's manor of Kinver.[4] The overlordship remained with the Prior of Dudley, who was himself holding it by 1255 of his religious superior the Prior of Wenlock (Salop.), and descended after the Reformation with the possessions of Dudley Priory until at least 1630 when it was held by Lord Dudley.[5]

Robert de Whiston, who probably held Little Saredon by 1251,[6] was holding it of the Prior of Dudley for 1 mark by 1255.[7] It was then still assessed at a hide, geldable, and paid 12d. to the sheriff's aid and 12d. to the view of frankpledge.[8] A Robert de Whiston was holding it in 1285,[9] and though still alive in 1291,[10] was dead by 1293 when his widow Beatrice, by then wife of Ralph de Wasteneys, was suing for dower in Little Saredon.[11] A Robert de Whiston was stated in 1300 to be holding the vill with William Trumwyn,[12] and about this time the capital messuage was held by Robert le Champion.[13] Robert son of Robert de Whiston occurs in 1322 or 1323.[14] By 1324 he had been succeeded by a John,[15] probably his son,[16] who was dead before 1333 when his widow Rose, by then the wife of Adam de Shareshill, was suing for dower in Little Saredon.[17] John was succeeded by his son, also John,[18] who as Sir John de Whiston granted in 1358 what was called his manor of Little Saredon to Sir William de Shareshill,[19] Sir John's widow Elizabeth quitclaiming her right in the manor in the following year.[20]

The manor then descended with Shareshill[21] until 1443 when Richard Harcourt and his wife Eleanor made a settlement reserving a life interest in Little Saredon to themselves with remainder to Richard Congreve and his issue.[22] In 1454 or 1455 Richard Congreve appointed attorneys to take seisin of the manor after the death of Eleanor,[23] but in 1457 he

[81] Dugd. *Baronage*, i. 747; *Foedera*, i. 420; Eyton, *Shropshire*, ii. 111; *D.N.B. sub* Gruffydd ab Madog.
[82] *Pat. R.* 1232–47, 430.
[83] *Rot. Hund.* (Rec. Com.), ii. 114.
[84] *D.N.B.*
[85] *S.H.C.* vi (1), 100, 220.
[86] Ibid. 183, 193; *Feud. Aids*, v. 3.
[87] *S.H.C.* vi (1), 220; ibid. 1911, 48–49, 52–53. William de la Pole was probably one of the 6 sons of Griffith ap Gwenwynen, lord of Upper Powys (with Welshpool as his headquarters), since in 1291 he received a grant of land from his brother Owen the son of Griffin of 'Wenunwyn', lord of Welshpool: *Cal. Chanc. R. Var.* 1277–1326, 171, 330; G. T. O. Bridgeman, 'Princes of Upper Powys', *Powysland Club* (1867).
[88] *Cal. Chanc. R. Var.* 1277–1326, 96.
[89] *S.H.C.* ix (1), 5.
[90] *Feud. Aids*, v. 16.
[91] *Cal. Inq. p.m.* vi, pp. 116–17.
[92] *S.H.C.* vii (1), 245.
[93] Ibid. xi. 163; W.S.L., S. MS. 201(1), p. 313.
[94] W.S.L., S. MS. 350A/40, f. 6a.
[95] Ibid.
[96] Ibid., ff. 6a–7a.
[97] *S.H.C.* xiii. 84, 90, 164, 176, 189, 203–4; ibid. xv. 14.
[98] W.S.L., S. MS. 201 (1), pp. 319, 320–1, 322–3; *S.H.C.* xv. 30; C.P. 25(2)/485, 13 Chas. I Mich.; S.R.O., D. 260/M/box 8, bdle. m, Great Saredon Ct. R.; White, *Dir. Staffs.* (1834).
[99] White, *Dir. Staffs.* (1851).
[1] *V.C.H. Staffs.* iv. 57, no. 272.

[2] Though Eyton, *Domesday Studies, Staffs.*, 73, suggested Penkridge.
[3] Dugd. *Mon.* v. 83.
[4] *S.H.C.* iv (1), 128.
[5] Ibid.; *Rot. Hund.* (Rec. Com.), ii. 114; *Feud. Aids*, v. 1; *S.H.C.* v (1), 178, where it is described as held of the Barony of Dudley; C 140/38; W.S.L., S.D. Beck 47; *V.C.H. Worcs.*, ii. 161; ibid. iii, 93, 101.
[6] *S.H.C.* iv (1), 123, 125, 128.
[7] *Rot. Hund.* (Rec. Com.), ii. 114.
[8] Ibid.
[9] *Feud. Aids*, v. 1. The use of the Christian name Robert apparently by four successive generations of the Whiston family (*S.H.C.* 1928, 60; W.S.L., S. MS. 350A/40 f. 9a) makes it difficult to trace the descent of the manor at this time.
[10] *S.H.C.* 1928, 160.
[11] Ibid. vi (1), 238.
[12] Ibid. v (1), 178.
[13] W.S.L., S. MS. 350A/40, f. 12a; *S.H.C.* 1931, 263.
[14] W.S.L., S. MS. 350A/40, f. 8a.
[15] Ibid.
[16] Ibid., f. 10a; *S.H.C.* 1911, 82–83.
[17] *S.H.C.* xi. 47, 50.
[18] Ibid.; W.S.L., S. MS. 350A/40, f. 11a.
[19] W.S.L., S. MS. 350A/40, f. 8a.
[20] Ibid.
[21] W.S.L., S. MS. 201 (1), pp. 320–21; *S.H.C.* xv. 30; ibid. xi. 208; C 137/4.
[22] *S.H.C.* xi. 234.
[23] W.S.L., S. MS. 350A/40, f. 11a.

was suing her executors for his rights there.[24] This may indicate a dispute over the devolution of the manor, although Richard made a settlement of at least the capital messuage in 1460 or 1461.[25] Little Saredon was returned as one of the manors held by Sir Robert Harcourt at his death in 1470[26] and was held by his son and heir John in 1475.[27] Francis Congreve was holding the manor by 1620[28] and was succeeded in 1630 by his son Richard,[29] to whom the manor was then released by the Crown.[30] Richard and his wife Anne conveyed the manor in 1641 to Edward son of Sir Edward Littleton,[31] in whose family it then descended, being held with Great Saredon as one manor in 1851.[32] In 1913 the estate was sold to R. G. Arblaster.[33] The Hall Farm was sold c. 1940 to Mr. Hawkins of Hawkins Tile Works, Cannock, who restored the house and renamed it Saredon Manor.[34]

The prebend of Shareshill in the collegiate church of Penkridge was valued at £10 in 1291.[35] In 1535 the prebend consisted of the site of the *PREBENDAL MANOR* and lands, valued at 20s., assised rents averaging 20s., tithe of grain averaging £3 a year, tithe of wool and lambs averaging 4 marks, other tithes averaging 33s. 4d., Easter offerings averaging 20s., and oblations averaging 10s.[36] Synodals of 6s. 8d. were due to the Dean of Penkridge every third year.[37] The lease of the prebend was granted to Edward Littleton in 1545 at a rent of £16 6s. 8d.[38] The prebend itself presumably descended with the rest of the collegiate possessions,[39] and in 1585 it passed to Edward Littleton of Pillaton,[40] grandson of the lessee of 1545. The prebend then descended in the Littleton family with Pillaton in Penkridge[41] until at least 1709.[42] Lord Hatherton was impropriator of the tithes of Shareshill in 1851.[43]

LESSER ESTATE. The William Trumwyn of Cannock who was named with Robert de Whiston in 1300 as holding the vill of Little Saredon[44] was, with his wife Emma, holding a messuage and carucate there in 1309.[45] His grandson, Sir William Trumwyn, released all the lands at 'Blakelye' called Saredon Wood in Little Saredon to John Trumwyn,

apparently his son, in 1342,[46] and John devised them to his brother Roger who in 1360 granted them to Richard de Wyrley.[47] In 1380 Richard's widow Katherine granted the messuage in Little Saredon called 'Blakelie' to John de Swynnerton,[48] and the estate then descended in the Swynnerton family until at least 1470, and probably until at least 1525.[49] Its subsequent descent is obscure until 1697, but it is known that a Mary Sanders lived at Black Lees in 1608.[50] In 1697 Collins Wolrich of Shrewsbury sold a messuage and lands in Little Saredon known as the Lees, the Black Lees, or the Great Black Lees, to Benjamin Hinds of Little Saredon, whose widow and son sold the estate in 1725 to Walter Duncalf of Albrighton (Salop.), as Hinds himself had intended to do before his death.[51] Duncalf mortgaged it in 1742 to Thomas Wenlock of Tong (Salop.).[52] By c. 1841 the Black Lees farm, owned and occupied by T. Stokes, was over 81 acres in extent.[53] The present Black Lees Farm is a brick farmhouse dating from c. 1800. A rectangular homestead moat,[54] lying about 300 yds. farther north, probably marks the site of the earlier messuage.

MILLS. William le Champion of Little Saredon, was holding a mill and a messuage there in 1331 and 1332.[55] There was a windmill in the centre of the township by 1832,[56] and this continued in use until at least 1872,[57] a portable steam engine being used in the corn-grinding for a few years after the use of wind-power had been discontinued. In 1942 the remains of the sails were removed, and the building was converted into a farm cottage by Mr. Hawkins of Hawkins Tile Works, Cannock.[58]

A mill at Great (or Bere) Saredon formed part of the estate there of William of Worcester and his wife Emma in 1288[59] and 1290[60] and their successors, William de la Pole and his wife Gladys, in 1293.[61] A water-mill on the Saredon Brook, which forms the boundary between Saredon and Hatherton (in St. Peter's, Wolverhampton), had been granted by 1388 by Sir William de Shareshill for life to William atte Mulnehous, who was then being sued by Sir William for not carrying out repairs to it.[62] This is presumably Saredon Mill described from 1444 as in Hatherton

24 *S.H.C.* N.S. iii. 221.
25 W.S.L., S. MS. 350A/40, f. 12a.
26 C 140/38.
27 W.S.L., S. MS. 350A/40, ff. 13a–14a.
28 *S.H.C.* N.S. vii. 214.
29 C 142/455, no. 72.
30 W.S.L., S.D. Beck 47.
31 C.P. 25(2)/486, 17 Chas. I East.
32 C.P. 25(2)/596, 1654 Trin.; S.R.O., D. 260/M/box 3, bdle. e, m. 4; *S.H.C.* 1928, 162; C.P. 43/490, rot. 164; C.P. 43/676, rot. 321; S.R.O., Gamekprs.' Deps.; White, *Dir. Staffs.* (1851).
33 Local inf.
34 Ibid. This house is probably to be identified with the capital messuage called 'Saraden Hall' mentioned in 1654: S.R.O., D. 260/M/box 3, bdle. e, m. 4; see p. 174.
35 *Tax. Eccl.* (Rec. Com.), 242.
36 *Valor Eccl.* (Rec. Com.), iii. 106.   37 Ibid.
38 *S.H.C.* 1950–1, 36 and n. 98.
39 See p. 111.
40 *S.H.C.* xv. 167.
41 C 142/455, no. 76; C.P. 25(2)/485, 8 Chas. I East.; C.P. 25(2)/486, 18 Chas. I Mich.; C.P. 25(2)/596, 1654 Trin.; C.P. 25(2)/725, 28 Chas. II Mich.; C.P. 43/490, rot. 164; see p. 119.
42 C.P. 43/506, rot. 98.
43 White, *Dir. Staffs.* (1851).
44 *S.H.C.* v (1), 178.

45 Ibid. 1911, 72–73.
46 W.S.L., D. 1790/A/7/1.
47 W.S.L., D. 1790/A/7/4; *S.H.C.* xiv (1), 105. In 1355 Roger, son of Roger Trumwyn deceased, was claiming a messuage and lands in Little Saredon against John, described as brother of the senior Roger, and others: *S.H.C.* xiii (1), 134.
48 W.S.L., D. 1790/A/7/7.
49 W.S.L., D. 1790/A/7/8, 9, 13, 16, 19, the latter two of which dated 1516 and 1525 are concerned only with pasture and meadow called 'Blakelie'; C 140/35; *S.H.C.* vii (2), 111–13; *Cal. Inq. p.m. Hen. VII*, ii, pp. 221–2.
50 See p. 180.
51 W.S.L. 29/46, bdle. 6; the messuage was described as a farmhouse in 1725.
52 Ibid.
53 Tithe Maps and Appt., Shareshill (copy in W.S.L.).
54 *V.C.H. Staffs.* i. 366.
55 W.S.L., S. MS. 350A/40, f. 10a.
56 Teesdale, *Map of Staffs.* (1832).
57 White, *Dir. Staffs.* (1834; 1851); Tithe Maps and Appt., Shareshill (copy in W.S.L.); *P.O. Dir. Staffs.* (1860; 1868; 1872).
53 Local inf.
59 *S.H.C.* vi (1), 183.
60 Ibid. 193.
61 Ibid. 1911, 48–49.
62 Ibid. xv. 11, 17.

and is therefore reserved for treatment under Hatherton in a subsequent volume.

Deepmoor Mill was situated on the Saredon Brook in the north-west corner of the parish by 1775[63] and described as a 'very powerful corn mill' in 1817.[64] The Moncktons owned the 'water corn mill and blade mill called Deepmore Mills' by 1829, and the mill continued in use until about 1900.[65] Parts of the millhouse date from the 17th century. The mill pool, now dry, lies to the west.

A quarter share in a water-mill in Shareshill seems to have formed part of the Black Lees estate by 1697.[66]

There were two fulling mills in Saredon township by 1704.[67]

WOODS. Shareshill and the Saredons lay within the royal forest of Cannock between at least 1167 and 1301.[68] After disafforestation there would have remained, however, a semi-encirclement of forest lands giving facilities for rough grazing on their fringes.

There was woodland ½ league square appurtenant to the manor of Shareshill in 1086,[69] while the wood of Great Saredon was formed from part of the royal forest by James de Audley and in 1271 was held by his sister Emma.[70] The wood of Little Saredon was mentioned c. 1300.[71] Tenants in Shareshill and Great Saredon were presented before the royal justices in 1286 for old and new assarts in the king's forest,[72] and in 1311 it was found that Gladys, widow of William de la Pole of Great Saredon, had taken 400 acres of waste at 'Calwehet' in Cannock Forest but was unable to cultivate it and draw profit since John de Swynnerton, steward of the forest, allowed the king's horses and deer to roam over the land.[73] The tenants of Great and Little Saredon seem to have been able to secure the lease of common rights in Cheslyn Hay within the forest to the east, and as a result there was a clash during the reign of Henry VIII between the inhabitants of Great Saredon and John Leveson of Wolverhampton who had inclosed the Hay as its owner.[74] Six hundred acres of the Hay were inclosed by an agreement of 1668 between Robert Leveson of Wolverhampton and the freeholders and copyholders of Great and Little Saredon and Great Wyrley (in Cannock),[75] and 256 acres of Cheslyn Common within the parish of Shareshill were inclosed in 1797 under an Act of 1792.[76]

AGRICULTURE. There seem to have been five open fields in Shareshill between about 1300 and 1703; Loddersford or Latherford Field, also known as Nether Field (probably situated to the north-west of the village where the name survives in Latherford House); Old Field (possibly situated to the south-east of the village where the name occurs in the Tithe Apportionment of c. 1841); Bromley, later Broomyhalf, Field; Hall Field; and Clay Field.[77] The process of consolidation of the strips in the open fields is indicated as early as 1363 when the lord of the manor paid a fine of 6s. 8d. for licence to exchange one acre for another, both in Shareshill, and valued at 4d.[78] In 1647 the penalties for each gap in the hedges of Clay Field, Hall Field, and Broomyhall Field were fixed at 4d. and for each missing gate 1s.[79] In 1701, when there were also numerous presentments for encroachment on the lord's waste, the penalties for those who did not hang the field gates and make up the field fences in the winter corn field by 20 September and in the barley field by 25 March were fixed at 1s. for each missing gate, 2d. for each gap, and 6d. for each missing perch of fence.[80] The penalty for keeping a colt over nine days old loose in the town fields or for tying a beast or horse on another's ground was 6d.[81] With regard to the five town meadows it was agreed in 1647 that they should be held in severalty after 10 August for a year, the meadows to be shared among six men each year and so in turn among all the inhabitants, the rate for each meadow being paid to the constable.[82] Each man was to have his hedges raised by 30 August.[83]

Three common fields in the manor of Great Saredon mentioned between at least 1461 and 1630 were the Church Field, the Mill Field, and the West Field.[84] Two field reeves were appointed in 1629 to supervise the fields.[85] In 1669 Thomas Burne was selling three closes inclosed from the West Field and the Mill Field.[86]

By 1654 there seem to have been no common fields in Little Saredon.[87]

It is not known when the common fields in the parish were inclosed. It was stated in 1817 that the land about the village of Shareshill was good loam, suited to grain, turnips, and pasture.[88] There were six farms in Shareshill in 1834 and eight in Great and Little Saredon.[89] By 1940 there were 22 farms, the main crops being turnips and barley.[90]

CHURCHES. There was a church at Shareshill by 1213.[91] It seems to have been appropriated to

[63] Yates, *Map of Staffs.* (1799), based on a survey made between 1769 and 1775.

[64] Pitt, *Staffs.* 259.

[65] W.S.L., D. 1813, bdle. 33; White, *Dir. Staffs.* (1834; 1851); Tithe Maps and Appt., Shareshill (copy in W.S.L.); P.O. *Dir. Staffs.* (1868; 1872; 1876); *Kelly's Dir. Staffs.* (1880, and subsequent edns. to 1900).

[66] C.P. 25(2)/873, 4 Wm. and Mary Trin.; C.P. 25(2)/874, 9 Wm. III.

[67] C.P. 25(2)/965, 2 Anne Hil.

[68] *S.H.C.* v. 178-9; ibid. 1912, 117-18; ibid. 1923, 294, 295, 300; *Select Pleas of the Forest*, ed. G. J. Turner (Selden Soc. xiii), p. cv.

[69] *V.C.H. Staffs.* iv. 53, no. 219.

[70] *S.H.C.* v (i), 153.

[71] Ibid. 1928, 158-9.

[72] Ibid. v (i), 169.

[73] Ibid. 1911, 311.

[74] Ibid. 1912, 117-18.

[75] Ibid. 1931, 73-74.

[76] Ibid. 93; S.R.O., Q/RDc 10.

[77] W.S.L., D. 1790/A/8/4, 6, 11, 12, 16, 22, 23, 27, 32, 34, 37-39, 41, 45, 47, 48, 54, 59, 60, 61, 68, 69, 74, 76, 83-86, 88, 91, 94, 97; S.R.O., D. 260, box 3, bdle. a; Lichfield D. and C. MS. Bk. liv, f. 129a. There was mention of the common land in Shareshill in 1213 (*S.H.C.* iii (1), 176-7) and of third-year fallow in about 1300: W.S.L., D. 1790/A/8/7.

[78] *S.H.C.* 1913, 176; *Cal. Pat.* 1361-4, 333.

[79] S.R.O., D. 260/M/box 3, bdle. a, Shareshill Ct. R.

[80] Ibid.   [81] Ibid.

[82] Ibid. The rates were 4s. for 2 of the meadows, 5s. for 2 of the others, and 12s. for the fifth.   [83] Ibid.

[84] S.R.O., D. 260/M/box II, bdle. d; ibid. box 8, bdle. m; W.S.L., D. 1790/A/7/17, 18; W.S.L. 45/30.

[85] S.R.O., D. 260/M/box 8, bdle. m.

[86] W.S.L., D. 1717, bdle. b.

[87] S.R.O., D. 260/M/box 3, bdle. e.

[88] Pitt, *Staffs.* 258.

[89] White, *Dir. Staffs.* (1834).

[90] *Kelly's Dir. Staffs.* (1940).

[91] *S.H.C.* iii. 176-7.

DUNSTON CHAPEL IN 1838
(replaced 1876–8)

SHARESHILL: the church from the south-east in 1837

Air view of Teddesley Hall in 1950 (demolished in 1954)

Park Gate Bridge, Staffordshire and Worcestershire Canal

TEDDESLEY HAY

Penkridge College in or after 1225, the year when the advowson was granted to the Dean of Penkridge by Robert Purcell,[92] and by 1535 all or most of the tithes were held by the Prebendary of Shareshill in Penkridge church.[93] No vicarage, however, was instituted, the church being served in 1548 by a stipendiary priest on behalf of the prebendary.[94] Shareshill church was apparently raised from the position of a chapel of ease to Penkridge to parochial status in 1551 when the lay rectors and the Vicar of Penkridge released to it the parochial right of burial.[95] A graveyard at Shareshill, however, had been mentioned c. 1300[96] and in 1455.[97] The benefice was still called a perpetual curacy in 1956.[98]

The advowson of the church was held in 1213 by Robert Purcell[99] who in 1225, after litigation, granted it to the Dean of Penkridge.[1] At the time of the dissolution of Penkridge College the priest was appointed by the Prebendary of Shareshill.[2] The advowson presumably passed to the Crown with the advowson of Penkridge with which it was granted in 1585 to Edward Littleton.[3] It descended in his family[4] until c. 1910 when it was acquired by the Bishop of Lichfield[5] who still held it in 1956.[6]

In 1548 the priest had a salary of £5 6s. and some glebe land and was ordered to go on serving the church at his old salary.[7] In 1604 the curate's stipend was £6,[8] but the minister was in receipt of £50 a year by 1646 when an augmentation of £50 out of the sequestered rectory was ordered.[9] In 1652, however, the minister's income was said to be only 16 nobles, and although further orders were given for its augmentation to £100 out of the sequestered tithes of Hilton and Featherstone (both in St. Peter's, Wolverhampton), the minister was complaining in 1656 of complete lack of means.[10] In 1780 the total income of the living was £31 6s. 8d., £14 being the interest on a grant from Queen Anne's Bounty and the rest derived from such miscellaneous and casual incidents as surplice fees and grants from charities.[11] After further augmentation the living was valued in 1796 at £66 19s. 6d.[12] The incumbent still benefits under the Alport Charity on condition of attending an annual service in Cannock parish church on the Feast of St. Barnabas (11 June), preaching a

sermon at this service in annual rotation with seven other beneficiaries, and residing in his benefice for at least 10 months in the year.[13]

A chapel, possibly founded from Shareshill, existed at Great Saredon in 1578.[14]

Henry Vernon of Hilton (St. Peter's, Wolverhampton), by will proved 1732, left a rent-charge of £2 on his estate at Hilton to be paid every New Year's Day to the minister of Shareshill as follows: £1 for preaching a sermon on the Feast of the Conversion of St. Paul (25 Jan.), on the subject of parental responsibility for instructing children early in the catechism and their religion, and for hearing the children's catechism that day; 10s. for such poor children as should say the catechism best; and 10s. for books of devotion for the children.[15] By 1823 £1 was paid for the sermon and £1 for bibles and prayer books for the poor.[16] Another fund, a rent-charge of £1 on land in Little Saredon, was then used to present bibles and prayer books and testaments to poor children of the parish who said the catechism well. This charity had lapsed in 1828 and proved irrecoverable.[17] By 1933 the sermon had lapsed and the vicar received only £1 on St. Thomas's Day which was used to buy bibles and prayer books for Shareshill children.[18] The payment was stopped in 1951, on the sale of the Vernon estate, but in 1953 liability was found to lie with Mr. R. L. Vernon. The rent charge was then redeemed and the proceeds invested in £40 stock.[19]

The church of *ST. LUKE AND ST. MARY THE VIRGIN*[20] was largely rebuilt c. 1742.[21] The tower, the base of which probably dates from the 14th century, is the only medieval feature that remains. An earlier rebuilding took place c. 1562 by Humphrey Swynnerton of Hilton and Swynnerton, who died at Hilton and was buried in the chancel in that year.[22] The upper stages of the tower date from the 16th century and may be part of his work. The belfry is pierced with two-light openings and has an embattled parapet with short angle pinnacles. Below the parapet is an enriched string bearing a variation of the lozenge design. The 14th-century tower arch has been partly blocked and the head recut to form a shouldered arch connecting the ringing-chamber

92 S.H.C. iv (1), 34, 222–3.
93 See p. 177.
94 S.H.C. 1915, 228–9.
95 W.S.L., S. MS. 201 (i), p. 423; S.H.C. 1915, 228, 229. In 1553 it was stated that the bishop's licence to bury had been purchased for £2: ibid. 229.
96 W.S.L., D. 1790/A/1/9.
97 Ibid. A/8/67.
98 The benefice was described as a vicarage in 1868 (Lich. Dioc. Ch. Cal. 1868) but since 1917 has reverted to its former designation: Lich. Dioc. Ch. Cal. (1917–1937); Lich. Dioc. Dir. (1938; 1955–6).
99 S.H.C. iii. 176–7.
1 Ibid. iv (1), 34, 222–3.
2 Ibid. 1915, 228–9.
3 Ibid. xv. 167; see p. 130.
4 C.P. 25(2)/484, 1 Chas. I Hil.; C.P. 25(2)/596, 1654 Trin.; C.P. 43/490, rot. 164; C.P 43/506, rot. 98; C.P. 43/676, rot. 321; W.S.L., Hand Morgan Coll., Littleton Papers, bdle. labelled 'Shareshill Curacy'; White, Dir. Staffs. (1834; 1851); Lich. Dioc. Ch. Cal. (1910).
5 Lich. Dioc. Ch. Cal. (1911).
6 Lich. Dioc. Dir. (1955–6).
7 S.H.C. 1915, 229.
8 Ibid.
9 Ibid. 203, 229.
10 Ibid. 229–30.
11 W.S.L., Hand Morgan Coll., Littleton Papers, bdle.

labelled 'Shareshill Curacy'. In the latter part of the 18th cent. at least 3 of the curates held the headmastership of Brewood Grammar School also: ibid.
12 Ibid.
13 See p. 64.
14 W.S.L. 45/30; Erdeswick, Staffs. ed. Harwood (1844), 162 note b. One of the common fields of Great Saredon was called Church Field (see p. 178), and a cottage in Great Saredon called the Chapel House occurs in 1528: S.R.O., D. 260/M/box II, bdle. d.
15 9th Rep. Com. Char. H.C. 258, p. 534 (1823), ix.
16 Ibid.
17 Ibid.; Benefactions Board in church, dated 1861; Staffs. Endowed Charities, Elem. Educ. [Cd. 2729], p. 110, H.C. (1906), xc.
18 Charity Com. files.
19 Charity Com. files.
20 It seems to have been dedicated to St. Luke during the Middle Ages at least (W.S.L., D. 1790/A/8/9; ibid. A/8/67), and to the Assumption of the Virgin by 1817: Pitt, Staffs. 256; White, Dir. Staffs. (1851). From 1895 the dedication is given as St. Mary the Virgin (Lich. Dioc. Ch. Cal. 1895), and from 1915 as St. Luke and St. Mary the Virgin: ibid. (1915); Lich. Dioc. Dir. (1955–6). In the 16th cent. there was a statue of St. Luke on the north side of the chancel: S.H.C. vii (2), 59.
21 Kelly's Dir. Staffs. (1884); see plate facing p. 178.
22 S.H.C. vii (2), 57.

with a later west gallery. The original vice staircase is sealed off and access to the ringing-chamber is now by an external stair and an 18th-century doorway on the west face of the tower. The body of the church, long and narrow on plan with an apse forming the sanctuary at the east end, is built of brick and dates entirely from the 18th century. Externally the south side has stone angle pilasters, a classical cornice, and a partly balustraded parapet. The round-headed windows have moulded architraves, panelled

took place at Hilton his body should be buried in Shareshill church 'in the chancel on the north side before the place where the image of St. Luke stood'.[26] In 1637, however, it is recorded that the tomb stood on the south side of the chancel.[27] Cassandra died in 1570 and was buried at Swynnerton.[28] On the north wall is an elaborate marble tablet flanked by cherubs commemorating Penelope (d. 1726) wife of Henry Vernon of Hilton. Other tablets commemorate John Morrall, vicar (d. 1700),

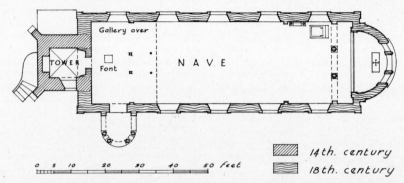

PLAN OF ST. LUKE'S AND ST. MARY THE VIRGIN'S CHURCH

jambs, sill brackets, and shaped aprons. There is a Tuscan porch with an elliptical front and a balustraded parapet. The south doorway has projecting quoins and voussoirs. The north side of the church is much plainer in treatment. The apse has a Venetian window with external details similar to those on the south side of the building.

Internally the apse is divided from the body of the church by an Ionic arcade of three bays with plaster decoration in the spandrels. The Venetian east window has a fluted Ionic order. There is a flat ceiling with plaster enrichments and a modillion cornice. The west gallery, originally supported on square posts, was later extended eastwards with additional supports in the form of iron columns. This alteration probably dates from 1842 when the church was restored.[23]

The fittings, including the altar rails and the painted royal arms, date largely from the 18th century. The original box pews have been altered and reduced in height. The font is dated 1861 and the east window has memorial glass of the same year. Painted boards carry the Commandments, the Creed, the Lord's Prayer, and a list of parish charities.

On window sills near the east end are two alabaster effigies representing Humphrey Swynnerton (d. 1562) and his wife Cassandra. These survive from an altar tomb[24] which was broken up at the 18th-century rebuilding of the church. From the style of the effigies it is thought that the tomb, which bore a memorial inscription and six shields of arms, was the work of the Royleys.[25] By his will of 1561 Humphrey Swynnerton directed that if his death

William Budworth, vicar and master of Brewood School (d. 1748), George B. Clare, vicar (d. 1859), and Robert Butcher, vicar (d. 1908).

In 1548 Shareshill chapel was said to have no plate or ornaments, but in 1553 it possessed one chalice, parcel gilt, and a maslyn censer.[29] In 1956 the plate consisted of a chalice, 1562; a paten with small wafer box as foot; a paten on foot, 1608, the gift of Mary Sanders of Black Lees; and a flagon and cover, 1759–60; all were of silver.[30]

In 1553 there was one bell with a small sanctus bell and a sacring bell,[31] a further bell having been sold for £4 with the assent of the parish. By 1889 there were four bells: (i) 1686; (ii) no inscription; (iii) 1624; (iv) 1632.[32] There is now a ring of six: 1899, J. Taylor & Co.[33]

The registers date from 1565.

In the 18th and early 19th centuries there was no parsonage house at Shareshill,[34] the incumbent in several cases being also the master at Brewood Grammar School and resident in that parish. In 1841 the inhabitants of Shareshill, 'being desirous of securing to the parish a resident minister', subscribed towards the erection of a parsonage house, Lord Hatherton giving £100 and an acre of land.[35] This house, which was built in 1845,[36] stands immediately west of the church. It has a gabled stucco front with 'Tudor' windows and ornamental barge-boards.

NONCONFORMITY. In 1703 William Swan's house in Little Saredon was certified as a Nonconformist place of worship,[37] and a 'constant meeting'

[23] White, *Dir. Staffs.* (1851), 479.
[24] *S.H.C.* vii (2), 57–58.
[25] *Trans. Birm. Arch. Soc.* lxx. 23–24.
[26] *S.H.C.* vii (2), 59.
[27] Ibid. 57–58, quoted from Dugdale's Ch. Notes, among Ashmolean MSS.
[28] Ibid. 59.
[29] Ibid. 1915, 228–9.
[30] Ex inf. the incumbent (1956).

[31] *S.H.C.* 1915, 229.
[32] C. Lynam, *Church Bells of Staffs.* 25 and pl. 113.
[33] A. E. Garbett, 'Church Bells of Staffs.' (*Trans. Old Stafford. Soc.* 1953–4), 18.
[34] Lich. Dioc. Regy., Reg. of non-residence licences 1804–18.
[35] *Staffs. Advertiser*, 3 July 1841.
[36] White, *Dir. Staffs.* (1851).
[37] Matthews, *Congregational Churches of Staffs.* 126.

of Nonconformists was reported at Saredon in 1717.[38] A monthly lecture at Mr. Swain's house at Little Saredon was conducted by an itinerant named 'Russel' apparently for the benefit of Protestant Dissenters who at other times worshipped at Wolverhampton.[39] Swain and Swan are probably the same person and the itinerant was Paul Russell who is mentioned as preaching every fortnight at Coseley (Seisdon hundred).[40] The last reference to this cause appears to be in 1738 when the house of Caleb Martin, Saredon Hall, was certified as a Presbyterian meeting house.[41] In 1851 there was said to be a small independent chapel, built in 1840, at Saredon,[42] but no further record of it has been found.

About 1895 a congregation of Primitive Methodists was meeting in the houses of W. J. Lycett, Manor Farm, Little Saredon, and Mr. Jarvis, Saredon Hill. After a period of open-air meetings an outhouse in Elms Lane, Shareshill, was fitted up as a chapel, c. 1900. Services and a Sunday school were held regularly until c. 1910. The building was later used as a library and for parish meetings but has since been demolished.[43]

PRIMARY SCHOOLS. In 1818 there was in the parish a dame's school for young children, as well as a school kept by a master in a house belonging to the parish.[44] The dame's school seems to have been situated in Little Saredon and to have continued at least until 1851.[45]

The parish school in Shareshill village, housed by 1841 in a building, now demolished, at the south end of the village,[46] was kept in 1851 by a mistress, with an attendance of about 70 children,[47] and was supported by voluntary contributions of the inhabitants and a small weekly payment by the pupils.[48] By 1853 the school had ceased to be held in the schoolhouse cottage which was then leased, the rent going to the Shareshill School Funds.[49] By 1865 it was held on the ground floor of a house at the corner of Hilton Lane,[50] and by 1871 in a building with accommodation for 42; the average attendance was then 27 boys and 35 girls.[51] A new building to the north-east of the village was opened in that year, 'a neat red-brick building', with a residence for a master, paid for by local subscriptions and a government grant.[52] The school was in receipt of a parliamentary grant by 1882 when attendance averaged 81 boys and girls.[53] By 1894 attendance had risen to 112.[54]

The building was enlarged in 1914 to take 160 children.[55] By 1930 the average attendance was 169 boys and girls including infants.[56] In 1954 the school became controlled[57] and is now Shareshill Church of England Voluntary Primary (Controlled) school,[58] with an average attendance of 150, under a master in 1955.[59]

CHARITIES FOR THE POOR. John Kempson and his mother, Mary, by will of 1678, gave land which in 1786 was producing 12s. for the poor of Shareshill.[60] Thomas Worsley bequeathed £10 to the poor of the parish before 1786 when it was producing 10s.[61] Both charities had lapsed by 1822.[62]

Sarah Knight of Cannock, by will of 1847, gave an annual income of £5 to the Minister of Shareshill for distribution to the poor of the parish.[63] The capital was represented by £166 13s. 4d. stock by 1868, and in 1932 the proceeds, £4 3s. 4d., were paid to 24 poor.[64] In 1956 the charity was distributed on 1 January to the old and infirm.[65]

A charity called Adcock's Dole was paid to the poor of the parish by 1861[66] and amounted to £1 2s. 4d. by 1932 when it was paid to 15 aged poor of Shareshill.[67] In 1956 the charity was distributed to the old and infirm on St. Thomas's Day (21 December).[68]

In 1697 Edward Littleton, as lord of the manor of Great Saredon, with Walter Littleton and freeholders and farmers of the manor conveyed to John Kempson a parcel of waste or common from which 5s. was to be paid each Midsummer Day to the Constable of Great Saredon for the use of the township.[69] This rent was carried to the account of the overseers of the poor by 1822,[70] but though still paid in 1895 it had lapsed by 1920.[71]

Tranter's Croft in Cheslyn Hay, leased by the parish officers of Saredon township in 1739 for 25s., was by 1822 producing £3 which was paid to the overseers.[72] The income by 1861 was 40s.[73] Land devised by one Southwell (or Southall) for poor

[38] Dr. Williams's Library, Evans MS.
[39] Matthews, op. cit. 127.
[40] Dr. Williams's Library, Evans MS.
[41] Matthews, op. cit. 127.
[42] White, Dir. Staffs. (1851), 480.
[43] Ex inf. Miss T. Jarvis, Shareshill Post Office (1956). There had been a parochial library, supported by voluntary contributions, from at least 1872 to 1896: P.O. Dir. Staffs. (1872); Kelly's Dir. Staffs. (1896).
[44] Digest of Returns to Sel. Cttee. on Education of Poor, H.C. 224, pp. 866, 875 (1819), ix (2).
[45] White, Dir. Staffs. (1834; 1851).
[46] Tithe Maps and Appt., Shareshill (copy in W.S.L.), no. 173, covering 20 perches.
[47] White, Dir. Staffs. (1851).
[48] P.O. Dir. Staffs. (1860).
[49] Staffs. Endowed Charities, Elem. Educ. [Cd. 2729], p. 110, H.C. (1906), xc.
[50] Ex inf. Miss T. Jarvis, Shareshill Post Office, whose father was at school there.
[51] Returns relating to Elem. Educ. H.C. 201, pp. 364–5 (1871), lv.
[52] Ibid.; P.O. Dir. Staffs. (1872); Staffs. Endowed Char. Elem. Educ. 110.
[53] Rep. of Educ. Cttee. of Council, 1882 [C. 3706–I], H.C. (1883), xxv.
[54] Return of Schools, 1893 [C. 7529], pp. 548–9, H.C.

(1894), lxv. The income from the endowments and subscriptions was then £38 12s. 7d. as against £143 16s. 3d. from grants.
[55] Kelly's Dir. Staffs. (1916).
[56] Staffs. Educ. Cttee. Minutes, Apr. 1930.
[57] Ibid. Nov. 1954; ex inf. Staffs. C.C. Educ. Dept.
[58] Staffs. Educ. Cttee. List of Schools, 1951 (corrected to 1955).
[59] Lich. Dioc. Dir. (1955–6).
[60] Abstract of Returns of Charitable Donations, 1786–8, H.C. 511, pp. 1120–1 (1816), xiv (2). A Mary Kempson, widow, was buried at Shareshill on 19 Feb. 1680/1: Shareshill Par. Reg., from transcript in W.S.L.
[61] Abstract 1786–8, 1120–1.
[62] 9th Rep. Com. Char. H.C. 258, p. 534 (1823), ix.
[63] Charity Com. files.
[64] Ibid.
[65] Ex inf. the Incumbent of Shareshill (1956).
[66] Board in Shareshill church dated 1861.
[67] Charity Com. files.
[68] Ex inf. the incumbent.
[69] 9th Rep. Com. Char. 534.
[70] Ibid.
[71] Charity Com. files.
[72] 9th Rep. Com. Char. 534.
[73] Board in church dated 1861.

widows of Saredon township was producing a rent of 12s. by 1786[74] and may be the Poor's Piece from which by 1822 payment due to the poor of Saredon had ceased[75] but which by 1861 was yielding 12s.[76] A Scheme of 1906 allowed the income of £2 12s. from Tranter's Croft and the Poor's Piece to be used for the poor of Saredon township in grants to hospitals and provident societies, payment of expenses for journeys made for reasons of health, grants of relief in kind, and temporary financial assistance in emergencies.[77] Tranter's Croft was sold c. 1948 and the money invested in £269 2s. 6d. stock.[78] In 1955 the income of the two charities was 12s. from Poor's Piece and £6 14s. 4d. interest.[79]

TEDDESLEY HAY

TEDDESLEY HAY, formerly a division of the forest of Cannock, is a civil parish lying five miles south of Stafford. Although part of the parish of Penkridge for the purpose of tithe by 1252,[1] Teddesley Hay was described as extra-parochial in 1817.[2] In 1300 the Hay was bounded by the River Penk on the west[3] where the present parish boundary is formed by the river and the road from Penkridge to Acton Trussell. The northern boundary in 1300 was formed by the 'Springewall' Brook as far as 'Springewall'.[4] It was probably the same as the present boundary which runs along Wellington Belt through Springslade Pool and down the Springslade.[5] The eastern boundary in 1300 followed 'the high road as far as the ditch of Saint Chadde'.[6] This probably corresponds to the present eastern boundary which runs along the Brocton–Cannock road between Springslade Lodge and Broadhurst Green and then along St. Chad's Ditch to St. Chad's Gate. The present parish boundary there turns due west, but in 1300 the eastern boundary of the Hay continued south along a road called 'Fethersti' to 'the Sholle' (Shoal Hill),[7] thus including Huntington (in Cannock parish) within Cannock Forest. The boundary of Gailey Hay[8] probably began at Shoal Hill.

Only three persons in Teddesley Hay were assessed for the Hearth Tax of 1666.[9] The population was 59 in 1811[10] and 136 in 1951.[11] The area is 2,625 acres.[12]

Much of the parish is occupied by Teddesley Park, formerly the seat of Lord Hatherton (see below). There is a small square entrenchment in the Park known as King Dick's Encampment, and a short iron sword or dagger, thought to be Roman, was found in the fosse in 1780.[13]

The parish is crossed by the main road from Stafford to Cannock. The western boundary of Teddesley Park is formed by the Staffordshire and Worcestershire canal which was keenly promoted by Sir Edward Littleton (d. 1812), the builder of Teddesley Hall.[14] It is crossed by three bridges within the parish. Shutthill Bridge and Parkgate Bridge,[15] each with an adjacent lock, are the original 18th-century bridges. New Bridge dates from c. 1825, probably as part of a new drive approach to Teddesley Hall.[16] It is of stone, now partly replaced by brick, and has a balustraded parapet terminating in octagonal piers.

Sir Edward Littleton, who seems to have undertaken extensive inclosing in Teddesley Hay after his succession in 1558,[17] was accused by Lord Stafford in 1561 of committing spoils there[18] and by the Earl of Oxford in 1569 of making inclosures which interfered with the pasture rights in the Hay of the earl's tenants in Acton Trussell and Bednall and with their common way through it for driving their cattle to 'Cannock Wood and Cannock Heath'.[19] A park in Teddesley Hay, mentioned in 1589,[20] and 'le coppy' there were held of the king by Sir Edward's son at his death in 1610,[21] and in 1675 the inhabitants of Penkridge and Bednall tried to have both park and coppice thrown open.[22] Common land in Teddesley Hay was inclosed in 1827 under the Act of 1814.[23]

The superiority of the cattle strain at Teddesley Park was noted in 1794 when the several hundred acres kept in hand by Sir Edward Littleton were mainly turf with little or no grain.[24] Sir Edward and his tenants had also been improving the breed of grey-faced hornless sheep, native to Cannock Chase, by crossing with Ross rams.[25] The 1st Lord Hatherton (d. 1863), who succeeded Sir Edward in 1812,[26] undertook an extensive development of his lands here.[27] By 1850, despite the gravelly nature of the soil and the neglected state of the land before he began his draining and irrigation, he was farming 1,700 acres with great success, producing good crops of wheat and barley and supporting 200 head of cattle, including a herd of Herefords, and 2,000

[74] Abstract, 1786–8, 1120–1. An Ann Southall, widow, of Great Saredon was buried at Shareshill on 20 Feb. 1692/3: Shareshill Par. Reg. from transcript in W.S.L.

[75] 9th Rep. Com. Char. 534.

[76] Board in church dated 1861.

[77] Charity Com. files.

[78] Ibid.

[79] Ibid.

[1] Close R. 1251–3, 128.

[2] W. Pitt, Topog. Hist. of Staffs. (1817), 257.

[3] S.H.C. v (1), 177.

[4] Ibid.

[5] The boundary ran along a field called Springwall Piece c. 1841: Tithe Maps and Appt., Penkridge (copy in W.S.L.).

[6] S.H.C. v (1), 177.

[7] Ibid.

[8] See p. 104.

[9] S.H.C. 1927, 71.

[10] V.C.H. Staffs. i. 320.

[11] Census, 1951, Staffs.

[12] Ibid.

[13] V.C.H. Staffs. i. 193; S.R.O., D. 260/M/E. 357.

[14] Pitt, Staffs. 257 For a portrait of Sir Edward in 1756 see plate facing p. 132.

[15] See plate facing p. 179.

[16] It had not been built by 1812: Tithe Maps and Appt., Penkridge (copy in W.S.L.), the map being a copy of one of 1812. It is similar in style to Bull Bridge, Penkridge (see p. 105) and St. Thomas's Bridge, Baswich: see p. 2.

[17] W.S.L., C.B. Littleton Transcripts.

[18] Cal. S.P. Dom. 1547–80, 180.

[19] W.S.L., C.B. Littleton Transcripts.

[20] 'Hatherton Charters' (S.H.C. 1928), 164–5.

[21] C 142/320, no. 71.

[22] S.R.O., D. 260/M/box 4, bdle. g.

[23] Penkridge Inclosure Act, 54 Geo. III, c. 50 (priv. act); S.R.O., Q/RDc 22.

[24] W. Pitt, General View of Agric. of Staffs. (1794), 49.

[25] Ibid. 53.

[26] Complete Peerage, vi. 394–5.

[27] W.S.L., S. 1549, Staffs. Parishes, Newspaper Cuttings, ii, Penkridge.

head of Southdown sheep.[28] There were 700 acres in regular cultivation, mainly on four-course rotation, and the rest was parkland, irrigated meadow, and some less developed high ground adjoining Cannock Chase.[29] Lord Hatherton also gave much encouragement to the tenant farmers of the district[30] and by 1860 had established a free agricultural college at Teddesley Hay, where 30 boys were educated spending most of the day on his farm and the rest in 'educational pursuits'.[31]

The broad-leaved woodland of Teddesley Hay was felled during the Second World War, but subsequently Lord Hatherton leased 641 acres, mainly to the east of the main road, to the Forestry Commission as an extension of the Cannock Chase State Forest.[32] Work was begun in 1950, the land being replanted with broad-leaved trees, mostly oak and beech.[33]

Thomas Lord Paget had iron works in Teddesley Hay by 1576,[34] the site of which may be indicated by the Springslade Pool on the northern boundary of the parish to the west of the main road. There was boring for coal in Teddesley Hay in 1686 and 1753,[35] and the National Coal Board had made a successful boring by 1951 at Springslade Pool.[36] There is now (1956) a gravel quarry on the site of the former Pottal Pool in the south of the parish.

THE HAY. Teddesley Hay formed a division of the royal forest of Cannock possibly by 1100[37] and certainly from 1236[38] until 1550.[39] In 1236 the custody was in the hands of Robert de Brok, lord of Pillaton (in Penkridge), who farmed his office for 2 marks a year and held the vill of Huntington by this service of keeping the Hay.[40] The custody followed the same descent as Huntington and Pillaton[41] until at least 1558,[42] after which date the office seems to have been discontinued.[43] The Hay was valued at £8 in 1293.[44] Leland, c. 1535, mentions 'a praty Chace by Pencriche of the Kinges where Littleton of Pillenhaul is foster by inheritance'.[45]

The Hay was granted by the Crown to John Dudley, Earl of Warwick, and his heirs in 1550,[46] and a grant of it was made in 1554 for life to his widow[47] who died the following year.[48] It subsequently passed

into the Littleton family, Sir Edward holding it of the king at his death in 1610.[49] Teddesley Hay descended in the family with Pillaton,[50] becoming the family seat in place of Pillaton soon after 1742[51] and being described as a manor in 1817[52] and 1827.[53] Such manorial rights as existed in 1940 were held by the 4th Lord Hatherton.[54] Some land was sold in 1947,[55] and a further 2,976 acres, along with the Hall, was sold in 1953.[56]

A moated site, now obliterated, lay about 200 yds. north-west of the Hall in 1754,[57] indicating the existence of a medieval house. In 1650 'Tedgley Lodge', probably this house or its successor, was occupied by Fisher Littleton, a kinsman of Sir Edward,[58] and in 1666 it was taxable for seven hearths.[59] The large 18th-century mansion known as Teddesley Hall was built by Sir Edward Littleton, the 4th baronet, who succeeded in 1742.[60] By 1754 he was already in occupation, but it is probable that the stable and service wings of the house were not yet completed.[61] The cost of building is said to have been largely defrayed by hoards of coins, found in 1742 and 1749 behind panelling at Pillaton Hall; these realized over £15,000.[62] The house remained the seat of the Littleton family but was no longer used as a residence after the death of the 3rd Lord Hatherton in 1930.[63] During the Second World War it was requisitioned and occupied by troops and prisoners. It then stood empty until its sale by the 5th Lord Hatherton in 1953. In 1954 the main house was demolished,[64] the stable and service wings being retained by the new owner for storage purposes.

In its original form[65] Teddesley Hall, built of red brick with stone dressings, consisted of a central house linked by curved screen walls to two flanking courtyard blocks, one containing stables, the other kitchens and service quarters. The house itself was a tall square building, having three stories and a basement. On all four sides there were seven windows to each of the upper floors, and the south-west or garden front had a projecting splayed bay as its central feature. On the ground floor a pedimented doorway with rusticated pilasters was approached by a double flight of steps. Internally the central room was octagonal and was enriched with contemporary

[28] Ibid.
[29] Ibid.
[30] Ibid.; *Staffs. Advertiser*, 11 Oct. 1856.
[31] *P.O. Dir. Staffs.* (1860).
[32] *Britain's Forests: Cannock Chase* (Forestry Commission, 1950), 7, map.
[33] Ibid. 7.
[34] W.S.L., D. 1734, Account Bks. for Iron Works, 1576–82; E 101/546/16.
[35] S.R.O., D. 260/M/E. 10.
[36] Ex inf. the National Coal Board, Cannock.
[37] *S.H.C.* 1928, 164.
[38] *Bk. of Fees*, 7.
[39] *Cal. Pat.* 1549–51, 365.
[40] *Bk. of Fees*, 7.
[41] See pp. 76, 119.
[42] C 142/124, no. 178. On the death of William de Engleton in 1398 the king granted the custody to William Walsale (*Cal. Pat.* 1396–9, 293), but by 1450 it had reverted to the hereditary claimant: C 139/137.
[43] The grant of the keepership to Lord Stafford in May 1558 (*Cal. Pat.* 1557–8, 254), was probably a grant of the reversion of the herbage and pannage: *Cal. S.P. Dom.* 1547–80, 165; *Cal. Pat.* 1560–3, 291–2; *S.H.C.* 1938, 81–82. The herbage and pannage passed to Sir Edward Littleton in 1567: *S.H.C.* xiii. 264.
[44] *S.H.C.* vi (1), 270.
[45] Leland, *Itin.* ed. Toulmin Smith, v (1910), 22.

[46] *Cal. Pat.* 1549–51, 365.
[47] Ibid. 1553–4, 129.
[48] *Complete Peerage*, ix. 726.
[49] *S.H.C.* xiii. 246; *Cal. S.P. Dom.* 1547–80, 180; *S.H.C.* 1939, 123; ibid. 1928, 164–5; C 142/320, no. 71.
[50] See p. 119.
[51] Burke, *Peerage* (1931), 1198.
[52] Pitt, *Staffs.* 257.
[53] S.R.O., Q/RDc 22.
[54] *Kelly's Dir. Staffs.* (1940).
[55] W.S.L., Sale Cat., B/2/10.
[56] Ex inf. Teddesley and Hatherton Estate Office, Penkridge (1955). The Hall was bought by Mr. E. Buxton of the Home Farm, Teddesley: *Staffs. Chronicle*, 5 Oct. 1954.
[57] S.R.O., D. 260/M/E. 353 (a, b), map 10. It is marked as 'site of old house'.
[58] *Cal. Cttee. for Compounding*, 2081.
[59] *S.H.C.* 1927, 71.
[60] Burke, *Peerage* (1931), 1198.
[61] S.R.O., D. 260/M/E. 353 (a, b), map 10, where the wings are shown in outline only.
[62] J. C. Tildesley, *Penkridge* (1886), 63; *S.H.C.* 1927, 34–36.
[63] Ex inf. Teddesley and Hatherton Estate Office.
[64] *Staffs. Chronicle*, 5 Oct. 1954.
[65] W.S.L., Staffs. Views, x, pp. 119–24; National Buildings Record Coll. Phot. 1953; S.R.O., D. 260/M/E. 368; see plate facing p. 179.

plasterwork. One of its arched niches contained an 18th-century organ. The flanking screen walls had a treatment of stone pilasters and oval piercings. The service blocks are of two stories, and each has a square central courtyard. The entrance court to the house lay between them. The plainness and height of the house, accentuated by falling ground to the south-west, gave it a stark appearance, and even in 1789 it was described as 'rather deficient in the usual graces of architecture'.[66] The name of the architect originally employed c. 1750 is doubtful, but it is known that Charles Cope Trubshaw (1715–72) of Haywood (Pirehill hundred) worked at Teddesley.[67] Between 1757 and 1759 William Baker (1705–71) of Audlem (Ches.) received sums from Sir Edward Littleton for drawing plans and 'in part for building his house at the Coppice'[68] (see below). It is probable that at this date Teddesley Hall had been standing for some years, and Baker's accounts may refer to the service wings only or to the farmhouse about a mile away at Teddesley Coppice. In 1814 schemes were submitted by Joseph Potter of Lichfield,[69] probably working in conjunction with Jeffrey Wyatt,[70] for adding a grandiose range on the garden side, but

these were never executed. In 1899 a billiard room was designed by Henry T. Hare,[71] and additions to the entrance front, including a first-floor Ionic colonnade, were probably of the same date.

A small farmhouse south of Parkgate Bridge and called Park Gate House c. 1841[72] was formerly known as Little Moor.[73] It is partly timber-framed and probably dates from the early 17th century. The Home Farm[74] and Teddesley Coppice are 18th-century houses, the latter described in 1860 as 'a neat unassuming mansion'.[75] 'Dairy House' at the Home Farm is an early-19th-century red-brick group consisting of two octagonal lodges with Gothic windows, connected by a low curved range of outbuildings. Many of the other buildings on the estate, including extensive agricultural buildings at the Home Farm, date from the time of the 1st Lord Hatherton (d. 1863). Keeper's Lodge at the southern boundary of the park is a mid-19th-century Italianate cottage of yellow brick with a low-pitched roof. A lodge at Teddesley Hall was designed by Francis Goodwin in 1835,[76] and other buildings on the estate may also have been his work. Many farms and cottages date from the later 19th century.

[66] Gent. Mag. 1789, lix. 1078.
[67] H. M. Colvin, Biog. Dict. of Eng. Architects, 624.
[68] S.H.C. 1950–1, 126.
[69] S.R.O., D. 260/M/E. 359–71.
[70] Ibid. E. 372. Wyatt made visits in 1814 and 1817, charging 2s. 6d. per mile for the journeys from London. His account totalled £232.
[71] S.R.O., D. 260/M/E. 373. Hare was architect of the

County Buildings, Stafford.
[72] Tithe Maps and Appt., Penkridge (copy in W.S.L.), no. 1292.
[73] S.R.O., D. 260/M/E. 353 (a), Map 10.
[74] Tithe Maps and Appt., Penkridge (copy in W.S.L.).
[75] P.O. Dir. Staffs. (1860); it was then the residence of Capt. Moseley.
[76] Francis Goodwin, Rural Architecture, i, suppl. pls. 1–4.

INDEX

The following abbreviations have been used, sometimes with the addition of the letter s to form the plural: Abp., Archbishop; adv., advowson; agric., agriculture; Alb., Albert; Alex., Alexander; And., Andrew; Ant., Anthony; Arth., Arthur; Bart., Bartholomew; Beat., Beatrice; Ben., Benjamin; Bp., Bishop; bro., brother; cast., castle; Cath., Catherine; ch., church; chant., chantry; chap., chapel; char., charity; Chas., Charles; Chris., Christopher; coll., college; ct., court; Ctss., Countess; d., died; Dan., Daniel; Dchss., Duchess; dom. arch., domestic architecture; Edm., Edmund; Edw., Edward; Eliz., Elizabeth; fam., family; fl., flourished; Fred., Frederick; Geo., George; Geoff., Geoffrey; Gil., Gilbert; grds., grandson; Hen., Henry; Herb., Herbert; Hosp., hospital; Humph., Humphrey; incl., inclosure; ind., industry; Jas., James; Jos., Joseph; Laur., Laurence; Lawr., Lawrence; Leon., Leonard; m., married; man., manor; Mat., Matthew; Mchnss., Marchioness; mkt., market; Nat., Nathaniel; neph., nephew; Nich., Nicholas; nonconf., nonconformity; par., parish; Phil., Philip; pop., population; prot., protestant; Revd., Reverend; Reyn., Reynold; Ric., Richard; riv., river; rly., railway; Rob., Robert; Rog., Roger; Rom., Roman; Rom. Cath., Roman Catholic; s., son; Sam., Samuel; sch., school; Sim., Simon; sis., sister; Steph., Stephen; stn., station; Thos., Thomas; vic., vicarage; Vct., Viscount; Vctss., Viscountess; w., wife; Wal., Walter; wid., widow; Wm., William.

Achi s. of Burtheimer, 27
Ackroyd, Rog., 7
Acton, Adam, 128; John de, 5, 13; Rob, 128
Acton Gate, *see* Castle Church
Acton Trussell (Actone), in Baswich, 1, 5, **11–17**, 103, 126, 144–6, 182; adv., 15; bridge, 11, 12, 15, 110, 146; chap., 7, 15, 17; char., 17; ch., 15–17; commons, 14; dom. arch., 12; farms, 14, 15; fields, 14; Gipsy Green, 12; incl., 12, 14; mans., 6 *n*, 12–14; mill, 11, 13 *n*, 14, 15, 146; Moat House, 12, 14, 16; sch., 12, 17; vic., 12, 15, 17; vicars, 16, 17
Adam s. of John, 27, 92
Adam s. of Maud, 124
Adam, Rob., 29
Adams, Ric., 124
Adbaston, *see* Flashbrook
Adcock, —, 181
Adleinere, Wm., 120
Adshed, Thos., 145
Africa, South, 133
Agricultural Executive Committee, 104
Agriculture and Fisheries, Min. of, 95
Ailric (fl. before 1066), 30, 117
Ailric, wid. of (fl. *c.* 1149), 27
Air Ministry, 158
Akesey, Beat., 89; Hugh de, 89
Albo Monasterio, Alan de, 117; Eve de, 117; Rog. de, 117
Albrighton (Salop.), 177
Albrighton Hussey (Salop.), 57
Alcock, A., 147
Alde (Alle), John de, 89
Aldenham, John de, 39, 40
Alle, *see* Alde
Allen, Revd. Edw., 96; Wm., 96
Alli (fl. before 1066), 120
Allsop (Alsop), Revd. Arth. Ric., 16, 17; Edith Mary, 9; Herb. T., 9; fam., 16
Alport, Eleanor, 64, 66, 96, 130; Thos., 60; Wm. (fl. 1567), 74; Wm. (d. 1721), 16, 40, 64, 66, 82, 130, 179
Alrewas, *see* Orgrave
Alric (fl. before 1066), 111
Alsop, *see* Allsop
Alstone, *see* Bradley
Alveton, Nichola, w. of John de, *see* Blund
Alvric (fl. 1086), 55
Amasal Ltd., 3
Anglesey, Marquess of, 5, 57; *and see* Paget
Anne, queen, 42
Ansell, —, 140
Ansger (fl. 1086), 86
Anson, Edw., 147; Geo., 5, 145, 146; Mary, 145 *n*; Thos. (fl. 1752), 145; Thos., Vct. Anson (d. 1818), 145, 146, 158, 165; Thos. Edw., Earl of Lichfield, 3, 5; Thos. Frances,

Earl of Lichfield (d. 1918), 3, 5, 165; Thos. Geo., Earl of Lichfield (d. 1892), 146 *n*, 148; Thos. Wm., Earl of Lichfield (d. 1854), 145, 158; Wm. (fl. 1617), 146, 147; Wm. (fl. 1658), 13; Wm. (fl. 1768), 160; — (fl. 1780), 158
Anson, Vct., *see* Anson, Thos.
Anzelark, Revd. Rob., 96
Apeton, *see* Bradley
Appleyard, E., 67
Arblaster, Jas., 60; R. G., 177
Archer, Mary, 44
Armishaw, Ralph, 164
Armitage, 149, 152, 155, 158 *n*, 173; Hawksyard, 57, 157; man., 155; *and see* Handsacre
Armstrong, Charlotte, 43
Arundel, Earl of, *see* Howard, Thos.
Ashebye, Joyce, 63
Aspley, in Brewood, 39; farm, 27; man., 27
Assent, Rog., 60
Astley, Thos., 30 *n*
Aston, Bridget, 123; Sir Edw. (fl. 1538), 59; Edw. (d. 1569), 6; Edw. (fl. 1584), 6; Eliz., 137; Isabel, w. of Rog. de, m. 2 Wm. de Chetwynd, 6; Joan, *see* Littleton; John de (d. by 1353), 6; John de (d. 1484), 6; John (d. 1523), 6; John (d. by 1595), 122; Marg., 123; Mary, 123; Ric., 123; Rob., 6; Rog. de (fl. 1307), 6, 59; Rog. de (d. before 1365), 6; Rog. (d. 1448), 6; Thos. (d. before 1413), 6; Thos. (fl. 1538), and his w. Bridget, 122; Thos. (fl. 1595), 123; Sir Thos. (fl. 1604), 123; Thos. (fl. 1638), 6; Wal. (fl. 1584), 6; Wal., Lord Aston (d. 1714), 60; Wm., 123; fam., 6, 59, 60
Aston, Lord, *see* Aston, Wal.
Aston (Warws.), 146
Aston, Wheaton, *see* Lapley
Atkinson, Revd. T. D., 165
Attewell, Ric., 184
Audlem (Ches.), 184
Audley, Emma, dau. of Hen. de, m. Griffin ap Madoc, 175, 176, 178; Sir Hen. de (fl. 1228), 57, 154; Hen. de (fl. 1243), 175; Jas. de, 57, 61, 154, 178; fam., 175
augmentations, court of, 54, 130
Ault, Jos., 81
Austin, John, 39
Avarne, Ellen, 171
Avery, Edw., 125
Avice (fl. before 1261), 120
Awnoilus, Wm., 27
Aysheton, Peter, 111, 130

Backhouse (or Chamberlain), Anne, 92; Francis, 92; Geo., and his w. Marg., 92, 93; John (fl. 1589), s. of

John, 92; John (fl. 1589), s. of Thos., 92; John (fl. 1608), s. of Geo., 92; Marg. (fl. 1562), w. of Thos., 92; Marg. (fl. 1588), w. of Geo., 92; Marg. (fl. 1688), *see* Fowler; Thos. (fl. 1562), 92; Thos. (fl. 1629), 93, 96, 99, 100
Baddeley, Geo., 11
Bagley, —, bellfounder, 66
Bagnall, Ric., 96
Bagnall & Sons Ltd., 101
Bagot, Anne, m. Thos. Lane, 34 *n*; Ascira, w. of Rob., 139; Edm., 139; Eleanor, w. of Wm. de, *see* Louvaine; Eliz., 66; Joan, 139; Hervey (fl. 1194), 113, 128; Hervey (fl. 1294), 89; Millicent, *see* Stafford; Sir Ralph, 139; Ric. (fl. 1279), 139; Ric. (fl. 1310), 142; Rob. (d. by 1249), 139, 144; Rob. (fl. 1276), 139; Wm. (d. by 1182), 139, 141; Wm. (d. by 1236), 139, 141; Wm. (fl. 1285), 139; Wm. (d. *c.* 1324), 89, 139; Wm., Lord Bagot (d. 1798), 10
Baillie (Bayley), Algernon Harold, 9; Wm., 124
Baker, John, 101; Wm., 184
Ball, Eliz., 75; Jack, 66
Bamford (Balmford), John, 163, 168; Wm., 165
Bangley, 106 *n*; Park, 128
Banks, E., 44
Barber (Barbor, Barbour), Catn., 172; Geo., 24, 35; Humph. (fl. 1487), 6, 90; Humph. (d. by 1531), 91 *n*; Jas., 35; John (fl. 1452), 90; John (fl. 1475), 6; John (fl. 1543), 91; John (fl. 1598), 145, 146; Joyce, *see* Eyton; Rob. (d. 1532), 6, 90; Rob. (fl. 1744), 31, 35; Thos., 88
Bardmerscote (Bermundeston), Hen. de, and his w. Ismannia, 111, 123
Bardolf, Amice, *see* Beverley; Rob., 109 *n*
Barentyn, Drew, 80
Barker, Thos., 106 *n*; Miss, 106 *n*; —, ironmaster, 21, 106 *n*
Barlow, John (d. *c.* 1804), 14; John (fl. 1819), 14; — (fl. *c.* 1562), 57
Barnaby, Revd. Thos., 97
Barnes, Sarah Jane, 67
Barnesley, Wm., 92
Barnett, Sam., 165
Barnfield, Sampson, 89
Bartlem, Edw., 115; Ric., 115
Barton, Hen. de (or Passelewe) (fl. 1325), 163; Hen. (fl. 1697), 61; Thos., 61
Barton, in Bradley, 88
Barwicke, Abraham, 46
Basset, Mrs. E., 124; Marg., *see* St. Pierre; Ralph (fl. 1295), 33; Ralph (d. 1390), Lord Basset of Drayton, 88

INDEX

Hamilton, Capt. Geo., 153
Hamlett, Geo., and sons, 3
Hammerwich, in St. Michael's, Lichfield, 64
Hamper, Wm., 86
Hampton, Ric. de, 60
Hamstall Ridware, 37
Hanbury, 171
Hand, Chas. Fred., 148; fam., 148
Handsacre, in Armitage, 152; man., 155
Handsworth, 90
Handy, Wm., 141
Hankeford, see Haukeford
Hankyn, Wm., 13
Hanson, Chas., 167
Harborne, 27
Harcourt, Isabel, 175; John (fl. 1476), 175, 177; Leon., 115 n; Marg., wid. of Rob., 175; Ric. (d. 1400), and his w. Marg., 175; Ric. (fl. 1406), 175; Ric. (fl. 1443), and his w. Eleanor, 176; Sir Rob. (d. 1470), 175, 177; Sir Rob. (d. by 1509), 175; Sir Sim., 27, 175; Sir Wal., 175; fam. 175
Harding, Esther, 9, 11
Hare, Cecil, architect, 9; Hen. T., 184
Harper, Thos., 36
Harpesfield, Edw., 156
Harris, Eliz., 38; Miss M., 167; Thos. (fl. 1666), 38; Thos., s. of Thos. (fl. 1666), 38
Harrison, Geoff., 7; Wm., 156, 157; Wm., messrs., 62, 78
Harte, Edw., 124
Hartley, Thos., 44
Hartshorn, Thos., 93
Haseley, see Baswich
Haszard, Mrs. Gerald, dau. of Capt. W. S. B. Levett, 3, 7
Hatherton, Lord, 182; and see Littleton
Hatherton, in St. Peter's, Wolverhampton, 54, 68, 77, 78, 104, 108, 119, 127, 177, 178; chap., 131; Colliery, 78; Hall, 71; mill, 177; vic., 135
Hatton (the Hattons), in Brewood, 18, 25, 27, 33, 38; House, 33; man., 32, 33
Haughton (Halghton, Halughton, Houghton), Marg., 93; Sir Rob., 118, 121; Thos., 138; Thos. de (fl. 1335), 93
Haughton, 88, 93 n, 143
Haukeford (Hankeford), Ric., 109; Sir Wm., 109
Havergal, Frances Ridley, 174; Wm. Hen., musical composer, 174
Havering, Ric. de, 111 n
Hawkins, Hen., Ltd., 63; Jos., 101; Thos. A., 101; —, 177
Hawkins Tile Works, 177
Hawksyard, see Armitage
Hayes, New, see Cannock
Haymes, Hen., 89
Haywood, 2, 8, 59, 61, 184; Chase, 59; man., 2, 5, 12, 13; park, 59
Hazel Slade, in Rugeley (later in Cannock), 49, 52 n, 64, 147, 149, 152; ch., 67, 72; nonconf. chap., 69, 70; sch., 72, 74
Hearn, John, 160
Heath (Heth), Thos., 51; Mrs., 17
Heath Hayes (Five Ways), in Cannock, 51, 62, 64; ch., 67; colliery, 62; nonconf. chap., 70, 71; sch., 73
Hedgeford, riv., 61
Hednesford (Edenesford, Hedenedford), in Cannock, 49, 51, 52, 54, 56, 57, 60–64, 69, 78, 152, 162; char., 74; ch., 64, 66, 72; collieries, 62, 63; Hill Top, 49, 73; Hills, 52;

inds., 62, 63; inn, 49, 53; Lodge, 52, 53; mkt., 62; nonconf., 69–71; Pye Green, 49; Rom. Cath., 68, 73; sch., 68, 72–74; Uxbridge Pit, 49, 62; West Hill, 64, 71, 74; and see Heath Hayes; Wimblebury
Hednesford, Old, in Cannock, 53, 69
Hellier, Thos. Shaw, 122, 127
Henney, John, 114; Wm., 114
Henry II, 21, 25, 155; as Duke of Normandy, 53, 57, 79 n, 81
Henry III, 54, 61, 95
Henry VIII, 88, 92, 118
Herbert, John, 133
Hercy, Eliz., see Stanley; John, 57
Hervey (fl. 1086), 114, 122, 174, 175
Hervy, Wm., 60
Heth, see Heath
Heyworth, Wm., Bp. of Coventry and Lichfield, 33
Hick, Edw., 78; Thos., 78
Hide, see Hyde
Higgot, John, 16
Higley, Ric., 48
Hille, Thos., 159
Hillier, A. N., 141
Hilton, in St. Peter's, Wolverhampton, 77, 130, 174, 179, 180; Park, 174
Hinde, Nat., 130
Hinds, Ben., 177
Hinton, Rog., 89, 99
Hitch, N., 43
Hitchecocke, Thos., 90
Hitchings, Revd. Gerard, 9; Mary, 9
Hodington, John de, 174; Kath., see Shareshill
Holford, Jas., 63
Holland, Dr. Chas., 122; Geo., 45; Wm., 45, 46, 122; fam., 43
Hollinhurst, Edw., w. of, 165; Ric., 153
Hollyhock, —, 98
Holmes, Wm. Lionel, and his w. Marg., 114
Holt, Jas., 140
Home Office, 90
Hook (Dorset), 89, 109, 140, 145
Hoord, Jane, m. Sir John Giffard, 43
Hopkins, Sam., 158; Sarah, 158, 162, 163, 165, 169, 170, 172
Hore, John, 31
Horsebrok, John de, 40
Horsebrook, see Brewood
Hose, Hugh, 108, 129; Wal., 108
Hoskins, Abraham, 93; Sarah, 93
Hothum, Wm. de, Abp. of Dublin, Dean of Penkridge, 117, 128
Hough, Wm., 60
Houghton, see Haughton
Howard, Chas., Earl of Nottingham, 80; Hen., Earl of Stafford (d. 1719), 87; Hen. Edw. John, Dean of Lichfield, 35, 40; Marg., m. Ric. Leveson, 80; Mary, see Stafford; Thos., Earl of Arundel, Earl Marshal (d. 1646), 87; Wm., Vct. Stafford (d. 1680), 85, 87; Cardinal, 87
Howell, Miss B., 45; Geo., 34
Hubball, Mrs. M., 45
Hugh s. of Ralph (fl. 1208), 91
Hugh s. of Wm., 124
Hull, Misses, 168 n
Hulme Trustees, 15
Huntedon, Alfred de, 75, 119; Brun de, 76, 119
Huntington (Estendone), in Cannock, 49, 51, 54, 64, 68, **75–77**, 126, 128, 182, 183; chap., 64; chars., 77; ch., 76, 77; colliery, 62, 75, 105; Farm, 75, 76; fields, 76; incl., 76; man., 75, 76; nonconf., 76; sch., 77; Shoal Hill, 59, 75

Hurd, John, 106; Ric., Bp. of Coventry and Lichfield, Bp. of Worcester, 26, 106
Hurleston, Rob., 162
Hussey, Alice, m. Rob. Boteler, 125; Anna, 125; Beat., see More; Dorothy, 125; Fowke (fl. 1724), 31, 32; John (fl. 1300), 109; John (fl. 1503), 109; Phineas, 31; Ric., 57; Thos., 109; Wal., 108; Wm. (fl. 1435), 125; Wm. (fl. 1480), 125; Wm. (d. 1532), 125, 126, 129; fam., 37, 109
Hyde (Hide), Eliz., m. Ric. Lane, 27, 32, 34; Giles, 27; Iseult, wid. of Thos. de la, 27, 34; Joan, wid. of Ralph, 27, 32, 34; Marg., w. of Thos. de la, 27; Nich., 27; Parnel, wid. of Thos. de Gypwich, 34; Ralph (d. by 1420), 27, 32, 34; Rog. de (fl. 1222), 35; Rog. de la (fl. before 1295), 33, 34; Thos. de la (d. 1314), 27, 34; Thos., s. of Thos. (fl. 1316), 34; Thos. de la (fl. 1341), 27, 32, 36; Thos. (fl. 1354), s. of Ralph, 27; Thos (fl. 1650), 58; Wal., s. of Rog. (fl. 1295), 33, 34; Wm. de la, 34
Hyde (Hyde Lee), see Castle Church
Hyde (la Hyde), in Brewood, 27, 28, 30, 33, 36, 38, 47; Farm, 34; man., 33, 34, 39; mill, 39.
Hyde, in Coppenhall, 138 n, 139, 140, 142; man., 139, 140

Icke, Wm., 38
India, 35
industries: agricultural machinery, 20; boots and shoes, 161; brass, 161; breweries, 24, 161; bricks and tiles, 3, 63, 101, 161, 173; carbon, 20, 106; chemicals, 161; coal-mining, 62, 63, 78, 101, 102, 149, 161, 183; edge-tools, 49, 61–63, 78; electrical, 63, 161; engineering, 24, 63, 161; hats, 161; iron, 20, 21, 63, 78, 106, 151, 161, 162; instruments, 63; jewellery, 63; lead, 101; lock-making, 20; malting, 20; quarrying, 106, 161, 183; salt, 3, 84; saw mills, 63; tanning, 161; tar-distilling, 20, 161
Inge, Mrs. C. B., 7; Revd. Francis Geo., 8, 9; Very Revd. W. R., 7
Ingestre, Vct., see Chetwynd-Talbot, John
Ingestre, 6, 88, 117, 157
Ingram, wid., 138; —, 106
Innocent II, pope, 26
Ireland, 93
Isabella, Queen, 108
Isham, Giles, 92
Italy, 165

Jackson, John, 175; Ric., 8
James I, 129
James II, 87
James, Edw. (fl. 1589), 114; Edw. (fl. 1663), 114; Edw. (fl. 1695), 135; John, 38; Mary Ann, 165; Rob., 114; Thos., 165
Jarvis, —, 181
Jeffries, —, 70
Jekyll, Sir Jos. and Lady, 15
Jellicoe, Wm., 31
Jenks, Mary, 168
Jennings, Wm., 92
Jerningham, Edw., 86, 98; Sir Geo., 98; Sir Geo. Wm., Lord Stafford (d. 1851), 86, 93, 95, 116; Sir Wm., 85, 87
Joan, queen of Hen. IV, 86

John, king, 18, 21, 26, 53, 114
John, Canon of Penkridge, 120
John, Chaplain of Penkridge, 110
John s. of Ralph, 27
John s. of Walron the Miller, 39
John, Adam s. of, 27, 92
Johnson, Lucy Emma, 15, 100; Dr. Sam., 152; —, 172
Jones, Norman, 9; Rob., 30
Jordan, clerk of Roger de Fécamp, 130
Joyce, N., 65
Juliana, dau. of Rose, 115
Justice, John, 61

Kanocbury, see Cannock
Keeling, Fred J., 43; fam., 133
Keen, Geo., 90; Wm., 90
Kempson, Revd. Hen., 43, 46; John, 181; Mary, 181
Kendrick, see Wood, Kendrick, and Williams
Kenefare, Osb. de, 176
Kenilworth, John de, 119; Marg. see Elmedon
Kenilworth (Warws.), 89, 97
Kent, Edw., 39
Kenysson, Revd. J. H., 135
Kibblestone, see Stone
Kiddemore (Kyrrymore), in Brewood, 18, 19, 27; Green, 18, 19, 24, 33, 38, 39
Kidderminster (Worcs.), 39
Kilkenny, Ric. de, 115
King, Greg., 36, 41 n, 91, 132 n, 133; Sir Roland, 25
Kinvaston, see Wolverhampton
Kinver, 176
Knevett, Thos., 93
Knight, Sarah, 75, 181
Knightley, John de, 80; Rob., 32, 39; Thos. (fl. 1473), 26, 39
Knowles, Mary, 152
Kyrrymore, see Kiddemore

Lakeham, Rob., 45
Lancashire Dynamo Electronic Products Ltd., 158
Landor (Lander), Anna, 164; Eliz. (fl. 1679), 6; Eliz. (d. 1753), 164; Eliz. (d. 1814), 165; Geo., 3, 6; Jos., and his w. Mary, 164; Mary, 165; Rob., 165; Thos., 164, 171; Thos., s. of Thos., 171 n; Wal., 164, 171; Wm., 165; Mrs. (fl. 1786), 100; fam., 153
Landywood, in Gt. Wyrley, 78; chap., 82; colliery, 78; farms, 77, 78; sch., 82
Landywood, Upper in Gt. Wyrley, 81
Lane, Anne (fl. 1517), w. of Ric., 43; Anne (fl. 1710), 156; Anne, see Bagot; Eliz., see Hyde; J. H. H. V., 7; J. N., 101; Jane, 34, 47; John (d. 1470), 32, 34; John (fl. 1547), 33; John (d. 1576), 34, 43 n; John (d. 1605), 28, 32–34; John (d. 1667), 34; John (d. 1748), 28, 30, 31, 34; John (d. 1782), 101; Marg., 43 n; Margery, 34; Ralph (d. 1477), 27, 34, Ric. (d. by 1439), 27, 30, 32–34, Ric. (d. 1517), 34, 43; Sarah, see Fowler; Thos. (d. 1589), 34; Thos. (d. 1660), 34; Thos. (d. 1715), 34; Thos. (fl. 1747), 34; Capt. (fl. 1680), 28; fam., 27, 30, 32–34
Langford, John, 137; Rob., 109.
Langley, C. O., 37
Langton, Wal., Bp. of Coventry and Lichfield, 26
Lansant, Eliz., see Trumwyn; Rog., 55
Lanthony Secunda (Glos.), abbey, 57

Lapley, 19, 64, 103; ch., 20; Wheaton Aston, 135, 137
Launder, see Lander
Lawson, Jas., 102
Leacroft, in Cannock, 49, 51, 52, 54–56, 60–62, 64; char., 74, 75; farms, 53, 56; Old Hall, 56, 65; pop., 49
Leche, John de, Abp. of Dublin, 111 n, 117
Ledsam, Joshua, 114, 123
Lee, Joan, w. of Wm., 175; Ric. de (fl. 1270), 92; Roland, Bp. of Coventry and Lichfield, 5, 7, 15, 26, 33, 38, 39, 113; and see Leigh; Leye
Leek, Thos., 45
Lees, John, 92; Lt. J. M., 16; Thos., 92
Leicester (Leics.), 27
Leigh, fam., 91; and see Lee; Leye
Leland, John, antiquary, 183
Lettice, w. of Adam, 27
Levedale, Geoff. de, 126 n; John of, 126 n; Steph. de, 126 n; Wm. of, 126 n
Levedale, in Penkridge, 88, 103, 108, 115, 124, 126, 127, 144; chap., 131; ch., 135; Hall (Old Hall), 115; man., 114–16; pop., 103; sch., 137
Levershed (Levereshoved), Eleanor, 31; Joan, 31; (Levershed), Thos. de, 31
Leveson, Anne, w. of Sir Wal., 175; Jas., 80, 92 n; Joan, m. 1 Wm. Skeffington, m. 2 Wm. Fowke, m. 3 Edw. Giffard, 43; John (d. 1575), 55, 101, 142, 178; Sir John (d. c. 1615), 80; Joyce (fl. 1554), w. of John, 142; Joyce (d. 1608), m. John Giffard, 43; Marg. see Howard; Sir Ric. (d. 1560), 80; Ric. (d. 1605), 80; Sir Ric. (d. 1661), 80; Rob., 101; Sarah, m. Chas. Fowler, 101; Thos. (fl. temp. Hen. VIII), 101; Thos. (d. 1594), 55, 57, 101; Thos. (fl. 1611), 175; Thos. (fl. 1621–39), 30, 61, 100, 101, 175; Wal. (d. 1602), 80; Sir Wal. (d. 1621), 39, 101, 175; fam., 101
Leveson-Gower, Geo., Duke of Sutherland, 80; Sir Thos., 80
Levett, Evelyn Honora, 9; Francis Mary, 164; Louisa, 10; Louisa Frances, 9, 164; Louisa Mary, 9; Lucy, see Byrd; Ric. (fl. 1817), 4, 10; Revd. Ric. (d. 1843), 4, 6, 9, 57; Ric. Byrd (fl. 1843), 9; Col. Ric. Byrd (d. 1888), 9; Lt. Ric. Byrd (d. 1917), 9; Capt. Wm. Swynnerton Byrd, 7–9; his dau., see Haszard, Mrs. Gerald; fam., 3, 6, 9, 10
Lewinus (fl. 1066), 55
Lewis, A. F., 120
Leye, Nich. s. of Thos. de la, 92; Thos. s. of Ric. de la, 92; and see Lee; Leigh
Lichfield, Earl of, 13; and see Anson
Lichfield, 26, 44, 51, 59, 68, 98, 105 n, 152, 162, 184; cath., 25, 27, 35, 106, 110; canons of, 33, 58; dean, dean and chapter of, 26, 27, 35, 36, 40, 58, 63, 65, 68, 157, 162, 163, 175, and see Collingwood; Dalham; Howard, Hen.; Woodhouse; prebends in, 7, 15, 40; precentor of, 162; vicars choral of, 40; char., 100 n; consistory ct., 135; M.P., see Weston, Sir Ric.; roads to, 2, 51, 56, 82–84, 91, 94, 149, 152 n; workhouse, 151; and see Hammerwich
Lichfield, bps., see Coventry and Lichfield, bps., 8
Lichfield Diocesan Soc., 99

Lilleburn, Hen. de, and his w. Isabel, 32
Lilleshall (Salop.), 80
Lillyman, Rob., 31
Linacres, John, 11
Linhill, see Lynehill
Linhull, see Lyne Hill
Linney, John, 69
Linton, Thos., 114
Lionell, see Lynehill
Litler, Emma O., 165; Revd. Rob., 164; Thos., 123
Littleton, Alice (d. 1529), see Wynnesbury; Alice (fl. c. 1574), see Cockayne; Ann, 138; Revd. the hon. Cecil J., 105, 172; Edw. (fl. 1533), 85, 88, 125, 129; Edw. (d. 1558), 60, 111, 115, 119, 123, 125, 126, 129, 133, 140, 177, 183; Sir Edw. (d. 1574), 14, 111, 114, 115, 119, 123, 133; Sir Edw. (d. 1610), 57, 76, 106, 111, 113–15, 119, 120, 124, 125, 129, 130, 133, 140, 142, 147, 179, 182, 183; Sir Edw. (d. 1629), 119, 120, 133, 137, 182; Sir Edw. (fl. 1657), 14, 15, 30, 61, 118 n, 119, 175, 177; Edw. (d. 1705), 135, 137, 181; Sir Edw. (d. 1742), 119, 133, 135; Sir Edw. (d. 1812), 15, 61, 110, 113, 114, 117, 119, 130 n, 136, 137, 182–4; Edw. (fl. 1818), 136; Edw. Chas, Lord Hatherton (d. 1944), 128, 175, 183; Edw. John (formerly Walhouse), Lord Hatherton (d. 1836), 12, 14, 15, 60, 62, 72 n, 81, 106, 110, 113–19, 120, 125, 133, 134, 136, 141, 176, 177, 182–4; Edw. Ric., Lord Hatherton (d. 1888), 72 n, 77, 102, 120, 131, 133, 136, 137; Edw. Thos., Lord Hatherton (succ. 1944), 110, 117, 119, 125, 129, 130, 183; Edw. Geo. Percy, Lord Hatherton (d. 1930), 62, 72 n, 76, 77, 111, 113–16, 120, 125, 140, 147, 183; Fisher, 119, 183; Helen, see Swynnerton; Isabel, see Wood; Sir Jas., 6; Joan, m. John Aston, 6; Marg. (fl. 1610), see Devereux; Marg. (d. 1627), 137; Marg., Lady Hatherton (d. 1897), 105, 138; Mary (fl. 1629), see Fisher; Mary (fl. c. 1642), 137; Ric., 118, 119, 131–3; Thos., 60; Wal. (fl. 1637), 162, 164; Wal. (fl. 1697), 181; Wm. (fl. 1635), 14; Wm. (fl. 1652), 137; Hon. Wm. (fl. 1778), 133; Lady (fl. 1754), 120; fam., 14, 76, 111, 113, 115–17, 119, 120, 124, 125, 130, 132–4, 138, 147, 148, 175, 177, 179, 183
Littleworth, see Cannock
Littywood, in Bradley, 87, 89, 109, 145; man., 140
Liverpool (Lancs.), 18, 19, 51, 103, 104, 149
Llandudno (Caernarv.), 143
Locker, Ric., 16; fam., 16
Loges, Eleanor, m. John de Peyto, 121; Eliz., w. of Ric. m. 2 John de Saundrestede, 79, 80, 121; Eliz., m. Nic. de Warrewyk, 79, 80; Hugh de (fl. 1215), 2, 79, 114 n, 120; Hugh de (d. 1268), 79, 116, 118; John de, 121, and see Warrewyk; Marg., see Brok; Ric. (fl. 1285), 118; Ric. de (d. 1293), 79–81; Ric. de (d. 1300), 79; Ric. de (fl. 1300), 118, 128; Ric., s. of Ric. de, 121
London (Loundres), Hen. of, Abp. of Dublin, Archdeacon of Stafford, 108, 110, 129; Hugh de, 154
London, 19, 30, 36, 45, 48, 51, 69, 91, 95, 103, 104, 109, 138, 145, 147 n, 149, 163; Clements' Inn, 56;

PRINTED IN GREAT BRITAIN

PRINTED IN GREAT BRITAIN
AT THE UNIVERSITY PRESS, OXFORD
BY VIVIAN RIDLER
PRINTER TO THE UNIVERSITY